Developing Windows™ Applications with Borland® C++ 3

Developing Windows™ Applications with Borland® C++ 3

James McCord

SAMS
A Division of Macmillan Computer Publishing
11711 North College, Carmel, Indiana 46032 USA

FIRST EDITION

International Standard Book Number: 0-672-30231-4

Library of Congress Catalog Card Number: 91-62355

94 93 92 91 4 3 2 1

Interpretation of the printing code: the rightmost double-digit number is the year of the book's printing; the rightmost single-digit number, the number of the book's printing. For example, a printing code of 91-1 shows that the first printing of the book occurred in 1991.

Trademarks

Screen reproductions in this book were created by means of the program Collage Plus from Inner Media, Inc., Hollis, NH.

Publisher
Richard K. Swadley

Publishing Manager
Joseph B. Wikert

Managing Editor
Neweleen Trebnik

Acquisitions Editor
Gregory Croy

Development Editor
Jennifer Flynn

Production Editors
Andy Saff
Rich Limacher

Copy Editors
Anne Clarke
Gayle Johnson

Technical Reviewer
Derrel Blain
Greg Guntle

Editorial Assistants
Molly Carmody
Rosemarie Graham
San Dee Phillips

Book Design
Michele Laseau

Cover Art
Held & Diedrich Design

Production Analyst
Mary Beth Wakefield

Production
Jeff Baker
Claudia Bell
Brad Chinn
Michelle Cleary
Mark Enochs
Brook A. Farling
Sandy Grieshop
Denny Hager
Audra Hershman
Betty Kish
Phil Kitchel
Bob LaRoche
Laurie Lee
Tad Ringo
Linda Seifert
Kevin Spear
Phil Worthington

Indexer
Jeanne Clark

Composed in ITC Garamond and MCP Digital
Printed in the United States of America

Overview

Contents

Preface

Borland C++ 3 is a powerful tool for the development of C, C++, and Windows applications. Borland C++ 3 offers full ANSI C compatibility, provides the features of C++, and includes the Resource Workshop. The Resource Workshop enables you to create and edit resources for Windows applications such as bitmaps, icons, cursors, dialog boxes, strings, menus, and accelerators.

My purpose in writing this book is to provide you, the programmer, with the information that you need to develop Windows applications using Borland C++ 3. This book introduces you to the basic programming concepts and principles involved in developing Windows applications.

This book provides three major categories of information that supplement the Borland C++ 3 documentation. The first category of information is Windows programming basics. This book introduces you to Windows and to the methods used for Windows application development. The second category of information deals with developing Windows applications using ObjectWindows. The ObjectWindows functions and classes are described in detail and numerous programming examples are provided. The third category of information is reference material for the hundreds of Windows functions, messages, and printer escapes.

The information contained in this book will provide you with the foundation that you need to develop Windows applications using Borland C++ 3.

Acknowledgments

I could not have completed this project without the help of many people. I would like to thank, most of all, my family, Jill, Josh, and Jamie, for their love and support. I would also like to thank the staff at SAMS for all their hard work on putting this book together. It takes a good team to put this much information together and I thank each person involved with this project. I would also like to thank Gary and Tony, two great officers and friends, for being there when I needed them. Last but not least, I thank T.B.T. for all the great things in my life.

Introduction

This book was developed to accomplish three primary objectives. The first objective is to provide you with a Windows programming foundation for developing Windows applications with Borland C++ 3. The second objective is to provide you with reference information and programming examples for using ObjectWindows for Windows application development. The third objective is to provide complete reference material on the Windows functions and messages so that you can continue to build on this Windows programming foundation.

To meet the objectives of this book, the chapters are divided into three sections. Part I, Chapters 1 to 10, introduces the fundamentals of developing Windows applications using Borland C++. The second part, Chapters 11 and 12, introduce the ObjectWindows features included with Borland C++ 3. Part III, which includes Chapters 13 to 19 and Appendixes A, B, and C, contains the reference information for each of the Windows functions and messages as well as the Whitewater Resource Toolkit and the Resource Workshop. The chapters contained in each section are described in the following paragraphs.

Part I—Windows Programming with Borland C++

Chapter One—Introduction to Windows

This chapter provides a fundamental introduction to the Windows environment and explains the ways that programming for Windows applications differs from programming for traditional MS-DOS applications.

Chapter Two—Windows Programming Basics

This chapter provides the foundation that you will need to develop Windows applications using Borland C++ 3. All the basic components of a Windows applications—including the `WinMain` function, the message loop, window procedures, and resource files—are explained.

Chapter Three—The Graphics Device Interface (GDI)

The capabilities of the Graphics Device Interface are addressed in this chapter. Topics covered include lines, brushes, pens, the device context, and text output. Several examples demonstrating the capabilities of the GDI are provided.

Chapter Four—Resources

This chapter introduces accelerator, bitmap, cursor, dialog box, icon, menu, and string resources. An example that creates and uses each type of resource is provided.

Chapter Five—The Keyboard and Windows

The principles of using the keyboard with Windows are addressed. Topics for this chapter include keyboard messages, character messages, character sets, and the caret.

Chapter Six—The Mouse and Windows

This chapter addresses the principles of using the mouse with Windows. The focus of this chapter is Windows mouse messages.

Chapter Seven—Windows and Child Windows

This chapter introduces the concepts of windows and child windows inside the Windows environment. This chapter specifically addresses the use of child window controls.

Chapter Eight—Memory Management and Windows

This chapter addresses Windows' use of local heaps, global heaps, and segments.

Chapter Nine—The Multiple Document Interface (MDI)

The Multiple Document Interface specification is discussed and demonstrated in this chapter.

Chapter Ten—Dynamic Libraries

This chapter presents the concepts and uses of dynamic link libraries. A dynamic link library is created and demonstrated.

Part II—Windows Programming with ObjectWindows

Chapter Eleven—Introduction to ObjectWindows for C++

This chapter introduces ObjectWindows and the ObjectWindows class hierarchy.

Chapter Twelve—Windows Programming Using ObjectWindows

This chapter introduces the fundamental concepts behind programming with ObjectWindows and provides numerous programmimg examples of Windows applications using ObjectWindows.

Part III—Reference

Chapter Thirteen—Windows Functions

This chapter provides reference material for each of the Windows functions. The functions are divided into three general categories: Window Manager Interface functions, Graphic Device Interface functions, and System Services Interface functions.

Chapter Fourteen—Windows Messages

This chapter provides reference material for each of the Windows messages. The messages are divided into appropriate categories.

Chapter Fifteen—Windows Printer Escapes

This chapter introduces the Windows printer escapes and provides reference information on each escape.

Chapter Sixteen—The Whitewater Resource Toolkit

This chapter introduces the editors of the Whitewater Resource Toolkit.

Chapter Seventeen—The Resource Workshop

This chapter includes the capabilities and features of the Resource Workshop.

Chapter Eighteen—ObjectWindow Classes

This chapter provides detailed reference information for each of the ObjectWindows classes. Reference information includes descriptions of each of the classes' data members and member functions.

Chapter Nineteen—ObjectWindow Functions

This chapter provides detailed reference information for each of the ObjectWindows functions.

I

Windows Programming with Borland C++

1

Introduction to Windows

Microsoft Windows is a graphical user interface environment for MS-DOS computers. Windows provides a multitasking environment that uses a consistent windowing and menu structure for its applications. Because the windowing and menu structure is consistent between applications, Windows applications are easier for the user to learn and use. The multitasking advantage of Windows enables you to run several applications at a time, especially those that are created for the Windows environment. However, Windows also provides the capability to run and multitask non-Windows MS-DOS applications. The Windows 3.0 environment is shown in Figure 1.1.

Microsoft Windows is "the" graphical user interface environment for MS-DOS machines. Although other graphical user interface environments exist, none can compare with Windows in popularity. Graphical user interfaces use bitmapped displays to convey information. Because the display is not limited to the ASCII character set, as is the case with traditional MS-DOS text-based programs, the image on the display accurately reflects the image produced on an output device such as a printer or plotter. This correlation between the screen image and the output image

is called *what-you-see-is-what-you-get* (WYSIWYG) and is one reason graphical user interfaces such as Windows have become so popular. Windows offers the user and the programmer several advantages, which are discussed later in this chapter.

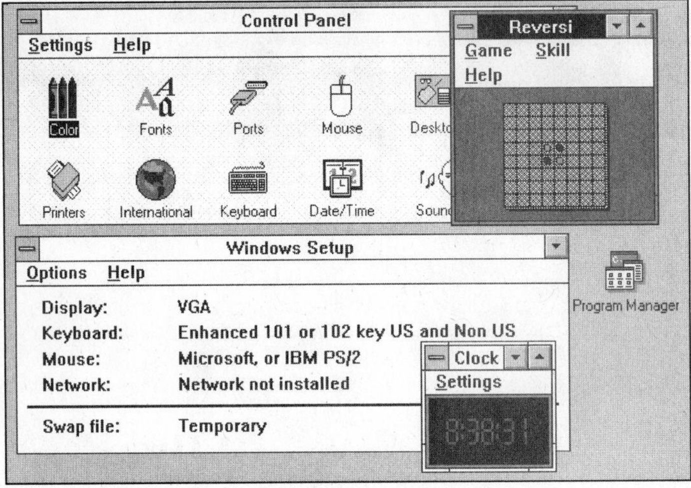

Figure 1.1. *The Windows environment.*

The History of Windows

Microsoft began working on the first version of Windows in 1983, and released Version 1.1 of Windows in 1985. This version was designed for a two-floppy 8088 IBM PC system with 256K of RAM. Windows 1.1 automatically tiled the application windows and supported pop-up windows.

In 1987, Microsoft released the next major version of Windows, numbered 2.0. This version contained a new user interface that supported overlapping windows. A major advantage to Windows 2.0 was the improved use of expanded memory. However, because Windows 2.0 only ran in real mode, the amount of memory that could be addressed was limited to one megabyte.

Microsoft released Windows Version 3.0 in 1990. This version of Windows added support for owner-draw menus, owner-draw list boxes, and owner-draw buttons. Additionally, when Windows 3.0 is run on a 80386 or 80486 machine, 16 megabytes of memory can be addressed. Windows 3.0 has become the standard graphical user interface for MS-DOS machines. Borland C++ contains features for designing and developing Windows 3.0 applications with either C or C++. The features and enhancements provided in Windows 3.0 are documented in the reference section of this book.

Why Windows?

The use of Windows and Windows applications offers many advantages to both the user and the programmer. Features such as point-and-click capabilities and multitasking are advantageous to the user. Features such as device-independent graphics and enhanced memory management are helpful for the programmer. The following paragraphs describe some of the advantages of Windows for the user and the programmer.

Advantages of Windows to the User

One advantage for users of Windows and Windows applications is the consistent user interface. Because most users work with several different software packages, each with its own user interface, the consistency of the user interface's design is very important. Each window in the Windows environment contains the same basic features. Because these basic features are consistent among applications, the user can adapt to new applications more easily.

Another advantage for the user is the use of graphics-based images to represent applications and data. Because Windows is a graphical user interface, graphics images represent physical data structures such as files, applications, windows, and directories. The user can manipulate these physical structures with a mouse by selecting, double clicking, dragging, and so forth. It is easier for the user to double click an icon that represents an application than it is to go to the appropriate directory and type the name of the file to launch.

What-you-see-is-what-you-get (WYSIWYG) is a major advantage to the user. For example, most text-based word-processing software packages use the read-only memory, basic input-output system (ROM BIOS) character sets for the screen display. Because the ROM BIOS character sets are not proportional and have no direct correlation to the font used by an application, the text displayed on the screen usually does not correspond to the resulting text output by the printer. However, because of WYSIWYG, Windows can treat text as a series of graphics images that are drawn onto the screen as they will appear when printed.

Windows provides the user with multitasking capabilities. Multitasking is very important to the user because it allows several applications to run at the same time. Therefore, you do not need to save the working file and exit the application to enter another application; you simply switch between applications. Multitasking is enhanced by Windows memory management capabilities. Windows 3.0 provides the user with access to up to 16 megabytes of extended memory. Because Windows provides access to all available memory resources, the user can optimize the system more easily.

Advantages of Windows to the Programmer

Many of the user's advantages in Windows are also the programmer's advantages. For example, the consistent user interface is a user advantage because the user interface among applications is similar. The programmer benefits from the consistent user interface because the basic interface design and tools already are established. Since the interface is basically the same for every application, the programmer can spend more time on the actual functionality of the application and less time on the interface design.

The basic design of the Windows graphical user interface is another advantage. The programmer can more easily design graphical representations of physical structures, such as files and directories, and provide features such as pop-up menus and dialog boxes that are easy to use. Windows also provides direct mouse and keyboard support, which significantly decreases application development time.

The memory management features of Windows provide a distinct advantage to the programmer. These features enable you to access more memory than you can using traditional MS-DOS applications so you can make the most of the system memory resources while maintaining flexibility in system design. Chapter 8, "Memory Management and Windows," provides more details on the memory management features of Windows.

Windows also provides the ability to develop device-independent graphics. Because well-designed Windows applications do not access the graphics hardware (the screen and printer) directly, Windows applications operate with any video subsystem or printer that has a Windows device driver. For the programmer, device-independent graphics means that code is not dependent on a certain system configuration. Further, each application's programmer does not need to develop device drivers for all the possible video displays, adapters, and printers.

Standard Components of a Window

A Windows application uses an application window for input and output to the screen. The Windows application creates the application window and has primary access to the window. The application and Windows, however, share the responsibility of managing the application window. Windows is responsible for managing the size, position, and components of the application window. The application maintains the primary responsibility of managing the client area (working area) of the application window. The application window contains some, and often all, of the following components:

- Window border
- Client area
- Control menu box
- Control menu
- Horizontal scroll bar
- Maximize box
- Menu bar
- Minimize box
- Title bar
- Vertical scroll bar

The application window for the Windows Notepad application is shown in Figure 1.2. The Notepad application window contains each of the components in the previous list. The following paragraphs describe each component of a typical application window.

The Border

The window border surrounds the outside edge of the application window. The window border contains three basic sets of components. The first set of components contains the window corners. The four window corners enable you to size the window vertically and horizontally at the same time. The second set of components contains the vertical sides of the border that enable you to size the window in the horizontal direction. The third set of components contains the horizontal sides of the border that enable you to size the window in the vertical direction.

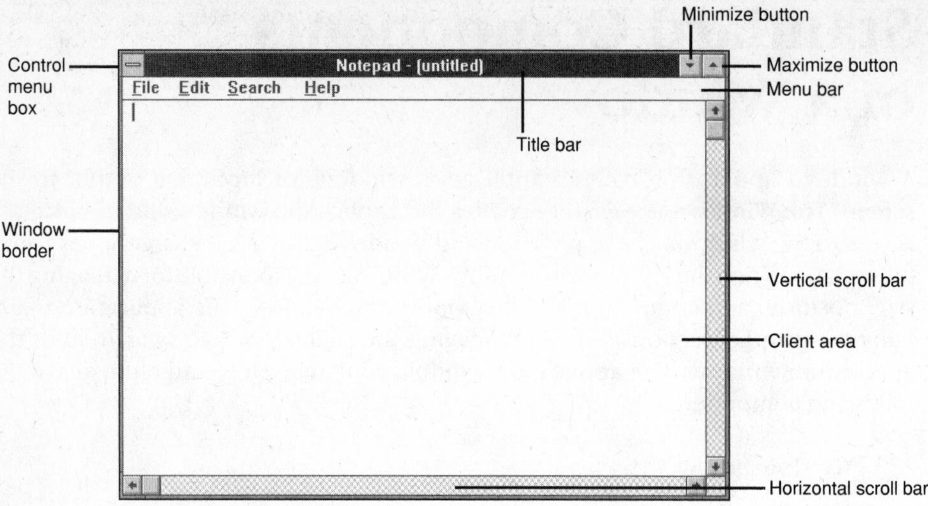

Figure 1.2. *The Notepad window.*

The Client Area

The client area is the physical part of the window that is not occupied by the menu bar, scroll bars, borders, or other components. The application uses the client area as its workspace. The application maintains the client area, and Windows maintains the position, size, and components of the application window.

The Control Menu

The control menu box is located in the upper-left corner of the application window. The control menu box provides access to the control menu.

Through the menu options of the control menu, you can restore, move, size, minimize, maximize, and close the application window. The control menu, which is also called the *system menu*, provides the primary access to the various components in the application window when the user either does not choose to use a mouse or does not have a mouse. The control menu for the Notepad application is shown in Figure 1.3.

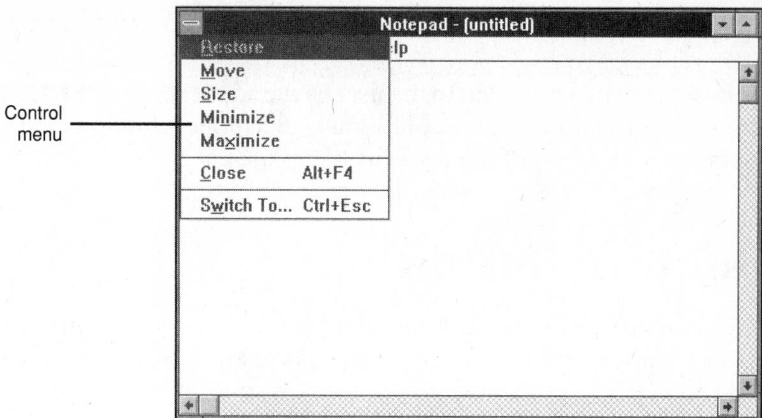

Figure 1.3. *The control menu.*

The Horizontal Scroll Bar

With the horizontal scroll bar, you can move through documents and images that are too large for the current size of the client area. The horizontal scroll bar contains three components. The first component is the left arrow, positioned at the left end of the scroll bar. Clicking this arrow displays a part of the document or image located to the left of the left window border. The second component is the right arrow, positioned at the right end of the scroll bar. Clicking this arrow displays a part of the document or image located to the right of the right window border. The last component indicates the thumb position of the current view area. The solid square in the scroll bar indicates the current view position relative to the far left and far right sides of the document or image.

The Maximize Button

The maximize button enlarges the application window to fill the screen. After you click the maximize button, it is replaced with the restore button. You can click the restore button to restore the window to its previous size. When the window is restored to its previous size, the restore button is replaced with the maximize button.

The Menu Bar

The menu bar lists the menus provided to the user by the application. The File, Edit, and Help menus are common to most applications. The application, however, can customize the number and type of menus available to the user.

The Minimize Button

The minimize button shrinks the application window to an icon. When you click the minimize button, the application is minimized (shrunk to an icon). Double-clicking the minimized window (the icon) restores the window to its previous size.

The Title Bar

The title bar lists the application name and often the active file name for the application window. The title bar of the active window is differentiated by color and/or intensity from inactive windows.

The Vertical Scroll Bar

By using the vertical scroll bar, you can move through documents and images that are too large for the current size of the client area. The vertical scroll bar contains three components. The first component is the up arrow positioned at the top of the scroll bar. Clicking this arrow displays a part of the document or image located above the top window border. The second component is the down arrow positioned at the bottom of the scroll bar. Clicking this arrow displays a part of the document or image located below the bottom window border. The last component indicates the thumb position of the current view area. The solid square in the scroll bar indicates the current view position relative to the top and bottom of the document or image.

Windows Functions

The Windows functions are the heart of the Windows application. Most MS-DOS applications written in C or C++ use the functions from the compiler's run-time library to interface with MS-DOS. Functions in the compiler's run-time libraries are oriented specifically for the development of MS-DOS applications running on the 80x86 architecture. Use Windows functions to take advantage of the capabilities of Windows and device-independence when developing Windows applications.

There is a wide range of Windows functions. Chapter 13 and Appendix A provide additional reference information for each of the functions from each of the function categories/subcategories. You should skim Chapter 13 to get an idea of the almost overwhelming number of Windows functions. Don't get too alarmed, however, because, as with most programming libraries, you may soon find a subset of functions that you can become familiar with and use over and over.

Windows Messages

Windows applications use Windows messages to communicate with other Windows applications and with the Windows system. Because Windows applications are message, or event, driven, it is important to understand how the Windows messages function. Chapter 14 and Appendix B provide reference information for each of the Windows messages and explain the usage of the Windows messages. Skim Chapter 14 to get a feel for the number of messages that Windows supports. As with the Windows functions, don't be too alarmed at the almost overwhelming number of messages, because you will use a small subset of these messages frequently and will quickly become familiar with the messages in this subset.

Hungarian Notation

Hungarian notation, a method of creating variable names, is commonly used by Windows programmers. Hungarian notation is named for the nationality of Microsoft programmer Charles Simonyi and is used extensively by Microsoft for application and operating system software.

Hungarian notation uses lowercase letters in the prefix of the variable name to indicate the data type of the variable. The remainder of the variable name describes how the variable functions. For example,

```
nCharacterCounter
```

specifies that the variable is an integer (`n`) and represents a character counter (`CharacterCounter`).

The Windows functions and messages listed in Chapters 13 and 14 commonly use the prefixes listed in Table 1.1 in variable and parameter names.

Table 1.1. Common prefixes for Windows variables.

Prefix	*Meaning*
`b`	Boolean (nonzero is true, 0 is false)
`c`	Character (one byte value)
`dw`	Long 32-bit unsigned integer
`f`	Bit flags packed into a 16-bit integer
`h`	16-bit handle
`l`	Long 32-bit integer
`lp`	Long 32-bit pointer
`n`	Short 16-bit integer
`p`	Short 16-bit pointer
`pt`	Coordinate pair (x and y) packed into an unsigned 32-bit integer
`rgb`	RGB color value packed into a 32-bit integer
`w`	Short 16-bit unsigned integer

Handles

Handles are fundamental to Windows programming; therefore, you must understand exactly what handles are. A *handle* is a unique integer value used by Windows to identify an object in an application such as a window, instance, menu, memory, output device, control, or file. For example, in a module definition file (explained later in this book), menu resources are defined and associated with handles. The first menu item of the first menu in the menu bar of an application, for example, might be assigned a handle of 100. The second menu item might be assigned a handle of 101. In the application source code, these menu items would be referenced by the handles 100 and 101. The Windows application usually can access the handle only, not the actual data the handle represents. Windows controls access to the data and, therefore, protects the data in the multitasking environment.

The Include File

Borland C++ provides the WINDOWS.H include file so that you can access the various Windows functions and messages from your C or C++ program. WINDOWS.H contains the definitions for the Windows constants, variables, data structures, and functions. All Windows applications must include the WINDOWS.H file in the source code.

2

Windows Programming Basics

Windows programming can be, quite honestly, a major headache to newcomers. Most programmers who are familiar with the traditional, sequential programming methodologies used with C are often not mentally prepared to meet the challenges of Windows programming. Many programmers have the following attitude when approaching Windows programming:

- "A Windows program can't be much different than a C program!"
- "I've programmed in C for years, so all I have to do is become familiar with the Windows functions!"
- "Windows? C? It's all the same!"

Unfortunately, it is this type of attitude that gives Windows programming the reputation of being very difficult for programmers.

Learning to program Windows, in itself, is no more difficult than learning the ins and outs of any structured language—you just have to learn the basic code structure and

programming methodologies. For most programmers, the biggest hurdle in learning Windows programming is that you must be willing to discard traditional programming methodologies and wholeheartedly adopt the Windows programming methodologies. If you approach Windows programming with an open mind, you will quickly adapt to the new programming concepts and methodologies.

This chapter gives you the whirlwind tour of Windows programming. The chapter begins with an introduction to event-driven programming, then introduces the basic concepts and methodologies for programming Windows applications using Borland C++, and ends by demonstrating these concepts and methodologies in a fundamental Windows program.

Event-Driven Programming

The majority of MS-DOS programs are written using sequential, procedure-driven programming methodologies. Sequential, procedure-driven programs have a distinct beginning, distinct procedures, and a distinct end. Therefore, the program directly controls the sequence of program events or procedures.

Windows programming methodologies differ from MS-DOS programming methodologies in that Windows programs are event-driven. Event-driven programs are not controlled by event sequence; event-driven programs are controlled by the occurrence of events. The following example quickly demonstrates the primary difference in sequential, procedure-driven programs and event-driven programs.

Suppose that you had to write a program that averages the grades of a class which had taken three tests during the semester. You have determined that the procedure for generating the averages is as follows:

1. Enter the names of the students.
2. Enter the grades for test one.
3. Enter the grades for test two.
4. Enter the grades for test three.
5. Calculate and display the averages.

In a sequential, procedure-driven program, the logic flow looks something like that shown in Figure 2.1. The program displays a screen that prompts you for the names of the students. After you enter the names of the students, the next screen prompts you for the grades for test one. Again, another screen prompts you for the grades for test two. After completing the grades for test two, a screen is displayed that enables you to enter grades for test three. After you enter test three grades, the final screen containing the calculated averages is displayed. This approach is very logical and follows a structured sequence of events. However, to use the program as intended, you must follow the procedure as designed. There is no room for exceptions such as changing a grade in step 3 once you are in step 5.

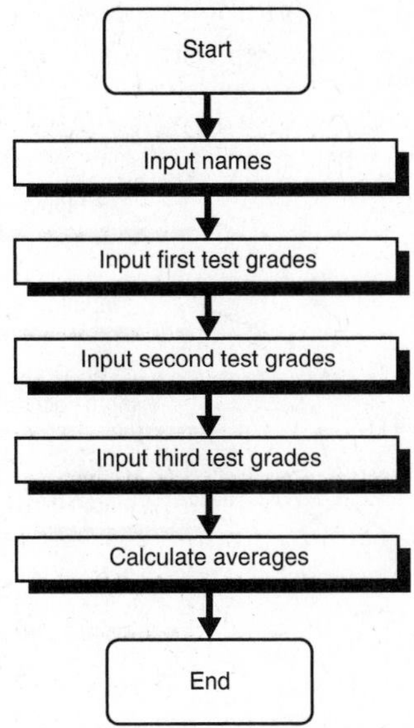

Figure 2.1. *Sequential, procedure-driven methodology.*

Although there are many ways to handle exceptions in sequential, procedure-driven programs such as the one just presented, exceptions also must follow sequential, procedure-driven architectures. Event-driven programs are designed to avoid the limitations of sequential, procedure-driven methodologies by processing events in a nonsequential manner.

Event-driven programming revolves around the generation and processing of messages. A message is information about an event that has occurred. For example, whenever a key or mouse button is pressed, a message is sent. Another message is sent when the key or mouse button is released. Your job as a Windows programmer involves, to a large extent, the sorting and managing of the Windows messages sent to and from the application that you are developing. Because Windows messages are event-driven, messages do not appear in any predefined order.

The previous example of a sequential, procedure-driven application can be easily implemented using event-driven methodologies. Figure 2.2 illustrates the methodology that would be used to implement the application with an event-driven architecture. The full functionality of the sequential, procedure-driven program is

still there; however, the user does not have to go through each step, in sequence, to calculate the grades. The user may skip around the various screens while adding or modifying data at each level. For example, with the event-driven application, you can enter grades for the third test without previously having entered the test scores for tests one and two. With the procedure-driven example, you could not do this. Event-driven programming methodologies provide many benefits and are very useful for applications that require extensive user interaction.

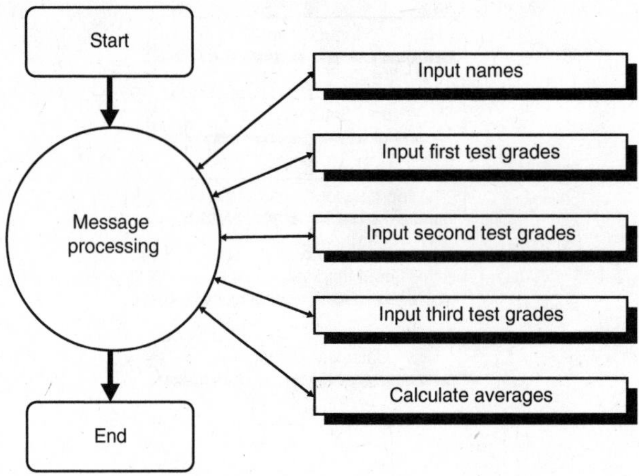

Figure 2.2. *Event-driven methodology.*

The *WinMain* Function

The `WinMain` function is the entry point for all Windows applications. There are three basic parts to the `WinMain` function: prodecure declaration, program initialization, and the message loop. The general form of the `WinMain` function follows.

```
int PASCAL WinMain (HANDLE hInstance, HANDLE hPrevInstance,
            LPSTR lpszCmdParam, int nCmdShow)

{
HWND hWnd;
MSG Message;
WNDCLASS WndClass;

if (!hPrevInstance)
     {
     WndClass.cbClsExtra = 0;
     WndClass.cbWndExtra = 0;
```

```
     WndClass.hbrBackground = GetStockObject(WHITE_BRUSH);
     WndClass.hCursor = LoadCursor(NULL, IDC_ARROW);
     WndClass.hIcon = LoadIcon (NULL, "END");
     WndClass.hInstance = hInstance;
     WndClass.lpfnWndProc = WndProc;
     WndClass.lpszClassName = "WIN_ONE";
     WndClass.lpszMenuName = NULL;
     WndClass.style = CS_HREDRAW ¦ CS_VREDRAW;

     RegisterClass (&WndClass);
     }

hWnd = CreateWindow ("WIN_ONE",        /* class name */
          "Fundamental Window",        /* Caption */
          WS_OVERLAPPEDWINDOW,         /* Style */
          CW_USEDEFAULT,               /* x position */
          0,                           /* y position */
          CW_USEDEFAULT,               /* cx - size */
          0,                           /* cy - size */
          NULL,                        /* Parent window */
          NULL,                        /* Menu */
          hInstance,                   /* Program Instance */
          NULL);                       /* Parameters */

ShowWindow (hWnd, nCmdShow);
while (GetMessage (&Message, 0, 0, 0))
     {
     TranslateMessage(&Message);
     DispatchMessage(&Message);
     }
return Message.wParam;
```

The procedure declaration for the `WinMain` function follows:

```
int PASCAL WinMain (HANDLE hInstance, HANDLE hPrevInstance,
                    LPSTR lpszCmdLine, int cmdShow);
```

`hInstance` is a handle identifying the program. `hPrevInstance` specifies the program that `hInstance` is related to, if any. Programs are considered related if they share the same module name. `lpszCmdLine` specifies the command-line arguments for the program. `cmdShow` specifies the state of the main window when the window is first opened.

Program initialization is the bulk of the `WinMain` function. In the example later in this chapter (Listing 2.2), the program initialization portion of the `WinMain` function involves the creation of a window. In the process of creating a window, you must define the window class. The first part of the initialization portion of the `WinMain` function defines the various members of a `WndClass` data structure. In this part of the code, you define the cursor used for the window, the brush used to fill the window background, the name of the window procedure, the window class style, the main menu of the window, and the class name. The program initialization portion of the example presented in Listing 2.2 follows:

```
if (!hPrevInstance)
     {
     WndClass.cbClsExtra = 0;
     WndClass.cbWndExtra = 0;
     WndClass.hbrBackground = GetStockObject(WHITE_BRUSH);
     WndClass.hCursor =  LoadCursor(NULL, IDC_ARROW);
     WndClass.hIcon = LoadIcon (NULL, "END");
     WndClass.hInstance = hInstance;
     WndClass.lpfnWndProc = WndProc;
     WndClass.lpszClassName = "WIN_ONE";
     WndClass.lpszMenuName = NULL;
     WndClass.style = CS_HREDRAW | CS_VREDRAW;

     RegisterClass (&WndClass);
     }

hWnd = CreateWindow ("WIN_ONE",       /* class name */
          "Fundamental Window",       /* Caption */
          WS_OVERLAPPEDWINDOW,        /* Style */
          CW_USEDEFAULT,              /* x position */
          0,                          /* y position */
          CW_USEDEFAULT,              /* cx - size */
          0,                          /* cy - size */
          NULL,                       /* Parent window */
          NULL,                       /* Menu */
          hInstance,                  /* Program Instance */
          NULL);                      /* Parameters */

ShowWindow (hWnd, nCmdShow);
```

The message loop of the `WinMain` function retrieves messages from the application queue and sends each message to the appropriate window function. The message loop from Listing 2.2 follows. More information on the message loop is provided in the following paragraphs.

```
while (GetMessage (&Message, 0, 0, 0))
     {
     TranslateMessage(&Message);
     DispatchMessage(&Message);
     }
```

The Message Loop

Windows applications receive input in the form of messages. These messages contain information about the device that generated the input, the current state of the keyboard, the position of the cursor, the state of the mouse, and the system time. Windows monitors all the input devices and places input messages into the system queue. Windows then copies the input messages from the system queue into the appropriate application queue. The application's message loop retrieves the messages from the application queue and sends each message to the appropriate window function. Figure 2.3 diagrams this message-handling process.

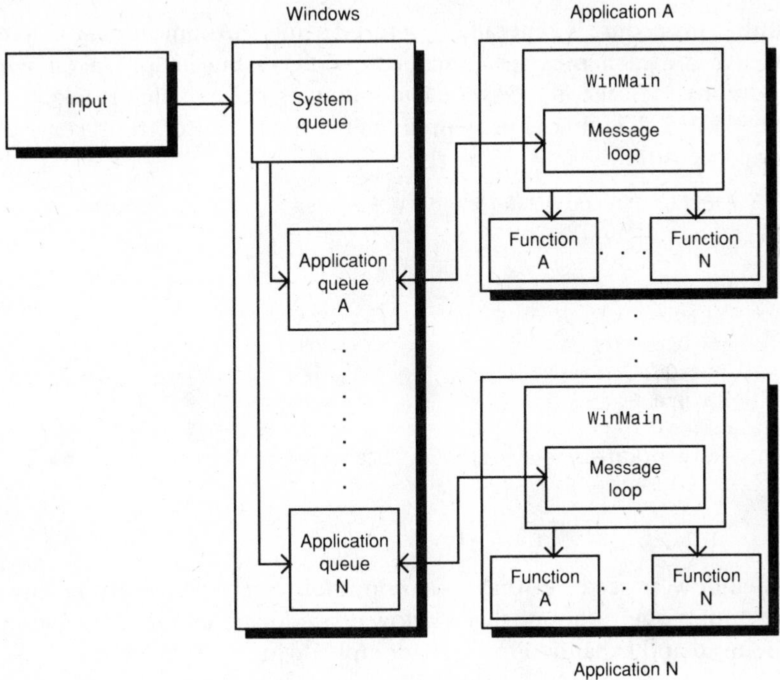

Figure 2.3. *Windows and the message loop.*

The message loop follows the general format of

```
while (GetMessage (&Message, NULL, 0, 0))
     {
     TranslateMessage (&Message);
     DispatchMessage (&Message);
     }
return Message.wParam;
```

In this message loop, `Message` refers to a data structure of type `MSG`. Chapter 13 provides information on the `GetMessage`, `TranslateMessage`, and `DispatchMessage` functions used in the message loop.

Window Procedures

Window procedures are functions that receive and process messages. The message loop is responsible for retrieving messages from the application queue and sending the message to the appropriate window procedures. The window procedure determines the action that is taken when a certain message is received.

The window procedure is generally structured using one or more `switch` statements with a case for each message. Each case reflects the action taken when the corresponding message is received. The following code, which is taken from the example (Listing 2.2) that is presented later in this chapter, represents a simple window procedure:

```
long FAR PASCAL WndProc (HWND hWnd, WORD iMessage, WORD wParam,
                LONG lParam)
{
switch (iMessage)
     {
     case WM_DESTROY:
          PostQuitMessage(0);
          return 0;
     default:
          return(DefWindowProc(hWnd, iMessage, wParam,
               lParam));
     }
}
```

In this window procedure, only one condition is checked—the receipt of the `WM_DESTROY` message. Although this window procedure is simple, the same structure could be used and expanded for more complex window procedures.

Using Projects to Develop Windows Applications

There are several ways to create a Windows application, including the use of the Integrated Development Environment (IDE) and Project Manager, the use of the command-line compiler, or the use of a makefile. Whatever method you use, the basic process and the results are the same.

The process for creating a Windows application includes the following basic steps as shown in Figure 2.4. C or C++ source files are compiled into object code using the Borland C++ compiler. The resulting object code is linked with definition and library files to form executable code. The resource compiler then binds the resource files with the executable code to create a Windows application.

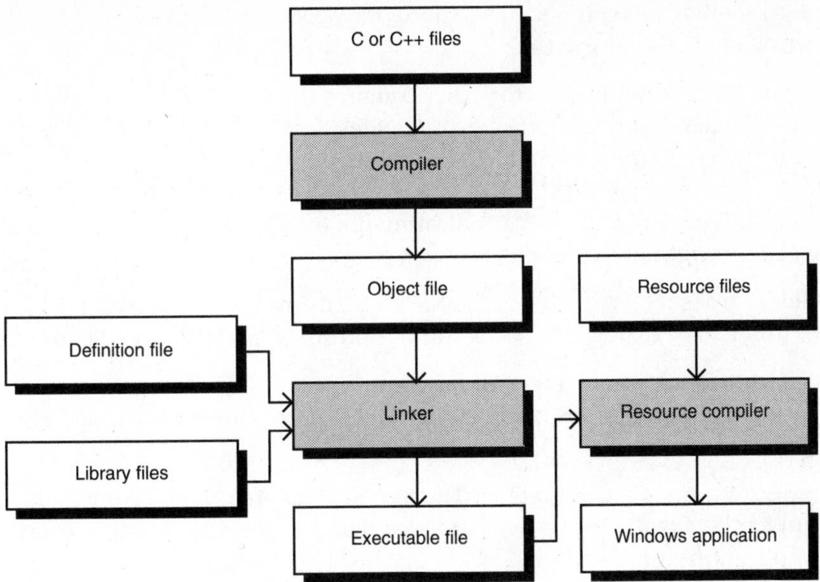

Figure 2.4. *Building a Windows application.*

If you are familiar with Borland C++ or have used Turbo C or Turbo C++, using projects to build applications is not a new concept. However, if you are new to Borland C++ or have never developed an application using the Project Manager features of the IDE, you need to understand the use of projects. The project is probably the most straightforward method for creating Windows applications from within the IDE. Therefore, this book uses the IDE and the Project Manager for developing all of the examples in this book.

When using the Project Manager and the IDE for creating Windows applications, you must follow ten basic steps:

> **Note:**
>
> This process is designed for use with DOS-based versions of the IDE. The process used for the Windows-based IDE is similar except for steps 2, 9, and 10. You can start the Windows-based IDE by double clicking the IDE icon. The compiled application can be run from the Program Manager.

1. Create all appropriate C or C++ source files, module definition files, and resource files. More information on these files is provided later in this chapter.

2. Start the IDE by typing **BC** (real mode for version 2.0 or 3.0) or **BCX** (protected mode for 2.0).

3. If you are not in the directory that contains the C or C++ source files, module definition files, and resource files, select `File ¦ Change dir` and change to the directory that contains these files. (The notation `File ¦ Change dir` means that you select the `File` menu and `Change dir` option. This convention for indicating the menus and options to select is used throughout this book.)

4. Select `Project ¦ Open`. Type the filename, using a .PRJ extension, in the `Project Name` dialog box. Click the `OK` button, or press Enter to continue.

5. Select `Project ¦ Add item`. Add the appropriate C or C++ source files, module definition files, and resource files. Close the `Project` dialog box when you are done.

6. Select `Options ¦ Application`. The `Set Application Options` dialog box will appear. Select `Windows App` to indicate that you are developing a Windows application.

7. Select `Compile ¦ Build all`. This selection builds the project into a Windows application.

8. If there are any errors, modify the appropriate file(s) and repeat step 7. After the project is successfully built, continue with step 9.

9. Exit the IDE by selecting `File ¦ Quit` or pressing Alt-X.

10. Run your program from inside Windows. Although there are several ways to run your application, the easiest way is to type

    ```
    win filename
    ```

    at the DOS prompt if your system is set up to run Windows. This loads into memory Windows, which will in turn load and run your application.

This process is relatively simple and provides you with access to the powerful features of the IDE and Project Manager. Again, this process is used for all the examples in this book. Each example contains a listing of the files used in the application project.

Your windows applications projects generally will contain three types of files: the C or C++ source code file(s), the module definition file, and the resource file(s). Each of these file types is discussed in the following sections.

The C or C++ Source Code File

The source code for the Windows application resides in the C or C++ source code file. As with traditional C or C++ projects, there may be more than one C or C++ file included in a project. The C or C++ source code file contains a combination of C and/or C++ keywords and functions, Windows functions, Windows messages, and references to include files such as windows.h.

The Module Definition File

The module definition file gives the linker specific information about the application's code and data segments, the size of the application's local heap, and the size of the application's program stack. When using the Borland C++ linker, you don't need to create the module definition file because the linker can determine this information. However, if you follow the C programming practices described in Part I of this book, most of your Windows applications will need the module definition file because its use is customary for developing Windows applications and enables you to specify settings for the application.

The following lines are included in the module definition file:

```
NAME
DESCRIPTION
EXETYPE
CODE
DATA
HEAPSIZE
STACKSIZE
EXPORTS
```

where

`NAME` defines a module as an executable.

`DESCRIPTION` adds the specified text to the executable.

`EXETYPE` indicates the type of program the linker should create. `WINDOWS` is used for Windows applications.

`CODE` provides information on the application's code segments. Possible values include `PRELOAD`, `FIXED`, `MOVEABLE`, and `DISCARDABLE`.

`DATA` provides information on the application's data segments. Possible values include `PRELOAD`, `MOVEABLE`, and `MULTIPLE`.

`HEAPSIZE` defines the initial size of the application's local heap.

`STACKSIZE` defines the size of the application's stack.

`EXPORTS` enables you to specify the window and dialog procedures for your application.

Listing 2.1 is a typical module definition file.

The Resource Files

Most Windows applications use resources such as icons, cursors, bitmaps, and dialog boxes. You can use the Whitewater Resource Toolkit or the Resource Workshop to create these resources. After a resource is created, it is stored in a resource file. Resource files created by the Resource Toolkit and the Resource Workshop are source files and must be compiled by the Resource Compiler and bound to the executable so they are available at run-time.

The Resource Compiler compiles the resource source file, binds the compiled file with the compiled .EXE or .DLL module, and generates a Windows-compatible application. When you use the Project Manager to develop Windows applications, the Resource Compiler is invoked automatically.

A Fundamental Windows Program

The example in Listing 2.1 and 2.2 demonstrates a fundamental window. A fundamental window is a window that can be sized, moved, closed, minimized, or maximized. The IDE and the Project Manager were used to create and build the project. The process for creating a Windows application, as described previously in this chapter, was used for this project. The project used to build this example is called WIN_ONE and contains the files WIN_ONE.C and WIN_ONE.DEF. The following project description summarizes the project. A similar summary is used for every example in this book. The window created with this example is shown in Figure 2.5.

Project Name: `WIN_ONE`
Files in Project: `WIN_ONE.C`
`WIN_ONE.DEF`

Listing 2.1. *The module definition file for the fundamental window example.*

```
NAME            WIN_ONE
DESCRIPTION     'Fundamental Window'
EXETYPE         WINDOWS
CODE            PRELOAD MOVEABLE
DATA            PRELOAD MOVEABLE MULTIPLE
HEAPSIZE        1024
STACKSIZE       5120
EXPORTS         WndProc
```

Listing 2.2. *C source code for the fundamental window example.*

```
#include <windows.h>
#include <stdlib.h>
#include <string.h>

long FAR PASCAL WndProc (HWND hWnd, WORD iMessage,
                WORD wParam, LONG lParam);

int PASCAL WinMain (HANDLE hInstance, HANDLE hPrevInstance,
              LPSTR lpszCmdParam, int nCmdShow)

{
HWND hWnd;
MSG Message;
WNDCLASS WndClass;

if (!hPrevInstance)
     {
     WndClass.cbClsExtra = 0;
     WndClass.cbWndExtra = 0;
     WndClass.hbrBackground = GetStockObject(WHITE_BRUSH);
     WndClass.hCursor = LoadCursor(NULL, IDC_ARROW);
     WndClass.hIcon = LoadIcon (NULL, "END");
     WndClass.hInstance = hInstance;
     WndClass.lpfnWndProc = WndProc;
     WndClass.lpszClassName = "WIN_ONE";
     WndClass.lpszMenuName = NULL;
     WndClass.style = CS_HREDRAW | CS_VREDRAW;

     RegisterClass (&WndClass);
     }

hWnd = CreateWindow ("WIN_ONE",      /* class name */
          "Fundamental Window",      /* Caption */
          WS_OVERLAPPEDWINDOW,       /* Style */
```

continues

Listing 2.2. continued

```
          CW_USEDEFAULT,               /* x position */
          0,                           /* y position */
          CW_USEDEFAULT,               /* cx - size */
          0,                           /* cy - size */
          NULL,                        /* Parent window */
          NULL,                        /* Menu */
          hInstance,                   /* Program Instance */
          NULL);                       /* Parameters */

ShowWindow (hWnd, nCmdShow);
while (GetMessage (&Message, 0, 0, 0))
     {
     TranslateMessage(&Message);
     DispatchMessage(&Message);
     }
return Message.wParam;
}

/****************************************************************/
/*              Window Procedure: WndProc                        */
/****************************************************************/

long FAR PASCAL WndProc (HWND hWnd, WORD iMessage, WORD wParam,
                LONG lParam)
{
switch (iMessage)
     {
     case WM_DESTROY:
          PostQuitMessage(0);
          return 0;
     default:
          return(DefWindowProc(hWnd, iMessage, wParam,
               lParam));
     }
}
```

As you can see from the size of the listings, a significant number of source code lines are required to generate even a fundamental window. The C source code file contains the `WinMain` and the `WndProc` functions. `WinMain`, which was explained earlier in this chapter, is the entry point for the application. `WndProc` is the window procedure for the window generated by the application. `WndProc` is responsible for processing the messages for the resulting window. A typical window procedure, such as in Listing 2.2, contains a `switch` statement. The actions of the window procedure are triggered by the receipt of certain messages. In Listing 2.2, `WndProc` monitors and provides actions for only one message, `WM_DESTROY`; however, most window procedures define actions for dozens of messages. When `WndProc` detects the `WM_DESTROY` message, the `PostQuitMessage` function is called and the window is terminated. All other messages sent to `WndProc` are handled by the default window procedure, `DefWndProc`. When working with window procedures, remember that only Windows calls `WndProc`; `WinMain` references `WndProc` but never calls `WndProc` directly.

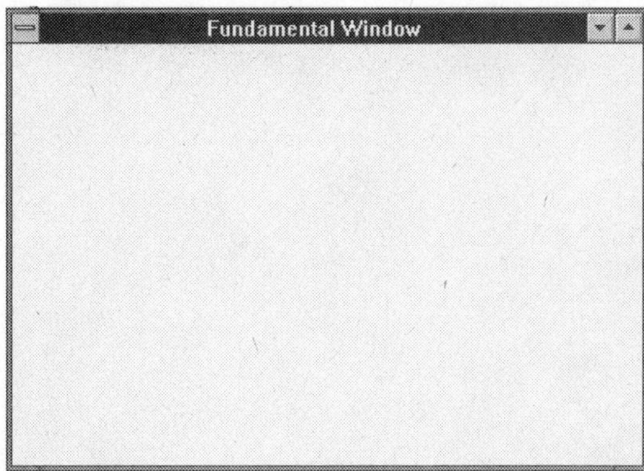

Figure 2.5. *The fundamental window.*

This example serves as the baseline for the remainder of the examples in this book.

3

The Graphics Device Interface (GDI)

The Windows Graphics Device Interface (GDI) is designed for device-independent graphics. Because many combinations of output and display devices can be part of a computer system, device-independent graphics enable you to program without being concerned about specific hardware configurations. Many MS-DOS software packages already include more than one executable file to meet different configuration requirements. For example, a software package may contain three executables: one for the Color Graphics Adapter (CGA), one for the Enhanced Graphics Adapter (EGA), and one for the Video Graphics Array (VGA).

Windows applications use the Graphics Device Interface and the Windows device drivers to support device-independent graphics. A device driver converts a general drawing command into the precise actions needed to implement the command on the specified output device. As long as the device driver for the output device is available to Windows, the programmer does not need to be overly concerned with the hardware configuration of the system. This chapter introduces the features and terminology of the Graphics Device Interface.

The Device Context

The device context is a set of attributes determining the location and appearance of GDI output for any device. The application cannot access the device context directly, but the application can use the device context's handle *indirectly* to access the device context and its attributes. A device context is created when the program requests the handle for a device context. The created device context contains default values for all of its attributes. Table 3.1 lists the default values for each of the device context attributes, any of which can be modified to meet the requirements of the application.

Table 3.1. The device context attributes.

Attribute	*Default*	*Related Function(s)*
Background color	White	`GetBkColor`, `SetBkColor`
Background mode	`OPAQUE`	`GetBkMode`, `SetBkMode`
Bitmap	none	`CreateBitmap`, `CreateBitmapIndirect`, `CreateCompatibleBitmap`, `SelectObject`
Brush	`WHITE_BRUSH`	`CreateBrushIndirect`, `CreateDIBPatternBrush`, `CreateHatchBrush`, `CreatePatternBrush`, `CreateSolidBrush`, `SelectObject`
Brush origin	(0,0)	`GetBrushOrg`, `SetBrushOrg`, `UnrealizeObject`
Clipping region	Display surface	`ExcludeClipRect`, `IntersectClipRect`, `OffsetClipRgn`, `SelectClipRgn`
Color palette	`DEFAULT_PALETTE`	`CreatePalette`, `RealizePalette`, `SelectPalette`
Current pen position	(0,0)	`GetCurrentPosition`, `LineTo`, `MoveTo`
Drawing mode	`R2_COPYPEN`	`GetROP2`, `SetROP2`
Font	`SYSTEM_FONT`	`CreateFont`, `CreateFontIndirect`, `SelectObject`
Intercharacter spacing	0	`GetTextCharacterExtra`, `SetTextCharacterExtra`
Mapping mode	`MM_TEXT`	`GetMapMode`, `SetMapMode`
Pen	`BLACK_PEN`	`CreatePen`, `CreatePenIndirect`, `SelectObject`
Polygon filling mode	`ALTERNATE`	`GetPolyFillMode`, `SetPolyFillMode`
Stretching mode	`BLACKONWHITE`	`SetStretchBltMode`
Text color	Black	`GetTextColor`, `SetTextColor`

Attribute	*Default*	*Related Function(s)*
Viewport extent	(1,1)	`GetViewportExt`, `SetMapMode`, `SetViewportExt`
Viewport origin	(0,0)	`GetViewportOrg`, `OffsetViewportOrg`, `SetViewportOrg`
Window extents	(1,1)	`GetWindowExt`, `SetMapMode`, `SetWindowExt`
Window origin	(0,0)	`GetWindowOrg`, `OffsetWindowOrg`, `SetWindowOrg`

The Mapping Mode

The *mapping mode* affects the appearance of output on the display device and defines the unit of measure used to transform logical units into device units. The mapping mode also defines the orientation of the device's x- and y-axes. The mapping modes defined by Windows are listed in Table 3.2.

Table 3.2. Windows mapping modes.

Mapping Mode	*Logical Unit*
`MM_ANISOTROPIC`	x and y are arbitrary units where x and y can be scaled independently
`MM_HIENGLISH`	.001 inch
`MM_HIMETRIC`	.01 mm
`MM_ISOTROPIC`	x and y are arbitrary units where x and y are scaled uniformly
`MM_LOENGLISH`	.01 inch
`MM_LOMETRIC`	.1 mm
`MM_TEXT`	Pixel
`MM_TWIPS`	1/1440 inch

The mapping mode you choose for your application is important. The `MM_TEXT` mapping mode is most commonly used and quite sufficient for most purposes. However, by using the `MM_TEXT` mode, which is based on the pixel, you may get surprising results. For example, a 100-pixel by 100-pixel image on a VGA screen does not have the same size or appearance as a 100-pixel by 100-pixel image on a CGA screen. Therefore, the results may not be what you desire. The various mapping

modes offer unique advantages and disadvantages, such as direct mapping to pixels, arbitrary scaling, and scaling by inches or millimeters. The requirements of the application indicate the best mapping mode to choose.

The Drawing Coordinates

Windows uses several coordinate systems, which are generally grouped under two classifications: device and logical.

There are three distinct *device* coordinate systems: the screen coordinate system, the whole-window coordinate system, and the client area coordinate system. These device coordinate systems express units of measurement in terms of pixels. Remember that pixels only change relative to video mode; units of measurement change relative to the device context selected as indicated in Table 3.1.

The *screen coordinate system* uses the entire screen. The upper-left corner of the screen is the origin of the coordinate system. The x-axis increases from left to right; the y-axis increases from top to bottom. Screen coordinates are generally used with functions that move objects relative to a physical location on the screen.

The *whole-window coordinate system* uses the entire physical size of a window including the window border. The upper-left corner of the window border is the origin of the coordinate system. The x-axis increases from left to right; the y-axis increases from top to bottom. Programmers might use the whole window system when they want to access the entire window to do something unusual like creating icons on the window's border—in other words, not very often.

The *client area coordinate system* is the most commonly used coordinate system. The client area is the working area of the window and excludes the window borders, the Menu bar, and the scroll bars. Because your program generally manipulates only the client area, the client area coordinate system is appropriate for most applications. The upper-left corner of the client area is the origin of the coordinate system. The x-axis increases from left to right; the y-axis increases from top to bottom.

The other grouping of coordinate systems is the *logical coordinate system*. The mapping mode specifies how the *logical* units specified in GDI functions are converted to device coordinates. Logical units are associated with a window, and device coordinates are associated with a viewport, which usually is the same as the client area. The logical units of a window are expressed in units specified by the mapping mode. Before an object can be drawn, Windows must translate these logical units to one of the device coordinate systems.

GDI Graphics and Points

The GDI is designed for graphic output and contains many functions for displaying graphics such as lines, arcs, and points. The most fundamental element in computer graphics is the point. Therefore, the point is a good subject for beginning this discussion of GDI graphics.

The GDI `SetPixel` function draws a point on the screen, which is the same as illuminating a pixel on the screen because the pixel is the most fundamental screen element. The point example in Listings 3.1 and 3.2 uses the `SetPixel` function to draw a series of alternating blue and red dots in the window's client area.

The point example builds on the fundamental window example from Chapter 2. The only changes made to the `WinMain` function for the point example are the changing of the window caption and the name of the window class. The point example's window procedure, `WndProc`, differs in one major way from the window procedure in the fundamental window example from Chapter 2.

`WndProc` for the point example adds to the capabilities of `WndProc` for the fundamental window example by defining actions for the Windows message `WM_PAINT`. The `WM_PAINT` message is sent to the window procedure when the window first is created and whenever the window is sized. The code that is nested to define the actions for the `WM_PAINT` message is executed whenever the window procedure receives the `WM_PAINT` message. As a result, dots are drawn in the client area of the window with the `SetPixel` function when the window is created and each time the window is sized. You can see the effects of responding to the `WM_PAINT` message by sizing the window created by the code in Listings 3.1 and 3.2. The window resulting from the code in Listings 3.1 and 3.2 is shown in Figure 3.1. Chapter 13 provides additional information on the `SetPixel` function. Chapter 14 provide additional information on the `WM_PAINT` message.

Note: This example, as well as the remaining examples in this chapter, use the `MM_ANISOTROPIC` mapping mode. The `MM_ANISOTROPIC` mode allows the x- and y-coordinates to be scaled independently. The `SetWindowExt` and `SetViewportExt` functions can be used to specify the units, orientation, and scaling of the axes.

As Chapter 2 mentioned, the Integrated Development Environment (IDE) and the Project Manager are used in all the examples of this book for code development. The following information describes the files used for the points example project. The project name is `WIN_PT`. The files that are included in the project are `WIN_PT.C` and `WIN_PT.DEF`.

Project Name:	`WIN_PT`
Files in Project:	`WIN_PT.C`
	`WIN_PT.DEF`

Listing 3.1. The definition file for the point drawing example.

```
NAME           WIN_PT
DESCRIPTION    'Point Example'
EXETYPE        WINDOWS
CODE           PRELOAD MOVEABLE
DATA           PRELOAD MOVEABLE MULTIPLE
HEAPSIZE       1024
STACKSIZE      5120
EXPORTS        WndProc
```

Listing 3.2. The C source file for the point drawing example.

```
#include <windows.h>
#include <stdlib.h>
#include <string.h>

long FAR PASCAL WndProc (HWND hWnd, WORD iMessage,
                WORD wParam, LONG lParam);

int PASCAL WinMain (HANDLE hInstance, HANDLE hPrevInstance,
              LPSTR lpszCmdParam, int nCmdShow)

{
HWND hWnd;
MSG Message;
WNDCLASS WndClass;

if (!hPrevInstance)
     {
     WndClass.cbClsExtra = 0;
     WndClass.cbWndExtra = 0;
     WndClass.hbrBackground = GetStockObject(WHITE_BRUSH);
     WndClass.hCursor =  LoadCursor(NULL, IDC_ARROW);
     WndClass.hIcon = LoadIcon (NULL, "END");
     WndClass.hInstance = hInstance;
     WndClass.lpfnWndProc = WndProc;
     WndClass.lpszClassName = "WIN_PT";
     WndClass.lpszMenuName = NULL;
     WndClass.style = CS_HREDRAW ¦ CS_VREDRAW;

     RegisterClass (&WndClass);
     }

hWnd = CreateWindow ("WIN_PT",           /* class name */
                    "Point Example",    /* Caption */
                    WS_OVERLAPPEDWINDOW,     /* Style */
```

```
                    CW_USEDEFAULT,       /* x position */
                    0,                   /* y position */
                    CW_USEDEFAULT,       /* cx - size */
                    0,                   /* cy - size */
                    NULL,                /* Parent window */
                    NULL,                /* Menu */
                    hInstance,           /* Program Instance */
                    NULL);               /* Parameters */

ShowWindow (hWnd, nCmdShow);
while (GetMessage (&Message, 0, 0, 0))
     {
     TranslateMessage(&Message);
     DispatchMessage(&Message);
     }
return Message.wParam;
}

/*************************************************************/
/*              Window Procedure: WndProc                    */
/*************************************************************/

long FAR PASCAL WndProc (HWND hWnd, WORD iMessage, WORD wParam,
                LONG lParam)
{
HDC hDC;
PAINTSTRUCT PtStr;
int x, y;

switch (iMessage)
     {
     case WM_PAINT:

          hDC = BeginPaint(hWnd, &PtStr);
          SetMapMode (hDC, MM_ANISOTROPIC);
          for (x=0; x<640; x=x+10)
               {
               for (y=0; y<480; y=y+10)
                 {
                 SetPixel (hDC,x,y,RGB(255,0,0));
                 SetPixel (hDC,x+5,y,RGB(0,0,255));
                 SetPixel (hDC,x,y+5,RGB(0,0,255));
                 SetPixel (hDC,x+5,y+5,RGB(255,0,0));
                 }
               }
          EndPaint(hWnd,&PtStr);
          return 0;
```

continues

Listing 3.2. continued

```
    case WM_DESTROY:

         PostQuitMessage(0);
         return 0;

    default:

         return(DefWindowProc(hWnd, iMessage, wParam,
              lParam));
    }
}
```

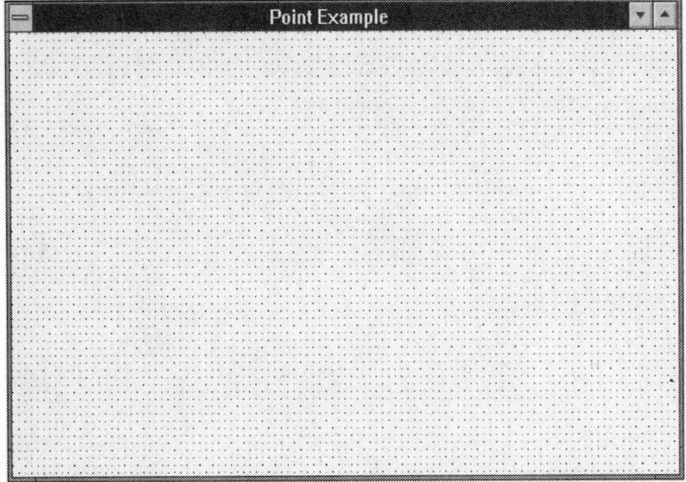

Figure 3.1. Point drawing example.

Drawing Lines

The GDI also provides functions for drawing lines. The functions `LineTo` and `Polyline` are provided to draw straight lines. The `Arc` function is provided to draw elliptical lines. The appearance of the lines drawn by these functions depends on the current pen and the drawing mode. These terms are described later in this chapter. For now, you should focus on how to use these functions.

The `LineTo` function is the most basic line drawing function. The `LineTo` function draws a line from the current pen position to the specified point. The `MoveTo` function often is used to move the pen position before the `LineTo` function is called.

The line drawing example in Listings 3.3 and 3.4 demonstrates the use of the `MoveTo` and `LineTo` functions to draw a series of red, green, and blue lines. This example is structured like the point drawing example presented previously in this chapter. In the line drawing example, however, the `MoveTo` and `LineTo` functions are used to create the lines for the example.

One major difference between the point example and the line drawing example is that the line drawing example defines and uses three colored pens. The `CreatePenIndirect` function is used to create a red, blue, and green logical pen. The `SelectObject` function is used to select one of the created pens prior to drawing a line. The `MoveTo` function is used to move the current pen position prior to each call to the `LineTo` function. When the `MoveTo` function is called, the pen is moved but no drawing takes place. When the `LineTo` function is called, a line is drawn using the currently selected pen. Figure 3.2 shows the window created by Listings 3.3 and 3.4.

The description of the project for the line drawing example follows:

Project Name: `WIN_LINE`
Files in Project: `WIN_LINE.C`
`WIN_LINE.DEF`

Listing 3.3. *The definition file for the line drawing example.*

```
NAME            WIN_LINE
DESCRIPTION     'Line Drawing Example'
EXETYPE         WINDOWS
CODE            PRELOAD MOVEABLE
DATA            PRELOAD MOVEABLE MULTIPLE
HEAPSIZE        1024
STACKSIZE       5120
EXPORTS         WndProc
```

Listing 3.4. *The C source file for the line drawing example.*

```
#include <windows.h>
#include <stdlib.h>
#include <string.h>

long FAR PASCAL WndProc (HWND hWnd, WORD iMessage,
                WORD wParam, LONG lParam);

int PASCAL WinMain (HANDLE hInstance, HANDLE hPrevInstance,
              LPSTR lpszCmdParam, int nCmdShow)

{
```

continues

Listing 3.4. continued

```
HWND hWnd;
MSG Message;
WNDCLASS WndClass;

if (!hPrevInstance)
     {
     WndClass.cbClsExtra = 0;
     WndClass.cbWndExtra = 0;
     WndClass.hbrBackground = GetStockObject(WHITE_BRUSH);
     WndClass.hCursor =  LoadCursor(NULL, IDC_ARROW);
     WndClass.hIcon = LoadIcon (NULL, "END");
     WndClass.hInstance = hInstance;
     WndClass.lpfnWndProc = WndProc;
     WndClass.lpszClassName = "WIN_LINE";
     WndClass.lpszMenuName = NULL;
     WndClass.style = CS_HREDRAW ¦ CS_VREDRAW;

     RegisterClass (&WndClass);
     }

hWnd = CreateWindow ("WIN_LINE",    /* class name */
                     "Line Drawing Example", /* Caption */
                     WS_OVERLAPPEDWINDOW,    /* Style */
                     CW_USEDEFAULT, /* x position */
                     0,             /* y position */
                     CW_USEDEFAULT, /* cx - size */
                     0,             /* cy - size */
                     NULL,          /* Parent window */
                     NULL,          /* Menu */
                     hInstance,     /* Program Instance */
                     NULL);         /* Parameters */

ShowWindow (hWnd, nCmdShow);
while (GetMessage (&Message, 0, 0, 0))
     {
     TranslateMessage(&Message);
     DispatchMessage(&Message);
     }
return Message.wParam;
}

/*****************************************************************/
/*                Window Procedure: WndProc                      */
/*****************************************************************/

long FAR PASCAL WndProc (HWND hWnd, WORD iMessage, WORD wParam,
                LONG lParam)
{
```

```
static LOGPEN lpBlue = {PS_SOLID, 1, 1, RGB(0,0,255)},
           lpGreen = {PS_SOLID, 1, 1, RGB(0,255,0)},
           lpRed = {PS_SOLID, 1, 1, RGB(255,0,0)};
HDC hDC;
HPEN hBluePen, hGreenPen, hRedPen;
PAINTSTRUCT PtStr;
short x;

switch (iMessage)
     {
     case WM_PAINT:

          hDC = BeginPaint(hWnd, &PtStr);
          hBluePen = CreatePenIndirect(&lpBlue);
          hGreenPen = CreatePenIndirect(&lpGreen);
          hRedPen = CreatePenIndirect(&lpRed);
          for (x=1; x<640; x=x+2)
               {
               SelectObject(hDC,hBluePen);
               MoveTo(hDC,x,100);
               LineTo(hDC,x,150);
               SelectObject(hDC,hGreenPen);
               MoveTo(hDC,x,150);
               LineTo(hDC,x,200);
               SelectObject(hDC,hRedPen);
               MoveTo(hDC,x,200);
               LineTo(hDC,x,250);
               }

          EndPaint(hWnd, &PtStr);
          DeleteObject(hBluePen);
          DeleteObject(hGreenPen);
          DeleteObject(hRedPen);
          return 0;

     case WM_DESTROY:

          PostQuitMessage(0);
          return 0;

     default:

          return(DefWindowProc(hWnd, iMessage, wParam,
               lParam));
     }
}
```

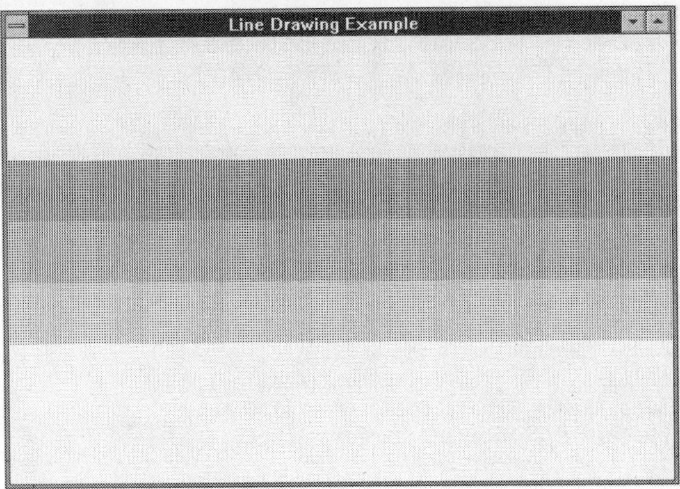

***Figure 3.2.** Line drawing example.*

The `Polyline` function enables you to connect an array of points with lines. The `Polyline` function often is more convenient to use than the `MoveTo` and `LineTo` functions because it enables you to express all the points in an array. The code structure shown in the line drawing example could be used for the `Polyline` function. The only changes to the code that would be necessary are the addition of a defined array containing the points to draw and a call to the `Polyline` function in place of the `MoveTo` and `LineTo` function calls.

The `Arc` function draws an elliptical arc. The arc resulting from this function is actually part of an underlying ellipse whose points are calculated but are not actually drawn. The underlying ellipse is specified by the coordinates in the parameters passed to the `Arc` function in X1, Y1, X2, and Y2 (see Chapter 13 concerning the `Arc` function). These parameters specify the corners of a rectangle that bind the underlying ellipse. The starting point of the ellipse is specified by two other parameters, X3 and Y3. The arc begins at the point where the line—beginning at center of the underlying ellipse and extending to the point specified in X3 and Y3—intersects the ellipse. The arc is then drawn in a counterclockwise direction until it reaches the point where the line—drawn between the center of the underlying ellipse and the point specified by two additional parameters, X4 and Y4—intersects the ellipse.

The arc drawing example in Listings 3.5 and 3.6 demonstrates the use of the `Arc` function to create an ellipse consisting of four colored line segments. This example is very similar to the previous line drawing example. The listing creates four colored pens by using the `CreatePenIndirect` function, selected with the `SelectObject` function, and uses the pens to draw four different colored arcs that join to form an ellipse. The resulting ellipse contains one red, green, blue, and black elliptical line. Figure 3.3 shows the window resulting from this example.

The description of the project for the arc drawing example follows:

Project Name:	`WIN_ARC`
Files in Project:	`WIN_ARC.C`
	`WIN_ARC.DEF`

Listing 3.5. *The definition file for the arc drawing example.*

```
NAME            WIN_ARC
DESCRIPTION     'Arc Drawing Example'
EXETYPE         WINDOWS
CODE            PRELOAD MOVEABLE
DATA            PRELOAD MOVEABLE MULTIPLE
HEAPSIZE        1024
STACKSIZE       5120
EXPORTS         WndProc
```

Listing 3.6. *The C source file for the arc drawing example.*

```
#include <windows.h>
#include <stdlib.h>
#include <string.h>

long FAR PASCAL WndProc (HWND hWnd, WORD iMessage,
                WORD wParam, LONG lParam);

int PASCAL WinMain (HANDLE hInstance, HANDLE hPrevInstance,
              LPSTR lpszCmdParam, int nCmdShow)

{
HWND hWnd;
MSG Message;
WNDCLASS WndClass;

if (!hPrevInstance)
     {
     WndClass.cbClsExtra = 0;
```

continues

Listing 3.6. continued

```
     WndClass.cbWndExtra = 0;
     WndClass.hbrBackground = GetStockObject(WHITE_BRUSH);
     WndClass.hCursor =  LoadCursor(NULL, IDC_ARROW);
     WndClass.hIcon = LoadIcon (NULL, "END");
     WndClass.hInstance = hInstance;
     WndClass.lpfnWndProc = WndProc;
     WndClass.lpszClassName = "WIN_ARC";
     WndClass.lpszMenuName = NULL;
     WndClass.style = CS_HREDRAW ¦ CS_VREDRAW;

     RegisterClass (&WndClass);
     }

hWnd = CreateWindow ("WIN_ARC",        /* class name */
          "Arc Drawing Example",       /* Caption */
          WS_OVERLAPPEDWINDOW,         /* Style */
          CW_USEDEFAULT,               /* x position */
          0,                           /* y position */
          CW_USEDEFAULT,               /* cx - size */
          0,                           /* cy - size */
          NULL,                        /* Parent window */
          NULL,                        /* Menu */
          hInstance,                   /* Program Instance */
          NULL);                       /* Parameters */

ShowWindow (hWnd, nCmdShow);
while (GetMessage (&Message, 0, 0, 0))
     {
     TranslateMessage(&Message);
     DispatchMessage(&Message);
     }
return Message.wParam;
}

/*****************************************************************/
/*               Window Procedure: WndProc                      */
/*****************************************************************/

long FAR PASCAL WndProc (HWND hWnd, WORD iMessage, WORD wParam,
                  LONG lParam)
{
static LOGPEN lpBlue = {PS_SOLID, 1, 1, RGB(0,0,255)},
           lpGreen = {PS_SOLID, 1, 1, RGB(0,255,0)},
           lpRed = {PS_SOLID, 1, 1, RGB(255,0,0)},
```

```
            lpBlack = {PS_SOLID, 1, 1, RGB(0,0,0)};
HDC hDC;
HPEN hBluePen, hGreenPen, hRedPen, hBlackPen;
PAINTSTRUCT PtStr;

switch (iMessage)
     {
     case WM_PAINT:

          hDC = BeginPaint(hWnd, &PtStr);
          hBluePen = CreatePenIndirect(&lpBlue);
          hGreenPen = CreatePenIndirect(&lpGreen);
          hRedPen = CreatePenIndirect(&lpRed);
          hBlackPen = CreatePenIndirect(&lpBlack);

          SelectObject(hDC,hBluePen);
          Arc(hDC,50,50,200,200,200,50,50,50);

          SelectObject(hDC,hGreenPen);
          Arc(hDC,50,50,200,200,50,50,50,200);

          SelectObject(hDC,hRedPen);
          Arc(hDC,50,50,200,200,50,200,200,200);

          SelectObject(hDC,hBlackPen);
          Arc(hDC,50,50,200,200,200,200,200,50);

          EndPaint(hWnd, &PtStr);
          DeleteObject(hBluePen);
          DeleteObject(hGreenPen);
          DeleteObject(hRedPen);
          DeleteObject(hBlackPen);
          return 0;

     case WM_DESTROY:

          PostQuitMessage(0);
          return 0;

     default:

          return(DefWindowProc(hWnd, iMessage, wParam,
               lParam));
     }
}
```

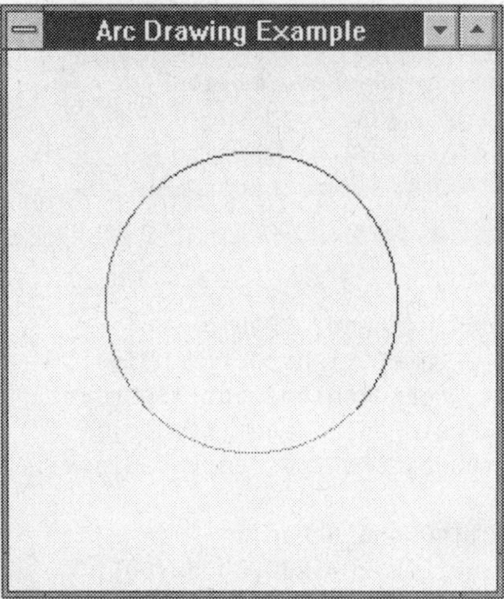

Figure 3.3. *Arc drawing example.*

Chapter 13 provides additional information on the `LineTo`, `MoveTo`, `Arc`, and `Polyline` functions.

Pens

The line drawing functions, as well as some other functions, use the *pen*, which specifies the color, width, and style of the line to be drawn. By default, the pen draws a solid black line that is one pixel wide. You can select predefined pens—called *stock pens*—by using the `GetStockObject` function, or you can create your own pens by using the `CreatePen` or `CreatePenIndirect` functions. Table 3.3 lists the stock pens that you can select with the `GetStockObject` function.

Table 3.3. *Stock pens.*

Pen	*Meaning*
`BLACK_PEN`	Black pen
`NULL_PEN`	Null pen (nothing is drawn)
`WHITE_PEN`	White pen

The CreatePen and CreatePenIndirect functions enable you to create a pen with a specified color, width, and style. You can specify the color of the pen by using the RGB macro, which enables you to specify the mix of red, green, and blue intensities for the color (see Chapter 13 for more information on the RGB macro). The pen width is specified in logical units. You can select the style of the pen from one of the values listed in Table 3.4 and defined in windows.h.

Table 3.4. Pen styles.

Style	*Value*
PS_SOLID	0
PS_DASH	1
PS_DOT	2
PS_DASHDOT	3
PS_DASHDOTDOT	4
PS_NULL	5
PS_INSIDEFRAME	6

The previous examples in this chapter used the CreatePenIndirect function to create the pens used for drawing lines. You should review these previous examples to see how pens are created and used. Chapter 13 provides additional information on the GetStockObject, CreatePen, and CreatePenIndirect functions.

Drawing Modes

The *drawing mode* affects the appearance of lines. It defines the way the color of the pen is combined with the color that already exists at the pen location. This combination of the pixel patterns of the pen and destination is called a *binary raster operation*, or ROP2.

The default drawing mode is R2_COPYPEN, which behaves as you might expect a pen to behave. The color of the pen is copied "as is" onto the drawing surface. For most purposes, this mode is sufficient. However, you often can benefit from using other modes to achieve certain effects. For example, you may need to use another mode whenever you require the same pen to draw black on a white background and white on a black background. The various drawing modes, listed in Table 3.5, provide numerous line drawing combinations, such as this one just described.

Table 3.5. Drawing modes.

Mode	*Pixel Color*
R2_BLACK	Black
R2_COPYPEN	The pen color
R2_MASKNOTPEN	Combination of the common colors of the display and the inverse of the pen
R2_MASKPEN	Combination of the common colors of the pen and the display
R2_MASKPENNOT	Combination of the common colors of the pen and the inverse of the display color
R2_MERGENOTPEN	Combination of the display color and the inverse of the pen color
R2_MERGEPEN	Combination of the pen and display colors
R2_MERGEPENNOT	Combination of the pen color and inverse of display color
R2_NOP	Not changed
R2_NOT	Inverse of display color
R2_NOTCOPYPEN	Inverse of pen color
R2_NOTMASKPEN	Inverse of R2_MASKPEN
R2_NOTMERGEPEN	Inverse of R2_MERGEPEN
R2_NOTXORPEN	Inverse of R2_XORPEN color
R2_WHITE	White
R2_XORPEN	Combination of the colors in the pen and in the display but not both

The GetROP2 and SetROP2 functions retrieve and set the drawing mode, respectively. Chapter 13 provides additional information on these functions.

Creating Filled Areas

Windows creates filled figures by first drawing the border of the figure using the current pen and then filling in the figure with the current brush. The procedures for drawing and filling the figure are explained later in this section. Right now you should focus on the functions used to create filled figures (see Table 3.6). Chapter 13 provides full reference information for each of the functions listed in Table 3.6.

Table 3.6. Functions for drawing filled figures.

Function	*Figure*
`Chord`	Chord
`DrawFocusRect`	Rectangle that indicates focus (which represents the primary selection)
`Ellipse`	Ellipse
`Pie`	Pie
`Polygon`	Polygon
`PolyPolygon`	Series of closed polygons
`Rectangle`	Rectangle
`RoundRect`	Rounded rectangle

Drawing the Borders

The filled figures example in Listings 3.7 and 3.8 demonstrates the `Pie`, `Ellipse`, `Rectangle`, `Chord`, and `RoundRect` functions. The code structure for this example follows the code structure from the previous examples in this chapter (the line drawing example, arc drawing example, and so on). In this example, a pen and brush are selected using stock objects. The `GetStockObject` function is used to select the `BLACK_PEN` object as the pen and `DKGRAY_BRUSH` object as the brush. The `Pie`, `Ellipse`, `Rectangle`, `Chord`, and `RoundRect` functions are then called to draw the filled figures using the specified pen and brush. Figure 3.4 shows the window resulting from this example.

The description of the project for the filled figures example follows:

Project Name: `WIN_FIGS`
Files in Project: `WIN_FIGS.C`
`WIN_FIGS.DEF`

Listing 3.7. The definition file for the filled figures example.

```
NAME          WIN_FIGS
DESCRIPTION   'Filled Figures Example'
EXETYPE       WINDOWS
CODE          PRELOAD MOVEABLE
DATA          PRELOAD MOVEABLE MULTIPLE
HEAPSIZE      1024
STACKSIZE     5120
EXPORTS       WndProc
```

Listing 3.8. The C source file for the filled figures example.

```
#include <windows.h>
#include <stdlib.h>
#include <string.h>

long FAR PASCAL WndProc (HWND hWnd, WORD iMessage,
                WORD wParam, LONG lParam);

int PASCAL WinMain (HANDLE hInstance, HANDLE hPrevInstance,
              LPSTR lpszCmdParam, int nCmdShow)

{
HWND hWnd;
MSG Message;
WNDCLASS WndClass;

if (!hPrevInstance)
     {
     WndClass.cbClsExtra = 0;
     WndClass.cbWndExtra = 0;
     WndClass.hbrBackground = GetStockObject(WHITE_BRUSH);
     WndClass.hCursor =  LoadCursor(NULL, IDC_ARROW);
     WndClass.hIcon = LoadIcon (NULL, "END");
     WndClass.hInstance = hInstance;
     WndClass.lpfnWndProc = WndProc;
     WndClass.lpszClassName = "WIN_FIGS";
     WndClass.lpszMenuName = NULL;
     WndClass.style = CS_HREDRAW ¦ CS_VREDRAW;

     RegisterClass (&WndClass);
     }

hWnd = CreateWindow ("WIN_FIGS",     /* class name */
          "Filled Figures Example", /* Caption */
          WS_OVERLAPPEDWINDOW,      /* Style */
          CW_USEDEFAULT,            /* x position */
          0,                        /* y position */
          CW_USEDEFAULT,            /* cx - size */
          0,                        /* cy - size */
          NULL,                     /* Parent window */
          NULL,                     /* Menu */
          hInstance,                /* Program Instance */
          NULL);                    /* Parameters */

ShowWindow (hWnd, nCmdShow);
while (GetMessage (&Message, 0, 0, 0))
     {
     TranslateMessage(&Message);
     DispatchMessage(&Message);
     }
```

```
return Message.wParam;
}

/***************************************************************/
/*              Window Procedure: WndProc                      */
/***************************************************************/

long FAR PASCAL WndProc (HWND hWnd, WORD iMessage, WORD wParam,
                LONG lParam)
{
HDC hDC;
HBRUSH hBrush;
HPEN hPen;
PAINTSTRUCT PtStr;

switch (iMessage)
     {
     case WM_PAINT:

          hDC = BeginPaint (hWnd,&PtStr);

          SetMapMode(hDC, MM_ANISOTROPIC);

          hPen = GetStockObject(BLACK_PEN);
          hBrush = GetStockObject(DKGRAY_BRUSH);
          SelectObject(hDC,hBrush);
          SelectObject(hDC,hPen);

          Rectangle (hDC,50,50,100,100);
          RoundRect (hDC,50,150,100,200,15,15);
          Ellipse (hDC,150,50,200,100);
          Chord (hDC,150,150,200,200,150,150,200,200);
          Pie (hDC,250,50,300,100,250,50,300,50);

          EndPaint(hWnd,&PtStr);
          return 0;

     case WM_DESTROY:

          PostQuitMessage(0);
          return 0;

      default:

           return(DefWindowProc(hWnd, iMessage, wParam,
               lParam));
     }
}
```

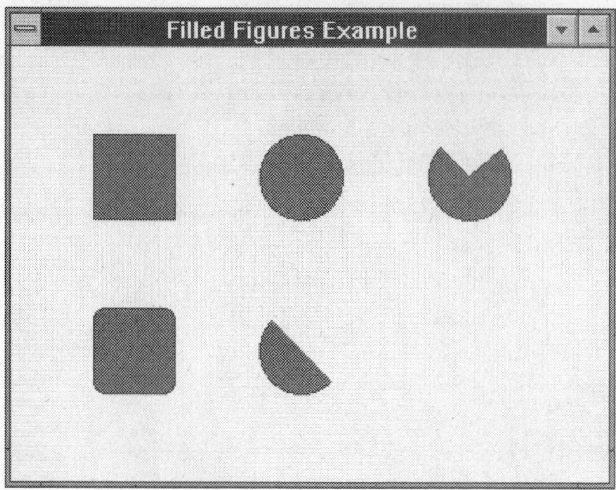

Figure 3.4. *Filled figures example.*

Filling the Area

The figures created by the functions in Table 3.6 are filled with the current brush. You can choose the brush in two ways:

- Select a predefined stock brush by using the `GetStockObject` function
- Create a brush by using the `CreateSolidBrush`, `CreateHatchBrush`, `CreatePatternBrush`, or `CreateBrushIndirect` functions

If you select a predefined stock brush by using the `GetStockObject` function, seven brushes are available. Table 3.7 lists these brushes. Listings 3.7 and 3.8 use the `GetStockObject` function to select the dark gray stock brush. These listings also demonstrate the use of the selected stock brush for filling a figure.

Table 3.7. Stock brushes.

Brush	*Meaning*
`BLACK_BRUSH`	Black brush
`DKGRAY_BRUSH`	Dark gray brush
`GRAY_BRUSH`	Gray brush
`HOLLOW_BRUSH`	Hollow brush (which draws borders but does not fill them)
`LTGRAY_BRUSH`	Light gray brush
`NULL_BRUSH`	Null brush
`WHITE_BRUSH`	White brush

You can create your own brush with the `CreateSolidBrush`, `CreateHatchBrush`, `CreatePatternBrush`, or `CreateBrushIndirect` functions. Chapter 13 provides reference information on the use of each of these functions. A brush that you create is used just like a stock brush. The fill example in Listings 3.9 and 3.10 demonstrates how to create and select brushes of your own design. The fill example follows the same format as the previous examples in this chapter. The fill example, however, differs from these previous examples because four hatched brushes are created and used. The `CreateHatchBrush` function is used to create four brushes, each consisting of a differect fill pattern and fill color. In turn, each brush is selected and a rectangle is drawn using the current pen and filled using the current brush. Like the previous examples, the client area (and the filled figures) is redrawn each time the window is sized. Figure 3.5 shows the window resulting from the listings.

The description of the project for the fill example follows:

Project Name:	`WIN_FILL`
Files in Project:	`WIN_FILL.C`
	`WIN_FILL.DEF`

Listing 3.9. The definition file for the fill example.

```
NAME            WIN_FILL
DESCRIPTION     'Fill Example'
EXETYPE         WINDOWS
CODE            PRELOAD MOVEABLE
DATA            PRELOAD MOVEABLE MULTIPLE
HEAPSIZE        1024
STACKSIZE       5120
EXPORTS         WndProc
```

Listing 3.10. The C source file for the fill example.

```
#include <windows.h>
#include <stdlib.h>
#include <string.h>

long FAR PASCAL WndProc (HWND hWnd, WORD iMessage,
                WORD wParam, LONG lParam);

int PASCAL WinMain (HANDLE hInstance, HANDLE hPrevInstance,
              LPSTR lpszCmdParam, int nCmdShow)

{
HWND hWnd;
MSG Message;
WNDCLASS WndClass;

if (!hPrevInstance)
     {
     WndClass.cbClsExtra = 0;
     WndClass.cbWndExtra = 0;
     WndClass.hbrBackground = GetStockObject(WHITE_BRUSH);
     WndClass.hCursor =  LoadCursor(NULL, IDC_ARROW);
     WndClass.hIcon = LoadIcon (NULL, "END");
     WndClass.hInstance = hInstance;
     WndClass.lpfnWndProc = WndProc;
     WndClass.lpszClassName = "WIN_FILL";
     WndClass.lpszMenuName = NULL;
     WndClass.style = CS_HREDRAW ¦ CS_VREDRAW;

     RegisterClass (&WndClass);
     }

hWnd = CreateWindow ("WIN_FILL",        /* class name */
          "Fill Example",               /* Caption */
          WS_OVERLAPPEDWINDOW,          /* Style */
          CW_USEDEFAULT,                /* x position */
          0,                            /* y position */
          CW_USEDEFAULT,                /* cx - size */
          0,                            /* cy - size */
          NULL,                         /* Parent window */
          NULL,                         /* Menu */
          hInstance,                    /* Program Instance */
          NULL);                        /* Parameters */

ShowWindow (hWnd, nCmdShow);
while (GetMessage (&Message, 0, 0, 0))
     {
     TranslateMessage(&Message);
```

```
    DispatchMessage(&Message);
    }
return Message.wParam;
}

/***************************************************************/
/*              Window Procedure: WndProc                      */
/***************************************************************/

long FAR PASCAL WndProc (HWND hWnd, WORD iMessage, WORD wParam,
                LONG lParam)
{

switch (iMessage)
    {
    static HBRUSH hBrush[4];
    static LOGPEN lpBlack = {PS_SOLID,1,1,RGB(0,0,0)};
    HPEN hBlackPen;
    HDC hDC;
    PAINTSTRUCT PtStr;


    case WM_PAINT:

        hBlackPen = CreatePenIndirect(&lpBlack);

        hBrush[0] = CreateHatchBrush(HS_HORIZONTAL,
                 RGB(0,0,0));
        hBrush[1] = CreateHatchBrush(HS_VERTICAL,
                 RGB(255,0,0));
        hBrush[2] = CreateHatchBrush(HS_FDIAGONAL,
                 RGB(0,255,0));
        hBrush[3] = CreateHatchBrush(HS_BDIAGONAL,
                 RGB(0,0,255));

        hDC = BeginPaint(hWnd, &PtStr);

        SelectObject(hDC, hBlackPen);
        SelectObject(hDC, hBrush[0]);
        Rectangle(hDC,10,10,100,200);

        SelectObject(hDC, hBlackPen);
        SelectObject(hDC, hBrush[1]);
        Rectangle(hDC,110,10,200,200);

        SelectObject(hDC, hBlackPen);
        SelectObject(hDC, hBrush[2]);
        Rectangle(hDC,210,10,300,200);
```

continues

Listing 3.10. continued

```
        SelectObject(hDC, hBlackPen);
        SelectObject(hDC, hBrush[3]);
        Rectangle(hDC,310,10,400,200);

        EndPaint(hWnd, &PtStr);

        DeleteObject(hBlackPen);
        DeleteObject(hBrush[0]);
        DeleteObject(hBrush[1]);
        DeleteObject(hBrush[2]);
        DeleteObject(hBrush[3]);

        return 0;

    case WM_DESTROY:

        PostQuitMessage(0);
        return 0;

    default:

        return(DefWindowProc(hWnd, iMessage, wParam,
            lParam));
    }
}
```

The use of brushes is not limited to the filled figures listed in Table 3.6. You can use the `FloodFill`, `FillRect`, and `FillRgn` functions to fill various shapes and types of figures. Chapter 13 provides reference information on the `FloodFill`, `FillRect`, and `FillRgn` functions.

Text and Fonts

Windows often uses the Graphics Device Interface for text output. If you have programmed MS-DOS applications, you may think immediately that "graphics" in the Graphics Device Interface and "text" in text output do not mix. MS-DOS applications use two primary modes of operation for the video hardware: graphics and text. *Graphics* mode displays device dependent graphics objects; *text* mode displays text characters. With Windows you don't have this distinction between text and graphics. *Everything* in Windows, in a sense, is treated like a graphics object.

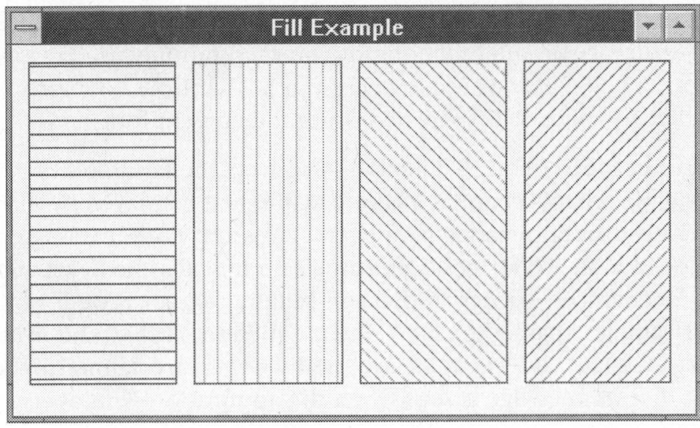

Figure 3.5. *Fill example.*

Text characters in Windows are drawn according to a selected font. A *font* contains specific information on the shape and appearance of each character, number, and punctuation mark in a character set. By using defined device-independent font sets, Windows can maintain its device independence while providing the benefits of *what-you-see-is-what-you-get* (WYSIWYG), which means that the text drawn on-screen generally looks the same as it does when drawn by other output devices such as printers or plotters.

Text Drawing Functions

Windows provides several functions for displaying text. These functions are listed in Table 3.8.

Table 3.8. *Text drawing functions.*

Function	*Meaning*
`DrawText`	Draws formatted text in the specified rectangle
`ExtTextOut`	Writes a character string, using the current font, inside a rectangular region
`GrayString`	Writes a string using gray text
`TabbedTextOut`	Writes a character string with expanded tabs
`TextOut`	Writes a character string using the current font

Although all of the functions listed in Table 3.8 can be used to display text, `TextOut` and `TabbedTextOut`, both GDI functions, are most commonly used in an application for text output. The `TextOut` example in Listings 3.11 and 3.12 demonstrates how to use the `TextOut` function to display text using the current font.

The `TextOut` example in Listing 3.11 and 3.12 follows the same code structure as the previous examples of this chapter. Therefore, the text displayed by this example is redrawn each time the application window receives a `WM_PAINT` message. In response to the receipt of a `WM_PAINT` message, this example calls the `TextOut` function to display the 30 character strings in the text buffer, `textbuf`. You'll notice that the positional parameters passed to the `TextOut` function, `nXChar` and `nYChar`, are not defined in the `WM_PAINT` code; instead, `nXChar` and `nYChar` are defined in the `WM_CREATE` code. The `WM_CREATE` message is sent when the application window is created. It is often a good idea to define initial values for the application's variables when responding the `WM_CREATE` message. Figure 3.6 shows the window resulting from the `TextOut` example.

The description of the project for the `TextOut` example follows:

Project Name:	`WIN_TXT`
Files in Project:	`WIN_TXT.C`
	`WIN_TXT.DEF`

Listing 3.11. ***The definition file for the*** `TextOut` ***example.***

```
NAME            WIN_TXT
DESCRIPTION     'TextOut Example'
EXETYPE         WINDOWS
CODE            PRELOAD MOVEABLE
DATA            PRELOAD MOVEABLE MULTIPLE
HEAPSIZE        1024
STACKSIZE       5120
EXPORTS         WndProc
```

Listing 3.12. ***The C source file for the*** `TextOut` ***example.***

```
#include <windows.h>
#include <stdlib.h>
#include <string.h>

long FAR PASCAL WndProc (HWND hWnd, WORD iMessage,
                WORD wParam, LONG lParam);

int PASCAL WinMain (HANDLE hInstance, HANDLE hPrevInstance,
              LPSTR lpszCmdParam, int nCmdShow)
```

```
{
HWND hWnd;
MSG Message;
WNDCLASS WndClass;

if (!hPrevInstance)
      {
      WndClass.cbClsExtra = 0;
      WndClass.cbWndExtra = 0;
      WndClass.hbrBackground = GetStockObject(WHITE_BRUSH);
      WndClass.hCursor =  LoadCursor(NULL, IDC_ARROW);
      WndClass.hIcon = LoadIcon (NULL, "END");
      WndClass.hInstance = hInstance;
      WndClass.lpfnWndProc = WndProc;
      WndClass.lpszClassName = "WIN_TXT";
      WndClass.lpszMenuName = NULL;
      WndClass.style = CS_HREDRAW ¦ CS_VREDRAW;

      RegisterClass (&WndClass);
      }

hWnd = CreateWindow ("WIN_TXT",        /* class name */
          "TextOut Example",           /* Caption */
          WS_OVERLAPPEDWINDOW,         /* Style */
          CW_USEDEFAULT,               /* x position */
          0,                           /* y position */
          CW_USEDEFAULT,               /* cx - size */
          0,                           /* cy - size */
          NULL,                        /* Parent window */
          NULL,                        /* Menu */
          hInstance,                   /* Program Instance */
          NULL);                       /* Parameters */

ShowWindow (hWnd, nCmdShow);
while (GetMessage (&Message, 0, 0, 0))
      {
      TranslateMessage(&Message);
      DispatchMessage(&Message);
      }
return Message.wParam;
}

/****************************************************************/
/*               Window Procedure: WndProc                      */
/****************************************************************/

long FAR PASCAL WndProc (HWND hWnd, WORD iMessage, WORD wParam,
                LONG lParam)
{
```

continues

Listing 3.12. continued

```
static short nXChar, nCaps, nYChar;
HDC hDC;
short x;
PAINTSTRUCT PtStr;
TEXTMETRIC tm;
short LnCount = 30;
static char *textbuf[] =
      {"One",
      "Two",
      "Three",
      "Four",
      "Five",
      "Six",
      "Seven",
      "Eight",
      "Nine",
      "Ten",
      "Eleven",
      "Twelve",
      "Thirteen",
      "Fourteen",
      "Fifteen",
      "Sixteen",
      "Seventeen",
      "Eighteen",
      "Nineteen",
      "Twenty",
      "Twenty-one",
      "Twenty-two",
      "Twenty-three",
      "Twenty-four",
      "Twenty-five",
      "Twenty-six",
      "Twenty-seven",
      "Twenty-eight",
      "Twenty-nine",
      "Thirty"};

switch (iMessage)
      {

      case WM_CREATE:

            hDC = GetDC(hWnd);

            GetTextMetrics(hDC,&tm);
            nXChar = tm.tmAveCharWidth;
            nYChar = tm.tmHeight + tm.tmExternalLeading;
```

```
            nCaps = (tm.tmPitchAndFamily & 1 ?3 : 2) *
                 nXChar/2;

            ReleaseDC(hWnd, hDC);
            return 0;

       case WM_PAINT:

            hDC = BeginPaint(hWnd, &PtStr);

            for (x=0; x<LnCount; x=x+1)
                 {
                 TextOut(hDC,nXChar,nYChar * (1+x),
                   textbuf[x],lstrlen(textbuf[x]));
                 }

            EndPaint(hWnd, &PtStr);
            return 0;


       case WM_DESTROY:

            PostQuitMessage(0);
            return 0;

       default:

            return(DefWindowProc(hWnd, iMessage, wParam,
                 lParam));
       }
}
```

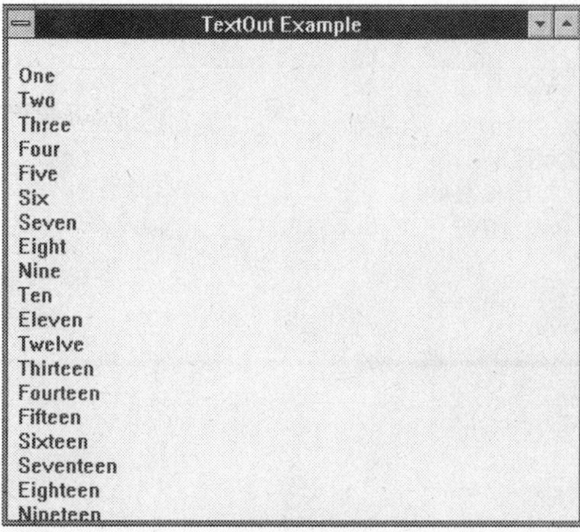

Figure 3.6. *Text output using* `TextOut`.

As Figure 3.6 shows, the example in Listings 3.11 and 3.12 has some limitations. The example displays 30 lines of text; however, not all of these lines can be seen. Because the window has no scroll bar, you cannot view the portion of the text that extends beyond the borders of the window—which is a serious limitation. Therefore, an example that uses both vertical and horizontal scroll bars is presented later in the chapter. For now, however, you need to focus on another method for sending text to a device.

The `TabbedTextOut` example in Listings 3.13 and 3.14 demonstrates how to use the `TabbedTextOut` function for displaying text in the current font and with extended tabs. The `TabbedTextOut` example is almost identical to the `TextOut` example demonstrated previously in this chapter. There are, however, two major differences: the use of the `TabbedTextOut` function and the addition of a tab indicator (`\t`) to the text buffer.

If you compare the code in Listings 3.13 and 3.14 (the `TabbedTextOut` example) to the code in Listings 3.11 and 3.12 (the `TextOut` example), you will notice that the text buffer defined for the `TabbedTextOut` example differs from the text buffer defined for the `TextOut` example. The difference in these text buffers is the addition of tab indicators (`\t`) and a column of additional text to the buffer for the `TabbedTextOut` example. The tab indicator (`\t`) tells the `TabbedTextOut` function to tab over before displaying the text following the indicator. Figure 3.7 shows the window resulting from the `TabbedTextOut` example. Once again, the resulting window has no scroll bars and some of the text sent to the window can't be seen.

The description of the project for the `TabbedTextOut` example follows:

Project Name:	`WIN_TTXT`
Files in Project:	`WIN_TTXT.C`
	`WIN_TTXT.DEF`

Listing 3.13. *The definition file for the* `TabbedTextOut` *example.*

```
NAME            WIN_TTXT
DESCRIPTION     'TabbedTextOut Example'
EXETYPE         WINDOWS
CODE            PRELOAD MOVEABLE
DATA            PRELOAD MOVEABLE MULTIPLE
HEAPSIZE        1024
STACKSIZE       5120
EXPORTS         WndProc
```

Listing 3.14. The C source file for the `TabbedTextOut` example.

```
#include <windows.h>
#include <stdlib.h>
#include <string.h>

long FAR PASCAL WndProc (HWND hWnd, WORD iMessage,
                WORD wParam, LONG lParam);

int PASCAL WinMain (HANDLE hInstance, HANDLE hPrevInstance,
              LPSTR lpszCmdParam, int nCmdShow)

{
HWND hWnd;
MSG Message;
WNDCLASS WndClass;

if (!hPrevInstance)
     {
     WndClass.cbClsExtra = 0;
     WndClass.cbWndExtra = 0;
     WndClass.hbrBackground = GetStockObject(WHITE_BRUSH);
     WndClass.hCursor =  LoadCursor(NULL, IDC_ARROW);
     WndClass.hIcon = LoadIcon (NULL, "END");
     WndClass.hInstance = hInstance;
     WndClass.lpfnWndProc = WndProc;
     WndClass.lpszClassName = "WIN_TTXT";
     WndClass.lpszMenuName = NULL;
     WndClass.style = CS_HREDRAW | CS_VREDRAW;

     RegisterClass (&WndClass);
     }

hWnd = CreateWindow ("WIN_TTXT",        /* class name */
          "TabbedTextOut Example",   /* Caption */
          WS_OVERLAPPEDWINDOW,       /* Style */
          CW_USEDEFAULT,             /* x position */
          0,                         /* y position */
          CW_USEDEFAULT,             /* cx - size */
          0,                         /* cy - size */
          NULL,                      /* Parent window */
          NULL,                      /* Menu */
          hInstance,                 /* Program Instance */
          NULL);                     /* Parameters */

ShowWindow (hWnd, nCmdShow);
```

continues

Listing 3.14. continued

```
while (GetMessage (&Message, 0, 0, 0))
     {
     TranslateMessage(&Message);
     DispatchMessage(&Message);
     }
return Message.wParam;
}

/****************************************************************/
/*               Window Procedure: WndProc                      */
/****************************************************************/

long FAR PASCAL WndProc (HWND hWnd, WORD iMessage, WORD wParam,
                LONG lParam)
{
int nXText, nYText, nHeight, nTab;
HDC hDC;
short x;
DWORD dwExt;
PAINTSTRUCT PtStr;
short LnCount = 30;
static char *textbuf[] =
     {"One \t1",
     "Two \t2",
     "Three \t3",
     "Four \t4",
     "Five \t5",
     "Six \t6",
     "Seven \t7",
     "Eight \t8",
     "Nine \t9",
     "Ten \t10",
     "Eleven \t11",
     "Twelve \t12",
     "Thirteen \t13",
     "Fourteen \t14",
     "Fifteen \t15",
     "Sixteen \t16",
     "Seventeen \t17",
     "Eighteen \t18",
     "Nineteen \t19",
     "Twenty \t20",
     "Twenty-one \t21",
     "Twenty-two \t22",
     "Twenty-three \t23",
```

```
        "Twenty-four \t24",
        "Twenty-five \t25",
        "Twenty-six \t26",
        "Twenty-seven \t27",
        "Twenty-eight \t28",
        "Twenty-nine \t29",
        "Thirty \t30"};

switch (iMessage)
     {

     case WM_PAINT:

          hDC = BeginPaint(hWnd, &PtStr);

          dwExt = GetTextExtent(hDC,"S",1);
          nHeight = HIWORD(dwExt);
          nYText = nHeight;
          nXText = LOWORD(dwExt);
          nTab = 25 * LOWORD(dwExt);
          for (x=0; x<LnCount; x=x+1)
               {
               TabbedTextOut(hDC,nXText,nYText,
                 textbuf[x],lstrlen(textbuf[x]),1,
                 &nTab, nXText);
               nYText = nYText + nHeight;
               }

          EndPaint(hWnd, &PtStr);
          return 0;


     case WM_DESTROY:

          PostQuitMessage(0);
          return 0;

     default:

          return(DefWindowProc(hWnd, iMessage, wParam,
               lParam));
     }
}
```

TabbedTextOut Example

One	1
Two	2
Three	3
Four	4
Five	5
Six	6
Seven	7
Eight	8
Nine	9
Ten	10
Eleven	11
Twelve	12
Thirteen	13
Fourteen	14
Fifteen	15
Sixteen	16
Seventeen	17
Eighteen	18
Nineteen	19
Twenty	20
Twenty-one	21

Figure 3.7. *Text output using* `TabbedTextOut`.

The remaining functions in Table 3.8 can generate results similar to those produced by the preceding two examples. Chapter 13 provides reference information on each text output function listed in Table 3.8.

Device Context Attributes for Text

As was mentioned previously in this chapter, the device context is a set of attributes that determine the location and appearance of GDI output for a device. The application cannot access the device context directly; however, the application can use the handle of the device context to indirectly access the device context and its attributes. A device context is created when the program requests the handle for a device context. The created device context contains default values for all of its attributes. Table 3.1 listed all the device context attributes. Those that affect text are listed in Table 3.9.

Table 3.9. The device context attributes that affect text.

Attribute	*Default*	*Related Function(s)*
Background color	White	`GetBkColor`, `SetBkColor`
Background mode	`OPAQUE`	`GetBkMode`, `SetBkMode`
Font	`SYSTEM_FONT`	`CreateFont`, `CreateFontIndirect`, `SelectObject`
Intercharacter spacing	0	`GetTextCharacterExtra`, `SetTextCharacterExtra`
Text color	Black	`GetTextColor`, `SetTextColor`

The *background color* attribute specifies the color that is used to fill the areas around, inside, and between characters. This attribute also is used to fill both the areas between hatches in a hatched brush pattern and the spaces in a styled line pattern. The current background color attribute can be retrieved with the `GetBkColor` function and set with the `SetBkColor` function.

The *background mode* is set to either `OPAQUE` or `TRANSPARENT`. The default setting, `OPAQUE`, turns on the background color. Setting the background mode to `TRANSPARENT` turns off the background color. The `GetBkMode` function retrieves the current background mode. The `SetBkMode` function sets the background mode.

The *font attribute* specifies the current font. A font contains the patterns that specify the shape, size, and appearance of the text characters. Fonts are discussed in more detail later in the chapter.

The *intercharacter spacing* attribute specifies the number of logical units to insert between characters. The `GetTextCharacterExtra` function retrieves the current setting of the intercharacter spacing attribute. The `SetTextCharacterExtra` function sets the intercharacter spacing attribute.

The *text color* attribute specifies the color used to draw the text. This attribute must be a pure color (with no color shades created using hatched or dithered patterns) and is defined using the `SetTextColor` function. The `GetTextColor` function retrieves the current text color.

Using Fonts

A font describes the size, shape, and appearance of the text you display. In other words, the font contains a specific description of each character in a character set. There are two fundamental types of fonts: logical and physical. *Logical* fonts define

a character set and are device-independent. *Physical* fonts are designed for a specific device and are, therefore, device-dependent. Logical fonts are more difficult to develop but provide flexibility in use because they are device-independent and often scalable. Physical fonts are easier to develop, but of course, are less flexible because they are device-dependent. Although physical fonts are sometimes scalable, the font resolution is generally poor at larger scales.

You can create logical fonts by using the `CreateFont` or `CreateFontIndirect` functions. The font example in Listings 3.15 and 3.16 demonstrates the use of the `CreateFontIndirect` function to create Times Roman and Helvetica logical fonts.

The font example follows the code structure of the `TabbedTextOut` example. The code to notice in this example is the code written to respond to the `WM_CREATE` and `WM_PAINT` messages. The `WM_CREATE` code, which is executed when the window is created, creates the fonts used for the example with the `CreateFontIndirect` function. The `CreateFontIndirect` function accepts a data structure of type `LOGFONT`, which describes the font to create. The six lines of code that directly precede each `CreateFontIndirect` function call initialize the `LOGFONT` data structure passed to the `CreateFontIndirect` function.

The `WM_PAINT` code selects each font created in the `WM_CREATE` code and displays a line of text. Figure 3.8 shows the window created by the font example. Chapter 13 provides reference information on the `CreateFont` and `CreateFontIndirect` functions. Table 3.10 lists the font families and typefaces for the GDI.

The description of the project for the font example follows:

Project Name:	`WIN_FONT`
Files in Project:	`WIN_FONT.C`
	`WIN_FONT.DEF`

Listing 3.15. The definition file for the font example.

```
NAME            WIN_FONT
DESCRIPTION     'Font Example'
EXETYPE         WINDOWS
CODE            PRELOAD MOVEABLE
DATA            PRELOAD MOVEABLE MULTIPLE
HEAPSIZE        1024
STACKSIZE       5120
EXPORTS         WndProc
```

Listing 3.16. The C source file for the font example.

```
#include <windows.h>
#include <stdlib.h>
#include <string.h>

long FAR PASCAL WndProc (HWND hWnd, WORD iMessage,
                WORD wParam, LONG lParam);

int PASCAL WinMain (HANDLE hInstance, HANDLE hPrevInstance,
              LPSTR lpszCmdParam, int nCmdShow)

{
HWND hWnd;
MSG Message;
WNDCLASS WndClass;

if (!hPrevInstance)
     {
     WndClass.cbClsExtra = 0;
     WndClass.cbWndExtra = 0;
     WndClass.hbrBackground = GetStockObject(WHITE_BRUSH);
     WndClass.hCursor =  LoadCursor(NULL, IDC_ARROW);
     WndClass.hIcon = LoadIcon (NULL, "END");
     WndClass.hInstance = hInstance;
     WndClass.lpfnWndProc = WndProc;
     WndClass.lpszClassName = "WIN_FONT";
     WndClass.lpszMenuName = NULL;
     WndClass.style = CS_HREDRAW ¦ CS_VREDRAW;

     RegisterClass (&WndClass);
     }

hWnd = CreateWindow ("WIN_FONT",     /* class name */
          "Font Example",            /* Caption */
          WS_OVERLAPPEDWINDOW,       /* Style */
          CW_USEDEFAULT,             /* x position */
          0,                         /* y position */
          CW_USEDEFAULT,             /* cx - size */
          0,                         /* cy - size */
          NULL,                      /* Parent window */
          NULL,                      /* Menu */
          hInstance,                 /* Program Instance */
          NULL);                     /* Parameters */

ShowWindow (hWnd, nCmdShow);
while (GetMessage (&Message, 0, 0, 0))
     {
     TranslateMessage(&Message);
```

continues

Listing 3.16. continued

```
     DispatchMessage(&Message);
     }
return Message.wParam;
}

/**************************************************************/
/*              Window Procedure: WndProc                     */
/**************************************************************/

long FAR PASCAL WndProc (HWND hWnd, WORD iMessage, WORD wParam,
                LONG lParam)
{
static HANDLE hTmsRmn;
static HANDLE hHelv;
LOGFONT LogFont;
HDC hDC;
PAINTSTRUCT PtStr;

switch (iMessage)
     {

     case WM_CREATE:

          memset(&LogFont,0,sizeof(LOGFONT));
          LogFont.lfHeight = 25;
          LogFont.lfWidth = 15;
          LogFont.lfUnderline = 1;
          LogFont.lfItalic = 1;
          lstrcpy (LogFont.lfFaceName,"Helv");
          hHelv = CreateFontIndirect(&LogFont);

          memset(&LogFont,0,sizeof(LOGFONT));
          LogFont.lfHeight = 25;
          LogFont.lfWidth = 15;
          LogFont.lfUnderline = 1;
          LogFont.lfItalic = 1;
          lstrcpy(LogFont.lfFaceName,"Tms Rmn");
          hTmsRmn = CreateFontIndirect(&LogFont);

          return 0;

     case WM_PAINT:

          hDC = BeginPaint (hWnd, &PtStr);
```

```
        SelectObject(hDC, hHelv);
        TextOut(hDC,20,20,
            "Helvetica - Underlined and Italics",34);

        SelectObject(hDC, hTmsRmn);
        TextOut(hDC,20,100,
            "Times Roman - Underlined and Italics",36);

        EndPaint(hWnd,&PtStr);
        return 0;

    case WM_DESTROY:

        DeleteObject(hHelv);
        DeleteObject(hTmsRmn);

        PostQuitMessage(0);
        return 0;

    default:

        return(DefWindowProc(hWnd, iMessage, wParam,
            lParam));
    }
}
```

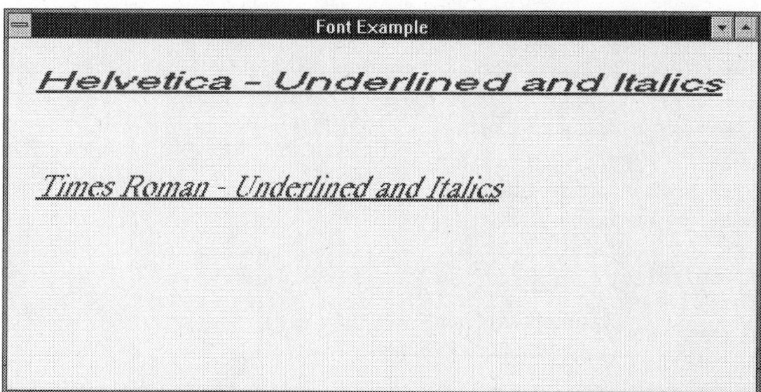

Figure 3.8. *Font example.*

Table 3.10. GDI font families and typefaces.

Font Family	*Font Family Constant*	*Typefaces*	*Description*
Dontcare	`FF_DONTCARE`	System	Used when font information is not available or is not important
Decorative	`FF_DECORATIVE`	Symbol	Novelty fonts
Modern	`FF_MODERN`	Courier, Modern,	Constant stroke Terminalwidth font, may or may not have serifs
Roman	`FF_ROMAN`	Roman, Times	Variable stroke Roman width font with serifs
Script	`FF_SCRIPT`	Script	Resembles handwriting
Swiss	`FF_SWISS`	Helvetica, System	Variable stroke width font without serifs

Text Metrics

The values that describe a font are called the *text metrics* of the font. The `GetTextMetrics` function retrieves a font's text metrics and places them in a data structure of type `TEXTMETRIC`, as follows:

```
typedef struct tagTEXTMETRIC {
     short int tmHeight;
     short int tmAscent;
     short int tmDescent;
     short int tmInternalLeading;
     short int tmExternalLeading;
     short int tmAveCharWidth;
     short int tmMaxCharWidth;
     short int tmWeight
     BYTE tmItalic;
     BYTE tmUnderlined;
     BYTE tmStruckOut;
     BYTE tmFirstChar;
     BYTE tmLastChar;
     BYTE tmDefaultChar;
     BYTE tmBreakChar;
     BYTE tmPitchAndFamily;
     BYTE tmCharSet;
     short int tmOverhang;
     short int tmDigitizedAspectX;
     short int tmDigitizedAspectY;
} TEXTMETRIC;
```

where:

`tmHeight` is the character height

`tmAscent` is the character ascent (units above baseline)

`tmDescent` is the character descent (units below baseline)

`tmInternalLeading` is the amount of space at the top of the character height specified by `tmHeight`

`tmExternalLeading` is the amount of space added between rows

`tmAveCharWidth` is the average character width

`tmMaxCharWidth` is the width of the widest character

`tmWeight` is the font weight

`tmItalic` is nonzero if the font is italic

`tmUnderlined` is nonzero if the font is underlined

`tmStruckOut` is nonzero if the font is struck out

`tmFirstChar` is first character defined for the font

`tmLastChar` is the last character defined for the font

`tmDefaultChar` is the character substituted for characters not in the font

`tmBreakChar` is the character used for word breaks

`tmPitchAndFamily` is the pitch (low-order bit) and family (four high-order bits) of the font

`tmCharSet` is the character set for the font

`tmOverhang` is the extra width added to some synthesized fonts

`tmDigitizedAspectX` is the horizontal aspect of the device the font was designed for

`tmDigitizedAspectY` is the vertical aspect of the device the font was designed for

Although most of the fields of the `TEXTMETRIC` data structure are easy to understand, some need further explanation. Figure 3.9 includes several graphical definitions of a font character cell.

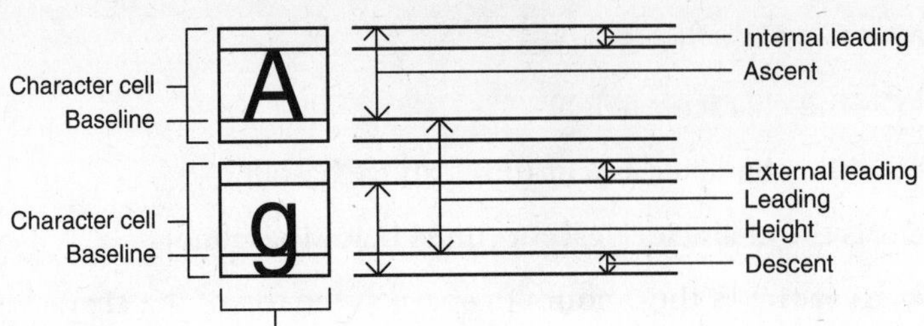

Figure 3.9. Character cell dimensions.

Aligning Text

The majority of the text functions listed in Table 3.8 require that the coordinates to a point be passed in the function's argument list. For example, the following line of code from the font example uses the coordinates (20,100) to define the reference point for the text.

```
TextOut(hDC,20,100,"Times Roman - Underlined and Italics",36);
```

The function uses the coordinates of the specified point and the current text alignment to draw the text string. The current text alignment specifies how the string is drawn relative to the passed coordinates. The `SetTextAlign` function sets the current text alignment. (See Chapter 13 for more information on the `SetTextAlign` function.) Table 3.11 lists the horizontal, vertical, and update flags for the `SetTextAlign` function. The default settings for the text alignment flags are `TA_LEFT` (horizontal), `TA_TOP` (vertical), and `TA_NOUPDATECP` (update).

Table 3.11. Text alignment flags.

Value	*Meaning*
Horizontal Flags	
`TA_CENTER`	Alignment of y-axis and center of bounding rectangle
`TA_LEFT`	Alignment of y-axis and left side of bounding rectangle
`TA_RIGHT`	Alignment of y-axis and right side of bounding rectangle
Vertical Flags	
`TA_BASELINE`	Alignment of x-axis and baseline of font within the bounding rectangle
`TA_BOTTOM`	Alignment of x-axis and bottom of bounding rectangle
`TA_TOP`	Alignment of x-axis and top of bounding rectangle

Update Flags

TA_NOUPDATECP	Current position is not updated
TA_UPDATECP	Current position is updated

Note: The default values for these flags are TA_LEFT, TA_TOP, *and* TA_NOUPDATECP.

Scrolling Text Windows

This chapter has presented several examples that displayed text in a window. These examples used a window without scroll bars and, therefore, contained lines of text that could not be viewed. The scrolling text example in Listings 3.17 and 3.18 demonstrates the use of the vertical and horizontal scroll bars for text scrolling.

The first thing that you should notice about this example is that the window class definition in the `WinMain` function differs in one major way from the previous examples in this chapter: because this example requires the use of scroll bars, the `WS_VSCROLL` and `WS_HSCROLL` styles are used.

The next thing that you should notice about this example is that the window procedure is quite long and responds to several messages that have not yet been presented: `WM_SIZE`, `WM_HSCROLL`, and `WM_VSCROLL`. Additional messages that are monitored include `WM_CREATE` and `WM_PAINT`.

The `WM_CREATE` code defines initial values for several of the parameters used to track the text positions. The `WM_SIZE` code defines the scrolling ranges for the vertical and horizontal scroll bars each time the window is sized. The `WM_PAINT` code draws the text that is to be scrolled.

The most interesting code in the example is the code for the `WM_VSCROLL` and `WM_HSCROLL` messages. Both of these message code segments consist of additional `switch` statements that monitor the scroll bar code that is contained in the `wParam` parameter of the appropriate message. The nested `switch` statement determines the direction and amount of scrolling that takes place.

Figure 3.10 shows the window resulting from Listings 3.17 and 3.18. Notice that although each character string displayed in the window contains the same number of characters, the right margin of the text is not aligned. This is because the font used to display the text was a proportional font, which means that the width of each character varies. If a fixed font had been used, the right margin of the text would have been aligned. This example is based on the discussion of scroll bars by Charles Petzold in his book *Programming Windows: The Microsoft Guide to Writing Applications for Windows 3, 2nd Edition,* published in 1990 by Microsoft Press.

The description of the project for the scrolling text example follows:

Project Name: `WIN_SCR`
Files in Project: `WIN_SCR.C`
`WIN_SCR.DEF`

Listing 3.17. The definition file for the scolling text example.

```
NAME            WIN_SCR
DESCRIPTION     'Text Scrolling Example'
EXETYPE         WINDOWS
CODE            PRELOAD MOVEABLE
DATA            PRELOAD MOVEABLE MULTIPLE
HEAPSIZE        1024
STACKSIZE       5120
EXPORTS         WndProc
```

Listing 3.18. The C source file for the scrolling text example.

```
#include <windows.h>
#include <stdlib.h>
#include <string.h>

long FAR PASCAL WndProc (HWND hWnd, WORD iMessage,
                WORD wParam, LONG lParam);

int PASCAL WinMain (HANDLE hInstance, HANDLE hPrevInstance,
              LPSTR lpszCmdParam, int nCmdShow)

{
HWND hWnd;
MSG Message;
WNDCLASS WndClass;

if (!hPrevInstance)
     {
     WndClass.cbClsExtra = 0;
     WndClass.cbWndExtra = 0;
     WndClass.hbrBackground = GetStockObject(WHITE_BRUSH);
     WndClass.hCursor =  LoadCursor(NULL, IDC_ARROW);
     WndClass.hIcon = LoadIcon (NULL, "END");
     WndClass.hInstance = hInstance;
     WndClass.lpfnWndProc = WndProc;
     WndClass.lpszClassName = "WIN_SCR";
     WndClass.lpszMenuName = NULL;
     WndClass.style = CS_HREDRAW | CS_VREDRAW;
```

```
     RegisterClass (&WndClass);
     }

hWnd = CreateWindow ("WIN_SCR",        /* class name */
         "Text Scrolling Example",   /* Caption */
         WS_OVERLAPPEDWINDOW ¦
         WS_VSCROLL ¦ WS_HSCROLL,    /* Style */
         CW_USEDEFAULT,              /* x position */
         0,                          /* y position */
         CW_USEDEFAULT,              /* cx - size */
         0,                          /* cy - size */
         NULL,                       /* Parent window */
         NULL,                       /* Menu */
         hInstance,                  /* Program Instance */
         NULL);                      /* Parameters */

ShowWindow (hWnd, nCmdShow);
UpdateWindow (hWnd);
while (GetMessage (&Message, 0, 0, 0))
     {
     TranslateMessage(&Message);
     DispatchMessage(&Message);
     }
return Message.wParam;
}

/*****************************************************************/
/*           Window Procedure: WndProc                           */
/*****************************************************************/

long FAR PASCAL WndProc (HWND hWnd, WORD iMessage, WORD wParam,
               LONG lParam)
{
static short nXChar, nYChar, nCaps, nXClnt, nYClnt, nMaxWidth,
     nVPos, nVMax, nHPos, nHMax;
HDC hDC;
short x, y, z, nBegin, nEnd, nVInc, nHInc;
PAINTSTRUCT PtStr;
TEXTMETRIC tm;
short LnCount = 30;
static char *textbuf[] =
    {"One.........................................1",
     "Two.........................................2",
     "Three.......................................3",
     "Four........................................4",
     "Five........................................5",
     "Six.........................................6",
     "Seven.......................................7",
     "Eight.......................................8",
```

continues

Listing 3.18. continued

```
        "Nine.........................................9",
        "Ten.........................................10",
        "Eleven......................................11",
        "Twelve......................................12",
        "Thirteen....................................13",
        "Fourteen....................................14",
        "Fifteen.....................................15",
        "Sixteen.....................................16",
        "Seventeen...................................17",
        "Eighteen....................................18",
        "Nineteen....................................19",
        "Twenty......................................20",
        "Twenty-one..................................21",
        "Twenty-two..................................22",
        "Twenty-three................................23",
        "Twenty-four.................................24",
        "Twenty-five.................................25",
        "Twenty-six..................................26",
        "Twenty-seven................................27",
        "Twenty-eight................................28",
        "Twenty-nine.................................29",
        "Thirty......................................30"};

switch (iMessage)
     {

     case WM_CREATE:

          hDC = GetDC(hWnd);

          GetTextMetrics(hDC,&tm);
          nXChar = tm.tmAveCharWidth;
          nYChar = tm.tmHeight + tm.tmExternalLeading;
          nCaps = (tm.tmPitchAndFamily & 1 ? 3 : 2) *
               nXChar/2;


          ReleaseDC(hWnd, hDC);
          nMaxWidth = 40 * nXChar + 18 * nCaps;
          return 0;

     case WM_SIZE:

          nYClnt = HIWORD(lParam);
          nXClnt = LOWORD(lParam);
```

```
          nVMax = max(0,LnCount+2-nYClnt/nYChar);
          nVPos = min(nVPos,nVMax);

          SetScrollRange(hWnd,SB_VERT,0,nVMax,FALSE);
          SetScrollPos(hWnd,SB_VERT,nVPos,TRUE);

          nHMax = max(0,2+(nMaxWidth-nXClnt)/nXChar);
          nHPos = min(nHPos,nHMax);

          SetScrollRange(hWnd,SB_HORZ,0,nHMax,FALSE);
          SetScrollPos(hWnd,SB_HORZ,nHPos,TRUE);
          return 0;

     case WM_HSCROLL:

          switch(wParam)
               {
               case SB_LINEUP:
                    nHInc = -1;
                    break;
               case SB_LINEDOWN:
                    nHInc = 1;
                    break;
               case SB_PAGEUP:
                    nHInc = -8;
                    break;
               case SB_PAGEDOWN:
                    nHInc = 8;
                    break;
               case SB_THUMBPOSITION:
                    nHInc = LOWORD(lParam)-nHPos;
                    break;
               default:
                    nHInc = 0;
               }
          if (nHInc == max(-nHPos,min(nHInc,nHMax-nHPos)))
               {
               nHPos = nHPos + nHInc;
               ScrollWindow(hWnd,-nXChar*nHInc,0,
                    NULL,NULL);
               SetScrollPos(hWnd,SB_HORZ,nHPos,TRUE);
               }
          return 0;

     case WM_VSCROLL:

          switch(wParam)
               {
               case SB_TOP:
                    nVInc = -nVPos;
```

continues

Listing 3.18. continued

```
                    break;
                case SB_BOTTOM:
                    nVInc = nVMax - nVPos;
                    break;
                case SB_LINEUP:
                    nVInc = -1;
                    break;
                case SB_LINEDOWN:
                    nVInc = 1;
                    break;
                case SB_PAGEUP:
                    nVInc = min(-1,-nYClnt/nYChar);
                    break;
                case SB_PAGEDOWN:
                    nVInc = max(1,nYClnt/nYChar);
                    break;
                case SB_THUMBPOSITION:
                    nVInc = LOWORD(lParam)-nVPos;
                    break;
                default:
                    nVInc = 0;
                }
            if (nVInc == max(-nVPos,min(nVInc,nVMax-nVPos)))
                {
                nVPos = nVPos + nVInc;
                ScrollWindow(hWnd,0,-nYChar*nVInc,
                    NULL,NULL);
                SetScrollPos(hWnd,SB_VERT,nVPos,TRUE);
                UpdateWindow(hWnd);
                }
            return 0;

        case WM_PAINT:

            hDC = BeginPaint(hWnd, &PtStr);

            nBegin = max(0,nVPos +
               PtStr.rcPaint.top / nYChar-1);
            nEnd = min(LnCount,nVPos +
               PtStr.rcPaint.bottom / nYChar);
            for (z=nBegin; z<nEnd; z=z+1)
                {
                x = nXChar * (1-nHPos);
                y = nYChar * (1-nVPos+z);

                TextOut(hDC,x,y,textbuf[z],
                   lstrlen(textbuf[z]));
                }
```

```
            EndPaint(hWnd, &PtStr);
            return 0;

        case WM_DESTROY:

            PostQuitMessage(0);
            return 0;

        default:

            return(DefWindowProc(hWnd, iMessage, wParam,
                lParam));
        }
    }
```

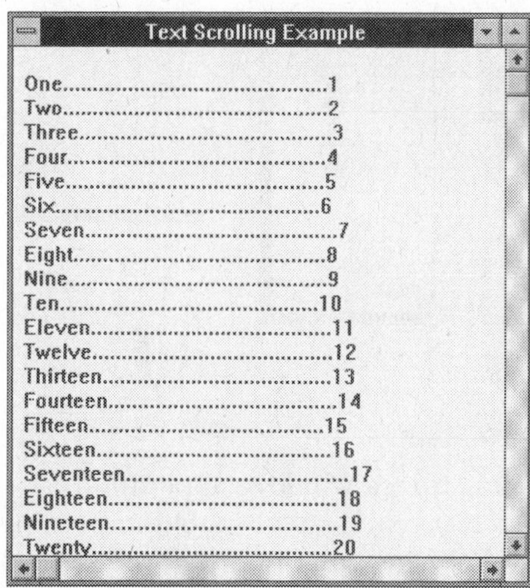

Figure 3.10. *Scrolling text example.*

Printing

As this chapter has mentioned several times, the GDI is designed to be device-independent. Therefore, in theory, the method for printing text on the printer is the same as that for displaying text on the screen. Unfortunately, things are not quite as straightforward as that.

The same GDI functions used to create text and graphics on a screen are used to print text and graphics on a printer. However, there are fundamental differences in the way both devices operate. For example, not all printers support graphics, and others do not contain enough memory to print a full page of graphics. To account for the differences between printers and the screen, the GDI function `Escape` is provided. An application can use the `Escape` function to access the features of a printer device and to retrieve and modify printer settings. Chapter 13 provides additional information on the `Escape` function. Chapter 15 provides reference information for each of the printer escape subfunctions supported by `Escape`.

Sending output to the printer follows the basic steps outlined in Figure 3.11. The application calls the `Escape` function which, in turn, is handled by the GDI module. The GDI module calls the `Control` function, which is the printer device driver's equivalent of the `Escape` function and which is also handled by the printer device driver. This driver, with the help of the GDI module, activates the Print Manager.

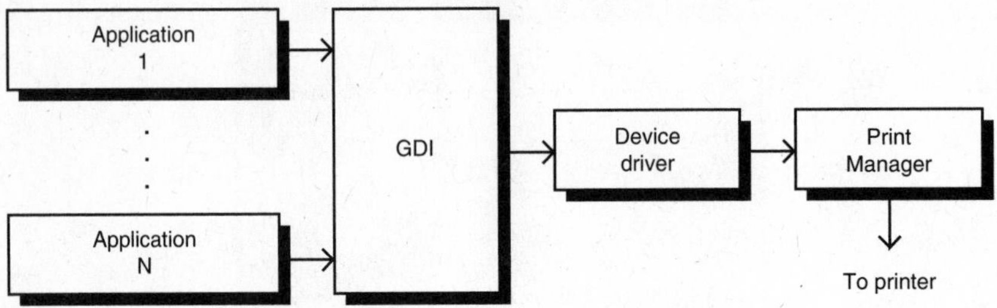

Figure 3.11. *Printer output.*

A full discussion of printing from a Windows application can be found in *Microsoft Windows Programmer's Reference, 1990,* published by Microsoft Press. Again, Chapter 15 of this book contains descriptions of the subfunctions for the `Escape` function.

4

Resources

Resources are read-only data stored in an application's .EXE file or in a library's .DLL file. Windows uses several different types of resources, including cursors, bitmaps, strings, accelerators, icons, dialog boxes, and menus. You can use the Whitewater Resource Toolkit or the Resource Workshop to create and edit many types of resources used by Windows applications.

This chapter introduces the accelerator, bitmap, cursor, dialog box, icon, menu, and string resources. For each of these types, the resource itself is created—using the Whitewater Resource Toolkit or the Resource Workshop—and incorporated in an example demonstrating the use of that resource.

Using Accelerators

An *accelerator* is a key or key combination used to select a menu item or invoke a command. Using accelerators enables you to access menu items or commands more quickly and conveniently than you can with other methods, such as using pull-down menus.

You can use the Accelerator editor of the Whitewater Resource Toolkit to create *accelerator resources* (Chapter 16 provides specific information on the features of the Accelerator editor) or you can use the Accelerator editor of the Resource Workshop (see Chapter 17).

The accelerator example in Listings 4.1, 4.2, and 4.3 demonstrates the use of accelerators and includes three files: a C source file, a module definition file, and a resource script file. The accelerator table shown in the *resource script file* (Listing 4.3) was created with the Accelerator editor of the Whitewater Resource Toolkit and saved as an .RC file. Figure 4.1 shows the accelerator resource as it was created with the Accelerator editor.

Accelerator: C:\BORLANDC\WIN_ACC.RES A_RESOURCE

File Edit Header Help

Type	Key	Code	Shift	Ctrl	Alt	Value	Invert
Virtkey	A	65	No	No	No	1	No
Virtkey	B	66	No	No	No	2	No
Virtkey	C	67	No	No	No	3	No
Virtkey	D	68	No	No	No	4	No
Virtkey	E	69	No	No	No	5	No
Virtkey	F	70	No	No	No	6	No
Virtkey	G	71	No	No	No	7	No
Virtkey	H	72	No	No	No	8	No
Virtkey	I	73	No	No	No	9	No

Figure 4.1. *The accelerator resource.*

The accelerators defined for this example are the A, B, C, D, E, F, G, H, and I keys. Whenever you press one of these keys, a message box is displayed that echoes the ID number of the accelerator (see Figure 4.2). For this example, the accelerators are not tied to the selection of menu items. However, accelerators are generally used as alternatives to selecting items from a menu.

The code structure of this example is similar to code structures already presented in this chapter. The message box that appears when you press an accelerator key is displayed in response to the `WM_COMMAND` message.

The following lines, preceding the program listing, show the name of this project as well as the files used to create the accelerator example.

Project Name:	`WIN_ACC`
Files in Project:	`WIN_ACC.C`
	`WIN_ACC.DEF`
	`WIN_ACC.RC`

Listing 4.1. The definition file for the accelerator example.

```
NAME            WIN_ACC
DESCRIPTION     'Accelerator Example'
EXETYPE         WINDOWS
CODE            PRELOAD MOVEABLE
DATA            PRELOAD MOVEABLE MULTIPLE
HEAPSIZE        1024
STACKSIZE       5120
EXPORTS         WndProc
```

Listing 4.2. The C source file for the accelerator example.

```
#include <windows.h>
#include <stdlib.h>
#include <string.h>

long FAR PASCAL WndProc (HWND hWnd, WORD iMessage,
                WORD wParam, LONG lParam);

int PASCAL WinMain (HANDLE hInstance, HANDLE hPrevInstance,
              LPSTR lpszCmdParam, int nCmdShow)

{
HWND hWnd;
MSG Message;
WNDCLASS WndClass;
HANDLE hAccel;

if (!hPrevInstance)
     {
     WndClass.cbClsExtra = 0;
     WndClass.cbWndExtra = 0;
     WndClass.hbrBackground = GetStockObject(WHITE_BRUSH);
     WndClass.hCursor =  LoadCursor(NULL, IDC_ARROW);
     WndClass.hIcon = LoadIcon (NULL, "END");
     WndClass.hInstance = hInstance;
     WndClass.lpfnWndProc = WndProc;
     WndClass.lpszClassName = "WIN_ACC";
     WndClass.lpszMenuName = NULL;
     WndClass.style = CS_HREDRAW ¦ CS_VREDRAW;

     RegisterClass (&WndClass);
     }

hWnd = CreateWindow ("WIN_ACC",        /* class name */
         "Accelerator Example",      /* Caption */
          WS_OVERLAPPEDWINDOW,        /* Style */
```

continues

Listing 4.2. continued

```
          CW_USEDEFAULT,                /* x position */
          0,                            /* y position */
          CW_USEDEFAULT,                /* cx - size */
          0,                            /* cy - size */
          NULL,                         /* Parent window */
          NULL,                         /* Menu */
          hInstance,                    /* Program Instance*/
          NULL);                        /* Parameters */

ShowWindow (hWnd, nCmdShow);

hAccel = LoadAccelerators(hInstance,"A_RESOURCE");

while (GetMessage (&Message, 0, 0, 0))
     {
     if (!TranslateAccelerator(hWnd,hAccel,&Message))
          {
          TranslateMessage(&Message);
          DispatchMessage(&Message);
          }
     }
return Message.wParam;
}

/*************************************************************/
/*              Window Procedure: WndProc                    */
/*************************************************************/

long FAR PASCAL WndProc (HWND hWnd, WORD iMessage, WORD wParam,
                LONG lParam)
{
char textout[40];

switch (iMessage)
     {
     case WM_COMMAND:

          wsprintf(textout,"Accelerator ID = %d",wParam);
          MessageBox(hWnd,textout,"Accelerator!",MB_OK);
          return 0;


     case WM_DESTROY:

          PostQuitMessage(0);
          return 0;
```

```
        default:

            return(DefWindowProc(hWnd, iMessage, wParam,
                lParam));
        }
}
```

Listing 4.3. The resource file for the accelerator example.

```
A_RESOURCE ACCELERATORS
BEGIN
  "A", 1, VIRTKEY, NOINVERT
  "B", 2, VIRTKEY, NOINVERT
  "C", 3, VIRTKEY, NOINVERT
  "D", 4, VIRTKEY, NOINVERT
  "E", 5, VIRTKEY, NOINVERT
  "F", 6, VIRTKEY, NOINVERT
  "G", 7, VIRTKEY, NOINVERT
  "H", 8, VIRTKEY, NOINVERT
  "I", 9, VIRTKEY, NOINVERT
END
```

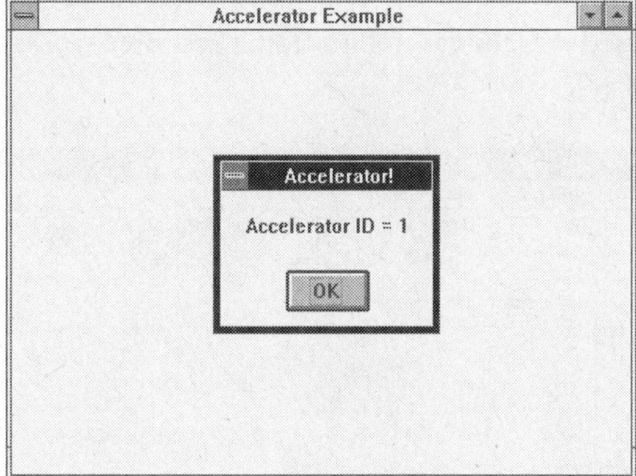

***Figure 4.2.** Accelerator example.*

Using Bitmaps

A *bitmap* is a data series that represents a graphical object. An application uses the bitmap to draw predefined objects quickly onto the screen. The two basic types of bitmaps are the device-dependent bitmap and the device-independent bitmap.

Device-dependent bitmaps are closely tied to a particular output display device, because there is a close correlation between the bits of the bitmaps and the pixels of the output display device. *Device-independent bitmaps*, on the other hand, are not closely tied to a particular display device, because they represent the appearance of the image and not the correlation of the bitmap bits and the pixels of the output device.

You can use preexisting bitmaps or create your own. You can create bitmaps with the Bitmap editor of the Whitewater Resource Toolkit (Chapter 16 provides more information on the features and tools of the Bitmap editor) or the Paint editor of the Resource Workshop (see Chapter 17).

The four bitmap resources used in Listings 4.4, 4.5, and 4.6 were created with the Bitmap editor of the Whitewater Resource Toolkit and the Paint editor of the Resource Workshop. The football and basketball bitmap resources, created with the Bitmap editor and used for the bitmap example, are shown in Figures 4.3 and 4.4, respectively. The baseball and golf ball bitmap resources used for the bitmap example were created with the Paint editor of the Resource Workshop and are shown in Figures 4.5 and 4.6, respectively.

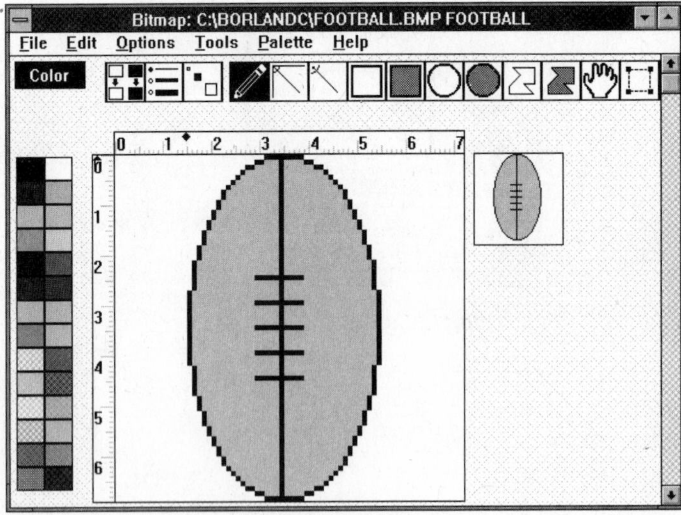

Figure 4.3. *The football bitmap resource.*

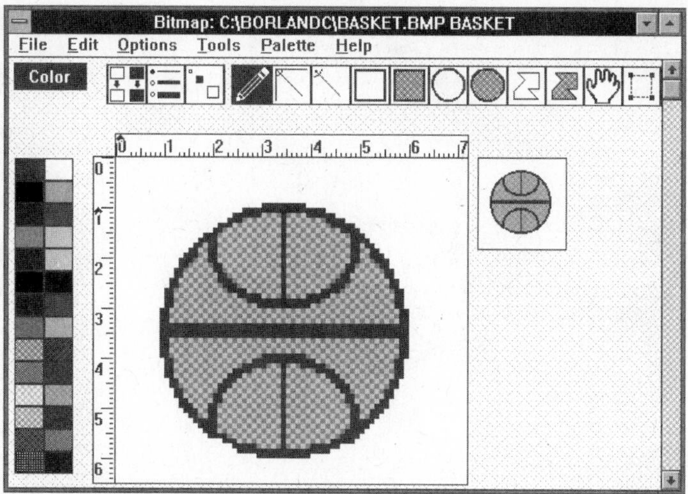

Figure 4.4. *The basketball bitmap resource.*

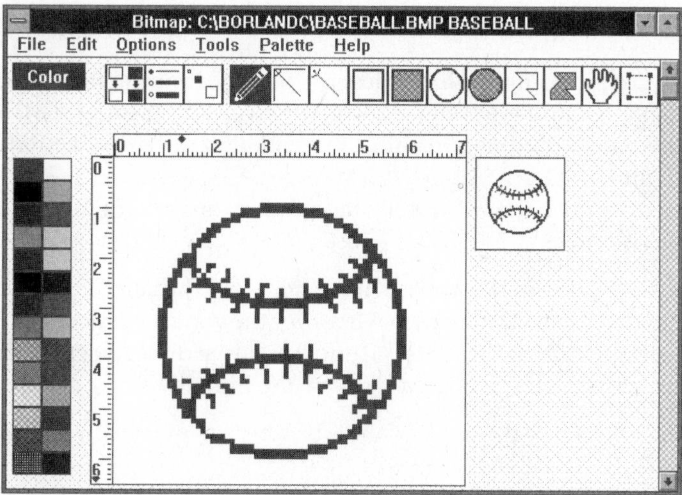

Figure 4.5. *The baseball bitmap resource.*

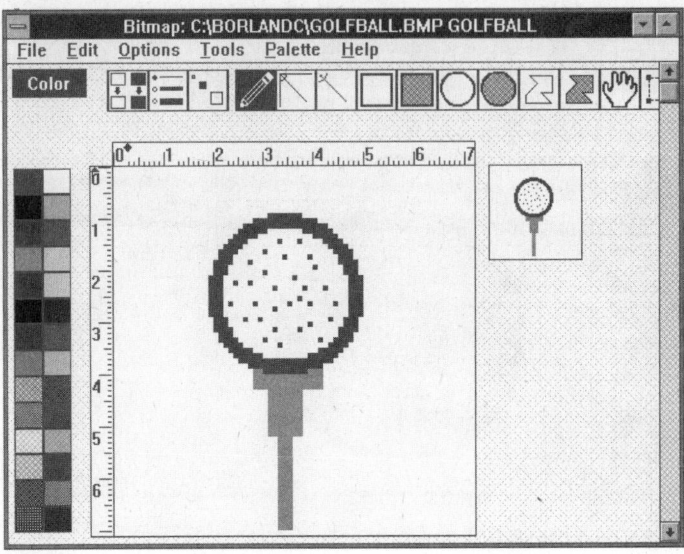

Figure 4.6. *The golf ball bitmap resource.*

The bitmap example contains three files: a module definition file (Listing 4.4), a C source code file (Listing 4.5), and a resource script file (Listing 4.6). The bitmap example loads the four bitmap resources specified in the resource script (.RC) file and displays these bitmaps. Figure 4.7 shows the window created by the bitmap example. This example demonstrates a straightforward procedure for loading and using bitmap resources.

The bitmaps are loaded in the `WinMain` function using the `LoadBitmap` function. The bitmaps are then drawn on the screen whenever the window procedure receives the `WM_PAINT` message. The `SelectObject` function is used to select the appropriate bitmap. The `BitBlt` function is used to draw the bitmap.

The following lines show the project name as well as files used to create the bitmap example.

Project Name:	`WIN_BIT`
Files in Project:	`WIN_BIT.C`
	`WIN_BIT.DEF`
	`WIN_BIT.RC`

Listing 4.4. *The definition file for the bitmap example.*

```
NAME            WIN_BIT
DESCRIPTION     'Bitmap Example'
EXETYPE         WINDOWS
```

```
CODE           PRELOAD MOVEABLE
DATA           PRELOAD MOVEABLE MULTIPLE
HEAPSIZE       1024
STACKSIZE      5120
EXPORTS        WndProc
```

Listing 4.5. The C source file for the bitmap example.

```
#include <windows.h>
#include <stdlib.h>
#include <string.h>

static HANDLE hFootball;
static HANDLE hBasketball;
static HANDLE hGolfball;
static HANDLE hBaseball;

long FAR PASCAL WndProc (HWND hWnd, WORD iMessage,
                WORD wParam, LONG lParam);

int PASCAL WinMain (HANDLE hInstance, HANDLE hPrevInstance,
              LPSTR lpszCmdParam, int nCmdShow)

{
HWND hWnd;
MSG Message;
WNDCLASS WndClass;

if (!hPrevInstance)
     {
     WndClass.cbClsExtra = 0;
     WndClass.cbWndExtra = 0;
     WndClass.hbrBackground = GetStockObject(WHITE_BRUSH);
     WndClass.hCursor =  LoadCursor(NULL, IDC_ARROW);
     WndClass.hIcon = LoadIcon (NULL, "END");
     WndClass.hInstance = hInstance;
     WndClass.lpfnWndProc = WndProc;
     WndClass.lpszClassName = "WIN_BIT";
     WndClass.lpszMenuName = NULL;
     WndClass.style = CS_HREDRAW ¦ CS_VREDRAW;

     RegisterClass (&WndClass);
     }

hWnd = CreateWindow ("WIN_BIT",      /* class name */
         "Bitmap Example",         /* Caption */
          WS_OVERLAPPEDWINDOW,      /* Style */
```

continues

Listing 4.5. continued

```
            CW_USEDEFAULT,                /* x position */
            0,                            /* y position */
            CW_USEDEFAULT,                /* cx - size */
            0,                            /* cy - size */
            NULL,                         /* Parent window */
            NULL,                         /* Menu */
            hInstance,                    /* Program Instance */
            NULL);                        /* Parameters */

hFootball = LoadBitmap(hInstance,"FOOTBALL");
hBasketball = LoadBitmap(hInstance,"BASKET");
hGolfball = LoadBitmap(hInstance,"GOLFBALL");
hBaseball = LoadBitmap(hInstance,"BASEBALL");

ShowWindow (hWnd, nCmdShow);
UpdateWindow (hWnd);
while (GetMessage (&Message, 0, 0, 0))
     {
     TranslateMessage(&Message);
     DispatchMessage(&Message);
     }
return Message.wParam;
}

/****************************************************************/
/*              Window Procedure: WndProc                       */
/****************************************************************/

long FAR PASCAL WndProc (HWND hWnd, WORD iMessage, WORD wParam,
                LONG lParam)
{
HDC hDC, hMemDC;
short x, y;
PAINTSTRUCT PtStr;

switch (iMessage)
     {

     case WM_PAINT:

          hDC = BeginPaint(hWnd, &PtStr);
          hMemDC = CreateCompatibleDC(hDC);
          for (y=30; y<300; y=y+80)
              {
              SelectObject(hMemDC,hFootball);
              BitBlt(hDC,30,y,72,72,hMemDC,0,0,SRCCOPY);
              SelectObject(hMemDC,hBasketball);
              BitBlt(hDC,130,y,72,72,hMemDC,0,0,SRCCOPY);
```

```
                SelectObject(hMemDC,hGolfball);
                BitBlt(hDC,230,y,72,72,hMemDC,0,0,SRCCOPY);
                SelectObject(hMemDC,hBaseball);
                BitBlt(hDC,330,y,72,72,hMemDC,0,0,SRCCOPY);
                }
            DeleteDC(hMemDC);
            EndPaint(hWnd, &PtStr);
            return 0;

        case WM_DESTROY:

            DeleteObject(hFootball);
            DeleteObject(hBaseball);
            DeleteObject(hBasketball);
            DeleteObject(hGolfball);
            PostQuitMessage(0);
            return 0;

        default:

            return(DefWindowProc(hWnd, iMessage, wParam,
                lParam));
        }
}
```

Listing 4.6. The resource file for the bitmap example.

```
FOOTBALL BITMAP FOOTBALL.BMP
BASKET   BITMAP BASKET.BMP
GOLFBALL BITMAP GOLFBALL.BMP
BASEBALL BITMAP BASEBALL.BMP
```

Using Cursors

A *cursor* is a special 32-by-32-pixel bitmap used to indicate the positions where mouse actions occur. Windows has several predefined cursor types, which are listed in Table 4.1. In addition to using the predefined cursors, you can create your own cursors by using the Cursor editor of the Whitewater Resource Toolkit. (See Chapter 16 for information on the features and tools of the Cursor editor.) You also can use the Paint editor of the Resource Workshop to create cursor resources.

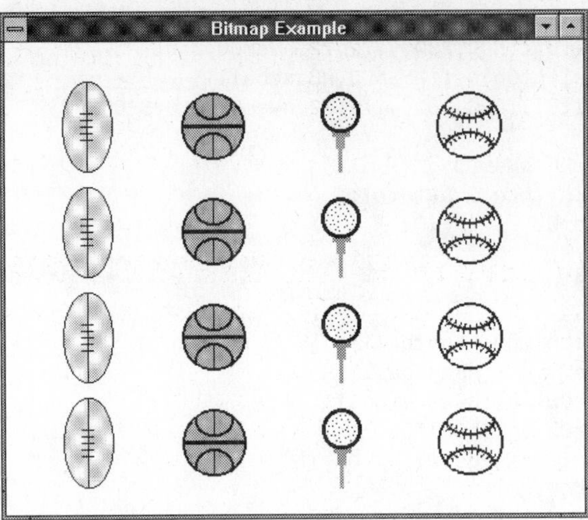

Figure 4.7. *Bitmap example.*

Table 4.1. *Predefined cursor types.*

Constant	*Meaning*
IDC_ARROW	Arrow cursor
IDC_CROSS	Crosshair cursor
IDC_IBEAM	I-beam text cursor
IDC_ICON	Empty icon
IDC_SIZE	Square with small square in lower right corner
IDC_SIZENESW	Cursor with arrows pointing northeast and southwest
IDC_SIZENS	Cursor with arrows pointing north and south
IDC_SIZENWSE	Cursor with arrows pointing northwest and southeast
IDC_SIZEWE	Cursor with arrows pointing west and east
IDC_UPARROW	Vertical arrow cursor
IDC_WAIT	Hourglass cursor

The cursor example in Listings 4.7, 4.8, and 4.9 uses a cursor resource created with the Cursor editor of the Whitewater Resource Toolkit, saved in .CUR format, and included in the resource script file. Figure 4.8 shows the cursor created with the Cursor editor and used in the cursor example.

The cursor example contains three files: the module definition file (Listing 4.7), a C source code file (Listing 4.8), and a resource script file (Listing 4.9). This example loads the cursor resource shown in Figure 4.8 by specifying it as the default cursor for the window class (see the `WndClass.hCursor` line of the `WinMain` function). In this cursor example, the cursor resource is used whenever the current mouse position is within the application window.

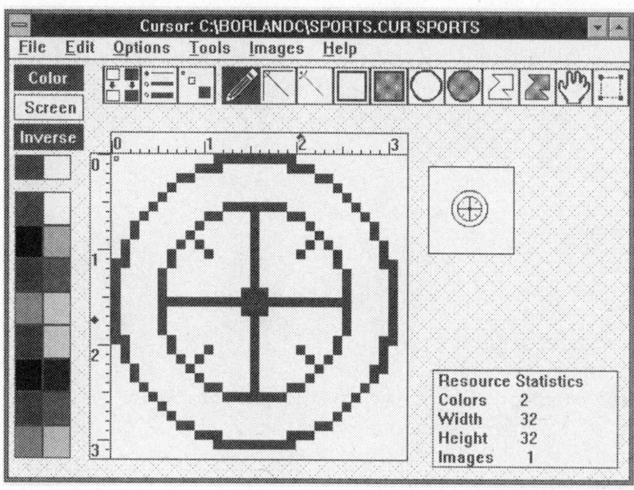

***Figure 4.8.** The cursor resource.*

The following lines show the project name as well as files used to create the cursor.

Project Name: `WIN_CUR`
Files in Project: `WIN_CUR.C`
`WIN_CUR.DEF`
`WIN_CUR.RC`

***Listing 4.7.** The definition file for the cursor example.*

```
NAME            WIN_CUR
DESCRIPTION     'Cursor Example'
EXETYPE         WINDOWS
CODE            PRELOAD MOVEABLE
DATA            PRELOAD MOVEABLE MULTIPLE
HEAPSIZE        1024
STACKSIZE       5120
EXPORTS         WndProc
```

Listing 4.8. The C source file for the cursor example.

```
#include <windows.h>
#include <stdlib.h>
#include <string.h>

long FAR PASCAL WndProc (HWND hWnd, WORD iMessage,
                WORD wParam, LONG lParam);

int PASCAL WinMain (HANDLE hInstance, HANDLE hPrevInstance,
              LPSTR lpszCmdParam, int nCmdShow)

{
HWND hWnd;
MSG Message;
WNDCLASS WndClass;

if (!hPrevInstance)
     {
     WndClass.cbClsExtra = 0;
     WndClass.cbWndExtra = 0;
     WndClass.hbrBackground = GetStockObject(WHITE_BRUSH);
     WndClass.hCursor =  LoadCursor(hInstance,"SPORTS");
     WndClass.hIcon = LoadIcon (NULL, "END");
     WndClass.hInstance = hInstance;
     WndClass.lpfnWndProc = WndProc;
     WndClass.lpszClassName = "WIN_CUR";
     WndClass.lpszMenuName = NULL;
     WndClass.style = CS_HREDRAW ¦ CS_VREDRAW;

     RegisterClass (&WndClass);
     }

hWnd = CreateWindow ("WIN_CUR",   /* class name */
         "Cursor Example",      /* Caption */
         WS_OVERLAPPEDWINDOW,   /* Style */
         CW_USEDEFAULT,         /* x position */
         0,                     /* y position */
         CW_USEDEFAULT,         /* cx - size */
         0,                     /* cy - size */
         NULL,                  /* Parent window */
         NULL,                  /* Menu */
         hInstance,             /* Program Instance */
         NULL);                 /* Parameters */

ShowWindow(hWnd,nCmdShow);
UpdateWindow(hWnd);
while (GetMessage (&Message, 0, 0, 0))
     {
```

```
     TranslateMessage(&Message);
     DispatchMessage(&Message);
     }
return Message.wParam;
}

/****************************************************************/
/*              Window Procedure: WndProc                       */
/****************************************************************/

long FAR PASCAL WndProc (HWND hWnd, WORD iMessage, WORD wParam,
             LONG lParam)
{
switch (iMessage)
     {
     case WM_DESTROY:
          PostQuitMessage(0);
          return 0;
     default:
          return(DefWindowProc(hWnd, iMessage, wParam,
               lParam));
     }
}
```

Listing 4.9. The resource file for the cursor example.

```
SPORTS CURSOR SPORTS.CUR
```

Using Dialog Boxes

A *dialog box* is a pop-up window indicating that the application expects some input from, or interaction with, the user. A dialog box enables you to choose from a series of options, each corresponding to a *control* that can consist of such things as radio buttons, checkboxes, input fields, and list boxes.

The examples demonstrated so far in this book have contained two primary elements: the `WinMain` function and the window procedure. Applications that contain a dialog box, however, contain another basic element, the *dialog function*, which is similar to the window procedure except that it processes messages for the dialog box. There are two basic types of dialog boxes: modal and modeless.

A *modal dialog box* disables the parent window and does not let the user return to the parent window until the user makes the appropriate dialog box selections. When

a modal dialog box is initiated, the message loop for the dialog box processes messages from the application queue and does not return to the `WinMain` function.

A *modeless dialog box*, in contrast to the modal dialog box, does not disable the parent window. The modeless dialog box receives input from the message loop of the `WinMain` function and does not contain its own message loop. Your use of modal vs. modeless dialog boxes depends on the application and the desired implementation. You can implement the exact same dialog box (as seen by the user) using either modal or modeless.

You can create dialog boxes by using the Dialog Box editor of the Whitewater Resource Toolkit or the Dialog editor of the Resource Workshop. These editors contain a variety of tools that you can use to design effective dialog boxes. (See Chapters 16 and 17 for more information on the features and tools of the Dialog Box and Dialog editors.) The Dialog Box editor of the Whitewater Resource Toolkit was used to create the dialog box for the dialog box example in Listings 4.10, 4.11, and 4.12. Figure 4.9 shows the dialog box created with the Dialog Box editor and used in the dialog box example.

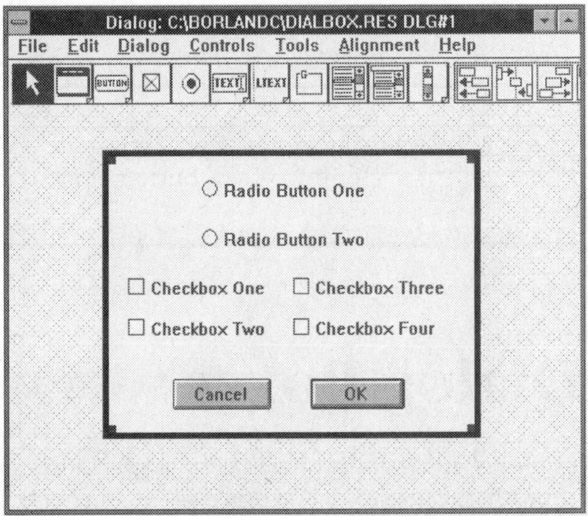

***Figure 4.9.** The dialog box resource.*

The dialog box example contains three files: the module definition file (Listing 4.10), a C source code file (Listing 4.11), and a resource script file (Listing 4.12). This example contains a `Help` menu with a `Dialog Box Demo` menu item. (See the "Using Menus" section later in this chapter for more information on creating menus.) When this menu item is selected, the dialog box created with the Dialog Box editor pops up. You then can select or deselect the controls of that dialog box. Figure 4.10 shows the window and dialog box generated by the dialog box example.

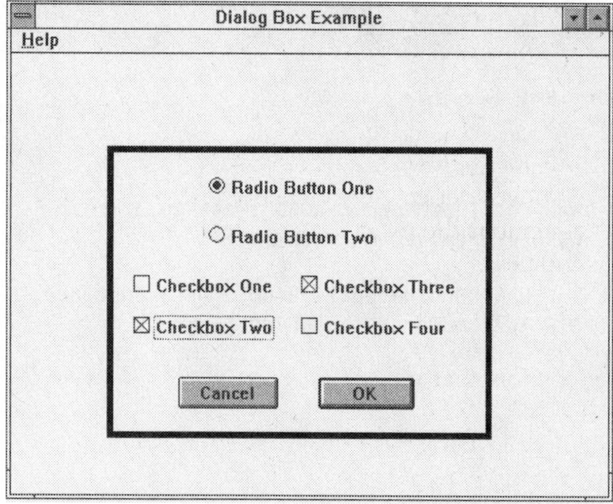

Figure 4.10. *Dialog box example.*

The dialog box format is different from the previously presented examples. The dialog box example contains the usual `WinMain` function and window procedure. However, this example also contains an additional procedure, the dialog procedure, that defines the actions for the dialog buttons. The dialog buttons are referenced in the dialog procedure by the ID defined for each button in the dialog resource.

The following lines show the project name as well as files used to create the dialog box example.

Project Name:	`WIN_DLG`
Files in Project:	`WIN_DLG.C`
	`WIN_DLG.DEF`
	`WIN_DLG.RC`

Listing 4.10. *The definition file for the dialog box example.*

```
NAME           WIN_DLG
DESCRIPTION    'Dialog Box Example'
EXETYPE        WINDOWS
CODE           PRELOAD MOVEABLE
DATA           PRELOAD MOVEABLE MULTIPLE
HEAPSIZE       1024
STACKSIZE      5120
EXPORTS        WndProc
               DlgProc
```

Listing 4.11. The C source file for the dialog box example.

```
#include <windows.h>
#include <stdlib.h>
#include <string.h>

long FAR PASCAL WndProc (HWND hWnd, WORD iMessage,
                WORD wParam, LONG lParam);

int PASCAL WinMain (HANDLE hInstance, HANDLE hPrevInstance,
              LPSTR lpszCmdParam, int nCmdShow)

#define DLG_DEMO 1

{
HWND hWnd;
MSG Message;
WNDCLASS WndClass;

if (!hPrevInstance)
     {
     WndClass.cbClsExtra = 0;
     WndClass.cbWndExtra = 0;
     WndClass.hbrBackground = GetStockObject(WHITE_BRUSH);
     WndClass.hCursor =  LoadCursor(NULL, IDC_ARROW);
     WndClass.hIcon = LoadIcon (NULL, "END");
     WndClass.hInstance = hInstance;
     WndClass.lpfnWndProc = WndProc;
     WndClass.lpszClassName = "WIN_DLG";
     WndClass.lpszMenuName = "DlgMenu";
     WndClass.style = CS_HREDRAW ¦ CS_VREDRAW;

     RegisterClass (&WndClass);
     }

hWnd = CreateWindow ("WIN_DLG",      /* class name */
          "Dialog Box Example",      /* Caption */
          WS_OVERLAPPEDWINDOW,       /* Style */
          CW_USEDEFAULT,             /* x position */
          0,                         /* y position */
          CW_USEDEFAULT,             /* cx - size */
          0,                         /* cy - size */
          NULL,                      /* Parent window */
          NULL,                      /* Menu */
          hInstance,                 /* Program Instance */
          NULL);                     /* Parameters */

ShowWindow(hWnd,nCmdShow);
UpdateWindow(hWnd);
while (GetMessage (&Message, 0, 0, 0))
```

```
     {
     TranslateMessage(&Message);
     DispatchMessage(&Message);
     }
return Message.wParam;
}

/****************************************************************/
/*              Dialog Procedure: DlgProc                       */
/****************************************************************/

BOOL FAR PASCAL DlgProc(HWND hDlg, WORD iMessage, WORD wParam,
               LONG lParam)
{
WORD status;

switch(iMessage)
     {
     case WM_INITDIALOG:

          CheckDlgButton(hDlg,101,1);
          return TRUE;

     case WM_COMMAND:

          switch(wParam)
            {
            case 101:
              status = IsDlgButtonChecked(hDlg,101);
              if (status == 0)
                CheckDlgButton(hDlg,101,1);
              else
                CheckDlgButton(hDlg,101,0);
              return TRUE;

            case 102:
               status = IsDlgButtonChecked(hDlg,102);
              if (status == 0)
                CheckDlgButton(hDlg,102,1);
              else
                CheckDlgButton(hDlg,102,0);
              return TRUE;

            case 103:
               status = IsDlgButtonChecked(hDlg,103);
             if (status == 0)
                CheckDlgButton(hDlg,103,1);
              else
                CheckDlgButton(hDlg,103,0);
              return TRUE;
```

continues

Listing 4.11. continued

```
            case 104:
               status = IsDlgButtonChecked(hDlg,104);
              if (status == 0)
                CheckDlgButton(hDlg,104,1);
              else
                CheckDlgButton(hDlg,104,0);
              return TRUE;

            case 105:
               status = IsDlgButtonChecked(hDlg,105);
              if (status == 0)
                CheckDlgButton(hDlg,105,1);
              else
                CheckDlgButton(hDlg,105,0);
              return TRUE;

            case 106:
               status = IsDlgButtonChecked(hDlg,106);
              if (status == 0)
                CheckDlgButton(hDlg,106,1);
              else
                CheckDlgButton(hDlg,106,0);
              return TRUE;

            case 107:
              EndDialog(hDlg,FALSE);
              return TRUE;

            case 108:
              EndDialog(hDlg,TRUE);
              return TRUE;

            }
            break;
      }
return FALSE;
}

/*****************************************************************/
/*               Window Procedure: WndProc                       */
/*****************************************************************/

long FAR PASCAL WndProc (HWND hWnd, WORD iMessage, WORD wParam,
                LONG lParam)
{
static FARPROC lpfnDlgProc;
static HANDLE hInstance;
```

```
switch (iMessage)
     {
     case WM_CREATE:

         hInstance = ((LPCREATESTRUCT)lParam)->hInstance;
         lpfnDlgProc = MakeProcInstance(DlgProc,hInstance);
         return 0;

     case WM_COMMAND:

         switch(wParam)
          {
          case DLG_DEMO:
               if(DialogBox(hInstance,"DLG#1",hWnd,
                  lpfnDlgProc));
                  InvalidateRect(hWnd,NULL,TRUE);
               return 0;
          }
         break;

     case WM_DESTROY:

         PostQuitMessage(0);
         return 0;

     }

return(DefWindowProc(hWnd,iMessage,wParam,lParam));
}
```

Listing 4.12. *The resource file for the dialog box example.*

```
#include <windows.h>
#define DLG_DEMO 1

DLG#1 DIALOG DISCARDABLE LOADONCALL PURE MOVEABLE 42, 38, 148,
108 STYLE WS_POPUP ¦ WS_DLGFRAME ¦ WS_SYSMENU
  BEGIN
  CONTROL "Radio Button One" 101, "BUTTON", WS_CHILD ¦
     WS_VISIBLE ¦ 0x4L, 38, 6, 74, 14
  CONTROL "Radio Button Two" 102, "BUTTON", WS_CHILD ¦
     WS_VISIBLE ¦ 0x4L, 38, 25, 74, 14
  CONTROL "Checkbox One" 103, "BUTTON", WS_CHILD ¦
     WS_VISIBLE ¦ WS_TABSTOP ¦ 0x2L, 8, 45, 64, 12
  CONTROL "Checkbox Two" 104, "BUTTON", WS_CHILD ¦
     WS_VISIBLE ¦ WS_TABSTOP ¦ 0x2L, 8, 61, 64, 12
  CONTROL "Checkbox Three" 105, "BUTTON", WS_CHILD ¦
     WS_VISIBLE ¦ WS_TABSTOP ¦ 0x2L, 75, 45, 72, 12
```

continues

Listing 4.12. continued

```
  CONTROL "Checkbox Four" 106, "BUTTON", WS_CHILD ¦
    WS_VISIBLE ¦ WS_TABSTOP ¦ 0x2L, 75, 61, 68, 12
  CONTROL "Cancel" 107, "BUTTON", WS_CHILD ¦
    WS_VISIBLE ¦ WS_TABSTOP, 26, 87, 40, 12
  CONTROL "OK" 108, "BUTTON", WS_CHILD ¦
    WS_VISIBLE ¦ WS_TABSTOP ¦ 0x1L, 82, 87, 38, 12
  END

DlgMenu MENU
  {
  POPUP "&Help"
    {
    MENUITEM "&Dialog Demo",  DLG_DEMO
    }
  }
```

Using Icons

An *icon* is a specialized bitmap that represents a minimized application. Double clicking the icon that represents a minimized application opens that application window.

You can create icons by using the Icon editor of the Whitewater Resource Toolkit or the Paint editor of the Resource Workshop. The Icon editor contains a variety of tools for this purpose. (See Chapter 16 for more information on the features and tools of the Icon editor.) The Paint editor of the Resource Workshop was used to create the icon used for the icon example in Listings 4.13, 4.14, and 4.15. The icon created with the Paint editor and used in the icon example is shown in Figure 4.11.

The icon example contains three files: the module definition file (Listing 4.13), a C source code file (Listing 4.14), and a resource script file (Listing 4.15). This example is basically the same example as the bitmap example demonstrated earlier in the chapter. The only difference is that the icon shown in Figure 4.11 represents the application when the window is minimized. This example loads the icon resource by specifying it as the default icon for the window class. (See the `WndClass.hIcon` line of the `WinMain` function.) Figure 4.12 shows the minimized window and icon generated by the icon example.

The following lines show the project name as well as files used to create the icon example.

Project Name:	`WIN_ICO`
Files in Project:	`WIN_ICO.C`
	`WIN_ICO.DEF`
	`WIN_ICO.RC`

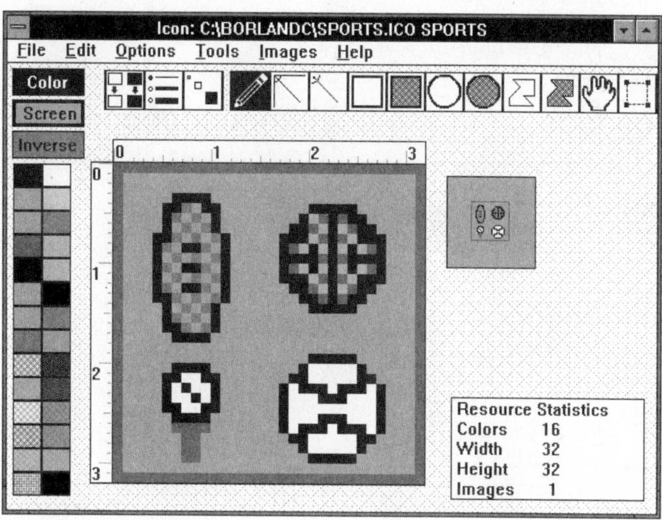

Figure 4.11. *The icon resource.*

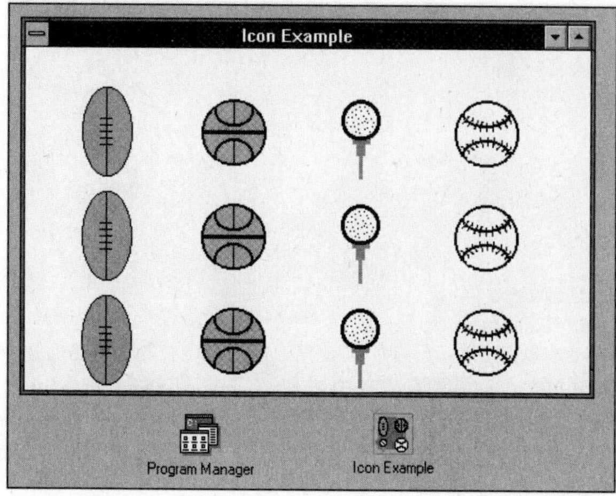

Figure 4.12. *Icon example.*

Listing 4.13. The definition file for the icon example.

```
NAME            WIN_ICO
DESCRIPTION     'Icon Example'
EXETYPE         WINDOWS
CODE            PRELOAD MOVEABLE
DATA            PRELOAD MOVEABLE MULTIPLE
HEAPSIZE        1024
STACKSIZE       5120
EXPORTS         WndProc
```

Listing 4.14. The C source file for the icon example.

```
#include <windows.h>
#include <stdlib.h>
#include <string.h>

static HANDLE hFootball;
static HANDLE hBasketball;
static HANDLE hGolfball;
static HANDLE hBaseball;

long FAR PASCAL WndProc (HWND hWnd, WORD iMessage,
                WORD wParam, LONG lParam);

int PASCAL WinMain (HANDLE hInstance, HANDLE hPrevInstance,
              LPSTR lpszCmdParam, int nCmdShow)

{
HWND hWnd;
MSG Message;
WNDCLASS WndClass;

if (!hPrevInstance)
     {
     WndClass.cbClsExtra = 0;
     WndClass.cbWndExtra = 0;
     WndClass.hbrBackground = GetStockObject(WHITE_BRUSH);
     WndClass.hCursor =  LoadCursor(NULL, IDC_ARROW);
     WndClass.hIcon = LoadIcon (hInstance, "A_RESOURCE");
     WndClass.hInstance = hInstance;
     WndClass.lpfnWndProc = WndProc;
     WndClass.lpszClassName = "WIN_ICO";
     WndClass.lpszMenuName = NULL;
     WndClass.style = CS_HREDRAW ¦ CS_VREDRAW;

     RegisterClass (&WndClass);
     }
```

```
hWnd = CreateWindow ("WIN_ICO",       /* class name */
         "Icon Example",              /* Caption */
         WS_OVERLAPPEDWINDOW,         /* Style */
         CW_USEDEFAULT,               /* x position */
         0,                           /* y position */
         CW_USEDEFAULT,               /* cx - size */
         0,                           /* cy - size */
         NULL,                        /* Parent window */
         NULL,                        /* Menu */
         hInstance,                   /* Program Instance */
         NULL);                       /* Parameters */

hFootball = LoadBitmap(hInstance,"FOOTBALL");
hBasketball = LoadBitmap(hInstance,"BASKET");
hGolfball = LoadBitmap(hInstance,"GOLFBALL");
hBaseball = LoadBitmap(hInstance,"BASEBALL");

ShowWindow (hWnd, nCmdShow);
UpdateWindow (hWnd);
while (GetMessage (&Message, 0, 0, 0))
     {
     TranslateMessage(&Message);
     DispatchMessage(&Message);
     }
return Message.wParam;
}

/*************************************************************/
/*             Window Procedure: WndProc                     */
/*************************************************************/

long FAR PASCAL WndProc (HWND hWnd, WORD iMessage, WORD wParam,
              LONG lParam)
{
HDC hDC, hMemDC;
short x, y;
PAINTSTRUCT PtStr;

switch (iMessage)
     {

    case WM_PAINT:

         hDC = BeginPaint(hWnd, &PtStr);
         hMemDC = CreateCompatibleDC(hDC);
         for (y=30; y<300; y=y+80)
             {
             SelectObject(hMemDC,hFootball);
             BitBlt(hDC,30,y,72,72,hMemDC,0,0,SRCCOPY);
```

continues

Listing 4.14. continued

```
                SelectObject(hMemDC,hBasketball);
                BitBlt(hDC,130,y,72,72,hMemDC,0,0,SRCCOPY);
                SelectObject(hMemDC,hGolfball);
                BitBlt(hDC,230,y,72,72,hMemDC,0,0,SRCCOPY);
                SelectObject(hMemDC,hBaseball);
                BitBlt(hDC,330,y,72,72,hMemDC,0,0,SRCCOPY);
                }
            DeleteDC(hMemDC);
            EndPaint(hWnd, &PtStr);
            return 0;

        case WM_DESTROY:

            DeleteObject(hFootball);
            DeleteObject(hBaseball);
            DeleteObject(hBasketball);
            DeleteObject(hGolfball);
            PostQuitMessage(0);
            return 0;

        default:

            return(DefWindowProc(hWnd, iMessage, wParam,
                lParam));
        }
}
```

Listing 4.15. The resource file for the icon example.

```
FOOTBALL   BITMAP FOOTBALL.BMP
BASKET     BITMAP BASKET.BMP
GOLFBALL   BITMAP GOLFBALL.BMP
BASEBALL   BITMAP BASEBALL.BMP
A_RESOURCE ICON   SPORTS.ICO
```

Using Menus

A *menu* is a list of application menu items, or commands, that the user can select. A *menu resource* defines the menus that appear on the application's Menu bar. The menu resource also defines the menu items for each of the menus on the Menu bar. Menu items can be represented with either text or bitmaps.

You can create menus by using the Menu editor of the Whitewater Resource Toolkit or the Menu editor of the Resource Workshop. The Menu editors contain a variety of tools for designing and creating menus. (See Chapters 16 and 17 for more information on the features and tools of the Menu editors.) The Menu editor of the Resource Workshop was used to create the menu used for the menu example in Listings 4.16, 4.17, and 4.18. The Resource Toolkit compiles the .RES file. Figure 4.13 shows the menus created with the Menu editor and used in the menu example.

The menu example contains three files: the module definition file (Listing 4.16), a C source code file (Listing 4.17), and a resource script file (Listing 4.18). This example contains several menus, each containing at least one menu item. Whenever you select a menu item, a message box appears that echoes the name of the menu item you selected. Figure 4.14 shows the window and message box generated by the menu example.

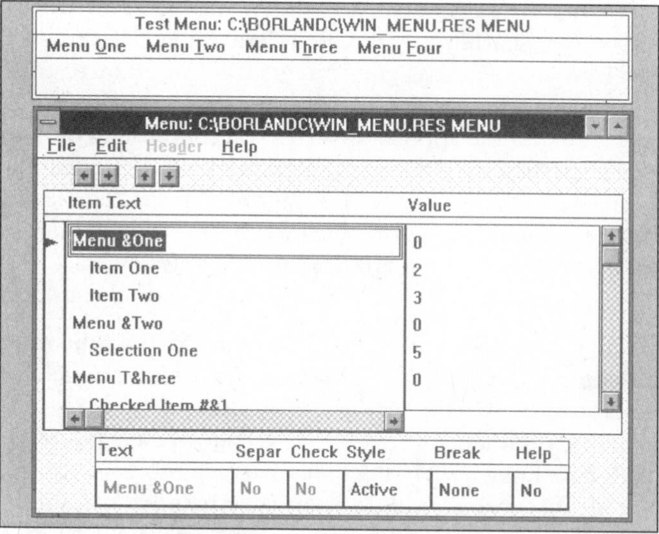

Figure 4.13. *The menu resource.*

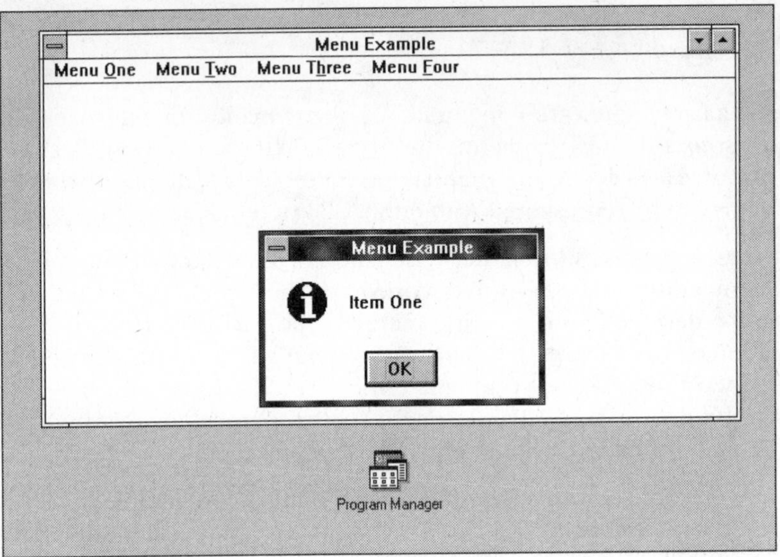

Figure 4.14. *Menu example.*

There are several steps that you must accomplish in order to add a menu to your application. The first step, of course, is to define the menu resource. As you define the menu resource, you arbitrarily define unique integer IDs to each of the menu items. Top-level menus are not assigned integer IDs. The menu resource used for the menu example is shown in Figure 4.13. The next step is to define the created menu resource as the menu for the application. This is accomplished by naming the menu resource as the default menu in the `WndClass.lpszMenuName` line of the window class defined in the `WinMain` function of the application. By declaring the menu in this line of the window class, the menu automatically appears as the application menu. The last step in adding a menu to your application is to define the actions for the menu items.

When you create a menu resource, you are merely defining the menus and menu items. The functionality and actions of the menu items are not defined in the menu resource; they are defined in the window procedure of the application. The action for the menu items is defined in the `WM_COMMAND` code of the window procedure. The `WM_COMMAND` code contains a *switch* statement that contains cases for each of the menu item IDs. The code that corresponds to a particular menu item ID defines the actions for that menu item. Although this example merely displays a message box whenever a menu item is selected, you can program a menu item to perform almost any task.

The following lines show the project name as well as files used to create the menu example.

Project Name: WIN_MENU
Files in Project: WIN_MENU.C
WIN_MENU.DEF
WIN_MENU.RC

Listing 4.16. The definition file for the menu example.

```
NAME            WIN_MENU
DESCRIPTION     'Menu Example'
EXETYPE         WINDOWS
CODE            PRELOAD MOVEABLE
DATA            PRELOAD MOVEABLE MULTIPLE
HEAPSIZE        1024
STACKSIZE       5120
EXPORTS         WndProc
```

Listing 4.17. The C source file for the menu example.

```
#include <windows.h>
#include <stdlib.h>
#include <string.h>

BOOL CheckOne = MF_CHECKED;
BOOL CheckTwo = MF_CHECKED;

long FAR PASCAL WndProc (HWND hWnd, WORD iMessage,
                WORD wParam, LONG lParam);

int PASCAL WinMain (HANDLE hInstance, HANDLE hPrevInstance,
              LPSTR lpszCmdParam, int nCmdShow)

{
HWND hWnd;
MSG Message;
WNDCLASS WndClass;

if (!hPrevInstance)
     {
     WndClass.cbClsExtra = 0;
     WndClass.cbWndExtra = 0;
     WndClass.hbrBackground = GetStockObject(WHITE_BRUSH);
     WndClass.hCursor =  LoadCursor(NULL, IDC_ARROW);
     WndClass.hIcon = LoadIcon (NULL, "END");
     WndClass.hInstance = hInstance;
     WndClass.lpfnWndProc = WndProc;
    WndClass.lpszClassName = "WIN_MENU";
```

continues

Listing 4.17. continued

```
     WndClass.lpszMenuName = "MENU";
     WndClass.style = CS_HREDRAW ¦ CS_VREDRAW;

     RegisterClass (&WndClass);
     }

hWnd = CreateWindow ("WIN_MENU",   /* class name */
          "Menu Example",          /* Caption */
          WS_OVERLAPPEDWINDOW,     /* Style */
          CW_USEDEFAULT,           /* x position */
          0,                       /* y position */
          CW_USEDEFAULT,           /* cx - size */
          0,                       /* cy - size */
          NULL,                    /* Parent window */
          NULL,                    /* Menu */
          hInstance,               /* Program Instance */
          NULL);                   /* Parameters */

ShowWindow(hWnd,nCmdShow);
UpdateWindow(hWnd);
while (GetMessage (&Message, 0, 0, 0))
     {
     TranslateMessage(&Message);
     DispatchMessage(&Message);
     }
return Message.wParam;
}

/****************************************************************/
/*              Window Procedure: WndProc                       */
/****************************************************************/

long FAR PASCAL WndProc (HWND hWnd, WORD iMessage, WORD wParam,
                LONG lParam)
{
HMENU hMenu;

switch (iMessage)
     {
     case WM_COMMAND:
       hMenu = GetMenu(hWnd);

       switch(wParam)
         {
         case 2:
          MessageBox(hWnd,"Item One","Menu Example",
                MB_ICONINFORMATION¦MB_OK);
          return 0;
```

```
        case 3:
         MessageBox(hWnd,"Item Two","Menu Example",
                 MB_ICONINFORMATION¦MB_OK);
         return 0;

        case 5:
         MessageBox(hWnd,"Selection One","Menu Example",
                 MB_ICONINFORMATION¦MB_OK);
         return 0;

        case 7:
         if (CheckOne == MF_CHECKED)
            {
            CheckMenuItem(hMenu,7,MF_BYCOMMAND ¦
                    MF_UNCHECKED);
            CheckOne = MF_UNCHECKED;
            }
            else
            {
            CheckMenuItem(hMenu,7,MF_BYCOMMAND ¦
                    MF_CHECKED);
            CheckOne = MF_CHECKED;
            }
         return 0;

        case 8:
         if (CheckTwo == MF_CHECKED)
            {
            CheckMenuItem(hMenu,8,MF_BYCOMMAND ¦
                    MF_UNCHECKED);
            CheckTwo = MF_UNCHECKED;
            }
         else
            {
            CheckMenuItem(hMenu,8,MF_BYCOMMAND ¦
                    MF_CHECKED);
            CheckTwo = MF_CHECKED;
            }
         return 0;

        case 10:
         MessageBox(hWnd,"Menu Item One","Menu Example",
            MB_ICONINFORMATION¦MB_OK);
         return 0;

        case 11:
         MessageBox(hWnd,"Menu Item Two","Menu Example",
                 MB_ICONINFORMATION¦MB_OK);
        return 0;
        }
    break;
```

continues

Listing 4.17. continued

```
    case WM_DESTROY:

      PostQuitMessage(0);
      return 0;

    default:

      return(DefWindowProc(hWnd, iMessage, wParam,
         lParam));
    }
}
```

Listing 4.18. The resource file for the menu example.

```
MENU  MENU LOADONCALL MOVEABLE PURE DISCARDABLE
BEGIN
  POPUP "Menu &One"
  BEGIN
    MenuItem  "Item One", 2
    MenuItem  "Item Two", 3
  END
  POPUP "Menu &Two"
  BEGIN
    MenuItem  "Selection One", 5
  END
  POPUP "Menu T&hree"
  BEGIN
    MenuItem  "Checked Item #&1", 7, CHECKED
    MenuItem  "Checked Item #&2", 8, CHECKED
  END
  POPUP "Menu &Four"
  BEGIN
    MenuItem  "Menu Item One", 10
    MenuItem  "Menu Item Two", 11
  END
END
```

Using Strings

String resources are text strings that an application can use for menu item names, error messages, dialog box control names, and so forth. String resources are maintained in the resource file of the application. Because the text strings used in an application are all in one location, you can locate and modify the strings easily. Therefore, if you want to display a different string (for example, an error message), you would not need to modify the C source file of the application. You merely modify the line of text in the resource file.

You can create string resources by using the String editor of the Whitewater Resource Toolkit or the String editor of the Resource Workshop. These editors contain a string table where you can define string resources. (See Chapters 16 and 17 for more information on the features of the String editors.) The String editor of the Whitewater Resource Toolkit was used to create the strings in the string example in Listings 4.19, 4.20, and 4.21. Figure 4.15 shows the string table created with the String editor of the Whitewater Resource Toolkit and used in the string example.

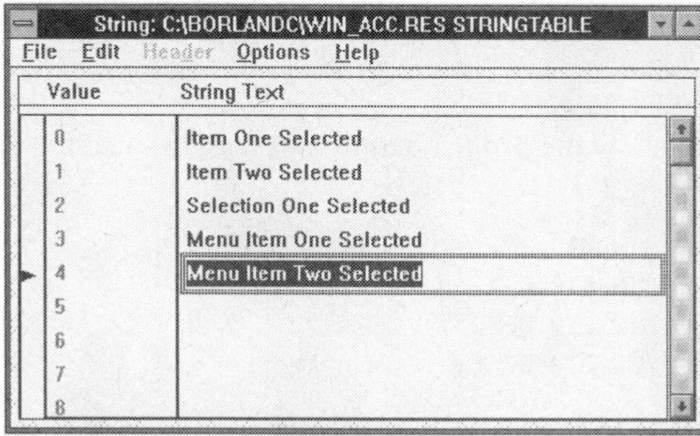

***Figure 4.15**. The string resource.*

The string example contains three files: the module definition file (Listing 4.19), a C source code file (Listing 4.20), and a resource script file (Listing 4.21). This example is the basically the same as the menu example (a message box appears each time a menu item is selected). The difference is that this example uses references to a string table for the message displayed in the resulting message box. Figure 4.16 shows the window and message box generated by the string example.

There are three basic steps for using string tables in an application. The first step is to create the string table. You can create the string table with the String editor or with a simple text editor. The second step is to load the desired string from the string table. This example uses the `LoadString` function to load a string from the string table. The last step is to display the string. In this example, the messages for the message boxes (that are displayed when a menu item is selected) are defined in the string table. The `LoadString` function copies the specified string for the menu item into a buffer, which is then used in the `MessageBox` function to display the specified string.

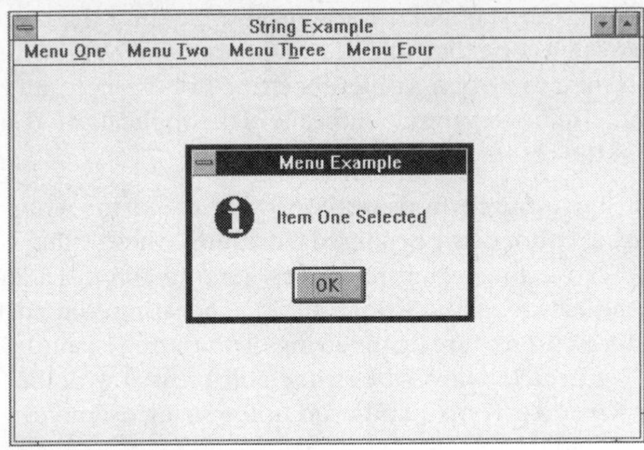

Figure 4.16. *String example.*

The following lines show the project name as well as files used to create the string example.

Project Name:	WIN_STR
Files in Project:	WIN_STR.C
	WIN_STR.DEF
	WIN_STR.RC

Listing 4.19. ***The definition file for the string example.***

```
NAME            WIN_STR
DESCRIPTION     'String Example'
EXETYPE         WINDOWS
CODE            PRELOAD MOVEABLE
DATA            PRELOAD MOVEABLE MULTIPLE
HEAPSIZE        1024
STACKSIZE       5120
EXPORTS         WndProc
```

Listing 4.20. ***The C source file for the string example.***

```
#include <windows.h>
#include <stdlib.h>
#include <string.h>

BOOL CheckOne = MF_CHECKED;
BOOL CheckTwo = MF_CHECKED;
HANDLE hIns;
```

```
long FAR PASCAL WndProc (HWND hWnd, WORD iMessage,
                WORD wParam, LONG lParam);

int PASCAL WinMain (HANDLE hInstance, HANDLE hPrevInstance,
              LPSTR lpszCmdParam, int nCmdShow)

{
HWND hWnd;
MSG Message;
WNDCLASS WndClass;

if (!hPrevInstance)
     {
     WndClass.cbClsExtra = 0;
     WndClass.cbWndExtra = 0;
     WndClass.hbrBackground = GetStockObject(WHITE_BRUSH);
     WndClass.hCursor =  LoadCursor(NULL, IDC_ARROW);
     WndClass.hIcon = LoadIcon (NULL, "END");
     WndClass.hInstance = hInstance;
     WndClass.lpfnWndProc = WndProc;
     WndClass.lpszClassName = "WIN_STR";
     WndClass.lpszMenuName = "MENU";
     WndClass.style = CS_HREDRAW ¦ CS_VREDRAW;

     RegisterClass (&WndClass);
     }

hIns = hInstance;
hWnd = CreateWindow ("WIN_STR",     /* class name */
          "String Example",         /* Caption */
          WS_OVERLAPPEDWINDOW,      /* Style */
          CW_USEDEFAULT,            /* x position */
          0,                        /* y position */
          CW_USEDEFAULT,            /* cx - size */
          0,                        /* cy - size */
          NULL,                     /* Parent window */
          NULL,                     /* Menu */
          hInstance,                /* Program Instance */
          NULL);                    /* Parameters */

ShowWindow(hWnd,nCmdShow);
UpdateWindow(hWnd);
while (GetMessage (&Message, 0, 0, 0))
     {
     TranslateMessage(&Message);
     DispatchMessage(&Message);
     }
return Message.wParam;
}
```

continues

Listing 4.20. continued

```
/*****************************************************************/
/*              Window Procedure: WndProc                       */
/*****************************************************************/

long FAR PASCAL WndProc (HWND hWnd, WORD iMessage, WORD wParam,
                LONG lParam)
{
HMENU hMenu;
char buffer[25];

switch (iMessage)
     {
     case WM_COMMAND:
       hMenu = GetMenu(hWnd);

       switch(wParam)
         {
         case 2:
          LoadString(hIns,0,buffer,25);
          MessageBox(hWnd,buffer,"Menu Example",
                  MB_ICONINFORMATION¦MB_OK);
          return 0;

         case 3:
          LoadString(hIns,1,buffer,25);
          MessageBox(hWnd,buffer,"Menu Example",
                  MB_ICONINFORMATION¦MB_OK);
          return 0;

         case 5:
          LoadString(hIns,2,buffer,25);
          MessageBox(hWnd,buffer,"Menu Example",
                  MB_ICONINFORMATION¦MB_OK);
          return 0;

         case 7:
          if (CheckOne == MF_CHECKED)
             {
             CheckMenuItem(hMenu,7,MF_BYCOMMAND ¦
                     MF_UNCHECKED);
             CheckOne = MF_UNCHECKED;
             }
          else
             {
             CheckMenuItem(hMenu,7,MF_BYCOMMAND ¦
```

```
                MF_CHECKED);
            CheckOne = MF_CHECKED;
            }
         return 0;

        case 8:
         if (CheckTwo == MF_CHECKED)
            {
            CheckMenuItem(hMenu,8,MF_BYCOMMAND ¦
                    MF_UNCHECKED);
            CheckTwo = MF_UNCHECKED;
            }

         else
            {
            CheckMenuItem(hMenu,8,MF_BYCOMMAND ¦
                    MF_CHECKED);
            CheckTwo = MF_CHECKED;
            }
         return 0;

        case 10:
         LoadString(hIns,3,buffer,25);
         MessageBox(hWnd,buffer,"Menu Example",
                 MB_ICONINFORMATION¦MB_OK);
         return 0;

        case 11:
         LoadString(hIns,4,buffer,25);
         MessageBox(hWnd,buffer,"Menu Example",
                 MB_ICONINFORMATION¦MB_OK);
         return 0;
        }
     break;

     case WM_DESTROY:

       PostQuitMessage(0);
       return 0;

     default:

    return(DefWindowProc(hWnd, iMessage, wParam,
         lParam));
     }
}
```

Listing 4.21. The resource file for the string example.

```
STRINGTABLE LOADONCALL MOVEABLE PURE DISCARDABLE
BEGIN
  0,  "Item One Selected"
  1,  "Item Two Selected"
  2,  "Selection One Selected"
  3,  "Menu Item One Selected"
  4,  "Menu Item Two Selected"
END

MENU  MENU LOADONCALL MOVEABLE PURE DISCARDABLE
BEGIN
  POPUP "Menu &One"
  BEGIN
    MenuItem  "Item One", 2
    MenuItem  "Item Two", 3
  END
  POPUP "Menu &Two"
  BEGIN
    MenuItem  "Selection One", 5
  END
  POPUP "Menu T&hree"
  BEGIN
    MenuItem  "Checked Item #&1", 7, CHECKED
    MenuItem  "Checked Item #&2", 8, CHECKED
  END
  POPUP "Menu &Four"
  BEGIN
    MenuItem  "Menu Item One", 10
    MenuItem  "Menu Item Two", 11
  END
END
```

5

The Keyboard and Windows

The keyboard is a very important input device for Windows applications. Although Windows supports the mouse in its graphical "point-and-click" environment, you do not need to use or even install the mouse to operate Windows successfully. Therefore, you should think of the keyboard as the primary input device. Well-designed Windows applications, however, always support both the mouse and the keyboard for input and cursor manipulation.

This chapter introduces the basic concepts and programming principles that you must consider when developing user interfaces that use the keyboard as the primary input device. Remember that well-designed applications should support both the mouse and the keyboard. Chapter 6 addresses using the mouse as an input device.

Keyboard Input

A Windows application receives input from the keyboard in the following manner. When you press or release a key, the keyboard device driver passes the appropriate

keyboard messages to Windows. The keyboard messages are placed in the system queue and then sent to the message queue of the appropriate application. The application's window procedure then processes the messages. Figure 5.1 shows this procedure.

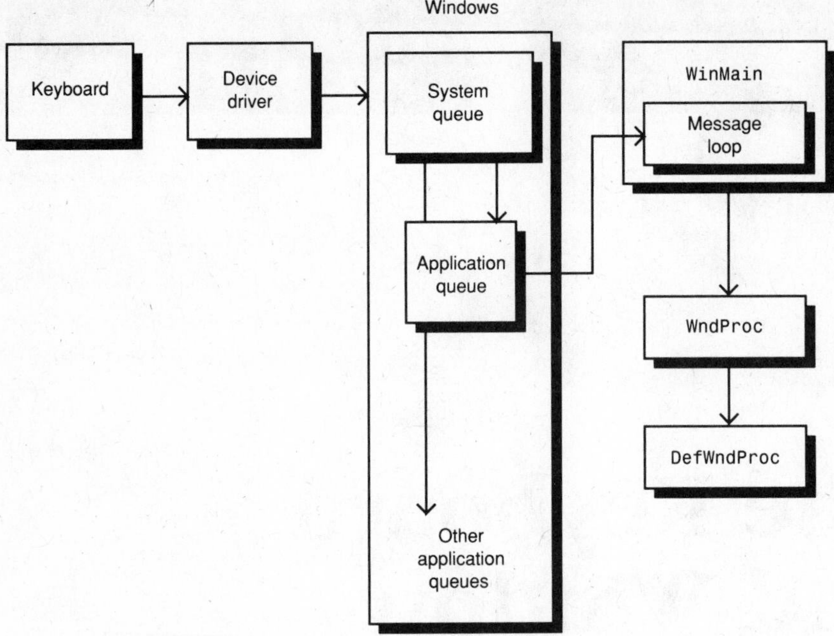

Figure 5.1. *Keyboard input.*

After receiving input from the keyboard, Windows must determine which application should receive the input. Windows solves this problem by sending input messages to the window that has the "input focus," which is either the active window or a "child" of the active window. The window that has the input focus is the targeted recipient of all input messages. The user can distinguish the *active window* in several ways. If the active window has a caption bar, the bar is highlighted. If the active window has a dialog frame, the frame is highlighted. A *child window* that has the input focus usually contains a blinking cursor or caret, and the parent window must be active.

Keyboard Messages

Keyboard input is divided into two categories: keystrokes and characters. Whenever you press or release a key, a *keystroke message* is generated. When a keystroke combination occurs that results in a displayable character, a *character message* is generated—assuming you are using the traditional message loop that contains the `TranslateMessage` function, as follows:

```
while (GetMessage (&Message, 0, 0, 0))
     {
     TranslateMessage(&Message);
     DispatchMessage(&Message);
     }
return Message.wParam;
```

For example, if you press the A key, two keystroke messages—one for pressing and one for releasing the key—are generated. However, an additional character message is also sent because the keystroke combination results in a displayable character, the letter *A.* (You learn more about this later in the chapter.)

There are two general types of keystroke messages: system and non-system. Table 5.1 lists these messages. *System messages* correspond only to keystrokes that use the Alt key and invoke options from the application or system menus. *Non-system messages* correspond to virtually all other keystrokes.

Table 5.1. Keystroke messages.

Message	*Type*	*Meaning*
`WM_KEYDOWN`	Non-system	Non-system key is pressed
`WM_KEYUP`	Non-system	Non-system key is released
`WM_SYSKEYDOWN`	System	System key is pressed
`WM_SYSKEYUP`	System	System key is released

lParam

The keystroke message contains vital information on the keystroke in its two variables, `wParam` and `lParam`. The 32-bit `lParam` variable of the keystroke message is divided into the following six fields:

- Repeat count (bits 0 to 15)
- OEM scan code (bits 16 to 23)
- Extended key flag (bit 24)
- Context code (bit 29)

- Previous key state (bit 30)
- Transition state (bit 31)

(Note: Bits 25 to 28 are reserved.)

The *repeat count* is the number of keystrokes that the message represents. The repeat count is one, except when the key is held down. The window procedure often is not fast enough to process the key-down messages that result from a key being pressed and held down. When this happens, Windows combines several key-down messages and then increments the repeat count.

The *OEM scan code* is the scan code value sent from the keyboard. Because this field is device-dependent, the value generally is ignored.

The *context code* is set to 1 if the Alt key is pressed. Otherwise, the context code is set to 0.

The *previous key state* helps to determine whether the message is the result of automated typing actions, such as those generated when you hold down a key. The previous key state is 0 if the key was previously up, and 1 if the key was previously down.

The *transition state* indicates whether the key is being pressed or released. The transition state is set to 0 when the key is being pressed down—`WM_KEYDOWN` or `WM_SYSKEYDOWN` key messages. The transition state is set to 1 when the key is being released—`WM_KEYUP` or `WM_SYSKEYUP` key messages.

wParam

The `wParam` parameter of the keystroke message contains the virtual key code that identifies the pressed key. The virtual key code is the device-dependent scan code converted by the Windows system to a device-independent form. Virtual keys are device-independent and are defined in the windows.h include file. Table 5.2 lists the virtual keys and their constants.

Character Messages

The customary message loop of the `WinMain` function contains the `TranslateMessage` function, which translates keystroke messages into character messages. Again, there are two types of character messages: non-system and system. Table 5.3 lists the character messages.

Table 5.2. The virtual key codes.

Decimal	*Hex*	*Constant*	*Key*
1	01	VK_LBUTTON	
2	02	VK_RBUTTON	
3	03	VK_CANCEL	Ctrl-break
4	04	VK_MBUTTON	
8	08	VK_BACK	Backspace
9	09	VK_TAB	Tab
12	0C	VK_CLEAR	Numeric keypad 5 with Num Lock off
13	0D	VK_RETURN	Enter
16	10	VK_SHIFT	Shift
17	11	VK_CONTROL	Ctrl
18	12	VK_MENU	Alt
19	13	VK_PAUSE	Pause
20	14	VK_CAPITAL	Caps Lock
27	1B	VK_ESCAPE	Esc
32	20	VK_SPACE	Space bar
33	21	VK_PRIOR	PgUp
34	22	VK_NEXT	PgDn
35	23	VK_END	End
36	24	VK_HOME	Home
37	25	VK_LEFT	Left arrow
38	26	VK_UP	Up arrow
39	27	VK_RIGHT	Right arrow
40	28	VK_DOWN	Down arrow
41	29	VK_SELECT	
42	2A	VK_PRINT	
43	2B	VK_EXECUTE	
44	2C	VK_SNAPSHOT	PrtSc
45	2D	VK_INSERT	Ins
46	2E	VK_DELETE	Del
47	2F	VK_HELP	
48–57	30–39	VK_0 to VK_9	0 to 9 on main keyboard
65–90	41–5A	VK_A to VK_Z	A to Z

continues

Table 5.2. continued

Decimal	*Hex*	*Constant*	*Key*
96–105	60–69	VK_NUMPAD0 to VK_NUMPAD9	Numeric keypad 0 to numeric keypad 9 (Num Lock on)
106	6A	VK_MULTIPLY	* on numeric keypad
107	6B	VK_ADD	+ on numeric keypad
108	6C	VK_SEPARATOR	
109	6D	VK_SUBTRACT	– on numeric keypad
110	6E	VK_DECIMAL	. on numeric keypad
111	6F	VK_DIVIDE	/ on numeric keypad
112–123	70–7B	VK_F1 to VK_F12	F1 to F12
124	7C	VK_F13	
125	7D	VK_F14	
126	7E	VK_F15	
127	7F	VK_F16	
144	90	VK_NUMLOCK	Num Lock

Table 5.3. Character messages.

Message	*Type*	*Meaning*
WM_CHAR	Non-system	Non-system character
WM_DEADCHAR	Non-system	Non-system dead character *
WM_SYSCHAR	System	System character
WM_SYSDEADCHAR	System	System dead character *

**Dead characters* do not display characters but modify the display of other characters.

The character messages contain the same two variables as the keyboard messages, `wParam` and `lParam`. For the character message, `lParam` is the same as `lParam` for keyboard messages. For the character message, however, `wParam` differs from `wParam` for the keyboard message. For character messages, `wParam` contains the ASCII code for the character.

Character Sets

Windows supports two extended character sets: OEM and ANSI. The *OEM character set* is the IBM character set with which MS-DOS programmers are familiar. However, Windows applications seldom use the OEM character set. Instead, Windows applications most frequently use the *ANSI character set*. Windows provides several functions for the conversion between character sets. Table 5.4 lists these functions and explains their conversions.

Table 5.4. Conversion functions.

Function	*Meaning*
`AnsiToOem`	Converts an ANSI string to an OEM character string
`AnsiToOemBuff`	Converts an ANSI string in a buffer to an OEM string
`OemToAnsi`	Converts an OEM character string to an ANSI string
`OemToAnsiBuff`	Converts an OEM character string in a buffer to an ANSI string

The Caret

Windows uses the caret to indicate the current text position. In many environments, the term *cursor* or *text cursor* refers to the current text position. In Windows, however, the term *caret* refers to the current text position and the term *cursor* refers to the current mouse position. The caret is a system resource that is shared between applications, so the Windows environment has only one caret. Only the window that has the input focus can display the caret. The keyboard example in Listings 5.1 and 5.2 demonstrates the use of the caret and the keyboard messages.

The Keyboard Example

The keyboard example in Listings 5.1 and 5.2 demonstrates the use of the caret and keyboard messages for the input and editing of a line of text. This example shows the caret and maintains its position relative to the line of text.

The keyboard example demonstrates how you can create a simple single-line text editor. This example enables you to enter text, and it provides the basic capabilities of an editor. The Left- and Right-arrow keys enable you to move the caret. The End, Del, and Home keys enable you, respectively, to move the caret to the end of the line, to delete a character at the caret, and to move the caret to the beginning of the line.

The `WinMain` function of this example is similar to what you have already seen in this book. The window procedure, however, contains two significant differences. The window procedure contains the standard switch statement and checks for two keyboard input cases: `WM_CHAR` and `WM_KEYDOWN`. The code for `WM_CHAR` monitors input and checks to make sure that the input is valid. The `WM_KEYDOWN` code updates the caret position and performs the appropriate screen updates for the key that was pressed. Figure 5.2 shows the window created by the keyboard example.

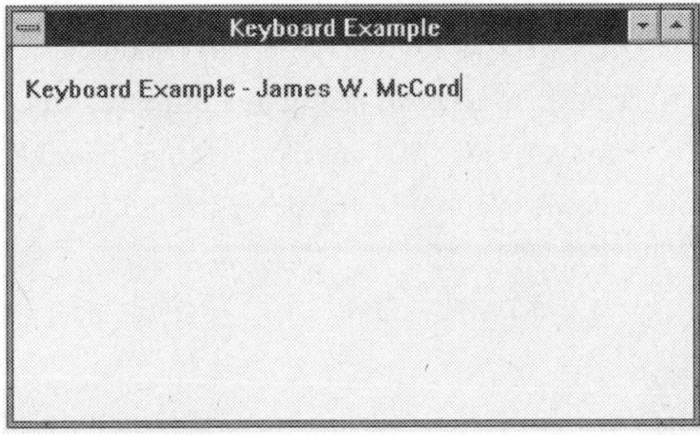

Figure 5.2. *The keyboard example.*

The following lines show the project name as well as files used to create the keyboard example.

Project Name:	`WIN_KEY`
Files in Project:	`WIN_KEY.C`
	`WIN_KEY.DEF`

Listing 5.1. *The definition file for the keyboard example.*

```
NAME            WIN_KEY
DESCRIPTION     'Keyboard Example'
EXETYPE         WINDOWS
CODE            PRELOAD MOVEABLE
DATA            PRELOAD MOVEABLE MULTIPLE
HEAPSIZE        1024
STACKSIZE       5120
EXPORTS         WndProc
```

Listing 5.2. *The C source file for the keyboard example.*

```
#include <windows.h>
#include <stdlib.h>
#include <string.h>

long FAR PASCAL WndProc (HWND hWnd, WORD iMessage,
                WORD wParam, LONG lParam);

void NEAR PASCAL CaretPos(HWND hWnd, int nArrayPos,
                 char *cCharBuf, int *xCaret,
                 int *yCaret, int nCharWidth);

int PASCAL WinMain (HANDLE hInstance, HANDLE hPrevInstance,
              LPSTR lpszCmdParam, int nCmdShow)

{
HWND hWnd;
MSG Message;
WNDCLASS WndClass;

if (!hPrevInstance)
     {
     WndClass.cbClsExtra = 0;
     WndClass.cbWndExtra = 0;
     WndClass.hbrBackground = GetStockObject(WHITE_BRUSH);
     WndClass.hCursor =  LoadCursor(NULL, IDC_ARROW);
     WndClass.hIcon = LoadIcon (NULL, "END");
     WndClass.hInstance = hInstance;
     WndClass.lpfnWndProc = WndProc;
     WndClass.lpszClassName = "WIN_KEY";
     WndClass.lpszMenuName = NULL;
     WndClass.style = CS_HREDRAW ¦ CS_VREDRAW;
```

continues

Listing 5.2. continued

```
     RegisterClass (&WndClass);
     }

hWnd = CreateWindow ("WIN_KEY",      /* class name */
          "Keyboard Example",        /* Caption */
          WS_OVERLAPPEDWINDOW,       /* Style */
          CW_USEDEFAULT,             /* x position */
          0,                         /* y position */
          CW_USEDEFAULT,             /* cx - size */
          0,                         /* cy - size */
          NULL,                      /* Parent window */
          NULL,                      /* Menu */
          hInstance,                 /* Program Instance */
          NULL);                     /* Parameters */

ShowWindow(hWnd,nCmdShow);
while (GetMessage (&Message, 0, 0, 0))
     {
     TranslateMessage(&Message);
     DispatchMessage(&Message);
     }
return Message.wParam;
}

/****************************************************************/
/*              Window Procedure: WndProc                      */
/****************************************************************/

long FAR PASCAL WndProc (HWND hWnd, WORD iMessage, WORD wParam,
                LONG lParam)
{
#define BufSize 40
static unsigned char cCharBuf[BufSize];
static int nNumChar = 0;
static int nArrayPos = 0;
static int nLnHeight;
static int nCharWidth;
static int xCaret, yCaret;
int x;
HDC hDC;
TEXTMETRIC tm;
PAINTSTRUCT PtStr;

switch (iMessage)
     {
     case WM_CHAR:
          {
```

```
        if (wParam == VK_BACK)
           {
           if (nArrayPos == 0)
              MessageBox(hWnd,"Can't Backspace",NULL,
                     MB_OK);
           else
              {
              nArrayPos = nArrayPos - 1;
              CaretPos(hWnd,nArrayPos,cCharBuf,
                  &xCaret,&yCaret,nCharWidth);
              for (x=nArrayPos; x<nNumChar; x=x+1)
              cCharBuf[x]=cCharBuf[x+1];
              nNumChar= nNumChar - 1;
              InvalidateRect(hWnd,NULL,TRUE);
              }
            break;
            }

        if (wParam <= VK_ESCAPE)
           {
           MessageBox(hWnd,"Try another key",NULL,
                   MB_OK);
           break;
           }

        if (nNumChar >= 40)
           {
           MessageBox(hWnd,"Buffer is full",NULL,
                   MB_OK);
           break;
           }

        for (x=nNumChar;x>nArrayPos;x=x-1)
           cCharBuf[x] = cCharBuf[x-1];
        cCharBuf[nArrayPos] = (unsigned char)wParam;
        nArrayPos = nArrayPos + 1;
        nNumChar = nNumChar + 1;
        CaretPos(hWnd,nArrayPos,cCharBuf,&xCaret,
           &yCaret,nCharWidth);
        InvalidateRect(hWnd,NULL,TRUE);
        }
        break;


    case WM_CREATE:
        {
        hDC = GetDC(hWnd);
        GetTextMetrics(hDC,&tm);
```

continues

Listing 5.2. continued

```
        nLnHeight = tm.tmHeight + tm.tmExternalLeading;
        nCharWidth = tm.tmAveCharWidth;
        yCaret = nLnHeight;
        ReleaseDC(hWnd,hDC);
        }
        break;

    case WM_SETFOCUS:

        CreateCaret(hWnd,0,0,nLnHeight);
        CaretPos(hWnd,nArrayPos,cCharBuf,&xCaret,
            &yCaret,nCharWidth);
        ShowCaret(hWnd);
        break;

    case WM_KILLFOCUS:

        DestroyCaret();
        break;

    case WM_KEYDOWN:
        {
        switch(wParam)
          {
          case VK_END:
            nArrayPos = nNumChar;
            CaretPos(hWnd,nArrayPos,cCharBuf,&xCaret,
               &yCaret,nCharWidth);
            break;;

          case VK_HOME:
            nArrayPos = 0;
            CaretPos(hWnd,nArrayPos,cCharBuf,&xCaret,
             &yCaret,nCharWidth);
            break;

          case VK_DELETE:
            if(nArrayPos == nNumChar)
              MessageBox(hWnd,"End of Buffer",NULL,
                   MB_OK);
            else
              {
              for (x=nArrayPos; x<nNumChar; x=x+1)
              cCharBuf[x] = cCharBuf[x+1];
              nNumChar = nNumChar - 1;
              InvalidateRect(hWnd,NULL,TRUE);
              }
            break;
```

```
            case VK_LEFT:
              if (nArrayPos > 0)
                {
                nArrayPos = nArrayPos - 1;
                CaretPos(hWnd,nArrayPos,cCharBuf,&xCaret,
                  &yCaret,nCharWidth);
                }
              else
                MessageBox(hWnd,"Can't move left",NULL,
                     MB_OK);
              break;

            case VK_RIGHT:
              if (nArrayPos < nNumChar)
               {
               nArrayPos = nArrayPos + 1;
               CaretPos(hWnd,nArrayPos,cCharBuf,&xCaret,
                     &yCaret,nCharWidth);
               }
              else
               MessageBox(hWnd,"At end of buffer",NULL,
                       MB_OK);
              break;
            }
          }
          break;

     case WM_PAINT:
          {
          hDC = BeginPaint(hWnd,&PtStr);
          TextOut(hDC,nCharWidth,nLnHeight,cCharBuf,
               nNumChar);
          EndPaint(hWnd,&PtStr);
          }
          break;

     case WM_DESTROY:

          PostQuitMessage(0);
          break;

     default:
          return(DefWindowProc(hWnd,iMessage,wParam,
                         lParam));
     }
return 0;
}
```

continues

Listing 5.2. continued

```
void NEAR PASCAL CaretPos(HWND hWnd, int nArrayPos,
                 char *cCharBuf, int *xCaret,
                 int *yCaret, int nCharWidth)
{
DWORD dWord;
HDC hDC;

hDC = GetDC(hWnd);
dWord = GetTextExtent(hDC,cCharBuf,nArrayPos);
ReleaseDC(hWnd,hDC);
*xCaret = LOWORD(dWord) + nCharWidth;
SetCaretPos(*xCaret,*yCaret);
}
```

6

The Mouse and Windows

Many people associate the mouse with Windows. This association is natural because graphical user interfaces such as Windows offer the "point-and-click" advantage. Sometimes the Microsoft Mouse is bundled with the Windows software product. As a Windows programmer you are tempted to assume that the user has a mouse—but don't count on it. As Chapter 5 mentioned, Windows can be installed and operated successfully without a mouse. Therefore, a well-designed Windows program supports the mouse but does not require one.

This chapter introduces the basics of using the mouse as an input device. By combining the information provided in this chapter with the keyboard information in Chapter 5, you can design an effective interface for your Windows application that can be manipulated with either the keyboard or the mouse.

Mouse Input

Most programmers are familiar with the basic operations of the mouse. The cursor, a special bit map, indicates the current mouse position on the screen. Table 6.1 lists the cursors that Windows has predefined. The mouse cursor moves as the mouse moves and the mouse buttons provide input. The actions resulting from the mouse input depend on the mouse position and the mouse button pressed. Several actions can be taken with the mouse buttons, including clicking, double clicking, and dragging.

Table 6.1. Predefined cursors.

Constant	*Meaning*
IDC_ARROW	Arrow cursor
IDC_CROSS	Crosshair cursor
IDC_IBEAM	I-beam text cursor
IDC_ICON	Empty icon
IDC_SIZE	Square with small square in lower right corner
IDC_SIZENESW	Cursor with arrows pointing northeast and southwest
IDC_SIZENS	Cursor with arrows pointing north and south
IDC_SIZENWSE	Cursor with arrows pointing northwest and southeast
IDC_SIZEWE	Cursor with arrows pointing west and east
IDC_UPARROW	Vertical arrow cursor
IDC_WAIT	Hourglass cursor

Clicking is the pressing and releasing of a mouse button. Clicking can be used to select objects and initiate program commands. *Double clicking* is the pressing and releasing of a mouse button two times in a short time period (1/2 second is the default setting for Windows). Double clicking activates the default action of the selected item. *Dragging* refers to pressing the mouse button and moving the mouse while the mouse button is still pressed. Dragging often is used for selecting menu items and for moving objects.

Windows receives mouse input through the mouse device driver. The mouse driver, if installed, is loaded when Windows starts (unless the device driver already is loaded) and determines whether a mouse is present. If a mouse is present, the device driver notifies Windows of any mouse event. A window receives a mouse event (in the form of a message) whenever the mouse event occurs within the window. The window receiving the mouse event does not have to be active or have the input focus.

Mouse Messages

The window procedure of a Windows application is notified of a mouse event by a mouse message. There are three general classifications of mouse messages: the hit test message, non-client area messages, and client area messages.

The Hit Test Message

The hit test message is sent before any client or non-client mouse messages. Each time the mouse is moved, the message, `WM_NCHITTEST`, is sent to the window that contains the cursor to determine the position and region of the mouse (see Chapter 14, "Windows Messages," for more information). The `lParam` parameter of the `WM_NCHITTEST` message contains the x and y screen coordinates of the cursor at the time that the message was sent.

The `WM_NCHITTEST` message usually is passed to the `DefWindowProc` function. The return value of the `DefWindowProc` function indicates the area containing the cursor. The `DefWindowProc` function returns one of the hit test values listed in Table 6.2.

Table 6.2. Hit test codes.

Hit Test Code	*Meaning*
HTBOTTOM	Lower horizontal window border
HTBOTTOMLEFT	Lower left corner of window border
HTBOTTOMRIGHT	Lower right corner of window border
HTCAPTION	Caption area
HTCLIENT	Client area
HTERROR	Screen background or window dividing line—produces a beep on error
HTGROWBOX	Size box
HTHSCROLL	Horizontal scroll bar
HTLEFT	Left window border
HTMENU	Menu area
HTNOWHERE	Screen background or window dividing line
HTREDUCE	Minimize box
HTRIGHT	Right window border
HTSIZE	Size box

continues

Table 6.2. continued

Hit Test Code	Meaning
HTSYSMENU	Control menu box
HTTOP	Upper horizontal window border
HTTOPLEFT	Upper left corner of window border
HTTOPRIGHT	Upper right corner of window border
HTTRANSPARENT	Window covered by another window
HTVSCROLL	Vertical scroll bar
HTZOOM	Maximize box

The `WM_NCHITTEST` message generates all other mouse messages. Either a client area or non-client area message is generated, depending on the value that the `DefWindowProc` function returns.

Client Area Mouse Messages

When a mouse event occurs in the client area, a client area mouse message is generated. Table 6.3 lists the client area mouse messages.

Table 6.3. Client area mouse messages.

Message	Meaning
WM_LBUTTONDOWN	The left mouse button was pressed in the client area
WM_LBUTTONUP	The left mouse button was released in the client area
WM_LBUTTONDBLCLK	The left mouse button was double clicked in the client area
WM_MBUTTONDOWN	The middle mouse button was pressed in the client area
WM_MBUTTONUP	The middle mouse button was released in the client area
WM_MBUTTONDBLCLK	The middle mouse button was double clicked in the client area
WM_MOUSEMOVE	The mouse was moved in the client area
WM_RBUTTONDOWN	The right mouse button was pressed in the client area
WM_RBUTTONUP	The right mouse button was released in the client area
WM_RBUTTONDBLCLK	The right mouse button was double clicked in the client area

The lParam parameter of each of the client area messages contains the mouse position. The low-order word of the parameter consists of the x-coordinate of the mouse position; the high-order word of lParam contains the y-coordinate of the mouse position. The coordinates expressed in lParam are relative to the upper-left corner of the window.

The wParam parameter of the client area messages contains a value that indicates the status of the various virtual keys. The wParam parameter can be a combination of the values listed in Table 6.4.

Table 6.4. wParam values.

Value	Meaning
MK_CONTROL	Ctrl key is down
MK_LBUTTON	Left button is down
MK_MBUTTON	Middle button is down
MK_RBUTTON	Right button is down
MK_SHIFT	Shift key is down

By using the lParam and wParam parameters of the client area mouse messages, you can determine the mouse postion and status of the mouse keys.

Non-Client Area Mouse Messages

Whenever a mouse event occurs at a location other than in the client area but still inside the window (such as the menu, caption bar, or scroll bar), a non-client area message is generated. Table 6.5 lists the non-client area mouse messages. Non-client area messages usually are not handled by the application but instead are sent to DefWindowProc.

The lParam parameter of the non-client area mouse messages contains the screen coordinates of the mouse position at the time that the message was generated. The low-order word of lParam contains the horizontal coordinate of the mouse position; the high-order word of lParam contains the vertical coordinate of the mouse position.

The wParam parameter of the non-client area mouse messages contains the value determined at the time that the WM_NCHITTEST message was generated. This value indicates the non-client area at which the cursor was located when the message was generated. Table 6.3 lists the possible values for wParam.

Table 6.5. Non-client area mouse messages.

Message	*Meaning*
WM_LBUTTONDOWN	The left mouse button was pressed in a non-client area
WM_LBUTTONUP	The left mouse button was released in a non-client area
WM_LBUTTONDBLCLK	The left mouse button was double clicked in a non-client area
WM_MBUTTONDOWN	The middle mouse button was pressed in a non-client area
WM_MBUTTONUP	The middle mouse button was released in a non-client area
WM_MBUTTONDBLCLK	The middle mouse button was double clicked in a non-client area
WM_MOUSEMOVE	The mouse was moved in a non-client area
WM_RBUTTONDOWN	The right mouse button was pressed in a non-client area
WM_RBUTTONUP	The right mouse button was released in a non-client area
WM_RBUTTONDBLCLK	The right mouse button was double clicked in a non-client area

By using the `lParam` and `wParam` parameters of the non-client area mouse messages, you can determine the mouse position and non-client area associated with the message.

Mouse Example

The mouse example in Listings 6.1 and 6.2 demonstrates one way that you can monitor mouse movements. The example monitors the non-client area message `WM_MOUSEMOVE` and determines whether the mouse is located within the one of nine predefined rectangular regions. Anytime the cursor moves within one of the regions, a new cursor is displayed. Ten different cursors can be displayed in this example.

The `WinMain` function follows the same format as the examples previously presented in this book. The window procedure, however, differs from previous examples. The window procedure for the mouse example checks for the `WM_MOUSEMOVE` message. When the `WM_MOUSEMOVE` message is received by the window procedure, the `WM_MOUSEMOVE` code determines the mouse position. If the mouse position is within any one of nine predefined areas, the cursor is changed using the `LoadCursor` and `SetCursor` functions.

The following lines show the project name as well as files used to create the mouse example.

Project Name: WIN_MOUS
Files in Project: WIN_MOUS.C
WIN_MOUS.DEF

Listing 6.1. *The definition file for the mouse example.*

```
NAME            WIN_MOUS
DESCRIPTION     'Mouse Example'
EXETYPE         WINDOWS
CODE            PRELOAD MOVEABLE
DATA            PRELOAD MOVEABLE MULTIPLE
HEAPSIZE        1024
STACKSIZE       5120
EXPORTS         WndProc
```

Listing 6.2. *The C source file for the mouse example.*

```
#include <windows.h>
#include <stdlib.h>
#include <string.h>

long FAR PASCAL WndProc (HWND hWnd, WORD iMessage,
                WORD wParam, LONG lParam);

int PASCAL WinMain (HANDLE hInstance, HANDLE hPrevInstance,
              LPSTR lpszCmdParam, int nCmdShow)

{
HWND hWnd;
MSG Message;
WNDCLASS WndClass;

if (!hPrevInstance)
     {
     WndClass.cbClsExtra = 0;
     WndClass.cbWndExtra = 0;
     WndClass.hbrBackground = GetStockObject(WHITE_BRUSH);
     WndClass.hCursor = NULL;
     WndClass.hIcon = LoadIcon (NULL, "END");
     WndClass.hInstance = hInstance;
     WndClass.lpfnWndProc = WndProc;
     WndClass.lpszClassName = "WIN_MOUS";
     WndClass.lpszMenuName = NULL;
     WndClass.style = CS_HREDRAW | CS_VREDRAW;
```

continues

Listing 6.2. continued

```
     RegisterClass (&WndClass);
     }

hWnd = CreateWindow ("WIN_MOUS",     /* class name */
          "Mouse Example",           /* Caption */
          WS_OVERLAPPEDWINDOW,       /* Style */
          CW_USEDEFAULT,             /* x position */
          0,                         /* y position */
          CW_USEDEFAULT,             /* cx - size */
          0,                         /* cy - size */
          NULL,                      /* Parent window */
          NULL,                      /* Menu */
          hInstance,                 /* Program Instance */
          NULL);                     /* Parameters */

ShowWindow (hWnd, nCmdShow);
UpdateWindow(hWnd);
while (GetMessage (&Message, 0, 0, 0))
     {
     TranslateMessage(&Message);
     DispatchMessage(&Message);
     }
return Message.wParam;
}

/***************************************************************/
/*             Window Procedure: WndProc                       */
/***************************************************************/

long FAR PASCAL WndProc (HWND hWnd, WORD iMessage, WORD wParam,
                LONG lParam)
{
HDC hDC;
PAINTSTRUCT PtStr;
WORD x, y;
HCURSOR hCursor;

switch (iMessage)
     {

     case WM_MOUSEMOVE:

        x = LOWORD(lParam);
        y = HIWORD(lParam);

        if (x>=50 && x<=200 && y>=50 && y<=200)
          {
```

```
if (x>=50 && x<=100 && y>=50 && y<=100)
{
hCursor = LoadCursor(NULL,IDC_CROSS);
SetCursor(hCursor);
}

if (x>=100 && x<=150 && y>=50 && y<=100)
{
hCursor = LoadCursor(NULL,IDC_IBEAM);
SetCursor(hCursor);
}

if (x>=150 && x<=200 && y>=50 && y<=100)
{
hCursor = LoadCursor(NULL,IDC_SIZE);
SetCursor(hCursor);
}

if (x>=50 && x<=100 && y>=100 && y<=150)
{
hCursor = LoadCursor(NULL,IDC_SIZENESW);
SetCursor(hCursor);
}

if (x>=100 && x<=150 && y>=100 && y<=150)
{
hCursor = LoadCursor(NULL,IDC_SIZENS);
SetCursor(hCursor);
}

if (x>=150 && x<=200 && y>=100 && y<=150)
{
hCursor = LoadCursor(NULL,IDC_SIZENWSE);
SetCursor(hCursor);
}

if (x>=50 && x<=100 && y>=150 && y<=200)
{
hCursor = LoadCursor(NULL,IDC_SIZEWE);
SetCursor(hCursor);
}

if (x>=100 && x<=150 && y>=150 && y<=200)
{
hCursor = LoadCursor(NULL,IDC_UPARROW);
SetCursor(hCursor);
}
```

continues

Listing 6.2. continued

```
          if (x>=150 && x<=200 && y>=150 && y<=200)
          {
          hCursor = LoadCursor(NULL,IDC_WAIT);
          SetCursor(hCursor);
          }
          }
        else
          {
          hCursor = LoadCursor(NULL,IDC_ARROW);
          SetCursor(hCursor);
          }
        return 0;

     case WM_DESTROY:

          PostQuitMessage(0);
          return 0;

     default:

          return(DefWindowProc(hWnd, iMessage, wParam,
               lParam));
     }
}
```

7

Windows and Child Windows

Unlike most previous examples in this book, consisting of only one window, most Windows applications actually consist of several windows. Applications that operate under the multiple document interface (MDI) standard create a unique window for each document in the program. Other applications create multiple windows in the form of edit controls, list boxes, buttons, and so forth.

This chapter focuses on the creation and use of parent and child windows. However, the following discussion on child windows is limited to the application of child window controls only. Chapter 9 discusses the use of child windows that follow the MDI standard.

Creating a Window

Creating a window consists of two basic steps: creating a window class and creating the window itself.

Step 1: Defining Window Classes

A *window class* provides the information required to create a window, including the name of window procedure that processes the messages for the window. The examples in this book have registered the window class by using code similar to the following:

```
WNDCLASS WndClass;

if (!hPrevInstance)
     {
     WndClass.cbClsExtra = 0;
     WndClass.cbWndExtra = 0;
     WndClass.hbrBackground = GetStockObject(WHITE_BRUSH);
     WndClass.hCursor =  LoadCursor(NULL, IDC_ARROW);
     WndClass.hIcon = LoadIcon (NULL, "END");
     WndClass.hInstance = hInstance;
     WndClass.lpfnWndProc = WndProc;
     WndClass.lpszClassName = "WIN_ONE";
     WndClass.lpszMenuName = NULL;
     WndClass.style = CS_HREDRAW ¦ CS_VREDRAW;

     RegisterClass (&WndClass);
     }
```

In this block of code, you are defining the fields of a `WNDCLASS` data structure called `WndClass`. To better understand this code, you must examine the `WNDCLASS` data structure that follows:

```
typedef struct tagWNDCLASS {
     WORD style;
     long (FAR PASCAL *lpfnWndProc)();
     int cbClsExtra;
     int cbWndExtra;
     HANDLE hInstance;
     HICON hIcon;
     HCURSOR hCursor;
     HBRUSH hbrBackground;
     LPSTR lpszMenuName;
     LPSTR lpszClassName;
} WNDCLASS;
```

The fields of the `WNDCLASS` structure are as follows:

- `style` defines the class style. The `style` field can be any combination (using bitwise OR) of the following values:

Value	*Meaning*
CS_BYTEALIGNCLIENT	Aligns a window's client area to the byte boundary in the horizontal direction
CS_BYTEALIGNWINDOW	Aligns a window to the byte boundary in the horizontal direction
CS_CLASSDC	Gives the window class its own display context
CS_DBLCLKS	Sends double-click messages to a window
CS_GLOBALCLASS	Indicates that the window class is an application global class
CS_HREDRAW	Redraws the window if the horizontal window size is changed
CS_NOCLOSE	Disables the close option on the `System` menu
CS_OWNDC	Gives each window its own device context
CS_PARENTDC	Gives the display context of the parent window to the window class
CS_SAVEBITS	Saves the part of the screen image that is covered by a window
CS_VREDRAW	Redraws the window if the vertical window size is changed

- `lpfnWndProc` specifies a pointer to the window function.
- `cbClsExtra` indicates the number of bytes to allocate following the window class structure.
- `hInstance` specifies the class module. This field cannot be set to NULL.
- `hIcon` specifies the class icon. This field can be set to NULL or to specify the handle of an icon resource. When `hIcon` is set to NULL, its application must draw the icon.
- `hCursor` specifies the class cursor. This field either should identify the handle of a cursor resource or be set to NULL. When the field is set to NULL, the application must specify the cursor shape.
- `hbrBackground` specifies the class background brush. This field is set to either the handle of a physical brush or to a color value. If the field specifies a color value, 1 must be added; for example, `COLOR_BACKGROUND + 1`. The color values are the following:

COLOR_ACTIVEBORDER	COLOR_HIGHLIGHTTEXT
COLOR_ACTIVECAPTION	COLOR_INACTIVEBORDER
COLOR_APPWORKSPACE	COLOR_INACTIVECAPTION
COLOR_BACKGROUND	COLOR_MENU
COLOR_BTNFACE	COLOR_MENUTEXT
COLOR_BTNSHADOW	COLOR_SCROLLBAR
COLOR_BTNTEXT	COLOR_WINDOW
COLOR_CAPTIONTEXT	COLOR_WINDOWFRAME
COLOR_GRAYTEXT	COLOR_WINDOWTEXT
COLOR_HIGHLIGHT	

- `lpszMenuName` contains a pointer to the string that specifies the resource name of the class menu. If this field is set to NULL, the windows of the class have no default menu.

- `lpszClassName` contains a pointer to the string that specifies the name of the window class.

As you can see from the number of fields in the `WNDCLASS` structure and from the number of possibilities for each field, the window class is very flexible. When you create a window class, you are, in effect, creating an object class and engaging in a type of object-oriented programming. By creating the window class, you can easily make several windows without redefining the many values contained in the `WNDCLASS` structure for each window.

Step 2: Creating the Window Itself

After the window class is defined, your next step in creating a window is, of course, to create the window itself. You use two Windows functions when creating a window. The first is the `CreateWindow` function, and its syntax is as follows:

```
HWND CreateWindow(lpClassName, lpWindowName, dwStyle, X, Y,
                  nWidth, nHeight, hWndParent, hMenu, hInstance,
                  lpParam)
```

Table 7.1 describes the parameters used in `CreateWindow` function.

Table 7.1. `CreateWindow` *parameters.*

Parameter	Type	Description
lpClassname	LPSTR	Pointer to a null-terminated character string that names the window class
lpWindowName	LPSTR	Pointer to a null-terminated character string that represents the window name
dwStyle	DWORD	The style of window to create
X	int	Initial horizontal position of the window's upper-left corner, expressed in screen coordinates
Y	int	Initial vertical position of the window's upper-left corner, expressed in screen coordinates
nWidth	int	Window width in device units
nHeight	int	Window height in device units
hWndParent	HWND	Parent or owner of the window to create
hMenu	HMENU	Menu or child window identifier
hInstance	HANDLE	Instance of module associated with the window
lpParam	LPSTR	Value passed to the window through the `CREATESTRUCT` data structure referenced by the `lParam` parameter of the `WM_CREATE` message

The fundamental window example in Chapter 2 uses the following call to the `CreateWindow` function to create the basic window. The `CreateWindow` function usually is followed by the `ShowWindow` function, which makes the created window visible.

```
hWnd = CreateWindow ("WIN_ONE",      /* class name */
         "Fundamental Window",       /* Caption */
         WS_OVERLAPPEDWINDOW,        /* Style */
         CW_USEDEFAULT,              /* x position */
         0,                          /* y position */
         CW_USEDEFAULT,              /* cx - size */
         0,                          /* cy - size */
         NULL,                       /* Parent window */
         NULL,                       /* Menu */
         hInstance,                  /* Program Instance */
         NULL);                      /* Parameters */
```

The other function used to create a window is the `CreateWindowEx` function, which is similar to the `CreateWindow` function except that `CreateWindowEx` provides several extended style bits. The syntax for the `CreateWindowEx` function is as follows:

```
HWND CreateWindowEx(dwExStyle, lpClassName, lpWindowName,
                    dwStyle, X, Y, nWidth, nHeight, hWndParent,
                    hMenu, hInstance, lpParam)
```

Table 7.2 describes the additional style bits.

Table 7.2. `CreateWindowEx` style bits.

Parameter	Type	Description
`dwExStyle`	`DWORD`	Extended style for the window to create. The following values are used for `dwExStyle`: • `WS_EX_DLGMODALFRAME` creates a window with a double border. The window contains a title bar if `WS_CAPTION` is specified in `dwStyle` • `WS_EX_NOPARENTNOTIFY` creates a child window that will not send the `WM_PARENTNOTIFY` message to the parent window when the child window is created or destroyed.
`lpClassname`	`LPSTR`	Pointer to a null-terminated character string that names the window class
`lpWindowName`	`LPSTR`	Pointer to a null-terminated character string that represents the window name
`dwStyle`	`DWORD`	The style of window to create
`X`	`int`	Initial horizontal position of the window's upper-left corner, expressed in screen coordinates
`Y`	`int`	Initial vertical position of the window's upper-left corner, expressed in screen coordinates
`nWidth`	`int`	Window width in device units
`nHeight`	`int`	Window height in device units
`hWndParent`	`HWND`	Parent or owner of the window to create
`hMenu`	`HMENU`	Menu or child window identifier
`hInstance`	`HANDLE`	Instance of module associated with the window
`lpParam`	`LPSTR`	Value passed to the window through the `CREATESTRUCT` data structure referenced by the `lParam` parameter of the `WM_CREATE` message

With the exception of the `dwExStyle` parameter of the `CreateWindowEx` function, the `CreateWindow` and `CreateWindowEx` functions share the same parameters. Although most of the parameters are fairly self-explanatory, the `lpClassName` and `dwStyle` parameters each have a variety of constants that can be associated with them. The lpClassName parameter specifies the class name. Windows has several predefined public window classes. Table 7.3 lists the values you can use to specify one of the public window classes for the lpClassName parameter.

All of the window classes listed in Table 7.3, with the exception of MDICLIENT, correspond to child window controls. In this chapter, a "child window" refers to a child window *control*. Chapter 9 further discusses child windows and the MDI.

Table 7.3. Values for lpClassName.

Value	*Meaning*
BUTTON	A small, rectangular child window representing a two-state button that can turned on or off
COMBOBOX	A control that contains a selection field and edit control
EDIT	A rectangular child window that accepts user input
LISTBOX	A list of character strings
MDICLIENT	An MDI client window
SCROLLBAR	A rectangle containing a direction arrow at either end and a position indicator
STATIC	A simple text field, box, or rectangle

The dwStyle parameter specifies the style for the created window. Table 7.4 lists the values that you can combine for dwStyle by using bitwise OR.

Table 7.4. Styles.

Value	*Meaning*
	Window Styles
DS_LOCALEDIT	Specifies that edit controls in the dialog box will use all memory in the application's data segment
DS_MODALFRAME	Creates a dialog box with a modal dialog box frame
DS_NOIDLEMSG	Suppresses WM_ENTERIDLE messages while the dialog box is displayed
DS_SYSMODAL	Creates a system modal dialog box
WS_BORDER	Creates a window with a border
WS_CAPTION	Creates a window with a Title bar; cannot be used with WS_DLGFRAME
WS_CHILD	Creates a child window; cannot be used with WS_POPUP
WS_CHILDWINDOW	Creates a child window with style WS_CHILD
WS_CLIPCHILDREN	Excludes the area occupied by child windows when drawing within the parent window

continues

Table 7.4. continued

Value	Meaning
	Window Styles
WS_CLIPSIBLINGS	Clips child windows relative to each other; for use with WS_CHILD only
WS_DISABLED	Creates a window that is disabled
WS_DLGFRAME	Creates a window with a double border and no title
WS_GROUP	Defines the first control from a group that the user can move from one control to another with the direction keys
WS_HSCROLL	Creates a window with a horizontal scroll bar
WS_ICONIC	Creates an iconic window
WS_MAXIMIZE	Creates a window that is to be maximized
WS_MAXIMIZEBOX	Creates a window with a maximize box
WS_MINIMIZE	Creates a window that is minimum size
WS_MINIMIZEBOX	Creates a window with a minimize box
WS_OVERLAPPEDWINDOW	Creates an overlapped window with styles WS_OVERLAPPED, WS_CAPTION, WS_SYSMENU, WS_THICKFRAME, WS_MINIMIZEBOX, and WS_MAXIMIZEBOX
WS_POPUP	Creates a pop-up window; cannot be used with WS_CHILD
WS_POPUPWINDOW	Creates a pop-up window with styles WS_BORDER, WS_POPUP, and WS_SYSMENU
WS_SYSMENU	Creates a window with a System menu box in the Title bar
WS_TABSTOP	Specifies the controls that a user can move to with the Tab key
WS_THICKFRAME	Creates a window with a thick frame
WS_VISIBLE	Creates a visible overlapped or pop-up window
	BUTTON Class Control Styles
BS_AUTOCHECK	Creates a small rectangular button that may be checked; button toggles when clicked
BS_AUTORADIOBUTTON	Creates a small circular button that can be checked; when clicked, the checkmarks are removed from the other radio buttons in the group
BS_AUTO3STATE	Creates a small rectangular button that changes state when clicked; supports three states: on, off, or grayed
BS_CHECKBOX	Creates a small rectangular button that may be checked
BS_DEFPUSHBUTTON	Designates a button as the default button by its bold border
BS_GROUPBOX	Groups the buttons in the designated rectangle

Value	Meaning
BS_LEFTTEXT	Forces text to appear on the left side (the right side is the default) for styles BS_CHECKBOX, BS_RADIOBUTTON, and BS_3STATE
BS_OWNERDRAW	Designates an owner draw button; parent is notified when the button is clicked
BS_PUSHBUTTON	Designates a button containing the specified text
BS_RADIOBUTTON	Creates a small circular button that can be checked
BS_3STATE	Creates a small rectangular button that may be checked; supports three states: on, off, and grayed
	COMBOBOX Class Control Styles
CBS_AUTOHSCROLL	Scrolls the text in the edit control to the right when text reaches the end of the line
CBS_DROPDOWN	Displays the list box only when the icon beside the selection field is selected
CBS_DROPDOWNLIST	Like CBS_DROPDOWN; edit control, however, is replaced by a static text item that displays the current selection from the list box
CBS_HASSTRINGS	Designates that owner-draw combo box contains items that consist of strings
CBS_OEMCONVERT	Converts text from combo box edit control from ANSI to OEM and back to ANSI
CBS_OWNERDRAWFIXED	Designates that the list box owner draws the contents of the list box; contents are all the same height
CBS_OWNERDRAWVARIABLE	Designates that the list box owner draws the contents of the list box; contents are not all the same height
CBS_SIMPLE	Always displays the list box
CBS_SORT	Automatically sorts strings entered in the list box
	EDIT Class Control Styles
ES_AUTOHSCROLL	Automatically scrolls text to the right 10 spaces when the end of the line is reached
ES_AUTOVSCROLL	Automatically scrolls the text up one page when Enter is pressed on the last line
ES_CENTER	Centers text in a multiline edit control
ES_LEFT	Left justifies text
ES_LOWERCASE	Displays all entered characters as lowercase
ES_MULTILINE	Multiline edit control
ES_NOHIDESEL	Disables the default action of hiding the selection when control loses the input focus and inverting the selection when the control receives the input focus

continues

Table 7.4. continued

Value	*Meaning*
	EDIT Class Control Styles
ES_OEMCONVERT	Converts text in the edit control from ANSI to OEM to ANSI
ES_PASSWORD	Displays asterisk (*) for each character entered into the edit control
ES_RIGHT	Right justifies text in a multiline edit control
ES_UPPERCASE	Displays all entered characters as uppercase
	LISTBOX Class Control Styles
LBS_EXTENDEDSEL	Enables user to select multiple selections from the list box
LBS_HASSTRINGS	Creates a owner draw list box contains items made up of strings
LBS_MULTICOLUMN	Creates a multicolumn list box with horizontal scroll
LBS_MULTIPLESEL	Toggles the string selection each time a string is clicked or double clicked; multiple selections can be made
LBS_NOINTEGRALHEIGHT	Creates a list box that has the exact size specified by the application creating the list box
LBS_NOREDRAW	Does not redraw the list box after modification
LBS_NOTIFY	Sends an input message to the parent when a string is clicked or double clicked
LBS_OWNERDRAWVARIABLE	Enables the list box owner to draw the contents of the list box
LBS_SORT	Alphabetically sorts strings in the list box
LBS_STANDARD	Alphabetically sorts strings in the list box and sends an input message to the parent window when a string is clicked or double clicked
LBS_USETABSTOPS	Enables a list box to recognize tab characters when drawing strings
LBS_WANTKEYBOARDINPUT	Sends WM_VKEYTOITEM or WM_CHARTOITEM message to the owner of the list box when a key is pressed while the list box has the input focus
	SCROLLBAR Class Control Styles
SBS_BOTTOMALIGN	Aligns the bottom edge of scroll bar with the bottom edge of the rectangle specified by X, Y, nWidth, and nHeight from the CreateWindow function; used with SBS_HORIZON
SBS_HORZ	Creates a horizontal scroll bar
SBS_LEFTALIGN	Aligns the left edge of scroll bar with the left edge of the rectangle specified by X, Y, nWidth, and nHeight from the CreateWindow function; used with SBS_VERT

Value	Meaning
SBS_RIGHTALIGN	Aligns the right edge of scroll bar with the right edge of the rectangle specified by X, Y, nWidth, and nHeight from the CreateWindow function; used with SBS_VERT
SBS_SIZEBOX	Specifies a size box
SBS_SIZEBOXBOTTOMRIGHTALIGN	Aligns the lower-right corner of size box with the lower-right corner of the rectangle specified by X, Y, nWidth, and nHeight from the CreateWindow function; used with SBS_SIZEBOX
SBS_SIZEBOXTOPLEFTALIGN	Aligns the upper-left corner of size box with the upper-left corner of the rectangle specified by X, Y, nWidth, and nHeight from the CreateWindow function; used with SBS_SIZEBOX
SBS_TOPALIGN	Aligns the top edge of scroll bar with the top edge of the rectangle specified by X, Y, nWidth, and nHeight from the CreateWindow function; used with SBS_HORIZON
SBS_VERT	Creates a vertical scroll bar
STATIC Class Control Styles	
SS_BLACKFRAME	Colors the frame of a box with same color as window frames
SS_BLACKRECT	Fills a rectangle with same color as window frames
SS_CENTER	Creates a simple rectangle with text centered in rectangle; wraps text to next line if necessary
SS_GRAYFRAME	Colors the frame of a box with same color as screen background
SS_GRAYRECT	Fills a rectangle with the same color as screen background
SS_ICON	Displays an icon in the dialog box
SS_LEFT	Creates a simple rectangle with text left-justified inside the rectangle; wraps text to next line if necessary
SS_LEFTNOWORDWRAP	Creates a simple rectangle with text left-justified inside the rectangle; does not wrap text to the next line
SS_NOPREFIX	Without this style, the & character is interpreted as an accelerator prefix character
SS_RIGHT	Creates a simple rectangle with text right-justified inside the rectangle; wraps text to the next line if necessary

continues

Table 7.4. continued

Value	*Meaning*
SS_SIMPLE	Creates a simple rectangle with text left-justified; the text cannot be altered
SS_USERITEM	Creates a user-defined item
SS_WHITEFRAME	Draws the frame of a box in same color as the window background
SS_WHITERECT	Fills a rectangle with the same color as the window background

The `CreateWindow` and `CreateWindowEx` functions provide a great deal of flexibility in the specification of a window. The various window and control styles, when combined with the various predefined window classes, provide numerous child window control combinations.

Although the process of creating a window requires only two steps, these steps require much work. To get the most out of your Windows application, it is important that you understand the capabilities provided by Windows for the window creation process. By carefully reviewing the basic concepts of and the features provided by the `WNDCLASS` data structure, the `CreateWindow` function, and the `CreateWindowEx` function, you should be able to create the window that is best for your application.

Child Window Controls

You create child window controls by using the same basic process you used to develop top-level windows. The remainder of this chapter discusses these controls. However, do not confuse child window controls with child windows that follow the MDI standard, which are discussed in Chapter 9.

The discussion of the `CreateWindow` and `CreateWindowEx` functions introduced several predefined window classes. The window classes that pertain to child window controls are listed as follows:

- `BUTTON` is a small rectangular child window representing a two-state button that can turned on or off.
- `COMBOBOX` is a control that contains a selection field and an edit control.
- `EDIT` is a rectangular child window that accepts user input.
- `LISTBOX` is a list of character strings.

- `SCROLLBAR` is a rectangle containing a direction arrow at either end and a position indicator.
- `STATIC` is a simple text field, box, or rectangle.

As the list of predefined classes indicates, child window controls are in the form of buttons, combo boxes, edit boxes, list boxes, scroll bars, and text fields. You can place child window controls inside dialog boxes or on the surfaces of normal overlapped window client areas.

A child window control communicates with its parent window by sending a `WM_COMMAND` message to the parent. The `WM_COMMAND` message contains three pieces of information. The `wParam` parameter of the message contains the ID of the child window. The low-order word of the `lParam` parameter of the message contains the handle of the child window. The high-order word of the `lParam` parameter of the message contains the notification code. The *notification codes* inform the parent window of the actions that occur within a control.

The following paragraphs briefly describe each of the child window control types. Each description includes a list of the notification codes that apply to that control type.

Button controls—You select a button by clicking on the control. The several button types include push buttons, check boxes, radio buttons, and group boxes. The following notification codes are associated with buttons:

Notification Code	*Meaning*
`BN_CLICKED`	Specifies that a button has been clicked
`BN_DOUBLECLICKED`	Specifies that a owner draw or radio button has been double clicked

Edit controls—Rectangular child windows that accept input from the user, edit controls are often used to enable the user to type in a file name or keyword. The following notification codes are associated with edit controls:

Notification Code	*Meaning*
`EN_CHANGE`	Indicates that an action changed the content of the text
`EN_ERRSPACE`	Specifies that an edit control is out of space
`EN_HSCROLL`	Specifies that the horizontal scroll bar was clicked and is active
`EN_KILLFOCUS`	Specifies that the edit control has lost the input focus
`EN_MAXTEXT`	Specifies that the inserted text exceeds the limits for the edit control
`EN_SETFOCUS`	Specifies that the edit control has received the input focus
`EN_UPDATE`	Specifies that the edit control will display altered text
`EN_VSCROLL`	Specifies that the vertical scroll bar was clicked and is active

List box controls—A list of character strings, the list box control often is used to display a list of options such as files or directories that can be selected. The following notification codes are associated with list box controls:

Notification Code	*Meaning*
LBN_DBLCLK	Specifies that a string was double clicked
LBN_ERRSPACE	Specifies that there is no more system memory
LBN_KILLFOCUS	Specifies that the list box has lost the input focus
LBN_SELCHANGE	Specifies that the selection was changed
LBN_SETFOCUS	Specifies that the list box has received the input focus

Combo box controls—A combo box contains a selection field and an edit control. The following notification codes are associated with combo boxes:

Notification Code	*Meaning*
CBN_DBLCLK	Sent when a string is double clicked
CBN_DROPDOWN	Sent to the owner of the combo box when a list box is to be dropped down
CBN_EDITCHANGE	Sent when the text in the edit control is modified
CBN_EDITUPDATE	Specifies that the edit control will display altered text
CBN_ERRSPACE	Sent when there is no more system memory
CBN_KILLFOCUS	Specifies that the combo box no longer has the input focus
CBN_SELCHANGE	Specifies that the selection was modified
CBN_SETFOCUS	Specifies that the combo box received the input focus

Scroll bar controls—Rectangles containing a direction arrow at either end and a position indicator, scroll bars are used to position fields of text or graphics that are too large for the current client area. There are no notification codes associated with scroll bar controls.

Static controls—A simple text field, box, or rectangle, the static control can display messages. There are no notification codes associated with static controls.

Child Window Example

The child window example in Listings 7.1 and 7.2 demonstrates how you can use child window controls to display three buttons. The first button is a three-state button that automatically cycles between the states when clicked. The second button is a simple push-button. The last button is a check box that is automatically checked or unchecked.

The buttons are created when the WM_CREATE message is received by the window procedure. The three buttons are then created using the CreateWindow function, and the created buttons can be selected by the user. However, this child window example has not defined any actions for the buttons. To modify this example, you must make the window procedure respond to the WM_COMMAND message.

A child window control communicates with its parent window by sending a WM_COMMAND message to the parent that contains three pieces of information. The wParam parameter of the message contains the ID of the child window. The low-order word of the lParam parameter of the message contains the handle of the child window. The high-order word of the lParam parameter of the message contains the *notification code*, which informs the parent window of the actions that occur within a control. By evaluating the information sent from the control, the application can be coded to respond accordingly. Figure 7.1 shows the application window and button controls created by this example.

The following lines show the project name as well as files used to create the child window example.

Project Name: WIN_CHLD
Files in Project: WIN_CHLD.C
WIN_CHLD.DEF

Listing 7.1. *The definition file for the child window example.*

```
NAME           WIN_CHLD
DESCRIPTION    'Child Window Example'
EXETYPE        WINDOWS
CODE           PRELOAD MOVEABLE
DATA           PRELOAD MOVEABLE MULTIPLE
HEAPSIZE       1024
STACKSIZE      5120
EXPORTS        WndProc
```

Listing 7.2. *The C source file for the child window example.*

```
#include <windows.h>
#include <stdlib.h>
#include <string.h>

long FAR PASCAL WndProc (HWND hWnd, WORD iMessage,
                WORD wParam, LONG lParam);

int PASCAL WinMain (HANDLE hInstance, HANDLE hPrevInstance,
              LPSTR lpszCmdParam, int nCmdShow)
```

continues

Listing 7.2. continued

```
{
HWND hWnd;
MSG Message;
WNDCLASS WndClass;

if (!hPrevInstance)
     {
     WndClass.cbClsExtra = 0;
     WndClass.cbWndExtra = 0;
     WndClass.hbrBackground = GetStockObject(WHITE_BRUSH);
     WndClass.hCursor =  LoadCursor(NULL, IDC_ARROW);
     WndClass.hIcon = LoadIcon (NULL, "END");
     WndClass.hInstance = hInstance;
     WndClass.lpfnWndProc = WndProc;
     WndClass.lpszClassName = "WIN_CHLD";
     WndClass.lpszMenuName = NULL;
     WndClass.style = CS_HREDRAW ¦ CS_VREDRAW;

     RegisterClass (&WndClass);
     }

hWnd = CreateWindow ("WIN_CHLD",     /* class name */
          "Child Window Example",    /* Caption */
          WS_OVERLAPPEDWINDOW,       /* Style */
          CW_USEDEFAULT,             /* x position */
          0,                         /* y position */
          CW_USEDEFAULT,             /* cx - size */
          0,                         /* cy - size */
          NULL,                      /* Parent window */
          NULL,                      /* Menu */
          hInstance,                 /* Program Instance */
          NULL);                     /* Parameters */

ShowWindow(hWnd,nCmdShow);
UpdateWindow(hWnd);
while (GetMessage (&Message, 0, 0, 0))
     {
     TranslateMessage(&Message);
     DispatchMessage(&Message);
     }
return Message.wParam;
}

/****************************************************************/
/*              Window Procedure: WndProc                       */
/****************************************************************/

long FAR PASCAL WndProc (HWND hWnd, WORD iMessage, WORD wParam,
                 LONG lParam)
```

```
{
HDC hDC;
HWND hWndButton;


switch (iMessage)
      {
      case WM_CREATE:

            CreateWindow("BUTTON","AUTO3STATE",
              WS_CHILD ¦ WS_VISIBLE ¦ BS_AUTO3STATE,
              100,50,200,50,hWnd,0,
              ((LPCREATESTRUCT)lParam)->hInstance,
              NULL);
            CreateWindow("BUTTON","PUSHBUTTON",
              WS_CHILD ¦ WS_VISIBLE ¦ BS_PUSHBUTTON,
              100,125,200,50,hWnd,0,
              ((LPCREATESTRUCT)lParam)->hInstance,
              NULL);
            CreateWindow("BUTTON","AUTOCHECKBOX",
              WS_CHILD ¦ WS_VISIBLE ¦ BS_AUTOCHECKBOX,
              100,200,200,50,hWnd,0,
              ((LPCREATESTRUCT)lParam)->hInstance,
              NULL);
            return 0;

      case WM_DESTROY:

            PostQuitMessage(0);
            return 0;
      }
return(DefWindowProc(hWnd, iMessage, wParam, lParam));
}
```

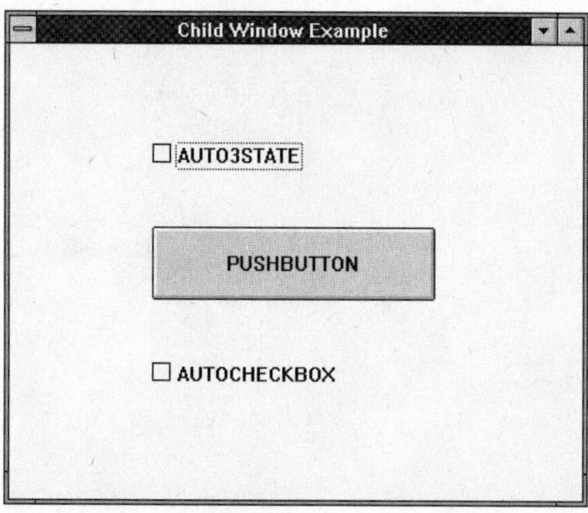

Figure 7.1. *The child window example.*

8

Memory Management and Windows

Windows is a multitasking environment. Because multiple tasks can run at the same time, Windows must carefully manage the system memory so that the memory required by an application is available without affecting the operations of the other tasks. This chapter introduces Windows memory management.

Before getting any further into this chapter, you need to quickly review the way that the Intel 8086 family of microprocessors organizes memory into segments. To begin this review, however, you also must review the basic operating modes for Windows: *real mode*, *standard mode*, and *386 enhanced mode*. These terms appear several times during the discussion of memory management and are briefly described as follows:

- Windows *real mode* is designed for machines with less than 1MB of memory. In real mode, Windows can take advantage of expanded memory that follows the Lotus-Intel-Microsoft Expanded Memory Specification 4.0.

- Windows *standard mode* is designed for 80286 machines with at least 1MB of memory or 80386 machines with less than 2MB of memory. Windows standard mode provides the advantages of 80286 protected mode and can address up to 16MB of conventional and extended memory.
- Windows *386 enhanced mode* is designed for 80386 machines with greater than 2MB of memory. The 386 enhanced mode provides the advantages of standard mode while adding the feature of virtual memory and accommodating virtual DOS machines.

Now that we have reviewed the Windows operating modes, we can begin the discussion of segments and memory addresses.

The microprocessor uses a physical address to read from and write to physical memory. Programmers use the logical address to access physical memory. The logical address consists of two parts. The first part of the logical address is the *segment identifier*. The segment identifier is a 16-bit value that specifies the segment of memory to access. The second part of the logical address is the *offset*. The offset specifies a byte number within the segment. The microprocessor converts the logical address specified by the segment identifier and the offset to a physical address.

In the real mode, the logical address corresponds directly to the physical address. The 20-bit physical address is determined by adding the 16-bit offset and the 16-bit segment address (shifted left four bits) as follows:

```
Offset                      xxxxxxxxxxxxxxxx
Segment                 + xxxxxxxxxxxxxxxx0000
                        ----------------------
20-bit Physical Address   xxxxxxxxxxxxxxxxxxxx
```

In the standard mode, the logical address does not correspond to the physical address. Instead the logical address references the physical address through a descriptor table. The same is true for the 386 enhanced mode. The portion of the logical address referred to as the segment identifier for the real mode is called the *segment selector* for the standard and 386 enhanced modes. The segment selector identifies the segment from an array of segment information records called *segment descriptors*.

The Local and Global Heaps

Windows allocates blocks of memory for an application from either the global or local heap. The *global heap* is memory available to all applications. The *local heap* is memory that is restricted for use by only one application.

The global heap is the memory that Windows controls. The global heap begins at the position at which Windows is loaded into memory and includes the remainder of the available memory. When Windows starts, memory blocks for the code and data are allocated. The memory remaining after the allocation of the memory blocks for the code and data—called *free memory*—can be used by applications. The global heap often is used for allocating large memory blocks; however, any size of memory block can be allocated.

Blocks of memory are allocated in the global heap according to the following guidelines, which are illustrated in Figure 8.1:

- Fixed segments are allocated from the bottom up.
- Discardable segments are allocated from the bottom down.
- Moveable, nondiscardable data segments are allocated between fixed segments and discardable segments.
- The largest block of free memory usually is located below the discardable segments.

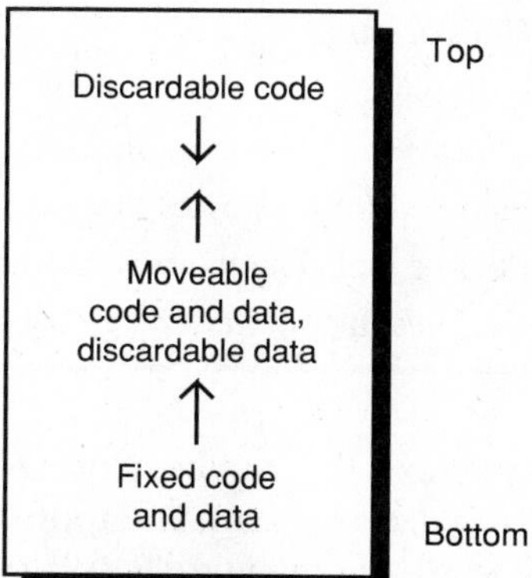

Figure 8.1. *Global memory.*

Windows provides several functions for managing global memory. Table 8.1 lists these functions. Chapter 13 provides additional information on the use of each of the functions listed in Table 8.1.

Table 8.1. Global memory management functions.

Function	Meaning
`GetFreeSpace`	Gets the number of bytes available in the global heap
`GlobalAlloc`	Allocates memory from the global heap
`GlobalCompact`	Compacts global memory
`GlobalDiscard`	Discards global memory
`GlobalDosAlloc`	Allocates global memory
`GlobalDosFree`	Frees global memory allocated with `GlobalDosAlloc`
`GlobalFix`	Keeps a global memory block from being moved in linear memory
`GlobalFlags`	Gets the flags and lock count of a memory block
`GlobalFree`	Removes a global block and invalidates the handle
`GlobalHandle`	Gets the handle of a global memory object
`GlobalLock`	Gets the pointer for a handle to a global memory block
`GlobalLRUNewest`	Moves a global memory object to the newest least-recently-used (LRU) position
`GlobalLRUOldest`	Moves a global memory object to the oldest least-recently-used (LRU) position
`GlobalNotify`	Installs a notification procedure
`GlobalReAlloc`	Reallocates a global memory block
`GlobalSize`	Gets the number of bytes in a global memory block
`GlobalUnfix`	Unlocks a global memory block
`GlobalUnlock`	Invalidates the pointer to a global memory block

The local heap contains memory that can be allocated only by the application and is located in the application's data segment. The application's data segment contains three other types of data as shown in Figure 8.2.

From top to bottom, as Figure 8.2 shows, the types of data in the application's data segment are the local heap, the stack, the static data, and the task header. The local heap contains all local dynamic data (data allocated using `LocalAlloc`). The stack stores automatic data (variables allocated in the stack when a function is called). Static data refers to all of the variables that are declared to be either `static` or `extern`. The task header contains 16 bytes of information about the application.

The guidelines for allocating memory in the local heap are similar to those used for allocating memory in the global heap. These guidelines (shown in Figure 8.3) are the following:

1. Fixed blocks are located at the bottom of the local heap.
2. Discardable blocks are allocated from the top of the local heap.
3. Nondiscardable, moveable blocks of memory are allocated above the fixed blocks.
4. The largest block of free memory usually is located below the discardable segments.

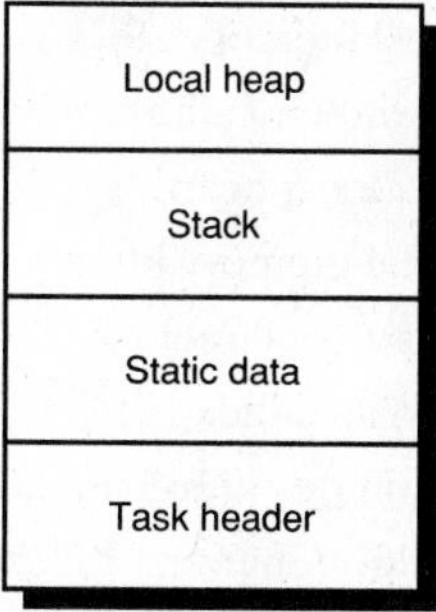

Figure 8.2. *The application's data segment.*

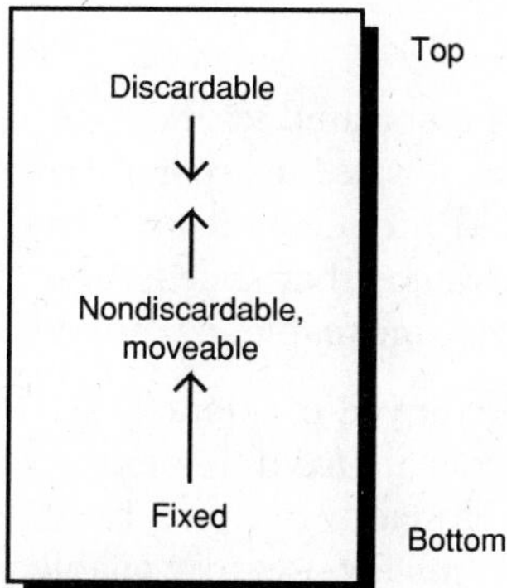

Figure 8.3. *The local heap.*

Windows provides several functions for managing local memory. Table 8.2 lists these functions. Chapter 13 provides additional information on the use of each of the functions listed in Table 8.2.

Table 8.2. Local memory management functions.

Function	*Meaning*
`LocalAlloc`	Allocates memory from the local heap
`LocalCompact`	Compacts local memory
`LocalDiscard`	Discards local memory when the lock count is zero
`LocalFlags`	Gets the memory type of a local memory block
`LocalFree`	Frees a local memory block when the lock count is zero
`LocalHandle`	Gets the handle of a local memory block
`LocalInit`	Initializes a local heap
`LocalLock`	Locks a local memory block
`LocalReAlloc`	Reallocates a local memory block
`LocalShrink`	Shrinks the local heap
`LocalSize`	Gets the number of bytes in a local memory block
`LocalUnlock`	Unlocks a local memory block

Segments

A block of memory that is associated with a particular segment address is called a *segment*. Segments can vary in size but are limited to 64KB blocks. The memory that Windows controls is divided into segments of varying sizes. Each segment controlled by Windows contains attributes that specify how the segment is to be treated. A segment can be either fixed, moveable, or moveable and discardable.

Fixed segments cannot be moved in memory. Although most segments are moveable, in some cases segments are fixed. For example, when a far pointer references a segment, the segment is fixed. Because fixed segments cannot be moved or discarded, fixed segments quickly use up available memory. Therefore, you should limit the number of fixed segments.

Moveable segments can be moved in memory. When moveable memory is allocated, a handle that identifies the memory segment is created. Applications use the handle to identify the memory block. Windows uses the handle to locate the memory address of the segment. Windows can relocate moveable segments to make the most efficient use of the memory available on the system.

Moveable segments can be specified as discardable. Windows can remove moveable, discardable segments from memory to make room for memory requests. When the segment is needed, the segment is loaded back into memory from the disk. Code segments are often defined as moveable, discardable segments because code is not changed. Therefore, when the code must be executed, it is reloaded into memory. Resources are another example of memory blocks that often are marked as moveable, discardable segments.

Table 8.3 lists several functions that Windows provides for dealing with segments. Chapter 13 provides additional information on the use of each of the functions listed in Table 8.3.

Table 8.3. Segment functions.

Function	*Meaning*
`AllocDStoCSAlias`	Returns a code segment selector from the specified data segment selector
`AllocSelector`	Allocates a new selector
`ChangeSelector`	Generates a code or data selector
`DefineHandleTable`	Creates a private handle table in an application's data segment
`FreeSelector`	Frees a selector
`GetCodeInfo`	Gets code segment information
`GlobalFix`	Keeps a global memory block from being moved in linear memory
`GlobalPageLock`	Page locks the memory associated with the specified global selector
`GlobalPageUnlock`	Decreases the page lock count for a block of memory
`GlobalUnfix`	Unlocks a global memory block
`LockSegment`	Locks the specified data segment
`UnlockSegment`	Unlocks the specified data segment

9

The Multiple Document Interface (MDI)

Windows provides the Multiple Document Interface (MDI) specification for applications dealing with documents. The MDI specification standardizes the methods for displaying and manipulating multiple documents from a single application. This chapter introduces the components of an MDI application, the MDI message loop, and the MDI messages.

MDI Applications

MDI applications contain one main window, called the *frame window*, which is similar to most application windows except that the frame window's client area itself contains a child window. This window, called the *client window*, is the background

where the other child windows are placed. Each document created by the MDI application has its own window—a child window—that can be moved, minimized, and maximized. However, this child window is restricted to the area of the client window. Figure 9.1 illustrates the components of an MDI application.

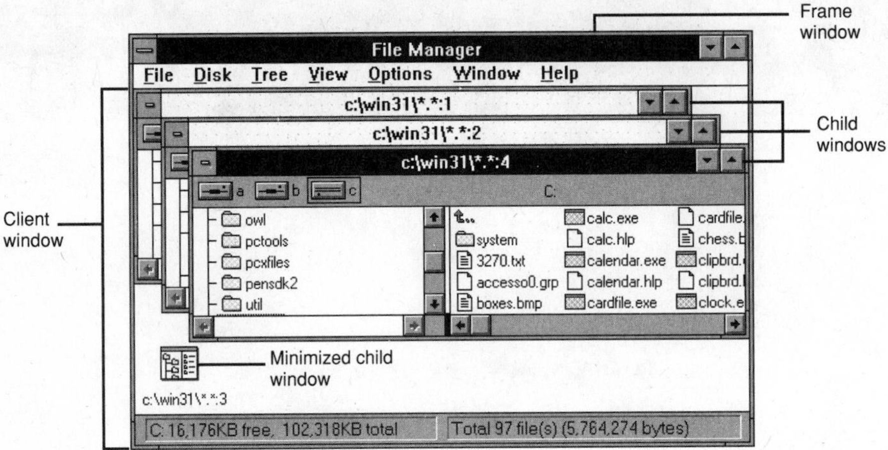

Figure 9.1. *The MDI application.*

The MDI interface is controlled by the passing of messages up and down the heirarchy of windows. The MDI hierarchy begins at the frame window and extends downward to the client window and to its child windows.

The general process for developing an MDI application is about the same as for almost any other Windows application. However, the differences in the code structure between the traditional Windows application and the MDI application makes the development of the MDI application more difficult.

One noticeable difference between the traditional Windows application and the MDI application occurs during initialization. MDI applications, in general, register at least two window classes. The first window class is for the frame window of the MDI application. The second class—and any other subsequent class—is for the child windows of the MDI application. It is not necessary to register a class for the client window, because Windows has a predefined class for this purpose. When you define the window classes, keep the following in mind:

- The class structure should have an icon, because child windows can be minimized.
- The menu name should be set to NULL.
- Additional space should be reserved in the class structure for storing data associated with the window.

The following code is from the MDI example presented later in this chapter. The window class for the frame window is defined first and then registered using the `RegisterClass` function. The window class for the child window follows, and it is also registered using the `RegisterClass` function.

```
if (!hPrevInstance)
     {
     WndClass.cbClsExtra = 0;
     WndClass.cbWndExtra = 0;
     WndClass.hbrBackground = GetStockObject(WHITE_BRUSH);
     WndClass.hCursor =  LoadCursor(NULL, IDC_ARROW);
     WndClass.hIcon = LoadIcon (NULL, IDI_APPLICATION);
     WndClass.hInstance = hInstance;
     WndClass.lpfnWndProc = FrameWndProc;
     WndClass.lpszClassName = "WIN_MDI:FRAME";
     WndClass.lpszMenuName = NULL;
     WndClass.style = CS_HREDRAW ¦ CS_VREDRAW;

     RegisterClass (&WndClass);

     WndClass.cbClsExtra = 0;
     WndClass.cbWndExtra = sizeof(LOCALHANDLE);
     WndClass.hbrBackground = GetStockObject(WHITE_BRUSH);
     WndClass.hCursor =  LoadCursor(NULL, IDC_ARROW);
     WndClass.hIcon = LoadIcon (NULL, IDI_APPLICATION);
     WndClass.hInstance = hInstance;
     WndClass.lpfnWndProc = DocWndProc;
     WndClass.lpszClassName = "WIN_MDI:DOC";
     WndClass.lpszMenuName = NULL;
     WndClass.style = CS_HREDRAW ¦ CS_VREDRAW;

     RegisterClass (&WndClass);
     }
```

The MDI Message Loop

The message loop is another difference between MDI and typical Windows applications. MDI-application message loops use the `TranslateMDISysAccel` function, which is added to the message loop to translate child window accelerators. The reason the MDI message loop differs from the typical Windows application message loop is that system-menu accelerators for MDI child windows respond to the Ctrl key instead of the Alt key.

The message loop for an MDI application usually is structured as follows:

```
while (GetMessage (&Message, NULL, 0, 0))
  {
  if (!TranslateMDISysAccel(hWndClient,&Message) &&
      !TranslateAccelerator(hWndFrame,hAccel,&Message))
     {
     TranslateMessage(&Message);
     DispatchMessage(&Message);
     }
  }
```

The MDI example in Listings 9.1, 9.2, and 9.3 demonstrates how this message loop is implemented.

MDI Messages

MDI applications control child windows by sending messages to the client window. Windows provides 11 MDI messages to control the child windows of MDI applications. Table 9.1 lists the MDI messages and briefly describes each one. Chapter 14 provides additional information on the use of each of these messages.

Table 9.1. *MDI messages.*

Message	*Meaning*
WM_MDIACTIVATE	Activates a child window
WM_MDICASCADE	Arranges child windows in a cascade fashion
WM_MDICREATE	Creates a child window
WM_MDIDESTROY	Closes a child window
WM_MDIGETACTIVE	Gets the active MDI child window
WM_MDIICONARRANGE	Arranges minimized child windows
WM_MDIMAXIMIZE	Maximizes an MDI child window
WM_MDINEXT	Makes the next child window active
WM_MDIRESTORE	Restores a child window
WM_MDISETMENU	Replaces the menu of the Window pop-up menu, an MDI frame window, or both
WM_MDITILE	Arranges child windows in a tiled format

Frame and Child Window Functions

Typical MDI applications contain at least two window functions. The first window function is for the frame window of the application. The second and every subseqent window function controls the various child window classes specified in `WinMain`.

The frame window procedure of an MDI application is similar to the main window procedure of a typical Windows application. However, there are some differences. The most noticeable difference is that the frame window procedure passes all the messages it does not handle to the `DefFrameProc` function. Typical Windows applications pass all of their unhandled messages to the `DefWindowProc` function.

Child window procedures of MDI applications also differ from window procedures of typical Windows applications. Like the frame window procedure, the most noticeable difference is that child window procedures in an MDI application pass all messages that it does not handle to the `DefMDIChildProc` function. Typical window procedures pass all their unhandled messages to the `DefWindowProc` function.

MDI Example

The MDI example presented in Listings 9.1, 9.2, and 9.3 demonstrates how to use the MDI to create a document. Three files are required to create this example. The first file is the *module definition file*. One thing that you should notice about this module definition file (as opposed to other module definition files you have seen in previous examples) is that two window functions are listed after `EXPORTS`: `FrameWndProc` and `DocWndProc`. `FrameWndProc` is the window procedure for the frame window. `DocWndProc` is the window procedure for the document.

The second file is the *C source file*. The overall structure of this example is, for the most part, similar to previous examples demonstrated in the book. However, you should notice some differences: one is that two window classes are defined; and one class is defined for the frame window, while another class is defined for the document child window.

The third file in the project is the *resource script file*, which specifies the menus used by the frame and child windows as well as the accelerators for the application.

When this example is executed, the first thing that appears on-screen is the frame window of the application, as shown in Figure 9.2. The menu bar of the frame window contains one menu: `File`, which offers two selections—`New Document` and

`Exit`. Selecting `Exit` from the frame window menu enables you to exit the application. Selecting `New Document` opens a document child window, as shown in Figure 9.3. When the child window is opened, notice that the Menu bar contains the menus and menu options defined for the document child window (see Figure 9.3).

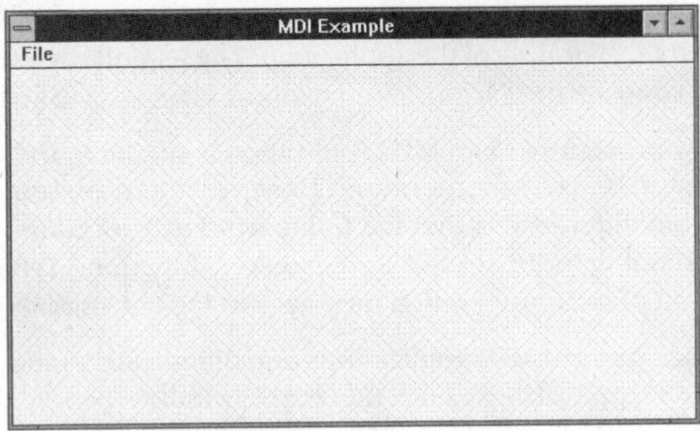

Figure 9.2. *The frame window of the MDI example.*

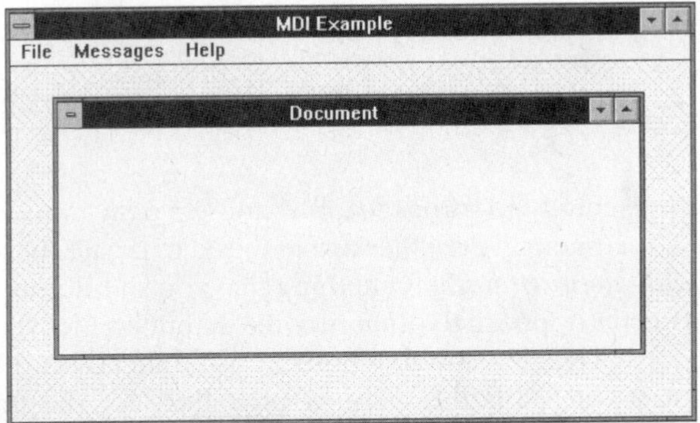

Figure 9.3. *The child window of the MDI example.*

Child windows can be minimized or maximized. The document child window shown in Figure 9.3 can be *maximized*, as shown in Figure 9.4, or *minimized*, as shown in Figure 9.5. There are a few things you should notice when the child window is either minimized or maximized.

When a child window is minimized, the menu for the child window is still active and the actions resulting from various menu item selections are still active. In Figure 9.5, a message box is displayed that results from selecting the `Message 1` menu item of the `Messages` menu while the document child window is minimized.

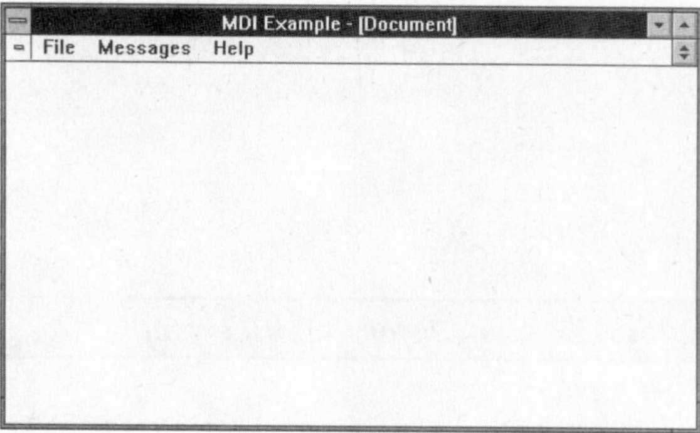

Figure 9.4. *The maximized child window of the MDI example.*

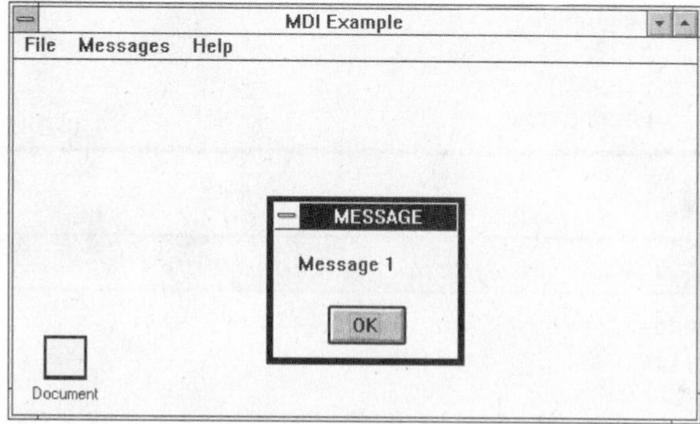

Figure 9.5. *The minimized child window of the MDI example.*

When the child window is maximized, a restore button appears in the upper-right corner of the child window (see Figure 9.4). Additionally, a button that enables you to select the system menu for the child window appears below the system menu of the frame window. You may remember, from the discussion of message loops for MDI applications, that the system menu of the child window is selected with the Ctrl key, and the system menu of the frame window is selected with the Alt key. It is important to keep this in mind when using the keyboard to select options from the system menus.

The last thing you should notice on the maximized child window is that the name of the child window appears on the caption line of the frame window—along with the name of the frame window.

The following lines show the project name as well as files used to create the MDI example.

Project Name:	`WIN_MDI`
Files in Project:	`WIN_MDI.DEF`
	`WIN_MDI.C`
	`WIN_MDI.RC`

Listing 9.1. *The definition file for the MDI example.*

```
NAME            WIN_MDI
DESCRIPTION     'MDI Example'
EXETYPE         WINDOWS
CODE            PRELOAD MOVEABLE
DATA            PRELOAD MOVEABLE MULTIPLE
HEAPSIZE        1024
STACKSIZE       5120
EXPORTS         FrameWndProc
                DocWndProc
```

Listing 9.2. *The C source file for the MDI example.*

```
#include <windows.h>
#include <stdlib.h>
#include <string.h>

long FAR PASCAL FrameWndProc (HWND hWnd, WORD iMessage,
                WORD wParam, LONG lParam);

long FAR PASCAL DocWndProc (HWND hWnd, WORD iMessage,
                WORD wParam, LONG lParam);

HANDLE hInst;
HMENU hMenu, hMenuDoc;
HMENU hMenuWin, hMenuDocWin;
typedef struct
  {
  int x;
  int y;
  }
  DOCDATA;

typedef DOCDATA NEAR *NPDOCDATA;

int PASCAL WinMain (HANDLE hInstance, HANDLE hPrevInstance,
              LPSTR lpszCmdParam, int nCmdShow)
```

```
{
HWND hWndFrame, hWndClient;
HANDLE hAccel;
MSG Message;
WNDCLASS WndClass;
hInst = hInstance;

if (!hPrevInstance)
     {
     WndClass.cbClsExtra = 0;
     WndClass.cbWndExtra = 0;
     WndClass.hbrBackground = GetStockObject(WHITE_BRUSH);
     WndClass.hCursor =  LoadCursor(NULL, IDC_ARROW);
     WndClass.hIcon = LoadIcon (NULL, IDI_APPLICATION);
     WndClass.hInstance = hInstance;
     WndClass.lpfnWndProc = FrameWndProc;
     WndClass.lpszClassName = "WIN_MDI:FRAME";
     WndClass.lpszMenuName = NULL;
     WndClass.style = CS_HREDRAW ¦ CS_VREDRAW;

     RegisterClass (&WndClass);

     WndClass.cbClsExtra = 0;
     WndClass.cbWndExtra = sizeof(LOCALHANDLE);
     WndClass.hbrBackground = GetStockObject(WHITE_BRUSH);
     WndClass.hCursor =  LoadCursor(NULL, IDC_ARROW);
     WndClass.hIcon = LoadIcon (NULL, IDI_APPLICATION);
     WndClass.hInstance = hInstance;
     WndClass.lpfnWndProc = DocWndProc;
     WndClass.lpszClassName = "WIN_MDI:DOC";
     WndClass.lpszMenuName = NULL;
     WndClass.style = CS_HREDRAW ¦ CS_VREDRAW;

     RegisterClass (&WndClass);
     }

hMenu = LoadMenu(hInst, "MdiMenu");
hMenuDoc = LoadMenu(hInst, "MdiMenuDoc");

hMenuWin = GetSubMenu(hMenu,0);
hMenuDocWin = GetSubMenu(hMenu,1);

hAccel = LoadAccelerators(hInst,"MdiAccel");

hWndFrame = CreateWindow ("WIN_MDI:FRAME", /* class name */
          "MDI Example",          /* Caption */
          WS_OVERLAPPEDWINDOW ¦
          WS_CLIPCHILDREN,        /* Style */
          CW_USEDEFAULT,          /* x position */
          CW_USEDEFAULT,          /* y position */
```

continues

Listing 9.2. continued

```
          CW_USEDEFAULT,            /* cx - size */
          CW_USEDEFAULT,            /* cy - size */
          NULL,                     /* Parent window */
          hMenu,                    /* Menu */
          hInstance,                /* Program Instance */
          NULL);                    /* Parameters */

hWndClient = GetWindow(hWndFrame,GW_CHILD);

ShowWindow (hWndFrame, nCmdShow);
UpdateWindow (hWndFrame);

while (GetMessage (&Message, NULL, 0, 0))
  {
  if (!TranslateMDISysAccel(hWndClient,&Message) &&
      !TranslateAccelerator(hWndFrame,hAccel,&Message))
     {
     TranslateMessage(&Message);
     DispatchMessage(&Message);
     }
  }
return Message.wParam;
}

/***************************************************************/
/*               Window Procedure: FrameWndProc                */
/***************************************************************/

long FAR PASCAL FrameWndProc (HWND hWnd, WORD iMessage,
                     WORD wParam, LONG lParam)
{
static HWND hWndClient;
HWND hWndChild;
CLIENTCREATESTRUCT clcr;
MDICREATESTRUCT mdi;

switch (iMessage)
     {
     case WM_CREATE:

          clcr.hWindowMenu = hMenuWin;
          clcr.idFirstChild = 100;

          hWndClient = CreateWindow("MDICLIENT",NULL,
                   WS_CHILD|WS_CLIPCHILDREN|
                   WS_VISIBLE,0,0,0,0,hWnd,1,hInst,
                   (LPSTR)&clcr);
          return 0;
```

```
case WM_COMMAND:

  switch(wParam)
     {
     case 10:
       mdi.szClass = "WIN_MDI:DOC";
       mdi.szTitle = "Document";
       mdi.hOwner = hInst;
       mdi.x = CW_USEDEFAULT;
       mdi.y = CW_USEDEFAULT;
       mdi.cx = CW_USEDEFAULT;
       mdi.cy = CW_USEDEFAULT;
       mdi.style = 0;
       mdi.lParam = NULL;
       hWndChild = SendMessage(hWndClient,
        WM_MDICREATE,0,
        (LONG)(LPMDICREATESTRUCT)&mdi);
       return 0;

     case 11:
       SendMessage(hWnd,WM_CLOSE,0,0L);
       return 0;

     case 30:
       MessageBox(hWnd,"Help 1","HELP",MB_OK);
       return 0;

     case 31:
       MessageBox(hWnd,"Help 2","HELP",MB_OK);
       return 0;

     case 32:
       MessageBox(hWnd,"Help 3","HELP",MB_OK);
       return 0;

     case 33:
       MessageBox(hWnd,"Help 4","HELP",MB_OK);
       return 0;

     default:
       hWndChild = LOWORD(SendMessage(hWndClient,
             WM_MDIGETACTIVE,0,0L));
       if(IsWindow(hWndChild))
       SendMessage(hWndChild,WM_COMMAND,wParam,
             lParam);
       break;
     }
  break;
```

continues

Listing 9.2. continued

```
     case WM_QUERYENDSESSION:

     case WM_CLOSE:

     case WM_DESTROY:
          PostQuitMessage(0);
          return 0;

     }
return DefFrameProc(hWnd,hWndClient,iMessage,wParam,lParam);
}

/*****************************************************************/
/*              Window Procedure: DocWndProc                     */
/*****************************************************************/

long FAR PASCAL DocWndProc (HWND hWnd, WORD iMessage,
                    WORD wParam, LONG lParam)
{
static HWND hWndClient, hWndFrame;
HDC hDC;
HMENU hMenu;
LOCALHANDLE hDocData;
NPDOCDATA npDocData;

switch(iMessage)
     {
     case WM_CREATE:
          hDocData = LocalAlloc(LMEM_MOVEABLE ¦
                 LMEM_ZEROINIT,sizeof(DOCDATA));
          npDocData = (NPDOCDATA)LocalLock(hDocData);
          npDocData->x = 10;
          npDocData->y = 10;
          LocalUnlock(hDocData);
          SetWindowWord(hWnd,0,hDocData);
          hWndClient = GetParent(hWnd);
          hWndFrame = GetParent(hWndClient);
          return 0;

     case WM_COMMAND:
       switch(wParam)
          {
          case 20:
            MessageBox(hWnd,"Message 1","MESSAGE",
                 MB_OK);
            return 0;
```

```
        case 21:
          MessageBox(hWnd,"Message 2","MESSAGE",
               MB_OK);
          return 0;

        case 22:
          MessageBox(hWnd,"Message 3","MESSAGE",
               MB_OK);
          return 0;

        case 23:
          MessageBox(hWnd,"Message 4","MESSAGE",
               MB_OK);
          return 0;

        case 25:
          MessageBox(hWnd,"Message 5","MESSAGE",
               MB_OK);
          return 0;

        default:
          return 0;
        }

    case WM_MDIACTIVATE:
        if(wParam == TRUE)
        SendMessage(hWndClient,WM_MDISETMENU,0,
                MAKELONG(hMenuDoc,hMenuDocWin));
        if(wParam == FALSE)
        SendMessage(hWndClient,WM_MDISETMENU,0,
                MAKELONG(hMenu,hMenuWin));
        DrawMenuBar(hWndFrame);
        return 0;

    case WM_QUERYENDSESSION:

    case WM_CLOSE:
        MessageBox(hWnd,"Close Disabled","STOP",
             MB_ICONSTOP|MB_OK);
        return 0;

    case WM_DESTROY:
        hDocData = GetWindowWord(hWnd,0);
        LocalFree(hDocData);
        return 0;
    }
return DefMDIChildProc(hWnd,iMessage,wParam,lParam);
}
```

Listing 9.3. The resource file for the MDI example.

```
#include <windows.h>
MdiMenu MENU
  {
  POPUP "File"
     {
     MENUITEM "New Document", 10
     MENUITEM "Exit",         11
     }
  }


MdiMenuDoc MENU
  {
  POPUP "File"
     {
     MENUITEM "Exit",         11
     }
  POPUP "Messages",
     {
     MENUITEM "Message 1",    20
     MENUITEM "Message 2",    21
     MENUITEM "Message 3",    22
     MENUITEM "Message 4",    23
     MENUITEM "Message 5",    24
     }
  POPUP "Help",
     {
     MENUITEM "Help 1",       30
     MENUITEM "Help 2",       31
     MENUITEM "Help 3",       32
     MENUITEM "Help 4",       33
     }
  }

MdiAccel ACCELERATORS
  {
  VK_F1,20,VIRTKEY,SHIFT
  VK_F2,30,VIRTKEY,SHIFT
  }
```

10

Dynamic Libraries

Dynamic link libraries (DLLs) enable Windows applications to share resources and code. A DLL is actually an executable module that contains functions which can be used by all Windows applications. DLLs are similar to the C run-time libraries that you regularly use when developing C code. DLLs differ from C run-time libraries, however, because DLLs are linked with the application at run-time (dynamic linking). C run-time libraries are linked using a linker when the executable is built (static linking). This chapter introduces dynamic link libraries and their use for Windows application development.

Static Versus Dynamic Linking

If you have developed MS-DOS applications using Borland C++, you are familiar with Borland's C run-time library and the many functions that it provides. To use one of the functions provided in the C run-time library, you must include the header file that contains the function prototype and any constants defined for the function in your C source file. After you include the header file, you then can use the function to develop the application code. When you create the executable, the C source code

is compiled into object code using the compiler. The linker then links object code with the run-time library to create the executable code. Using the linker to link the C run-time library is called *static linking*.

Static linking advantageously provides a set of functions that is available to all applications. The application is not required to include the source code for these functions because the linker will copy the appropriate information to the application's executable file during linking.

Although static linking works well for the MS-DOS environments where only one application runs at a time, static linking is not efficient for multitasking environments such as Windows. Because applications share memory resources in a multitasking environment, static linking often results in wasted memory. An example of such waste is two applications using ten of the same functions from a C run-time library. With static linking, the functions are copied into each application during linking. The result is two copies of each of the ten functions in memory—wasted memory. With dynamic linking, applications share resources and functions. This results in the efficient use of memory and system resources.

Import Libraries

An import library has special importance when working with DLLs. The import library helps Windows find code in the DLL. The import library contains the information that connects application modules and DLL modules. An application module is the application's .EXE file and contains the application code. The DLL module is the library module containing the library code and usually has the extension .DLL, .DRV, .FON, or .EXE.

Import libraries are used along with static link libraries to resolve references to external routines. As was mentioned before, when the application references a function from a static link library, the code for the function is copied to the application's executable during linking. However, when the application references a function from a dynamic link library, the linker does not copy the function's code. The linker instead copies information from the import library to indicate the location where the required code can be found during run-time.

The DLL Code Structure

When you use Borland C++ to create a dynamic link library, you follow the same basic steps (outlined in Chapter 2) that you follow to create a Windows application.

The main difference, however, is that in step 6 you select the `Windows DLL` option under `Options ¦ Applications` instead of `Windows App`. The steps to create a Windows DLL follow:

1. Create all appropriate C or C++ source files, module definition files, and resource files.
2. Start the IDE by typing `BC` (real mode) or `BCX` (protected mode).
3. If you are not in the directory that contains the C or C++ source files, module definition files, and resource files, select `File ¦ Change dir` and change to the directory that contains these files.
4. Select `Project ¦ Open`. Type the file name, using a .PRJ extension, in the Project Name dialog box. Click the `OK` button, or press Enter to continue.
5. Select `Project ¦ Add item`. Add the appropriate C or C++ source files, module definition files, and resource files. Close the Project dialog box when you are done.
6. Select `Options ¦ Application`. The Set Application Options dialog box appears. Select `Windows DLL` to indicate that you are developing a Windows dynamic link library.
7. Select `Compile ¦ Build all`. This selection builds the project into a Windows dynamic link library.
8. If there are any errors, modify each appropriate file and repeat step 7. After the project is successfully built, continue with step 9.
9. Exit the IDE by selecting `File ¦ Quit` or by pressing Alt-X.
10. Create a Windows program that uses your DLL.

You still can use the Project Manager to develop the DLL. As with Windows applications, the DLL requires two files that you must create: the C source code file and the module definition file.

The C source code file is very different from the C source code files that you have seen so far in this book. The following code outline represents the basic code structure of the C source file for a DLL. This code structure is described in *Microsoft Windows Software Development Kit—Guide to Programming*, published (1990) by Microsoft Corporation.

```
#include <windows.h>

int FAR PASCAL LibMain(HANDLE hInstance, WORD wDataSeg,
                       WORD wHeapSize, LPSTR lpszCmdLine)
{
```

```
   /*                                      */
   /*     DLL Initialization               */
   /*                                      */

if (cbHeapSize != 0)    /* if MOVEABLE data segment */
   UnlockData(0);

return(1);
}

VOID FAR PASCAL MinRoutine(int iParam1, int iParam2)
{
char cLocalVariable;    /* Local variables on stack */

     /*                                   */
     /*         MinRoutine Code           */
     /*                                   */
}

VOID FAR PASCAL WEP(int iParam)
{
if (nParameter == WEP_SYSTEMEXIT)
   {
   /* System shutdown in progress - respond accordingly */
   return(1);
   }
else
   {if(nParameter == WEP_FREE_DLL)
      {
      /* DLL use count is zero - DLL is free */
      return(1);
      }
    else
      {
      /* ignore undefined value */
      return(1);
      }
   }
}
```

This code structure has three basic components. The first is the `LibMain` function, which is the main entry point for a Windows DLL and is responsible for initializing the DLL. The second component is the `MinRoutine` function, which is simply a representative function in this code structure. The DLL code structure can contain one or more functions; it does not need to have the `MinRoutine` function. The last component of the code structure is the `WEP` (Windows Exit Procedure) function. The `WEP` function, although not necessary, enables the user to define cleanup activities before the DLL is unloaded from memory.

The module definition file is another file that is required for creating DLLs. The module definition file used for DLLs is similar to the module definition files used for Windows applications. It contains the following eight entries:

- `LIBRARY` specifies that the module is a DLL. The library name follows the `LIBRARY` keyword.
- `DESCRIPTION` is a string that describes the DLL.
- `EXETYPE WINDOWS` is required for Windows applications and DLLs.
- `STUB` specifies the DOS 2.x program that is copied into the body of the library's executable file. When a Windows application is run from DOS instead of Windows, the specified executable stub is executed. If the `STUB` statement is not used, an executable stub is assigned automatically. Most applications use the WINSTUB.EXE executable file for the executable stub.
- `CODE` defines the memory attributes of the library's code segments.
- `DATA` defines the memory attributes of the library's data segment.
- `HEAPSIZE` defines the initial size of the local heap for the DLL.
- `EXPORTS` specifies the functions used as entry points from applications or other DLLs.

Creating a DLL

Listings 10.1 and 10.2 demonstrate the creation of a DLL containing two functions: `XBox` and `SlashBox`. The `XBox` function creates a box that has diagonal lines connecting the opposite corners. The `SlashBox` function creates a box that has one diagonal line connecting the upper-left and lower-right corners. Two files were necessary to create the DLL. Listing 10.1 shows the module definition file. The C source code file, shown in Listing 10.2, contains the functions `XBox` and `SlashBox`.

The following lines show the project name as well as files used to create the DLL.

Project Name:	`WIN_DLL`
Files in Project:	`WIN_DLL.DEF`
	`WIN_DLL.C`

Listing 10.1. The definition file for the DLL.

```
LIBRARY         WIN_DLL
DESCRIPTION     'DLL for DLL Example'
EXETYPE         WINDOWS
CODE            PRELOAD MOVEABLE DISCARDABLE
DATA            PRELOAD MOVEABLE SINGLE
HEAPSIZE        1024
EXPORTS         XBox
                SlashBox
```

Listing 10.2. The C source file for the DLL.

```
#include <windows.h>

int FAR PASCAL LibMain(HANDLE hInstance, WORD wDataSeg,
                       WORD wHeapSize, LPSTR lpszCmdLine)
{
if(wHeapSize != 0)
   UnlockData(0);
return 1;
}

int FAR PASCAL XBox(HDC hDC,int X,int Y)
{
MoveTo(hDC,X,Y);
LineTo(hDC,X+25,Y);
LineTo(hDC,X+25,Y+25);
LineTo(hDC,X,Y+25);
LineTo(hDC,X,Y);
LineTo(hDC,X+25,Y+25);
MoveTo(hDC,X+25,Y);
LineTo(hDC,X,Y+25);
return 1;
}

int FAR PASCAL SlashBox(HDC hDC,int X,int Y)
{
MoveTo(hDC,X,Y);
LineTo(hDC,X+25,Y);
LineTo(hDC,X+25,Y+25);
LineTo(hDC,X,Y+25);
LineTo(hDC,X,Y);
LineTo(hDC,X+25,Y+25);
return 1;
}
```

Using the DLL from a Windows Application

The purpose of a DLL is to provide functions that several Windows applications can use. The `XBox` and `SlashBox` functions of the DLL in Listings 10.1 and 10.2 are used in the DLL example in Listings 10.3 and 10.4. Two files are required for this demonstration. The module definition file of this example (Listing 10.3) looks similar to the module definition files of the previous examples in this book. There is one difference to note, however. The module definition file for this example uses the `IMPORTS` function to specify that the `XBox` and `SlashBox` functions are part of the WIN_DLL dynamic link library and that these functions are necessary for the application.

The C source file in Listing 10.4 is similar to the C source file of the previous examples in this book. The only items of special interest are the function prototypes of the `XBox` and `SlashBox` functions. When the window procedure receives the WM_PAINT message, the `XBox` and `SlashBox` functions are used to draw figures. The DLL example displays nine boxes created with the `XBox` and `SlashBox` functions. Figure 10.1 shows the output of the DLL example.

The following lines show the project name as well as files used to create the DLL example.

Project Name:	`WIN_DLLE`
Files in Project:	`WIN_DLLE.DEF`
	`WIN_DLLE.C`

***Listing 10.3.** The definition file for the DLL example.*

```
NAME            WIN_DLLE
DESCRIPTION     'DLL Example'
EXETYPE         WINDOWS
CODE            PRELOAD MOVEABLE
DATA            PRELOAD MOVEABLE MULTIPLE
HEAPSIZE        1024
STACKSIZE       5120
EXPORTS         WndProc
IMPORTS         WIN_DLL.XBox
                WIN_DLL.SlashBox
```

Listing 10.4. The C source file for the DLL example.

```
#include <windows.h>
#include <stdlib.h>
#include <string.h>

long FAR PASCAL WndProc (HWND hWnd, WORD iMessage,
                WORD wParam, LONG lParam);

int FAR PASCAL XBox(HDC hDC,int X,int Y);

int FAR PASCAL SlashBox(HDC hDC,int X,int Y);

int PASCAL WinMain (HANDLE hInstance, HANDLE hPrevInstance,
              LPSTR lpszCmdParam, int nCmdShow)

{
HWND hWnd;
MSG Message;
WNDCLASS WndClass;

if (!hPrevInstance)
     {
     WndClass.cbClsExtra = 0;
     WndClass.cbWndExtra = 0;
     WndClass.hbrBackground = GetStockObject(WHITE_BRUSH);
     WndClass.hCursor =  LoadCursor(NULL, IDC_ARROW);
     WndClass.hIcon = LoadIcon (NULL, IDI_APPLICATION);
     WndClass.hInstance = hInstance;
     WndClass.lpfnWndProc = WndProc;
     WndClass.lpszClassName = "WIN_DLLE";
     WndClass.lpszMenuName = NULL;
     WndClass.style = CS_HREDRAW ¦ CS_VREDRAW;

     RegisterClass (&WndClass);
     }

hWnd = CreateWindow ("WIN_DLLE",  /* class name */
          "DLL Example",          /* Caption */
          WS_OVERLAPPEDWINDOW,    /* Style */
          CW_USEDEFAULT,          /* x position */
          0,                      /* y position */
          CW_USEDEFAULT,          /* cx - size */
          0,                      /* cy - size */
          NULL,                   /* Parent window */
          NULL,                   /* Menu */
          hInstance,              /* Program Instance */
          NULL);                  /* Parameters */
```

```
ShowWindow (hWnd, nCmdShow);
while (GetMessage (&Message, 0, 0, 0))
     {
     TranslateMessage(&Message);
     DispatchMessage(&Message);
     }
return Message.wParam;
}

/***************************************************************/
/*                Window Procedure: WndProc                    */
/***************************************************************/

long FAR PASCAL WndProc (HWND hWnd, WORD iMessage, WORD wParam,
                LONG lParam)
{
HDC hDC;
HPEN hPen;
PAINTSTRUCT PtStr;

switch (iMessage)
     {
     case WM_PAINT:

          hDC = BeginPaint (hWnd,&PtStr);

          SetMapMode(hDC, MM_ANISOTROPIC);

          hPen = GetStockObject(BLACK_PEN);
          SelectObject(hDC,hPen);

          XBox(hDC,50,50);
          SlashBox(hDC,100,50);
          XBox(hDC,150,50);
          SlashBox(hDC,50,100);
          XBox(hDC,100,100);
          SlashBox(hDC,150,100);
          XBox(hDC,50,150);
          SlashBox(hDC,100,150);
          XBox(hDC,150,150);

          EndPaint(hWnd,&PtStr);
          return 0;

     case WM_DESTROY:
```

continues

Listing 10.4. continued

```
            PostQuitMessage(0);
            return 0;

        default:

            return(DefWindowProc(hWnd, iMessage, wParam,
                lParam));
        }
}
```

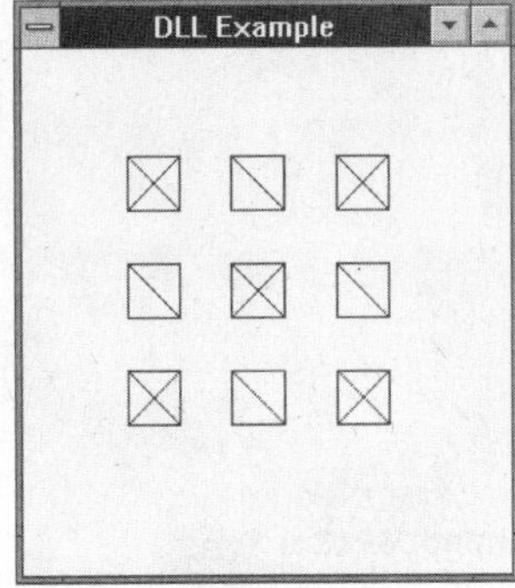

Figure 10.1. *The DLL example.*

II

Windows Programming with ObjectWindows

11

Introduction to ObjectWindows for C++

Part I of this book introduced traditional Windows programming, whose techniques utilize the C language. Although traditional Windows programs are modular, the resulting code sometimes becomes very long and cumbersome. Part II of the book introduces object-oriented programming techniques and Borland's ObjectWindows for developing Windows applications.

But before you get too far into object-oriented Windows programming using ObjectWindows, you first need to review the basics of object-oriented programming and the C++ language.

Object-Oriented Programming for C++

Object-oriented programming is a relatively new programming methodology. A computer environment is modeled as a collection of objects that interact with each other through messages. Object-oriented programming makes a program more modular and maintainable.

Object-oriented programs, of course, contain objects. Objects contain properties and behaviors. Properties are not directly accessible from outside the object. Instead, the properties are manipulated by the behaviors of the object. The behaviors of the object are invoked when a message is received by the object. This is confusing for newcomers to object-oriented programming, so let's take this one step at a time.

First, we will define an *object*. In the real world, an object has properties and behaviors. For example, a basketball is round and usually orange (its properties) and can be dribbled, passed, or shot (its behaviors). In the programming world, an object also has properties and behaviors. For example, in a graphics application, a circle is described by certain data such as its center, color, radius, and fill pattern (its properties), and can be created, moved, sized, or deleted (its behaviors). Objects in a program can represent the physical entities, such as circles and rectangles, or the more abstract entities, such as stacks and complex data structures.

Object-oriented programming has several characteristics and advantages. First, because objects contain properties and behaviors, objects support modular programming. Modular programming supports ease of development and maintainability of code. The other characteristics and advantages of object-oriented programming involve the properties of encapsulation, inheritance, and polymorphism. The following sections explain these properties.

Encapsulation

Encapsulation is described in the Borland C++ tutorial as combining a data structure with the functions (actions or methods) dedicated to manipulating the data. Encapsulation is achieved by means of a new structuring and data-typing mechanism, the *class*.

To simplify this definition, encapsulation is the practice of using classes to link data and the code used to manipulate the data. In the traditional C programming style, data is usually kept in data structures; functions are then created to manipulate the data. This style is shown as follows:

```
struct data_items
     {
     int a;
     int b;
     int c;
     };

void manipulate_data (int x, int y, int z)
{
data_items.a = data_items.a + x;
data_items.b = data_items.b + y;
data_items.c = data_items.c + z;
}
```

This structure and function then is put into a source file, compiled separately, and treated as a module. The problem with this method is that even though the structure and function are created to be used together, the data can be accessed without using the described function.

The property of encapsulation solves this problem. Encapsulation is provided in C++ by the `struct`, `union`, and `class` keywords. These keywords let you combine data and functions into a class entity. The data items are called data members, whereas the functions are called member functions.

The following is an example of a class:

```
class Circle {
     int x;
     int y;
     int radius;

     int DrawCircle (int a, int b, int rad);
     int DeleteCircle (int a, int b, int rad);
};
```

The data members of the class are `x`, `y`, and `radius`. The member functions of the class are `DrawCircle` and `DeleteCircle`.

By defining the class `Circle`, the properties of the object cannot be directly accessed from outside the object. Only the behaviors of the object, `DrawCircle` and `DeleteCircle`, can manipulate the data. The behaviors of the object can be invoked only by sending a message to the object. By defining an object in this way, the implementation details of the object are not visible to, or accessible by, the outside. This is encapsulation, which leads to modular programming and maintainable, reusable code.

Inheritance

Inheritance is described in the Borland C++ tutorial as building new, derived classes that inherit the data and functions from one or more previously defined base classes, while possibly redefining or adding new data and actions. This creates a hierarchy of classes.

In other words, inheritance is the ability to create a class that has the properties and behaviors of another class. For example, suppose that you start with a class called DOG. This class has several properties, including four legs, a tail, two eyes, two ears, a mouth, and a nose. Under this class you can add classes that provide more specific information.

For our purposes we'll add the `BigDog` class and the `LittleDog` class. The `BigDog` class has the properties of heavy and tall. The `LittleDog` class has the properties of light and short. You could add more classes that provide even more detail. For example, `LongHairBigDog`, `ShortHairBigDog`, `LongHairLittleDog`, and `ShortHairLittleDog` classes could be added. The `LongHairBigDog` and `LongHairLittleDog` classes add the property of long hair. The `ShortHairBigDog` and `ShortHairLittleDog` classes add the property of short hair.

Additional classes could be added which provide even more specifics. We'll add the `IrishSetter` class and the `Chihuahua` class. The `IrishSetter` class adds the property of red hair. The `Chihuahua` class adds the properties of very small and nervous. This hierarchy is shown in Figure 11.1. By developing a hierarchy, it is possible to classify and inherit properties of objects.

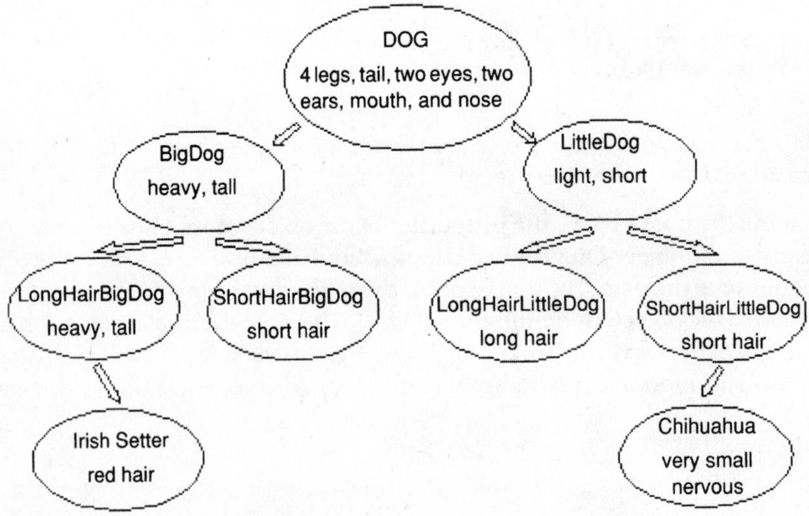

Figure 11.1. *The DOG hierarchy.*

Now let's look at applying this hierarchy. An Irish Setter, for example, has the property of red hair as determined from the derived class `IrishSetter`. Derived classes inherit properties from other classes, called ***base classes***. Therefore, the Irish Setter also has the property of the `LongHairBigDog` class, which is long hair. The `LongHairBigDog` class also inherits properties from the `BigDog` class which, in turn, inherits properties from the DOG class. Therefore, you can determine that the Irish Setter has long red hair, is heavy and tall, and has two ears, two eyes, a tail, a mouth, a nose, and four legs. Similarly, you can determine that the Chihuahua is very small and nervous, has short hair, is light and short, and has two ears, two eyes, a tail, a mouth, a nose, and four legs.

Although this is a simple illustration of inheritance, it provides a basic understanding of the power of inheritance. The ability to inherit properties from other classes enables you to generalize data and properties, thus improving programmer efficiency and reducing redundancy in code.

The following example demonstrates the use of the C++ features of inheritance and encapsulation for the implementation of a graphics program:

```
#include <graphics.h>
#include <stdio.h>
#include <stdlib.h>
#include <conio.h>

class Circle {
protected:
   int X;
   int Y;
   int Rad;
public:
   Circle (int InitX, int InitY, int InitRad)
      {X = InitX; Y = InitY; Rad = InitRad;}
};

class SolidCircle : public Circle {
protected:
   int Color;
public:
   SolidCircle (int InitX, int InitY, int InitRad,
   int InitColor);
};

class ShadedCircle : public Circle {
protected:
   int Color;
public:
   ShadedCircle (int InitX, int InitY, int InitRad,
   int InitColor);
};
```

```
SolidCircle::SolidCircle(int InitX, int InitY, int InitRad,
   int InitColor) : Circle (InitX, InitY, InitRad) {
   setfillstyle (SOLID_FILL, InitColor);
   fillellipse (InitX, InitY, InitRad, InitRad);
};

ShadedCircle::ShadedCircle(int InitX, int InitY, int InitRad,
   int InitColor) : Circle (InitX, InitY, InitRad) {
   setfillstyle (HATCH_FILL, InitColor);
   fillellipse (InitX, InitY, InitRad, InitRad);
};


int main()
{
int gdriver = VGA;
int gmode = VGAHI;

int x, y, color, rad, selection;

registerbgidriver(EGAVGA_driver);
registerbgifont(sansserif_font);

initgraph(&gdriver,&gmode,"");

do
{
x = random (639);
y = random (479);
rad = random (51);
color = random (15);
selection = random (2);

if (selection == 0)
     ShadedCircle (x, y, rad + 5, color + 1);
else
     SolidCircle (x, y, rad + 5, color + 1);

} while (! kbhit());

closegraph();
return 0;
}
```

The program begins by declaring the class `Circle`. The `Circle` class demonstrates the properties of encapsulation through its data `X`, `Y`, and `Rad`. Inheritance is demonstrated by the two derived classes, `ShadedCircle` and `SolidCircle`, of the base class `Circle`.

The program randomly selects the horizontal and vertical coordinates for the center position of a circle. The radius and fill color are then randomly selected. A selection is then made to determine which type of circle will be drawn—either a shaded or solid circle. The shaded or solid circle is then drawn. This continues until a key is pressed.

Polymorphism

Polymorphism is described in the Borland C++ tutorial as giving an action one name or symbol that is shared up and down a class hierarchy, with each class in the hierarchy implementing the action in a way appropriate to itself.

Very simply stated, polymorphism, in C++, is the ability to create several versions of the same function or operator. The Borland C++ Run-Time Library contains several functions that have been "overloaded" to work with various data types. Look at the following function prototypes, for example:

```
int square (int value);
float square (float value);
double square (double square);
```

Each function is designed to accept and return a particular data type: int, float, or double; however, each function is called `square`. In C, you can have only one function with a given name. In C++, on the other hand, function overloading is fully supported as long as the argument lists differ. Therefore, if you call `square` while passing an integer value, the proper function will be called and an integer value will be returned. Similarly, if you call `square` with a float or double value, a float or double value, respectively, will be returned.

The ability to overload functions and operators provides greater flexibility in program design.

The following example demonstrates the overloading of a function:

```
#include <stdio.h>
#include <stdlib.h>
#include <conio.h>
#include <iostream.h>

class squared {
public:
  int squ(int);
  double squ(double);
  long squ(long);
};
```

```
int squared::squ(int intval)
{
   int result;

   result = intval * intval;
   return (result);
}

double squared::squ(double dblval)
{
   double result;

   result = dblval * dblval;
   return (result);
}

long squared::squ(long longval)
{
   long result;

   result = longval * longval;
   return (result);
}


int main()
{
squared value;

clrscr();
cout << "The square of 3 is " << value.squ(3) << endl;
cout << "The square of 3.5 is " << value.squ(3.5) << endl;
cout << "The square of 6L is " << value.squ(6L) << endl;

return 0;
}
```

In this example, the class `squared` has three functions called `squ` associated with it. Each function is designed to work with either int, double, or long values. When the function `squ` is called, the value passed as a parameter determines which version of the `squ` function is executed.

Polymorphism is also known as late, or dynamic, binding and is often accomplished using virtual functions.

Now that you have reviewed the basics of object-oriented programming, take a look at Borland's ObjectWindows, an object-oriented library that enables you to take full advantage of object-oriented programming features.

Object-Oriented Windows Programming with ObjectWindows

ObjectWindows is an object-oriented library that incorporates the advantages of object-oriented programming to make programming Windows applications easier for you. With ObjectWindows all major Windows elements, including windows themselves, are treated as objects with defined behaviors, attributes, and data. The three most significant features of ObjectWindows are:

- The encapsulation of window information
- The abstraction of many of the Windows functions
- Automatic message response

The encapsulation of window information is significant in that the behaviors, attributes, and data for the window, dialog box, and control objects (known as *interface objects*) are defined by ObjectWindows. While ObjectWindows defines the behavior, attributes, and data for interface objects, it is still up to Windows to implement the physical representation of the objects (what you see in the display). The physical representation of the interface objects depends upon Windows structures that are known as *interface elements*.

The interface elements' handle is the thread that binds the interface object and the interface element. When the `Create` member function of an interface object is called, the interface element is created and the handle to the element is returned. The `HWindow` data member of the interface object is used to store the handle to the interface element. You must understand the distinction and bond between interface objects and elements to take full advantage of the features that ObjectWindows offers. Once you understand the basics of ObjectWindows, you can simplify Windows application development by using ObjectWindows' many features.

Another significant feature of ObjectWindows is the abstraction of many Windows functions. Using member functions that abstract a called Windows function makes programming easier for you, because it provides a built-in interface to that function. There are approximately 600 Windows functions and, unfortunately, not all 600 functions are abstracted. However, you can call Windows functions directly, and many of the parameters you need to call a Windows function are already stored in the data members of the interface objects.

Automatic message response is another significant feature of ObjectWindows. Windows requires its applications to respond to Windows messages that are sent to it. With traditional Windows programming as presented in Part I, a `switch` statement is used to respond to messages. With ObjectWindows, however, Windows messages are handled by object member function calls. A member function can be defined for each message that must be handled. Therefore, when your object receives a message, the appropriate member function is called automatically.

You have briefly reviewed the significant features of ObjectWindows. Now you should look at the hierarchy of ObjectWindows classes. Once you review the ObjectWindows hierarchy, you can look more closely at classes that comprise the ObjectWindows library.

The ObjectWindows Hierarchy

ObjectWindows is a library of hierarchical classes that enable you to take advantage of the object-oriented feature of inheritance. The ObjectWindows classes contain data members and member functions that make Windows programming easier. Figure 11.2 illustrates the ObjectWindows hierarchy. The ObjectWindows classes and ObjectWindows member functions are explained in detail in the ObjectWindows Classes and ObjectWindows Functions chapters of this book.

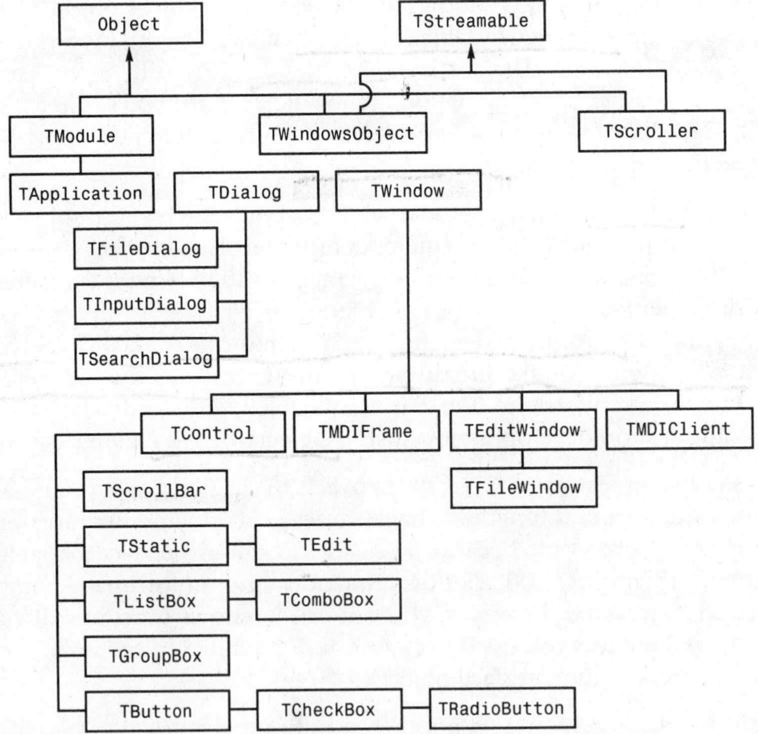

Figure 11.2. *The ObjectWindows hierarchy.*

The remainder of this chapter provides additional information on the base class `Object` and `ObjectWindows` application objects, interface objects, window objects, dialog objects, control objects, MDI objects, and `Scroller` objects.

Object

Before you look at application objects, interface objects, window objects, dialog objects, control objects, MDI objects, or `Scroller` objects, you should look at the base class that defines the behaviors, data, and attributes for derived classes. The `Object` class is the base class for all ObjectWindows derived classes. `Object` is an abstract class that defines the behaviors of a derived object and provides the structures for type checking and encapsulation. The `Object` class has the following data members and member functions:

Data Members:

`ZERO` handles problems when the `new` operator cannot allocate space for an object

Member Functions:

Two `Object` constructors

`Object` destructor

`firstThat` finds the first object in the container that meets the specified conditions

`forEach` iterates through each object in the container

`hashValue` returns a hash value

`isA` returns a unique class identifier for the class

`isAssociation` returns zero for the base `Object` class

`isEqual` is a pure virtual function for derived classes

`isSortable` determines whether or not an object is derived from the class `Sortable`

`lastThat` is identical to `firstThat` for noncontainer objects

`nameOf` enables derived classes to return a class ID string

`new` allocates the specified number of bytes for an object

`printOn` writes the printable representation of the object on a stream

Chapter 18, "ObjectWindows Classes," and Chapter 19, "ObjectWindows Functions," provide reference information for the data members and member functions of the `Object` class.

Application Objects

Every Windows application developed using ObjectWindows must define an application class derived from `TApplication`. The resulting application object encapsulates the application's behavior including the creation and display of the main window, the initialization of the first instance of an application, the initialization of every subsequent instance of an application, the processing of messages for the application, and the closing of the application.

For the derived application class, you must define the construction of the main window object and redefine the behaviors for the initialization of instances, the processing of messages, and the closing of the application. Before you go any further into the details of creating and defining the application object, you should quickly review the `TApplication` object.

TApplication

`TApplication` defines the behavior of ObjectWindows applications and provides the structure for the application. All ObjectWindows applications derive an application class from `TApplication`. `TApplication` contains the following data members and member functions:

Data Members:

`HAccTable` stores the handle to the current Windows accelerator table

`hPrevInstance` defines the handle of the previous instance of the application

`KBHandlerWnd` points to the active window if the keyboard handler for the window is enabled

`MainWindow` points to the main window of the application

`nCmdShow` specifies whether the application should be displayed as an icon or as an open window

Member Functions:

`TApplication` constructor constructs the `TApplication` object

`~TApplication()` destructor destroys the `TApplication` object

`CanClose` determines whether the application can close

`IdleAction` can be redefined to perform special functions when the application is idle

`InitApplication` makes the initializations required for the first executing instance of the application

`InitInstance` makes the initializations required for all executing instances of the application

`InitMainWindow` constructs a generic `TWindow` class using the application name

`isA` redefines the pure virtual function in class `Object`. This function returns the class ID of `TApplication`

`MessageLoop` manages the message loop of the application

`nameOf` redefines the pure virtual function in class `Object`

`ProcessAccels` processes accelerator messages

`ProcessAppMsg` calls `ProcessDlgMsg`, `ProcessMDIAccels`, and `ProcessAccels` for the processing of modeless dialog messages, MDI accelerator messages, and accelerator messages, respectively

`ProcessDlgMsg` provides message processing of keyboard input for modeless dialog boxes and windows with controls

`ProcessMDIAccels` processes accelerator messages for MDI applications

`Run` initializes the instance and executes the application

`SetKBHandler` enables keyboard handling for the specified window

Chapter 18, "ObjectWindows Classes," and Chapter 19, "ObjectWindows Functions," provide reference information for the data members and member functions of the `TApplication` class.

The Application's Main Program

All ObjectWindows applications contain a main program that controls the application. For most applications, this main program contains three statements in the format shown in the following code:

```
int PASCAL WinMain(HANDLE hInstance, HANDLE hPrevInstance,
                   LPSTR lpCmdLine, int nCmdShow)
{
```

```
    TAppExample AppExample("Application Example" ,hInstance,
        hPrevInstance, lpCmdLine, nCmdShow);
    AppExample.Run();
    return AppExample.Status;
}
```

The first statement of the main program calls the constructor to construct the application object. When the constructor is called, the data members of the application object are initialized.

The second statement of the main program calls the `Run` member function, which calls `InitApplication` and `InitInstance`. `InitApplication` initializes the first instance of the application. `InitInstance` initializes each instance of the application. After `Run` has called `InitApplication` and `InitInstance`, `InitMainWindow` is called to create a main window. `InitMainWindow` is generally redefined for each application. Lastly, the `Run` member function calls `MessageLoop`. `MessageLoop` receives and processes Windows messages sent to the application.

The third statement of the main program returns the final status of the application. Zero is generally used to represent a normal closing of the application. A nonzero value usually indicates that an error has occurred.

As the three statements indicate, there are three basic steps that occur in the main window:

- The initialization of the application
- The execution of the application
- The termination of the application

The following paragraphs describe each of these steps in more detail.

Initializing Applications

As previously described, the main program generally consists of three statements. Of these three statements, the first two contribute to the initialization of the application. The main window is described in the following paragraphs.

The first statement of the main program called the constructor to the application object. However, before you can call the constructor to the application object, you must first define an application class derived from `TApplication`. The following code demonstrates how this can be done:

```
class TAppExample : public TApplication
{
```

```
public:
     TAppExample(LPSTR AName, HANDLE hInstance, HANDLE hPrevInstance,
          LPSTR lpCmdLine, int nCmdShow): TApplication(AName, hInstance,
          hPrevInstance, lpCmdLine, nCmdShow) {};
     virtual void InitMainWindow();
};
```

In this example you are creating an application class, `TAppExample`, that is derived from `TApplication`. When you create an application object, you must define an `InitMainWindow` member function that constructs and initializes the main window object. Once created, the main window object can be referenced by the `MainWindow` data member. The following code demonstrates how to you can define the `InitMainWindow` member function:

```
void TAppEx::InitMainWindow()
{
     MainWindow = new TAppExWindow(NULL, "Main Window");
}
```

The second statement of the main program calls the `Run` member function which, in turn, calls `InitApplication` and `InitInstance`. `InitInstance`, again in turn, calls `InitMainWindow`. Therefore, it is obvious that the second statement of the main program plays an important role in application initialization. Since the `Run` member function first calls `InitApplication`, you should look at what happens when you call `InitApplication`.

When the application is executed for the first time (referring to the first time the application has been run since all instances of the application have been terminated), you may want some special initialization of the application to take place. `InitApplication` can be defined to manage the first-time initialization of the application. Subsequent instances of the application do not call `InitApplication`.

The next function that gets called by the `Run` member function is `InitInstance`, which performs initialization for each instance of the application. `InitInstance` also calls `InitMainWindow`, which function must have been previously defined. The previous paragraphs provide an example of a definition for `InitMainWindow`.

Once all the initializations for the application have been completed, the application is ready to execute.

Executing Applications

Although the second statement of the main program contributes to the initialization of the application, it also executes the application. The `Run` member function of the application object calls the `MessageLoop` member function. When the `MessageLoop`

function is called, the interactive portion of your application begins. Once the `MessageLoop` function begins processing the messages sent to the application, the application is able to consistently interact with Windows and respond to the messages that are sent to it. The `MessageLoop` function that is inherited by the application works well for most applications and does not need to be modified. However, if you want special message handling for dialog box, accelerator, or MDI messages, you can redefine `MessageLoop`.

`MessageLoop` calls the `ProcessDlgMsg`, `ProcessAccels`, and `ProcessMDIAccels` member functions for the processing of modeless dialog messages, accelerator messages, and MDI accelerator messages, respectively. If your application does not use modeless dialog boxes, accelerators, or MDI accelerators, it may be beneficial for you to redefine `MessageLoop` to elimate these unnecessary function calls since they require time to execute.

Terminating Applications

The application terminates when the main window is closed. However, before the main window can be closed, the application must exit `MessageLoop` and agree to terminate. When the user attempts to close an application, the `WM_CLOSE` message is sent to the main window of the application. The `CloseWindow` member function of the main window object is then called. `CloseWindow` calls the `CanClose` member function of the application object to determine if it is all right to close the application. The application's `CanClose` function returns the result of its call to the `CanClose` function of the main window object. If all agree to close, the application terminates. The third statement of the main program returns the final status of the application.

Interface Objects

Interface objects represent windows, dialog boxes, and controls. As mentioned at the beginning of this chapter, interface objects usually have a corresponding interface element. The interface object provides the functions and data members for initializing, creating, manipulating, and terminating the interface element.

Interface elements are treated as a child window of the parent window. For example, a dialog box is often a child window of the main window. In this case the main window would be the parent window. The dialog box often contains, for example, a list box. The list box contained in the dialog box is considered to be a child window of the dialog box.

Before you go any further into the discussion of interface objects, you should briefly review the class that binds the three basic types of interface objects defined by ObjectWindows, `TWindowsObject`.

TWindowsObject

Derived from `Object`, `TWindowsObject` is an abstract class that defines the behaviors that all interface objects share and maintains a list of child windows. By defining the common behaviors of windows, dialog boxes, and controls and maintaining a list of child windows, `TWindowsObject` enables interface objects to inherit object behaviors and provides a central location for the maintenance of the child window list. `TWindowsObject` contains the following data members and member functions:

Data Members:

`DefaultProc` holds the address of the default window procedure

`HWindow` specifies the handle of the interface element associated with the interface object

`Parent` points to the interface object that acts as the parent window for the interface object

`Status` can indicate an error in the initialization of an interface object

`Title` points to the caption for the window

`TransferBuffer` points to a buffer used to transfer data

Member Functions:

Two `TWindowsObject` constructors

`TWindowsObject` destructor

`AfterDispatchHandler` is called by `DispatchAMessage` after responding to a message

`BeforeDispatchHandler` is called by `DispatchAMessage` before invoking a message response

`build` invokes the `TWindowsObject` constructor and constructs an object of type `TWindowsObject` before reading its data members from a stream

`CanClose` determines whether the associated interface element can be closed by calling the `CanClose` member functions of each of the child windows

`ChildWithID` returns the pointer to the child window from child window list that has the specified ID

CloseWindow calls ShutDownWindow to close the window

CMExit is called when a menu item with an ID of CM_EXIT is selected

Create is a pure virtual function

CreateChildren creates child windows from the child list

DefChildProc handles incoming child-ID-based messages by default

DefCommandProc, by default, handles command-based messages

DefNotificationProc provides the default processing of notification messages and passes these notification messages to the parent as a child-ID-based message

DefWndProc handles default message processing

Destroy calls an associated interface element

DisableAutoCreate disables the autocreate feature

DisableTransfer disables the transfer of state data to and from the transfer buffer

DispatchAMessage dispatches Windows messages to the appropriate response member function

DispatchScroll dispatches messages from scroll bar controls

DrawItem is called when a control or menu item needs to be redrawn

EnableAutoCreate enables the autocreate feature

EnableKBHandler enables windows and modeless dialog boxes to provide a keyboard interface to child controls

EnableTransfer enables the transfer of state data to and from the transfer buffer

FirstThat calls the specified test function for each child window in ChildList

FirstThat calls the specified test function for each child window in ChildList and takes a member function as a parameter

ForEach calls the specified function and passes each child window in ChildList as an argument

ForEach function is like the previous ForEach function except that this function takes a member function as a parameter

GetApplication gets the pointer to the TApplication object that is associated with this

`GetChildPtr` reads a reference to a pointer to a child window from the specified stream

`GetChildren` reads child windows from the specified stream into the child list

`GetClassName` returns the Windows registration class name and must be redefined for derived classes

`GetClient` returns NULL for non-MDI interface objects

`GetFirstChild` returns the pointer to the first child window in the child list for the interface object

`GetId` returns –1 by default

`GetInstance` returns the instance thunk of the window

`GetLastChild` returns the pointer to the last child window in the child list for the interface object

`GetModule` returns the pointer to the `TModule` that owns the object

`GetSiblingPtr` is used only during a `read` operation to references written by a call to `PutSiblingPtr`

`GetWindowClass` is redefined by derived classes

`hashValue` redefines the pure virtual function in class `Object`

`isA` redefines the pure virtual function in class `Object` and should be redefined to return a unique class ID

`isEqual` redefines the pure virtual function in class `Object`

`IsFlagSet` returns TRUE if the bit flag of the `Flags` data member with the specified mask is set

`nameOf` is a pure virtual function

`Next` returns a pointer to the next window in the child window list

`printOn` must be redefined by all objects derived from the base class object

`Previous` returns a pointer to the previous window in the child window list

`PutChildPtr` writes a child window to the specified output stream

`PutChildren` reads child windows from the specified stream and adds the windows to `ChildList`

`PutSiblingPtr` writes the reference to a sibling window to the specified output stream `read` creates an object instance and calls `GetChildren` to read in the child windows

`Register` registers the Windows registration class of `this`

`RemoveClient` removes the specified client window from the child list

`SetCaption` defines the caption of the interface element as the value specified in `ATitle`

`SetFlags` sets the bit flag of the `Flags` data member with the specified mask according to the value specified in `OnOff`

`SetParent` sets `Parent` to the parent window specified in `NewParent`, removes `this` from the child list of the previous parent, and adds `this` to the child list of the new parent

`SetTransferBuffer` sets `TransferBuffer` to the buffer specified in `ATransferBuffer`

`SetupWindow` attempts to create an associated interface element for each child window in `ChildList` that has the autocreate feature enabled

`Show` displays the interface element as specified in `ShowCmd`

`ShutDownWindow` destroys the associated interface element

`Transfer` transfers data to and from the buffer referenced by `DataPtr`

`TransferData` transfers data between the buffer and the interface object's child windows that have the `WM_TRANSFER` flag set

`WMActivate` enables keyboard handling if requested when a `WM_ACTIVATE` message is detected

`WMClose` calls `CloseWindow` to close the window

`WMCommand` calls the appropriate member functions when command-based, child-ID-based, or notify-based messages are detected

`WMDestroy` handles the `WM_DESTROY` message

`WMDrawItem` dispatches the `WM_DRAWITEM` message for drawable controls

`WMHScroll` calls `DispatchScroll` in response to a `WM_HSCROLL` message

`WMNCDestroy` handles the `WM_NCDESTROY` message

`WMQueryEndSession` calls the appropriate `CanClose` function to determine whether the session can close

`WMVScroll` calls `DispatchScroll` in response to the detection of vertical scroll bar messages

`write` writes `Title`, `Status`, flags, and `CreateOrder` and calls `PutChildren` to write out child windows

Chapter 18, "ObjectWindows Classes," and Chapter 19, "ObjectWindows Functions," provide reference information for the data members and member functions of the `TWindowsObject` class.

It is important to note that the three primary types of interface objects are derived from `TWindowsObject`: windows, dialog boxes, and controls. Each of these interface types is discussed in more detail later in this chapter.

Window Objects

Window objects are interface objects that are associated with window elements. The basic behaviors of window objects are defined in the `TWindow` class. `TWindow` is derived from `TWindowsObject` and has four classes derived from it: `TMDIFrame`, `TMDIClient`, `TControl`, and `TEditWindow`. The following paragraphs briefly explain the `TWindow` class.

Using Window Objects

A window object is an interface object and has a corresponding interface element. In order to create a window, you must first define the object and then create the interface element.

ObjectWindows defines a data structure `TWindowAttr` that contains the creation attributes for the window object. The `TWindowAttr` data structure follows:

```
struct_CLASSTYPE TWindowAttr {
     DWORD Style;
     DWORD ExStyle;
     int X, Y, W, H;
     LPSTR Menu;
     int Id;
     LPSTR Param;
     };
```

where

`Style` is a combination of one or more of the following window style constants:

WS_BORDER

WS_CAPTION

WS_CHILD

WS_CHILDWINDOW

WS_CLIPCHILDREN

WS_CLIPSIBLINGS

WS_DISABLED

WS_DLGFRAME

WS_GROUP

WS_HSCROLL

WS_ICONIC

WS_MAXIMIZE

WS_MAXIMIZEBOX

WS_MINIMIZE

WS_MINIMIZEBOX

WS_OVERLAPPED

WS_OVERLAPPEDWINDOW

WS_POPUP

WS_POPUPWINDOW

WS_SIZEBOX

WS_SYSMENU

WS_TABSTOP

WS_THICKFRAME

WS_TILED

WS_TILEDWINDOW

WS_VISIBLE

WS_VSCROLL

`ExStyle` specifies any extended styles. The extended styles follow:

WS_EX_DLGMODALFRAME

WS_EXNOPARENTNOTIFY

`X` is the x screen coordinate of the upper-left corner of the window

`Y` is the y screen coordinate of the upper-left corner of the window

`W` is the width of the window

`H` is the height of the window

`Param` contains a value passed to the window when it is created

`Menu` contains the resource identifier for parent windows

`Id` holds the child window ID for child windows or the resource identifier for dialog boxes

TWindow

`TWindow` is an ObjectWindows class that defines the behaviors for the main window and pop-up windows. In general, the main window of an application is an instance of a derived class of `TWindow`. However, you can create an instance of `TWindow`. The window defined from the TWindow class is a generic, captioned window that can be minimized, maximized, moved, sized, and closed. The TWindow class contains the following data members and member functions:

Data Members:

Attr references a TWindowAttr structure that specifies the attributes used to create the window including the control ID, menu, text, and style

FocusChildHandle is the child window handle of the child window that had the focus when the window was last activated

Scroller points to the TScroller object used for display scrolling

Member Functions:

Three TWindow constructors

TWindow destructor

AssignMenu sets Attr.Menu to the specified menu name

AssignMenu calls the previous AssignMenu function and passes the specifed menu ID

build invokes the TWindow constructor and constructs an object of type TWindow before reading its data members from a stream

Create creates an interface object associated with the TWindow object

GetClassName returns "OWLWindow", the default Windows registration class name for TWindow

GetWindowClass places the default values for the registration attributes into the window class structure referenced by AWndClass

isA redefines the pure virtual function in class Object

nameOf redefines the pure virtual function in class Object

Paint stores derived types that define Paint member functions

read uses TWindowsObject::read to read the base TWindowsObject object

SetupWindow initializes the new window

WMActivate gives a window a keyboard interface when it is being activated or deactivated

WMCreate calls SetupWindow when the WM_CREATE message is detected

WMHScroll handles horizontal scroll bar events

WMLButtonDown responds to WM_LBUTTONDOWN messages

`WMMove` saves the new window coordinates when a `WM_MOVE` message is detected

`WMPaint` calls `Paint` when a `WM_PAINT` message is detected

`WMSize` calls `SetPageSize` when a window with scrollers has been sized

`WMVScroll` calls `DispatchScroll` when the `WM_VSCROLL` message is detected from a scroll bar control

`write` uses `TWindowsObject::write` to write the base `TWindowsObject` object

Chapter 18, "ObjectWindows Classes," and Chapter 19, "ObjectWindows Functions," provide reference information for the data members and member functions of the `TWindow` class.

To define the attributes for your window you must first derive a class from `TWindow` and call the constructor of the base class. For example:

```
class TExampleWindow : public TWindow
{
TExampleWindow(PTWindowsObject AParent, LPSTR ATitle) :
     TWindow(AParent, ATitle) {};
};
```

Once this has been done, you can directly modify the attributes of the window object by defining the `Attr` data member. As an example, you could specify the menu for your window as follows:

```
TExampleWindow::TExampleWindow(PTWindowsObject AParent,
     LPSTR ATitle) : TWindow(AParent, ATitle)
{
AssignMenu("MENUNAME");
}
```

Using Window Elements

Once the window object has been defined, you must create the window element. Fortunately, you do not have to explicitly create the window element because the window element is generally created automatically when either the application is started (main windows) or the `SetupWindow` member function of a parent window is called (child windows). It is, however, a good idea quickly to review the process involved in creating the window element.

The window element is created by calling the `MakeWindow` member function of the application object while passing the window object. `MakeWindow`, in turn, calls

ValidWindow and Create. The ValidWindow function determines whether the window object is valid. If valid, MakeWindow continues and calls Create to create the window element.

Creating Window Classes

Now that you have learned to create the window object and the window element, you may find it necessary to define your own window class that has a specified background, icon, menu, and cursor. In the process of creating the window object, you can define certain attributes, called creation attributes, for each window. Creation attributes include those attributes contained in the TWindowAttr data structure. However, other attributes, including the icon, menu, and background cannot be defined for each window. Instead, these attributes can only be defined for a window class.

When you decide to modify the attributes (other than creation attributes) of a window, a new window class must be associated with that window. Two member functions of the window must be redefined to accomplish this task of association. The first member function to redefine is GetClassName. The GetClassName function returns the name of the window class. For example:

```
LPSTR TCursorWindow::GetClassName()
{
return "CursorWindow";
}
```

The second function to redefine is the GetWindowClass function. When you redefine the GetWindowClass function, you specify the modified attributes as in the following example, which redefines the cursor:

```
void TCursorWindow::GetWindowClass(WNDCLASS _FAR & AWndClass)
{
TWindow::GetWindowClass(AWndClass);
AWndClass.hCursor = LoadCursor(0, IDC_CROSS);
}
```

GetWindowClass receives a WNDCLASS data structure and defines the attributes of the structure relative to what you have specified.

Now that you know how to create window objects, window elements, and window classes, you should look at two classes derived from TWindow: TEditWindow and TFileWindow.

TEditWindow

TEditWindow enables you easily to create an edit window that enables the user to enter and modify the text. Edit windows do not, however, enable you to read and write files. The text of the edit window is contained and controlled in a child TEdit control that completely fills the client area of the edit window. The Editor data member of TEditWindow references the instance of TEdit. The search and replace capabilities of the edit window are provided by TEditWindow and are not a part of TEdit.

TEditWindow defines a window object that enables the user to enter and edit text. The TEditWindow class is derived from TWindow and has one derived class, TFileWindow. TEditWindow contains the following data members and member functions:

Data Members:

Editor points to a multiline edit control that provides text editing for the edit window

IsReplaceOp is TRUE when the next search will also perform a replace

SearchStruct is a transfer buffer used with TSearchDialog

Member Functions:

Two TEditWindow constructors

build invokes the TEditWindow constructor and constructs an object of type TEditWindow before reading its data members from a stream

CMEditFind initiates a text search and displays a search dialog box when a Find menu item is selected

CMEditFindNext initiates a text search when a Find Next menu item is selected

CMEditReplace initiates a text search and replace operation and displays a search dialog box when a Replace menu item is selected

DoSearch offers search functions using the options and features in SearchStruct

read calls TWindow::read to read in the base TWindow object

WMSetFocus sets the focus to Editor edit control when the WM_SETFOCUS message is detected

WMSize sizes the Editor edit control to the TEditWindow's client area when the WM_SIZE message is detected

write calls TWindow::write to write out the base TWindow object and then PutChildPtr to write out the edit control child window

Chapter 18, "ObjectWindows Classes," and Chapter 19, "ObjectWindows Functions," provide reference information for the data members and member functions of the `TEditWindow` class.

TFileWindow

`TFileWindow` enables you to easily create a file editing window. Since `TFileWindow` is derived from `TEditWindow`, the file editing window is similar to the edit window. The primary difference is that the file editing window enables the user to open a new file, open an existing file, save a file under its current name, save a file under a new name; the member functions of `TFileWindow` provide these capabilities.

`TFileWindow` defines an editing window that enables the user to read, write, and edit files. `TFileWindow` contains the following data members and member functions:

Data Members:

`FileName` is the name of the file being edited

`IsNewFile` indicates whether the file being edited is a new file or a previously opened file

Member Functions:

Two `TFileWindow` constructors

`TFileWindow` destructor

`build` invokes the `TFileWindow` constructor and constructs an object of type `TFileWindow` before reading its data members from a stream

`CanClear` determines whether it is all right to clear the text in the editor

`CanClose` determines whether it is all right to close the file

`CMFileNew` calls `NewFile` when a "New" command with a `CM_FILENEW` ID is detected

`CMFileOpen` calls `Open` when an "Open" command with a `CM_FILEOPEN` ID is detected

`CMFileSave` calls `Save` when a "Save" command with a `CM_FILESAVE` ID is detected

`CMFileSaveAs` calls `SaveAs` when a "SaveAs" command with a `CM_FILESAVEAS` ID is detected

`NewFile` calls `CanClear` to determine whether the current text in the editor can be cleared, and if so opens a new file

`Open` calls `CanClear` to determine whether the current text in the editor can be cleared, and if so displays a file dialog box that enables the user to select a file

`Read` reads the contents of a file into the editor and sets `IsNewFile` to FALSE

`read` calls `TEditWindow::read` to read in the base `TEditWindow` object

`ReplaceWith` replaces the current file in the editor with the specified file

`Save` saves the current file

`SaveAs` saves the current file by using a file name retrieved from the user

`SetFileName` sets the `FileName` data member and modifies the window caption

`SetupWindow` establishes the edit window's Editor edit control

`Write` saves the contents of the editor to the file specified in `FileName`

`write` calls `TEditWindow::write` to write out the base `TEditWindow` object and then writes out `FileName`

Chapter 18, "ObjectWindows Classes," and Chapter 19, "ObjectWindows Functions," provide reference information for the data members and member functions of the `TFileWindow` class.

Dialog Objects

Dialog boxes are special purpose child windows that are used as user interfaces input-related tasks. Dialog boxes are defined in resource files and are referenced in an application by the dialog box ID specified in the resource file. The `TDialog` class is defined by ObjectWindows to create and support dialog boxes.

TDialog

Dialog objects can either be modal or modeless. A modeless dialog box, in effect, is the same as displaying a window. A modal dialog box, on the other hand, disables the parent window and receives all input.

You create modeless dialog boxes by using the `MakeWindow` member function of the application object, as the following example shows:

```
GetModule()->MakeWindow(new TExampleDialog(this,"Dialog"));
```

Modal dialog boxes are created using the `ExecDialog` member function of the application object. For example:

```
GetModule()->ExecDialog(new TExampleDialog(this, "Dialog"));
```

`TDialog` has two members functions, `Ok` and `Cancel`, that are predefined to let you close the dialog box. To use these member functions, the `Ok` and `Cancel` buttons of your dialog box should use the button IDs IDOK and IDCANCEL, respectively. If you want, you can define your own member functions for closing your dialog box.

To manipulate the controls of the dialog box, you must define your own controls and actions. The predefined control classes are not used with dialog boxes. They are for use inside windows other than dialog boxes. The dialog box example in Chapter 12, "Windows Programming Using ObjectWindows," demonstrates one way that you can create a dialog box and define the actions for the controls of the dialog box.

There are three derived classes of `TDialog` that provide special dialog boxes: `TFileDialog`, `TInputDialog`, and `TSearchDialog`. These classes are discussed in the following paragraphs.

`TDialog` is the base class for derived classes that create modal and modeless dialog boxes. `TDialog` is derived from `TWindowsObject` and has three derived classes, `TFileDialog`, `TInputDialog`, and `TSearchDialog`. `TDialog` contains the following data members and member functions:

Data Members:

`Attr` stores the attributes used to create the dialog box

`IsModal` indicates whether the dialog box is modal or modeless

Member Functions:

Three `TDialog` constructors

`TDialog` destructor

`build` invokes the `TDialog` constructor and constructs an object of type `TDialog` before reading its data members from a stream

`Cancel` calls `CloseWindow` using IDCANCEL when the `Cancel` button for the dialog box is selected

`CloseWindow` calls either `TWindowsObject::CloseWindow` when `this` is a modeless dialog box or `CanClose` for a modal dialog box to determine whether the dialog box can be shut; this function returns the specified return value

CloseWindow calls either TWindowsObject::CloseWindow when this is a modeless dialog box or CloseWindow for a modal dialog box to determine whether the dialog box can be shut; this function returns ARetValue

Create creates a modeless dialog box associated with the object

Destroy destroys the interface element associated with TDialog, and passes a value for a modal dialog box

Destroy destroys the interface element associated with TDialog, and passes a value for a modeless dialog box

Execute executes the modal dialog box associated with TDialog

GetClassName returns the name of the default Windows class for modal dialog boxes

GetItemHandle returns the handle of the dialog control that has the ID specified in DlgItemID

GetWindowClass fills AWndClass (a WNDCLASS structure) with the registration attributes for TDialog

isA redefines the pure virtual function in class Object

nameOf redefines the pure virtual function in class Object. This function returns “TDialog”, the class ID string for TDialog.

Ok calls CloseWindow when the Ok button of the dialog box is selected, and passes IDOK

read calls TWindowsObject::read to read in the base TWindowsObject object

SendDlgItemMsg sends the control message (AMsg) to the dialog box control that has the ID specified in DlgItemID

SetCaption calls TWindowsObject::SetCaption unless ATitle is –1

SetupWindow calls SetCaption and TWindowsObject::SetupWindow to set up the dialog box

ShutDownWindow calls TWindowsObject::ShutDownWindow for modeless dialog boxes or Destroy (passing IDCANCEL) for modal dialog boxes to shut down the dialog box

ShutDownWindow calls TWindowsObject::ShutDownWindow for modeless dialog boxes or Destroy (passing ARetValue) for modal dialog boxes to shut down the dialog box

WMClose handles the WM_CLOSE message

WMInitDialog calls SetupWindow and is automatically called before the dialog box is displayed

`WMQueryEndSession` responds when Windows attempts to shut down

`write` calls `TWindowsObject::write` to write out the base `TWindowsObject` object

Chapter 18, "ObjectWindows Classes," and Chapter 19, "ObjectWindows Functions," provide reference information for the data members and member functions of the `TDialog` class.

TFileDialog

The file dialog is a special dialog that prompts the user for a file name. The file dialog contains an input line, two list boxes, and two buttons. One list box contains a listing of all the files in the current directory. The other list box specifies the directories visible from the current directory. The two buttons are `Ok` and `Cancel`.

The file dialog box constructor requires that the parent window, the resource identifier (`SD_FILEOPEN` or `SD_FILESAVE`), and the file name or mask be specified. As the previous line indicates, there are two types of file dialog boxes. The first is the `Open` dialog box (specified by `SD_FILEOPEN`). The second is the `Save` dialog box (specified by `SD_FILESAVE`).

The following code creates an open file dialog box using `"*.*"` as the file mask:

```
char NAME[MAXPATH];
_fstrcpy(NAME, "*.*");
GetApplication()->ExecDialog(new TFileDialog(this, SD_FILEOPEN, NAME));
```

The following code creates a save file dialog using `"DUMMY.DOC"` as the file mask:

```
char NAME[MAXPATH];
_Fstrcpy(NAME, "*.*");
GetApplication()->ExecDialog(new TFileDialog(this, SD_FILESAVE, NAME));
```

`TFileDialog` defines a dialog box that enables the user to select a file. `TFileDialog` is derived from `TDialog` and contains the following data members and member functions:

Data Members:

`Extension` holds the file name extension

`FilePath` points to the buffer that returns the file name defined by the user

`FileSpec` contains the current file name

`PathName` contains the current file path

Member Functions:

Two `TFileDialog` constructors

`build` invokes the `TFileDialog` constructor and constructs an object of type `TFileDialog` before reading its data members from a stream

`CanClose` returns TRUE when the user entered a valid file name

`HandleDList` responds to messages from the directory list box, calling `UpdateListBoxes` when an entry is double clicked and `UpdateFileName` otherwise

`HandleFList` responds to messages from the file list box and calls `UpdateFileName` when the list box selection changes

`HandleFName` responds to messages from the edit control and enables the `Ok` button when the edit control contains text

`SelectFileName` selects text from the edit control and sets the focus to the edit control

`SetupWindow` calls `UpDateListBoxes`, `SelectFileName`, and `TWindowsObject::SetupWindow` to set up the dialog box

`UpdateFileName` sets the text of the edit control to `PathName` and selects the text

`UpdateListBoxes` updates the file and directory list boxes

Chapter 18, "ObjectWindows Classes," and Chapter 19, "ObjectWindows Functions," provide reference information for the data members and member functions of the `TFileDialog` class.

TInputDialog

An input dialog contains a single input line and two buttons. The user can enter a single line of text in the input line. The two buttons in the input dialog are `Ok` and `Cancel`.

The constructor for the input dialog accepts five parameters: the parent window, the dialog caption, the prompt text, the buffer where input is placed, and the size of the input buffer. The following code creates an input dialog with the "Input" caption and the "Enter Text" prompt.

```
PTInputDialog InDlg;
char Txt[79];
```

```
strcpy[Txt,""];
InDlg = new TInputDialog(this,"Input","Enter Text", Txt,
        sizeof(Txt));
```

TInputDialog defines a dialog box that enables the user to enter a single line of text. TInputDialog is derived from TDialog and contains the following data members and member functions:

Data Members:

Buffer is a pointer to a buffer that returns the text entered by the user

BufferSize stores the size of Buffer

Prompt points the input dialog box prompt

Member Functions:

Two TInputDialog constructor

build invokes the TInputDialog constructor and constructs an object of type TInputDialog before reading its data members from a stream

read calls TDialog::read to read in the base TDialog object

SetupWindow calls TDialog::SetupWindow to set up the window and limit the number of characters that can be input to BufferSize minus 1

TransferData transfers input dialog data

write calls TDialog::write to write out the base TDialog object

Chapter 18, "ObjectWindows Classes," and Chapter 19, "ObjectWindows Functions," provide reference information for the data members and member functions of the TInputDialog class.

TSearchDialog

TSearchDialog is derived from TDialog and provides search-and-replace options for the user. TSearchDialog uses a data structure of type TSearchStruct to transfer data. Two resource definitions (a search dialog and a replace dialog) are provided in STDWNDS.DLG. TSearchDialog contains only the TSearchDialog constructor.

Control Objects

Control objects are special windows that serve as user interface elements. Control objects include buttons, scroll bars, list boxes, check boxes, group boxes, edit controls, MDI client controls, and radio buttons. The abstract class `TControl` is the base class for the control objects.

TControl

`TControl` defines member functions for the creation of controls and the processing of messages for derived classes. `TControl` is derived from `TWindow` and has five derived classes: `TButton`, `TScrollBar`, `TStatic`, `TListBox`, and `TGroupBox`. `TControl` contains the following data members and member functions:

Data Members:

None

Member Functions:

Three `TControl` constructors

`GetId` returns the window ID, `Attr.Id`

`ODADrawEntire` responds when notified that a drawable control needs to be redrawn

`ODAFocus` responds when notified that the focus has been given to or taken from the drawable control

`ODASelect` responds when notified that the selection state of the drawable control has changed

`WMDrawItem` responds to the `WM_DRAWITEM` message that is sent when the drawable control needs to be redrawn

`WMPaint` calls `DefWndProc` for painting

Chapter 18, "ObjectWindows Classes," and Chapter 19, "ObjectWindows Functions," provide reference information for the data members and member functions of the `TControl` class. The following paragraphs describe each of the derived classes of `TControl` and describe the various control objects.

TButton

There are two types of button objects. The first type of button object is the standard push-button, `BS_PUSHBUTTON`. The second type of button is the default push-button, `BS_DEFPUSHBUTTON`. The default push-button is surrounded by a bold border and represents the default action.

The `TButton` constructor requires the following parameters: the parent window, the control ID, the button text, the location of the button, the size of the button, and a `TRUE/FALSE` flag indicating whether this button is the default. The following constructs a default button called "Default" (Note: `ID_PushButton` represents the constant for the button ID):

```
PushButton = new TButton(this, ID_PushButton, "Default", 50,
             50, 50, 25, TRUE);
```

The `TButton` class defines push-button interfaces and is derived from `TControl`. `TButton` contains the following data members and member functions:

Data Members:

None

Member Functions:

Three `TButton` constructors

`build` constructs an object of type `TButton` before reading its member from an input stream

`GetClassName` returns "BUTTON", the name of `TButton`'s Windows registration class

Chapter 18, "ObjectWindows Classes," and Chapter 19, "ObjectWindows Functions," provide reference information for the data members and member functions of the `TButton` class.

TListBox

List box controls provide a list of items that the user can select from. The member functions of `TListBox` can be used to create list boxes, modify the list of the list box, retrieve information about the list, and determine the item that the user has selected.

The `TListBox` constructor requires the following parameters: the parent window, the control ID, the location of the control, and the size of the control. The `TListBox` constructor invokes the `TControl` constructor and adds the `LBS_STANDARD` style to the default styles for the list box in `Attr.Style`. Using `LBS_STANDARD`, the list box

alphabetizes the items of the list, notifies the parent of all list box events, is surrounded by a border, and contains a vertical scroll bar. The following code constructs a list box where `ID_ListBox` is a reference to the constant for the list box ID:

```
ListBox = new TListBox(this, ID_ListBox, 50, 50, 200, 100);
```

The `TListBox` class defines an interface object that represents a Windows list box. `TListBox` is used to create and manage list boxes. `TListBox` is derived from `TControl` and contains the following data members and member functions. `TComboBox` is derived from `TListBox`.

Data Members:

None

Member Functions:

Three `TListBox` constructors

`AddString` adds the string specified in `AString` to the list box

`build` invokes the `TListBox` constructor and constructs an object of type `TListBox` before reading its data members from a stream

`ClearList` clears all list items

`DeleteString` deletes the list item at the location specified by `Index`

`FindExactString` searches the list box for a string that exactly matches the string specified in `AString`

`FindString` searches the list box for a string that begins with the string specified in `AString`

`GetClassName` returns "LISTBOX"

`GetCount` returns the number of list box items when successful

`GetMsgID` returns the Windows list box message ID associated with the specified ObjectWindows message ID

`GetSelIndex` returns the position of the currently selected item when successful

`GetSelString` places the currently selected list item in `AString`

`GetString` copies the item at the location specified in `Index` to `AString`

`GetStringLen`, when successful, returns the length of the item at the location specified in `Index`

`InsertString` inserts the string specified in `AString` at the list position specified in `Index`

`SetSelIndex`, when successful, selects the item at the position specified in `Index`

`SetSelString` selects the list box item that matches `AString`

`Transfer` uses the buffer pointed to by `DataPtr` to transfer data

Chapter 18, "ObjectWindows Classes," and Chapter 19, "ObjectWindows Functions," provide reference information for the data members and member functions of the `TListBox` class.

TComboBox

A combo box control is a combination of a list box and an edit control. A combo box control can be any one of three types: simple, drop-down, or drop-down list.

The first type is a simple combo box (`CBS_SIMPLE`). A simple combo box contains an edit control and a list box. The list box of a simple combo box cannot be hidden.

The second type is a drop-down combo box (`CBS_DROPDOWN`). A drop-down combo box is similar to a simple combo box. The difference lies in the list box. With a drop-down combo box, the list area is hidden until the user selects the down-arrow to the right of the list area. The list area is hidden again after the user makes a selection.

The third type is a drop-down list combo box (`CBS_DROPDOWNLIST`). The drop-down list combo box behaves like the drop-down combo box with the exception that the edit control does not accept input directly. Only text from the list items can be displayed in the edit control.

The `TComboBox` constructor requires the following parameters: the parent window, the control ID, the control location, the control size, the combo box type (`CBS_SIMPLE`, `CBS_DROPDOWN`, or `CBS_DROPDOWNLIST`), and the edit control text length. The following code constructs a simple combo box where `ID_ComboBox` represents the constant for the control ID:

```
ComboBox = new TComboBox(this, ID_ComboBox, 50, 50, 100, 150,
           CBS_SIMPLE, 40);
```

The `TComboBox` class represents a Windows combo box interface. `TComboBox` is derived from `TListBox` and contains the following data members and member functions:

Data Members:

`TextLen` specifies the length of the buffer used for the edit control of the combo box

Member Functions:

Three `TComboBox` constructors

`build` constructs an object of type `TComboBox` before reading its data members from a stream

`GetClassName` returns "COMBOBOX"

`GetMsgID` returns the message ID of the Windows combo box message that is associated with the ObjectWindows message ID

`HideList` hides the list of a drop-down or drop-down list combo box

`nameOf` redefines the pure virtual function in class `Object`

`read` calls `TListBox::read` to read in the base `TListBox` object

`SetupWindow` limits the length of the text in the edit control to `TextLen` minus 1 when setting up the combo box

`ShowList` shows the list of a drop-down or drop-down list combo box

`Transfer` moves data to and from a transfer buffer pointed to by `DataPtr`

`write` calls `TListBox::write` to write out the base `TListBox` object

Chapter 18, "ObjectWindows Classes," and Chapter 19, "ObjectWindows Functions," provide reference information for the data members and member functions of the `TComboBox` class.

TCheckBox

A check box control offers the user a selection and represents the state of the selection—either on or off (some check box controls can have a third state—grayed). By default, check boxes are toggled between states when they are selected.

The `TCheckBox` constructor requires the following parameters: the parent window, the control ID, the text associated with the check box, the location of the check box, the size of the check box, and an `AGroup` parameter that helps to group check and radio boxes. The following code creates the required `AGroup` parameter and a check box:

```
GroupBox = new TGroupBox(this, ID_GroupBox, "Group", 50, 50,
           100, 100);

CheckBox = new TCheckBox(this, ID_CheckBox, "Box One", 300,
           200, 50, 50, GroupBox);
```

The TCheckBox class represents a Windows check box interface. TCheckBox is derived from TControl and contains the following data members and member functions. TRadioButton is derived from TCheckBox.

Data Members:

Group is a pointer to the TGroupBox control object that groups the check box with other check boxes and radio buttons

Member Functions:

Three TCheckBox constructors

BNClicked responds to notification messages indicating that the check box was clicked

build constructs an object of type TCheckBox before reading its data members from an input stream

Check places the check box into the checked state by calling SetCheck

GetCheck determines the check state of the check box

read calls TWindow::read to read in the base TWindow object

SetCheck sets the state of the check box to the state specified in CheckFlag—which can be BF_UNCHECKED (box is unchecked), BF_CHECKED (box is checked), or BF_GRAYED (box is grayed)

Toggle toggles between the states of the check box

Transfer transfers the state of the check box to or from the location pointed to by DataPtr

Uncheck places the check box in an unchecked state by calling SetCheck

write calls TWindow::write to write the base TWindow object

Chapter 18, "ObjectWindows Classes," and Chapter 19, "ObjectWindows Functions," provide reference information for the data members and member functions of the TCheckBox class.

TRadioButton

A radio button control offers the user a selection and represents the state of the selection—either on or off (some check box controls can have a third state—grayed). By default, radio buttons are toggled between states when they are selected. Radio buttons are usually grouped to provide the user with a choice of mutually exclusive buttons.

The `TRadioButton` constructor requires the following parameters: the parent window, the control ID, the text associated with the radio button, the location of the button, the size of the button, and an `AGroup` parameter that helps to group check and radio boxes. The following code creates the required `AGroup` parameter and a radio button:

```
GroupBox = new TGroupBox(this, ID_GroupBox, "Group", 50, 50,
           100, 100);

RadioButton = new TRadioButton(this, ID_RadioButton, "Box One",
              300, 200, 50, 50, GroupBox);
```

The `TRadioButton` class represents a Windows radio button. A radio button is a two-state button; it can either be checked or unchecked. `TRadioButton` is derived from `TCheckBox` and contains the following data members and member functions:

Data Members:

None

Member Functions:

Three `TRadioButton` constructors

`build` invokes the `TRadioButton` constructor and constructs an object of type `TRadioButton` before reading its data members from a stream

Chapter 18, "ObjectWindows Classes," and Chapter 19, "ObjectWindows Functions," provide reference information for the data members and member functions of the `Object` class.

TGroupBox

Group box controls simply group a series of controls with a captioned rectangle. The controls within the group box are visually grouped; however, they are not logically grouped. Logical grouping means that the controls are mutually exclusive. The `WS_GROUP` style for the controls is the only indicator of the logical grouping of controls.

Although group boxes do not logically group controls, they do enable you to define a group response method for the parent window. The group box accepts notification messages from the individual controls and converts the messages to group notification messages.

The `TGroupBox` constructor requires the following parameters: the parent window, the control ID, the text for the group box, the group box location, and the group box size. The following code constructs a group box:

```
GroupBox = new TGroupBox(this, ID_GroupBox, "Options", 50, 50,
         100, 100);
```

The `TGroupBox` class represents group box elements. `TGroupBox` is derived from `TControl` and contains the following data members and member functions:

Data Members:

> `NotifyParent` indicates whether the parent should be notified when one of the group box's selection boxes has changed state

Member Functions:

> Three `TGroupBox` constructors
>
> `build` invokes the `TGroupBox` constructor and constructs an object of type `TGroupBox` before reading its data members from a stream
>
> `GetClassName` returns "BUTTON"
>
> `read` calls `TWindow::read` to read in the base `TGroupBox` object
>
> `SelectionChanged` notifies the parent window of a group box that a change has been made in the group box *only* if `NotifyParent` is TRUE
>
> `write` calls `TWindow::write` to write out the base `TGroupBox` object

Chapter 18, "ObjectWindows Classes," and Chapter 19, "ObjectWindows Functions," provide reference information for the data members and member functions of the `TGroupBox` class.

TStatic

Static controls are graphics or text that can be displayed in the window. Static controls are not selected or modified by the user and do not need unique IDs. Static controls are often used to display "for your information" data.

The `TStatic` constructor requires the following parameters: the parent window, the control ID, the control text, the control location, the control size, and the text length. The following code constructs a static text control. Note: –1 is the ID you should use for static IDs.

```
StaticText = new TStatic(this, -1, "Static Text", 50, 50, 100, 100, 12);
```

The `TStatic` class represents a static text interface element and provides functions for the management of the element. `TStatic` is derived from `TControl` and has one derived class, `TEdit`. `TStatic` contains the following data members and member functions:

Data Members:

`TextLen` specifies the size of the text buffer for the static control

Member Functions:

Three `TStatic` constructors

`build` invokes the `TStatic` constructor and constructs an object of type `TStatic` before reading its data members from a stream

`Clear` clears the text of the static control

`GetClassName` returns "STATIC"

`GetText` returns the text of the static control in `ATextString`

`nameOf` redefines the pure virtual function in class `Object`

`read` calls `TWindow::read` to read in the base `TWindow` object

`SetText` sets the text of the static control to the string specified in `ATextString`

`Transfer` transfers text to and from the buffer pointed to by `DataPtr`

`write` calls `TWindow::write` to write out the base `TWindow` object

Chapter 18, "ObjectWindows Classes," and Chapter 19, "ObjectWindows Functions," provide reference information for the data members and member functions of the `TStatic` class.

TEdit

Edit controls enable the user to input text and can be used by a program. Edit controls enable you to cut, copy, and paste using the clipboard and provide many of the features found in text editors.

The `TEdit` constructor requires the following parameters: the parent window, the control ID, the control text, the control location, the control size, the maximum number of characters for the edit control, and a `TRUE/FALSE` flag that indicates whether this is a multiline edit control. By default, edit controls have the following styles: `WS_CHILD`, `WS_VISIBLE`, `WS_TABSTOP`, `ES_LEFT`, `ES_AUTOHSCROLL`, and `WS_BORDER`. Multiline edit controls have the following additional styles: `ES_MULTILINE`, `ES_AUTOVSCROLL`, `WS_HSCROLL`, and `WS_VSCROLL`.

The following code constructs a single line edit control that can handle up to 80 characters:

```
SingleEdit = new TEdit(this, ID_SingleEdit, "Single Edit", 50,
             50, 100, 100, 80, FALSE);
```

The following code constructs a multline edit control that can handle up to 300 characters:

```
MultiEdit = new TEdit(this, ID_MultiEdit, "Multi Edit", 50,
          50, 100, 100, 300, TRUE);
```

The `TEdit` class is the Windows edit control interface and provides the features of a text editor. `TEdit` is derived from `TStatic` and contains the following data members and member functions:

Data Members:

None

Member Functions:

Three `TEdit` constructors

`build` invokes the `TEditWindow` constructor and constructs an object of type `TEditWindow` before reading its data members from a stream

`CanUndo` indicates whether it is possible to undo the last edit

`ClearModify` resets the edit control change flag

`CMEditClear` calls `Clear` when a menu item with menu ID `CM_EDITCLEAR` is selected

`CMEditCopy` calls `Copy` when a menu item with menu ID `CM_EDITCOPY` is selected

`CMEditCut` calls `Cut` when a menu item with the menu ID `CM_EDITCUT` is selected

`CMEditDelete` calls `DeleteSelection` when a menu item with menu ID `CM_EDITDELETE` is selected

`CMEditPaste` calls `Paste` when a menu item with menu ID `CM_EDITPASTE` is selected

`CMEditUndo` calls `Undo` when a menu item with menu ID `CM_EDITUNDO` is selected

`Copy` copies the selected text to the clipboard

`Cut` deletes the selected text and copies it to the clipboard

`DeleteLine` deletes the line of text specified in `LineNumber`

`DeleteSelection` deletes the selected text

`DeleteSubText` deletes the text between the text positions specified in `StartPos` and `EndPos`

`ENErrSpace` sounds a beep when the edit control cannot allocate more memory

`GetClassName` returns "EDIT"

`GetLine` gets a line of text from the edit control

`GetLineFromPos` gets the line number from a multiline edit control of the line that contains the character position specified in `CharPos`

`GetLineIndex` returns the number of characters prior to the specified line number in a multiline edit control

`GetLineLength` gets the number of characters in a line of text from a multiline edit control

`GetNumLines` gets the number of lines in a multiline edit control

`GetSelection` returns the starting and ending positions of the selected text in `StartPos` and `EndPos`, respectively

`GetSubText` gets the text specified by `StartPos` and `EndPos` and returns the text to `ATextString`

`Insert` inserts the text in `ATextString` into the edit control at the current cursor position

`IsModified` indicates whether the text in the edit control has been modified

`Paste` places the text in the clipboard into the edit control at the current cursor position

`Scroll` scrolls the multiline edit control horizontally or vertically

`Search` searches for the text specified in `AText`

`SetSelection` defines the current text selection

`SetupWindow` defines the limit for the number of characters in the edit control as `TextLen` minus 1

`Undo` performs an "undo" on the last edit

Chapter 18, "ObjectWindows Classes," and Chapter 19, "ObjectWindows Functions," provide reference information for the data members and member functions of the `TStatic` class.

TScrollBar

Scroll bar controls indicate position relative to a specified range. Scroll bar controls are stand-alone scroll bars and should not be confused with window scroll bars.

Scroll bars can be either horizontal or vertical and practically any width and length. `TScrollBar` defines several member functions that enable you to customize and monitor scroll bars.

The `TScrollBar` constructor invokes the `TControl` constructor and adds `SBS_HORIZ` and `SBS_VERT` to the styles for the scroll bar. The parameters required for the `TScrollBar` constructor are: the parent window, the control ID, the control location, the control size, and a `TRUE/FALSE` flag that indicates whether this is a horizontal scroll bar.

The following code constructs a horizontal scroll bar:

```
HorzScroll = new TScrollBar(this, ID_HorzScroll, 50, 50, 100, 30, TRUE);
```

The following code constructs a vertical scroll bar:

```
VertScroll = new TScrollBar(this, ID_VertScroll, 50, 50, 30, 100, FALSE);
```

The `TScrollBar` class represents and manages stand-alone horizontal and vertical scroll bars. `TScrollBar` is derived from `TControl` and contains the following data members and member functions:

Data Members:

`LineMagnitude` specifies the number of range units that the scroll bar is scrolled when one of the scroll bar arrows is clicked

`PageMagnitude` specifies the number of range units that the scroll bar is scrolled when the scrolling area of the scroll bar is clicked

Member Functions:

Three `TScrollBar` constructors

`build` invokes the `TScrollBar` constructor and constructs an object of type `TScrollBar` before reading its data members from a stream

`DeltaPos` changes the thumb position of the scroll bar by calling `SetPosition`

`GetClassName` returns "SCROLLBAR"

`GetPosition` returns the thumb position of the scroll bar

`GetRange` returns the scroll bar range in `LoVal` and `HiVal`

`read` calls `TWindow::read` to read in the base `TWindow` object

`SBBottom` calls `SetPosition` to move the scroll thumb to the bottom of the scroll bar for vertical scroll bars or to the right for horizontal scroll bars

`SBLineDown` calls `SetPosition` to move the scroll thumb down for vertical scroll bars or right for horizontal scroll bars

SBLineUp calls SetPosition to move the scroll thumb up for vertical scroll bars or left for horizontal scroll bars

SBPageDown calls SetPosition to move the scroll thumb down for vertical scroll bars or right for horizontal scroll bars

SBPageUp calls SetPosition to move the scroll thumb up for vertical scroll bars or left for horizontal scroll bars

SBThumbPosition calls SetPosition to move the scroll thumb

SBThumbTrack calls SetPosition to move the scroll thumb to a new position as it is being dragged

SBTop calls SetPosition to move the scroll thumb to the top for vertical scroll bars or the left for horizontal scroll bars

SetPosition moves the thumb position to the position specified in ThumbPos

SetRange sets to scroll bar range to the values specified in LoVal and HiVal

SetupWindow defines the scroll bar range as 0 to 100

Transfer uses the data buffer pointed to by DataPtr to transfer scroll bar information

write calls TWindow::write to write out the base TWindow object

Chapter 18, "ObjectWindows Classes," and Chapter 19, "ObjectWindows Functions," provide reference information for the data members and member functions of the TScrollBar class.

MDI Objects

Part I of this book discussed the multiple document interface standard for Windows. ObjectWindows defines two classes for the creation of MDI applications: TMDIFrame and TMDIClient. These classes are described in the following paragraphs. The following chapter provides an example of an MDI application using ObjectWindows.

TMDIFrame

The TMDIFrame class represents Multiple Document Interface (MDI) frame windows, the main windows for MDI applications. TMDIFrame is derived from TWindow and contains the following data members and member functions:

Data Members:

ChildMenuPos stores the top-level menu position for the MDI window

ClientWnd is a pointer to the TMDIFrame client window

Member Functions:

Three TMDIFrame constructors

TMDIFrame destructor

ArrangeIcons calls the ArrangeIcons member function of the client window to arrange the iconized MDI child windows along the bottom of the client window

build invokes the TMDIFrame constructor and constructs an object of type TMDIFrame before reading its data members from a stream

CascadeChildren calls the CascadeChildren member function of the client window to arrange the MDI child windows that are not iconized in an overlapping style

CloseChildren calls the CanClose member function of each MDI child window and closes all the child windows if possible

CMArrangeIcons calls ArrangeIcons when a menu item with a CM_ARRANGEICONS ID is selected

CMCascadeChildren calls CascadeChildren when a menu item with a CM_CASCADECHILDREN ID is selected

CMCloseChildren calls CloseChildren when a menu item with a CM_CLOSECHILDREN ID is selected

CMCreateChild calls CreateChild when a menu item with a CM_CREATECHILD ID is selected

CMTileChildren calls TileChildren when a menu item with a CM_TILECHILDREN ID is selected

CreateChild creates a MDI child window and returns a pointer to the created child window

GetClassName returns "OWLMDIFrame"

GetClient returns the pointer to the client window stored in ClientWnd

GetWindowClass calls TWindow::GetWindowClass and sets AWndClass.Style to 0

InitChild constructs an instance of TWindow as an MDI child window

InitClientWindow constructs the MDI client window as an instance of TMDIClient

read calls TWindow::read to read in the base TWindow object

SetupWindow calls InitClientWindow to construct an MDI client window and creates the interface element

TileChildren calls the TileChildren member function of the client window to size and arrange the MDI child windows that are not iconized in a nonoverlapping style

write calls TWindow::write to write out the base TWindow object

Chapter 18, "ObjectWindows Classes," and Chapter 19, "ObjectWindows Functions," provide reference information for the data members and member functions of the TMDIWindow class.

The frame window of an MDI application is also the application's main window. The TMDIFrame constructor creates the frame window and requires two parameters: the title for the MDI frame window and the handle to an MDI-style menu.

The TMDIFrame constructor calls InitClientWindow to construct the TMDIClient object that serves as the MDI client window. The MDI client window is created by SetupWindow. The TMDIClient class follows.

TMDIClient

The TMDIClient class represents Multiple Document Interface (MDI) client windows and manages the MDI client area and the MDI child windows. TMDIClient is derived from TControl and contains the following data members and member functions:

Data Members:

ClientAttr stores the attributes of the MDI client window

Member Functions:

Three TMDIClient constructors

TMDIClient destructor

ArrangeIcons aligns MDI child window icons along the bottom of the MDI client window

build invokes the TMDIClient constructor and constructs an object of type TMDIClient before reading its data members from a stream

CascadeChildren adjusts the size of all MDI child windows that are not minimized and arranges them in an overlapping style

GetClassName returns "MDICLIENT"

read calls TWindow::read to read the base TWindow object

TileChildren adjusts the size of all MDI child windows that are not minimized and arranges them in a nonoverlapping, tiled style

WMPaint redefines TWindow::WMPaint to call DefWndProc

write calls TWindow::write to write out the base TWindow object

Chapter 18, "ObjectWindows Classes," and Chapter 19, "ObjectWindows Functions," provide reference information for the data members and member functions of the TMDIClient class.

Scroller Objects

For many applications you must provide vertical or horizontal scroll bars to view areas that are too large for the current window. The TScroller class adds functionality to the scroll bars of a window and can even provide a window with auto-scrolling features. Auto-scrolling refers to the window's capability to scroll when the mouse is dragged from the inside of the window to the outside.

TScroller

The TScroller class provides automated scrolling for window displays. TScroller is usually associated with scroll bars; however, TScroller works with windows without scroll bars. TScroller is derived from TControl and contains the following data members and member functions.

Data Members:

AutoMode indicates whether auto-scrolling is in effect

AutoOrg indicates whether the origin of the client area should automatically be offset when preparing the area for painting

ClassHashValue contains the hash value of the last constructed instance of TScroller

HasHScrollBar is TRUE when the owner window has a horizontal scroll bar

HasVScrollBar is TRUE when the owner window has a vertical scroll bar

InstanceHashValue contains the hash value of this

`TrackMode` indicates whether the display should be scrolled as the scroll thumb is dragged

`Window` points to the owner window

`XLine` specifies the number of horizontal scroll units to move when the scroll arrow is clicked

`XPage` specifies the number of horizontal scroll units to move when the thumb area of the scroll bar is clicked

`XPos` is the horizontal position of the scroller in horizontal scroll units

`XRange` is the maximum number of horizontal scroll units for the window

`XUnit` is the horizontal logical scroll unit used by `TScroller`

`YLine` is the number of vertical units scrolled when the scroll arrow is clicked

`YPage` is the number of vertical units scrolled when the thumb area of the scroll bar is clicked

`YPos` is the current vertical position of the scroller

`YRange` is the maximum number of vertical scroll units for the window

`YUnit` is the vertical logical scroll unit used by `TScroller`

Member Functions:

Two `TScroller` constructors

`TScroller` destructor

`AutoScroll` scrolls the display of the owner window when the mouse is dragged from the inside of the window to the outside

`BeginView` sets the origin of the owner window's paint display context relative to the current scroller position when `AutoOrg` is TRUE

`build` invokes the `TScroller` constructor and constructs an object of type `TScroller` before reading its data members from a stream

`EndView` updates the scroll bar positions to correspond to the position of `TScroller`

`hashValue` redefines the pure virtual function in class `Object`

`HScroll` calls `ScrollTo` to handle the specified horizontal scroll event

`isA` must be redefined by all objects derived from the base class object

`isEqual` redefines the pure virtual function in class `Object`

`IsVisibleRect` determines whether any part of the specified rectangle is visible in the owner window

`nameOf` must be redefined by all objects derived from the base class object

`printOn` must be redefined by all objects derived from the base class object

`read` reads `AutoMode`, `AutoOrg`, `HasHScrollBar`, `HasVScrollBar`, `TrackMode`, `XLine`, `XPage`, `XPos`, `XRange`, `XUnit`, `YLine`, `YPage`, `YPos`, `YRange`, and `YUnit`

`ScrollBy` calls `ScrollTo` to scroll the display the amount specified in `Dx` and `Dy`

`ScrollTo` scrolls the display to the specified position

`SetPageSize` sets the page width and height to the size of the client area of the owner window

`SetRange` sets the scroll ranges of `TScroller` to those specified and calls `SetSBarRange` to coordinate the ranges of the owner window scroll bars

`SetSBarRange` sets the range of the scroll bars for the owner window to fit within the range specified for `TScroller`

`SetUnits` defines the data members `XUnit` and `YUnit`

`VScroll` calls `ScrollTo` to handle the specified vertical scroll event

`write` writes `AutoMode`, `AutoOrg`, `HasHScrollBar`, `HasVScrollBar`, `TrackMode`, `XLine`, `XPage`, `XPos`, `XRange`, `XUnit`, `YLine`, `YPage`, `YPos`, `YRange`, and `YUnit`

`XRangeValue` converts a horizontal scroll value to a horizontal range value

`XScrollValue` converts a horizontal range value to a horizontal scroll value

`YRangeValue` converts a vertical scroll value to a vertical range value

`YScrollValue` converts a vertical range value to a vertical scroll value

The data members of the `TScroller` define the characteristics of the scrolling action. Chapter 18, "ObjectWindows Classes," and Chapter 19, "ObjectWindows Functions," provide reference information for the data members and member functions of the `TScroller` class.

12

Windows Programming Using ObjectWindows

This chapter introduces you to programming Windows applications using ObjectWindows. Part I of the book already demonstrated many basic Windows programming concepts contained in this chapter. However, these concepts are reintroduced here in a new light, through the use of object-oriented procedures and ObjectWindows features. This chapter begins with the basic application structure of a Windows program using ObjectWindows and the steps involved in creating the application. Then you learn how to create several Windows applications by using the structures and steps described.

Windows Application Structure Using ObjectWindows

The code structure of a Windows application developed using ObjectWindows differs from the Windows application code structure presented in Part I. ObjectWindows application code uses the features of ObjectWindows classes and takes advantage of object-oriented programming. By using these features and advantages, you usually find that the resulting code is less lengthy and quicker to develop. In addition, you can spend more time on the functionality of the program and less time on the structure, since ObjectWindows has defined the majority of Windows structures that are required to be defined for each application when you use traditional Windows programming styles.

With a traditional Windows program, there are three fundamental parts to the application: the `WinMain` function, the message loop, and the window procedures. With ObjectWindows applications, these elements are still present; however, ObjectWindows has already defined objects that enable you to avoid most of the difficulties involved with defining these elements. The following paragraphs review each of these components and describe how each is implemented and handled in ObjectWindows applications.

The *WinMain* Function

As Chapter 11, "Introduction to ObjectWindows Programming for C++," describes, all ObjectWindows applications contain a `WinMain` function that controls the application. For most applications this main program contains three statements in the format shown in the following code. In general, you do not deviate from this structure.

```
int PASCAL WinMain(HANDLE hInstance, HANDLE hPrevInstance,
                   LPSTR lpCmdLine, int nCmdShow)
{
    TAppExample AppExample("Application Example", hInstance, hInstance,
        lpCmdLine, nCmdShow);
    AppExample.Run();
    return AppExample.Status;
}
```

The first statement of the main program calls the constructor that constructs the application object. When the constructor is called, the data members of the application object are initialized. The application object is referenced by the global variable `Application`.

The second statement of the main program calls the Run member function which, in turn, calls InitApplication and InitInstance. InitApplication initializes the first instance of the application. InitInstance initializes each instance of the application. After Run has called InitApplication and InitInstance, InitMainWindow is called to create a main window. InitMainWindow is generally redefined for the application. Lastly, the Run member function calls MessageLoop, which receives and processes Windows messages sent to the application.

The main program's third statement returns the final status of the application. Zero is generally used to represent a normal closing of the application. A nonzero value usually indicates that an error has occurred.

The Message Loop

In traditional Windows programming styles, the message loop is part of the WinMain function and has the following format:

```
while (GetMessage (&Message, 0, 0, 0))
{
TranslateMessage(&Message);
DispatchMessage(&Message);
}
```

For ObjectWindows applications, the Run member function of the application automatically calls the MessageLoop member function. MessageLoop automatically processes messages and runs until the application is closed. There is no need to define MessageLoop because ObjectWindows has already taken care of it.

Window Procedures

Traditional Windows programming styles use a window procedure to give a window functionality. The window procedure generally consists of at least one switch statement (often nested switch statements) that handles the various incoming messages. The following is an example of a fundamental window procedure using traditional Windows programming styles is as follows:

```
long FAR PASCAL WndProc (HWND hWnd, WORD iMessage, WORD
    wParam, LONG lParam)
{
    switch (iMessage)
        {
        case WM_DESTROY:
            PostQuitMessage(0);
            return 0;
```

```
            default:
                  return(DefWindowProc(hWnd, iMessage,
                  wParam, lParam));
            }
}
```

With ObjectWindows, you do not define a window procedure, as previously shown. Instead, you simply define or redefine member functions for the window object. These member functions handle the various messages directed at the window object. Again ObjectWindows has eliminated a lot of the work required to add functionality to window objects. The procedures of defining and redefining window object member functions are demonstrated throughout this chapter.

Project Files

The creation of a Windows application requires several files. The files you most commonly utilize with traditional Windows programming methods include the C source file, the resource file, and the module definition file. The most common way to handle these files during application development is through the use of the Project Manager and the Integrated Development Environment (IDE). The Project Manager and IDE were used extensively in Part I to develop the program examples. A typical Windows project would contain a module definition file (.DEF), a resource file (.RC), and a C source file (.C).

As with Windows applications developed using traditional programming styles, ObjectWindows applications are commonly developed using the Project Manager and the IDE. A typical ObjectWindows project contains a module definition file, a resource file, a C++ source file, and library files. These files are described in more detail in the following paragraphs.

The Module Definition File

The module definition file gives the linker specific information about the application's code and data segments, the size of the application's local heap, and the size of the application's program stack. When you use the Borland C++ linker, it is not really necessary to create the module definition file since the linker is able to determine that information. With traditional Windows programming styles, it is customary, although not necessary, to include the module definition file. With ObjectWindows, however, most projects do not define one but instead use the predefined ObjectWindows definition file OWL.DEF. If you decide to define a module definition file with your ObjectWindows application, this quick description should help you:

```
NAME
DESCRIPTION
EXETYPE
CODE
DATA
HEAPSIZE
STACKSIZE
```

where

`NAME` defines a module as an executable

`DESCRIPTION` adds the specified text to the executable

`EXETYPE` indicates the type of program the linker should create; `WINDOWS` is used for Windows applications

`CODE` provides information on the application's code segments; possible values include `PRELOAD`, `FIXED`, `MOVEABLE`, and `DISCARDABLE`

`DATA` provides information on the application's data segments; possible values include `PRELOAD`, `MOVEABLE`, and `MULTIPLE`

`HEAPSIZE` defines the initial size of the application's local heap

`STACKSIZE` defines the size of the application's stack

Resource Files

Resource files define resources such as menus, dialog boxes, icons, bitmaps, and accelerator tables. Although many things differ between the use of traditional Windows programming styles and the use of ObjectWindows, the resource file is not one of them. You define resource files using the exact same method that you use for applications developed with traditional programming styles for ObjectWindows applications. You can also use the Whitewater Resource Toolkit or the Resource Workshop effectively to generate the resources required for both programming styles.

C++ Source Files

The C++ source file contains the actual code for the application. Since this file is a C++ file, it should contain such items as class definitions and member function definitions. It is in this file that the actual functionality of the application is defined. The examples that appear later in this chapter provide numerous C++ source file listings.

Library Files, DLLs, and Import Libraries

ObjectWindows applications often contain two library files, one for the ObjectWindows library and one for the container class library. The actual library files included in the project depends on the memory model you are using. Table 12.1 lists files that are used for the memory models specified.

Table 12.1. *ObjectWindows library files.*

Memory Model	*ObjectWindows Library*	*Container Class Library*
Small	OWLWS.LIB	TCLASSWS.LIB
Medium	OWLWM.LIB	TCLASSWM.LIB
Compact	OWLWC.LIB	TCLASSWC.LIB
Large	OWLWL.LIB	TCLASSWL.LIB

For example, if you are using the small memory model, you should include the OWLWS.LIB and TCLASSWS.LIB files in your project.

Several dynamic link libraries (DLLs) and import libraries are available for use with your ObjectWindows application. Table 12.2 lists these libraries.

Table 12.2. *DLLs and import libraries.*

Type	*DLL*	*Import Library*
ObjectWindows	OWL.DLL	OWL.BIB
Borland C++	BCRTL.DLL	CRTLL.LIB

If you want your application to use either DLL, you must link the appropriate import library. If you use either of the DLLs, you must use the large memory model and smart callbacks (the `-ml` and `-WS` options).

Using the IDE with ObjectWindows

When the topic of developing Windows applications using Borland C++ was introduced in Part I, there were three different development methods mentioned. These three methods involved the use of the command-line compiler, the Integrated Development Environment (IDE), and the MAKE utility. Using the IDE and its Program Manager features was selected as the most desirable method for developing Windows applications because this choice offers a more straightforward, procedural approach to development.

The process presented for Windows development in Part I, however, is not directly applicable to ObjectWindows development. For this reason you must define a procedure for building the ObjectWindows application using the features of the IDE and the Program Manager. All ObjectWindows examples in this book have been created using the IDE, the Project Manager, and the following procedure.

When you use the IDE and the Project Manager to develop Windows applications with ObjectWindows, you must follow several basic steps:

> **Note:**
>
> This procedure is designed for use with the DOS-based version of the IDE. The process used for the Windows-based IDE is similar except for steps 1 and 12. You can start the Windows-based IDE by double clicking the IDE icon. The compiled application can be run from the Program Manager.

1. Start the IDE by typing **`BC`** (real mode for version 2.0 or 3.0) or **`BCX`** (protected mode for version 3.0).
2. Create the appropriate C++ source files, module definition files (if desired), and resource files.
3. Move to the directory that contains the C++ source files, module definition files, and resource files. Select `File ¦ Change dir` (the `File` menu, `Change dir` option) to change directories.
4. Select `Project ¦ Open`. Type the file name, using a .PRJ extension, into the Project Name box. Click the `Ok` button or press Enter to continue.
5. Select `Project ¦ Add Item`. Add the appropriate C++ source files, module definition files, and resource files. You can also include the correct ObjectWindows library and the ObjectWindows container class for the

memory model you are using (for example, OWLWS.LIB and TCLASSWS.LIB for the small memory model). If you are using the ObjectWindows or Borland C++ DLLs, you also must add the appropriate import library. Close the `Project` dialog box when you are done.

6. Select `Options | Application`. The `Set Applications Options` dialog box should appear. Select `Windows App` to indicate that you are developing a Windows application.
7. Select `Options | Compiler` to specify any compiler options you might want to use.
8. Select `Options | Linker` to specify any linker options you want to use.
9. Select `Options | Directories` to define the location of the include and library directories for both ObjectWindows and Borland C++.
10. Select `Compile | Build all`. This selection should build the project into a Windows application.
11. If there are any errors, review the steps to make sure that you have not made a mistake or forgotten anything, correct any file(s) that must be modified, and repeat step 10. Once the project has been successfully built, continue with step 12.
12. Run your program from inside Windows. Although there are several ways to run your application, the easiest way is to type

    ```
    win filename
    ```

    at the DOS prompt (where *`filename`* represents the name of your Windows application executable file).

    This process is rather painless and enables you to take full advantage of the IDE and Project Manager features.

Programming Examples Using ObjectWindows

The remainder of this chapter provides examples on programming with ObjectWindows. Each example contains a full description of the example code and operation.

Basic Window Example

A good way to begin the examples portion of the chapter is to show a minimal ObjectWindows application. This example displays a window that can respond to events, be resized and moved, manage child windows, and be closed. Note that nothing is displayed inside the client area of the resulting window.

This example, as well as all examples in this chapter, have been created using a project. The project used to build this example is called OBJ_BAS and contains the files OBJ_BAS.CPP, OWL.DEF, OWL.LIB, and CRTLL.LIB. The following project description summarizes the project. A similar summary is used for every example in this chapter.

Project Name: `OBJ_BAS`
Files in Project: `OBJ_BAS.CPP`
`OWL.DEF`
`OWL.LIB`
`CRTLL.LIB`

Because this example is the fundamental structure used for all the examples in this book, it is important that you understand each component of the code. You should look at each component of the example code individually.

The program begins by including the owl.h header file. Every ObjectWindows program must include this header file.

```
#include <owl.h>
```

The next component of the code, shown as follows, defines a new application class `TBasicDemo`, derived from `TApplication`. An instance of the derived class should be constructed in `WinMain`. `WinMain` appears later in the code. At a minimum, the derived class must redefine the member function `InitMainWindow`. The `InitMainWindow` function is called automatically and constructs the window object that should be the main window of the application.

```
class TBasicDemo : public TApplication
{
public:
     TBasicDemo(LPSTR AName HANDLE hInstance, HANDLE hPrevInstance,
          LPSTR lpCmdLine, intCmdShow) :
          TApplication(AName, hInstance, hPrevInstance, lpCmdLine,
               nCmdShow) {};
     virtual void InitMainWindow();
};
```

The following component of code defines the `InitMainWindow` function of the application object `TBasicDemo` (`TBasicDemo::InitMainWindow`). The main window object, in this case, is constructed as an instance of `TWindow`. In the remaining examples, however, the main window object should be constructed as an instance of a derived class of `TWindow` or some other ObjectWindows class.

```
void TBasicDemo::InitMainWindow()
{
MainWindow = new TWindow(NULL, "Basic Window
      Demonstration");
}
```

The last component of code, shown as follows, is the main program of the application. In this section, an instance of the derived class `TBasicDemo` is constructed. All application initializations are made and the message loop is entered. The application exits from the message loop and returns the final status of the application as it closes.

```
int PASCAL WinMain(HANDLE hInstance, HANDLE hPrevInstance,
     LPSTR lpCmdLine, int nCmdShow)
{
TBasicDemo BasicDemo("Basic Window", hInstance, hPrevInstance, lpCmdLine,
     nCmdShow);
BasicDemo.Run();
return(BasicDemo.Status);
}
```

This basic structure is followed throughout the chapter's remaining examples. Listing 12.1 contains the complete code for the basic window example. Figure 12.1 illustrates the output of this example.

Listing 12.1. Basic window example.

```
#include <owl.h>

class TBasicDemo : public TApplication
{
public:
     TBasicDemo(LPSTR AName, HANDLE hInstance, HANDLE
        hPrevInstance, LPSTR lpCmdLine, int nCmdShow) :
        TApplication(AName, hInstance, hPrevInstance,
        lpCmdLine, nCmdShow) {};
     virtual void InitMainWindow();
};


void TBasicDemo::InitMainWindow()
{
MainWindow = new TWindow(NULL, "Basic Window Demonstration");
}

int PASCAL WinMain(HANDLE hInstance, HANDLE hPrevInstance,
```

```
     LPSTR lpCmdLine, int nCmdShow)
{
TBasicDemo BasicDemo("Basic Window", hInstance, hPrevInstance,
     lpCmdLine, nCmdShow);
BasicDemo.Run();
return(BasicDemo.Status);
}
```

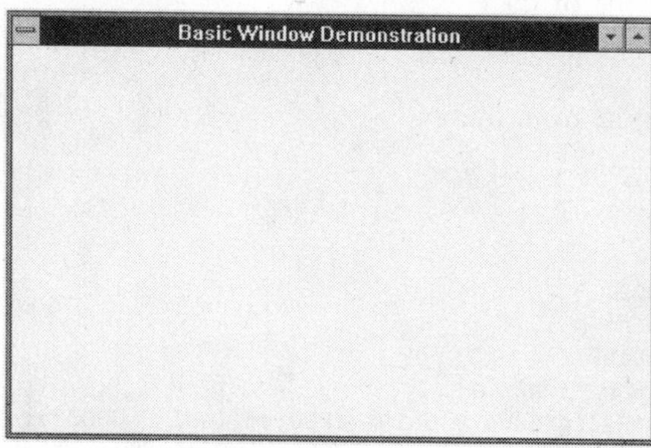

***Figure 12.1.** Basic window example.*

For comparison purposes, the fundamental window example from Part I is included in Listings 12.2 and 12.3. As you can see, ObjectWindows insulates you from the majority of the work required to create a basic window application. The project WIN_ONE was used to create this example.

Project Name: `WIN_ONE`
Files in Project: `WIN_ONE.C`
`WIN_ONE.DEF`

***Listing 12.2.** The module definition file for the fundamental window example.*

```
NAME           WIN_ONE
DESCRIPTION    'Fundamental Window'
EXETYPE        WINDOWS
CODE           PRELOAD MOVEABLE
DATA           PRELOAD MOVEABLE MULTIPLE
HEAPSIZE       1024
STACKSIZE      5120
```

Listing 12.3. C source code for the fundamental window example.

```
#include <windows.h>
#include <stdlib.h>
#include <string.h>

long FAR PASCAL WndProc (HWND hWnd, WORD iMessage,
                WORD wParam, LONG lParam);

int PASCAL WinMain (HANDLE hInstance, HANDLE hPrevInstance,
              LPSTR lpszCmdParam, int nCmdShow)

{
HWND hWnd;
MSG Message;
WNDCLASS WndClass;

if (!hPrevInstance)
     {
     WndClass.cbClsExtra = 0;
     WndClass.cbWndExtra = 0;
     WndClass.hbrBackground = GetStockObject(WHITE_BRUSH);
     WndClass.hCursor =  LoadCursor(NULL, IDC_ARROW);
     WndClass.hIcon = LoadIcon (NULL, "END");
     WndClass.hInstance = hInstance;
     WndClass.lpfnWndProc = WndProc;
     WndClass.lpszClassName = "WIN_ONE";
     WndClass.lpszMenuName = NULL;
     WndClass.style = CS_HREDRAW ¦ CS_VREDRAW;

     RegisterClass (&WndClass);
     }

hWnd = CreateWindow ("WIN_ONE",           /* class name */
          "Fundamental Window",           /* Caption */
          WS_OVERLAPPEDWINDOW,            /* Style */
          CW_USEDEFAULT,                  /* x position */
          0,                              /* y position */
          CW_USEDEFAULT,                  /* cx - size */
          0,                              /* cy - size */
          NULL,                           /* Parent window */
          NULL,                           /* Menu */
          hInstance,                      /* Program Instance */
          NULL);                          /* Parameters */

ShowWindow (hWnd, nCmdShow);
while (GetMessage (&Message, 0, 0, 0))
     {
     TranslateMessage(&Message);
     DispatchMessage(&Message);
```

```
    }
return Message.wParam;
}

/**************************************************************/
/*            Window Procedure: WndProc                      */
/**************************************************************/

long FAR PASCAL WndProc (HWND hWnd, WORD iMessage, WORD wParam,
                LONG lParam)
{
switch (iMessage)
        {
    case WM_DESTROY:
        PostQuitMessage(0);
        return 0;
    default:
        return(DefWindowProc(hWnd, iMessage, wParam,
            lParam));
    }
}
```

Line Drawing Example

The line drawing example introduces a few concepts beyond the basic window example. In this example, you are using the GDI functions to create pens and draw lines. In addition, you are defining the member function `Paint` to monitor the `WM_PAINT` message. Therefore, when you start the program and every time the window is sized, the specified lines are drawn in the client area. The OBJ_LINE project was used to create this example. The code for the C++ source file is provided in Listing 12.4. The output of this example is shown in Figure 12.2.

Project Name: `OBJ_LINE`

Files in Project: `OBJ_LINE.CPP`
`OWL.DEF`
`OWL.LIB`
`CRTLL.LIB`

Listing 12.4. Line drawing example.

```
#include <owl.h>

class TLineDemo : public TApplication
{
```

continues

Listing 12.4. continued

```
public:
     TLineDemo(LPSTR AName, HANDLE hInstance, HANDLE
        hPrevInstance, LPSTR lpCmdLine, int nCmdShow) :
        TApplication(AName, hInstance, hPrevInstance,
        lpCmdLine, nCmdShow) {};
     virtual void InitMainWindow();
};

_CLASSDEF(TLineWindow)

class TLineWindow : public TWindow
{
public:
     TLineWindow(PTWindowsObject AParent, LPSTR ATitle) :
        TWindow(AParent, ATitle) {};
     virtual void Paint(HDC PaintDC, PAINTSTRUCT _FAR &
        PaintInfo);
};


void TLineWindow::Paint(HDC PaintDC, PAINTSTRUCT _FAR &)
{

     static LOGPEN lpBlue = {PS_SOLID, 1, 1, RGB(0,0,255)},
                lpRed = {PS_SOLID, 1, 1, RGB(255,0,0)};
     HPEN hBluePen;
     HPEN hRedPen;
     int x1;
     int x2 = 300;

     hBluePen = CreatePenIndirect(&lpBlue);
     hRedPen = CreatePenIndirect(&lpRed);
     for (x1=50; x1<300; x1=x1+5)
       {
       SelectObject(PaintDC, hBluePen);
       MoveTo(PaintDC, x1, 50);
       LineTo(PaintDC, x2, 150);
       SelectObject(PaintDC, hRedPen);
       MoveTo(PaintDC, x2, 50);
       LineTo(PaintDC, x1, 150);
       x2 = x2 - 5;
       }
}


void TLineDemo::InitMainWindow()
```

```
{
MainWindow = new TLineWindow(NULL, "Line Drawing Demonstration");
}


int PASCAL WinMain(HANDLE hInstance, HANDLE hPrevInstance,
     LPSTR lpCmdLine, int nCmdShow)
{
TLineDemo LineDemo("Line Demo Window", hInstance,
   hPrevInstance, lpCmdLine, nCmdShow);
LineDemo.Run();
return(LineDemo.Status);
}
```

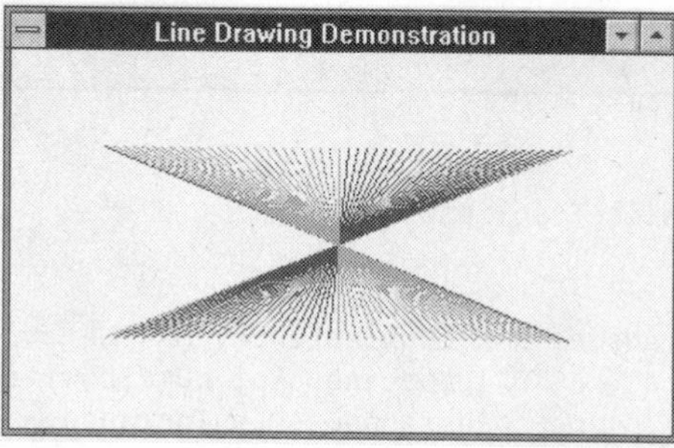

Figure 12.2. *Line drawing example.*

The program begins much like the basic window example. A derived class of TApplication—TLineDemo—is defined in the first component of the code. The second component of code, however, differs from the basic window example in that it defines a derived class of TWindow—TLineWindow. The main window object should be constructed from an instance of the derived class TLineWindow. As was already mentioned in the basic window example discussion, the main window object is usually an instance of a derived class of an ObjectWindows class. TLineWindow expects the member function Paint to be redefined.

The third component of code redefines the Paint member function of TLineWindow (TLineWindow::Paint). This member function defines and creates two pens and uses these pens to draw a series of blue and red lines. Each time the main window receives the WM_PAINT message, the Paint member function should be called.

The next component constructs the main window object as an instance of TLineWindow. The NULL parameter indicates that this is to be the main window. The second parameter, "Line Drawing Demonstration," specifies the window title.

The last component is the main program. The main program follows the same principal format as described in the basic window example.

Arc Drawing Example

The arc drawing example is very similar to that of the line drawing. In this example, you are using the GDI functions to create pens and draw arcs. Again, you are redefining the member function `Paint` to monitor the `WM_PAINT` message. The OBJ_ARC project was used to create this example. The code for the C++ source file is provided in Listing 12.5.

Project Name:	`OBJ_ARC`
Files in Project:	`OBJ_ARC.CPP`
	`OWL.DEF`
	`OWL.LIB`
	`CRTLL.LIB`

Listing 12.5. *Arc drawing example.*

```
#include <owl.h>

class TArcDemo : public TApplication
{
public:
     TArcDemo(LPSTR AName, HANDLE hInstance, HANDLE
        hPrevInstance, LPSTR lpCmdLine, int nCmdShow) :
        TApplication(AName, hInstance, hPrevInstance,
        lpCmdLine, nCmdShow) {};
     virtual void InitMainWindow();
};

_CLASSDEF(TArcWindow)

class TArcWindow : public TWindow
{
public:
     TArcWindow(PTWindowsObject AParent, LPSTR ATitle) :
        TWindow(AParent, ATitle) {};
     virtual void Paint(HDC PaintDC, PAINTSTRUCT _FAR &
        PaintInfo);
};


void TArcWindow::Paint(HDC PaintDC, PAINTSTRUCT _FAR &)
{

     static LOGPEN lpBlue = {PS_SOLID, 1, 1, RGB(0,0,255)},
                   lpRed = {PS_SOLID, 1, 1, RGB(255,0,0)};
     HPEN hBluePen;
     HPEN hRedPen;
```

```
        int x1;
        int y1 = 50;
        int x2 = 350;
        int y2 = 250;

        hBluePen = CreatePenIndirect(&lpBlue);
        hRedPen = CreatePenIndirect(&lpRed);
        for (x1=50; x1<200; x1=x1+5)
          {
          SelectObject(PaintDC, hBluePen);
          Arc(PaintDC, x1, y1, 200, 150, 200, 150, 50, 150);
          SelectObject(PaintDC, hRedPen);
          Arc(PaintDC, 200, 150, x2, y2, 200, 150, 350, 150);
          y1 = y1 + 3;
          x2 = x2 - 5;
          y2 = y2 - 3;
          }
}


void TArcDemo::InitMainWindow()
{
MainWindow = new TArcWindow(NULL, "Arc Demonstration");
}


int PASCAL WinMain(HANDLE hInstance, HANDLE hPrevInstance,
     LPSTR lpCmdLine, int nCmdShow)
{
TArcDemo ArcDemo("Arc Demo Window", hInstance, hPrevInstance,
   lpCmdLine, nCmdShow);
ArcDemo.Run();
return ArcDemo.Status;
}
```

A derived class of `TApplication`—`TArcDemo`—is defined in the first component of the code. The second component of the code defines a derived class of `TWindow`—`TArcWindow`. The main window object is to be constructed from an instance of the derived class `TArcWindow` that expects the member function `Paint` to be redefined.

The third component of code redefines the `Paint` member function of `TArcWindow` (`TArcWindow::Paint`). This member function defines and creates two pens and uses these pens to draw a series of blue and red arcs.

The next component constructs the main window object as an instance of `TArcWindow`. The NULL parameter indicates that this is to be the main window. The second parameter, "Arc Demonstration," specifies the window title.

The last component is the main program, which follows the same principal format as described in the basic window example. The output of this example is shown in Figure 12.3.

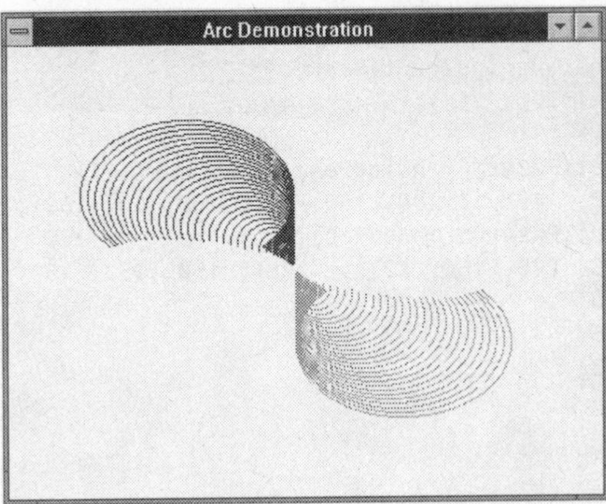

Figure 12.3. *Arc drawing example.*

Filled Figures Example

The filled figure example is very similar to the previous two examples. In this example, you are using the GDI functions to create brushes and draw several filled figures including a rectangle, a rounded rectangle, a circle, a chorded circle, and a pie-shaped wedge. Again, you are defining the member function `Paint` to monitor the `WM_PAINT` message. The OBJ_FIG project was used to create this example. Listing 12.6 shows the code for this C++ source file.

Project Name:	`OBJ_FIG`
Files in Project:	`OBJ_FIG.CPP`
	`OWL.DEF`
	`OWL.LIB`
	`CRTLL.LIB`

Listing 12.6. Filled figures example.

```
#include <owl.h>

class TFiguresDemo : public TApplication
{
public:
     TFiguresDemo(LPSTR AName, HANDLE hInstance, HANDLE
        hPrevInstance, LPSTR lpCmdLine, int nCmdShow) :
        TApplication(AName, hInstance, hPrevInstance,
        lpCmdLine, nCmdShow) {};
     virtual void InitMainWindow();
};

_CLASSDEF(TFiguresWindow)

class TFiguresWindow : public TWindow
{
public:
     TFiguresWindow(PTWindowsObject AParent, LPSTR ATitle) :
        TWindow(AParent, ATitle) {};
     virtual void Paint(HDC PaintDC, PAINTSTRUCT _FAR
        & PaintInfo);
};


void TFiguresWindow::Paint(HDC PaintDC, PAINTSTRUCT _FAR &)
{
     static HBRUSH hBrush[2];
     hBrush[0] = CreateHatchBrush(HS_HORIZONTAL,
                    RGB(0,0,0));
     hBrush[1] = CreateHatchBrush(HS_VERTICAL,
                    RGB(255,0,0));

     SelectObject(PaintDC,hBrush[0]);
     Rectangle (PaintDC,50,50,100,100);

     SelectObject(PaintDC,hBrush[1]);
     RoundRect (PaintDC,50,150,100,200,15,15);
     Ellipse (PaintDC,150,50,200,100);

     SelectObject(PaintDC,hBrush[0]);
     Chord (PaintDC,150,150,200,200,150,150,200,200);
     Pie (PaintDC,250,50,300,100,250,50,300,50);

}
```

continues

Listing 12.6. continued

```
void TFiguresDemo::InitMainWindow()
{
MainWindow = new TFiguresWindow(NULL, "Figures Demonstration");
}


int PASCAL WinMain(HANDLE hInstance, HANDLE hPrevInstance,
     LPSTR lpCmdLine, int nCmdShow)
{
TFiguresDemo FiguresDemo("Figures Demo Window", hInstance,
   hPrevInstance, lpCmdLine, nCmdShow);
FiguresDemo.Run();
return(FiguresDemo.Status);
}
```

A derived class of `TApplication`—`TFiguresDemo`—is defined in the first component of the code. The second component of the code defines a derived class of `TWindow`: `TFiguresWindow`. `TFiguresWindow` expects the member function `Paint` to be redefined.

The third component of code redefines the `Paint` member function of `TFiguresWindow` (`TFiguresWindow::Paint`). This member function defines and creates two brushes and uses these brushes when drawing the filled figures.

The next component constructs the main window object as an instance of `TFiguresWindow`. The NULL parameter indicates that this is to be the main window. The second parameter, "Figures Demonstration," specifies the window title.

The last component is the main program that follows the same principal format as described in the basic window example. The output of this example is shown in Figure 12.4.

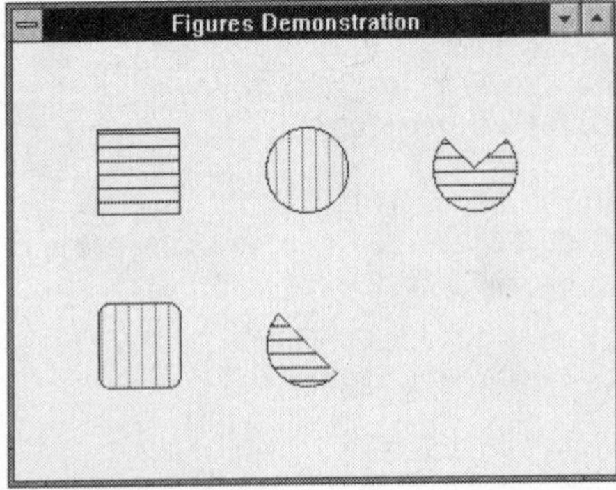

Figure 12.4. *Filled figures example.*

TextOut Example

The `TextOut` example demonstrates how you can generate text in the client area. In this example, you are using the `TextOut` function to display text. This example writes the specified text in response to the `WM_PAINT` message. Therefore, you must redefine the member function `Paint` to draw the text in response to the `WM_PAINT` message. The OBJ_TXT project was used to create this example. Listing 12.7 shows the code for this C++ source file.

Project Name:	`OBJ_TXT`
Files in Project:	`OBJ_TXT.CPP`
	`OWL.DEF`
	`OWL.LIB`
	`CRTLL.LIB`

Listing 12.7. *`TextOut` example.*

```
#include <owl.h>

class TTextOutDemo : public TApplication
{
public:
     TTextOutDemo(LPSTR AName, HANDLE hInstance, HANDLE
        hPrevInstance, LPSTR lpCmdLine, int nCmdShow) :
        TApplication(AName, hInstance, hPrevInstance,
        lpCmdLine, nCmdShow) {};
     virtual void InitMainWindow();
};

_CLASSDEF(TTextOutWindow)

class TTextOutWindow : public TWindow
{
public:
     TTextOutWindow(PTWindowsObject AParent, LPSTR ATitle) :
        TWindow(AParent, ATitle) {};
     virtual void Paint(HDC PaintDC, PAINTSTRUCT _FAR &
        PaintInfo);
};


void TTextOutWindow::Paint(HDC PaintDC, PAINTSTRUCT _FAR &)
{
```

continues

Listing 12.7. continued

```
    int nXText, nYText, nHeight;
    short x;
    DWORD dwExt;
    short LnCount = 15;
    static char *textbuf[] =
        {"One",
        "Two",
        "Three",
        "Four",
        "Five",
        "Six",
        "Seven",
        "Eight",
        "Nine",
        "Ten",
        "Eleven",
        "Twelve",
        "Thirteen",
        "Fourteen",
        "Fifteen"};

        dwExt = GetTextExtent(PaintDC,"S",1);
        nHeight = HIWORD(dwExt);
        nYText = nHeight;
        nXText = LOWORD(dwExt);
        for (x=0; x<LnCount; x=x+1)
            {
            TextOut(PaintDC,nXText,nYText,
              textbuf[x],lstrlen(textbuf[x]));
            nYText = nYText + nHeight;
            }

}


void TTextOutDemo::InitMainWindow()
{
MainWindow = new TTextOutWindow(NULL, "TextOut Demonstration");
}


int PASCAL WinMain(HANDLE hInstance, HANDLE hPrevInstance,
    LPSTR lpCmdLine, int nCmdShow)
{
```

```
TTextOutDemo TextOutDemo("TextOut Demo Window", hInstance,
   hPrevInstance, lpCmdLine, nCmdShow);
TextOutDemo.Run();
return(TextOutDemo.Status);
}
```

A derived class of `TApplication`—`TTextOutDemo`—is defined in the first component of the code. The second component of the code defines a derived class of `TWindow`—`TTextOutWindow`—that expects the member function `Paint` to be redefined.

The third component of code redefines the `Paint` member function of `TTextOutWindow` (`TTextOutWindow::Paint`). This member function defines and displays the 15 specified lines of text. Every time the `WM_PAINT` message is received, the text is redrawn.

The next component constructs the main window object as an instance of `TTextOutWindow`. The NULL parameter indicates that this is to be the main window. The second parameter, "TextOut Demonstration," specifies the window title.

The last component is the main program, which follows the same principal format as described in the basic window example. The output of this example is shown in Figure 12.5.

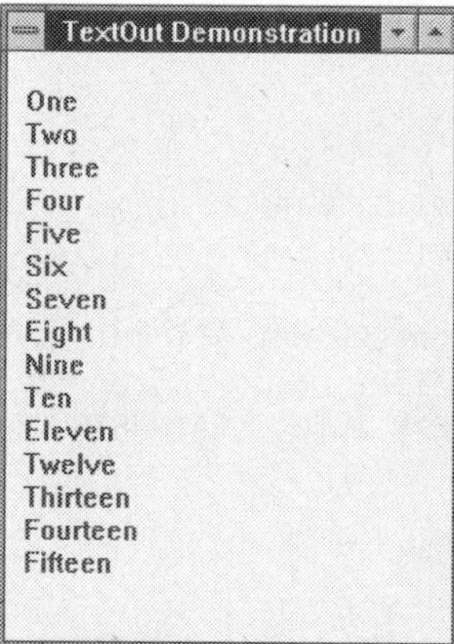

Figure 12.5. *`TextOut` example.*

TabbedTextOut Example

The `TabbedTextOut` example is similar to the `TextOut` example, except that the `TabbedTextOut` example demonstrates how you can generate tabbed text in the client area. In this example, you are using the `TabbedTextOut` function to display text. Again,

this example writes the specified text in response to the `WM_PAINT` message. Therefore, you must redefine the member function `Paint` to draw text in response to the `WM_PAINT` message. The OBJ_TTXT project was used to create this example. The code for the C++ source file is provided in Listing 12.8.

Project Name:	OBJ_TTXT
Files in Project:	OBJ_TTXT.CPP
	OWL.DEF
	OWL.LIB
	CRTLL.LIB

Listing 12.8. `TabbedTextOut` **example.**

```
#include <owl.h>

class TTTextOutDemo : public TApplication
{
public:
     TTTextOutDemo(LPSTR AName, HANDLE hInstance, HANDLE
        hPrevInstance, LPSTR lpCmdLine, int nCmdShow) :
        TApplication(AName, hInstance, hPrevInstance,
        lpCmdLine, nCmdShow) {};
     virtual void InitMainWindow();
};

_CLASSDEF(TTTextOutWindow)

class TTTextOutWindow : public TWindow
{
public:
     TTTextOutWindow(PTWindowsObject AParent, LPSTR ATitle) :
        TWindow(AParent, ATitle) {};
     virtual void Paint(HDC PaintDC, PAINTSTRUCT _FAR &
        PaintInfo);
};


void TTTextOutWindow::Paint(HDC PaintDC, PAINTSTRUCT _FAR &)
{

     int nXText, nYText, nHeight, nTab;
     short x;
     DWORD dwExt;
     short LnCount = 13;
     static char *textbuf[] =
          {"Number \tPlayer",
          "______ \t______",
          "One \tJim",
```

```
          "Two \tSue",
          "Three \tJohn",
          "Four \tMary",
          "Five \tSally",
          "Six \tGary",
          "Seven \tKenny",
          "Eight \tDonna",
          "Nine \tTony",
          "Ten \tKim",
          "Eleven \tWes"};

          dwExt = GetTextExtent(PaintDC,"S",1);
          nHeight = HIWORD(dwExt);
          nYText = nHeight;
          nXText = LOWORD(dwExt);
          nTab = 25 * LOWORD(dwExt);
          for (x=0; x<LnCount; x=x+1)
               {
               TabbedTextOut(PaintDC,nXText,nYText,
                 textbuf[x],lstrlen(textbuf[x]),1,
                 &nTab,nXText);
               nYText = nYText + nHeight;
               }
}


void TTTextOutDemo::InitMainWindow()
{
MainWindow = new TTTextOutWindow(NULL, "TabbedTextOut Demonstration");
}


int PASCAL WinMain(HANDLE hInstance, HANDLE hPrevInstance,
     LPSTR lpCmdLine, int nCmdShow)
{
TTTextOutDemo TTextOutDemo("TTextOut Demo Window",
   hInstance, hPrevInstance, lpCmdLine, nCmdShow);
TTextOutDemo.Run();
return(TTextOutDemo.Status);
}
```

A derived class of TApplication—TTTextOutDemo—is defined in the first component of the code. The second component of the code defines a derived class of TWindow—TTTextOutWindow—that expects the member function Paint to be redefined.

The third component of code redefines the Paint member function of TTTextOutWindow (TTTextOutWindow::Paint). This member function defines and displays the 15 tabbed lines of text. Every time the WM_PAINT message is received, the text is redrawn.

The next component constructs the main window object as an instance of `TTextOutWindow`. The NULL parameter indicates that this is to be the main window. The second parameter, "TabbedTextOut Demonstration," specifies the window title.

The last component is the main program, which follows the same principal format as described in the basic window example. The output of this example is shown in Figure 12.6.

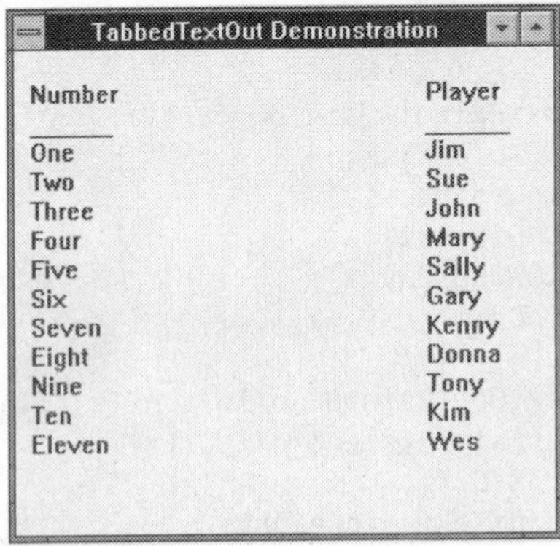

Figure 12.6. *`TabbedTextOut` example.*

Scroller Example

The scroller example demonstrates the use the scrolling features of `TScroller`. This example begins by drawing an ellipse that is larger than the current window. The features of `TScroller` enable you to scroll the image both horizontally and vertically. The OBJ_SCRL project was used to create this example. The code for the C++ source file is provided in Listing 12.9.

Project Name: `OBJ_SCRL`

Files in Project: `OBJ_SCRL.CPP`
`OWL.DEF`
`OWL.LIB`
`CRTLL.LIB`

Listing 12.9. *Scroller example.*

```
#include <owl.h>

class TScrollerDemo : public TApplication
{
```

```
public:
     TScrollerDemo(LPSTR AName, HANDLE hInstance, HANDLE
        hPrevInstance, LPSTR lpCmdLine, int nCmdShow) :
        TApplication(AName, hInstance, hPrevInstance,
        lpCmdLine, nCmdShow) {};
     virtual void InitMainWindow();
};

_CLASSDEF(TScrollerWindow)

class TScrollerWindow : public TWindow
{
public:
     TScrollerWindow(LPSTR ATitle);
     virtual void Paint(HDC PaintDC, PAINTSTRUCT _FAR &
        PaintInfo);
};


TScrollerWindow::TScrollerWindow(LPSTR ATitle) :
     TWindow(NULL, ATitle)
{
     Attr.Style |= WS_VSCROLL | WS_HSCROLL;
     Scroller = new TScroller(this,5,5,100,100);
}

void TScrollerWindow::Paint(HDC PaintDC, PAINTSTRUCT _FAR &)
{
Ellipse(PaintDC,50,50,500,500);
}


void TScrollerDemo::InitMainWindow()
{
MainWindow = new TScrollerWindow("Scroller Demonstration");
}


int PASCAL WinMain(HANDLE hInstance, HANDLE hPrevInstance,
     LPSTR lpCmdLine, int nCmdShow)
{
TScrollerDemo ScrollerDemo("Scroller Demo Window", hInstance,
   hPrevInstance, lpCmdLine, nCmdShow);
ScrollerDemo.Run();
return(ScrollerDemo.Status);
}
```

A derived class of TApplication—TScrollerDemo—is defined in the first component of the code. The second component of the code defines a derived class of TWindow—TScrollerWindow—that expects the member function Paint to be redefined.

The third component of code is unlike any of the components in the previous examples. This component is a constructor for a TScrollerWindow, defines the scroll styles, and constructs the Scroller object.

The fourth component of code redefines the Paint member function of TScrollerWindow (TScrollerWindow::Paint). This member function generates the oversized ellipse.

The next component constructs the main window object as an instance of TScrollerWindow. The second parameter, "Scroller Demonstration," specifies the window title.

The last component is the main program, which follows the same principal format as described in the basic window example. The output of this example is shown in Figure 12.7.

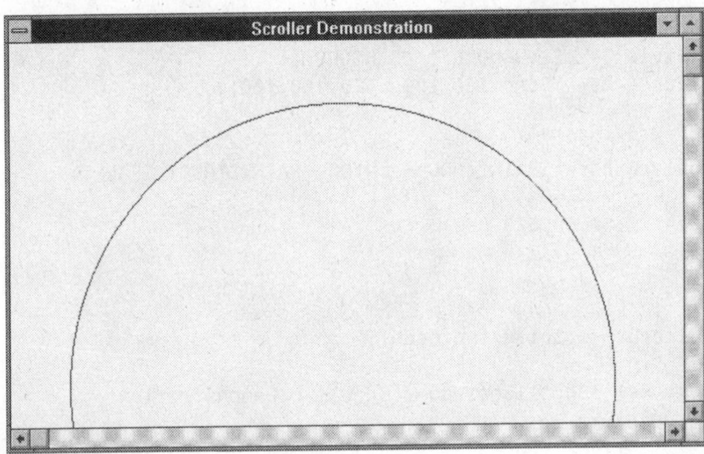

Figure 12.7. *Scroller example.*

Accelerator Example

The accelerator example demonstrates several new concepts. The first new concept is the use of accelerator and menu resources. Another concept is using and defining the InitInstance member function of the application object. Lastly, this example demonstrates the methods for defining actions for menu item and accelerator selection. The OBJ_ACC project was used to create this example. Listing 12.10 shows the resource file for this project. The code for the C++ source file is provided in Listing 12.11.

Project Name: `OBJ_ACC`

Files in Project: `OBJ_ACC.CPP`
`OBJ_ACC.RC`
`OWL.DEF`
`OWL.LIB`
`CRTLL.LIB`

Listing 12.10. *Resource file for the accelerator example.*

```
ACC_TABLE ACCELERATORS
BEGIN
  "1", 1, VIRTKEY, NOINVERT
  "2", 2, VIRTKEY, NOINVERT
  "3", 3, VIRTKEY, NOINVERT
  "4", 4, VIRTKEY, NOINVERT
  "5", 5, VIRTKEY, NOINVERT
  "6", 6, VIRTKEY, NOINVERT
  "7", 7, VIRTKEY, NOINVERT
END

MENU  MENU LOADONCALL MOVEABLE PURE DISCARDABLE
BEGIN
  POPUP "Menu One"
  BEGIN
    MenuItem  "Item One", 1
    MenuItem  "Item Two", 2
  END
  POPUP "Menu Two"
  BEGIN
    MenuItem  "Selection One", 3
  END
  POPUP "Menu Three"
  BEGIN
    MenuItem  "Checked Item #1", 4, CHECKED
    MenuItem  "Checked Item #2", 5, CHECKED
  END
  POPUP "Menu Four"
  BEGIN
    MenuItem  "Menu Item One", 6
    MenuItem  "Menu Item Two", 7
  END
END
```

Listing 12.11. C++ source file for the accelerator example.

```
#include <owl.h>

#define CM_ONEONE 1
#define CM_ONETWO 2
#define CM_TWOONE 3
#define CM_THREEONE 4
#define CM_THREETWO 5
#define CM_FOURONE 6
#define CM_FOURTWO 7

class TAcceleratorDemo : public TApplication
{
public:
     TAcceleratorDemo(LPSTR AName, HANDLE hInstance, HANDLE
        hPrevInstance, LPSTR lpCmdLine, int nCmdShow) :
        TApplication(AName, hInstance, hPrevInstance,
        lpCmdLine, nCmdShow) {};
     virtual void InitMainWindow();
     virtual void InitInstance();
};

_CLASSDEF(TAcceleratorWindow)

class TAcceleratorWindow : public TWindow
{
public:
     TAcceleratorWindow(PTWindowsObject AParent, LPSTR ATitle);
     virtual void CMOneOne(RTMessage Msg) =
          [CM_FIRST + CM_ONEONE];
     virtual void CMOneTwo(RTMessage Msg) =
          [CM_FIRST + CM_ONETWO];
     virtual void CMTwoOne(RTMessage Msg) =
          [CM_FIRST + CM_TWOONE];
     virtual void CMThreeOne(RTMessage Msg) =
          [CM_FIRST + CM_THREEONE];
     virtual void CMThreeTwo(RTMessage Msg) =
          [CM_FIRST + CM_THREETWO];
     virtual void CMFourOne(RTMessage Msg) =
          [CM_FIRST + CM_FOURONE];
     virtual void CMFourTwo(RTMessage Msg) =
          [CM_FIRST + CM_FOURTWO];
};


TAcceleratorWindow::TAcceleratorWindow(PTWindowsObject AParent,
     LPSTR ATitle) : TWindow(AParent, ATitle)
{
```

```
AssignMenu("MENU");
};

void TAcceleratorDemo::InitMainWindow()
{
MainWindow = new TAcceleratorWindow(NULL,"Accelerators");
}

void TAcceleratorDemo::InitInstance()
{
TApplication::InitInstance();
HAccTable = LoadAccelerators(hInstance, "ACC_TABLE");
}

void TAcceleratorWindow::CMOneOne(RTMessage)
{
     MessageBox(HWindow,"Menu One - Item One",
       "Accelerator = 1",MB_OK);
}

void TAcceleratorWindow::CMOneTwo(RTMessage)
{
     MessageBox(HWindow,"Menu One - Item Two",
       "Accelerator = 2",MB_OK);
}


void TAcceleratorWindow::CMTwoOne(RTMessage)
{
     MessageBox(HWindow,"Menu Two - Selection One",
       "Accelerator = 3",MB_OK);
}


void TAcceleratorWindow::CMThreeOne(RTMessage)
{
     MessageBox(HWindow,"Menu Three - Checked Item #1",
       "Accelerator = 4",MB_OK);
}


void TAcceleratorWindow::CMThreeTwo(RTMessage)
{
     MessageBox(HWindow,"Menu Three - Checked Item #2",
       "Accelerator = 5",MB_OK);
}
```

continues

Listing 12.11. continued

```
void TAcceleratorWindow::CMFourOne(RTMessage)
{
     MessageBox(HWindow,"Menu Four - Menu Item One",
        "Accelerator = 6",MB_OK);
}


void TAcceleratorWindow::CMFourTwo(RTMessage)
{
     MessageBox(HWindow,"Menu Four - Menu Item Two",
        "Accelerator = 7",MB_OK);
}


int PASCAL WinMain(HANDLE hInstance, HANDLE hPrevInstance,
     LPSTR lpCmdLine, int nCmdShow)
{
TAcceleratorDemo AcceleratorDemo("Accelerators Window",
   hInstance, hPrevInstance, lpCmdLine, nCmdShow);
AcceleratorDemo.Run();
return(AcceleratorDemo.Status);
}
```

You should first review the resource file that defines four menus: Menu One, Menu Two, Menu Three, and Menu Four. Menu One contains two items: Item One and Item Two. Menu Two contains one item: Selection One. Menu Three contains two items: Checked Item #1 and Checked Item #2. Menu Four contains two items: Menu Item One and Menu Item Two. Accelerators, keys ranging from 1 to 7, have been defined for each menu item.

Now you should examine the C++ source file. A derived class of `TApplication`—`TAcceleratorDemo`—is defined in the first component of the code. The second component of the code defines a derived class of `TWindow`—`TAcceleratorWindow`—that expects the seven member functions to be defined. Each member function should define the action for a corresponding menu item or accelerator selection.

The third component of the code constructs a `TAcceleratorWindow` and loads the specified menu.

The next component constructs the main window object as an instance of `TAcceleratorWindow`. The NULL parameter indicates that this is to be the main window. The second parameter, "Accelerators," specifies the window title.

The next component defines the `InitInstance` member function of the application object. This member function initializes each application instance and loads the specified accelerator table.

The seven code components following the definition of the `InitInstance` member function of the application object define the actions to be taken for each of the menu items. The member functions correspond to an appropriate menu item (for example, `CMOneOne` corresponds to Item One of Menu One). The member functions are automatically called in response to the command messages sent when a menu item is selected. Although these member functions only display message boxes, they could easily be redefined to perform more intricate, detailed operations.

The last component is the main program that follows the same principal format as described in the basic window example. The output of this example is shown in Figure 12.8.

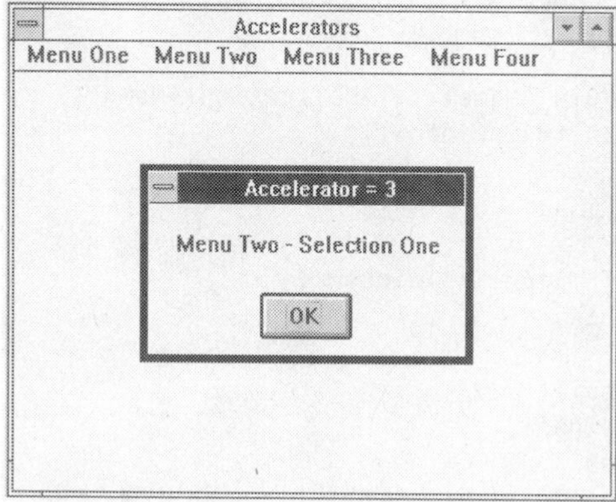

Figure 12.8. *The accelerator example.*

Bitmap Example

The bitmap example demonstrates the use of bitmap resources by loading and displaying the specified bitmaps. The bitmaps used in this example were created for the bitmap example demonstrated in Chapter 4. With this example, you are once again defining the member function `Paint` to respond to the `WM_PAINT` message. The OBJ_BIT project was used to create this example. The code for the resource file is provided in Listing 12.12. The code for the C++ source file is provided in Listing 12.13.

Project Name:	`OBJ_BIT`
Files in Project:	`OBJ_BIT.CPP`
	`OBJ_BIT.RC`
	`OWL.DEF`
	`OWL.LIB`
	`CRTLL.LIB`

Listing 12.12. *Resource file for the bitmap example.*

```
FOOTBALL BITMAP FOOTBALL.BMP
BASKET   BITMAP BASKET.BMP
GOLFBALL BITMAP GOLFBALL.BMP
BASEBALL BITMAP BASEBALL.BMP
```

Listing 12.13. *C++ source file for the bitmap example.*

```
#include <owl.h>

class TBitmapDemo : public TApplication
{
public:
     TBitmapDemo(LPSTR AName) : TApplication(AName){}
     virtual void InitMainWindow();
};


class TBitmapWindow : public TWindow
{
public:
     HBITMAP hFootball;
     HBITMAP hBasketball;
     HBITMAP hGolfball;
     HBITMAP hBaseball;

     TBitmapWindow(PWindowsObject AParent, LPSTR ATitle) :
        TWindow(AParent, ATitle) {};
     virtual void Paint(HDC PaintDC, PAINTSTRUCT& PaintInfo);
};


void TBitmapWindow::Paint(HDC PaintDC, PAINTSTRUCT& PaintInfo)
{
     HDC hMemDC;

     hMemDC = CreateCompatibleDC(PaintInfo.hdc);

     hFootball = LoadBitmap(Application->hInstance,
          "FOOTBALL");
     hBasketball = LoadBitmap(Application->hInstance,
          "BASKET");
     hGolfball = LoadBitmap(Application->hInstance,
          "GOLFBALL");
     hBaseball = LoadBitmap(Application->hInstance,
          "BASEBALL");
```

```
        SelectObject(hMemDC,hFootball);
        BitBlt(PaintDC,30,50,72,72,hMemDC,0,0,SRCCOPY);

        SelectObject(hMemDC,hBasketball);
        BitBlt(PaintDC,130,100,72,72,hMemDC,0,0,SRCCOPY);

        SelectObject(hMemDC,hGolfball);
        BitBlt(PaintDC,230,150,72,72,hMemDC,0,0,SRCCOPY);

        SelectObject(hMemDC,hBaseball);
        BitBlt(PaintDC,330,200,72,72,hMemDC,0,0,SRCCOPY);

    DeleteDC(hMemDC);
}


void TBitmapDemo::InitMainWindow()
{
MainWindow = new TBitmapWindow(NULL, "Bitmap Demonstration");
}


int PASCAL WinMain(HANDLE hInstance, HANDLE hPrevInstance,
     LPSTR lpCmdLine, int nCmdShow)
{
TBitmapDemo BitmapDemo("Bitmap Window");
BitmapDemo.Run();
return(BitmapDemo.Status);
}
```

The resource file of this project simply defines four bitmaps that were previously created using the Whitewater Resource Toolkit and the Resource Workshop.

In the source file, a derived class of `TApplication`—`TBitmapDemo`—is defined in the first component of the code. The second component of the code defines a derived class of `TWindow`—`TBitmapWindow`—that creates the handles for the bitmaps and expects the member function `Paint` to be redefined.

The third component of the code redefines the `Paint` member function of `TBitmapWindow` (`TBitmapWindow::Paint`). This member function loads and displays the bitmaps defined in the resource file.

The next component constructs the main window object as an instance of `TBitmapWindow`. The NULL parameter indicates that this is to be the main window. The second parameter, "Bitmap Demonstration," specifies the window title.

The last component is the main program, which follows the same principal format as described in the basic window example. The output of this example is shown in Figure 12.9.

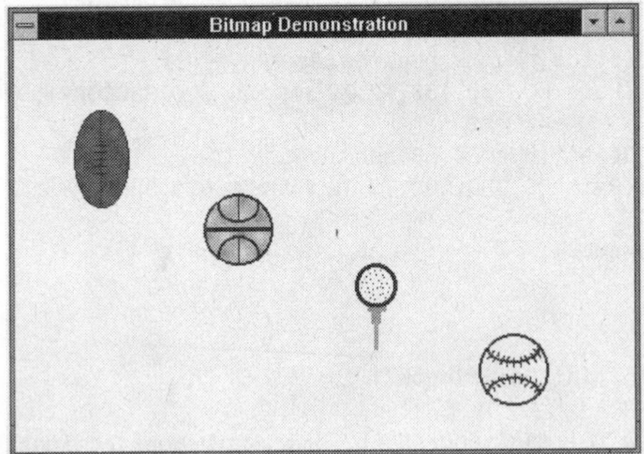

Figure 12.9. *The bitmap example.*

Cursor Example

This example demonstrates how you can redefine the cursor (that is, modify the predefined cursor or redefine the predefined cursor). Whenever the cursor is located inside the client area of the main window, the cursor is changed to the specified shape. The OBJ_CUR project was used to create this example. The code for the C++ source file is provided in Listing 12.14.

Project Name:	`OBJ_CUR`
Files in Project:	`OBJ_CUR.CPP`
	`OWL.DEF`
	`OWL.LIB`
	`CRTTL.LIB`

Listing 12.14. *The cursor example.*

```
#include <owl.h>

class TCursorDemo : public TApplication
{
public:
    TCursorDemo(LPSTR AName, HANDLE hInstance, HANDLE
```

```
        hPrevInstance, LPSTR lpCmdLine, int nCmdShow) :
        TApplication(AName, hInstance, hPrevInstance,
        lpCmdLine, nCmdShow) {};
     virtual void InitMainWindow();
};

_CLASSDEF(TCursorWindow)

class TCursorWindow : public TWindow
{
public:
     TCursorWindow(PTWindowsObject AParent, LPSTR AName) :
       TWindow (AParent, AName) {};
     virtual void GetWindowClass(WNDCLASS& AWndClass);
};

void TCursorWindow::GetWindowClass(WNDCLASS _FAR & AWndClass)
{
     TWindow::GetWindowClass(AWndClass);
     AWndClass.hCursor = LoadCursor(0, IDC_CROSS);
}


void TCursorDemo::InitMainWindow()
{
MainWindow = new TCursorWindow(NULL, "Cursor Demonstration");
}

int PASCAL WinMain(HANDLE hInstance, HANDLE hPrevInstance,
     LPSTR lpCmdLine, int nCmdShow)
{
TCursorDemo CursorDemo("Cursor Window", hInstance,
   hPrevInstance, lpCmdLine, nCmdShow);
CursorDemo.Run();
return(CursorDemo.Status);
}
```

A derived class of TApplication—TCursorDemo—is defined in the first component of the code. The second component of the code defines a derived class of TWindow—TCursorWindow—that expects the member function GetWindowClass to be redefined.

The third component of the code redefines the GetWindowClass member function of TCursorWindow (TCursorWindow::GetWindowClass). This member function loads the specified cursor.

The next component constructs the main window object as an instance of TCursorWindow. The NULL parameter indicates that this is to be the main window. The second parameter, "Cursor Demonstration," specifies the window title.

The last component is the main program, which follows the same principal format as described in the basic window example earlier in this chapter.

Dialog Example

The dialog example is similar in many respects to the accelerator example: it uses a resource file and demonstrates the methods for defining the actions of dialog controls, such as buttons. The OBJ_DLG project was used to create this example. Listing 12.15 shows the resource file for this project. The code for the C++ source file is provided in Listing 12.16.

Project Name: `OBJ_DLG`
Files in Project: `OBJ_DLG.CPP`
`OWL.DEF`
`OWL.LIB`
`CRTLL.LIB`

Listing 12.15. Resource file for the dialog example.

```
#include <windows.h>
#define DLG_DEMO 1

DLG#1 DIALOG DISCARDABLE LOADONCALL PURE MOVEABLE 42, 38, 148, 108 STYLE
WS_POPUP ¦ WS_DLGFRAME ¦ WS_SYSMENU
  BEGIN
  CONTROL "Radio Button One" 101, "BUTTON", WS_CHILD ¦
     WS_VISIBLE ¦ 0x4L, 38, 6, 74, 14
  CONTROL "Radio Button Two" 102, "BUTTON", WS_CHILD ¦
     WS_VISIBLE ¦ 0x4L, 38, 25, 74, 14
  CONTROL "Checkbox One" 103, "BUTTON", WS_CHILD ¦
     WS_VISIBLE ¦ WS_TABSTOP ¦ 0x2L, 8, 45, 64, 12
  CONTROL "Checkbox Two" 104, "BUTTON", WS_CHILD ¦
     WS_VISIBLE ¦ WS_TABSTOP ¦ 0x2L, 8, 61, 64, 12
  CONTROL "Checkbox Three" 105, "BUTTON", WS_CHILD ¦
     WS_VISIBLE ¦ WS_TABSTOP ¦ 0x2L, 75, 45, 72, 12
  CONTROL "Checkbox Four" 106, "BUTTON", WS_CHILD ¦
     WS_VISIBLE ¦ WS_TABSTOP ¦ 0x2L, 75, 61, 68, 12
  CONTROL "Cancel" 107, "BUTTON", WS_CHILD ¦
     WS_VISIBLE ¦ WS_TABSTOP, 26, 87, 40, 12
  CONTROL "OK" 108, "BUTTON", WS_CHILD ¦
     WS_VISIBLE ¦ WS_TABSTOP ¦ 0x1L, 82, 87, 38, 12
  END

DlgMenu MENU
  {
```

```
  POPUP "&Help"
    {
    MENUITEM "Dialog Demo",  DLG_DEMO
    }
  }
```

Listing 12.16. C++ source file for the dialog example.

```
#include <owl.h>
#include <dialog.h>

#define CM_DLG 1
#define ID_RADIOONE 101
#define ID_RADIOTWO 102
#define ID_CHECKONE 103
#define ID_CHECKTWO 104
#define ID_CHECKTHREE 105
#define ID_CHECKFOUR 106
#define ID_MYCANCEL 107
#define ID_MYOK 108

class TDlg : public TDialog
{
public:
     TDlg(PTWindowsObject AParent, LPSTR AName)
          : TDialog(AParent, AName) {};
     virtual void RadioOne(RTMessage Msg) =
          [ID_FIRST + ID_RADIOONE];
     virtual void RadioTwo(RTMessage Msg) =
          [ID_FIRST + ID_RADIOTWO];
     virtual void CheckOne(RTMessage Msg) =
          [ID_FIRST + ID_CHECKONE];
     virtual void CheckTwo(RTMessage Msg) =
          [ID_FIRST + ID_CHECKTWO];
     virtual void CheckThree(RTMessage Msg) =
          [ID_FIRST + ID_CHECKTHREE];
     virtual void CheckFour(RTMessage Msg) =
          [ID_FIRST + ID_CHECKFOUR];
     virtual void MyCancel(RTMessage Msg) =
          [ID_FIRST + ID_MYCANCEL];
     virtual void MyOk(RTMessage Msg) =
          [ID_FIRST + ID_MYOK];

};

_CLASSDEF(TDlgWindow)

class TDlgWindow : public TWindow
{
```

continues

Listing 12.16. continued

```
public:
  TDlgWindow(PTWindowsObject AParent, LPSTR ATitle);
  virtual void CMDlg(RTMessage Msg) =
    [CM_FIRST + CM_DLG];
};


class TDlgApp : public TApplication
{
public:
  TDlgApp(LPSTR AName, HANDLE hInstance, HANDLE
        hPrevInstance, LPSTR lpCmdLine, int nCmdShow) :
        TApplication(AName, hInstance, hPrevInstance,
        lpCmdLine, nCmdShow) {};
  virtual void InitMainWindow();
};


void TDlg::RadioOne(RTMessage)
{
WORD status;

status = IsDlgButtonChecked(HWindow,101);
if (status == 0)
     CheckDlgButton(HWindow,101,1);
else
     CheckDlgButton(HWindow,101,0);
}


void TDlg::RadioTwo(RTMessage)
{
WORD status;

status = IsDlgButtonChecked(HWindow,102);
if (status == 0)
     CheckDlgButton(HWindow,102,1);
else
     CheckDlgButton(HWindow,102,0);
}


void TDlg::CheckOne(RTMessage)
{
WORD status;
```

```
status = IsDlgButtonChecked(HWindow,103);
if (status == 0)
     CheckDlgButton(HWindow,103,1);
else
     CheckDlgButton(HWindow,103,0);
}


void TDlg::CheckTwo(RTMessage)
{
WORD status;

status = IsDlgButtonChecked(HWindow,104);
if (status == 0)
     CheckDlgButton(HWindow,104,1);
else
     CheckDlgButton(HWindow,104,0);
}


void TDlg::CheckThree(RTMessage)
{
WORD status;

status = IsDlgButtonChecked(HWindow,105);
if (status == 0)
     CheckDlgButton(HWindow,105,1);
else
     CheckDlgButton(HWindow,105,0);
}


void TDlg::CheckFour(RTMessage)
{
WORD status;

status = IsDlgButtonChecked(HWindow,106);
if (status == 0)
     CheckDlgButton(HWindow,106,1);
else
     CheckDlgButton(HWindow,106,0);
}

void TDlg::MyCancel(RTMessage)
{
CloseWindow(0);
}
```

continues

Listing 12.16. continued

```
void TDlg::MyOk(RTMessage)
{
CloseWindow(0);
}


TDlgWindow::TDlgWindow(PTWindowsObject AParent, LPSTR Title)
  : TWindow(AParent, Title)
{
AssignMenu("DlgMenu");
}


void TDlgWindow::CMDlg(RTMessage)
{
GetApplication()->ExecDialog(new TDlg(this, "DLG#1"));
}


void TDlgApp::InitMainWindow()
{
MainWindow = new TDlgWindow(NULL, "Dialogs");
}


int PASCAL WinMain(HANDLE hInstance, HANDLE hPrevInstance,
             LPSTR lpCmdLine, int nCmdShow)
{
  TDlgApp DlgApp("Dialogs", hInstance, hPrevInstance,
    lpCmdLine, nCmdShow);
  DlgApp.Run();
  return (DlgApp.Status);
}
```

You should first review the resource file. The resource file defines one menu with one menu item. The resource file also defines four check boxes, two radio buttons, an `OK` button, and a `Cancel` button for the dialog box.

Now you should examine the C++ source file. The first component of the code defines a derived class of `TDialog`—`TDlg`—that expects eight member functions to be defined, one for each of the buttons in the dialog box. Each member function should define the action for the corresponding button.

The second code component defines a derived class of `TWindow`—`TDlgWindow`. The `CMDlg` function is expected to be defined and should launch the dialog box when the one menu item is selected.

A derived class of `TApplication`—`TDlgApp`—is defined in the next component of the code.

The next eight code segments define the member functions for `TDlg`. Each function defines the default action for its corresponding button. For the radio buttons and check boxes, the state of the button is toggled. For the `OK` and `Cancel` buttons, the dialog box is terminated.

The next component of code constructs a `TDlgWindow` and loads the specified menu. The component following the `TDlgWindow` constructor defines the action for the `CMDlg` member function of `TDlgWindow`. When the appropriate menu item is selected, the dialog box is launched.

The next component constructs the main window object as an instance of `TDlgWindow`. The NULL parameter indicates that this is to be the main window. The second parameter, "Dialogs," specifies the window title.

The last component is the main program, which follows the same principal format as described in the basic window example earlier in this chapter. The output of this example is shown in Figure 12.10.

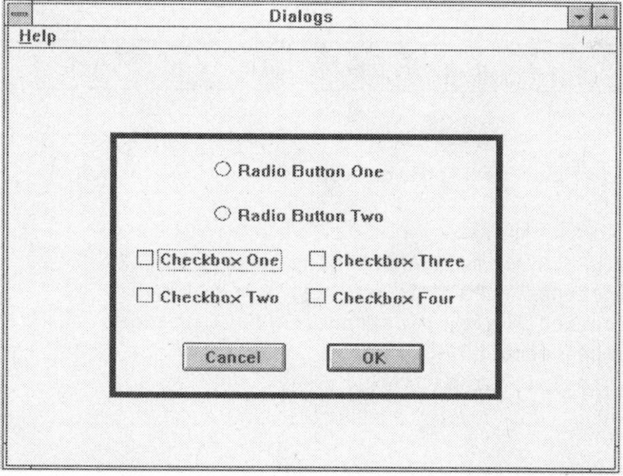

Figure 12.10. *The dialog example.*

Icon Example

The icon example is almost identical to the bitmap example. The only difference is that the icon example uses an icon created in Listings 4.13, 4.14, and 4.15 to represent the minimized application. The OBJ_ICON project was used to create this example. The code for the resource file is provided in Listing 12.17. The code for the C++ source file is provided in Listing 12.18. Figure 12.11 shows the output of this example.

Project Name: OBJ_ICON
Files in Project: OBJ_ICON.CPP
OBJ_ICON.RC
OWL.DEF
OWL.LIB
CRTLL.LIB

Listing 12.17. *Resource file for the icon example.*

```
FOOTBALL    BITMAP FOOTBALL.BMP
BASKET      BITMAP BASKET.BMP
GOLFBALL    BITMAP GOLFBALL.BMP
BASEBALL    BITMAP BASEBALL.BMP
SPORTS      ICON   SPORTS.ICO
```

Listing 12.18. *C++ source file for the icon example.*

```
#include <owl.h>

class TIconDemo : public TApplication
{
public:
     TIconDemo(LPSTR AName, HANDLE hInstance, HANDLE
        hPrevInstance, LPSTR lpCmdLine, int nCmdShow) :
        TApplication(AName, hInstance, hPrevInstance,
        lpCmdLine, nCmdShow) {};
     virtual void InitMainWindow();
};

_CLASSDEF(TIconWindow)

class TIconWindow : public TWindow
{
public:
     HBITMAP hFootball;
     HBITMAP hBasketball;
```

```
     HBITMAP hGolfball;
     HBITMAP hBaseball;

     TIconWindow(PTWindowsObject AParent, LPSTR AName) :
       TWindow (AParent, AName) {};
     virtual void GetWindowClass(WNDCLASS _FAR &
       AWndClass);
     virtual void Paint(HDC PaintDC, PAINTSTRUCT _FAR &
       PaintInfo);
};

void TIconWindow::GetWindowClass(WNDCLASS _FAR & AWndClass)
{
     TWindow::GetWindowClass(AWndClass);
     AWndClass.hIcon =  LoadIcon(GetApplication()->
        hInstance, "SPORTS");
}


void TIconWindow::Paint(HDC PaintDC, PAINTSTRUCT _FAR &
               PaintInfo)
{
     HDC hMemDC;

     hMemDC = CreateCompatibleDC(PaintInfo.hdc);

     hFootball = LoadBitmap(GetApplication()->
          hInstance,"FOOTBALL");
     hBasketball = LoadBitmap(GetApplication()->
          hInstance,"BASKET");
     hGolfball = LoadBitmap(GetApplication()->
          hInstance,"GOLFBALL");
     hBaseball = LoadBitmap(GetApplication()->
          hInstance,"BASEBALL");

     SelectObject(hMemDC,hFootball);
     BitBlt(PaintDC,30,50,72,72,hMemDC,0,0,SRCCOPY);

     SelectObject(hMemDC,hBasketball);
     BitBlt(PaintDC,130,100,72,72,hMemDC,0,0,SRCCOPY);

     SelectObject(hMemDC,hGolfball);
     BitBlt(PaintDC,230,150,72,72,hMemDC,0,0,SRCCOPY);

     SelectObject(hMemDC,hBaseball);
     BitBlt(PaintDC,330,200,72,72,hMemDC,0,0,SRCCOPY);

     DeleteDC(hMemDC);
}
```

continues

Listing 12.18. continued

```
void TIconDemo::InitMainWindow()
{
MainWindow = new TIconWindow(NULL, "Icon Demonstration");
}

int PASCAL WinMain(HANDLE hInstance, HANDLE hPrevInstance,
     LPSTR lpCmdLine, int nCmdShow)
{
TIconDemo IconDemo("Icon Window", hInstance, hPrevInstance,
   lpCmdLine, nCmdShow);
IconDemo.Run();
return(IconDemo.Status);
}
```

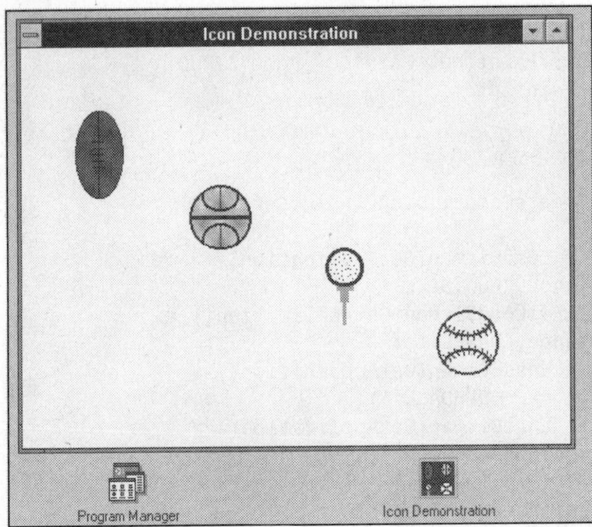

Figure 12.11. *The icon example.*

The resource file of this project simply defines four bitmaps and one icon that were previously created using the Whitewater Resource Toolkit and the Resource Workshop.

In the source file, a derived class of `TApplication`—`TIconDemo`—is defined in the first component of the code. The second component of the code defines a derived class of `TWindow`—`TIconWindow`—that creates handles for the bitmaps and expects the member functions `Paint` and `GetWindowClass` to be redefined.

The third code component redefines the `GetWindowClass` member function of `TIconWindow`. This member function loads the icon used to represent the minimized application.

The next component of the code redefines the `Paint` member function of `TIconWindow`. This member function loads and displays the bitmaps defined in the resource file.

The next component constructs the main window object as an instance of `TIconWindow`. The NULL parameter indicates that this is to be the main window. The second parameter, "Icon Demonstration," specifies the window title.

The last component is the main program that follows the same principal format as described in the basic window example earlier in this chapter. The output of this example is shown in Figure 12.11.

Menu Example

The menu example loads a menu resource and defines responses for each of the menu items. Each time a menu item is selected, a message box is displayed. The OBJ_MENU project was used to create this example. Listing 12.19 shows the resource file for this project. The code for the C++ source file is provided in Listing 12.20.

Project Name: `OBJ_MENU`
Files in Project: `OBJ_MENU.CPP`
`OBJ_MENU.RC`
`OWL.DEF`
`OWL.LIB`
`CTRLL.LIB`

Listing 12.19. Resource file for the menu example.

```
MENU  MENU LOADONCALL MOVEABLE PURE DISCARDABLE
BEGIN
  POPUP "Player One"
  BEGIN
    MenuItem  "Bob", 1
    MenuItem  "Mary", 2
    MenuItem  "John", 3
  END
  POPUP "Player Two"
  BEGIN
    MenuItem  "Gary", 4
    MenuItem  "Sue", 5
    MenuItem  "Jane", 6
  END
```

continues

Listing 12.19. continued

```
  POPUP "Game"
  BEGIN
    MenuItem  "Checkers", 7
    MenuItem  "Chess", 8
  END
END
```

Listing 12.20. C++ source file for the menu example.

```
#include <owl.h>

#define CM_BOB 1
#define CM_MARY 2
#define CM_JOHN 3
#define CM_GARY 4
#define CM_SUE 5
#define CM_JANE 6
#define CM_CHECKERS 7
#define CM_CHESS 8

class TMenuDemo : public TApplication
{

public:
     TMenuDemo(LPSTR AName, HANDLE hInstance, HANDLE
        hPrevInstance, LPSTR lpCmdLine, int nCmdShow) :
        TApplication(AName, hInstance, hPrevInstance,
        lpCmdLine, nCmdShow) {};
     virtual void InitMainWindow();
     virtual void InitInstance();
};

_CLASSDEF(TMenuWindow)

class TMenuWindow : public TWindow
{
public:
     TMenuWindow(PTWindowsObject AParent, LPSTR ATitle);
     virtual void CMBob(RTMessage Msg) =
          [CM_FIRST + CM_BOB];
     virtual void CMMary(RTMessage Msg) =
          [CM_FIRST + CM_MARY];
     virtual void CMJohn(RTMessage Msg) =
          [CM_FIRST + CM_JOHN];
     virtual void CMGary(RTMessage Msg) =
          [CM_FIRST + CM_GARY];
```

```
     virtual void CMSue(RTMessage Msg) =
          [CM_FIRST + CM_SUE];
     virtual void CMJane(RTMessage Msg) =
          [CM_FIRST + CM_JANE];
     virtual void CMCheckers(RTMessage Msg) =
          [CM_FIRST + CM_CHECKERS];
     virtual void CMChess(RTMessage Msg) =
          [CM_FIRST + CM_CHESS];
};


TMenuWindow::TMenuWindow(PTWindowsObject AParent,
     LPSTR ATitle) : TWindow(AParent, ATitle)
{
AssignMenu("MENU");
};

void TMenuDemo::InitMainWindow()
{
MainWindow = new TMenuWindow(NULL,"Menus");
}

void TMenuDemo::InitInstance()
{
TApplication::InitInstance();
}

void TMenuWindow::CMBob(RTMessage)
{
MessageBox(HWindow, "Bob","Player One",MB_OK);
}

void TMenuWindow::CMMary(RTMessage)
{
MessageBox(HWindow, "Mary","Player One",MB_OK);
}


void TMenuWindow::CMJohn(RTMessage)
{
MessageBox(HWindow, "John","Player One",MB_OK);
}


void TMenuWindow::CMGary(RTMessage)
{
MessageBox(HWindow, "Gary","Player Two",MB_OK);
}
```

continues

Listing 12.20. continued

```
void TMenuWindow::CMSue(RTMessage)
{
MessageBox(HWindow, "Sue","Player Two",MB_OK);
}


void TMenuWindow::CMJane(RTMessage)
{
MessageBox(HWindow, "Jane","Player Two",MB_OK);
}


void TMenuWindow::CMCheckers(RTMessage)
{
MessageBox(HWindow, "Checkers","Game",MB_OK);
}


void TMenuWindow::CMChess(RTMessage)
{
MessageBox(HWindow, "Chess","Game",MB_OK);
}

int PASCAL WinMain(HANDLE hInstance, HANDLE hPrevInstance,
     LPSTR lpCmdLine, int nCmdShow)
{
TMenuDemo MenuDemo("Menu Window", hInstance, hPrevInstance,
   lpCmdLine, nCmdShow);
MenuDemo.Run();
return(MenuDemo.Status);
}
```

You should quickly review the resource file. The resource file defines three menus: Player One, Player Two, and Game. Player One contains three items: Bob, Mary, and John. Player Two contains three items: Gary, Sue, and Jane. Game contains two items: Checkers and Chess.

Now you should examine the C++ source file. A derived class of `TApplication`—`TMenuDemo`—is defined in the first component of the code. The second component of the code defines a derived class of `TWindow`—`TMenuWindow`—that expects eight member functions to be defined. Each member function should define the action for a corresponding menu item selection.

The third component of the code constructs a `TMenuWindow`, loads the specified menu, and sets the state of each menu item.

The next component constructs the main window object as an instance of `TAcceleratorWindow`. The NULL parameter indicates that this is to be the main window. The second parameter, "Menus," specifies the window title.

The next component defines the `InitInstance` member function of the application object. This member function actually does nothing; however, it is included to indicate the location where an accelerator table would be loaded if one were defined and required.

The next eight code components define the actions to be taken for each of the menu items. The member functions correspond to an appropriate menu item. The member functions are automatically called in response to the command messages sent when a menu item is selected. Although these member functions only display message boxes, they could easily be redefined to perform more intricate, detailed operations.

The last component is the main program, which follows the same principal format as described in the basic window example. The output of this example is shown in Figure 12.12.

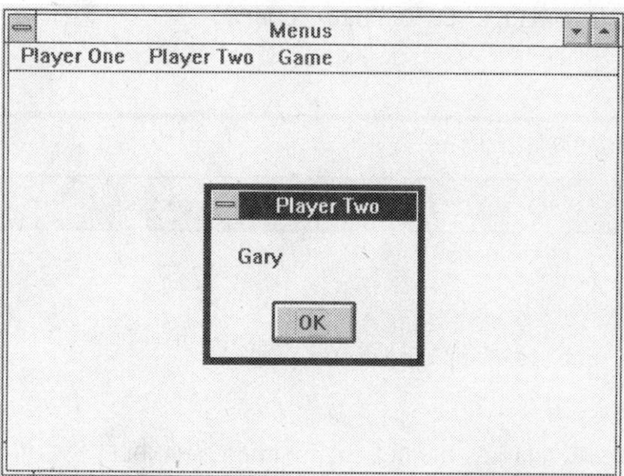

Figure 12.12. *The menu example.*

MDI Example

This example demonstrates a simple MDI application. Child windows can be created, tiled, cascaded, minimized, maximized, arranged, and closed. The OBJ_MDI project was used to create this example. Listing 12.21 shows the resource file for this project. The code for the C++ source file is provided in Listing 12.22.

Project Name: `OBJ_MDI`

Files in Project:
```
OBJ_MDI.CPP
OBJ_MDI.RC
OWL.DEF
OWL.LIB
CTRLL.LIB
```

Listing 12.21. Resource file for the MDI example.

```
#include <windows.h>
#include <owlrc.h>

MENU  MENU
BEGIN
  POPUP "MDI Menu"
  BEGIN
    MENUITEM  "Create Child", CM_CREATECHILD,
    MENUITEM  "Tile", CM_TILECHILDREN,
    MENUITEM  "Cascade", CM_CASCADECHILDREN,
    MENUITEM  "Arrange Icons", CM_ARRANGEICONS,
    MENUITEM  "Close All", CM_CLOSECHILDREN,
  END
END
```

Listing 12.22. C++ source file for the MDI example.

```
#include <owl.h>
#include <mdi.h>

class TMDIDemo : public TApplication
{
public:
     TMDIDemo(LPSTR AName, HANDLE hInstance, HANDLE
        hPrevInstance, LPSTR lpCmdLine, int nCmdShow) :
        TApplication(AName, hInstance, hPrevInstance,
        lpCmdLine, nCmdShow) {};
     virtual void InitMainWindow();
};

class TMDIDemoFrame : public TMDIFrame
{
WORD ChildNum;

public:
     TMDIDemoFrame(LPSTR ATitle, LPSTR AMenu);
```

```
    virtual PTWindowsObject InitChild();
};


void TMDIDemo::InitMainWindow()
{
MainWindow = new TMDIDemoFrame("MDI","MENU");
}


TMDIDemoFrame::TMDIDemoFrame(LPSTR ATitle, LPSTR AMenu)
          : TMDIFrame(ATitle, AMenu) {};


PTWindowsObject TMDIDemoFrame::InitChild()
{
return new TWindow(this, "Child");
}


int PASCAL WinMain(HANDLE hInstance, HANDLE hPrevInstance,
     LPSTR lpCmdLine, int nCmdShow)
{
TMDIDemo MDIDemo("MDI Demo Window", hInstance, hPrevInstance,
   lpCmdLine, nCmdShow);
MDIDemo.Run();
return(MDIDemo.Status);
}
```

The resource file defines the menu for the MDI application. The menu contains five items: Create Child, Tile, Cascade, Arrange Icons, and Close All.

The source file begins by defining a derived class of `TApplication`—`TMDIDemo`. The second code segment of the file defines a derived class of `TMDIWindow`—`TMDIDemoWindow`. The member function `InitChild` is expected to be redefined.

The next component constructs the main window object as an instance of `TMDIDemoWindow` and loads the menu. The next code segment constructs a `TMDIDemoWindow` and defines `ChildNum`. The definition of `TMDIDemoWindow::InitChild` follows. Lastly, the main program is called.

You may have noticed that although a menu was defined, no member functions were defined to handle the actions required of the menu items. ObjectWindows defines several member functions that automatically handle the manipulation of MDI child windows including the creation, tiling, and cascading of child windows and the arranging of icons. This saves you a great deal of work! To realize the amount of work that ObjectWindows can save, you should review the MDI example in Chapter 9.

An MDI application is very flexible and several *screen dumps* (that is, "dumps" of screens or screen shots) of the resulting application have been included. Figure 12.13 illustrates one open window and one minimized window. Figure 12.14 illustrates the result of choosing the Arrange Icons menu item with several minimized child windows. Figure 12.15 illustrates the results of the Tile menu item with four open windows. Figure 12.16 illustrates the results of the Cascade menu item when four windows are open. Figure 12.17 illustrates a maximized MDI child window.

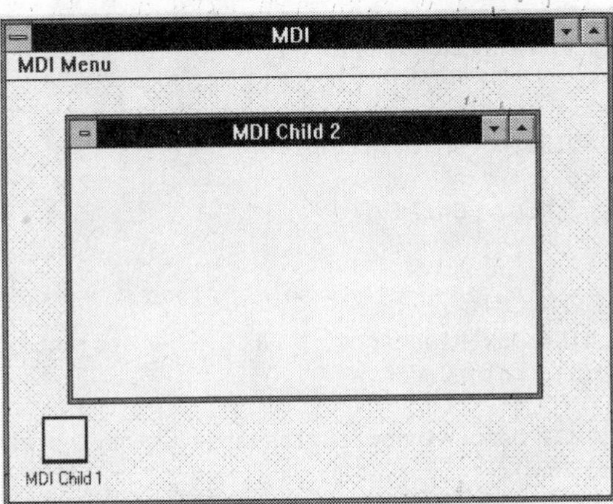

Figure 12.13. *The MDI example.*

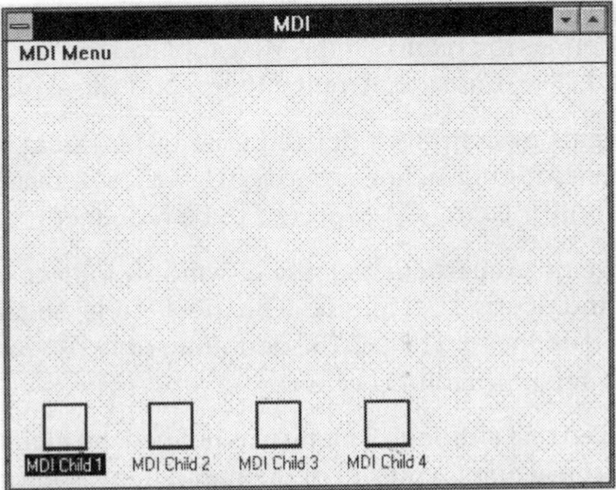

Figure 12.14. *The Arrange Icons option of the MDI example.*

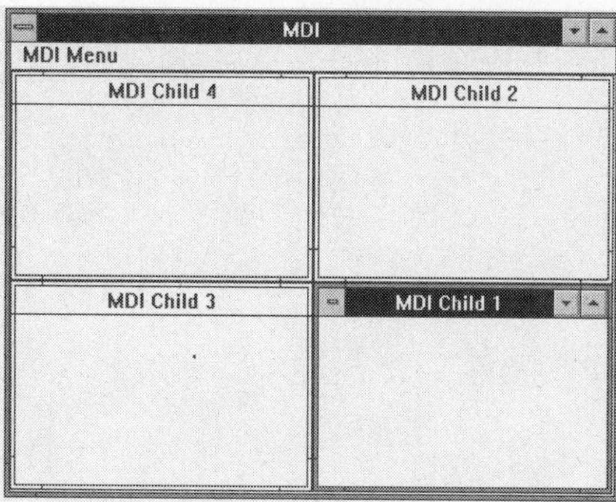

Figure 12.15. *The Tile option of the MDI example.*

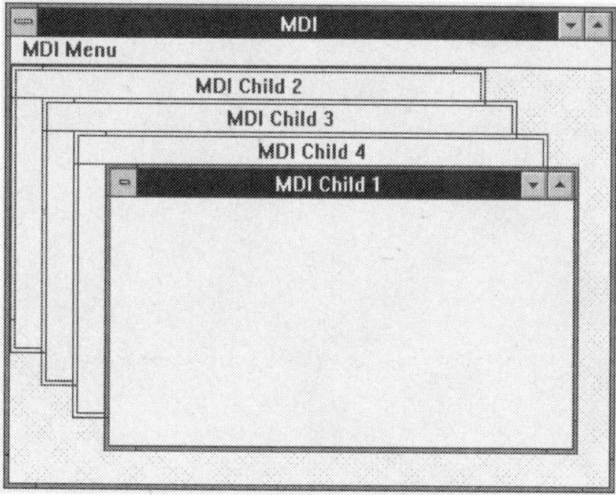

Figure 12.16. *The Cascade option of the MDI example.*

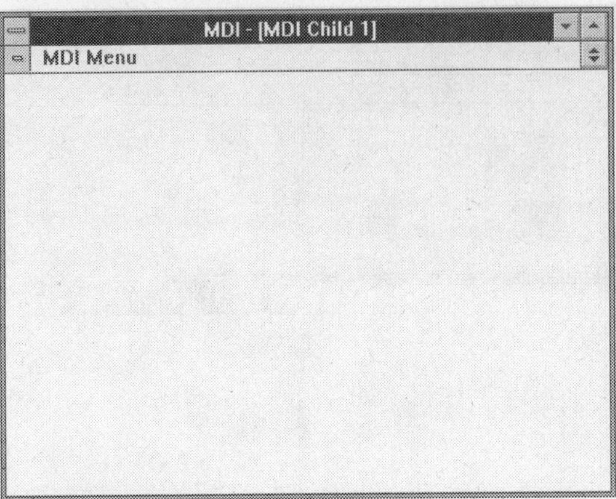

Figure 12.17. *A maximized MDI child window.*

III

Reference

13

Windows Functions

This chapter introduces the Windows functions. Windows functions are part of the C or C++ programs generated with Borland C++ when creating Windows applications. These functions let you take advantage of the Windows user interface, graphics, and memory management capabilities.

The Windows functions will be presented in three broad categories: Window Manager Interface functions, Graphics Device Interface functions, and System Services Interface functions. Each of these categories is further divided into subcategories.

Appendix A lists the Windows functions alphabetically. The function category and a brief function description is provided for each listed function. This list lets you review the relationships between function categories quickly as it indexes the location of each function's description.

Each function is described in the following format:

FunctionName

Syntax:

This section gives the syntax for the function.

Parameter, Type, and Description:

This section lists each of the function's parameters, with the parameter type and a brief description of its function.

Description:

This section gives a full description of the function.

Return Value:

This section describes the function's return value, if any.

This format provides helpful information on the purpose and use of the Windows functions.

Windows Data Types

The functions listed in this chapter and the messages listed in Chapter 14 refer to various data types used by Windows. These data types include:

Data Type	*Meaning*
BOOL	16-bit Boolean value
BYTE	8-bit unsigned integer
char	ASCII character or 8-bit signed integer
DWORD	32-bit unsigned integer or segment/offset address
FAR	Data-type attribute used to create a long pointer
FARPROC	Long pointer to a function retrieved by calling MakeProcInstance
GLOBALHANDLE	Global memory handle—16-bit index
HANDLE	General handle—16-bit index
HBITMAP	Bitmap handle—16-bit index
HBRUSH	Brush handle—16-bit index
HCURSOR	Cursor handle—16-bit index
HDC	Display context handle—16-bit index
HFONT	Font handle—16-bit index
HICON	Icon handle—16-bit index

Data Type	*Meaning*
HMENU	Menu handle—16-bit index
HPALETTE	Palette handle—16-bit index
HPEN	Pen handle—16-bit index
HRGN	Region handle—16-bit index
HSTR	String handle—16-bit index
int	16-bit signed integer
LOCALHANDLE	Local memory handle—16-bit index
long	32-bit signed integer
LONG	32-bit signed integer
LPBITMAP	Long pointer to BITMAP data structure
LPBITMAPCOREHEADER	Long pointer to BITMAPCOREHEADER data structure
LPBITMAPCOREINFO	Long pointer to BITMAPCOREINFO data structure
LPBITMAPFILEHEADER	Long pointer to BITMAPFILEHEADER data structure
LPBITMAPINFO	Long pointer to BITMAPINFO data structure
LPBITMAPINFOHEADER	Long pointer to BITMAPINFOHEADER data structure
LPCOMPAREITEMSTRUCT	Long pointer to COMPAREITEMSTRUCT data structure
LPCREATESTRUCT	Long pointer to CREATESTRUCT data structure
LPDELETEITEMSTRUCT	Long pointer to DELETEITEMSTRUCT data structure
LPDRAWITEMSTRUCT	Long pointer to DRAWITEMSTRUCT data structure
LPHANDLETABLE	Long pointer to HANDLETABLE data structure
LPINT	Long pointer to 16-bit signed integer
LPLOGBRUSH	Long pointer to LOGBRUSH data structure
LPLOGFONT	Long pointer to LOGFONT data structure
LPLOGPALETTE	Long pointer to LOGPALETTE data structure
LPLOGPEN	Long pointer to LOGPEN data structure
LPMEASUREITEMSTRUCT	Long pointer to MEASUREITEMSTRUCT data structure
LPMETAFILEPICT	Long pointer to METAFILEPICT data structure
LPMSG	Long pointer to MSG data structure
LPOFSTRUCT	Long pointer to OFSTRUCT data structure
LPPAINTSTRUCT	Long pointer to PAINTSTRUCT data structure
LPPALETTEENTRY	Long pointer to PALETTEENTRY data structure
LPPOINT	Long pointer to POINT data structure
LPRECT	Long pointer to RECT data structure
LPRESOURCELIST	Long pointer to one or more RESOURCESTRUCT data structures
LPSTR	Long pointer to a character string

Data Type	*Meaning*
`LPTEXTMETRIC`	Long pointer to `TEXTMETRIC` data structure
`LPVOID`	Long pointer to an undefined data type
`LPWNDCLASS`	Long pointer to `WNDCLASS` data structure
`NEAR`	Data type attribute used to create a short pointer
`NPSTR`	Near pointer to a character string
`PINT`	Pointer to a 16-bit signed integer
`PSTR`	Pointer to a character string
`PWORD`	Pointer to a 16-bit unsigned integer
`short`	16-bit signed integer
`void`	Empty value
`WORD`	16-bit unsigned integer

The rest of this chapter describes the Windows functions for the Window Manager Interface, the Graphics Device Interface, and the System Services Interface.

Window Manager Interface Functions

Window Manager Interface functions let you process messages, create a window, size and move a window, perform system output, and do many other window-oriented tasks. The Window Manager Interface functions are divided into the following subcategories (documented in Appendix A):

- Caret
- Clipboard
- Cursor
- Dialog Box
- Display and Movement
- Error
- Hardware
- Information
- Input
- Menu
- Message
- Painting
- Property
- Rectangle
- Scrolling
- System
- Window Creation

Caret Functions

A caret is a blinking line, block, or bitmap that indicates a location inside the window's client area. The caret can be practically any pattern and any color.

The caret is shown by inverting the pixels of a rectangular region, which is defined in logical units. The inverted pixels are restored to their original values at specified intervals to give the caret a blinking effect. The interval between inversion and restoration of the caret pixels is called the ***blink time***.

Only one caret shape can be active at any one time. The active caret is shared among applications. Therefore, a window should manipulate the caret only when that window has the input focus. The `CreateBitmap` function creates the bitmap for a caret. The `LoadBitmap` function loads an application resource for the caret. You can create the bitmaps for the caret with the Whitewater Resource Toolkit, which is included with Borland C++.

The following functions are categorized as Caret functions for the Window Manager Interface:

Function	*Meaning*
`CreateCaret`	Creates a caret
`DestroyCaret`	Destroys a caret
`GetCaretBlinkTime`	Gets the caret blink time
`GetCaretPos`	Gets the position of the caret
`HideCaret`	Removes the caret from a window
`SetCaretBlinkTime`	Sets the caret blink time
`SetCaretPos`	Moves the caret to the specified position
`ShowCaret`	Displays a new caret or redisplays a hidden caret

The rest of this section provides detailed information on each of the functions in this list.

CreateCaret

Syntax:

```
void CreateCaret(hWnd, hBitmap, nWidth, nHeight)
```

Parameter, Type, and Description:

`hWnd`	`HWND`	The window that owns the caret

`hBitmap`	`HBITMAP`	Bitmap identification for the caret shape. When `Bitmap` = NULL, the caret is solid. When `Bitmap` = 1, the caret is gray.
`nWidth`	`int`	Width of the caret in logical units
`nHeight`	`int`	Height of the caret in logical units

Description:

The `CreateCaret` function creates a new shape for the system caret. The caret is owned by the window specified in `hWnd`.

`Bitmap` defines the new shape of the caret. When `hBitmap` is a bitmap handle created with `CreateBitmap`, `CreateDIBitmap`, or `LoadBitmap`, `nWidth` and `nHeight` are determined automatically. For any other value of `Bitmap`, `nWidth` and `nHeight` define the number of logical units in the caret's width and height, respectively. By setting `nWidth` and/or `nHeight` to 0, the width and/or height of the caret are automatically set to the dimensions of the window's border.

Return Value:

There is no return value.

DestroyCaret

Syntax:

```
void DestroyCaret()
```

Description:

The `DestroyCaret` function destroys the current caret shape. The caret is destroyed only if a window in the current task owns the caret. In the process of destroying the caret this function both frees the caret from the window that owns it and clears it from the screen.

Return Value:

There is no return value.

GetCaretBlinkTime

Syntax:

```
WORD GetCaretBlinkTime()
```

Description:

The `GetCaretBlinkTime` function gets the blink rate of the caret, measured in milliseconds.

Return Value:

The `GetCaretBlinkTime` function returns the caret blink rate, measured in milliseconds.

GetCaretPos

Syntax:

```
void GetCaretPos(lpPoint)
```

Parameter, Type, and Description:

`lpPoint`	`LPPOINT`	Pointer to the `POINT` data structure that stores the retrieved screen coordinates

Description:

The `GetCaretPos` function retrieves the screen coordinates of the caret's current position. `lpPoint` points to the data structure of type `POINT` that holds the retrieved coordinates. The `POINT` structure is:

```
typedef struct tagPOINT {
     int x;
     int y;
} POINT;
```

where:

`x` specifies the horizontal coordinate of the caret position

`y` specifies the vertical coordinate of the caret position

Return Value:

There is no return value.

HideCaret

Syntax:

```
void HideCaret(hWnd)
```

Parameter, Type, and Description:

`hWnd`	`HWND`	The window that owns the caret

Description:

The `HideCaret` function removes the caret from the screen. The caret shape is not destroyed; the `ShowCaret` function can redisplay the caret on the screen.

`hWnd` specifies the window that owns the caret. When `hWnd` is NULL, the caret is hidden only if a window in the current task owns the caret.

For every call to the `HideCaret` function, there must be a corresponding call to the `ShowCaret` function before the caret will be made visible. For example, if you call `HideCaret` three times, you must also call `ShowCaret` three times before the caret is shown.

Return Value:

There is no return value.

SetCaretBlinkTime

Syntax:

```
void SetCaretBlinkTime(wMSeconds)
```

Parameter, Type, and Description:

`wMSeconds`	`WORD`	New blink rate, measured in milliseconds

Description:

The `SetCaretBlinkTime` function defines the caret blink rate. The blink rate is set to the number of milliseconds specified in `wMSeconds`.

Return Value:

There is no return value.

SetCaretPos

Syntax:

```
void SetCaretPos(X, Y)
```

Parameter, Type, and Description:

`X`	`int`	Horizontal logical coordinate
`Y`	`int`	Vertical logical coordinate

Description:

The `SetCaretPos` function places the caret at the position specified in `X` and `Y`. `X` and `Y` are expressed in logical coordinates. The caret is moved only if it's owned by a window in the current task.

Return Value:

There is no return value.

ShowCaret

Syntax:

```
void ShowCaret(hWnd)
```

Parameter, Type, and Description:

`hWnd`	`HWND`	Window that owns the caret

Description:

The `ShowCaret` function displays the caret at its current position. The caret is not shown if:

- A shape is not defined
- The caret was hidden two or more times
- The caret is not owned by the window in `hWnd`
- `hWnd` is NULL and no window in the current task owns the caret

The `ShowCaret` function must be called for every call to the `HideCaret` function before the caret will be shown. For example, if you call `HideCaret` three times, you must also call `ShowCaret` three times before the caret is shown.

Return Value:

There is no return value.

Clipboard Functions

The clipboard is provided by Windows as temporary storage. The clipboard enables you to exchange data among applications and provides cut-and-paste capabilities for applications. The following functions are classified as Clipboard functions for the Window Manager Interface:

Function	*Meaning*
`ChangeClipboardChain`	Removes a window from the clipboard viewer chain
`CloseClipboard`	Closes the clipboard
`CountClipboardFormats`	Gets the number of formats the clipboard can render
`EmptyClipboard`	Empties the clipboard
`EnumClipboardFormats`	Enumerates all the clipboard formats available
`GetClipboardData`	Gets data from the clipboard
`GetClipboardFormatName`	Gets the format for the clipboard
`GetClipboardOwner`	Gets the window handle associated with the clipboard owner
`GetClipboardViewer`	Gets the handle of the first window in the clipboard viewer chain
`GetPriorityClipboardFormat`	Gets data in the first format from a prioritized format list
`IsClipboardFormatAvailable`	Determines whether data is available in the specified format
`OpenClipboard`	Opens the clipboard
`RegisterClipboardFormat`	Registers a new clipboard format
`SetClipboardData`	Copies a handle for data
`SetClipboardViewer`	Adds a handle to the clipboard viewer chain

The rest of this section provides detailed information on each of the functions in this list.

ChangeClipboardChain

Syntax:

```
BOOL ChangeClipboardChain(hWnd, hWndNext)
```

Parameter, Type, and Description:

`hWnd`	`HWND`	Window to be removed from the chain
`hWndNext`	`HWND`	Window following `hWnd`

Description:

The `ChangeClipboardChain` function removes the window specified in `hWnd` from the clipboard chain of viewers. The window specified in `hWndNext` follows the window specified in `hWnd` on the clipboard chain of viewers.

Return Value:

The `ChangeClipboardChain` function returns a nonzero value when the window in `hWnd` is found and removed. A return value of zero indicates that the window in `hWnd` was not found and removed.

CloseClipboard

Syntax:

```
BOOL CloseClipboard()
```

Description:

The `CloseClipboard` function closes the clipboard. To let other applications access and use the clipboard, you should call this function after a window is finished using the clipboard.

Return Value:

The `CloseClipboard` function returns a nonzero value if the clipboard is closed. A return value of zero indicates that the clipboard is not closed.

CountClipboardFormats

Syntax:

```
int CountClipboardFormats()
```

Description:

The `CountClipboardFormats` function gets the number of formats the clipboard can render.

Return Value:

The `CountClipboardFormats` function returns the number of data formats in the clipboard.

EmptyClipboard

Syntax:

```
BOOL EmptyClipboard()
```

Description:

The `EmptyClipboard` function empties the clipboard. All data handles in the clipboard are freed. Ownership of the clipboard is assigned to the window that has currently opened the clipboard. The clipboard must be open when calling this function.

Return Value:

The `EmptyClipboard` function returns a nonzero value when the clipboard is emptied. A return code of zero indicates that this function can't empty the clipboard.

EnumClipboardFormats

Syntax:

```
WORD EnumClipboardFormats(wFormat)
```

Parameter, Type, and Description:

`wFormat`	`WORD`	Known available format

Description:

The `EnumClipboardFormats` function enumerates the available formats that belong to the clipboard.

To use this function, the clipboard must be open.

Return Value:

The return value depends on the setting of `wFormat`:

- When `wFormat` is zero, this function returns the first format in the clipboard format list.
- When `wFormat` specifies a known format, this function returns the next available format.

- When `wFormat` specifies the last available format or the clipboard is not open, this function returns a zero.

GetClipboardData

Syntax:

```
HANDLE GetClipboardData(wFormat)
```

Parameter, Type, and Description:

`wFormat`	`WORD`	Data format

Description:

The `GetClipboardData` function gets clipboard data in the format specified in `wFormat`. Determine the formats available for the clipboard by using the `EnumClipboardFormats` function. Two text formats are supported: `CF_TEXT` (the default), and `CF_OEMTEXT` (used for non-Windows applications).

Return Value:

The `GetClipboardData` function returns the identifier for the block containing the clipboard data. NULL indicates an error.

GetClipboardFormatName

Syntax:

```
int GetClipboardFormatName(wFormat, lpFormatName, nMaxCount)
```

Parameter, Type, and Description:

`wFormat`	`WORD`	Format type to retrieve
`lpFormatName`	`LPSTR`	Pointer to buffer where format name is copied
`nMaxCount`	`int`	Maximum number of bytes for the format name

Description:

The `GetClipboardFormatName` function gets the name of the format specified in `wFormat`, which cannot specify any of the predefined clipboard formats. `lpFormatName` points to the buffer where the format name will be stored. `nMaxCount` specifies the maximum length of the buffer.

Return Value:

The `GetClipboardFormatName` function returns the number of bytes copied to the buffer. A return value of zero indicates that the requested format is invalid.

GetClipboardOwner

Syntax:

```
HWND GetClipboardOwner()
```

Description:

The `GetClipboardOwner` function gets the handle of the clipboard's current owner.

Return Value:

The `GetClipboardOwner` function returns the identifier for the window that currently owns the clipboard. A NULL return value indicates that no window owns the clipboard.

GetClipboardViewer

Syntax:

```
HWND GetClipboardViewer()
```

Description:

The `GetClipboardViewer` function retrieves the handle of the first window in the clipboard viewer chain.

Return Value:

The `GetClipboardViewer` function returns the retrieved window handle. A NULL return value indicates that no viewer is in the clipboard viewer chain.

GetPriorityClipboardFormat

Syntax:

```
int GetPriorityClipboardFormat(lpPriorityList, nCount)
```

Parameter, Type, and Description:

`lpPriorityList`	`WORD FAR *`	Pointer to list of clipboard formats in priority order
`nCount`	`int`	Number of items in priority list

Description:

The `GetPriorityClipboardFormat` function retrieves the first entry in the prioritized clipboard format list. `lpPriorityList` points to the array that contains the list of prioritized clipboard formats. `nCount` specifies the number of items in the priority list.

Return Value:

The `GetPriorityClipboardFormat` function returns the clipboard format with the highest priority from the clipboard format list. A NULL return value indicates that no data exists in the clipboard. A return value of –1 indicates that the data in the clipboard doesn't match any format in the clipboard format list.

IsClipboardFormatAvailable

Syntax:

```
BOOL IsClipboardFormatAvailable(wFormat)
```

Parameter, Type, and Description:

`wFormat`	`WORD`	Clipboard format—must be registered

Description:

The `IsClipboardFormatAvailable` function determines whether data of a specified format exists on the clipboard. `wFormat` specifies the clipboard format to check for.

Return Value:

The `IsClipboardFormatAvailable` function returns TRUE when data matching the specified format exists in the clipboard. A return value of FALSE indicates that no matching data is found.

OpenClipboard

Syntax:

```
BOOL OpenClipboard(hWnd)
```

Parameter, Type, and Description:

`hWnd`	`HWND`	Window to access the clipboard

Description:

The `OpenClipboard` function allows the window specified in `hWnd` to gain access to the contents of the clipboard. No other application can modify the clipboard until the `CloseClipboard` function is called.

Return Value:

The `OpenClipboard` function returns a nonzero value when the clipboard is opened. A return value of zero indicates that the clipboard cannot be opened or is being used by another application.

RegisterClipboardFormat

Syntax:

```
WORD RegisterClipboardFormat(lpFormatName)
```

Parameter, Type, and Description:

`lpFormatName`	`LPSTR`	Name of the new clipboard format

Description:

The `RegisterClipboardFormat` function registers a new clipboard format. `lpFormatName` points to the name of the new format. The name is a null-terminated character string. The new format will be added to the format list for the clipboard.

Return Value:

The `RegisterClipboardFormat` function returns a value identifying the new clipboard format when the format is registered. This value will be in the range 0xC000 to 0xFFFF.

A return value of zero indicates that the format cannot be registered.

SetClipboardData

Syntax:

```
HANDLE SetClipboardData(wFormat, hMem)
```

Parameter, Type, and Description:

wFormat	WORD	Data format
hMem	HANDLE	Global memory block containing data

Description:

The SetClipboardData function defines a data handle for the data specified in hMem. After the SetClipboardData function is called, the specified data becomes the property of the clipboard.

wFormat specifies the format of the data. Format values for wFormat can be any obtained with the RegisterClipboardFormat function or from the following list:

Format	*Meaning*
CF_BITMAP	Handle to a bitmap
CF_DIB	Block containing a BITMAPINFO data structure and the bitmap
CF_DIF	Software Art's Data Interchange Format
CF_DSPBITMAP	Bitmap format corresponding to a private format
CF_DSPMETAFILEPICT	Metafile format corresponding to a private format
CF_DSPTEXT	Text display format corresponding to a private format
CF_METAFILEPICT	Metafile defined by the METAFILEPICT structure
CF_OEMTEXT	Text format using the OEM character set
CF_OWNERDISPLAY	Owner display format
CF_PALETTE	Color palette handle
CF_PRIVATEFIRST	Used for private formats to CF_PRIVATELAST
CF_SYLK	Microsoft Symbolic Link Format
CF_TEXT	Text format
CF_TIFF	Tag Image File Format

Return Value:

The SetClipboardData function returns the data handle for the specified data.

SetClipboardViewer

Syntax:

```
HWND SetClipboardViewer(hWnd)
```

Parameter, Type, and Description:

hWnd	HWND	Window to be added to chain

Description:

The SetClipboardViewer function puts the window specified in hWnd on the chain of windows notified when the clipboard is modified. This function is notified by the WM_DRAWCLIPBOARD message when the contents of the clipboard are modified.

Return Value:

The SetClipboardViewer function returns the handle for the next window in the chain. This value should be used to respond to clipboard-viewer chain messages.

Cursor Functions

Cursor functions manipulate the various aspects of the cursor. The cursor is a bitmap indicating the current position of the mouse. Windows automatically moves the cursor whenever mouse input is received. The following functions are categorized as Cursor functions for the Window Manager Interface:

Function	*Meaning*
ClipCursor	Confines the cursor to a rectangular region
CreateCursor	Creates a cursor from two bit-masks
DestroyCursor	Destroys a cursor
GetCursorPos	Gets the screen coordinates of the cursor position
LoadCursor	Loads a cursor from a resource file
SetCursor	Sets the shape of the cursor
SetCursorPos	Moves the cursor to the specified position
ShowCursor	Either increases or decreases the cursor display count

The rest of this section provides detailed information on each of the functions in this list.

ClipCursor

Syntax:

```
void ClipCursor(lpRect)
```

Parameter, Type, and Description:

lpRect	LPRECT	Pointer to RECT data structure that contains the rectangle coordinates

Description:

The ClipCursor function restricts the movement of the cursor to the rectangular region defined by lpRect. lpRect points to a structure of type RECT, which holds the screen coordinates of the upper-left and lower-right corners of the rectangular region. When lpRect is set to NULL, the confining rectangular region is defined as the entire screen.

The RECT structure is:

```
typedef struct tagRECT{
     int left;
     int top;
     int right;
     int bottom;
} RECT;
```

where:

left is the x-coordinate of the upper-left corner

top is the y-coordinate of the upper-left corner

right is the x-coordinate of the lower-right corner

bottom is the y-coordinate of the lower-right corner

Return Value:

There is no return value.

CreateCursor

Syntax:

```
HCURSOR CreateCursor(hInstance, nXhotspot, nYhotspot, nWidth,
                     nHeight, lpANDbitPlane, lpXORbitPlane)
```

Parameter, Type, and Description:

hInstance	HANDLE	Module creating the cursor
nXhotspot	int	Horizontal position of hotspot
nYhotspot	int	Vertical position of hotspot
nWidth	int	Cursor width in pixels

`nHeight`	`int`	Cursor height in pixels
`lpANDbitPlane`	`LPSTR`	Pointer to the array containing an AND mask for the cursor
`lpXORbitPlane`	`LPSTR`	Pointer to the array containing an XOR mask for the cursor

Description:

The `CreateCursor` function creates the specified cursor. `hInstance` specifies the module that is creating the cursor. The cursor hotspot is defined by the horizontal and vertical positions specified in `nXhotspot` and `nYhotspot`, respectively. `nWidth` defines the cursor width in pixels. `nHeight` defines the cursor height in pixels. `lpANDbitPlane` points to the array that contains the AND mask for the cursor. `lpXORbitPlane` points to the array which contains the XOR mask for the cursor.

Return Value:

The `CreateCursor` function returns the handle of the created cursor. A NULL return value indicates that the cursor was not created.

DestroyCursor

Syntax:

```
BOOL DestroyCursor(hCursor)
```

Parameter, Type, and Description:

`hCursor`	`HCURSOR`	Cursor to be destroyed

Description:

The `DestroyCursor` function destroys the cursor specified in `hCursor`. `hCursor` should only identify a cursor created by the `CreateCursor` function. Do not use `DestroyCursor` to destroy cursors not created with the `CreateCursor` function.

Return Value:

The `DestroyCursor` function returns a nonzero value when the cursor is destroyed. A return value of zero indicates that the cursor was not destroyed.

GetCursorPos

Syntax:

```
void GetCursorPos(lpPoint)
```

Parameter, Type, and Description:

lpPoint	LPPOINT	Pointer to POINT data structure where the cursor coordinates are stored

Description:

The GetCursorPos function retrieves the screen coordinates of the current cursor position. These screen coordinates then are placed in a structure of type POINT, pointed to by lpPoint. The POINT structure is:

```
typedef struct tagPOINT {
     int x;
     int y;
} POINT;
```

where:

x is the x screen coordinate of the cursor

y is the y screen coordinate of the cursor

Return Value:

There is no return value.

LoadCursor

Syntax:

```
HCURSOR LoadCursor(hInstance, lpCursorName)
```

Parameter, Type, and Description:

hInstance	HANDLE	Module whose executable contains the cursor
lpCursorName	LPSTR	Pointer to the name of the cursor resource

Description:

The LoadCursor function loads the cursor specified in lpCursorName. lpCursorName points to a null-terminated character string that holds the name of the cursor resource.

hInstance specifies the module that has the executable file containing the cursor resource.

Access the predefined Windows cursors with the LoadCursor function by setting hInstance to NULL and lpCursorName to one of these values:

Constant	*Meaning*
`IDC_ARROW`	Arrow cursor
`IDC_CROSS`	Cross hair cursor
`IDC_IBEAM`	I-beam text cursor
`IDC_ICON`	Empty icon
`IDC_SIZE`	Square with small square in lower-right corner
`IDC_SIZENESW`	Cursor with arrows pointing northeast and southwest
`IDC_SIZENS`	Cursor with arrows pointing north and south
`IDC_SIZENWSE`	Cursor with arrows pointing northwest and southeast
`IDC_SIZEWE`	Cursor with arrows pointing west and east
`IDC_UPARROW`	Vertical arrow cursor
`IDC_WAIT`	Hourglass cursor

Return Value:

The `LoadCursor` function returns the handle of the loaded cursor. A NULL return value indicates that the cursor is not loaded.

Note: If `lpCursorName` specifies a resource type other than a cursor resource, the return value will be an invalid cursor handle.

SetCursor

Syntax:

```
HCURSOR SetCursor(hCursor)
```

Parameter, Type, and Description:

`hCursor`	`HCURSOR`	Cursor resource

Description:

The `SetCursor` function redefines the shape of the cursor. The cursor is set to the shape specified in `hCursor`. `hCursor` must identify a resource that has been loaded with the `LoadCursor` function. If `hCursor` is NULL, the cursor is removed from the screen.

Return Value:

The `SetCursor` function returns the handle identifying the previous cursor shape. A NULL return value indicates that no previous shape exists.

SetCursorPos

Syntax:

```
void SetCursorPos(X, Y)
```

Parameter, Type, and Description:

X	int	X screen coordinate of cursor
Y	int	Y screen coordinate of cursor

Description:

The `SetCursorPos` function places the cursor at the screen coordinates specified in `X` and `Y`. `X` specifies the horizontal screen coordinate of the cursor; `Y` specifies the vertical screen coordinate of the cursor.

Return Value:

There is no return value.

ShowCursor

Syntax:

```
int ShowCursor(bShow)
```

Parameter, Type, and Description:

bShow	BOOL	Effect on display count

Description:

The `ShowCursor` function either hides or shows the cursor, depending on the setting of the cursor display counter. The cursor display counter is an internally maintained value that you modify by calling the `ShowCursor` function.

The direction of the modification is determined by `bShow`. The initial value of the display counter is zero when a mouse is installed and –1 when no mouse is installed. If `bShow` is a nonzero value, the display counter is incremented when `ShowCursor` is called. If `bShow` is zero, the display counter is decremented when `ShowCursor` is called. Whenever the display counter is equal to or greater than zero, the cursor is displayed.

Return Value:

The `ShowCursor` function returns the value of the cursor display counter.

Dialog Box Functions

Many applications use dialog boxes for user input. Using a dialog box is often advantageous because it can be customized for specialized input and destroyed after use.

There are three basic types of dialog boxes:

- The *modeless* dialog box accepts user input and lets the user return to the previous task without removing the dialog box.
- The *modal* dialog box accepts user input but requires the user respond to any requests in the dialog box before continuing. Only the parent window of the modal dialog box is disabled.
- The *system modal* dialog box is like a modal box, except that all windows are disabled.

Windows provides a series of functions for the manipulation of dialog boxes and their corresponding controls. The following functions are categorized as dialog box functions for the Window Manager Interface:

Function	*Meaning*
`CheckDlgButton`	Modifies the state of a button
`CheckRadioButton`	Puts a check beside a button while removing the check from all other buttons in the group
`CreateDialog`	Creates a modeless dialog box
`CreateDialogIndirect`	Creates a modeless dialog box from a template
`CreateDialogIndirectParam`	Creates a modeless dialog box from a template and passes initialization data
`CreateDialogParam`	Creates a modeless dialog box and passes initialization data
`DefDlgProc`	Processes messages that a dialog box with a private window class cannot process
`DialogBox`	Creates a modal dialog box
`DialogBoxIndirect`	Creates a modal dialog box from a template
`DialogBoxIndirectParam`	Creates a modal dialog box from a template and passes initialization data
`DialogBoxParam`	Creates a modal dialog box and passes initialization data
`DlgDirList`	Fills the list box with file names that match the specified path
`DlgDirListComboBox`	Fills a combo box with file names that match the specified path

Function	*Meaning*
`DlgDirSelect`	Copies the current selection of a list box to a string
`DlgDirSelectComboBox`	Copies the current selection of a combo box to a string
`EndDialog`	Terminates a modal dialog box
`GetDialogBaseUnits`	Gets the base dialog units
`GetDlgCtrlID`	Gets the ID value of a control window
`GetDlgItem`	Gets the handle of an item from the specified dialog box
`GetDlgItemInt`	Converts the item's control text to an integer
`GetDlgItemText`	Copies an item's control text to a string
`GetNextDlgGroupItem`	Gets the handle for the next item in the group
`GetNextDlgTabItem`	Gets the handle of the next or previous item
`IsDialogMessage`	Determines whether a message is sent to the specified dialog box
`IsDlgButtonChecked`	Determines whether a button is checked
`MapDialogRect`	Converts dialog box coordinates to client coordinates
`SendDlgItemMessage`	Sends a message to a dialog box item
`SetDlgItemInt`	Sets the caption or text for an item to a string representing an integer
`SetDlgItemText`	Sets the caption or text for an item to a string

The rest of this section provides detailed information on each of the functions in this list.

CheckDlgButton

Syntax:

```
void CheckDlgButton(hDlg, nIDButton, wCheck)
```

Parameter, Type, and Description:

`hDlg`	`HWND`	Dialog box containing the button
`nIDButton`	`int`	Button to modify
`wCheck`	`WORD`	Setting for the button

Description:

The CheckDlgButton function alters the setting of a button in the dialog box specified by hDlg. The button to modify is specified in nIDButton.

wCheck defines the new setting for the specified button:

- When wCheck is a nonzero value, this function places a check mark next to the button.
- When wCheck is zero, this function removes any check mark next to the button.

For three-state buttons:

- When wCheck is 1, this function places a check mark next to the button.
- When wCheck is 0, this function removes any check mark next to the button.
- When wCheck is 2, this function grays the button.

The CheckDlgButton function sends the BM_SETCHECK message to the button.

Return Value:

There is no return value.

CheckRadioButton

Syntax:

```
void CheckRadioButton(hDlg, nIDFirstButton, nIDLastButton, nIDCheckButton)
```

Parameter, Type, and Description:

hDlg	HWND	Dialog box
nIDFirstButton	int	First radio button in a group
nIDLastButton	int	Last radio button in a group
nIDCheckButton	int	Radio button to be checked

Description:

The CheckRadioButton function places a check mark next to the radio button specified in nIDCheckButton. Any check marks next to any other radio buttons in the group of buttons defined by nIDFirstButton and nIDLastButton are removed.

hDlg specifies the dialog box containing the radio buttons.

This function sends the BM_SETCHECK message to the radio-button control.

Return Value:

There is no return value.

CreateDialog

Syntax:

```
HWND CreateDialog(hInstance, lpTemplateName, hWndParent, lpDialogFunc)
```

Parameter, Type, and Description:

hInstance	HANDLE	Instance of module containing the dialog box template
lpTemplateName	LPSTR	Name of the dialog box
hWndParent	HWND	Window that owns the dialog box
lpDialogFunc	FARPROC	Procedure instance address for dialog function

Description:

The `CreateDialog` function creates a dialog box. `hInstance` specifies the instance of the module whose executable file contains the dialog-box template. The size, style, and controls for the dialog box are specified in `lpTemplateName`. `hWndParent` specifies the window that owns the dialog box.

`lpDialogFunc` points to the dialog function. The dialog function must follow these conventions and formats:

Syntax:

```
BOOL FAR PASCAL DialogFunc(hDlg, wMsg, wParam, lParam)
```

Parameter, Type, and Description:

hDlg	HWND	Dialog box receiving the message
wMsg	WORD	Message Number
wParam	WORD	16 bits of message-dependent information
lParam	DWORD	32 bits of message-dependent information

Description:

Use `DialogFunc` only when the dialog class is used for the dialog box. Do not use the `DefWindowProc` function with this function to process unwanted messages.

The name DialogFunc is simply a holder for the real function name; you must export the real name by using the EXPORTS statement.

Return Value:

The DialogFunc function returns a nonzero value when the message is handled. A return value of zero:

- Indicates that the function cannot handle the message
- When the WM_INITDIALOG message is sent, indicates that the function calls the SetFocus function

Return Value:

The CreateDialog function returns the window handle of the created dialog box. A NULL return value indicates that the dialog box was not created.

CreateDialogIndirect

Syntax:

```
HWND CreateDialogIndirect(hInstance, lpDialogTemplate,
                          hWndParent, lpDialogFunc)
```

Parameter, Type, and Description:

hInstance	HANDLE	Instance of a module containing the dialog box template
lpDialogTemplate	LPSTR	Points to a DLGTEMPLATE data structure containing the template size, style, control, and so on
hWndParent	HWND	Window that owns the dialog box
lpDialogFunc	FARPROC	Procedure instance address of dialog function

Description:

The CreateDialogIndirect function creates a modeless dialog box. hInstance specifies the instance of the module whose executable file contains the dialog-box template. hWndParent specifies the window that owns the dialog box.

lpDialogTemplate points to a data structure of type DLGTEMPLATE, which specifies the size, style, and controls for the dialog box. The DLGTEMPLATE structure is:

```
typedef struct {
     long dtStyle;
     BYTE dtItemCount;
```

```
    int dtX;
    int dtY;
    int dtCX;
    int dtCY;
    char dtMenuName[];
    char dtClassName[];
    char dtCaptionText[];
} DLGTEMPLATE;
```

where:

`dtStyle` is the dialog box style and can be any one of the following:

Style	*Value*
DS_LOCALEDIT	Text storage for edit controls will be allocated in the application's local data segment
DS_SYSMODAL	System-modal dialog box
DS_MODALFRAME	Dialog box with modal dialog box border
DS_ABSALIGN	dtX and dtY are relative to screen
DS_SETFONT	A font other than the system font will be used in the dialog box
DS_NOIDLEMSG	WM_ENTERIDLE message will not be sent to the dialog box owner while the box is being displayed

`dtItemCount` is the number of items in the dialog box.

`dtX` is the x-coordinate of the upper-left corner of the dialog box, specified in units of one-fourth the dialog base width unit.

`dtY` is the y-coordinate of the upper-left corner of the dialog box, specified in units of one-eighth the dialog base width unit.

`dtCX` is the width of the dialog box, specified in units of one-fourth the dialog base width unit.

`dtCY` is the height of the dialog box, specified in units of one-eighth the dialog base width unit.

`dtMenuName` is the name of the menu for the dialog box.

`dtClassName` is the name of the class for the dialog box.

`dtCaptionText[]` is the caption for the dialog box.

`lpDialogFunc` points to the dialog function. The dialog function must follow these conventions and formats:

Syntax:

```
BOOL FAR PASCAL DialogFunc(hDlg, wMsg, wParam, lParam)
```

Parameter, Type, and Description:

`hDlg`	`HWND`	Dialog box receiving the message
`wMsg`	`WORD`	Message number
`wParam`	`WORD`	16 bits of message-dependent information
`lParam`	`DWORD`	32 bits of message-dependent information

Description:

Use `DialogFunc` only when the dialog class is used for the dialog box. Do not use the `DefWindowProc` function with this function to process unwanted messages.

The name `DialogFunc` is simply a holder for the real function name; you must export the real name by using the `EXPORTS` statement.

Return Value:

The `DialogFunc` function returns a nonzero value when the message is handled. A return value of zero:

- Indicates that the function cannot handle the message
- When the `WM_INITDIALOG` message is sent, indicates that the function calls the `SetFocus` function

Return Value:

The `CreateDialogIndirect` function returns the window handle of the created dialog box. A NULL return value indicates that the dialog box was not created.

CreateDialogIndirectParam

Syntax:

```
HWND CreateDialogIndirectParam(hInstance, lpDialogTemplate,
                               hWndParent, lpDialogFunc,
                               dwInitParam)
```

Parameter, Type, and Description:

`hInstance`	`HANDLE`	Instance of a module containing the dialog box template
`lpDialogTemplate`	`LPSTR`	Points to a DLGTEMPLATE data structure containing the template size, style, control, and so on

hWndParent	HWND	Window that owns the dialog box
lpDialogFunc	FARPROC	Procedure instance address of dialog function
dwInitParam	DWORD	32-bit value passed to the dialog function when the dialog box is created

Description:

The `CreateDialogIndirectParam` function creates a modeless dialog box. `hWndParent` specifies the window that owns the dialog box.

`hInstance` specifies the instance of the module whose executable file contains the dialog-box template.

`lpDialogTemplate` points to a data structure of type `DLGTEMPLATE`, which specifies the size, style, and controls for the dialog box. The `DLGTEMPLATE` structure is:

```
typedef struct {
     long dtStyle;
     BYTE dtItemCount;
     int dtX;
     int dtY;
     int dtCX;
     int dtCY;
     char dtMenuName[];
     char dtClassName[];
     char dtCaptionText[];
} DLGTEMPLATE;
```

where:

`dtStyle` is the dialog box style and can be any one of the following:

Style	*Value*
DS_LOCALEDIT	Text storage for edit controls will be allocated in the application's local data segment
DS_SYSMODAL	System-modal dialog box
DS_MODALFRAME	Dialog box with modal dialog box border
DS_ABSALIGN	`dtX` and `dtY` are relative to screen
DS_SETFONT	A font other than the system font will be used in the dialog box
DS_NOIDLEMSG	`WM_ENTERIDLE` message will not be sent to the dialog box owner while the box is being displayed

`dtItemCount` is the number of items in the dialog box.

`dtX` is the x-coordinate of the upper-left corner of the dialog box, specified in units of one-fourth the dialog base width unit.

dtY is the y-coordinate of the upper-left corner of the dialog box, specified in units of one-eighth the dialog base width unit.

dtCX is the width of the dialog box, specified in units of one-fourth the dialog base width unit.

dtCY is the height of the dialog box, specified in units of one-eighth the dialog base width unit.

dtMenuName is the name of the menu for the dialog box.

dtClassName is the name of the class for the dialog box.

dtCaptionText[] is the caption for the dialog box.

dwInitParam is a 32-bit value passed to the dialog function to initialize dialog-box controls. lpDialogFunc points to the dialog function. The dialog function must follow these conventions and formats:

Syntax:

```
BOOL FAR PASCAL DialogFunc(hDlg, wMsg, wParam, lParam)
```

Parameter, Type, and Description:

hDlg	HWND	Dialog box receiving the message
wMsg	WORD	Message number
wParam	WORD	16 bits of message-dependent information
lParam	DWORD	32 bits of message-dependent information

Description:

Use DialogFunc only when the dialog class is used for the dialog box. Do not use the DefWindowProc function with this function to process unwanted messages.

The name DialogFunc is simply a holder for the real function name; you must export the real name by using the EXPORTS statement.

Return Value:

The DialogFunc function returns a nonzero value when the message is handled. A return value of zero:

- Indicates that the function cannot handle the message
- When the WM_INITDIALOG message is sent, indicates that the function calls the SetFocus function

Return Value:

The `CreateDialogIndirectParam` function returns the handle of the created dialog box. A return value of NULL indicates that this function cannot create the dialog box or controls.

CreateDialogParam

Syntax:

```
HWND CreateDialogParam(hInstance, lpTemplateName, hWndParent,
                       lpDialogFunc, dwInitParam)
```

Parameter, Type, and Description:

`hInstance`	`HANDLE`	Instance of a module containing the dialog box template
`lpTemplateName`	`LPSTR`	Pointer to name of the dialog box
`hWndParent`	`HWND`	Window that owns the dialog box
`lpDialogFunc`	`FARPROC`	Procedure instance address of dialog function
`dwInitParam`	`DWORD`	32-bit value passed to the dialog function

Description:

The `CreateDialogParam` function creates a MODELESS dialog box. `hInstance` specifies the instance of the module whose executable file contains the dialog box template. The size, style, and controls for the dialog box are specified in `lpTemplateName`. `hWndParent` specifies the window that owns the dialog box.

`CreateDialogParamdwInitParam` is a 32-bit value passed to the dialog function to initialize dialog box controls.

`lpDialogFunc` points to the dialog function. The dialog function must follow these conventions and formats:

Syntax:

```
BOOL FAR PASCAL DialogFunc(hDlg, wMsg, wParam, lParam)
```

Parameter, Type, and Description:

`hDlg`	`HWND`	Dialog box receiving the message
`wMsg`	`WORD`	Message number
`wParam`	`WORD`	16 bits of message-dependent information
`lParam`	`DWORD`	32 bits of message-dependent information

Description:

Use DialogFunc only when the dialog class is used for the dialog box. Do not use the DefWindowProc function with this function to process unwanted messages.

The name DialogFunc is simply a holder for the real function name; you must export the real name by using the EXPORTS statement.

Return Value:

The DialogFunc function returns a nonzero value when the message is handled. A return value of zero:

- Indicates that the function cannot handle the message
- When the WM_INITDIALOG message is sent, indicates that the function calls the SetFocus function

Return Value:

The CreateDialogParam function returns the window handle of the created dialog box. A NULL return value indicates that the dialog box was not created.

The window handle for the dialog box is returned if the dialog box is created. A value of –1 is returned if the dialog box is not created.

DefDlgProc

Syntax:

```
LONG DefDlgProc(hDlg, wMsg, wParam, lParam)
```

Parameter, Type, and Description:

hDlg	HWND	Dialog box
wMsg	WORD	Message number
wParam	WORD	16 bits of message-dependent information
lParam	DWORD	32 bits of message-dependent information

Description:

The DefDlgProc function processes Windows messages that the dialog box with a private window class, specified in hDlg, does not process. Window messages not processed by the window function must be passed to DefDlgProc.

Return Value:

The return value depends on the message sent and the result of the message processing.

DialogBox

Syntax:

```
int DialogBox(hInstance, lpTemplateName, hWndParent,
              lpDialogFunc)
```

Parameter, Type, and Description:

`hInstance`	`HANDLE`	Instance of a module containing the dialog box template
`lpTemplateName`	`LPSTR`	Pointer to null-terminated character string that contains the name of the dialog box template
`hWndParent`	`HWND`	Window that owns the dialog box
`lpDialogFunc`	`FARPROC`	Dialog function

Description:

The `DialogBox` function creates a modal dialog box. `hInstance` specifies the instance of the module whose executable file contains the dialog box template. `lpTemplateName` is a pointer to a null-terminated string that specifies the dialog box template. `hWndParent` specifies dialog box's owner.

`lpDialogFunc` points to a callback function that processes the messages sent to the dialog box. `DialogFunc` must follow these conventions and formats:

Syntax:

```
int FAR PASCAL DialogFunc(hDlg, wMsg, wParam, lParam)
```

Parameter, Type, and Description:

`hDlg`	`HWND`	Dialog box receiving the message
`wMsg`	`WORD`	Message number
`wParam`	`WORD`	16 bits of message-dependent information
`lParam`	`DWORD`	32 bits of message-dependent information

Description:

Use `DialogFunc` only when the dialog class is used for the dialog box. Do not use the `DefWindowProc` function with this function to process unwanted messages.

The name `DialogFunc` is simply a holder for the real function name; you must export the real name by using the `EXPORTS` statement.

Return Value:

The `DialogFunc` function returns a nonzero value when the message is handled. A return value of zero indicates that the function cannot handle the message.

Return Value:

After `DialogFunc` has finished processing, the dialog box is terminated with a call to the `EndDialog` function. The `DialogBox` function returns the result of the `EndDialog` function when the dialog box is created. A return value of –1 indicates that the function cannot create the dialog box.

DialogBoxIndirect

Syntax:

```
int DialogBoxIndirect(hInstance, hDialogTemplate, hWndParent,
                      lpDialogFunc)
```

Parameter, Type, and Description:

Parameter	Type	Description
hInstance	HANDLE	Instance of a module containing the dialog box template
hDialogTemplate	HANDLE	Points to DLGTEMPLATE data structure containing template size, style, control, and so on
hWndParent	HWND	Window that owns the dialog box
lpDialogFunc	FARPROC	Dialog function

Description:

The `DialogBoxIndirect` function creates a modal dialog box. `hInstance` specifies the instance of the module whose executable file contains the dialog box template. `hWndParent` specifies the window that owns the dialog box.

`hDialogTemplate` points to a data structure of type `DLGTEMPLATE`, which specifies the size, style, and controls for the dialog box. The `DLGTEMPLATE` structure is:

```
typedef struct {
     long dtStyle;
     BYTE dtItemCount;
     int dtX;
     int dtY;
     int dtCX;
     int dtCY;
```

```
    char dtMenuName[];
    char dtClassName[];
    char dtCaptionText[];
} DLGTEMPLATE;
```

where:

`dtStyle` is the dialog box style and can be any one of the following:

Style	*Value*
DS_LOCALEDIT	Text storage for edit controls will be allocated in the application's local data segment
DS_SYSMODAL	System-modal dialog box
DS_MODALFRAME	Dialog box with modal dialog box border
DS_ABSALIGN	dtX and dtY are relative to screen
DS_SETFONT	A font other than the system font will be used in the dialog box
DS_NOIDLEMSG	WM_ENTERIDLE message will not be sent to the dialog box owner while the box is being displayed

`dtItemCount` is the number of items in the dialog box.

`dtX` is the x-coordinate of the upper-left corner of the dialog box, specified in units of one-fourth the dialog base width unit.

`dtY` is the y-coordinate of the upper-left corner of the dialog box, specified in units of one-eighth the dialog base width unit.

`dtCX` is the width of the dialog box, specified in units of one-fourth the dialog base width unit.

`dtCY` is the height of the dialog box, specified in units of one-eighth the dialog base width unit.

`dtMenuName` is the name of the menu for the dialog box.

`dtClassName` is the name of the class for the dialog box.

`dtCaptionText` is the caption for the dialog box.

`lpDialogFunc` points to the dialog function. The dialog function must follow these conventions and formats:

Syntax:

```
BOOL FAR PASCAL DialogFunc(hDlg, wMsg, wParam, lParam)
```

Parameter, Type, and Description:

hDlg	HWND	Dialog box receiving the message
wMsg	WORD	Message number

`wParam`	`WORD`	16 bits of message-dependent information
`lParam`	`DWORD`	32 bits of message-dependent information

Description:

Use `DialogFunc` only when the dialog class is used for the dialog box. Do not use the `DefWindowProc` function with this function to process unwanted messages.

The name `DialogFunc` is simply a holder for the real function name; you must export the real name by using the `EXPORTS` statement.

Return Value:

The `DialogFunc` function returns a nonzero value when the message is handled. A return value of zero indicates that the function cannot handle the message.

Return Value:

After `DialogFunc` has finished processing, the dialog box is terminated with a call to the `EndDialog` function. The `DialogBoxIndirect` function returns the result of the `EndDialog` function when the dialog box is created. A return value of –1 indicates that the function cannot create the dialog box.

DialogBoxIndirectParam

Syntax:

```
int DialogBoxIndirectParam(hInstance, hDialogTemplate, hWndParent,
                           lpDialogFunc, dwInitParam)
```

Parameter, Type, and Description:

`hInstance`	`HANDLE`	Instance of a module containing the dialog box template
`hDialogTemplate`	`HANDLE`	Points to `DLGTEMPLATE` datastructure containing template size, style, control, and so on
`hWndParent`	`HWND`	Window that owns the dialog box
`lpDialogFunc`	`FARPROC`	Dialog function
`dwInitParam`	`DWORD`	32-bit value passed to the dialog function

Description:

The DialogBoxIndirectParam function creates a modal dialog box. hInstance specifies the instance of the module whose executable file contains the dialog box template. hWndParent specifies the window that owns the dialog box.

hDialogTemplate points to a data structure of type DLGTEMPLATE, which specifies the size, style, and controls for the dialog box. The DLGTEMPLATE structure is:

```
typedef struct {
     long dtStyle;
     BYTE dtItemCount;
     int dtX;
     int dtY;
     int dtCX;
     int dtCY;
     char dtMenuName[];
     char dtClassName[];
     char dtCaptionText[];
} DLGTEMPLATE;
```

where:

dtStyle is the dialog box style and can be any one of these:

Style	*Value*
DS_LOCALEDIT	Text storage for edit controls will be allocated in the application's local data segment
DS_SYSMODAL	System-modal dialog box
DS_MODALFRAME	Dialog box with modal dialog box border
DS_ABSALIGN	dtX and dtY are relative to screen
DS_SETFONT	A font other than the system font will be used in the dialog box
DS_NOIDLEMSG	WM_ENTERIDLE message will not be sent to the dialog box owner while the box is being displayed

dtItemCount is the number of items in the dialog box.

dtX is the x-coordinate of the upper-left corner of the dialog box, specified in units of one-fourth the dialog base width unit.

dtY is the y-coordinate of the upper-left corner of the dialog box, specified in units of one-eighth the dialog base width unit.

dtCX is the width of the dialog box, specified in units of one-fourth the dialog base width unit.

dtCY is the height of the dialog box, specified in units of one-eighth the dialog base width unit.

`dtMenuName` is the name of the menu for the dialog box.

`dtClassName` is the name of the class for the dialog box.

`dtCaptionText` is the caption for the dialog box.

Before the dialog box is displayed, this function sends the `WM_INITDIALOG` message to the dialog function. `dwInitParam` is passed to the dialog function as `lParam`. `lpDialogFunc` points to the dialog function. The dialog function must follow these conventions and formats:

Syntax:

```
BOOL FAR PASCAL DialogFunc(hDlg, wMsg, wParam, lParam)
```

Parameter, Type, and Description:

`hDlg`	`HWND`	Dialog box receiving message
`wMsg`	`WORD`	Message number
`wParam`	`WORD`	16 bits of message-dependent information
`lParam`	`DWORD`	32 bits of message-dependent information

Description:

Use `DialogFunc` only when the dialog class is used for the dialog box. Do not use the `DefWindowProc` function with this function to process unwanted messages.

The name `DialogFunc` is simply a holder for the real function name; you must export the real name by using the `EXPORTS` statement.

Return Value:

The `DialogFunc` function returns a nonzero value when the message is handled. A return value of zero indicates that the function cannot handle the message.

Return Value:

After `DialogFunc` has finished its processing, the dialog box is terminated with a call to the `EndDialog` function. When the `DialogBoxIndirectParam` function is successful, the `DialogBoxIndirectParam` function returns the result of the call to the `EndDialog` function. A return value of –1 indicates that the function cannot create the dialog box.

DialogBoxParam

Syntax:

```
int DialogBoxParam(hInstance, lpTemplateName, hWndParent,
                   lpDialogFunc, dwInitParam)
```

Parameter, Type, and Description:

hInstance	HANDLE	Instance of module containing the dialog box template
lpTemplateName	LPSTR	Name of dialog box
hWndParent	HWND	Window that owns the dialog box
lpDialogFunc	FARPROC	Dialog function
dwInitParam	DWORD	32-bit value passed to the dialog function

Description:

The DialogBoxParam function creates a modal dialog box. hInstance specifies the instance of the module whose executable file contains the dialog box template. The size, style, and controls for the dialog box are specified in lpTemplateName. hWndParent specifies the window that owns the dialog box.

dwInitParam is a 32-bit value passed to the dialog function to initialize dialog box controls.

lpDialogFunc points to the dialog function. The dialog function must follow these conventions and formats:

Syntax:

```
int FAR PASCAL DialogFunc(hDlg, wMsg, wParam, lParam)
```

Parameter, Type, and Description:

hDlg	HWND	Dialog box receiving message
wMsg	WORD	Message number
wParam	WORD	16 bits of message-dependent information
lParam	DWORD	32 bits of message-dependent information

Description:

Use DialogFunc only when the dialog class is used for the dialog box. Do not use the DefWindowProc function with this function to process unwanted messages.

The name DialogFunc is simply a holder for the real function name; you must export the real name by using the EXPORTS statement.

Return Value:

The DialogFunc function returns a nonzero value when the message is handled. A return value of zero indicates that the function cannot handle the message.

Return Value:

After DialogFunc has finished its processing, the dialog box is terminated with a call to the EndDialog function. When the DialogBoxParam function successful, the DialogBoxParam function returns the result of the call to the EndDialog function. A return value of –1 indicates that this function cannot create the dialog box.

DlgDirList

Syntax:

```
int DlgDirList(hDlg, lpPathSpec, nIDListBox, nIDStaticPath, wFiletype)
```

Parameter, Type, and Description:

hDlg	HWND	Dialog box containing list box
lpPathSpec	LPSTR	Pointer to string containing the path name
nIDListBox	int	Identifier for list box control
nIDStaticPath	int	Identifier for displaying the current drive and directory
wFiletype	WORD	DOS file attributes

Description:

The DlgDirList function fills a list box control with a file or directory listing. hDlg identifies the dialog box that contains the list box. nIDListBox specifies the list box control to fill.

lpPathSpec is a null-terminated character string specifying the pathname. The format for lpPathSpec is:

```
drive:\directory\directory\...\filename
```

The lpPathSpec path name may include wild cards. The DlgDirList function fills the list box with all file names matching the path name specified in lpPathSpec.

`nIDStaticPath` specifies the identifier of the static text control used for displaying the current drive and directory.

`wFiletype` specifies the DOS attributes of files to be displayed. The DOS attributes for the `wFiletype` parameter are:

Attribute	*Meaning*
0x0000	Read/Write data files without other attributes
0x0001	Read-only
0x0002	Hidden files
0x0004	System files
0x0010	Subdirectories
0x0020	Archives
0x2000	`LB_DIR` flag
0x4000	Drives
0x8000	Exclusive bit

In the directory list, square brackets ([ ]) enclose subdirectories; (-a-) denotes a drive, where "a" is the drive name.

This function sends the `LB_RESETCONTENT` and `LB_DIR` messages to the list box.

Return Value:

The `DlgDirList` function returns a nonzero value when the list box is filled. A return value of zero indicates that the search path specified is not valid.

DlgDirListComboBox

Syntax:

```
int DlgDirListComboBox(hDlg, lpPathSpec, nIDComboBox,
                       nIDStaticPath, wFiletype)
```

Parameter, Type, and Description:

`hDlg`	`HWND`	Dialog box containing a combo box
`lpPathSpec`	`LPSTR`	Pointer to string containing the path name
`nIDComboBox`	`int`	Identifier for a combo box control
`nIDStaticPath`	`int`	Identifier for displaying the current drive and directory
`wFiletype`	`WORD`	DOS file attributes

Description:

The DlgDirListComboBox function fills a list box of a combo box control with a file or directory listing. hDlg identifies the dialog box that contains the list box. nIDComboBox specifies the list box of the combo box to fill.

lpPathSpec is a null-terminated character string specifying the path name. The format for lpPathSpec is:

```
drive:\directory\directory\...\filename
```

The lpPathSpec path name may include wild cards. The DlgDirListComboBox function fills the list box with all file names matching the path name specified in lpPathSpec.

nIDStaticPath specifies the identifier of the static text control used for displaying the current drive and directory.

wFiletype specifies the DOS attributes of files to be displayed. The DOS attributes for the wFiletype parameter are:

Attribute	*Meaning*
0x0000	Read/Write data files without other attributes
0x0001	Read-only
0x0002	Hidden files
0x0004	System files
0x0010	Subdirectories
0x0020	Archives
0x2000	LB_DIR flag
0x4000	Drives
0x8000	Exclusive bit

In the directory list, square brackets ([]) enclose subdirectories; (-a-) denotes a drive, where "a" is the drive name.

This function sends the LB_RESETCONTENT and LB_DIR messages to the list box.

Return Value:

The DlgDirListComboBox function returns a nonzero return value when the listing is created. A return value of zero indicates that the search path specified is not valid.

DlgDirSelect

Syntax:

```
BOOL DlgDirSelect(hDlg, lpString, nIDListBox)
```

Parameter, Type, and Description:

`hDlg`	`HWND`	Dialog box containing the list box
`lpString`	`LPSTR`	Pointer to buffer to receive the path name
`nIDListBox`	`int`	ID of the list box control

Description:

The `DlgDirSelect` function gets the current selection from the list box and copies it into the buffer pointed to by `lpString`. `hDlg` specifies the dialog box containing the list box.

This function assumes that:

- The list box, specified by `nIDListBox`, has been filled
- The selection is a drive name, a directory name, or a file name

This function sends the `LB_GETCURSEL` and `LB_GETTEXT` messages to the list box.

Return Value:

The `DlgDirSelect` function returns the status of the current selection. A nonzero return value indicates the selection of a directory name. A return value of zero indicates all other selections.

DlgDirSelectComboBox

Syntax:

```
BOOL DlgDirSelectComboBox(hDlg, lpString, nIDComboBox)
```

Parameter, Type, and Description:

`hDlg`	`HWND`	Dialog box containing the combo box
`lpString`	`LPSTR`	Pointer to buffer to receive the path name
`nIDComboBox`	`int`	ID of the combo box control

Description:

The `DlgDirSelectComboBox` function gets the current selection from a list box in the combo box specified by `nIDComboBox`. `hDlg` specifies the dialog box that contains the combo box. `lpString` holds the retrieved list box selection.

This function assumes that:

- The list box specified by `nIDComboBox` has been filled
- The selection is a drive name, a directory name, or a file name

DlgDirSelectComboBox sends the CB_GETCURSEL and CB_GETLBTEXT messages to the combo box.

Return Value:

The DlgDirSelectComboBox returns the status of the current selection. A nonzero return value indicates that the current selection is a directory name. A return value of zero indicates all other selections.

EndDialog

Syntax:

```
void EndDialog(hDlg, nResult)
```

Parameter, Type, and Description:

hDlg	HWND	Dialog box to destroy
nResult	int	Value to be returned from dialog box

Description:

The EndDialog function removes a modal dialog box created with the DialogBox function. hDlg specifies the modal dialog box to destroy.

When the EndDialog function is called, an internal flag is set to indicate that the dialog box should be removed. When the dialog function ends, the dialog box is removed. The results of the EndDialog function are returned to the DialogBox function that created the dialog box. The EndDialog function must be used in the dialog function of the modal dialog box.

Return Value:

There is no return value.

GetDialogBaseUnits

Syntax:

```
LONG GetDialogBaseUnits()
```

Description:

The GetDialogBaseUnits function gets the dialog base units used by Windows when a dialog box is created. These units are useful for determining the average character width of the system font.

The returned dialog base units must be scaled to represent actual dialog units. The horizontal dialog unit is one-fourth the horizontal value returned by `GetDialogBaseUnits`. The vertical dialog unit is one-eighth the vertical value returned by `GetDialogBaseUnits`.

Return Value:

The `GetDialogBaseUnits` function returns a value representing the dialog base units. The high-order word contains the height of the current dialog base height unit in pixels. The low-order word contains the width of the current dialog base width unit in pixels.

GetDlgCtrlID

Syntax:

```
int GetDlgCtrlID(hWnd)
```

Parameter, Type, and Description:

`hWnd`	`HWND`	Child window handle

Description:

The `GetDlgCtrlID` function returns the child window ID for the child window specified in `hWnd`. Do not use this function when `hWnd` specifies a top-level window, since top-level windows have no ID.

Return Value:

The `GetDlgCtrlID` function returns the child window ID value. A NULL return value indicates that the child window specified in `hWnd` is not valid.

GetDlgItem

Syntax:

```
HWND GetDlgItem(hDlg, nIDDlgItem)
```

Parameter, Type, and Description:

`hDlg`	`HWND`	Dialog box containing the control
`nIDDlgItem`	`int`	ID of item to be retrieved

Description:

The `GetDlgItem` function gets the handle of the control specified by the integer ID in `nIDDlgItem`. The dialog box containing the control is specified in `hDlg`. This function is not limited to dialog boxes and can be used with any parent-child window pair.

Return Value:

The `GetDlgItem` function returns the handle for the specified control. A NULL return value indicates that no control with the specified ID exists.

GetDlgItemInt

Syntax:

```
WORD GetDlgItemInt(hDlg, nIDDlgItem, lpTranslated, bSigned)
```

Parameter, Type, and Description:

`hDlg`	`HWND`	Dialog box
`nIDDlgItem`	`int`	Dialog box item to be converted
`lpTranslated`	`BOOL FAR *`	Pointer to Boolean variable to receive the translated flag
`bSigned`	`BOOL`	Specifies whether the value is signed

Description:

The `GetDlgItemInt` function converts the text of the dialog box item specified in `nIDDlgItem` to an integer value. `nIDDlgItem` is contained in the dialog box specified by `hDlg`.

`lpTranslated` is set to a nonzero value when no conversion errors occur and to zero if a conversion error occurs.

`bSigned` indicates whether or not the item is signed. When `bSigned` is a nonzero value, the retrieved text of the specified item is checked for a minus sign.

White spaces at the beginning of the text are stripped and decimal digits are converted. Conversion stops when a non-numeric character is found or the end of the string is reached.

This function sends the `WM_GETTEXT` message to the control.

Return Value:

The `GetDlgItemInt` function returns the converted value of the text for the dialog box item. A return value of zero indicates that the converted value exceeds one of the following:

- 32,767 for signed values
- 65,535 for unsigned values

GetDlgItemText

Syntax:

```
int GetDlgItemText(hDlg, nIDDlgItem, lpString, nMaxCount)
```

Parameter, Type, and Description:

`hDlg`	`HWND`	Dialog box containing the control
`nIDDlgItem`	`int`	Item from which to retrieve text
`lpString`	`LPSTR`	Pointer to buffer to receive text
`nMaxCount`	`int`	Maximum number of bytes in string to be copied

Description:

The `GetDlgItemText` function gets the text associated with the control item specified in `nIDDlgItem`. `nIDDlgItem` is contained in the dialog box specified in `hDlg`.

The retrieved text is placed in the text buffer pointed to by `lpString`. The value specified in `nMaxCount` limits the length (in bytes) of the string copied into `lpString`.

This function sends the `WM_GETTEXT` message to the control item in `nIDDlgItem`.

Return Value:

The `GetDlgItemText` function returns the number of characters copied into `lpString`. A return value of zero indicates that no text is copied into `lpString`.

GetNextDlgGroupItem

Syntax:

```
HWND GetNextDlgGroupItem(hDlg, hCtl, bPrevious)
```

Parameter, Type, and Description:

`hDlg`	`HWND`	Dialog box being searched
`hCtl`	`HWND`	Control where search starts
`bPrevious`	`BOOL`	Specifies method of search

Description:

The `GetNextDlgGroupItem` function searches for the next control in the dialog box specified in `hDlg`. The control that contains the control specified in `hCtl` is searched. A control group has one or more controls of style `WS_GROUP`. The search for the next control begins with the control specified in `hCtl`. `bPrevious` controls the direction of the search. The previous control is returned when `bPrevious` is zero. The next control is returned when `bPrevious` is a nonzero value.

Return Value:

The `GetNextDlgGroupItem` function returns the handle of the next or previous control in the control group, depending on the setting of `bPrevious`:

- The previous control is returned when `bPrevious` is zero.
- The next control is returned when `bPrevious` is a nonzero value.

GetNextDlgTabItem

Syntax:

```
HWND GetNextDlgTabItem(hDlg, hCtl, bPrevious)
```

Parameter, Type, and Description:

`hDlg`	`HWND`	Dialog box to search
`hCtl`	`HWND`	Control where the search begins
`bPrevious`	`BOOL`	Specifies method of the search

Description:

The `GetNextDlgTabItem` function gets the handle of the next control of style `WS_TABSTOP` in the `hDlg` dialog box. The search for the next control begins with the control specified in `hCtl`.

`bPrevious` defines how the search will be conducted:

- If `bPrevious` is zero, `GetNextDlgTabItem` searches for the first preceding control of style `WS_TABSTOP`.

- If bPrevious is a nonzero value, GetNextDlgTabItem searches for the next control of style WS_TABSTOP.

Return Value:

The GetNextDlgTabItem function returns the handle of the previous or next control of style WS_TABSTOP. The control returned depends on the setting of bPrevious:

- The previous control is returned when bPrevious is zero.
- The next control is returned when bPrevious is a nonzero value.

IsDialogMessage

Syntax:

```
BOOL IsDialogMessage(hDlg, lpMsg)
```

Parameter, Type, and Description:

hDlg	HWND	Dialog box
lpMsg	LPMSG	Pointer to MSG data structure containing the message

Description:

The IsDialogMessage function determines whether or not a particular message is intended for a particular modeless dialog box. hDlg specifies the modeless dialog box.

lpMsg points to the MSG data structure containing the message. If the message is for the dialog box in hDlg, IsDialogMessage processes the message. During message processing IsDialogMessage checks for keyboard messages and processes these messages according to selection commands for the dialog box.

This function sends the WM_GETDLGCODE message to the dialog function.

The MSG data structure is:

```
typedef struct tagSG {
     HWND hwnd;
     WORD message;
     WORD wParam;
     LONG lParam;
     DWORD time;
     POINT pt;
} MSG;
```

where:

hwnd is the window receiving the message

`message` is the message

`wParam` is any additional information about the message

`lParam` is any additional information about the message

`time` is the time the message was posted

`pt` is the screen coordinates of the cursor when the message was posted

Return Value:

The `IsDialogMessage` function returns a nonzero value when the message in `lpMsg` is processed. A return value of zero indicates that the message is not processed.

IsDlgButtonChecked

Syntax:

```
WORD IsDlgButtonChecked(hDlg, nIDButton)
```

Parameter, Type, and Description:

`hDlg`	`HWND`	Dialog box containing button
`nIDButton`	`int`	Button control

Description:

The `IsDlgButtonChecked` function determines the state of the dialog button specified in `nIDButton`. `hDlg` specifies the dialog box containing the button in `nIDButton`.

`IsDlgButtonChecked` determines whether the button has been chcked (that is, whether a check mark was placed next to it). If the button is a three-state button, `IsDlgButtonChecked` determines whether the button is checked, not-checked, or gray.

This function sends the `BM_GETCHECK` message to the button control.

Return Value:

For two-state buttons:

The `IsDlgButtonChecked` function returns a nonzero value when the button is checked. A return value of zero indicates that there is no check mark beside the button.

For three-state buttons:

- A return value of 2 indicates that the three-state button is colored gray
- A return value of 1 indicates that the three-state button is checked

- As with normal buttons, a return value of 0 indicates that there is no check mark beside the button

MapDialogRect

Syntax:

```
void MapDialogRect(hDlg, lpRect)
```

Parameter, Type, and Description:

hDlg	HWND	Dialog box
lpRect	LPRECT	Pointer to RECT structure containing coordinates to convert

Description:

The MapDialogRect function converts dialog box units to screen units. lpRect points to the structure of type RECT, which contains the dialog box units to convert. hDlg specifies the dialog box for which unit conversion is to be accomplished.

Dialog box units are based on the average width and height of the system font. The horizontal dialog box unit is one-fourth the dialog base width unit. The vertical dialog box unit is one-eighth the dialog base height unit.

The dialog box units pointed to by lpRect are replaced with the converted screen units.

The RECT structure is:

```
typedef struct tagRECT {
     int left;
     int top;
     int right;
     int bottom;
} RECT;
```

where:

left is the x-coordinate of the upper-left corner

top is the y-coordinate of the upper-left corner

right is the x-coordinate of the lower-right corner

bottom is the y-coordinate of the lower-right corner

Return Value:

There is no return value.

SendDlgItemMessage

Syntax:

```
DWORD SendDlgItemMessage(hDlg, nIDDlgItem, wMsg, wParam, lParam)
```

Parameter, Type, and Description:

hDlg	HWND	Dialog box containing the control
nIDDlgItem	int	Item to receive message
wMsg	WORD	Message value
wParam	WORD	Additional message information
lParam	DWORD	Additional message information

Description:

The SendDlgItemMessage function sends a message to a control. The control that receives the message is specified in nIDDlgItem. The specified control is contained in the dialog box specified in hDlg.

wMsg contains the message value of the message that the function sends to the control. wParam and lParam contain additional information about the message in wMsg. (See Chapter 14 for more information on messages.)

Return Value:

The SendDlgItemMessage function returns the value returned by the control's window function. A return value of zero indicates that nIDDlgItem identifies an invalid control.

SetDlgItemInt

Syntax:

```
void SetDlgItemInt(hDlg, nIDDlgItem, wValue, bSigned)
```

Parameter, Type, and Description:

hDlg	HWND	Dialog box containing the control
nIDDlgItem	int	Control to be altered
wValue	WORD	Value to set
bSigned	BOOL	Specifies sign

Description:

The `SetDlgItemInt` function sets the text of a control to the specified value. The control to be altered is specified in `nIDDlgItem`. `hDlg` specifies the dialog box containing the control.

The text of the control is set to the string representing the integer value specified in `wValue`. The value in `wValue` is converted to a string of decimal digits. `bSigned` specifies whether or not `wValue` is signed: when `bSigned` is set to a nonzero value, `wValue` is signed.

This function sends the `WM_SETTEXT` message to the control.

Return Value:

There is no return value.

SetDlgItemText

Syntax:

```
void SetDlgItemText(hDlg, nIDDlgItem, lpString)
```

Parameter, Type, and Description:

`hDlg`	`HWND`	Dialog box containing the control
`nIDDlgItem`	`int`	Dialog box control
`lpString`	`LPSTR`	Pointer to text string for the control

Description:

The `SetDlgItemText` function sets the text of the control specified in `nIDDlgItem`. The specified control is contained in the dialog box defined in `hDlg`. The text of the control is set to the text string pointed to by `lpString`.

This function sends the `WM_SETTEXT` message to the control.

Return Value:

There is no return value.

Display and Movement Functions

Windows provides a set of functions that manipulate the number and position of windows on the display. These functions are called Display and Movement func-

tions. The following functions are categorized as Display and Movement functions for the Window Manager Interface:

Function	*Meaning*
`ArrangeIconicWindows`	Arranges minimized child windows
`BeginDeferWindowPos`	Allocates memory for `DeferWindowPos`
`BringWindowToTop`	Brings a window to the top of the stack
`CloseWindow`	Hides or minimizes a window
`DeferWindowPos`	Stores window position information for `EndDeferWindowPos`
`EndDeferWindowPos`	Used with `DeferWindowPos` to move or size one or more windows
`GetClientRect`	Gets the coordinates of a window's client area
`GetWindowRect`	Gets the coordinates of a window
`GetWindowText`	Copies the window caption to a buffer
`GetWindowTextLength`	Gets the number of characters in the window caption or text
`IsIconic`	Determines whether a window is open or closed
`IsWindowVisible`	Determines whether a window is visible
`IsZoomed`	Determines whether a window is zoomed
`MoveWindow`	Changes the size and position of a window
`OpenIcon`	Opens a window
`SetWindowPos`	Modifies a child or pop-up window's size, position, and ordering
`SetWindowText`	Defines the caption or text for a window
`ShowOwnedPopups`	Either shows or hides all pop-up windows
`ShowWindow`	Either displays or removes the window

The rest of this section provides detailed information on each of the functions in this list.

ArrangeIconicWindows

Syntax:

```
WORD ArrangeIconicWindows(hWnd)
```

Parameter, Type, and Description:

`hWnd`	`HWND`	Window handle

Description:

The `ArrangeIconicWindows` function arranges the minimized child windows for the window specified in `hWnd`.

Return Value:

When one or more minimized windows exist, this function returns the height of one row of icons. A return value of zero indicates that no minimized windows exist.

BeginDeferWindowPos

Syntax:

```
HANDLE BeginDeferWindowPos(nNumWindows)
```

Parameter, Type, and Description:

`nNumWindows`	`int`	Initial number of windows

Description:

The `BeginDeferWindowPos` function allocates memory for a data structure to contain the window positions of multiple windows. The amount of memory allocated depends on the number of windows specified in `nNumWindows`. Use this function with the `DeferWindowPos` and `EndDeferWindowPos` functions.

Return Value:

The `BeginDeferWindowPos` function returns the handle for the data structure. A NULL return value indicates that the function cannot allocate memory for the data structure.

BringWindowToTop

Syntax:

```
void BringWindowToTop(hWnd)
```

Parameter, Type, and Description:

`hWnd`	`HWND`	Window to be brought to the top

Description:

The `BringWindowToTop` function brings the pop-up or child window specified in `hWnd` to the top of the windows stack. Use this function to bring windows that are partially covered by other windows to the top of the stack.

Return Value:

There is no return value.

CloseWindow

Syntax:

```
void CloseWindow(hWnd)
```

Parameter, Type, and Description:

`hWnd`	`HWND`	Window to minimize

Description:

The `CloseWindow` function minimizes the window specified in `hWnd`. The function does not work on pop-up or child windows.

Return Value:

There is no return value.

DeferWindowPos

Syntax:

```
HANDLE DeferWindowPos(hWinPosInfo, hWnd, hWndInsertAfter,
                      x, y, cx, cy, wFlags)
```

Parameter, Type, and Description:

`hWinPosInfo`	`HANDLE`	Handle of window position data structure (Note: This value is returned by the `BeginDeferWindowPos` function)
`hWnd`	`HWND`	Update information on this window
`hWndInsertAfter`	`HWND`	Window following the window in `hWnd`
`x`	`int`	X-coordinate of window's upper-left corner
`y`	`int`	Y-coordinate of window's upper-left corner
`cx`	`int`	Window's new width
`cy`	`int`	Window's new height
`wFlags`	`WORD`	16-bit value affecting size and position of window

Description:

The DeferWindowPos function updates the window position data structure initialized by the BeginDeferWindowPos function and specified in hWinPosInfo. hWnd specifies the window for which the data structure is to be modified.

hWndInsertAfter identifies how the window in hWnd will be positioned:

- The window in hWnd is placed after the window in hWndInsertAfter when the SWP_NOZORDER flag is not set and hWndInsertAfter contains a valid window handle.
- The window in hWnd is placed at the top of the list when hWndInsertAfter is NULL.
- The window in hWnd is placed at the bottom of the list when hWndInsertAfter is 1.

The x and y arguments define the horizontal and vertical coordinates, respectively, of the upper-left corner of the new window position. The cx and cy parameters define the new width and height of the window, respectively.

wFlags is a 16-bit value affecting the size and position of the specified window. The following constants can be used with wFlags:

Constant	*Meaning*
SWP_DRAWFRAME	Window is framed
SWP_HIDEWINDOW	Window is hidden
SWP_NOACTIVATE	Window is not activated
SWP_NOMOVE	Position is not updated
SWP_NOREDRAW	Changes are not redrawn
SWP_NOSIZE	Size is not updated
SWP_NOZORDER	Ordering is not updated
SWP_SHOWWINDOW	Window is displayed

Return Value:

The DeferWindowPos function returns the handle for the updated window position data structure. A NULL return value indicates that DeferWindowPos cannot update the window position data structure.

EndDeferWindowPos

Syntax:

```
void EndDeferWindowPos(hWinPosInfo)
```

Parameter, Type, and Description:

hWinPosInfo	HANDLE	Handle for window position data structure (Note: This value is returned by either BeginDeferWindowPos or DeferWindowPos)

Description:

The EndDeferWindowPos function updates the size and position of the windows for which window position data exists in the window position data structure specified by hWinPosInfo. All updates occur in one screen-refresh cycle.

Return Value:

There is no return value.

GetClientRect

Syntax:

```
void GetClientRect(hWnd, lpRect)
```

Parameter, Type, and Description:

hWnd	HWND	Window associated with client area
lpRect	LPRECT	Pointer to RECT data structure where the coordinates of the client area are placed

Description:

The GetClientRect function places the client coordinates of a client area into the data structure pointed to by lpRect. hWnd specifies the window containing the client area. Client coordinates are defined in relation to the upper-left corner of the client area.

The data structure pointed to by lpRect is of type RECT. The RECT structure is:

```
typedef struct tagRECT {
     int left;
     int top;
     int right;
     int bottom;
} RECT;
```

where:

left is the x-coordinate of the upper-left corner

top is the y-coordinate of the upper-left corner

`right` is the x-coordinate of the lower-right corner

`bottom` is the y-coordinate of the lower-right corner

Return Value:

There is no return value.

GetWindowRect

Syntax:

```
void GetWindowRect(hWnd, lpRect)
```

Parameter, Type, and Description:

hWnd	HWND	Window handle
lpRect	LPRECT	Pointer to RECT data structure where the screen coordinates of the window are placed

Description:

The `GetWindowRect` function places the screen coordinates of the window specified in `hWnd` into the data structure pointed to by `lpRect`. Screen coordinates are expressed relative to the upper-left corner of the screen.

The data structure pointed to by `lpRect` is of type `RECT`. The `RECT` structure is:

```
typedef struct tagRECT {
     int left;
     int top;
     int right;
     int bottom;
} RECT;
```

where:

`left` is the x-coordinate of the upper-left corner

`top` is the y-coordinate of the upper-left corner

`right` is the x-coordinate of the lower-right corner

`bottom` is the y-coordinate of the lower-right corner

Return Value:

There is no return value.

GetWindowText

Syntax:

```
int GetWindowText(hWnd, lpString, nMaxCount)
```

Parameter, Type, and Description:

`hWnd`	`HWND`	Window or control handle
`lpString`	`LPSTR`	Pointer to buffer to store the caption
`nMaxCount`	`int`	Maximum number of characters to store

Description:

The `GetWindowText` function places the caption of the window, or the text of the control, into the buffer pointed to by `lpString`. `hWnd` specifies the control or window. `nMaxCount` specifies the maximum number of characters that will be placed into `lpString`.

This function sends the `WM_GETTEXT` message to the specified control or window.

Return Value:

The `GetWindowText` function returns the length of the copied string. A return value of zero indicates that the window has no caption, or the control has no text.

GetWindowTextLength

Syntax:

```
int GetWindowTextLength(hWnd)
```

Parameter, Type, and Description:

`hWnd`	`HWND`	Window or control handle

Description:

The `GetWindowTextLength` function returns the length of the caption for the window, or the length of the text for the control. `hWnd` specifies the control or window.

Return Value:

The `GetWindowTextLength` function returns the length of the caption or text. A return value of zero indicates that there is no caption or text.

IsIconic

Syntax:

```
BOOL IsIconic(hWnd)
```

Parameter, Type, and Description:

hWnd	HWND	Window handle

Description:

The `IsIconic` function determines whether or not the window specified in `hWnd` is minimized.

Return Value:

The `IsIconic` function returns a nonzero value when the window in `hWnd` is minimized. A return value of zero indicates that the window is not minimized.

IsWindowVisible

Syntax:

```
BOOL IsWindowVisible(hWnd)
```

Parameter, Type, and Description:

hWnd	HWND	Window handle

Description:

The `IsWindowVisible` function determines whether or not the window specified in `hWnd` has been made visible using the `ShowWindow` function. The window can be completely covered by child or pop-up windows and still be considered visible.

Return Value:

The `IsWindowVisible` function returns a nonzero value when the window in `hWnd` has been made visible. A return value of zero indicates that the window has not been made visible.

IsZoomed

Syntax:

```
BOOL IsZoomed(hWnd)
```

Parameter, Type, and Description:

hWnd	HWND	Window handle

Description:

The IsZoomed function determines whether or not the window specified in hWnd has been maximized.

Return Value:

The IsZoomed function returns a nonzero value when the window in hWnd has been maximized. A return value of zero indicates that the window has not been maximized.

MoveWindow

Syntax:

```
void MoveWindow(hWnd, X, Y, nWidth, nHeight, bRepaint)
```

Parameter, Type, and Description:

hWnd	HWND	Pop-up or child window
X	int	X-coordinate of upper-left corner of window
Y	int	Y-coordinate of upper-left corner of window
nWidth	int	New width of window
nHeight	int	New height of window
bRepaint	BOOL	Specifies whether the window is to be repainted after it is moved

Description:

The MoveWindow function sizes the pop-up or child window specified in hWnd. X and Y specify the horizontal and vertical coordinates, respectively, of the upper-left corner of the specified window. X and Y are expressed in screen coordinates for pop-up windows and in client coordinates for child windows. nWidth and nHeight express the new width and height, respectively, of the window.

bRepaint specifies whether or not the window will be repainted after moving:

- The window is repainted when bRepaint is a nonzero value.
- The window is not repainted when bRepaint is set to zero.

This function sends the WM_SIZE message to the window in hWnd.

Return Value:

There is no return value.

OpenIcon

Syntax:

```
BOOL OpenIcon(hWnd)
```

Parameter, Type, and Description:

hWnd	HWND	Window handle

Description:

The `OpenIcon` function displays the minimized window specified in `hWnd` in its original size and position.

Return Value:

The `OpenIcon` function returns a nonzero value when it displays the specified window. A return value of zero indicates that `OpenIcon` cannot display the specified window.

SetWindowPos

Syntax:

```
void SetWindowPos(hWnd, hWndInsertAfter, x, y, cx, cy, wFlags)
```

Parameter, Type, and Description:

hWnd	HWND	Window handle
hWndInsertAfter	HWND	Window in `hWnd` will be positioned after this window
x	int	x-coordinate of window's upper-left corner
y	int	y-coordinate of window's upper-left corner
cx	int	Window's new width
cy	int	Window's new height
wFlags	WORD	16-bit value affecting size and position of window

Description:

The `SetWindowPos` function alters the size, position, and order of the window specified in `hWnd`. `x` and `y` identify the horizontal and vertical coordinates, respectively, of the upper-left corner of the specified window. `cx` and `cy` specify the new width and height, respectively, of the window.

`hWndInsertAfter` specifies a window from the window manager's window list:

- The window in `hWnd` is placed after the window in `hWndInsertAfter` when the `SWP_NOZORDER` flag is not set and `hWndInsertAfter` contains a valid window handle.
- The window in `hWnd` is placed at the top of the window manager's list when `hWndInsertAfter` is NULL.
- The window in `hWnd` is placed at the bottom of the window manager's list when `hWndInsertAfter` is 1.

`wFlags` is a 16-bit value affecting the size and position of the specified window. The following constants can be used with `wFlags`:

Constant	*Meaning*
SWP_DRAWFRAME	Window is framed
SWP_HIDEWINDOW	Window is hidden
SWP_NOACTIVATE	Window is not activated
SWP_NOMOVE	Position is not updated
SWP_NOREDRAW	Changes are not redrawn
SWP_NOSIZE	Size is not updated
SWP_NOZORDER	Ordering is not updated
SWP_SHOWWINDOW	Window is displayed

Return Value:

There is no return value.

SetWindowText

Syntax:

```
void SetWindowText(hWnd, lpString)
```

Parameter, Type, and Description:

hWnd	HWND	Window or control handle
lpString	LPSTR	Pointer to string that contains the new text or caption

Description:

The `SetWindowText` function sets the caption of the window, or the text for the control. `hWnd` specifies the control or window. `lpString` points to the character string containing the new text or caption.

Return Value:

There is no return value.

ShowOwnedPopups

Syntax:

```
void ShowOwnedPopups(hWnd, fShow)
```

Parameter, Type, and Description:

`hWnd`	`HWND`	Window that owns the pop-up windows
`fShow`	`BOOL`	Specifies whether pop-up windows are to be hidden

Description:

The `ShowOwnedPopups` function either shows or hides the pop-up windows owned by the window specified in `hWnd`. `fShow` determines whether the pop-up windows will be shown or hidden:

- All visible pop-up windows will be hidden when `fShow` is zero.
- All hidden pop-up windows will be shown when `fShow` is a nonzero value.

Return Value:

There is no return value.

ShowWindow

Syntax:

```
BOOL ShowWindow(hWnd, nCmdShow)
```

Parameter, Type, and Description:

`hWnd`	`HWND`	Window handle
`nCmdShow`	`int`	Defines how the window is shown

Description:

The ShowWindow function either displays or removes the window specified in hWnd. nCmdShow specifies the way in which the function behaves. The constants used for nCmdShow are:

Constant	*Meaning*
SW_HIDE	Hides the window and another window becomes active
SW_MINIMIZE	Minimizes the window and the top level window becomes active
SW_RESTORE	Activates and displays the window
SW_SHOW	Activates and displays the window in its current size and position
SW_SHOWMAXIMIZED	Activates, displays, and maximizes the window
SW_SHOWMINIMIZED	Activates and displays the window as minimized
SW_SHOWMINNOACTIVE	Displays the window as minimized; the current window remains active
SW_SHOWNA	Displays the window in its current state
SW_SHOWNOACTIVE	Displays the window in its most recent size and position
SW_SHOWNORMAL	Activates and displays the window

Return Value:

The ShowWindow function returns a nonzero value if the window previously was visible. A return value of zero indicates that the window previously was hidden.

Error Functions

Microsoft Windows provides functions with which to indicate errors such as invalid input. These functions flash the specified window, send a beep to the system speaker, or display a message box with the specified text and options.

The following functions are categorized as Error functions for the Window Manager Interface:

Function	*Meaning*
FlashWindow	Flashes a window
MessageBeep	Sends a beep out the system speaker
MessageBox	Creates a window containing the specified caption and text

The rest of this section provides detailed information on each of the functions in this list.

FlashWindow

Syntax:

```
BOOL FlashWindow(hWnd, bInvert)
```

Parameter, Type, and Description:

hWnd	HWND	Window to flash
bInvert	BOOL	Specifies whether to flash the window or return it to its original state

Description:

The FlashWindow function flashes the window specified in hWnd. When the window is flashed, an inactive caption bar becomes active and an active caption bar becomes inactive. bInvert specifies whether the window should be flashed or returned to its original state:

- When bInvert is a nonzero value, the window is flashed from one state to another.
- When bInvert is zero, the window is returned to its original state.

Return Value:

The FlashWindow function returns a nonzero value when the window was active prior to calling FlashWindow. A return value of zero indicates that the window was inactive prior to calling FlashWindow.

MessageBeep

Syntax:

```
void MessageBeep(wType)
```

Parameter, Type, and Description:

wType	WORD	wType is not used. Always set wType to zero

Description:

The MessageBeep function sends a “beep” to the system speaker.

Return Value:

There is no return value.

MessageBox

Syntax:

```
int MessageBox(hWndParent, lpText, lpCaption, wType)
```

Parameter, Type, and Description:

hWndParent	HWND	Window that owns the message box
lpText	LPSTR	Pointer to string that contains the message to be displayed
lpCaption	LPSTR	Pointer to string that contains the caption for dialog box
wType	WORD	Contents of dialog box

Description:

The MessageBox function creates a message box containing a message, a caption, and a combination of icons and buttons. hWndParent specifies the owner of this message box. lpText contains the message to display. lpCaption contains the caption.

wType identifies the contents of the dialog box. wType can be any combination of the following constants:

Message Box Type	*Meaning*
MB_ABORTRETRYIGNORE	Message box contains three buttons: abort, retry, and ignore
MB_APPLMODAL	User must respond to message box before being allowed to continue work in the parent window
MB_DEFBUTTON1	Sets the first button to the default
MB_DEFBUTTON2	Sets the second button to the default
MB_DEFBUTTON3	Sets the third button to the default
MB_ICONASTERICK	Displays an icon showing an *i* inside a circle
MB_ICONEXCLAMATION	Displays the exclamation point icon
MB_ICONHAND	Displays a stop sign icon
MB_ICONINFORMATION	Displays an icon showing an *i* inside a circle
MB_ICONQUESTION	Displays a question mark icon
MB_ICONSTOP	Displays a stop sign icon
MB_OK	Displays only one button: the OK button
MB_OKCANCEL	Displays two buttons: OK and Cancel
MB_RETRYCANCEL	Displays two buttons: Retry and Cancel
MB_SYSTEMMODAL	Applications are halted until the user responds to the message box

Message Box Type	*Meaning*
MB_TASKMODAL	User must respond to the message box before continuing work in the parent window
MB_YESNO	Displays two buttons: Yes and No
MB_YESNOCANCEL	Displays three buttons: Yes, No, and Cancel

Combine constants by using the bitwise OR operator.

Return Value:

The MessageBox function returns zero when the dialog box is not created. If the dialog box is created, the return value is one of the following:

Return Value	*Meaning*
IDABORT	Abort button selected
IDCANCEL	Cancel button selected
IDIGNORE	Ignore button selected
IDNO	No button selected
IDOK	OK button selected
IDRETRY	Retry button selected
IDYES	Yes button selected

Hardware Functions

Windows hardware functions monitor or alter the state of the keyboard and mouse input devices. The following functions are categorized as Hardware functions for the Window Manager Interface:

Function	*Meaning*
EnableHardwareInput	Either enables or disables keyboard and mouse input
GetAsyncKeyState	Gets interrupt-level information on the key state
GetInputState	Determines whether there is any mouse or keyboard input
GetKBCodePage	Indicates the OEM/ANSI tables that are loaded
GetKeyboardState	Gets the state of the keyboard keys
GetKeyboardType	Gets the system keyboard type
GetKeyNameText	Gets the string that contains the name of a key
GetKeyState	Gets the state of a virtual key

Function	*Meaning*
`MapVirtualKey`	Gets the scan code, virtual key code, or ASCII value for the specified virtual key code or scan code
`OemKeyScan`	Maps OEM ASCII codes 0 to 0x0FF into the OEM scan codes and shift states
`SetKeyboardState`	Sets the state of keyboard keys
`VkKeyScan`	Converts the ANSI character to its corresponding virtual key code and shift state

The rest of this section provides detailed information on each of the functions in this list.

EnableHardwareInput

Syntax:

```
BOOL EnableHardwareInput(bEnableInput)
```

Parameter, Type, and Description:

`bEnableInput`	`BOOL`	Specifies whether function should save or discard input

Description:

The `EnableHardwareInput` function disables input from the mouse and keyboard. `bEnableInput` specifies whether input should be saved or discarded:

- If `bEnableInput` is a nonzero value, input is saved.
- If `bEnableInput` is zero, input is discarded.

Return Value:

The `EnableHardwareInput` function returns a nonzero value when input was enabled prior to the call. A return value of zero indicates that input was disabled prior to the call.

GetAsyncKeyState

Syntax:

```
int GetAsyncKeyState(vKey)
```

Parameter, Type, and Description:

`vKey`	`int`	Virtual key code value

Description:

The `GetAsyncKeyState` function gets the state of the key specified in `vKey`.

Return Value:

When the most significant bit of the returned value is set, the key is currently pressed down. When the least significant bit of the returned value is set, the key has been pressed since the last call to `GetAsyncKeyState`.

GetInputState

Syntax:

```
BOOL GetInputState()
```

Description:

The `GetInputState` function determines whether there's an input event that needs processing. This function checks mouse, keyboard, and timer events:

- Mouse events are generated every time the mouse is moved or a mouse button is pressed.
- Keyboard events are generated whenever a key is pressed.
- Timer events are generated at specified time intervals.

These events are stored in the system queue.

Return Value:

The `GetInputState` function returns a nonzero value when there is an input event that needs processing. A return value of zero indicates that no input event is detected.

GetKBCodePage

Syntax:

```
int GetKBCodePage()
```

Description:

The `GetKBCodePage` function determines which OEM/ANSI tables are loaded by Windows.

Return Value:

The `GetKBCodePage` function returns one of the following values to indicate which code page is currently loaded.

Return Value	*Meaning*
437	USA (default)—there is no OEMANSI.BIN in the Windows directory
850	International—OEMANSI.BIN = XLAT850.BIN
860	Portugal—OEMANSI.BIN = XLAT860.BIN
861	Iceland—OEMANSI.BIN = XLAT861.BIN
863	French Canadian—OEMANSI.BIN = XLAT863.BIN
865	Norway/Denmark—OEMANSI.BIN = XLAT865.BIN

GetKeyboardState

Syntax:

```
void GetKeyboardState(lpKeyState)
```

Parameter, Type, and Description:

`lpKeyState`	`BYTE FAR *`	Pointer to buffer of virtual key codes

Description:

The `GetKeyboardState` function determines the status of the 256 virtual keyboard keys and places this status into the buffer pointed to by `lpKeyState`. This buffer contains 256 bytes, one byte for each of the virtual keyboard keys.

The `GetKeyboardState` function copies the status of each virtual key as follows:

- If the high-order bit of the byte is set to 1, the key is down.
- If the high-order bit of the byte is set to 0, the key is up.
- If the low-order bit is set to 1, the key was pressed an odd number of times since start-up.
- If the low-order bit is set to 0, the key was pressed an even number of times since start-up.

Return Value:

There is no return value.

GetKeyboardType

Syntax:

```
int GetKeyboardType(nTypeFlag)
```

Parameter, Type, and Description:

`nTypeFlag`	`int`	Specifies whether a type or subtype of the keyboard is returned

Description:

The `GetKeyboardType` function gets the system keyboard type. The value of `nTypeFlag` specifies whether the function returns a type or subtype of the keyboard. The possible `nTypeFlag` values are:

Value	*Meaning*
0	The keyboard type is returned
1	The keyboard subtype is returned
2	The number of function keys on the keyboard is returned

Return Value:

The `GetKeyboardType` function returns a value corresponding to the `nTypeFlag` setting:

- If `nTypeFlag` is set to 0, a type is returned. The type is one of the following values:

Value	*Meaning*
1	IBM PC/XT or compatible keyboard (83 keys)
2	Olivetti M24 "ICO" keyboard (102 keys)
3	IBM AT or compatible keyboard (84 keys)
4	IBM enhanced or similar keyboard (101 or 102 keys)
5	Nokia 1050 or similar keyboard
6	Nokia 9140 or similar keyboard

- If `nTypeFlag` is set to 1, a subtype is returned. The value is OEM-dependent.
- If `nTypeFlag` is set to 2, the number of function keys on the keyboard is returned.
- Regardless of the value of `nTypeFlag`, a return code of zero indicates that the function cannot identify the system keyboard type.

GetKeyNameText

Syntax:

```
int GetKeyNameText(lParam, lpBuffer, nSize)
```

Parameter, Type, and Description:

lParam	DWORD	Keyboard message being processed
lpBuffer	LPSTR	Buffer to receive the key name
nSize	WORD	Maximum length of the name

Description:

The `GetKeyNameText` function gets the name of a key. `lParam` is a 32-bit parameter for the keyboard message being processed by the function. `lpBuffer` points to the buffer that will store the name of the key. `nSize` specifies the maximum length of the string, in bytes, and does not count the NULL terminator for the string. The keyboard driver maintains a list of names in the form of character strings.

Return Value:

The `GetKeyNameText` function returns the number of bytes copied to `lpBuffer`.

GetKeyState

Syntax:

```
int GetKeyState(nVirtKey)
```

Parameter, Type, and Description:

nVirtKey	int	Virtual key

Description:

The `GetKeyState` function gets the state of the key specified in `nVirtKey`. `nVirtKey` specifies the ASCII or virtual key code of the virtual key.

The virtual key codes and constants are as follows:

Decimal	*Hex*	*Constant*	*Key*
1	01	VK_LBUTTON	
2	02	VK_RBUTTON	
3	03	VK_CANCEL	Ctrl-break
4	04	VK_MBUTTON	

Decimal	Hex	Constant	Key
8	08	VK_BACK	Backspace
9	09	VK_TAB	Tab
12	0C	VK_CLEAR	Numeric keypad 5 with Num Lock off
13	0D	VK_RETURN	Enter
16	10	VK_SHIFT	Shift
17	11	VK_CONTROL	Ctrl
18	12	VK_MENU	Alt
19	13	VK_PAUSE	Pause
20	14	VK_CAPITAL	Caps Lock
27	1B	VK_ESCAPE	Esc
32	20	VK_SPACE	Space bar
33	21	VK_PRIOR	PgUp
34	22	VK_NEXT	PgDn
35	23	VK_END	End
36	24	VK_HOME	Home
37	25	VK_LEFT	Left arrow
38	26	VK_UP	Up arrow
39	27	VK_RIGHT	Right arrow
40	28	VK_DOWN	Down arrow
41	29	VK_SELECT	
42	2A	VK_PRINT	
43	2B	VK_EXECUTE	
44	2C	VK_SNAPSHOT	PrtSc
45	2D	VK_INSERT	Ins
46	2E	VK_DELETE	Del
47	2F	VK_HELP	
48–57	30–39	VK_0 to VK_9	0 to 9 on main keyboard
65–90	41–5A	VK_A to VK_Z	A to Z
96–105	60–69	VK_NUMPAD0 to VK_NUMPAD9	Numeric keypad 0 to numeric keypad 9 (Num Lock on)
106	6A	VK_MULTIPLY	* on numeric keypad
107	6B	VK_ADD	+ on numeric keypad
108	6C	VK_SEPARATOR	
109	6D	VK_SUBTRACT	– on numeric keypad
110	6E	VK_DECIMAL	. on numeric keypad
111	6F	VK_DIVIDE	/ on numeric keypad

Decimal	*Hex*	*Constant*	*Key*
112–123	70–7B	VK_F1 to VK_F12	F1 to F12
124	7C	VK_F13	
125	7D	VK_F14	
126	7E	VK_F15	
127	7F	VK_F16	
144	90	VK_NUMLOCK	Num Lock

Return Value:

The `GetKeyState` function returns the status of the specified virtual key:

- If the high-order bit of the byte is set to 1, the key is down.
- If the high-order bit of the byte is set to 0, the key is up.
- If the low-order bit is set to 1, the key was pressed an odd number of times since startup (indicating the key is toggled).
- If the low-order bit is set to 0, the key was pressed an even number of times since startup (indicating the key is untoggled).

MapVirtualKey

Syntax:

```
WORD MapVirtualKey(wCode, wMapType)
```

Parameter, Type, and Description:

`wCode`	`WORD`	Virtual key or scan code
`wMapType`	`WORD`	Type of mapping to perform

Description:

The `MapVirtualKey` function gets the scan code, virtual key code, or ASCII value for the virtual key code or scan code specified in `wCode`:

- When `wMapType` is set to 0, `wCode` must be a virtual key code.
- When `wMapType` is set to 1, `wCode` must be a scan code.
- When `wMapType` is set to 2, `wCode` must be a virtual key code.

Return Value:

The `MapVirtualKey` function returns the scan code, virtual key code, or ASCII value specified by `wMapType`:

- When `wMapType` is set to 0, the return code is the corresponding scan code.
- When `wMapType` is set to 1, the return code is the corresponding virtual key code.
- When `wMapType` is set to 2, the return code is the corresponding unshifted ASCII value.

OemKeyScan

Syntax:

```
DWORD OemKeyScan(wOemChar)
```

Parameter, Type, and Description:

`wOemChar`	`WORD`	ASCII value of an OEM character

Description:

The `OemKeyScan` function maps OEM ASCII codes into OEM scan codes and shift states. `wOemChar` specifies the ASCII value of the OEM character to map.

Return Value:

The `OemKeyScan` function returns information on the scan code and shift state of the specified character:

- The low-order word of the return value indicates the scan code of the OEM character.
- The high-order word of the return value contains flags that indicate the shift state as follows:

Bit	*Meaning*
2	Ctrl pressed
1	Shift pressed

- A return value of –1 in both the high- and low-order words indicates that the specified character is not defined in the OEM character tables.

SetKeyboardState

Syntax:

```
void SetKeyboardState(lpKeyState)
```

Parameter, Type, and Description:

`lpKeyState`	`BYTE FAR *`	Pointer to array containing keyboard key states

Description:

The `SetKeyboardState` function sets the Windows keyboard state table to the values in the 256-byte array pointed to by `lpKeyState`. The LEDs and BIOS flags for the Num Lock, Caps Lock, and Scroll Lock keys are set according to the corresponding values in the array.

Return Value:

There is no return value.

VkKeyScan

Syntax:

```
int VkKeyScan(cChar)
```

Parameter, Type, and Description:

`cChar`	`char`	ANSI character

Description:

The `VkKeyScan` function gets the virtual key code and shift state for the ANSI character specified in `cChar`.

Return Value:

The `VkKeyScan` function returns the virtual key code and shift state for the specified ANSI character:

- The low-order byte of the returned value specifies the virtual key code.
- The high-order byte of the returned value specifies the shift states, as follows:

Value	*Meaning*
0	No shift
1	Shifted character
2	Control character
6	Ctrl + Alt character
7	Shift + Ctrl + Alt character
3, 4, 5	Shift key combination not used for characters

- A return code of –1 in both the low- and high-order bytes indicates that no key code is found that matches the specified character.

Hook Functions

System hooks are shared resources that install Filter functions. Filter functions process events before they go to the application's message loop. The `SetWindowsHook` function specifies these Filter functions. Messages generated by a specific type of event are sent to Filter functions installed by the same type of hook. The following functions are categorized as Hook functions for the Window Manager Interface:

Function	*Meaning*
`CallMsgFilter`	Passes a message to the current filter function
`DefHookProc`	Calls the next function in the filter function chain
`SetWindowsHook`	Specifies a system filter function, an application filter function, or both
`UnhookWindowsHook`	Removes a filter function from the filter function chain

The rest of this section provides detailed information on each of the functions in this list.

CallMsgFilter

Syntax:

```
BOOL CallMsgFilter(lpMsg, nCode)
```

Parameter, Type, and Description:

`lpMsg`	`LPMSG`	Pointer to `MSG` data structure containing message
`nCode`	`int`	Specifies how the message is processed

Description:

The `CallMsgFilter` function passes the message pointed to by `lpMsg` to the current message filter function, set by the `SetWindowsHook` function. (See the description of `SetWindowsHook` in this chapter for more information.) The filter function uses `nCode` to determine how to process the message.

The message is stored in a data structure of type `MSG`. The `MSG` structure is:

```
typedef struct tagMSG {
     HWND hwnd;
     WORD message;
```

```
     WORD wParam;
     LONG lParam;
     DWORD time;
     POINT pt;
} MSG;
```

where:

hwnd is the window that receives the message

message is the message number

wParam is additional message information

lParam is additional message information

time is the time the message was posted

pt is the screen coordinates of the cursor position when the message was posted

Return Value:

The CallMsgFilter function returns FALSE when the message requires processing. If no further processing is required, the function returns TRUE.

DefHookProc

Syntax:

```
DWORD DefHookProc(code, wParam, lParam, lplpfnNextHook)
```

Parameter, Type, and Description:

code	int	Specifies how to process the message
wParam	WORD	Word parameter of the message
lParam	DWORD	Long parameter of the message
lplpfnNextHook	FARPROC FAR *	Pointer to memory location containing the FARPROC structure

Description:

The DefHookProc function calls the next function in the Hook function chain. Windows creates the Hook function chain when an application defines more than one Hook function using SetWindowsHook. lplpfnNextHook points to the memory location containing the FARPROC structure, which location is returned by the SetWindowsHook function. (See the description of SetWindowsHook in this chapter for more information.)

Return Value:

The `DefHookProc` function returns a value relating to the `code` parameter.

SetWindowsHook

Syntax:

```
FARPROC SetWindowsHook(nFilterType, lpFilterFunc)
```

Parameter, Type, and Description:

`nFilterType`	`int`	System hook to install
`lpFilterFunc`	`FARPROC`	Procedure instance address of the filter function

Description:

The `SetWindowsHook` function installs the system hook specified in `nFilterType`. `lpFilterFunc` is the procedure instance address of the filter function, which handles events before they go to the application's message loop.

The valid system hooks for `nFilterType` are:

System Hook	*Meaning*
WH_CALLWNDPROC	Window function filter installed
WH_GETMESSAGE	Message filter installed
WH_JOURNALPLAYBACK	Journaling playback filter installed
WH_JOURNALRECORD	Journaling record filter installed
WH_KEYBOARD	Keyboard filter installed
WH_MSGFILTER	Message filter installed
WH_SYSMSGFILTER	System wide message filter installed

Return Value:

The `SetWindowsHook` function returns the pointer to the previous procedure instance address for the previous filter function. NULL is returned if no previous filter was installed.

UnhookWindowsHook

Syntax:

```
BOOL UnhookWindowsHook(nHook, lpfnHook)
```

Parameter, Type, and Description:

nHook	int	Type of Hook function to remove
lpfnHook	FARPROC	Procedure instance address of the Hook function

Description:

The UnhookWindowsHook function removes the Hook function specified in lpfnHook. The type of Hook function to remove is specified in nHook.

The values used for nHook are:

Value	*Meaning*
WH_CALLWNDPROC	Window function filter
WH_GETMESSAGE	Message filter
WH_JOURNALPLAYBACK	Journaling playback filter
WH_JOURNALRECORD	Journaling record filter
WH_KEYBOARD	Keyboard filter
WH_MSGFILTER	Message filter

Return Value:

The UnhookWindowsHook returns a nonzero value when the specified Hook function is removed. A return value of zero indicates that the Hook function cannot be removed.

Information Functions

Microsoft Windows Information functions enable you to retrieve information pertaining to the number and position of the windows on the screen. The following functions are categorized as Information functions for the Window Manager Interface:

Function	*Meaning*
AnyPopup	Determines whether a pop-up window exists
ChildWindowFromPoint	Determines the pop-up window that contains the specified point
EnumChildWindows	Enumerates the child windows that belong to the specified parent window
EnumTaskWindows	Enumerates the windows associated with the specified task
EnumWindows	Enumerates the windows currently displayed

Function	*Meaning*
`FindWindow`	Gets the window handle for the specified class and caption
`GetDesktopWindow`	Gets the window handle for the Windows desktop window
`GetNextWindow`	Gets the handle for the next or previous window
`GetParent`	Gets the window handle for the parent window of the specified window
`GetTopWindow`	Gets the handle to the top-level child window
`GetWindow`	Gets a window handle from the window manager's list
`GetWindowTask`	Gets a task handle for the task associated with the window
`IsChild`	Determines whether a window is a descendant of the specified window
`IsWindow`	Determines whether a window is valid
`SetParent`	Sets the parent window for a child window
`WindowFromPoint`	Determines which window contains the specified point

The rest of this section provides detailed information on each of the functions in this list.

AnyPopup

Syntax:

None.

Description:

The `AnyPopUp` function determines whether any pop-up windows exist on the screen.

Return Value:

The `AnyPopUp` function returns a nonzero value when a pop-up window exists. A return value of zero indicates that no pop-up window exists.

ChildWindowFromPoint

Syntax:

```
HWND ChildWindowFromPoint(hWndParent, Point)
```

Parameter, Type, and Description:

hWndParent	HWND	Parent window
Point	POINT	Client coordinates of test point

Description:

The ChildWindowFromPoint function finds the child window containing the point specified in Point. Point specifies client coordinates. hWndParent specifies the parent window.

Return Value:

The value returned indicates the child window that contains the specified point.

- If the specified point lies within a child window, the ChildWindowFromPoint function returns the handle for the child window.
- If the point does not lie within a child window, but does lie inside the parent window, the ChildWindowFromPoint function returns the handle for the parent window.
- If the point does not lie within the parent window, the ChildWindowFromPoint function returns NULL.

EnumChildWindows

Syntax:

```
BOOL EnumChildWindows(hWndParent, lpEnumFunc, lParam)
```

Parameter, Type, and Description:

hWndParent	HWND	Parent window
lpEnumFunc	FARPROC	Procedure instance address of callback function
lParam	DWORD	Value to pass to callback function

Description:

The EnumChildWindows function enumerates the child windows for the parent window specified in hWndParent. The handle of each child window is passed to the callback function pointed to by lpEnumFunc. You create the value in lpEnumFunc by using MakeProcInstance. (See this chapter's description of the MakeProcInstance function for more information.) The callback function must follow these conventions and formats:

Syntax:

```
BOOL FAR PASCAL EnumFunc(hWnd, lParam)
```

Parameter, Type, and Description:

HWND	hWnd	Window handle
DWORD	lParam	Parameter in lParam from EnumChildWindows

Description:

EnumFunc is a placeholder for the actual function name, which you must export by using EXPORTS in the application's module definition file.

Return Value:

The callback function should return a nonzero value when enumeration is to continue. Set the return code to zero to stop enumeration.

Return Value:

The EnumChildWindows function returns a nonzero value when all child windows have been enumerated. A return value of zero indicates that the function cannot enumerate child windows.

EnumTaskWindows

Syntax:

```
BOOL EnumTaskWindows(hTask, lpEnumFunc, lParam)
```

Parameter, Type, and Description:

hTask	HANDLE	Task handle
lpEnumFunc	FARPROC	Procedure instance address for callback function
lParam	DWORD	Value to pass to callback function

Description:

The EnumTaskWindows function enumerates the windows associated with the task specified in hTask. The value used for hTask is returned by the GetCurrentTask function. lpEnumFunc points to the callback function. The structure of the callback function is:

Syntax:

```
BOOL FAR PASCAL EnumFunc(hWnd, lParam)
```

Parameter, Type, and Description:

hWnd	HWND	Window associated with current task
lParam	DWORD	Parameter in lParam from EnumTaskWindows

Description:

EnumFunc is a placeholder for the actual function name, which you must export by using EXPORTS in the application's module definition file.

Return Value:

The callback function should return a nonzero value to continue enumeration. Set the return code to zero to stop enumeration.

Return Value:

The EnumTaskWindows function returns a nonzero value when all windows associated with the task are enumerated. A return value of zero indicates that the function cannot enumerate all windows associated with the task.

EnumWindows

Syntax:

```
BOOL EnumWindows(lpEnumFunc, lParam)
```

Parameter, Type, and Description:

lpEnumFunc	FARPROC	Procedure instance address of callback function
lParam	DWORD	Value passed to callback function

Description:

The EnumWindows function enumerates the parent windows on the screen. The handle of each function is passed to the callback function pointed to by lpEnumFunc. The structure of the callback function is:

Syntax:

```
BOOL FAR PASCAL EnumFunc(hWnd, lParam)
```

Parameter, Type, and Description:

hWnd	HWND	Window handle
lParam	DWORD	Parameter in lParam from EnumWindows

Description:

EnumFunc is a placeholder for the actual function name, which you must export by using EXPORTS in the application's module definition file.

Return Value:

The callback function should return a nonzero value to continue enumeration. Set the return code to zero to stop enumeration.

Return Value:

The `EnumWindows` function returns a nonzero value when window enumeration has been completed. A return code of zero indicates that the function cannot enumerate the windows.

FindWindow

Syntax:

```
HWND FindWindow(lpClassName, lpWindowName)
```

Parameter, Type, and Description:

`lpClassName`	`LPSTR`	Pointer to string that contains the window class name
`lpWindowName`	`LPSTR`	Pointer to string that contains the window name

Description:

The `FindWindow` function returns the window handle of the window with the specified window class name and window name. `lpClassName` specifies the window class name. `lpWindowName` specifies the window name. `lpClassName` and `lpWindowName` point to null-terminated strings.

Return Value:

The `FindWindow` function returns the window handle of the window matching the specifications. If no matching window is found, `FindWindow` returns NULL.

GetDesktopWindow

Syntax:

```
HWND GetDesktopWindow()
```

Description:

The `GetDesktopWindow` function returns the window handle of the Windows desktop window.

Return Value:

The `GetDesktopWindow` function returns the handle to the Windows desktop window.

GetNextWindow

Syntax:

```
HWND    GetNextWindow(hWnd, wFlag)
```

Parameter, Type, and Description:

`hWnd`	`HWND`	Current window
`wFlag`	`WORD`	Specifies whether to get next or previous window handle

Description:

The `GetNextWindow` function returns the next, or previous, window in the window manager's list. `hWnd` specifies the current window, which can be either top-level or child window. `wFlag` specifies the return value. If `hWnd` is a handle to a child window, the function returns the handle of the next (previous) child window.

Return Value:

The `wFlag` setting determines whether the `GetNextWindow` function returns the previous or next window handle:

- If `wFlag` is `GW_HWNDNEXT`, the next window handle is returned.
- If `wFlag` is `GW_HWNDPREV`, the previous window handle is returned.

GetParent

Syntax:

```
HWND GetParent(hWnd)
```

Parameter, Type, and Description:

`hWnd`	`HWND`	Window handle

Description:

The `GetParent` function gets the handle for the parent window of the window specified in `hWnd`.

Return Value:

If the specified window has a parent, the `GetParent` function returns the window handle for the parent window. A NULL return value indicates that the specified window has no parent.

GetTopWindow

Syntax:

```
HWND GetTopWindow(hWnd)
```

Parameter, Type, and Description:

hWnd	HWND	Parent window

Description:

The `GetTopWindow` function gets the handle of the top-level child window for the parent window specified in `hWnd`.

Return Value:

The `GetTopWindow` function returns the handle of the top-level child window. A NULL return value indicates that the specified parent window has no child windows.

GetWindow

Syntax:

```
HWND GetWindow(hWnd, wCmd)
```

Parameter, Type, and Description:

hWnd	HWND	Window handle
wCmd	WORD	Window relationship

Description:

The `GetWindow` function returns the handle of the window that has the specified relationship with the window specified in `hWnd`. `wCmd` specifies the window relationship and can be one of the following values:

Value	*Meaning*
GW_CHILD	First child window
GW_HWNDFIRST	First sibling window for a child window, or first top-level window
GW_HWNDLAST	Last sibling window for a child window, or last top-level window
GW_HWNDNEXT	Next window on window manager's list
GW_HWNDPREV	Previous window on window manager's list
GW_OWNER	Window owner

Return Value:

If an appropriate window is found, the `GetWindow` function returns its window handle. A NULL return value indicates that no window is found or an error occurs.

GetWindowTask

Syntax:

```
HANDLE GetWindowTask(hWnd)
```

Parameter, Type, and Description:

`hWnd`	`HWND`	Window handle

Description:

The `GetWindowTask` function gets the handle of the task associated with the window specified in `hWnd`. Instances of applications are tasks, since each instance is executed as an independent unit.

Return Value:

The `GetWindowTask` function returns the handle of the associated task.

IsChild

Syntax:

```
BOOL IsChild(hWndParent, hWnd)
```

Parameter, Type, and Description:

`hWndParent`	`HWND`	Window handle of presumed parent window
`hWnd`	`HWND`	Window to check

Description:

The `IsChild` function determines whether the window in `hWnd` is a child window of the window specified in `hWndParent`.

Return Value:

The `IsChild` function returns TRUE when the window specified in `hWnd` is a child window, or descendant, of the window specified in `hWndParent`. A return value of FALSE indicates that the window specified in `hWnd` is not a child window of the window specified in `hWndParent`.

IsWindow

Syntax:

```
BOOL IsWindow(hWnd)
```

Parameter, Type, and Description:

hWnd	HWND	Window handle

Description:

The `IsWindow` function determines whether the window specified in `hWnd` is a valid window.

Return Value:

The `IsWindow` function returns a nonzero value when the specified window is a valid window. A return value of zero indicates that the specified window is not a valid window.

SetParent

Syntax:

```
HWND SetParent(hWndChild, hWndNewParent)
```

Parameter, Type, and Description:

hWndChild	HWND	Child Window
hWndNewParent	HWND	New parent window

Description:

The `SetParent` function sets the parent window of the child window in `hWndChild` to the window in `hWndNewParent`.

Return Value:

The `SetParent` function returns the window handle of the previous parent window for `hWndChild`.

WindowFromPoint

Syntax:

```
HWND WindowFromPoint(Point)
```

Parameter, Type, and Description:

`Point` `POINT` `POINT` data structure containing the specified point

Description:

The `WindowFromPoint` function determines which window contains the point specified in `Point`. The screen coordinates for the point are stored in a data structure of type `POINT`. The `POINT` structure is:

```
typedef struct tagPOINT {
    int x;
    int y;
} POINT;
```

where:

`x` is the horizontal coordinate of the point

`y` is the vertical coordinate of the point

Return Value:

The `WindowFromPoint` function returns the window handle of the window containing the point. A NULL return value indicates that no window contains the specified point.

Input Functions

Windows Input functions provide the interface to the system devices: the mouse, the keyboard, and the timer. The functions enable you to control these system devices and specify the way that Windows will handle input from these devices. The following functions are categorized as Input functions for the Window Manager Interface:

Function	*Meaning*
`EnableWindow`	Either enables or disables mouse and keyboard input for the application
`GetActiveWindow`	Gets the handle of the active window
`GetCapture`	Gets the handle of the window that has the mouse capture
`GetCurrentTime`	Gets the Windows time
`GetDoubleClickTime`	Gets the mouse double-click time
`GetFocus`	Gets the handle of the window that has the input focus
`GetSysModalWindow`	Gets the handle of a system modal window

Function	*Meaning*
`GetTickCount`	Gets the number of timer ticks that have occurred since the system was booted
`IsWindowEnabled`	Determines whether mouse and keyboard input is enabled for the specified window
`KillTimer`	Kills the specified timer event
`ReleaseCapture`	Releases the mouse capture
`SetActiveWindow`	Makes a window the active window
`SetCapture`	Gives the mouse capture to the specified window
`SetDoubleClickTime`	Sets the mouse double-click time
`SetFocus`	Gives the input focus to the specified window
`SetSysModalWindow`	Defines the specified window as a system modal window
`SetTimer`	Creates a system timer event
`SwapMouseButton`	Switches the left and right mouse buttons

The rest of this section provides detailed information on each of the functions in this list.

EnableWindow

Syntax:

```
BOOL EnableWindow(hWnd, bEnable)
```

Parameter, Type, and Description:

`hWnd`	`HWND`	Window handle
`bEnable`	`BOOL`	Specifies whether to enable or disable the window

Description:

The `EnableWindow` function enables or disables all mouse and keyboard input to the window specified in `hWnd`. `bEnable` specifies whether input is enabled or disabled:

- If `bEnable` is a nonzero value, input is enabled.
- If `bEnable` is zero, input is disabled.

Return Value:

The `EnableWindow` function returns a nonzero value when the input is either enabled or disabled, depending on the setting of `bEnable`. A return value of zero indicates that the function cannot enable, or disable, the input.

GetActiveWindow

Syntax:

```
HWND GetActiveWindow()
```

Description:

The `GetActiveWindow` function gets the handle of the active window. The active window either has the current input focus or has been made the active window by `SetActiveWindow`.

Return Value:

The `GetActiveWindow` function returns the handle of the active window

GetCapture

Syntax:

```
HWND GetCapture()
```

Description:

The `GetCapture` function gets the handle of the window that has the mouse capture. The retrieved handle identifies the window that receives the mouse input.

Return Value:

The `GetCapture` function returns the handle of the window that has the mouse capture. A NULL return value indicates that no window has the mouse capture.

GetCurrentTime

Syntax:

```
DWORD GetCurrentTime()
```

Description:

The `GetCurrentTime` function gets the number of milliseconds elapsed since the system booted. The retrieved time is called *Windows time*.

Return Value:

The `GetCurrentTime` function returns the number of milliseconds since the system was booted, called the Windows time.

GetDoubleClickTime

Syntax:

```
WORD GetDoubleClickTime()
```

Description:

The `GetDoubleClickTime` function gets the double-click time, measured in milliseconds. The double-click time is a specified maximum number of milliseconds between the first click of a button and the second click of the same button.

Return Value:

The `GetDoubleClickTime` function returns the double-click time, measured in milliseconds.

GetFocus

Syntax:

```
HWND GetFocus()
```

Description:

The `GetFocus` function gets the handle of the window that has the input focus.

Return Value:

The `GetFocus` function returns the handle of the window that has the input focus. NULL is a possible return value.

GetSysModalWindow

Syntax:

```
HWND GetSysModalWindow()
```

Description:

The `GetSysModalWindow` function gets the handle of a system modal window.

Return Value:

The `GetSysModalWindow` returns the window handle for the system modal window when a system modal window is found. A NULL return value indicates that no system modal window is found.

GetTickCount

Syntax:

```
DWORD GetTickCount()
```

Description:

The `GetTickCount` function gets the number of milliseconds elapsed since system start-up.

Return Value:

The `GetTickCount` function returns the number of milliseconds elapsed since system start-up.

IsWindowEnabled

Syntax:

```
BOOL IsWindowEnabled(hWnd)
```

Parameter, Type, and Description:

`hWnd`	`HWND`	Window handle

Description:

The `IsWindowEnabled` function determines whether mouse and keyboard input is enabled for the window specified in `hWnd`.

Return Value:

The `IsWindowEnabled` function returns a nonzero value when input is enabled. A return value of zero indicates that input is disabled.

KillTimer

Syntax:

```
BOOL KillTimer(hWnd, nIDEvent)
```

Parameter, Type, and Description:

`hWnd`	`HWND`	Window associated with timer
`nIDEvent`	`int`	Timer event

Description:

The `KillTimer` function terminates the timer event specified by `hWnd` and `nIDEvent`. `hWnd` specifies the window associated with the timer event. `nIDEvent` specifies the timer event.

Return Value:

The `KillTimer` function returns a nonzero value when the timer event is terminated. A return value of zero indicates that the timer event was not found.

ReleaseCapture

Syntax:

```
void ReleaseCapture()
```

Description:

The `ReleaseCapture` function restores normal input processing by releasing the mouse capture.

Return Value:

There is no return value.

SetActiveWindow

Syntax:

```
HWND SetActiveWindow(hWnd)
```

Parameter, Type, and Description:

`hWnd`	`HWND`	Top-level window to activate

Description:

The `SetActiveWindow` function designates the top-level window in `hWnd` as the active window. Use this function cautiously since standard Windows activation is bypassed.

Return Value:

The `SetActiveWindow` function returns the handle of the previously active window.

SetCapture

Syntax:

```
HWND SetCapture(hWnd)
```

Parameter, Type, and Description:

hWnd	HWND	Window to receive mouse input

Description:

The `SetCapture` function sends all subsequent mouse input to the window specified in `hWnd`.

Return Value:

The `SetCapture` function returns the handle of the window that previously had the mouse capture. A NULL return value indicates that no window previously had the mouse capture.

SetDoubleClickTime

Syntax:

```
void SetDoubleClickTime(wCount)
```

Parameter, Type, and Description:

wCount	WORD	Double-click time measured in milliseconds

Description:

The `SetDoubleClickTime` function defines the maximum number of milliseconds between two clicks of a button (a double click). `wCount` specifies the double-click time. If `wCount` is set to 0, `SetDoubleClickTime` uses the default double-click time of 500 milliseconds.

Return Value:

There is no return value.

SetFocus

Syntax:

```
HWND SetFocus(hWnd)
```

Parameter, Type, and Description:

`hWnd`	`HWND`	Window to receive keyboard input

Description:

The `SetFocus` function sends all keyboard input (the input focus) to the window specified in `hWnd`. When `hWnd` is NULL, all keyboard input is ignored. The `WM_KILLFOCUS` message is sent to the window that previously held the input focus. The `SetFocus` function sends the `WM_SETFOCUS` message to the window in `hWnd`.

Return Value:

The `SetFocus` function returns the handle of the window that previously held the input focus. A NULL return value indicates that no window previously held the input focus.

SetSysModalWindow

Syntax:

```
HWND SetSysModalWindow(hWnd)
```

Parameter, Type, and Description:

`hWnd`	`HWND`	Window to be made system modal

Description:

The `SetSysModalWindow` function makes the window specified in `hWnd` the system modal window.

Return Value:

The `SetSysModalWindow` function returns the handle of the previous system modal window.

SetTimer

Syntax:

```
WORD SetTimer(hWnd, nIDEvent, wElapse, lpTimerFunc)
```

Parameter, Type, and Description:

`hWnd`	`HWND`	Window associated with timer
`nIDEvent`	`int`	Timer event

wElapse	WORD	Time elapsed between timer events
lpTimerFunc	FARPROC	Procedure instance address of timer function

Description:

The SetTimer function creates a system timer event. hWnd specifies the window associated with the timer. When no window is associated with the timer, hWnd is set to NULL. When a window is associated with the timer, nIDEvent specifies the timer event. wElapse defines the number of milliseconds elapsed between timer events.

lpTimerFunc contains the procedure instance address of the function that processes the event. The WM_TIMER message is sent to the function specified in lpTimerFunc when a timer event occurs. The timer function must follow these conventions and formats:

Syntax:

```
WORD FAR PASCAL TimerFunc(hWnd, wMsg, nIDEvent, dwTime)
```

Parameter, Type, and Description:

hWnd	HWND	Window associated with timer event
wMsg	WORD	Specifies WM_TIMER message
nIDEvent	int	Timer identification
dwTime	DWORD	System time

Description:

TimerFunc is a placeholder for the function name that you must export by using EXPORTS in the application's module definition file. When lpTimerFunc is NULL, the WM_TIMER message is placed in the application queue.

Return Value:

The return value is application defined.

Return Value:

The SetTimer function returns the integer identifier for the new timer event. A return value of zero indicates that the timer could not be created.

SwapMouseButton

Syntax:

```
BOOL SwapMouseButton(bSwap)
```

Parameter, Type, and Description:

`bSwap`	`BOOL`	Specifies whether to reverse or restore mouse button meanings

Description:

The `SwapMouseButton` function redefines the way the left and right mouse buttons are interpreted:

- When `bSwap` is TRUE, the left mouse button generates right mouse button messages and the right mouse button generates left mouse button messages.
- When `bSwap` is FALSE, the mouse buttons are interpreted normally.

Return Value:

The `SwapMouseButton` function returns TRUE when the mouse buttons have been swapped. A return value of FALSE indicates that the buttons are set normally.

Menu Functions

Menus in a Windows application present the user with a choice of selections or items. The user selects from a menu by using a mouse or keyboard. The selection dictates the application's next action. Menu selections can contain a single entry or provide a pop-up menu that provides additional menu selections. The following functions are categorized as Menu functions for the Window Manager Interface:

Function	*Meaning*
`AppendMenu`	Appends a menu item to the menu
`CheckMenuItem`	Either puts or removes a check mark beside a pop-up menu item
`CreateMenu`	Creates an empty menu
`CreatePopupMenu`	Creates an empty pop-up menu
`DeleteMenu`	Deletes a menu item
`DestroyMenu`	Destroys a menu
`DrawMenuBar`	Redraws the Menu bar
`EnableMenuItem`	Sets the state of a menu item
`GetMenu`	Gets the menu handle for a window
`GetMenuCheckMarkDimensions`	Gets the dimensions of the default menu check mark bitmap
`GetMenuItemCount`	Gets the number of items in a menu
`GetMenuItemID`	Gets the ID for a menu item

Function	*Meaning*
`GetMenuState`	Gets the status for a menu item
`GetMenuString`	Copies a menu label to a string
`GetSubMenu`	Gets the menu handle for a pop-up menu
`GetSystemMenu`	Provides access to the System menu
`HiliteMenuItem`	Either highlights or removes the highlight from a top-level menu item
`InsertMenu`	Inserts a menu item into a menu
`LoadMenuIndirect`	Loads a menu resource
`ModifyMenu`	Modifies a menu item
`RemoveMenu`	Removes an item from a menu
`SetMenu`	Defines a new menu for the window
`SetMenuItemBitmaps`	Defines bitmaps for a menu item
`TrackPopupMenu`	Displays a pop-up menu at the specified position

The rest of this section provides detailed information on each of the functions in this list.

AppendMenu

Syntax:

```
BOOL AppendMenu(hMenu, wFlags, wIDNewItem, lpNewItem)
```

Parameter, Type, and Description:

`hMenu`	`HMENU`	Menu to modify
`wFlags`	`WORD`	State of new menu item
`wIDNewItem`	`WORD`	Command ID of new menu item, or menu handle of pop-up menu
`lpNewItem`	`LPSTR`	Content of new menu item

Description:

The `AppendMenu` function adds a new menu item at the end of the menu specified in `hMenu`. `wFlags` defines the state of the new menu item. The flags that may be set in `wFlags` are:

Value	*Meaning*
`MF_BITMAP`	Uses a bitmap as the item. The handle of the bitmap is in the low-order word of `lpNewItem`. This flag should not be used with `MF_STRING` or `MF_OWNERDRAW`.

Value	*Meaning*
MF_CHECKED	Puts a check mark next to the item. This flag should not be used with MF_UNCHECKED.
MF_DISABLED	Disables, but does not gray, the menu item. This flag should not be used with MF_ENABLED or MF_GRAYED.
MF_ENABLED	Enables the menu item. This flag should not be used with MF_DISABLED or MF_GRAYED.
MF_GRAYED	Disables and grays the menu item. This flag should not be used with MF_DISABLED or MF_ENABLED.
MF_MENUBARBREAK	Puts menu items on a new line. For pop-up menus, this flag puts the new item in a new column and separates the columns with a vertical line. This flag should not be used with MF_MENUBREAK.
MF_MENUBREAK	Puts menu items on a new line. For pop-up menus, puts the new item in a new column but does not separate the columns with a vertical line. This flag should not be used with MF_MENUBARBREAK.
MF_OWNERDRAW	Item is an owner-draw item. This flag should not be used with MF_BITMAP or MF_STRING.
MF_POPUP	Item has a pop-up menu associated with it. wIDNewItem specifies the handle of the pop-up window.
MF_SEPARATOR	Creates a horizontal line in a pop-up menu.
MF_STRING	Menu item is a character string. This flag should not be used with MF_BITMAP or MF_OWNERDRAW.
MF_UNCHECKED	No check mark is placed by the menu item. This flag should not be used with MF_CHECKED.

wIDNewItem contains the command ID of the menu item except when wFlags contains MF_POPUP. When wFlags contains MF_POPUP, wIDNewItem contains the menu handle of the pop-up menu.

lpNewItem determines the contents of the new menu item according to the setting of the flags in wFlags:

- If wFlags is set with MF_STRING, lpNewItem contains a long pointer to a null-terminated string.
- If wFlags is set with MF_BITMAP, lpNewItem contains the handle of the bitmap in its low-order word.
- If wFlags is set with MF_OWNERDRAW, lpNewItem contains the 32-bit value, supplied by the application, that provides data about the menu item.

Return Value:

TRUE is returned when successful. FALSE is returned when unsuccessful.

CheckMenuItem

Syntax:

```
BOOL CheckMenuItem(hMenu, wIDCheckItem, wCheck)
```

Parameter, Type, and Description:

hMenu	HMENU	Menu handle
wIDCheckItem	WORD	Menu item to check
wCheck	WORD	Specifies how to check menu item

Description:

The CheckMenuItem function either puts a check mark by or removes a check mark from the menu item in wIDCheckItem. The pop-up menu specified in hMenu contains the menu item in wIDCheckItem. wCheck specifies how to check the menu item. wCheck can be any combination of the following flags:

Flag	*Meaning*
MF_BYCOMMAND	wIDCheckItem specifies a menu-item ID. This flag cannot be used with MF_BYPOSITION.
MF_BYPOSITION	wIDCheckItem specifies the menu-item position. This flag cannot be used with MF_BYCOMMAND. The menu begins at zero.
MF_CHECKED	Places a check mark by the item.
MF_UNCHECKED	Removes a check mark from the item.

Combine flags by using the bitwise OR operator.

Note: Top-level menu items cannot be checked with this function.

Return Value:

The CheckMenuItem function returns the previous state of the button, either MF_CHECKED or MF_UNCHECKED. A return value of –1 indicates that the specified menu item is invalid.

CreateMenu

Syntax:

```
HMENU CreateMenu()
```

Description:

The CreateMenu function creates an empty menu. You add menu items to the menu by using AppendMenu or InsertMenu.

Return Value:

The CreateMenu function returns the handle of the new menu. A NULL return value indicates that the function cannot create the menu.

CreatePopupMenu

Syntax:

```
HMENU CreatePopupMenu()
```

Description:

The CreatePopupMenu function creates an empty pop-up menu. Menu items are added to the menu with AppendMenu or InsertMenu. The application is responsible for adding the pop-up menu to existing menus.

Return Value:

The CreatePopupMenu function returns the handle of the new pop-up window. A NULL return value indicates that the function cannot create the pop-up window.

DeleteMenu

Syntax:

```
BOOL DeleteMenu(hMenu, nPosition, wFlags)
```

Parameter, Type, and Description:

hMenu	HMENU	Menu to modify
nPosition	WORD	Menu item to delete
wFlags	WORD	Specifies how to interpret nPosition

Description:

The DeleteMenu function deletes a menu item from the menu specified in hMenu. nPosition identifies the menu item to delete. nPosition is interpreted according to the flag setting in wFlags:

- When wFlags is set to MF_BYPOSITION, nPosition identifies the menu item position.
- When wFlags is set to MF_BYCOMMAND, nPosition specifies the command ID of the menu item.

If the menu item in `nPosition` has a pop-up menu associated with it, the pop-up menu is automatically destroyed and all associated memory is freed.

Return Value:

The `DeleteMenu` function returns TRUE when the menu item is successfully deleted. A return value of FALSE indicates that the function cannot delete the menu item.

DestroyMenu

Syntax:

```
BOOL DestroyMenu(hMenu)
```

Parameter, Type, and Description:

`hMenu`	`HMENU`	Menu to destroy

Description:

The `DestroyMenu` function destroys the menu specified in `hMenu`. All memory associated with the menu is freed.

Return Value:

The `DestroyMenu` function returns a nonzero value when the menu is destroyed. A return value of zero indicates that the menu is not destroyed.

DrawMenuBar

Syntax:

```
void DrawMenuBar(hWnd)
```

Parameter, Type, and Description:

`hWnd`	`HWND`	Window containing menu to redraw

Description:

The `DrawMenuBar` function redraws the Menu bar associated with the window specified in `hWnd`.

Return Value:

There is no return value.

EnableMenuItem

Syntax:

```
BOOL EnableMenuItem(hMenu, wIDEnableItem, wEnable)
```

Parameter, Type, and Description:

hMenu	HMENU	Menu handle
wIDEnableItem	WORD	Menu item to check
wEnable	WORD	Specifies menu item setting

Description:

The EnableMenuItem function either enables, disables, or grays the menu item specified in wIDEnableItem. hMenu specifies the menu that contains the menu item. wEnable specifies the setting for the menu item and can be any combination of the following settings:

Value	*Meaning*
MF_BYCOMMAND	wIDEnableItem specifies a menu item ID. This value must not be used with MF_BYPOSITION.
MF_BYPOSITION	wIDEnableItem specifies the menu item position. This value must not be used with MF_BYCOMMAND.
MF_DISABLED	Disables the menu item. This value must not be used with MF_ENABLED or MF_GRAYED.
MF_ENABLED	Enables the menu item. This value must not be used with MF_DISABLED or MF_GRAYED.
MF_GRAYED	Grays the menu item. This value must not be used with MF_DISABLED or MF_ENABLED.

Combine settings by using the bitwise OR operator.

Return Value:

The EnableMenuItem function returns the previous state of the menu item. A return value of –1 indicates that the menu item is invalid.

GetMenu

Syntax:

```
HMENU GetMenu(hWnd)
```

Parameter, Type, and Description:

`hWnd`	`HWND`	Window containing menu

Description:

The `GetMenu` function gets the handle for the menu of the window specified in `hWnd`.

Return Value:

The `GetMenu` function returns the handle of the menu. A NULL return value indicates that the specified window has no menu.

GetMenuCheckMarkDimensions

Syntax:

```
DWORD GetMenuCheckMarkDimensions()
```

Description:

The `GetMenuCheckMarkDimensions` function gets the dimensions for the default check mark bitmap.

Return Value:

The `GetMenuCheckMarkDimensions` function returns the dimensions of the default check mark bitmap:

- The high-order word of the return value contains the height of the bitmap, in pixels.
- The low-order word of the return value contains the width of the bitmap, in pixels.

GetMenuItemCount

Syntax:

```
WORD GetMenuItemCount(hMenu)
```

Parameter, Type, and Description:

`hMenu`	`HMENU`	Menu handle

Description:

The `GetMenuItemCount` function gets the number of items in the top-level or pop-up menu specified in `hMenu`.

Return Value:

The `GetMenuItemCount` function returns the number of items in the specified menu. When unsuccessful, –1 is returned.

GetMenuItemID

Syntax:

```
WORD GetMenuItemID(hMenu, nPos)
```

Parameter, Type, and Description:

hMenu	HMENU	Pop-up menu containing the menu item
nPos	int	Position of menu item

Description:

The `GetMenuItemID` function gets the menu item ID for the menu item located at the position specified in `nPos`. `hMenu` specifies the menu that contains the menu item.

Return Value:

The `GetMenuItemID` function returns the menu item ID. A return value of –1 indicates that the `hMenu` is NULL, or `hMenu` specifies a pop-up menu.

GetMenuState

Syntax:

```
WORD GetMenuState(hMenu, wId, wFlags)
```

Parameter, Type, and Description:

hMenu	HMENU	Menu handle
wId	WORD	Menu item ID or position
wFlags	WORD	Flags indicating whether `wId` contains an item ID or position

Description:

The `GetMenuState` function either gets the status of a menu item or gets the number of items in a pop-up menu, depending on the setting of `hMenu`:

- When `hMenu` specifies a menu with an associated pop-up menu, `GetMenuState` retrieves the number of items in the pop-up menu.

- When `hMenu` specifies a pop-up menu, `GetMenuState` retrieves the status of the menu item.

`wId` specifies either a menu item ID or menu item position, depending on the flag settings in `wFlags`:

- If `wFlags` contains `MF_BYPOSITION`, `wId` contains a menu item position.
- If `wFlags` contains `MF_BYCOMMAND`, `wId` contains the menu item ID.

Return Value:

The `GetMenuState` function returns the status of a menu item or gets the number of items in a pop-up menu. When `wId` identifies a pop-up window:

- The high-order byte of the return value contains the number of items in the pop-up menu.
- The low-order byte contains the menu flags.

For all other cases, the return value identifies the status of the menu item. The status can be any combination of the following flags (using the Boolean OR):

Value	*Meaning*
MF_CHECKED	A check mark is placed next to menu item
MF_DISABLED	Disables the menu item
MF_ENABLED	Enables the menu item
MF_GRAYED	Grays and disables the menu item
MF_MENUBARBREAK	Menu item is placed on a new line. For pop-up menus, the item is placed in a new column with a vertical dividing line.
MF_MENUBREAK	Menu item is placed on a new line. For pop-up menus, the item is placed in a new column without a vertical dividing line.
MF_SEPARATOR	Creates a horizontal dividing line
MF_UNCHECKED	No check mark is placed next to the menu item

A return value of –1 indicates that the menu item does not exist.

GetMenuString

Syntax:

```
int GetMenuString(hMenu, wIDItem, lpString, nMaxCount, wFlag)
```

Parameter, Type, and Description:

hMenu	HMENU	Menu handle
wIDItem	WORD	Menu item ID or position

lpString	LPSTR	Pointer to buffer to receive label
nMaxCount	int	Maximum label length
wFlag	WORD	Specifies whether wIDItem contains a menu item ID or position

Description:

The GetMenuString function places the menu item label for the menu item in wIDItem into the buffer pointed to by lpString. hMenu specifies the menu containing the menu item. nMaxCount specifies the maximum number of characters to copy to lpString.

wIDItem contains either a menu item ID or position:

- When wFlag contains MF_BYPOSITION, wIDItem is a menu item position.
- When wFlag contains MF_BYCOMMAND, wFlag contains a menu item ID.

Return Value:

The GetMenuString function returns the number of bytes copied to lpString.

GetSubMenu

Syntax:

```
HMENU GetSubMenu(hMenu, nPos)
```

Parameter, Type, and Description:

hMenu	HMENU	Menu handle
nPos	int	Menu position of pop-up menu

Description:

The GetSubMenu function gets the handle for the pop-up menu specified by the menu position in nPos. hMenu identifies the menu that contains the pop-up menu.

Return Value:

The GetSubMenu function returns the menu handle for the pop-up menu. A NULL return value indicates that a pop-up menu does not exist at the specified position.

GetSystemMenu

Syntax:

```
HMENU GetSystemMenu(hWnd, bRevert)
```

Parameter, Type, and Description:

hWnd	HWND	Window to own System menu
bRevert	BOOL	Specifies copy or modify

Description:

The GetSystemMenu function provides access to the System menu. By using this function an application can copy and modify the System menu.

Return Value:

The return value of this function depends on the value of bRevert:

- When bRevert is a nonzero value and the System menu has been modified, the GetSystemMenu function returns the original System menu handle. The copy of the System menu owned by the window in hWnd is destroyed.
- When bRevert is a nonzero value and the System menu has not been modified, the GetSystemMenu function returns NULL.
- When bRevert is zero, the GetSystemMenu function returns the menu handle for the copy of the System menu owned by the window in hWnd.

HiliteMenuItem

Syntax:

```
BOOL HiliteMenuItem(hWnd, hMenu, wIDHiliteItem, wHilite)
```

Parameter, Type, and Description:

hWnd	HWND	Window containing the menu
hMenu	HMENU	Top-level menu containing item to highlight
wIDHiliteItem	WORD	Menu item ID or position
wHilite	WORD	Specifies whether menu item should be highlighted or not. Also specifies whether wIDHiliteItem contains a menu item ID or position.

Description:

The HiliteMenuItem function either highlights or removes the highlighting from a top-level menu item in the menu specified in hMenu. The specified menu is contained in the window in hWnd. wIDHiliteItem specifies either the menu item ID or the menu item position:

- wIDHiliteItem contains a menu item position when wHilite contains MF_BYPOSITION.

- `wIDHiliteItem` contains a menu item ID when `wHilite` contains `MF_BYCOMMAND`.

`wHilite` can be any of the following flags:

Value	*Meaning*
MF_BYCOMMAND	`wIDHiliteItem` contains a menu item ID
MF_BYPOSITION	`wIDHiliteItem` contains a menu item position
MF_HILITE	Highlights the menu item
MF_UNHILITE	Removes the highlight for the menu item

Combine flags by using the bitwise OR operator.

Return Value:

The `HiliteMenuItem` function returns a nonzero value if the item is highlighted. A return value of zero indicates that the item is not highlighted.

InsertMenu

Syntax:

```
BOOL InsertMenu(hMenu, nPosition, wFlags, wIDNewItem, lpNewItem)
```

Parameter, Type, and Description:

hMenu	HMENU	Menu to modify
nPosition	WORD	Menu item will be inserted prior to this menu item position
wFlags	WORD	Specifies state of new menu item
wIDNewItem	WORD	Menu item ID or menu handle
lpNewItem	LPSTR	Contents of new menu item

Description:

The `InsertMenu` function inserts a new menu item into the menu specified in `hMenu`. The new menu item is inserted into the position prior to the menu position specified in `nPosition`.

`wFlags` is a combination of values specifying the state of the new menu item and how `nPosition` is interpreted:

- When `wFlags` contains `MF_BYPOSITION`, `nPosition` contains a menu item position.
- When `wFlags` contains `MF_BYCOMMAND`, `nPosition` contains a menu item ID.

wIDNewItem contains the command ID of the menu item except when wFlags contains MF_POPUP. When wFlags contains MF_POPUP, wIDNewItem contains the menu handle of the pop-up menu.

The following flags can be set in wFlags:

Value	*Meaning*
MF_BITMAP	Uses a bitmap as the item. The handle of the bitmap is in the low-order word of lpNewItem. This flag should not be used with MF_STRING MF_OWNERDRAW, or MF_SEPARATOR.
MF_BYCOMMAND	nPosition contains a menu item command ID. This flag should not be used with MF_BYPOSITION
MF_BYPOSITION	nPosition contains a menu item position. This flag should not be used with MF_BYCOMMAND.
MF_CHECKED	Puts a check mark next to the item. This flag should not be used with MF_UNCHECKED.
MF_DISABLED	Disables, but does not gray, the menu item. This flag should not be used with MF_ENABLED or MF_GRAYED.
MF_ENABLED	Enables the menu item. This flag should not be used with MF_DISABLED or MF_GRAYED.
MF_GRAYED	Disables and grays the menu item. This flag should not be used with MF_DISABLED or MF_ENABLED.
MF_MENUBARBREAK	Puts menu items on a new line. For pop-up menus, puts the new item in a new column and separates the columns with a vertical line. This flag should not be used with MF_MENUBREAK.
MF_MENUBREAK	Puts menu items on a new line. For pop-up menus, this flag puts the new item in a new column but does not separate the columns with a vertical line. This flag should not be used with MF_MENUBARBREAK.
MF_OWNERDRAW	Item is an owner-draw item. This flag should not be used with MF_BITMAP or MF_STRING.
MF_POPUP	Item has a pop-up menu associated with it. wIDNewItem specifies the handle of the pop-up window.
MF_SEPARATOR	Creates a horizontal line in a pop-up menu.
MF_STRING	Menu item is a character string. This flag should not be used with MF_BITMAP or MF_OWNERDRAW.
MF_UNCHECKED	No check mark is placed by the menu item. This flag should not be used with MF_CHECKED.

Return Value:

The InsertMenu function returns TRUE when the new menu item is inserted in the menu specified in hMenu. A return value of FALSE indicates that the menu item is not inserted.

LoadMenuIndirect

Syntax:

```
HMENU LoadMenuIndirect(lpMenuTemplate)
```

Parameter, Type, and Description:

lpMenuTemplate	LPSTR	Pointer to the menu template

Description:

The LoadMenuIndirect function loads the menu specified in lpMenuTemplate into memory. lpMenuTemplate points to a menu template that contains a header and one or more MENUITEMTEMPLATE structures. The header and MENUITEMTEMPLATE structure are:

```
typedef struct {
    WORD versionNumber;
    WORD offset;
} MENUITEMTEMPLATEHEADER;
```

where:

versionNumber is the version number, usually zero

offset is the offset, in bytes, where the menu item list begins

```
typedef struct {
     WORD mtOption;
     WORD mtID;
     LPSTR mtString;
} MENUITEMTEMPLATE;
```

where:

mtOption is a combination of one or more of the following options:

Value	*Meaning*
MF_CHECKED	Check mark next to item
MF_END	Item is last item in menu
MF_GRAYED	Item is grayed and inactive
MF_HELP	Item has a vertical separator on its left
MF_MENUBARBREAK	Item is placed in a new column with a vertical separator
MF_MENUBREAK	Item is placed in a new column without a vertical separator
MF_OWNERDRAW	Owner draws menu item
MF_POPUP	Item displays a pop-up menu

mtID is the ID code for the menu (not for pop-up menus)

mtString points to the string that contains the name of the menu item

Return Value:

The `LoadMenuIndirect` function returns the menu handle when the menu specified in `lpMenuTemplate` is loaded into memory. A NULL return value indicates that the menu is not loaded.

ModifyMenu

Syntax:

```
BOOL ModifyMenu(hMenu, nPosition, wFlags, wIDNewItem, lpNewItem)
```

Parameter, Type, and Description:

`hMenu`	`HMENU`	Menu to be modified
`nPosition`	`WORD`	Menu item to modify
`wFlags`	`WORD`	Determines how `nPosition` is interpreted
`wIDNewItem`	`WORD`	Command ID of new menu item, or menu handle of pop-up menu
`lpNewItem`	`LPSTR`	Determines the contents of the modified menu item

Description:

The `ModifyMenu` function modifies an item from the menu specified in `hMenu`. `wFlags` defines the state of the modified menu item. The flags that may be set in `wFlags` are:

Value	*Meaning*
`MF_BITMAP`	Uses a bitmap as the item. The handle of the bitmap is in the low-order word of `lpNewItem`. This flag should not be used with `MF_STRING` `MF_OWNERDRAW` or `MF_SEPARATOR`.
`MF_BYCOMMAND`	`nPosition` contains a menu item command ID. This flag should not be used with `MF_BYPOSITION`.
`MF_BYPOSITION`	`nPosition` contains a menu item position. This flag should not be used with `MF_BYCOMMAND`.
`MF_CHECKED`	Puts a check mark next to the item. This flag should not be used with `MF_UNCHECKED`.
`MF_DISABLED`	Disables, but does not gray, the menu item. This flag should not be used with `MF_ENABLED` or `MF_GRAYED`.
`MF_ENABLED`	Enables the menu item. This flag should not be used with `MF_DISABLED` or `MF_GRAYED`.
`MF_GRAYED`	Disables and grays the menu item. This flag should not be used with `MF_DISABLED` or `MF_ENABLED`.

Value	*Meaning*
MF_MENUBARBREAK	Puts menu items on a new line. For pop-up menus, puts the new item in a new column and separates the columns with a vertical line. This flag should not be used with MF_MENUBREAK.
MF_MENUBREAK	Puts menu items on a new line. For pop-up menus, puts the new item in a new column but does not separate the columns with a vertical line. This flag should not be used with MF_MENUBARBREAK.
MF_OWNERDRAW	Item is an owner-draw item. This flag should not be used with MF_BITMAP or MF_STRING.
MF_POPUP	Item has a pop-up menu associated with it. wIDNewItem specifies the handle of the pop-up window.
MF_SEPARATOR	Creates a horizontal line in a pop-up menu.
MF_STRING	Menu item is a character string. This flag should not be used with MF_BITMAP or MF_OWNERDRAW.
MF_UNCHECKED	No check mark is placed by the menu item. This flag should not be used with MF_CHECKED.

nPosition specifies the menu item to modify or the command ID of the menu item, depending on the setting of the flags in wFlags:

- When wFlags contains MF_BYPOSITION, nPosition specifies the menu item position.
- When wFlags contains MF_BYCOMMAND, nPosition specifies the command ID of the menu item.

wIDNewItem contains the command ID of the menu item except when wFlags contains MF_POPUP. When wFlags contains MF_POPUP, wIDNewItem contains the menu handle of the pop-up menu.

lpNewItem determines the contents of the modified menu item according to the setting of the flags in wFlags:

- When wFlags contains MF_STRING, lpNewItem points to a string.
- When wFlags contains MF_BITMAP, lpNewItem contains the handle of a bitmap in its low-order word.
- When wFlags contains MF_OWNERDRAW, lpNewItem contains a 32-bit value supplied by the application

Return Value:

The ModifyMenu function returns TRUE when the menu item is modified. A return value of FALSE indicates that the menu item is unmodified.

RemoveMenu

Syntax:

```
BOOL RemoveMenu(hMenu, nPosition, wFlags)
```

Parameter, Type, and Description:

`hMenu`	`HMENU`	Menu to modify
`nPosition`	`WORD`	Menu item to remove
`wFlags`	`WORD`	Specifies meaning of `nPosition`

Description:

The `RemoveMenu` function deletes the menu item specified in `nPosition` from the menu specified in `hMenu`. The menu item specified in `nPosition` must have a pop-up menu associated with it. The handle for the pop-up menu is not destroyed and therefore can be reused.

`nPosition` is interpreted according to the flag setting in `wFlags`:

- When `wFlags` is set to `MF_BYPOSITION`, `nPosition` identifies the menu item position.
- When `wFlags` is set to `MF_BYCOMMAND`, `nPosition` specifies the command ID of the menu item.

Before the `RemoveMenu` function is called, use the `GetSubMenu` function to retrieve the handle of the pop-up menu. Call the `DrawMenuBar` function after the menu has been changed.

Return Value:

The `RemoveMenu` function returns TRUE when menu item is deleted. A return value of FALSE indicates that the menu item is not deleted.

SetMenu

Syntax:

```
BOOL SetMenu(hWnd, hMenu)
```

Parameter, Type, and Description:

`hWnd`	`HWND`	Window containing menu to modify
`hMenu`	`HMENU`	New menu

Description:

The SetMenu function sets the menu for the window specified in hWnd to the menu specified in hMenu. The window is redrawn when the function is called. If hMenu is set to NULL, the current menu for the window specified in hWnd is removed.

Return Value:

The SetMenu function returns a nonzero value when the menu is changed. A return value of zero indicates that the menu is not changed.

SetMenuItemBitmaps

Syntax:

```
BOOL SetMenuItemBitmaps(hMenu, nPosition, wFlags,
                        hBitmapUnchecked, hBitmapChecked)
```

Parameter, Type, and Description:

hMenu	HMENU	Menu to change
nPosition	WORD	Menu item to change
wFlags	WORD	Specifies meaning of nPosition
hBitmapUnchecked	HBITMAP	Bitmap to use when a menu item is not checked
hBitmapChecked	HBITMAP	Bitmap to use when the menu item is checked

Description:

The SetMenuItemBitmaps function defines the bitmaps associated with the menu item specified in nPosition from the menu specified in hMenu. nPosition is interpreted according to the flag setting in wFlags:

- When wFlags is set to MF_BYPOSITION, nPosition identifies the menu item position.
- When wFlags is set to MF_BYCOMMAND, nPosition specifies the command ID of the menu item.

hBitmapUnchecked and hBitmapChecked specify the bitmaps placed by the menu item when the item is unchecked and checked, respectively:

- When either hBitmapUnchecked or hBitmapChecked is NULL, nothing is displayed beside the menu item for the corresponding selection.
- When both are NULL, the default check mark is used when the menu item is checked and nothing is used when the menu item is unchecked.

Return Value:

The `SetMenuItemBitmaps` function returns TRUE when the bitmaps are defined. A return value of FALSE indicates that th bitmaps are not defined.

TrackPopupMenu

Syntax:

```
BOOL TrackPopupMenu(hMenu, wFlags, x, y, nReserved, hWnd, lpReserved)
```

Parameter, Type, and Description:

`hMenu`	`HMENU`	Pop-up menu to display
`wFlags`	`WORD`	Parameter is set to zero and is not used
`x`	`int`	Horizontal screen coordinate of upper-left corner of menu
`y`	`int`	Vertical screen coordinate of upper-left corner of menu
`nReserved`	`int`	Parameter is reserved and should be set to zero
`hWnd`	`HWND`	Window that owns the pop-up menu
`lpReserved`	`LPVOID`	Parameter is reserved and should be set to NULL

Description:

The `TrackPopupMenu` function places the pop-up menu specified in `hMenu` at the position specified in `x` and `y`. `TrackPopupMenu` tracks the menu and the selection of its items automatically. Obtain the handle of the pop-up menu with either the `CreatePopupMenu` or `GetSubMenu` function.

Return Value:

The `TrackPopupMenu` function returns TRUE when the pop-up menu is placed at the new position. A return value of FALSE indicates that the pop-up menu is not placed at the new position.

Message Functions

A Windows message is generated each time an input event occurs, such as a mouse event, a keyboard event, or a timer event. In general, the message is stored first in the system queue, then in the appropriate application queue. The application queue is a first-in-first-out queue. Some messages, however, are sent directly to the window function for the application. Windows sends messages in practically any sequence; therefore, the application should not depend on the order of the messages received.

Windows provides a set of functions for manipulating messages. The following functions are categorized as Message functions for the Window Manager Interface:

Function	*Meaning*
`CallWindowProc`	Sends message information to the specified function
`DispatchMessage`	Sends a message to the window function of the specified window
`GetMessage`	Gets a message
`GetMessagePos`	Gets the position of the mouse when the message was retrieved
`GetMessageTime`	Gets the time when the message was retrieved
`InSendMessage`	Determines whether the current window function is processing a message sent from `SendMessage`
`PeekMessage`	Checks the application queue
`PostAppMessage`	Sends a message to the application
`PostMessage`	Puts a message in the application queue
`PostQuitMessage`	Sends `WM_QUIT` to the application
`RegisterWindowMessage`	Defines a new, unique window message
`ReplyMessage`	Replies to a message
`SendMessage`	Sends a message
`SetMessageQueue`	Creates a new message queue
`TranslateAccelerator`	Translates keyboard accelerators
`TranslateMDISysAccel`	Translates MDI child window command accelerators
`TranslateMessage`	Translates virtual keystroke messages to character messages
`WaitMessage`	Yields control to other applications

The rest of this section provides detailed information on each of the functions in this list.

CallWindowProc

Syntax:

```
LONG CallWindowProc(lpPrevWndFunc, hWnd, wMsg, wParam, lParam)
```

Parameter, Type, and Description:

`lpPrevWndFunc`	`FARPROC`	Procedure instance address of the previous window function
`hWnd`	`HWND`	Window receiving the message
`wMsg`	`WORD`	Message number
`wParam`	`WORD`	Message-dependent information
`lParam`	`DWORD`	Message-dependent information

Description:

The `CallWindowProc` function is used for window subclassing and passes information to the function specified in `lpPrevWndFunc`. A subclass is created with the `SetWindowLong` function. A subclass is a window or set of windows that belong to the same window class. The messages for the subclass are processed by the specified function, or functions, prior to being processed by the window function for the class. (See this chapter's description of `SetWindowLong` for more information.)

Return Value:

The return value depends on the message sent. (See Chapter 14 for more information on Windows messages.)

DispatchMessage

Syntax:

```
LONG DispatchMessage(lpMsg)
```

Parameter, Type, and Description:

`lpMsg`	`LPMSG`	Pointer to `MSG` data structure containing message information from the Windows application queue

Description:

The `DispatchMessage` function sends the message specified by `lpMsg` to the window function of the specified window. `lpMsg` points to a data structure of type `MSG` that contains message information from the Windows application queue. The `MSG` structure is:

```
typedef struct tagMSG {
     HWND hwnd;
     WORD message;
     WORD wParam;
```

```
    LONG lParam;
    DWORD time;
    POINT pt;
} MSG;
```

where:

> hwnd is the window receiving the message
>
> message is the message number (refer to Chapter 14 for message definitions)
>
> wParam is additional message information
>
> lParam is additional message information
>
> time is the time the message was posted
>
> pt is the cursor position in screen coordinates

Return Value:

The DispatchMessage function returns the value returned from the window function, which can even be NULL.

GetMessage

Syntax:

```
BOOL GetMessage(lpMsg, hWnd, wMsgFilterMin, wMsgFilterMax)
```

Parameter, Type, and Description:

lpMsg	LPMSG	Pointer to MSG data structure containing message information from the Windows application queue
hWnd	HWND	Window receiving messages to be examined
wMsgFilterMin	WORD	Lowest message value to retrieve
wMsgFilterMax	WORD	Highest message value to retrieve

Description:

The GetMessage function places a message retrieved from the application queue into the data structure of type MSG, pointed to by lpMsg. The MSG data structure is:

```
typedef struct tagMSG {
    HWND hwnd;
    WORD message;
    WORD wParam;
    LONG lParam;
```

```
    DWORD time;
    POINT pt;
} MSG;
```

where:

> hwnd is the window receiving the message
>
> message is the message number
>
> wParam is additional message information
>
> lParam is additional message information
>
> time is the time the message was posted
>
> pt is the cursor position in screen coordinates

All messages retrieved are associated with the window specified in hWnd. wMsgFilterMin and wMsgFilterMax specify the range of message values that can be retrieved. The WM_KEYFIRST and WM_KEYLAST constants can specify that wMsgFilterMin and wMsgFilterMax, respectively, retrieve all keyboard-related messages. Similarly, WM_MOUSEFIRST and WM_MOUSELAST can retrieve all mouse related messages.

Return Value:

The GetMessage function returns a nonzero value when the message retrieved is not WM_QUIT. A return value of zero indicates that the message retrieved is WM_QUIT.

GetMessagePos

Syntax:

```
DWORD GetMessagePos()
```

Description:

The GetMessagePos function gets the value representing the screen coordinates of the cursor position where the last message retrieved by GetMessage occurred.

Return Value:

The GetMessagePos function returns a value representing the cursor position:

- The low-order word of the return value contains the horizontal coordinate of the cursor position.
- The high-order word of the return value contains the vertical coordinate of the cursor position.

GetMessageTime

Syntax:

```
DWORD GetMessageTime()
```

Description:

The `GetMessageTime` function gets the number of milliseconds elapsed from the time the system booted to the time the message was placed in the application queue (called the *message time*) for the last message retrieved by `GetMessage`.

Return Value:

The `GetMessageTime` function returns the message time, measured in milliseconds.

InSendMessage

Syntax:

```
BOOL InSendMessage()
```

Description:

The `InSendMessage` function determines whether the current window function is processing a message sent from the `SendMessage` function.

Return Value:

The `InSendMessage` function returns TRUE when the message being processed by the current window function is sent by `SendMessage`. A return value of FALSE indicates that the message that the current window function is processing was not sent by `SendMessage`.

PeekMessage

Syntax:

```
BOOL PeekMessage(lpMsg, hWnd, wMsgFilterMin, wMsgFilterMax,
                 wRemoveMsg)
```

Parameter, Type, and Description:

`lpMsg`	`LPMSG`	Pointer to `MSG` data structure containing message information from the Windows application queue

hWnd	HWND	Window receiving messages to be examined
wMsgFilterMin	WORD	Lowest message value to retrieve
wMsgFilterMax	WORD	Highest message value to retrieve
wRemoveMsg	WORD	Combination of PM_NOREMOVE, PM_NOYIELD, and PM_REMOVE flags

Description:

The PeekMessage function places a message retrieved from the application queue into the data structure of type MSG, pointed to by lpMsg. The MSG data structure is:

```
typedef struct tagMSG {
      HWND hwnd;
      WORD message;
      WORD wParam;
      LONG lParam;
      DWORD time;
      POINT pt;
} MSG;
```

where:

hwnd is the window receiving the message

message is the message number

wParam is additional message information

lParam is additional message information

time is the time the message was posted

pt is the cursor position in screen coordinates

All messages retrieved are associated with the window specified in hWnd. wMsgFilterMin and wMsgFilterMax specify the range of message values that can be retrieved. The WM_KEYFIRST and WM_KEYLAST constants can specify that wMsgFilterMin and wMsgFilterMax, respectively, retrieve all keyboard-related messages. Similarly, WM_MOUSEFIRST and WM_MOUSELAST can retrieve all mouse related messages.

wRemoveMsg is a combination of the following flags:

Value	*Meaning*
PM_NOREMOVE	Messages aren't removed from the queue after being processed by PeekMessage; not used with PM_REMOVE flag
PM_NOYIELD	Keeps the current task from yielding system resources to another task
PM_REMOVE	Messages are removed from the queue after being processed by PeekMessage; not used with PM_NOREMOVE flag

This function differs from `GetMessage` in that it doesn't wait for a message to be placed in the application queue before returning.

Return Value:

The `PeekMessage` function returns a nonzero value when a message is found. A return value of zero indicates that a message is not found.

PostAppMessage

Syntax:

```
BOOL PostAppMessage(hTask, wMsg, wParam, lParam)
```

Parameter, Type, and Description:

`hTask`	`HANDLE`	Task to receive message
`wMsg`	`WORD`	Type of message posted
`wParam`	`WORD`	Additional message information
`lParam`	`DWORD`	Additional message information

Description:

The `PostAppMessage` function posts a message to the application with the task handle specified in `hTask`. The function returns without waiting for the application to process the message.

Return Value:

The `PostAppMessage` function returns a nonzero value when the message is posted. A return value of zero indicates that the message is not posted.

PostMessage

Syntax:

```
BOOL PostMessage(hWnd, wMsg, wParam, lParam)
```

Parameter, Type, and Description:

`hWnd`	`HWND`	Window to receive message
`wMsg`	`WORD`	Type of message posted
`wParam`	`WORD`	Additional message information
`lParam`	`DWORD`	Additional message information

Description:

The `PostMessage` function places a message in the application queue of the window specified in `hWnd`. `PostMessage` does not wait for the window to process the message before returning.

Note: Do not use the `PostMessage` function to send a message to a control.

Return Value:

The `PostMessage` function returns a nonzero value when the message is posted. A return value of zero indicates that the message was not posted.

PostQuitMessage

Syntax:

```
void PostQuitMessage(nExitCode)
```

Parameter, Type, and Description:

`nExitCode`	`int`	Application exit code

Description:

The `PostQuitMessage` function posts the `WM_QUIT` message with the application. `PostQuitMessage` does not wait for the application to process the message before returning. This function informs Windows that the application wants to quit. `nExitCode` specifies the application exit code used as the `wParam` parameter for the `WM_QUIT` message.

Return Value:

There is no return value.

RegisterWindowMessage

Syntax:

```
WORD RegisterWindowMessage(lpString)
```

Parameter, Type, and Description:

`lpString`	`LPSTR`	Pointer to the message string to register

Description:

The `RegisterWindowMessage` function defines a new, unique window message. `lpString` specifies the message string to register. This function is often used to communicate between applications.

Return Value:

The `RegisterWindowMessage` function returns an unsigned short integer when the message is registered successfully. A return value of zero indicates that the message is not registered.

ReplyMessage

Syntax:

```
void ReplyMessage(lReply)
```

Parameter, Type, and Description:

`lReply`	`LONG`	Result of message processing

Description:

The `ReplyMessage` function replies to a message sent by the `SendMessage` function. Control is not returned to the function that called `SendMessage`. The window function receiving the message allows the task that called `SendMessage` to continue to execute. The task calling `ReplyMessage` also continues to execute.

Return Value:

There is no return value.

SendMessage

Syntax:

```
DWORD SendMessage(hWnd, wMsg, wParam, lParam)
```

Parameter, Type, and Description:

`hWnd`	`HWND`	Window to receive message
`wMsg`	`WORD`	Message to be sent
`wParam`	`WORD`	Additional message information
`lParam`	`DWORD`	Additional message information

Description:

The `SendMessage` function sends the message in `wMsg` to the window specified in `hWnd`, then waits for the message to be processed. The message is not placed in the destination application's queue. Windows handles the routing of messages. For more information about messages, see documentation contained in Chapter 14.

Return Value:

The `SendMessage` function returns the value returned by the window function receiving the message.

SetMessageQueue

Syntax:

```
BOOL SetMessageQueue(cMsg)
```

Parameter, Type, and Description:

`cMsg`	`int`	Maximum number of messages that a new queue can hold

Description:

The `SetMessageQueue` function creates a new message queue to hold the number of messages specified in `cMsg`. When the new queue is created, the old queue is destroyed. All messages in the old queue are also destroyed.

Return Value:

The `SetMessageQueue` function returns a nonzero value when a new queue is created. A return value of zero indicates that the new queue cannot be created.

TranslateAccelerator

Syntax:

```
int TranslateAccelerator(hWnd, hAccTable, lpMsg)
```

Parameter, Type, and Description:

`hWnd`	`HWND`	Window containing messages to be translated
`hAccTable`	`HANDLE`	Accelerator table
`lpMsg`	`LPMSG`	Pointer to retrieved message

Description:

The TranslateAccelerator function translates keyboard accelerators for use with menus commands. WM_KEYUP and WM_KEYDOWN messages are translated:

- To WM_COMMAND for all menu item accelerators except System menu accelerators
- To WM_SYSCOMMAND for System menu accelerators messages.

The WM_COMMAND or WM_SYSCOMMAND message is sent to the window, not to the application queue. The TranslateAccelerator function does not return until the message is processed. lpMsg points to a message retrieved with the GetMessage or PeekMessage function. The message must contain information from the Windows application queue and be an MSG data structure. (See descriptions for GetMessage and PeekMessage for more information.) The MSG data structure is:

```
typedef struct tagMSG {
     HWND hwnd;
     WORD message;
     WORD wParam;
     LONG lParam;
     DWORD time;
     POINT pt;
} MSG;
```

where:

hwnd is the window receiving the message

message is the message number

wParam is additional message information

lParam is additional message information

time is the time the message was posted

pt is the cursor position in screen coordinates

All messages retrieved are associated with the window specified in hWnd. wMsgFilterMin and wMsgFilterMax specify the range of message values that can be retrieved. The WM_KEYFIRST and WM_KEYLAST constants can specify that wMsgFilterMin and wMsgFilterMax, respectively, retrieve all keyboard-related messages. Similarly, WM_MOUSEFIRST and WM_MOUSELAST can retrieve all mouse related messages.

wRemoveMsg is a combination of the following flags:

Value	*Meaning*
PM_NOREMOVE	Messages aren't removed from the queue after being processed by PeekMessage; not used with PM_REMOVE flag

Value	Meaning
PM_NOYIELD	Keeps the current task from yielding system resources to another task
PM_REMOVE	Messages are removed from the queue after being processed by PeekMessage; not used with PM_NOREMOVE flag

This function differs from GetMessage in that it doesn't wait for a message to be placed in the application queue before returning.

Return Value:

The TranslateAccelerator function returns a nonzero value when translation is successful. A return value of zero indicates that translation is unsuccessful.

TranslateMDISysAccel

Syntax:

```
BOOL TranslateMDISysAccel(hWndClient, lpMsg)
```

Parameter, Type, and Description:

hWndClient	HWND	Parent MDI client window
lpMsg	LPMSG	Pointer to retrieved message

Description:

The TranslateMDISysAccel function translates keyboard accelerators for multiple document interface (MDI) child window System menu commands. WM_KEYUP and WM_KEYDOWN messages are translated to WM_SYSCOMMAND messages. lpMsg points to a message retrieved with the GetMessage or PeekMessage function. The message must contain information about the Windows application queue and be an MSG data structure. (See descriptions for GetMessage and PeekMessage for more information.) The MSG data structure is:

```
typedef struct tagMSG {
     HWND hwnd;
     WORD message;
     WORD wParam;
     LONG lParam;
     DWORD time;
     POINT pt;
} MSG;
```

where:

hwnd is the window receiving the message

`message` is the message number

`wParam` is additional message information

`lParam` is additional message information

`time` is the time the message was posted

`pt` is the cursor position in screen coordinates

All messages retrieved are associated with the window specified in `hWnd`. `wMsgFilterMin` and `wMsgFilterMax` specify the range of message values that can be retrieved. The `WM_KEYFIRST` and `WM_KEYLAST` constants can specify that `wMsgFilterMin` and `wMsgFilterMax`, respectively, retrieve all keyboard-related messages. Similarly, `WM_MOUSEFIRST` and `WM_MOUSELAST` can retrieve all mouse related messages.

`wRemoveMsg` is a combination of the following flags:

Value	*Meaning*
`PM_NOREMOVE`	Messages aren't removed from the queue after being processed by `PeekMessage`; not used with `PM_REMOVE` flag
`PM_NOYIELD`	Keeps the current task from yielding system resources to another task
`PM_REMOVE`	Messages are removed from the queue after being processed by `PeekMessage`; not used with `PM_NOREMOVE` flag

This function differs from `GetMessage` in that it doesn't wait for a message to be placed in the application queue before returning.

Return Value:

The `TranslateMDISysAccel` function returns TRUE when translation is successful. A return value of FALSE indicates that translation is not successful.

TranslateMessage

Syntax:

```
BOOL TranslateMessage(lpMsg)
```

Parameter, Type, and Description:

`lpMsg`	`LPMSG`	Pointer to retrieved message

Description:

The `TranslateMessage` function translates virtual key messages into character messages:

- WM_KEYDOWN, WM_KEYUP message combinations are translated to WM_CHAR or WM_DEADCHAR messages.
- WM_SYSKEYDOWN, WM_SYSKEYUP message combinations are translated to WM_SYSCHAR or WM_SYSDEADCHAR messages.

The translated character messages are posted to the application queue.

lpMsg points to a message retrieved with the GetMessage or PeekMessage function. The message must contain information about the Windows application queue and be an MSG data structure. (See descriptions for GetMessage and PeekMessage for more information.) The MSG data structure is:

```
typedef struct tagMSG {
     HWND hwnd;
     WORD message;
     WORD wParam;
     LONG lParam;
     DWORD time;
     POINT pt;
} MSG;
```

where:

hwnd is the window receiving the message

message is the message number

wParam is additional message information

lParam is additional message information

time is the time the message was posted

pt is the cursor position in screen coordinates

All messages retrieved are associated with the window specified in hWnd. wMsgFilterMin and wMsgFilterMax specify the range of message values that can be retrieved. The WM_KEYFIRST and WM_KEYLAST constants can specify that wMsgFilterMin and wMsgFilterMax, respectively, retrieve all keyboard-related messages. Similarly, WM_MOUSEFIRST and WM_MOUSELAST can retrieve all mouse related messages.

wRemoveMsg is a combination of the following flags:

Value	*Meaning*
PM_NOREMOVE	Messages aren't removed from the queue after being processed by PeekMessage; not used with PM_REMOVE flag
PM_NOYIELD	Keeps the current task from yielding system resources to another task
PM_REMOVE	Messages are removed from the queue after being processed by PeekMessage; not used with PM_NOREMOVE flag

This function differs from GetMessage in that it doesn't wait for a message to be placed in the application queue before returning.

Return Value:

The TranslateMessage function returns a nonzero value when translation is successful. A return value of zero indicates that translation is unsuccessful.

WaitMessage

Syntax:

```
void WaitMessage()
```

Description:

The WaitMessage function suspends the application when the application has no task to perform, yields control to another application, and the function returns only after a message has been placed in the application queue.

Return Value:

There is no return value.

Painting Functions

Windows provides functions used for simple graphics operations for the system display. The display system is shared by the applications running under Windows, so Windows must carefully manage the display to avoid conflicts between applications.

Use the display contexts to manage the system display. The display context enables each window to be treated as a separate display surface. An application can control the display surface of a window by obtaining the display context. The four types of display contexts are common, class, private, and window.

The *common* display context allows drawing in the window's client area. This is the default context for all windows. The default selections for the pen, brush, font, clipping area, and other attributes are used but can be modified.

The *class* display context is used when the window class has style CS_CLASSDC. All windows in the class use the class display context. The default selections for the pen, brush, font, clipping area, and other attributes are used but can be modified.

The *private* display context is used when the window class has style CS_OWNDC. Only the specified window uses the private display context. The default selections for the pen, brush, font, clipping area, and other attributes are used but can be modified.

The *window* display context does not limit drawing to the client area of the window; drawing can occur anywhere inside the window. The default selections for the pen, brush, font, clipping area, and other attributes are used but can be modified.

The following functions are categorized as Painting functions for the Window Manager Interface:

Function	*Meaning*
BeginPaint	Prepares a window for painting
CreateIcon	Creates an icon
DestroyIcon	Destroys an icon
DrawFocusRect	Draws a rectangle in the focus style
DrawIcon	Draws an icon
DrawText	Draws the specified string
EndPaint	Ends window repainting
ExcludeUpdateRgn	Prevents drawing in invalid window areas
FillRect	Fills a rectangle
FrameRect	Draws a border on the specified rectangle
GetDC	Gets the display context for a client area
GetUpdateRect	Gets the dimensions of the rectangle around the update region
GetUpdateRgn	Copies the update region of a window
GetWindowDC	Gets the display context for a window
GrayString	Writes a string in gray text
InvalidateRect	Defines a rectangle for repainting
InvalidateRgn	Defines a region for repainting
InvertRect	Inverts the bits of the specified rectangle
ReleaseDC	Releases the display context
UpdateWindow	Tells the application that the window needs repainting
ValidateRect	Validates the specified rectangle
ValidateRgn	Validates the specified region

The rest of this section provides detailed information on each of the functions in this list.

BeginPaint

Syntax:

```
HDC BeginPaint(hWnd, lpPaint)
```

Parameter, Type, and Description:

hWnd	HWND	Window to repaint
lpPaint	LPPAINTSTRUCT	Pointer to PAINTSTRUCT data structure that is to receive painting information

Description:

The BeginPaint function prepares the window in hWnd for painting. lpPaint points to a data structure of type PAINTSTRUCT, which the function fills with information about the painting. The PAINTSTRUCT structure is:

```
typedef struct tagPAINTSTRUCT {
     HDC hdc;
     BOOL fErase;
     RECT rcPaint;
     BOOL fRestore;
     BOOL fIncUpdate;
     BYTE rgbReserved[16];
} PAINTSTRUCT;
```

where:

hdc is the display context

fErase is nonzero if the background is to be redrawn, zero if the background will not be redrawn

rcPaint is a data structure containing the upper-left and lower-right corners of the rectangle to paint

fRestore is reserved for use by Windows

fIncUpdate is reserved for use by Windows

rgbReserved[16] is reserved for use by Windows

The application should call BeginPaint only in response to the WM_PAINT message and should have a corresponding EndPaint call.

Return Value:

The BeginPaint function returns the device context for the window in hWnd.

CreateIcon

Syntax:

```
HICON CreateIcon(hInstance, nWidth, nHeight, nPlanes, nBitsPixel,
                 lpANDbits, lpXORbits)
```

Parameter, Type, and Description:

hInstance	HANDLE	Instance of module creating the icon
nWidth	int	Width of icon in pixels
nHeight	int	Height of icon in pixels
nPlanes	BYTE	Number of planes in XOR mask of the icon
nBitsPixel	BYTE	Number of bits per pixel in XOR mask of the icon
lpANDbits	LPSTR	Pointer to an array containing the bits for the AND mask of the icon
lpXORbits	LPSTR	Pointer to an array containing the bits for the XOR mask of the icon

Description:

The `CreateIcon` function creates an icon with the specified height, width, and patterns.

Return Value:

The `CreateIcon` function returns the handle to the icon when successful. A NULL return value indicates that the icon is not created.

DestroyIcon

Syntax:

```
BOOL DestroyIcon(hIcon)
```

Parameter, Type, and Description:

hIcon	HICON	Icon to destroy

Description:

The `DestroyIcon` function destroys the icon specified by `hIcon`. The specified icon must have been created with `CreateIcon`.

Return Value:

The `DestroyIcon` function returns a nonzero value when the icon is destroyed. A return value of zero indicates that the icon is not destroyed.

DrawFocusRect

Syntax:

```
void DrawFocusRect(hDC, lpRect)
```

Parameter, Type, and Description:

hDC	HDC	Device context
lpRect	LPRECT	Pointer to RECT data structure containing coordinates of rectangle to draw

Description:

The `DrawFocusRect` function creates a rectangle in the style that indicates focus. `hDC` specifies the device context. `lpRect` points to a data structure of type `RECT`, which contains the coordinates of the rectangle to draw. The `RECT` structure is:

```
typedef struct tagRECT {
     int left;
     int top;
     int right;
     int bottom;
} RECT;
```

where:

`left` is the x-coordinate of the upper-left corner

`top` is the y-coordinate of the upper-left corner

`right` is the x-coordinate of the lower-right corner

`bottom` is the y-coordinate of the lower-right corner

`DrawFocusRect` uses XOR to draw the rectangle. Therefore, calling this function twice with the same parameters removes it from screen.

Return Value:

There is no return value.

DrawIcon

Syntax:

```
BOOL DrawIcon(hDC, X, Y, hIcon)
```

Parameter, Type, and Description:

`hDC`	`HDC`	Device context
`X`	`int`	Logical horizontal coordinate of upper-left corner of icon
`Y`	`int`	Logical vertical coordinate of upper-left corner of icon
`hIcon`	`HICON`	Icon to draw

Description:

The `DrawIcon` function draws the icon in `hIcon` at the location specified in `X` and `Y`. `hDC` specifies the device context. The icon specified in `hIcon` must have been loaded with the `LoadIcon` function; `X` and `Y` are dependent on the current mapping mode.

Return Value:

The `DrawIcon` message returns a nonzero value when the icon is drawn. A return value of zero indicates that the function cannot draw the icon.

DrawText

Syntax:

```
int DrawText(hDC, lpString, nCount, lpRect, wFormat)
```

Parameter, Type, and Description:

`hDC`	`HDC`	Device context
`lpString`	`LPSTR`	Pointer to string to draw
`nCount`	`int`	Number of bytes in the string
`lpRect`	`LPRECT`	Pointer to `RECT` data structure containing the logical coordinates of the rectangle where the text will be drawn
`wFormat`	`WORD`	Combination of text formats

Description:

The `DrawText` function draws the text in `lpString` inside the rectangle specified in `lpRect`. `nCount` can be set to –1 to indicate that `lpString` is a long pointer to a null-terminated string and the character count is to be determined automatically. `lpRect` points to a structure of type `RECT` that contains the logical coordinates of the rectangle where the text will be drawn. The `RECT` structure is:

```
typedef struct tagRECT {
     int left;
     int top;
     int right;
     int bottom;
} RECT;
```

where:

`left` is the x-coordinate of the upper-left corner

`top` is the y-coordinate of the upper-left corner

`right` is the x-coordinate of the lower-right corner

`bottom` is the y-coordinate of the lower-right corner

The device context in `hDC` specifies the font, text color, and background color used to draw the text. `wFormat` specifies the type of text formatting and can be any combination of the following values:

Value	*Meaning*
DT_BOTTOM	Bottom justifies text; used with DT_SINGLELINE
DT_CALCRECT	Determines the width and height of the rectangle
DT_CENTER	Centers text horizontally
DT_EXPANDTABS	Expands the size of tab characters (the default is 8)
DT_EXTERNALLEADING	Includes font external leading in line height
DT_LEFT	Left-justifies text
DT_NOCLIP	Draws text without clipping
DT_NOPREFIX	Does not allow the processing of prefix characters
DT_RIGHT	Right-justifies text
DT_SINGLELINE	Draws a single line only
DT_TABSTOP	Sets the number of characters in the tab stop to the value in the high-order byte of wFormat
DT_TOP	Top-justifies text—single line only
DT_VCENTER	Centers text vertically—single line only
DT_WORDBREAK	Allows lines to automatically be broken between words

Combine values by using bitwise OR operator.

Return Value:

The `DrawText` function returns the height of the text.

EndPaint

Syntax:

```
void EndPaint(hWnd, lpPaint)
```

Parameter, Type, and Description:

hWnd	HWND	Window to be repainted
lpPaint	LPPAINTSTRUCT	Pointer to PAINTSTRUCT data structure containing the paint information from the BeginPaint function

Description:

The EndPaint function ends the painting of the window specified in hWnd. lpPaint points to the data structure of type PAINTSTRUCT that contains the paint information from the BeginPaint function. The PAINTSTRUCT structure is:

```
typedef struct tagPAINTSTRUCT {
     HDC hdc;
     BOOL fErase;
     RECT rcPaint;
     BOOL fRestore;
     BOOL fIncUpdate;
     BYTE rgbReserved[16];
} PAINTSTRUCT;
```

where:

hdc is the display context

fErase is nonzero if the background is to be redrawn, zero if the background will not be redrawn

rcPaint specifies the upper-left and lower-right corners of the rectangle to paint

fRestore is reserved for use by Windows

fIncUpdate is reserved for use by Windows

rgbReserved[16] is reserved for use by Windows

Return Value:

There is no return value.

ExcludeUpdateRgn

Syntax:

```
int ExcludeUpdateRgn(hDC, hWnd)
```

Parameter, Type, and Description:

`hDC`	`HANDLE`	Device context associated with clipping region
`hWnd`	`HWND`	Window to update

Description:

The `ExcludeUpdateRgn` function disallows drawing inside an updated region in the window from a clipping region. `hWnd` specifies the window to update.

Return Value:

The `ExcludeUpdateRgn` function returns one of the following values to indicate the type of region resulting from the function call:

Value	*Meaning*
`COMPLEXREGION`	Region has overlapping borders
`ERROR`	Region cannot be created
`NULLREGION`	Region is empty
`SIMPLEREGION`	Region has no overlapping borders

FillRect

Syntax:

```
int FillRect(hDC, lpRect, hBrush)
```

Parameter, Type, and Description:

`hDC`	`HDC`	Device context
`lpRect`	`LPRECT`	Pointer to `RECT` data structure containing logical coordinates of rectangle to fill
`hBrush`	`HBRUSH`	Brush used to fill rectangle

Description:

The `FillRect` function fills the rectangle specified in `lpRect` by using the brush specified in `hBrush`. The left and top borders of the rectangle are filled; the right and bottom borders are not filled. `lpRect` points to a data structure of type `RECT` that contains the logical coordinates of the rectangle to fill. The `RECT` structure is:

```
typedef struct tagRECT {
     int left;
     int top;
     int right;
     int bottom;
} RECT;
```

where:

> `left` is the x-coordinate of the upper-left corner
>
> `top` is the y-coordinate of the upper-left corner
>
> `right` is the x-coordinate of the lower-right corner
>
> `bottom` is the y-coordinate of the lower-right corner

`hBrush` specifies the brush used to fill the rectangle. The specified brush should have been created previously with the `CreateHatchBrush`, `CreatePatternBrush`, or `CreateSolidBrush` function. The specified brush can also be retrieved using the `GetStockObject` function. `hDC` specifies the device context.

Return Value:

The return value has no significance and is not used.

FrameRect

Syntax:

```
int FrameRect(hDC, lpRect, hBrush)
```

Parameter, Type, and Description:

`hDC`	`HDC`	Device context
`lpRect`	`LPRECT`	Pointer to `RECT` data structure containing the logical coordinates of the rectangle
`hBrush`	`HBRUSH`	Brush used to frame the rectangle

Description:

The `FrameRect` function draws a border around the rectangle specified in `lpRect`. `lpRect` points to a data structure of type `RECT` containing the logical coordinates of the rectangle. The `RECT` structure is:

```
typedef struct tagRECT {
     int left;
     int top;
```

```
    int right;
    int bottom;
} RECT;
```

where:

`left` is the x-coordinate of the upper-left corner

`top` is the y-coordinate of the upper-left corner

`right` is the x-coordinate of the lower-right corner

`bottom` is the y-coordinate of the lower-right corner

`hBrush` specifies the brush used to draw the border. The specified brush should have been created previously with the `CreateHatchBrush`, `CreatePatternBrush`, or `CreateSolidBrush` function. The border is one logical unit wide and one logical unit high.

Return Value:

The return value has no significance and is not used.

GetDC

Syntax:

```
HDC GetDC(hWnd)
```

Parameter, Type, and Description:

`hWnd`	`HWND`	Window handle

Description:

The `GetDC` function gets the display context for the client area of the window specified in `hWnd`.

Return Value:

The `GetDC` function returns the identifier for the display context. A NULL return value indicates that the function cannot get the identifier for the display context.

GetUpdateRect

Syntax:

```
BOOL GetUpdateRect(hWnd, lpRect, bErase)
```

Parameter, Type, and Description:

`hWnd`	`HWND`	Window handle
`lpRect`	`LPRECT`	Pointer to `RECT` data structure receiving the client coordinates of the rectangle
`bErase`	`BOOL`	Indicates whether update region is to be erased

Description:

The `GetUpdateRect` function gets the coordinates of the smallest possible rectangle that encloses the update region of the window specified in `hWnd`. `lpRect` points to a data structure of type `RECT` that contains the coordinates of the rectangle. The `RECT` structure is:

```
typedef struct tagRECT {
     int left;
     int top;
     int right;
     int bottom;
} RECT;
```

where:

`left` is the x-coordinate of the upper-left corner

`top` is the y-coordinate of the upper-left corner

`right` is the x-coordinate of the lower-right corner

`bottom` is the y-coordinate of the lower-right corner

If the window in `hWnd` was created with style `CS_OWNDC` and a mapping mode other than `MM_TEXT`, logical coordinates are placed in the structure pointed to by `lpRect`. Otherwise, client coordinates are placed in the data structure. `bErase` specifies whether the update region is to be erased:

- When `bErase` is set to TRUE, the background of the update region is erased.
- When `bErase` is set to FALSE, the background of the update region is not erased.

Return Value:

The `GetUpdateRect` function returns a nonzero value if the update region is not empty. A return value of zero indicates that the update region is empty.

GetUpdateRgn

Syntax:

```
int GetUpdateRgn(hWnd, hRgn, fErase)
```

Parameter, Type, and Description:

hWnd	HWND	Window containing region to be updated
hRgn	HRGN	Update region
fErase	BOOL	Indicates whether the background should be erased and non-client areas of child windows drawn

Description:

The GetUpdateRgn function copies the update region of a window to the region specified by hRgn. Coordinates are expressed in client coordinates.

Return Value:

The GetUpdateRgn function returns one of the following values to indicate the type of resulting region:

Value	*Meaning*
COMPLEXREGION	Region has overlapping borders
ERROR	Region was not created
NULLREGION	Region is empty
SIMPLEREGION	Region has no overlapping borders

GetWindowDC

Syntax:

```
HDC GetWindowDC(hWnd)
```

Parameter, Type, and Description:

hWnd	HWND	Window handle

Description:

The GetWindowDC function retrieves the display context for the window specified in hWnd. The display context origin is in the upper-left corner of the window; therefore, painting is allowed anywhere in the window including caption bars, menus, and scroll bars.

Return Value:

The `GetWindowDC` function returns the display context. A NULL return value indicates that the function cannot get the display context.

GrayString

Syntax:

```
BOOL GrayString(hDC, hBrush, lpOutputFunc, lpData, nCount, X,
           Y, nWidth, nHeight)
```

Parameter, Type, and Description:

`hDC`	`HDC`	Device context
`hBrush`	`HBRUSH`	Brush used for graying
`lpOutputFunc`	`FARPROC`	Procedure instance address of the function drawing the string
`lpData`	`DWORD`	Long pointer to data that is sent to the output function
`nCount`	`int`	Number of characters to output
`X`	`int`	Logical horizontal coordinate of a rectangle enclosing the string
`Y`	`int`	Logical vertical coordinate of a rectangle enclosing the string
`nWidth`	`int`	Width of an enclosing rectangle in logical units
`nHeight`	`int`	Height of an enclosing rectangle in logical units

Description:

The `GrayString` function draws grayed text at the position specified in `X` and `Y`. `lpOutputFunc` is the procedure instance address of the application-supplied function used to draw the text. `lpOutputFunc` also can be set to NULL to indicate that the `TextOut` function should be used to draw the string. `nCount` is the number of characters to output. If `nCount` is set to zero, the length of the string is calculated automatically. If `nCount` is set to –1 and the function specified by `lpOutputFunc` returns zero, the text is displayed but not grayed. `nWidth` is the width of the enclosing rectangle, in logical units. If `nWidth` is set to zero, the width is calculated automatically. `nHeight` is the height of the enclosing rectangle, in logical units. If `nHeight` is set to zero, the height is calculated automatically.

The output function must follow these conventions and formats:

Syntax:

```
BOOL FAR PASCAL OutputFunc(hDC, lpData, nCount)
```

Parameter, Type, and Description:

`hDC`	`HDC`	Memory device context
`lpData`	`DWORD`	Points to the string to draw
`nCount`	`int`	The number of characters to output

Description:

`OutputFunc` is a placeholder for the actual function name, which the application supplies and you must export by using `EXPORTS` in the application's module-definition file.

Return Value:

The output function returns a nonzero when successful and zero when unsuccessful.

Return Value:

The `GrayString` function returns a nonzero value when the string is drawn. A return value of zero indicates that the string is not drawn.

InvalidateRect

Syntax:

```
void InvalidateRect(hWnd, lpRect, bErase)
```

Parameter, Type, and Description:

`hWnd`	`HWND`	Window handle
`lpRect`	`LPRECT`	Pointer to `RECT` data structure containing the client coordinates of the rectangle to add to the update region
`bErase`	`BOOL`	Indicates whether the background in the update region will be erased

Description:

The `InvalidateRect` function adds the client area in the rectangle specified in `lpRect` to the update region of the window in `hWnd`. This marks the specified area for painting when the next `WM_PAINT` message is sent. `bErase` specifies whether the background of the update region is erased:

- Set bErase to zero to leave the background unchanged.
- Set bErase to a nonzero value to erase the background.

lpRect points to a data structure of type RECT that contains the client coordinates of the rectangle to add to the update region. Set lpRect to NULL when the entire client area is to be added to the update region. The RECT structure is:

```
typedef struct tagRECT {
     int left;
     int top;
     int right;
     int bottom;
} RECT;
```

where:

left is the x-coordinate of the upper-left corner

top is the y-coordinate of the upper-left corner

right is the x-coordinate of the lower-right corner

bottom is the y-coordinate of the lower-right corner

Return Value:

There is no return value.

InvalidateRgn

Syntax:

```
void InvalidateRgn(hWnd, hRgn, bErase)
```

Parameter, Type, and Description:

hWnd	HWND	Window handle
hRgn	HRGN	Region to add to update region
bErase	BOOL	Indicates whether the background of the update region is to be erased

Description:

The InvalidateRgn function adds the client area of the region specified in hRgn to the update region of the window in hWnd. The added region is, therefore, marked for painting when the next WM_PAINT message is sent. bErase specifies whether the background of the update region is erased:

- Set bErase to a nonzero value to erase the background.
- Set bErase to zero to leave the background unchanged.

The region specified in hRgn must be created with one of the Region functions. (See "Region Functions" in this chapter for more information.)

Return Value:

There is no return value.

InvertRect

Syntax:

```
void InvertRect(hDC, lpRect)
```

Parameter, Type, and Description:

hDC	HDC	Device context
lpRect	LPRECT	Pointer to RECT data structure containing the logical coordinates of the rectangle to invert

Description:

The InvertRect function inverts the rectangle specified in lpRect. lpRect points to a data structure of type RECT that contains the logical coordinates of the rectangle to invert. The RECT structure is:

```
typedef struct tagRECT {
     int left;
     int top;
     int right;
     int bottom;
} RECT;
```

where:

left is the x-coordinate of the upper-left corner

top is the y-coordinate of the upper-left corner

right is the x-coordinate of the lower-right corner

bottom is the y-coordinate of the lower-right corner

Each pixel in the rectangle is inverted. The actual color of the inverted pixel depends on the colors available for the display.

Return Value:

There is no return value.

ReleaseDC

Syntax:

```
int ReleaseDC(hWnd, hDC)
```

Parameter, Type, and Description:

`hWnd`	`HWND`	Window handle
`hDC`	`HDC`	Device context to release

Description:

The `ReleaseDC` function releases the device context in `hDC` for the window in `hWnd`. Other applications then can use the device context. Only common or window device contexts can be released.

Return Value:

The `ReleaseDC` function returns zero when the device context is not released. A return value of 1 indicates that the device context is released.

UpdateWindow

Syntax:

```
void UpdateWindow(hWnd)
```

Parameter, Type, and Description:

`hWnd`	`HWND`	Window to update

Description:

The `UpdateWindow` function updates the client area of the window in `hWnd`. The function accomplishes the update by sending a `WM_PAINT` message to the window if the update region for the window is not empty. No message is sent if the update region is empty.

Return Value:

There is no return value.

ValidateRect

Syntax:

```
void ValidateRect(hWnd, lpRect)
```

Parameter, Type, and Description:

hWnd	HWND	Window handle
lpRect	LPRECT	Pointer to RECT structure containing the client coordinates of the rectangle to be removed from the update region

Description:

The ValidateRect function removes the rectangle specified in lpRect from the update region for the window in hWnd. lpRect points to the data structure of type RECT that contains the client coordinates of the rectangle to remove from the update region. The RECT structure is:

```
typedef struct tagRECT {
     int left;
     int top;
     int right;
     int bottom;
} RECT;
```

where:

left is the x-coordinate of the upper-left corner

top is the y-coordinate of the upper-left corner

right is the x-coordinate of the lower-right corner

bottom is the y-coordinate of the lower-right corner

If lpRect is set to NULL, the entire window is validated.

Return Value:

There is no return value.

ValidateRgn

Syntax:

```
void ValidateRgn(hWnd, hRgn)
```

Parameter, Type, and Description:

`hWnd`	`HWND`	Window handle
`hRgn`	`HRGN`	Region to be removed from the update region

Description:

The `ValidateRgn` function removes the region specified in `hRgn` from the update region of the window in `hWnd`. When `hRgn` is set to NULL, the entire window is validated. Otherwise, `hRgn` must have been created with one of the region functions.

Return Value:

There is no return value.

Property Functions

A property list contains data handles associated with a window. Each window has a property list. This list initially is empty but can have entries added. Each entry consists of an ANSI string and a data handle. The data handle identifies any object or memory block associated with the window. By maintaining a property list, you can easily access and modify data associated with a window. The following functions are categorized as Property functions for the Window Manager Interface:

Function	*Meaning*
`EnumProps`	Enumerates the window's properties
`GetProp`	Gets the handle for the specified string
`RemoveProp`	Removes the specified string from the property list
`SetProp`	Adds an entry to the property list

The rest of this section provides detailed information on each of the functions in this list.

EnumProps

Syntax:

```
int EnumProps(hWnd, lpEnumFunc)
```

Parameter, Type, and Description:

`hWnd`	`HWND`	Window for which property list to enumerate
`lpEnumFunc`	`FARPROC`	Procedure instance address of the callback function

Description:

The `EnumProps` function enumerates the entries in the property list of the window specified in `hWnd`. The callback function specified by `lpEnumFunc` enumerates the entries. The callback function should not yield control to other tasks or attempt to add properties.

This callback function for fixed data segments must follow these conventions and formats:

Syntax:

```
int FAR PASCAL EnumFunc(hWnd, lpString, hData)
```

Parameter, Type, and Description:

`hWnd`	`HWND`	Specifies the window that contains the property list
`lpString`	`LPSTR`	Pointer to the null-terminated string associated with the data handle when the property was set
`hData`	`HANDLE`	The data handle

Return Value:

The function must return a nonzero value to continue enumeration or a zero to stop enumeration.

The callback function for moveable data segments must follow these conventions and formats:

Syntax:

```
int FAR PASCAL EnumFunc(hWnd, nDummy, pString, hData)
```

Parameter, Type, and Description:

`hWnd`	`HWND`	The window that contains the property list
`nDummy`	`WORD`	A dummy parameter
`pString`	`PSTR`	Pointer to the null-terminated string associated with the data handle when the property was set
`hData`	`HANDLE`	The data handle

Description:

`EnumFunc` is a placeholder for the actual function name, which is supplied by the application and must be exported using `EXPORTS`.

Return Value:

The function must return a nonzero value to continue enumeration or zero to stop enumeration.

Return Value:

The `EnumProps` function returns the last value returned by the callback function. A return value of –1 indicates that the function did not find a property to enumerate.

GetProp

Syntax:

```
HANDLE GetProp(hWnd, lpString)
```

Parameter, Type, and Description:

`hWnd`	`HWND`	Window containing the property list
`lpString`	`LPSTR`	Pointer to null-terminated string or atom identifying a string

Description:

The `GetProp` function gets a data handle identified by `lpString` from the property list for the window specified in `hWnd`. `lpString` points to either a null-terminated string or an atom that identifies a string. When `lpString` specifies an atom, the atom (16-bits) is placed in the low-order word of `lpString`; the high-order word of `lpString` is set to zero.

Return Value:

The `GetProp` function returns the retrieved data handle. A NULL return value indicates that the function cannot retrieve the data handle.

RemoveProp

Syntax:

```
HANDLE RemoveProp(hWnd, lpString)
```

Parameter, Type, and Description:

`hWnd`	`HWND`	Window containing property list to modify
`lpString`	`LPSTR`	Pointer to null-terminated string or atom identifying the entry to remove

Description:

The `RemoveProp` function removes the entry specified in `lpString` from the property list of the window specified in `hWnd`. `lpString` points to either a null-terminated string or an atom that identifies a string. When `lpString` specifies an atom, the atom (16-bits) is placed in the low-order word of `lpString`; the high-order word of `lpString` is set to zero.

Return Value:

The `RemoveProp` function returns the handle to a specified string. A NULL return value indicates that the function cannot find the specified string.

SetProp

Syntax:

```
BOOL SetProp(hWnd, lpString, hData)
```

Parameter, Type, and Description:

`hWnd`	`HWND`	Window that contains the property list to receive the new entry
`lpString`	`LPSTR`	Pointer to null-terminated string or atom identifying the entry to add
`hData`	`HANDLE`	Data handle to be copied to property list

Description:

The `SetProp` function either adds or modifies the entry specified in `lpString` in the property list of the window specified in `hWnd`. `lpString` points to either a null-terminated string or an atom that identifies a string:

- When an entry matching `lpString` doesn't exist, an entry containing the string in `lpString` and the data handle in `hData` is added to the property list.
- When an entry matching `lpString` exists, the data handle in `hData` is assigned to the entry.
- When `lpString` specifies an atom, the atom (16-bits) is placed in the low-order word of `lpString`; the high-order word of `lpString` is set to zero.

Return Value:

The `SetProp` function returns a nonzero value if the data handle and string are added to the property list. A return value of zero indicates that the data handle and string are not added to the property list.

Rectangle Functions

Windows uses rectangles to specify certain areas of the display or window including the clipping area, client area, text area, and scroll area. Rectangles also are used for many other reasons. In Windows, rectangles are defined by the upper-left corner and lower-right corner. The dimensions of the rectangle are expressed in logical units. Rectangle functions are used to manipulate rectangles in a window's client area. The following functions are classified as Rectangle functions for the Window Manager Interface:

Function	*Meaning*
`CopyRect`	Copies a rectangle
`EqualRect`	Determines whether two rectangles are equal
`InflateRect`	Sizes the specified rectangle
`IntersectRect`	Determines the intersection of two rectangles
`IsRectEmpty`	Determines whether the rectangle is empty
`OffsetRect`	Moves a rectangle
`PtInRect`	Determines whether the specified point is within the rectangle
`SetRect`	Creates a new rectangle
`SetRectEmpty`	Creates an empty rectangle
`UnionRect`	Determines the union of two rectangles

CopyRect

Syntax:

```
int CopyRect(lpDestRect, lpSourceRect)
```

Parameter, Type, and Description:

`lpDestRect`	`LPRECT`	Pointer to `RECT` data structure containing coordinates of the destination rectangle
`lpSourceRect`	`LPRECT`	Pointer to `RECT` data structure containing coordinates of the source rectangle

Description:

The `CopyRect` function copies the rectangle specified in the data structure of type `RECT`, which is pointed to by `lpSourceRect`, to the data structure of type `RECT`, which is pointed to by `lpDestRect`. The `RECT` structure is:

```
typedef struct tagRECT {
     int left;
     int top;
     int right;
     int bottom;
} RECT;
```

where:

`left` is the x-coordinate of the upper-left corner

`top` is the y-coordinate of the upper-left corner

`right` is the x-coordinate of the lower-right corner

`bottom` is the y-coordinate of the lower-right corner

Return Value:

The return value has no significance and is not used.

EqualRect

Syntax:

`BOOL EqualRect(lpRect1, lpRect2)`

Parameter, Type, and Description:

lpRect1	LPRECT	Pointer to RECT data structure containing coordinates of the first rectangle
lpRect2	LPRECT	Pointer to RECT data structure containing coordinates of the second rectangle

Description:

The `EqualRect` function compares the two rectangles specified in `lpRect1` and `lpRect2`. `lpRect1` and `lpRect2` point to data structures of type `RECT` that contain the coordinates of the two rectangles to compare. The `RECT` structure is:

```
typedef struct tagRECT {
     int left;
     int top;
     int right;
     int bottom;
} RECT;
```

where:

`left` is the x-coordinate of the upper-left corner

`top` is the y-coordinate of the upper-left corner

`right` is the x-coordinate of the lower-right corner

`bottom` is the y-coordinate of the lower-right corner

Return Value:

The `EqualRect` function returns a nonzero value when the rectangles are the same. A return value of zero indicates that the rectangles are not the same.

InflateRect

Syntax:

```
void InflateRect(lpRect, X, Y)
```

Parameter, Type, and Description:

`lpRect`	`LPRECT`	Pointer to `RECT` data structure to modify
`X`	`int`	Amount to increase or decrease the width of the rectangle
`Y`	`int`	Amount to increase or decrease the height of the rectangle

Description:

The `InflateRect` function changes the size of the rectangle whose coordinates are stored in the data structure of type `RECT`, pointed to by `lpRect`. The `RECT` structure is:

```
typedef struct tagRECT {
     int left;
     int top;
     int right;
     int bottom;
} RECT;
```

where:

`left` is the x-coordinate of the upper-left corner

`top` is the y-coordinate of the upper-left corner

`right` is the x-coordinate of the lower-right corner

`bottom` is the y-coordinate of the lower-right corner

`X` indicates the amount that the width of the rectangle will change. `Y` indicates the amount that the height of the rectangle will change. A positive `X` or `Y` value increases the width and height, respectively. A negative `X` or `Y` value decreases the width and height, respectively. The coordinates of the rectangle must not exceed 32,676 or be less than –32,768.

Return Value:

There is no return value.

IntersectRect

Syntax:

```
int IntersectRect(lpDestRect, lpSrc1Rect, lpSrc2Rect)
```

Parameter, Type, and Description:

lpDestRect	LPRECT	Pointer to RECT data structure to receive the intersection
lpSrc1Rect	LPRECT	Pointer to RECT data structure containing a source rectangle
lpSrc2Rect	LPRECT	Pointer to RECT data structure containing a source rectangle

Description:

The IntersectRect function determines the intersection of the rectangles from lpSrc1Rect and lpSrc2Rect, and places the coordinates of the intersection rectangle in lpDestRect. lpDestRect, lpSrc1Rect, and lpSrc2Rect all point to a data structure of type RECT. The RECT structure is:

```
typedef struct tagRECT {
     int left;
     int top;
     int right;
     int bottom;
} RECT;
```

where:

left is the x-coordinate of the upper-left corner

top is the y-coordinate of the upper-left corner

right is the x-coordinate of the lower-right corner

bottom is the y-coordinate of the lower-right corner

Return Value:

The IntersectRect function returns a nonzero value when the intersection of the two source rectangles is not empty. A return value of zero indicates that the intersection is empty.

IsRectEmpty

Syntax:

```
BOOL IsRectEmpty(lpRect)
```

Parameter, Type, and Description:

lpRect	LPRECT	Pointer to RECT data structure containing the coordinates of the rectangle

Description:

The IsRectEmpty function checks the rectangle that is defined by the coordinates in the data structure of type RECT (this data structure is pointed to by lpRect). The function determines whether the rectangle is empty. The RECT data structure is:

```
typedef struct tagRECT {
     int left;
     int top;
     int right;
     int bottom;
} RECT;
```

where:

left is the x-coordinate of the upper-left corner

top is the y-coordinate of the upper-left corner

right is the x-coordinate of the lower-right corner

bottom is the y-coordinate of the lower-right corner

Return Value:

The IsRectEmpty function returns a nonzero value when the rectangle is empty. A return value of zero indicates that the rectangle is not empty.

OffsetRect

Syntax:

```
void OffsetRect(lpRect, X, Y)
```

Parameter, Type, and Description:

lpRect	LPRECT	Pointer to RECT data structure containing coordinates of the rectangle

X	int	Amount to move the rectangle horizontally
Y	int	Amount to move the rectangle vertically

Description:

The OffsetRect function moves the rectangle specified in lpRect the amount specified in X and Y. X specifies the amount to move in the horizontal direction. Y specifies the amount to move in the vertical direction. Positive values of X and Y move the rectangle right and down, respectively. Negative values of X and Y move the rectangle left and up, respectively. The coordinates of the rectangle must not exceed 32,767 or be less than –32,768. lpRect points to a data structure of type RECT. The RECT data structure follows:

```
typedef struct tagRECT {
     int left;
     int top;
     int right;
     int bottom;
} RECT;
```

where:

left is the x-coordinate of the upper-left corner

top is the y-coordinate of the upper-left corner

right is the x-coordinate of the lower-right corner

bottom is the y-coordinate of the lower-right corner

Return Value:

There is no return value.

PtInRect

Syntax:

```
BOOL PtInRect(lpRect, Point)
```

Parameter, Type, and Description:

lpRect	LPRECT	Pointer to RECT data structure containing the coordinates of the rectangle
Point	POINT	Pointer to POINT data structure containing the point to check

Description:

The `PtInRect` function determines whether the point in `Point` lies within the rectangle in `lpRect`. `lpRect` points to the data structure of type `RECT` that contains the coordinates for the rectangle. `Point` points to the data structure of type `POINT` that contains the coordinates of the point. The point is considered to be within the rectangle if it lies within the rectangle's borders or on the left or top borders. If the point is on the right or bottom borders, it is not considered to be inside the rectangle. The `RECT` and `POINT` data structures are:

```
typedef struct tagRECT {
     int left;
     int top;
     int right;
     int bottom;
} RECT;
```

where:

`left` is the x-coordinate of the upper-left corner

`top` is the y-coordinate of the upper-left corner

`right` is the x-coordinate of the lower-right corner

`bottom` is the y-coordinate of the lower-right corner

```
typedef struct tagPOINT {
     int x;
     int y;
} POINT;
```

where:

`x` is the horizontal coordinate of the point

`y` is the vertical coordinate of the point

Return Value:

The `PtInRect` function returns a nonzero value if the point lies within the given rectangle. A return value of zero indicates that the point does not lie within the given rectangle.

SetRect

Syntax:

```
void SetRect(lpRect, X1, Y1, X2, Y2)
```

Parameter, Type, and Description:

lpRect	LPRECT	Pointer to RECT data structure to receive the rectangle coordinates
X1	int	X-coordinate of the upper-left corner of the rectangle
Y1	int	Y-coordinate of the upper-left corner of the rectangle
X2	int	X-coordinate of the lower-right corner of the rectangle
Y2	int	Y-coordinate of lower-right corner of the rectangle

Description:

The SetRect function creates a new rectangle. The coordinates specified in X1, Y1, X2, and Y2 define the new rectangle. These coordinates are placed in the data structure of type RECT pointed to by lpRect. The RECT data structure is:

```
typedef struct tagRECT {
     int left;
     int top;
     int right;
     int bottom;
} RECT;
```

where:

left is the x-coordinate of the upper-left corner

top is the y-coordinate of the upper-left corner

right is the x-coordinate of the lower-right corner

bottom is the y-coordinate of the lower-right corner

Return Value:

There is no return value.

SetRectEmpty

Syntax:

```
void SetRectEmpty(lpRect)
```

Parameter, Type, and Description:

lpRect	LPRECT	Pointer to RECT data structure that receives the empty rectangle

Description:

The `SetRectEmpty` function creates an empty rectangle and stores the coordinates of the rectangle (all zero) in the data structure of type `RECT`, pointed to by `lpRect`. The `RECT` structure is:

```
typedef struct tagRECT {
     int left;
     int top;
     int right;
     int bottom;
} RECT;
```

where:

`left` is the x-coordinate of the upper-left corner

`top` is the y-coordinate of the upper-left corner

`right` is the x-coordinate of the lower-right corner

`bottom` is the y-coordinate of the lower-right corner

Return Value:

There is no return value.

UnionRect

Syntax:

```
int UnionRect(lpDestRect, lpSrc1Rect, lpSrc2Rect)
```

Parameter, Type, and Description:

`lpDestRect`	`LPRECT`	Pointer to `RECT` data structure that receives the union
`lpSrc1Rect`	`LPRECT`	Pointer to `RECT` data structure containing a source rectangle
`lpSrc2Rect`	`LPRECT`	Pointer to `RECT` data structure containing a source rectangle

Description:

The `UnionRect` function stores the coordinates of the smallest rectangle that contains both of the rectangles in `lpSrc1Rect` and `lpSrc2Rect` (the union of `lpSrc1Rect` and `lpSrc2Rect`) in `lpDestRect`. `lpDestRect`, `lpSrc1Rect`, and `lpSrc2Rect` all point to a structure of type `RECT` that contains the coordinates of the respective rectangle. The `RECT` structure is:

```
typedef struct tagRECT {
     int left;
     int top;
     int right;
     int bottom;
} RECT;
```

where:

`left` is the x-coordinate of the upper-left corner

`top` is the y-coordinate of the upper-left corner

`right` is the x-coordinate of the lower-right corner

`bottom` is the y-coordinate of the lower-right corner

Return Value:

The `UnionRect` function returns a nonzero value when the union of the rectangles is not empty. A return value of zero indicates that the union is empty.

Scrolling Functions

Scrolling occurs when data is moved in and out of the client area. The scroll bar is the primary tool used to allow the user to scroll the contents of the client area. The scroll bar is a part of the non-client area of the window and is created with the window. Both vertical and horizontal control bars can be created. The current display position of the contents, relative to the beginning and end of the contents being scrolled, is shown in the scroll bar thumb.

The scroll bar control is another tool to allow the user to scroll the contents of the client area. A scroll bar control is like a standard scroll bar but is not a part of the window. The scroll bar control can receive the input focus and permits the user to use the keyboard for scrolling.

Scrolling functions provide control over scroll bars and scroll bar controls. The following functions are categorized as Scrolling functions for the Window Manager Interface:

Function	*Meaning*
`GetScrollPos`	Gets the thumb position of a scroll bar
`GetScrollRange`	Gets the position range for a scroll bar
`ScrollDC`	Scrolls a rectangle horizontally and vertically
`ScrollWindow`	Moves the contents of the client area

Function	Meaning
SetScrollPos	Sets the thumb position of the scroll bar
SetScrollRange	Sets the position range for a scroll bar
ShowScrollBar	Either hides or displays a scroll bar

The rest of this section provides detailed information on each of the functions in this list.

GetScrollPos

Syntax:

```
int GetScrollPos(hWnd, nBar)
```

Parameter, Type, and Description:

hWnd	HWND	Window containing the scroll bars or scroll control
nBar	int	Scroll bar

Description:

The GetScrollPos function gets the thumb position of the scroll bar for the window specified in hWnd. nBar specifies the scroll bar to evaluate. The value for nBar is selected from the following values:

Value	Meaning
SB_CTL	Gets the position of a scroll bar control; hWnd must specify the window handle of a scroll bar control
SB_HORZ	Gets the position of the horizontal scroll bar
SB_VERT	Gets the position of the vertical scroll bar

The value returned by the GetScrollPos function is relative to the current scrolling range.

Return Value:

The GetScrollPos function returns the thumb position of the scroll bar. The returned value is relative to the scrolling range of the scroll bar. NULL is not a possible return value.

GetScrollRange

Syntax:

```
void GetScrollRange(hWnd, nBar, lpMinPos, lpMaxPos)
```

Parameter, Type, and Description:

`hWnd`	`HWND`	Window containing the scroll bars or scroll control
`nBar`	`int`	Scroll bar to retrieve
`lpMinPos`	`LPINT`	Pointer to the variable to receive the minimum position
`lpMaxPos`	`LPINT`	Pointer to the variable to receive the maximum position

Description:

The `GetScrollRange` function gets the minimum and maximum ranges for the scroll bar specified in `nBar` and places these values in `lpMinPos` and `lpMaxPos`, respectively. `nBar` specifies the scroll bar to retrieve. The values for `nBar` are:

Value	*Meaning*
`SB_CTL`	Gets the position of a scroll bar control; `hWnd` must specify the window handle of a scroll bar control
`SB_HORZ`	Gets the position of the horizontal scroll bar
`SB_VERT`	Gets the position of the vertical scroll bar

Return Value:

There is no return value.

ScrollDC

Syntax:

```
BOOL ScrollDC(hDC, dx, dy, lprcScroll, lprcClip, hrgnUpdate,
              lprcUpdate)
```

Parameter, Type, and Description:

`hDC`	`HDC`	Device context
`dx`	`int`	Number of horizontal scroll units
`dy`	`int`	Number of vertical scroll units
`lprcScroll`	`LPRECT`	Pointer to `RECT` structure that contains the coordinates of the scrolling rectangle

lprcClip	LPRECT	Pointer to RECT structure that contains the coordinates of the clipping region
hrgnUpdate	HRGN	Region that is uncovered by the scrolling—the region does not need to be rectangular
lprcUpdate	LPRECT	Pointer to RECT structure that contains the coordinates of the rectangle that bounds the update region

Description:

The ScrollDC function scrolls a rectangle of bits the amount specified in dx and dy. lprcScroll points to the data structure of type RECT that contains the coordinates of the rectangle to scroll. lprcClip and lprcUpdate both point to data structures of type RECT. The RECT structure is:

```
typedef struct tagRECT {
     int left;
     int top;
     int right;
     int bottom;
} RECT;
```

where:

left is the x-coordinate of the upper-left corner

top is the y-coordinate of the upper-left corner

right is the x-coordinate of the lower-right corner

bottom is the y-coordinate of the lower-right corner

Return Value:

The ScrollDC function returns a nonzero value when scrolling occurs. A return value of zero indicates that there was no scrolling.

ScrollWindow

Syntax:

```
void ScrollWindow(hWnd, XAmount, YAmout, lpRect, lpClipRect)
```

Parameter, Type, and Description:

hWnd	HWND	Window containing client area to scroll
XAmount	int	Number of device units to scroll horizontally
YAmount	int	Number of device units to scroll vertically

lpRect	LPRECT	Pointer to RECT data structure containing the coordinates of the area to scroll
lpClipRect	LPRECT	Pointer to RECT data structure containing the coordinates of the clipping rectangle to scroll

Description:

The ScrollWindow function scrolls the window in hWnd. The contents of the client area for the window in hWnd are moved the number of device units specified in XAmount and YAmount:

- XAmount describes the amount to scroll in the horizontal direction.
- YAmount describes the amount to scroll in the vertical direction.

Positive values for XAmount and YAmount move the client area right and down, respectively. Negative values for XAmount and YAmount move the client area left and up, respectively. lpRect and lpClipRect point to data structures of type RECT. The RECT data structure is:

```
typedef struct tagRECT {
     int left;
     int top;
     int right;
     int bottom;
} RECT;
```

where:

left is the x-coordinate of the upper-left corner

top is the y-coordinate of the upper-left corner

right is the x-coordinate of the lower-right corner

bottom is the y-coordinate of the lower-right corner

Set lpRect to NULL to scroll the entire client area. Set lpClipRect to NULL to scroll the entire window.

Return Value:

There is no return value.

SetScrollPos

Syntax:

```
int SetScrollPos(hWnd, nBar, nPos, bRedraw)
```

Parameter, Type, and Description:

hWnd	HWND	Window containing scroll bar to set
nBar	int	Scroll bar to set
nPos	int	New thumb position of scroll bar
bRedraw	BOOL	Set to nonzero if the scroll bar is to be redrawn

Description:

The SetScrollPos function sets the thumb position of the scroll bar specified in nBar to the position specified in nPos. The scroll bar is redrawn if bRedraw is set to a nonzero value. Set bRedraw to zero if the scroll bar is not to be redrawn. nBar is set to one of the following values:

Value	*Meaning*
SB_CTL	Sets the position of a scroll bar control; hWnd must specify the window handle of a scroll bar control
SB_HORZ	Sets the position of the horizontal scroll bar
SB_VERT	Sets the position of the vertical scroll bar

Return Value:

The SetScrollPos function returns the previous thumb position of the scroll bar. NULL is not a possible return value.

SetScrollRange

Syntax:

```
void SetScrollRange(hWnd, nBar, nMinPos, nMaxPos, bRedraw)
```

Parameter, Type, and Description:

hWnd	HWND	Window containing scroll bar to set
nBar	int	Scroll bar to set
nMinPos	int	Minimum scrolling position
nMaxPos	int	Maximum scrolling position
bRedraw	BOOL	Determines whether the scroll bar is redrawn

Description:

The SetScrollRange function defines the range of the scroll bar specified in nBar. The minimum and maximum positions for the scroll bar are defined by nMinPos and nMaxPos, respectively. bRedraw determines whether the scroll bar is redrawn:

- Set bRedraw to a nonzero value if the scroll bar is to be redrawn.
- Set bRedraw to zero if the scroll bar is not to be redrawn.

nBar is set to one of the following values:

Value	*Meaning*
SB_CTL	Sets the range of a scroll bar control; hWnd must specify the window handle of a scroll bar control
SB_HORZ	Sets the range of the horizontal scroll bar
SB_VERT	Sets the range of the vertical scroll bar

Return Value:

There is no return value.

ShowScrollBar

Syntax:

```
void ShowScrollBar(hWnd, wBar, bShow)
```

Parameter, Type, and Description:

hWnd	HWND	Window containing scroll bar or scroll bar control
wBar	WORD	Value indicating meaning of hWnd and scroll bar position
bShow	BOOL	Determines whether the scroll bar is hidden

Description:

The ShowScrollBar function either hides or shows the scroll bar in hWnd. bShow specifies whether the scroll bar is to be hidden or shown:

- Set bShow to zero to hide the scroll bar.
- Set bShow to a nonzero value to show the scroll bar.

wBar specifies the meaning of hWnd and the scroll bar position. wBar is set to one of the following values:

Value	*Meaning*
SB_BOTH	Hide/show both horizontal and vertical scroll bars; hWnd specifies a window containing a scroll bar in its non-client area
SB_CTL	Hide/show the scroll bar control; hWnd specifies the scroll bar control

Value	*Meaning*
SB_HORZ	Hide/show the horizontal scroll bar; hWnd specifies a window containing a scroll bar in its non-client area
SB_VERT	Hide/show the vertical scroll bar; hWnd specifies a window containing a scroll bar in its non-client area

Return Value:

There is no return value.

System Functions

Windows provides a set of functions used to retrieve information on system metrics, color, and time. These are the System functions. The following functions are categorized as System functions for the Window Manager Interface:

Function	*Meaning*
GetCurrentTime	Gets the elapsed time since the system was booted
GetSysColor	Gets the system color
GetSystemMetrics	Gets system metrics information
SetSysColors	Modifies system colors

The rest of this section provides detailed information on each of the functions in this list.

GetCurrentTime

Syntax:

```
DWORD GetCurrentTime()
```

Description:

The GetCurrentTime function gets the number of milliseconds elapsed since the system was booted, called the *current Windows time*.

Return Value:

The GetCurrentTime function returns the current Windows time, measured in milliseconds.

GetSysColor

Syntax:

```
DWORD GetSysColor(nIndex)
```

Parameter, Type, and Description:

`nIndex`	`int`	Display element

Description:

The `GetSysColor` function gets the current color for the display element specified in `nIndex`. The index values used for `nIndex` are:

Value	*Meaning*
`COLOR_ACTIVEBORDER`	Active window border
`COLOR_ACTIVECAPTION`	Active window caption
`COLOR_APPWORKSPACE`	Background color for MDI applications
`COLOR_BACKGROUND`	Desktop
`COLOR_BTNFACE`	Face shading for push buttons
`COLOR_BTNSHADOW`	Edge shading for push buttons
`COLOR_BTNTEXT`	Text on push buttons
`COLOR_CAPTIONTEXT`	Text for caption, size box, scroll bar arrow box
`COLOR_GRAYTEXT`	Grayed text
`COLOR_HIGHLIGHT`	Selected items in a control
`COLOR_HIGHLIGHTTEXT`	Text of selected items in a control
`COLOR_INACTIVEBORDER`	Inactive window border
`COLOR_INACTIVECAPTION`	Inactive window caption
`COLOR_MENU`	Menu background
`COLOR_MENUTEXT`	Text for menus
`COLOR_SCROLLBAR`	Gray area of the scroll bar
`COLOR_WINDOW`	Window background
`COLOR_WINDOWFRAME`	Window frame
`COLOR_WINDOWTEXT`	Text in windows

Return Value:

The `GetSysColor` function returns the RGB color value naming the color of the element in `nIndex`. NULL is not a possible return value.

GetSystemMetrics

Syntax:

```
int GetSystemMetrics(nIndex)
```

Parameter, Type, and Description:

`nIndex` `int` Specifies the system measurement to retrieve

Description:

The `GetSystemMetrics` function gets the size, or metrics, of the specified display element. `nIndex` specifies the system measurement to retrieve. Measurements are expressed in pixels. The following values are used for `nIndex`:

Value	*Meaning*
SM_CXSCREEN	Screen width
SM_CYSCREEN	Screen height
SM_CXFRAME	Width of window frame that can be sized
SM_CYFRAME	Height of window frame that can be sized
SM_CXHSCROLL	Width of arrow bitmap on the horizontal scroll bar
SM_CYHSCROLL	Height of arrow bitmap on the horizontal scroll bar
SM_CXVSCROLL	Width of arrow bitmap on the vertical scroll bar
SM_CYVSCROLL	Height of arrow bitmap on the vertical scroll bar
SM_CYCAPTION	Height of caption
SM_CXBORDER	Width of window frame that cannot be sized
SM_CYBORDER	Height of window frame that cannot be sized
SM_CXDLGFRAME	Width of frame for a window with style WS_DLGFRAME
SM_CYDLGFRAME	Height of frame for a window with style WS_DLGFRAME
SM_CXHTHUMB	Width of thumb box on the horizontal scroll bar
SM_CYVTHUMB	Height of thumb box on the vertical scroll bar
SM_CXICON	Width of icon
SM_CYICON	Height of icon
SM_CXCURSOR	Width of cursor
SM_CYCURSOR	Height of cursor
SM_CYMENU	Height of single line menu bar
SM_CXFULLSCREEN	Width of client area for full-screen window
SM_CYFULLSCREEN	Height of client area for full-screen window
SM_CYKANJIWINDOW	Height of Kanji window
SM_CXMINTRACK	Minimum tracking width of window

Value	Meaning
SM_CYMINTRACK	Minimum tracking height of window
SM_CXMIN	Minimum width of window
SM_CYMIN	Minimum height of window
SM_CXSIZE	Width of bitmaps in Title bar
SM_CYSIZE	Height of bitmaps in Title bar
SM_MOUSEPRESENT	Nonzero if mouse hardware is present
SM_DEBUG	Nonzero if Windows debugging version is executing
SM_SWAPBUTTON	Nonzero if left and right mouse buttons are swapped

Return Value:

The `GetSystemMetrics` function returns the system metric corresponding to `nIndex`.

SetSysColors

Syntax:

```
void SetSysColors(nChanges, lpSysColor, lpColorValues)
```

Parameter, Type, and Description:

nChanges	int	Number of system colors to change
lpSysColor	LPINT	Pointer to array of index values that indicate the display elements to change
lpColorValues	DWORD FAR *	Pointer to array of unsigned long integers containing the new RGB values for the display elements

Description:

The `SetSysColors` function sets the system color for the specified display elements. The number of elements to change is specified in `nChanges`. `lpSysColor` points to an array containing the index values for the display elements to change. The following values are used for values in `lpSysColor`:

Value	Meaning
COLOR_ACTIVEBORDER	Active window border
COLOR_ACTIVECAPTION	Active window caption
COLOR_APPWORKSPACE	Background color for MDI applications
COLOR_BACKGROUND	Desktop
COLOR_BTNFACE	Face shading for push buttons

Value	Meaning
COLOR_BTNSHADOW	Edge shading for push buttons
COLOR_BTNTEXT	Text on push buttons
COLOR_CAPTIONTEXT	Text for caption, size box, scroll bar arrow box
COLOR_GRAYTEXT	Grayed text
COLOR_HIGHLIGHT	Selected items in a control
COLOR_HIGHLIGHTTEXT	Text of selected items in a control
COLOR_INACTIVEBORDER	Inactive window border
COLOR_INACTIVECAPTION	Inactive window caption
COLOR_MENU	Menu background
COLOR_MENUTEXT	Text for menus
COLOR_SCROLLBAR	Gray area of the scroll bar
COLOR_WINDOW	Window background
COLOR_WINDOWFRAME	Window frame
COLOR_WINDOWTEXT	Text in windows

Return Value:

There is no return value.

Window Creation Functions

The first step in creating a window is to define or choose a window class. The window class defines the appearance and behavior of the window. The three types of window classes are the system global class, the application global class, and the application local class.

System global classes are available from Windows. Windows creates these classes on start-up. Applications can use these classes but cannot delete them.

The application creates the application global classes by using the CS_GLOBALCLASS style for the particular class. The created class then is available to all the applications in the system. All application global classes created by an application are destroyed when the application ends.

Application local classes are created by the application and are only available to the application.

After the class has been established, the class is registered. A window of that class type can then be created. Windows provides several functions for creating, destroying, modifying, and manipulating windows. These functions are called the Window Creation functions. The following functions are categorized as Window Creation functions for the Window Manager Interface:

Function	*Meaning*
`AdjustWindowRect`	Determines the window size for the specified client area
`AdjustWindowRectEx`	Determines the window size with extended style for the specified client area
`CreateWindow`	Creates a window
`CreateWindowEx`	Creates a window with extended style
`DefDlgProc`	Provides default processing for dialog box messages
`DefFrameProc`	Provides default processing for MDI frame window messages
`DefMDIChildProc`	Provides default processing for MDI child window messages
`DefWindowProc`	Provides default processing for window messages
`DestroyWindow`	Destroys a window
`GetClassInfo`	Gets information on the specified class
`GetClassLong`	Gets a long integer from a `WNDCLASS` structure
`GetClassName`	Gets a class name
`GetClassWord`	Gets a word from a `WNDCLASS` structure
`GetLastActivePopup`	Gets the most recently active pop-up window
`GetWindowLong`	Gets a long integer descriptor for the window
`GetWindowWord`	Gets a word descriptor for the window
`RegisterClass`	Registers the window class
`SetClassLong`	Replaces a long integer in a `WNDCLASS` structure
`SetClassWord`	Replaces a word in a `WNDCLASS` structure
`SetWindowLong`	Modifies an integer attribute
`SetWindowWord`	Modifies a word attribute
`UnregisterClass`	Removes a window class

The rest of this section provides detailed information on each of the functions in this list.

AdjustWindowRect

Syntax:

```
void AdjustWindowRect(lpRect, dwStyle, bMenu)
```

Parameter, Type, and Description:

`lpRect`	`LPRECT`	Pointer to `RECT` data structure containing coordinates of the client rectangle

dwStyle	DWORD	Window styles of the window containing the client rectangle
bMenu	BOOL	Indicates whether the window has a menu

Description:

The AdjustWindowRect function determines the size of the desired window rectangle based on the specified client rectangle size. The window rectangle can then be passed to CreateWindow to create a window with the new specified client area size. The client rectangle is the smallest rectangle that encloses the client area. The window rectangle is the smallest rectangle that encloses the window. lpRect points to a data structure or type RECT that contains the coordinates of the client rectangle. The RECT structure is:

```
typedef struct tagRECT {
     int left;
     int top;
     int right;
     int bottom;
} RECT;
```

where:

left is the x-coordinate of the upper-left corner

top is the y-coordinate of the upper-left corner

right is the x-coordinate of the lower-right corner

bottom is the y-coordinate of the lower-right corner

Return Value:

There is no return value.

AdjustWindowRectEx

Syntax:

```
void AdjustWindowRectEx(lpRect, dwStyle, bMenu, dwExStyle)
```

Parameter, Type, and Description:

lpRect	LPRECT	Pointer to RECT data structure containing coordinates of the client rectangle
dwStyle	DWORD	Window styles of the window containing the client rectangle

bMenu	BOOL	Indicates whether the window has a menu
dwExStyle	DWORD	Extended style of the window being created

Description:

The AdjustWindowRectEx function determines the desired window rectangle, considering the specified extended style, for the new specified client rectangle size. The window rectangle can then be passed to CreateWindowEx to create a window with the specified client area size. A client rectangle is the smallest rectangle that encloses the client area. A window rectangle is the smallest rectangle that encloses the window. The function itself assumes (by default) that the menu is a single-row menu. lpRect points to a data structure of type RECT that contains the coordinates of the client rectangle. The RECT structure is:

```
typedef struct tagRECT {
     int left;
     int top;
     int right;
     int bottom;
} RECT;
```

where:

left is the x-coordinate of the upper-left corner

top is the y-coordinate of the upper-left corner

right is the x-coordinate of the lower-right corner

bottom is the y-coordinate of the lower-right corner

Return Value:

There is no return value.

CreateWindow

Syntax:

```
HWND CreateWindow(lpClassName, lpWindowName, dwStyle, X, Y,
                  nWidth, nHeight, hWndParent, hMenu, hInstance, lpParam)
```

Parameter, Type, and Description:

lpClassname	LPSTR	Pointer to a null-terminated character string that names the window class
lpWindowName	LPSTR	Pointer to a null-terminated character string that represents the window name
dwStyle	DWORD	The style of window to create

`X`	`int`	Initial horizontal position of the window's upper-left corner, expressed in screen coordinates
`Y`	`int`	Initial vertical position of the window's upper-left corner, expressed in screen coordinates
`nWidth`	`int`	Window width in device units
`nHeight`	`int`	Window height in device units
`hWndParent`	`HWND`	Parent or owner of the window to create
`hMenu`	`HMENU`	Menu or child window identifier
`hInstance`	`HANDLE`	Instance of module associated with the window
`lpParam`	`LPSTR`	Pointer to value passed to the window through the `CREATESTRUCT` data structure; the structure is referenced by the `lParam` parameter of the `WM_CREATE` message

Description:

The `CreateWindow` function creates an overlapped, pop-up, or child window. `CreateWindow` sends the `WM_CREATE`, `WM_GETMINMAXINFO`, and `WM_NCCREATE` messages to the specified window. `lpClassName` points to a null-terminated string that names the window class. The following values can be used for `lpClassName`:

Value	*Meaning*
`BUTTON`	A small rectangular child window representing a two-state button that can turned on or off
`COMBOBOX`	A control that contains a selection field and edit control
`EDIT`	A rectangular child window that accepts user input
`LISTBOX`	A list of character strings
`MDICLIENT`	An MDI client window
`SCROLLBAR`	A rectangle containing a direction arrow at either end and a position indicator
`STATIC`	A simple text field, box, or rectangle

`lpWindowName` points to the string that represents the window name. `dwStyle` specifies the style for the created window and can be any combination of the following values:

Value	*Meaning*
	Window Styles
`DS_LOCALEDIT`	Specifies that edit controls in the dialog box will use memory in the application's data segment
`DS_MODALFRAME`	Creates a dialog box with a modal dialog box frame

Value	*Meaning*
	Window Styles
DS_NOIDLEMSG	Suppresses WM_ENTERIDLE messages while the dialog box is displayed
DS_SYSMODAL	Creates a system modal dialog box
WS_BORDER	Creates a window with a border
WS_CAPTION	Creates a window with a Title bar; cannot be used with WS_DLGFRAME
WS_CHILD	Creates a child window. Cannot be used with WS_POPUP
WS_CHILDWINDOW	Creates a child window with style WS_CHILD
WS_CLIPCHILDREN	Excludes the area occupied by child windows when drawing within the parent window
WS_CLIPSIBLINGS	Clips child windows relative to each other; for use with WS_CHILD only
WS_DISABLED	Creates a window that is disabled
WS_DLGFRAME	Creates a window with a double border and no title
WS_GROUP	Defines the first control from a group that the user can move from one control to another with the direction keys
WS_HSCROLL	Creates a window with a horizontal scroll bar
WS_ICONIC	Creates an iconic window
WS_MAXIMIZE	Creates a window that is to be maximized
WS_MAXIMIZEBOX	Creates a window with a maximize box
WS_MINIMIZE	Creates a window that is minimum size
WS_MINIMIZEBOX	Creates a window with a minimize box
WS_OVERLAPPED	Creates an overlapped window with a caption and border
WS_OVERLAPPEDWINDOW	Creates an overlapped window with styles WS_OVERLAPPED, WS_CAPTION, YSMENU, WS_THICKFRAME, WS_MINIMIZEBOX, and WS_MAXIMIZEBOX
WS_POPUP	Creates a pop-up window; cannot be used with WS_CHILD
WS_POPUPWINDOW	Creates a pop-up window with styles WS_BORDER, WS_POPUP, and WS_SYSMENU
WS_SYSMENU	Creates a window with a System menu box in the Title bar
WS_TABSTOP	Specifies the controls that a user can move to with the Tab key
WS_THICKFRAME	Creates a window with a thick frame

Value	Meaning
	Window Styles
WS_VISIBLE	Creates a visible overlapped or pop-up window
WS_VSCROLL	Creates a window with a vertical scroll bar
	BUTTON Class Control Styles
BS_AUTOCHECKBOX	Specifies a small rectangular button that may be checked; button toggles when clicked
BS_AUTORADIOBUTTON	Specifies a small circular button that can be checked; when clicked, the check marks are removed from the other radio buttons in the group
BS_AUTO3STATE	Specifies a small rectangular button that changes state when clicked; supports three states: on, off, or grayed
BS_CHECKBOX	Specifies a small rectangular button that may be checked
BS_DEFPUSHBUTTON	Designates a button as the default button by its bold border
BS_GROUPBOX	Groups the buttons in the designated rectangle
BS_LEFTTEXT	Forces text to appear on the left side (the right side is the default) for styles BS_CHECKBOX, BS_RADIOBUTTON, and BS_3STATE
BS_OWNERDRAW	Specifies an owner draw button; parent is notified when the button is clicked
BS_PUSHBUTTON	Specifies a button containing the specified text
BS_RADIOBUTTON	Specifies a small circular button that can be checked
BS_3STATE	Specifies a small rectangular button that may be checked; supports three states: on, off, and grayed
	COMBOBOX Class Control Styles
CBS_AUTOHSCROLL	Scrolls the text in the edit control to the right when text reaches the end of the line
CBS_DROPDOWN	Displays a list box only when the icon beside the selection field is selected
CBS_DROPDOWNLIST	Like CBS_DROPDOWN; edit control, however, is replaced by a static text item that displays the current selection from the list box
CBS_HASSTRINGS	Specifies that the owner-draw combo box contains items that consist of strings
CBS_OEMCONVERT	Converts text from combo box edit control from ANSI to OEM and back to ANSI
CBS_OWNERDRAWFIXED	Specifies that the list box owner draws the contents of the list box; contents are all the same height

Value	*Meaning*
	COMBOBOX Class Control Styles
CBS_OWNERDRAWVARIABLE	Specifies that the list box owner draws the contents of the list box; contents are not all the same height
CBS_SIMPLE	Permanently displays the list box
CBS_SORT	Automatically sorts strings entered in the list box
	EDIT Class Control Styles
ES_AUTOHSCROLL	Automatically scrolls text to the right 10 spaces when the end of the line is reached
ES_AUTOVSCROLL	Automatically scrolls the text up one page when Enter is pressed on the last line
ES_CENTER	Centers text in a multiline edit control
ES_LEFT	Left justifies text
ES_LOWERCASE	Displays all entered characters as lowercase
ES_MULTILINE	Permits multiline edit control
ES_NOHIDESEL	Disables the default action of hiding the selection when the control loses the input focus and inverting the selection when the control receives the input focus
ES_OEMCONVERT	Converts text in the edit control from ANSI to OEM to ANSI
ES_PASSWORD	Displays an asterisk (*) for each character entered into the edit control
ES_RIGHT	Right justifies text in a multiline edit control
ES_UPPERCASE	Displays all entered characters as uppercase
	LISTBOX Class Control Styles
LBS_EXTENDEDSEL	Enables the user to select multiple selections from the list box
LBS_HASSTRINGS	Specifies that the owner draw list box contains items made up of strings
LBS_MULTICOLUMN	Specifies a multicolumn list box with horizontal scroll
LBS_MULTIPLESEL	Toggles the string selection each time a string is clicked or double clicked; multiple selections can be made
LBS_NOINTEGRALHEIGHT	Specifies that the list box has the exact size indicated by the application creating the list box
LBS_NOREDRAW	Does not redraw the list box after modification

Value	*Meaning*
	LISTBOX Class Control Styles
`LBS_NOTIFY`	Sends the input message to the parent when a string is clicked or double clicked
`LBS_OWNERDRAWFIXED`	Specifies that the list box owner draws list box contents; all items in the list box are the same height
`LBS_OWNERDRAWVARIABLE`	Specifies that the list box owner draws the contents of the list box
`LBS_SORT`	Alphabetically sorts strings in the list box
`LBS_STANDARD`	Alphabetically sorts strings in the list box and sends an input message to the parent window when a string is clicked or double clicked
`LBS_USETABSTOPS`	Specifies that the list box recognize tab characters when drawing strings
`LBS_WANTKEYBOARDINPUT`	Sends a `WM_VKEYTOITEM` or `WM_CHARTOITEM` message to the owner of the list box when a key is pressed while the list box has the input focus
	SCROLLBAR Class Control Styles
`SBS_BOTTOMALIGN`	Aligns the bottom edge of scroll bar with the bottom edge of the rectangle specified by `X`, `Y`, `nWidth`, and `nHeight` from the `CreateWindow` function; used with `SBS_HORIZON`
`SBS_HORZ`	Specifies a horizontal scroll bar
`SBS_LEFTALIGN`	Aligns the left edge of scroll bar with the left edge of the rectangle specified by `X`, `Y`, `nWidth`, and `nHeight` from the `CreateWindow` function; used with `SBS_VERT`
`SBS_RIGHTALIGN`	Aligns the right edge of scroll bar with the right edge of the rectangle specified by `X`, `Y`, `nWidth`, and `nHeight` from the `CreateWindow` function; used with `SBS_VERT`
`SBS_SIZEBOX`	Specifies a size box
`SBS_SIZEBOXBOTTOMRIGHTALIGN`	Aligns the lower-right corner of a size box with the lower-right corner of the rectangle specified by `X`, `Y`, `nWidth`, and `nHeight` from the `CreateWindow` function; used with `SBS_SIZEBOX`
`SBS_SIZEBOXTOPLEFTALIGN`	Aligns the upper-left corner of a size box with the upper-left corner of the rectangle specified by `X`, `Y`, `nWidth`, and `nHeight` from the `CreateWindow` function; used with `SBS_SIZEBOX`

Value	*Meaning*
	SCROLLBAR Class Control Styles
SBS_TOPALIGN	Aligns the top edge of a scroll bar with the top edge of the rectangle specified by X, Y, nWidth, and nHeight from the CreateWindow function; used with SBS_HORIZON
SBS_VERT	Specifies a vertical scroll bar
	STATIC Class Control Styles
SS_BLACKFRAME	Draws a box's frame with same color as the window frames
SS_BLACKRECT	Fills a rectangle with the same color as the window frames
SS_CENTER	Creates a simple rectangle with text centered in rectangle; text is wrapped to next line if necessary
SS_GRAYFRAME	Draws a box's frame with same color as the screen background
SS_GRAYRECT	Fills a rectangle with the same color as the screen background
SS_ICON	Displays an icon in the dialog box
SS_LEFT	Creates a simple rectangle with text left justified inside the rectangle; text is wrapped to next line if necessary
SS_LEFTNOWORDWRAP	Creates a simple rectangle with text left justified inside the rectangle; text is not wrapped to the next line
SS_NOPREFIX	Without this style, the & character will be interpreted as an accelerator prefix character
SS_RIGHT	Creates a simple rectangle with text right justified inside the rectangle; text is wrapped to the next line if necessary
SS_SIMPLE	Creates a simple rectangle with text left justified; the text cannot be altered
SS_USERITEM	Designates a user-defined item
SS_WHITEFRAME	Draws a box with the frame in same color as the window background
SS_WHITERECT	Fills a rectangle with the same color as the window background

Combine values by using the bitwise OR operator.

Chapter 2, "Windows Programming Basics," and Chapter 7, "Windows and Child Windows," describe Windows and Windows classes in greater detail.

Return Value:

The `CreateWindow` function returns the window handle of the created window. A NULL return value indicates that the function cannot create the window.

CreateWindowEx

Syntax:

```
HWND CreateWindowEx(dwExStyle, lpClassName, lpWindowName,
                    dwStyle, X, Y, nWidth, nHeight, hWndParent,
                    hMenu, hInstance, lpParam)
```

Parameter, Type, and Description:

`dwExStyle`	`DWORD`	Extended style for the window to create
`lpClassname`	`LPSTR`	Pointer to a null-terminated character string that names the window class
`lpWindowName`	`LPSTR`	Pointer to a null-terminated character string that represents the window name
`dwStyle`	`DWORD`	The style of window to create
`X`	`int`	Initial horizontal position of the window's upper-left corner, expressed in screen coordinates
`Y`	`int`	Initial vertical position of the window's upper-left corner, expressed in screen coordinates
`nWidth`	`int`	Window width in device units
`nHeight`	`int`	Window height in device units
`hWndParent`	`HWND`	Parent or owner of the window to create
`hMenu`	`HMENU`	Menu or child window identifier
`hInstance`	`HANDLE`	Instance of module associated with the window
`lpParam`	`LPSTR`	Pointer to value passed to the window through the `CREATESTRUCT` data structure; the structure is referenced by the `lParam` parameter of the `WM_CREATE` message

Description:

The `CreateWindowEx` function creates an overlapped, pop-up, or child window using the specified extended style. `dwExStyle` specifies the extended style to use. The value for the extended style specified in `dwExStyle` is chosen from the following list:

Value	*Meaning*
WS_EX_DLGMODALFRAME	Window with a double border; the window contains a Title bar if WS_CAPTION is specified in dwStyle
WS_EX_NOPARENTNOTIFY	A child window with this style does not send the WM_PARENTNOTIFY message to the parent window when the child window is created or destroyed

The rest of the parameters for CreateWindowEx are the same as the parameters for CreateWindow. (See this chapter's description of CreateWindow for more information.)

Return Value:

The CreateWindowEx function returns the handle for the new window. A NULL return value indicates that the window cannot be created.

DefDlgProc

Syntax:

```
LONG DefDlgProc(hDlg, wMsg, wParam, lParam)
```

Parameter, Type, and Description:

hDlg	HWND	Dialog box
wMsg	WORD	Message number
wParam	WORD	Additional message information
lParam	DWORD	Additional message information

Description:

The DefDlgProc function processes Windows messages that the dialog box in hDlg with a private window class cannot process. Windows messages not processed by the window function must be passed to DefDlgProc.

Return Value:

The return value depends on the message processed.

DefFrameProc

Syntax:

```
LONG DefFrameProc(hWnd, hWndMDIClient, wMsg, wParam, lParam)
```

Parameter, Type, and Description:

`hWnd`	`HWND`	MDI frame window
`hWndMDIClient`	`HWND`	MDI client window
`wMsg`	`WORD`	Message number
`wParam`	`WORD`	Additional message information
`lParam`	`DWORD`	Additional message information

Description:

The `DefFrameProc` function processes the Windows messages that the window function of a multiple document interface (MDI) frame window cannot process. Windows messages not processed by the window function must be passed to the `DefFrameProc` function.

Return Value:

The return value depends on the message processed.

DefMDIChildProc

Syntax:

```
LONG DefMDIChildProc(hWnd, wMsg, wParam, lParam)
```

Parameter, Type, and Description:

`hWnd`	`HWND`	MDI child window
`wMsg`	`WORD`	Message number
`wParam`	`WORD`	Additional message information
`lParam`	`DWORD`	Additional message information

Description:

The `DefMDIChildProc` function processes the Windows messages that the window function of a multiple document interface (MDI) child window cannot process. Windows messages not processed by the window function must be passed to `DefMDIChildProc`.

Return Value:

The return value depends on the message processed.

DefWindowProc

Syntax:

```
LONG DefWindowProc(hWnd, wMsg, wParam, lParam)
```

Parameter, Type, and Description:

hWnd	HWND	Window passing message
wMsg	WORD	Message number
wParam	WORD	Additional message information
lParam	DWORD	Additional message information

Description:

The `DefWindowProc` function processes the Windows messages that the specified application cannot process. Windows messages not processed by the class window function must be passed to `DefWindowProc`.

Return Value:

The return value depends on the message processed.

DestroyWindow

Syntax:

```
BOOL DestroyWindow(hWnd)
```

Parameter, Type, and Description:

hWnd	HWND	Window to destroy

Description:

The `DestroyWindow` function destroys the window specified in `hWnd`. The window menu is destroyed, the application queue is flushed, outstanding timers are removed, clipboard ownership is removed, and the `WM_DESTROY` and `WM_NCDESTROY` messages are sent to the window. If a parent window is specified, the child windows of the parent window are destroyed as well.

Return Value:

The `DestroyWindow` function returns a nonzero value if the window is destroyed. A return value of zero indicates that the window is not destroyed.

GetClassInfo

Syntax:

```
BOOL GetClassInfo(hInstance, lpClassName, lpWndClass)
```

Parameter, Type, and Description:

`hInstance`	`HANDLE`	Instance of the application that created the class
`lpClassName`	`LPSTR`	Pointer to string that contains the name of class
`lpWndClass`	`LPWNDCLASS`	Pointer to `WNDCLASS` structure where class information will be copied

Description:

The `GetClassInfo` function gets information about the class specified by `lpClassName`. `hInstance` specifies the instance of the application that created the class. The class information is copied into the data structure of type `WNDCLASS` pointed to by `lpWndClass`.

Return Value:

The `GetClassInfo` function returns TRUE if a matching class is found and successfully copied into the structure. A return value of FALSE indicates that a matching class is not found.

GetClassLong

Syntax:

```
LONG GetClassLong(hWnd, nIndex)
```

Parameter, Type, and Description:

`hWnd`	`HWND`	Window handle
`nIndex`	`int`	Byte offset of value to retrieve

Description:

The `GetClassLong` function gets the long value specified in `nIndex` from the `WNDCLASS` structure for the window in `hWnd`. `nIndex` specifies the byte offset of the value to retrieve. `nIndex` also can be set to `GCL_WNDPROC` to retrieve a long pointer to the window function.

Return Value:

The `GetClassLong` function returns the value retrieved from the `WNDCLASS` structure.

GetClassName

Syntax:

```
int GetClassName(hWnd, lpClassName, nMaxCount)
```

Parameter, Type, and Description:

hWnd	HWND	Window handle
lpClassName	LPSTR	Pointer to buffer to receive class name
nMaxCount	int	Maximum number of bytes to store in lpClassName

Description:

The GetClassName function gets the class name of the window specified in hWnd. lpClassName points to the buffer that stores the class name. nMaxCount specifies the maximum number of bytes copied to lpClassName.

Return Value:

The GetClassName function returns the number of characters copied to lpClassName. Zero is returned when the class name is invalid.

GetClassWord

Syntax:

```
WORD GetClassWord(hWnd, nIndex)
```

Parameter, Type, and Description:

hWnd	HWND	Window handle
nIndex	int	Byte offset of value to be retrieved

Description:

The GetClassWord function gets the word identified by nIndex from the WNDCLASS structure for the window in hWnd. nIndex specifies the byte offset of the value to be retrieved. nIndex also can be set to any of the following values:

Value	*Meaning*
GCW_CBCLSEXTRA	Get number of bytes of additional class information available
GCW_CBWNDEXTRA	Get number of bytes of additional window information available
GCW_HBRBACKGROUND	Get the handle for the background brush

Value	*Meaning*
`GCW_HCURSOR`	Get the handle for the cursor
`GCW_HICON`	Get the handle for the icon
`GCW_HMODULE`	Get the handle for the module
`GCW_STYLE`	Get the window-class style bits

Return Value:

The `GetClassWord` function returns the value retrieved from the `WNDCLASS` structure.

GetLastActivePopup

Syntax:

```
HWND GetLastActivePopup(hwndOwner)
```

Parameter, Type, and Description:

`hwndOwner`	`HWND`	Owner window

Description:

The `GetLastActivePopup` function gets the pop-up window that most recently was active for the window specified in `hwndOwner`.

Return Value:

The `GetLastActivePopup` function returns the handle of the pop-up window that most recently was active.

GetWindowLong

Syntax:

```
LONG GetWindowLong(hWnd, nIndex)
```

Parameter, Type, and Description:

`hWnd`	`HWND`	Window handle
`nIndex`	`int`	Byte offset of value to retrieve

Description:

The `GetWindowLong` function gets information about the window identified in `hWnd`. `nIndex` specifies the byte offset of the value to be retrieved. `nIndex` also can be set to one of the following values:

Value	Meaning
GWL_EXSTYLE	Extended window style
GWL_STYLE	Window style
GWL_WNDPROC	Long pointer to the window function

Return Value:

The GetWindowLong function returns the specified window information.

GetWindowWord

Syntax:

```
WORD GetWindowWord(hWnd, nIndex)
```

Parameter, Type, and Description:

hWnd	HWND	Window handle
nIndex	int	Byte offset of value to retrieve

Description:

The GetWindowWord function gets information about the window identified in hWnd. nIndex specifies the byte offset of the value to retrieve. nIndex also can be set to one of the following values:

Value	Meaning
GWW_HINSTANCE	Instance handle of module that owns the window
GWW_HWNDPARENT	Handle of the parent window
GWW_ID	Control ID of the child window

Return Value:

The GetWindowWord function returns the retrieved information.

RegisterClass

Syntax:

```
BOOL RegisterClass(lpWndClass)
```

Parameter, Type, and Description:

lpWndClass	LPWNDCLASS	Pointer to the WNDCLASS structure that contains the class attributes

Description:

The `RegisterClass` function registers a window class. `lpWndClass` points to a data structure of type `WNDCLASS` that contains the attributes for the window class.

Return Value:

The `RegisterClass` function returns a nonzero value if the class is successfully registered. A return value of zero indicates that the class is not registered.

SetClassLong

Syntax:

```
LONG SetClassLong(hWnd, nIndex, dwNewLong)
```

Parameter, Type, and Description:

hWnd	HWND	Window handle
nIndex	int	Byte offset of word to change
dwNewLong	DWORD	New value

Description:

The `SetClassLong` function sets the value identified by `nIndex` to the value specified in `dwNewLong`. `nIndex` specifies the byte offset of the value to change from the `WNDCLASS` data structure. `nIndex` also can be set to the following values:

Value	*Meaning*
GCL_MENUNAME	Sets a new long pointer to a menu name
GCL_WNDPROC	Sets a new long pointer to a window function

Return Value:

The `SetClassLong` function returns the previous value of the changed long integer.

SetClassWord

Syntax:

```
WORD SetClassWord(hWnd, nIndex, wNewWord)
```

Parameter, Type, and Description:

hWnd	HWND	Window handle
nIndex	int	Byte offset of the word to change
wNewWord	WORD	New value

Description:

The SetClassWord function sets the value identified by nIndex to the value specified in hwNewWord. nIndex specifies the byte offset of the word to change from the WNDCLASS data structure. nIndex also can be set to the following values:

Value	*Meaning*
GCW_CBCLSEXTRA	Sets two new bytes of additional window class data
GCW_CBWNDEXTRA	Sets two new bytes of additional window call data
GCW_HBRBACKGROUND	Sets a new handle to a background brush
GCW_HCURSOR	Sets a new handle to a cursor
GCW_HICON	Sets a new handle to an icon
GCW_STYLE	Sets a new style bit for the window class

Return Value:

The SetClassWord function returns the previous value of the specified word.

SetWindowLong

Syntax:

```
LONG SetWindowLong(hWnd, nIndex, dwNewLong)
```

Parameter, Type, and Description:

hWnd	HWND	Window handle
nIndex	int	Byte offset of the attribute to change
dwNewLong	DWORD	New value

Description:

The SetWindowLong function sets the attribute value identified by nIndex to the value specified in dwNewLong. nIndex specifies the byte offset of the attribute to change. nIndex also can be set to the following values:

Value	*Meaning*
GWL_EXSTYLE	Sets a new extended window style
GWL_STYLE	Sets a new window style
GWL_WNDPROC	Sets a new long pointer to the window procedure

Return Value:

The `SetWindowLong` function returns the previous value of the specified long integer.

SetWindowWord

Syntax:

```
WORD SetWindowWord(hWnd, nIndex, wNewWord)
```

Parameter, Type, and Description:

`hWnd`	`HWND`	Window handle
`nIndex`	`int`	Byte offset of the word to change
`wNewWord`	`WORD`	New value

Description:

The `SetWindowWord` function sets the attribute identified by `nIndex` to the value specified in `wNewWord`. `nIndex` specifies the byte offset of the attribute to change. `nIndex` also can be set to the following values:

Value	*Meaning*
`GWW_HINSTANCE`	Instance handle of the module that owns the window
`GWW_ID`	Control ID of the child window

Return Value:

The `SetWindowWord` function returns the previous value of the specified word.

UnregisterClass

Syntax:

```
BOOL UnregisterClass(lpClassName, hInstance)
```

Parameter, Type, and Description:

`lpClassName`	`LPSTR`	Pointer to string containing the class name
`hInstance`	`HANDLE`	Instance of module that created the class

Description:

The UnregisterClass function removes the window class, whose name is specified in lpClassName, from the window class table. hInstance identifies the module that created the class.

Return Value:

The UnregisterClass function returns TRUE when the window class is successfully removed. A return value of FALSE indicates that the function cannot remove the window class.

Graphics Device Interface Functions

Graphics Device Interface functions provide operations that generate graphics objects, such as bitmaps, lines, text, rectangles, and ellipses, for many types of output devices. The graphics objects generated can be device-specific or device-independent. The Graphics Device Interface functions are divided into the following subcategories (documented in Appendix A):

Bitmap	Environment
Clipping	Font
Color Palette	Line Output
Coordinate	Mapping
Device Context	Metafile
Drawing Attribute	Printer Control
Drawing Tool	Region
Ellipse and Polygon	Text

Bitmap Functions

Bitmaps are used extensively in Windows. A bitmap is a series of bits that define the appearance of a section of the display surface. The bits specify the color and pattern of the corresponding pixels on the display. Because bitmaps can be stored in memory, they can be placed on the display quickly and used for drawings, menus,

charts, and so on. The following functions are categorized as Bitmap functions for the Graphics Device Interface:

Function	*Meaning*
`BitBlt`	Copies a bitmap from a source to the specified device
`CreateBitmap`	Creates a bitmap
`CreateBitmapIndirect`	Creates a bitmap using the data in a `BITMAP` structure
`CreateCompatibleBitmap`	Creates a bitmap compatible with the specified device
`CreateDIBitmap`	Creates a device-specific memory bitmap
`CreateDiscardableBitmap`	Creates a bitmap that is discardable and compatible with the specified device
`ExtFloodFill`	Fills the specified display surface
`FloodFill`	Fills the display area surrounded by the specified border
`GetBitmapBits`	Gets the bitmap bits for the specified bitmap
`GetBitmapDimension`	Gets the dimensions for the specified bitmap
`GetDIBits`	Gets the bits for a device-independent bitmap
`GetPixel`	Gets the RGB value for a pixel
`LoadBitmap`	Loads the specified bitmap
`PatBlt`	Creates a bit pattern
`SetBitmapBits`	Sets the bits for a bitmap
`SetBitmapDimension`	Defines the dimensions of a bitmap
`SetDIBits`	Sets the bits for a device-independent bitmap
`SetDIBitsToDevice`	Sets bits on a device directly from a device-independent bitmap
`SetPixel`	Defines the RGB value for a pixel
`StretchBlt`	Copies the bitmap to a destination device
`StretchDIBits`	Copies the device-independent bitmap to a destination device

The rest of this section provides detailed information on each of the functions in this list.

BitBlt

Syntax:

```
BOOL BitBlt(hDestDC, X, Y, nWidth, nHeight, hSrcDC, XSrc, YSrc,dwRop)
```

Parameter, Type, and Description:

`hDestDC`	`HDC`	Device context to receive the bitmap
`X`	`int`	Logical x-coordinate of the upper-left corner of the destination
`Y`	`int`	Logical y-coordinate of the upper-left corner of the destination
`nWidth`	`int`	Width of the destination rectangle in logical units
`nHeight`	`int`	Height of the destination rectangle in logical units
`hSrcDC`	`HDC`	Device context from which the bitmap will be copied
`XSrc`	`int`	Logical x-coordinate of the upper-left corner of the bitmap
`YSrc`	`int`	Logical y-coordinate of the upper-left corner of the bitmap
`dwRop`	`DWORD`	Raster operation to perform

Description:

The `BitBlt` function copies a bitmap from the source device to the destination device. `hSrcDC` specifies the source device. `hDestDC` specifies the destination device. `dwRop` specifies the raster operation to perform. The raster operation specifies how the source and destination will be combined. The following values can be used for `dwRop`:

Value	*Meaning*
`BLACKNESS`	Makes all output black
`DSTINVERT`	Inverts the destination bitmap
`MERGECOPY`	Uses Boolean AND to combine the pattern and source bitmap
`MERGEPAINT`	Uses Boolean OR to combine the inverted source bitmap with the destination bitmap
`NOTSRCCOPY`	Copies the inverted source bitmap to the destination
`NOTSRCERASE`	Uses Boolean OR to combine the destination and source, then inverts the combination
`PATCOPY`	Copies the pattern to the destination bitmap
`PATINVERT`	Uses Boolean XOR to combine the destination bitmap with the pattern
`PATPAINT`	Uses Boolean OR to combine the inverted source with the pattern, then uses Boolean OR to combine the result of the previous operation with the destination

Value	*Meaning*
SRCAND	Uses Boolean AND to combine the source and destination bitmaps
SRCCOPY	Copies the source bitmap to the destination
SRCERASE	Uses Boolean AND to combine the inverted destination bitmap with the source bitmap
SRCINVERT	Uses Boolean XOR to combine the source and destination bitmaps
SRCPAINT	Uses Boolean OR to combine the source and destination bitmaps
WHITENESS	Makes all output white

Return Value:

The `BitBlt` function returns a nonzero value when the bitmap is drawn. A return value of zero indicates that the function cannot draw the bitmap.

CreateBitmap

Syntax:

```
HBITMAP CreateBitmap(nWidth, nHeight, nPlanes, nBitCount, lpBits)
```

Parameter, Type, and Description:

nWidth	int	Width of the bitmap in pixels
nHeight	int	Height of the bitmap in pixels
nPlanes	BYTE	Number of color planes in the bitmap
nBitCount	BYTE	Number of color bits per pixel
lpBits	LPSTR	Pointer to an array that contains the bit values for the bitmap

Description:

The `CreateBitmap` function creates a bitmap with the specified parameters. The resulting bitmap is device dependent. `nWidth` and `nHeight` specify the size of the bitmap, in pixels. `nPlanes` specifies the number of color planes in the bitmap. `nBitCount` defines the number of color bits per pixel for the display. `lpBits` points to an array that contains the bit values for the bitmap. `lpBits` can be set to NULL. When `lpBits` is NULL, the bitmap is uninitialized.

Return Value:

The `CreateBitmap` function returns the handle of the created bitmap. A NULL return value indicates that the function cannot create the bitmap.

CreateBitmapIndirect

Syntax:

```
HBITMAP CreateBitmapIndirect(lpBitmap)
```

Parameter, Type, and Description:

lpBitmap	BITMAP FAR *	Pointer to BITMAP data structure that contains bitmap information

Description:

The CreateBitmapIndirect function creates a bitmap by using the parameters in the data structure of type BITMAP, pointed to by lpBitmap. The BITMAP structure is:

```
typedef struct tagBITMAP {
     short bmType;
     short bmWidth;
     short bmHeight;
     short bmWidthBytes;
     BYTE bmPlanes;
     BYTE bmBitsPixel;
     LPSTR bmBits;
} BITMAP;
```

where:

bmType is the bitmap type (zero for logical bitmaps)

bmWidth is the bitmap width in pixels

bmHeight is the bitmap height in pixels

bmWidthBytes is the number of bytes in each raster line

bmPlanes is the number of color planes in the bitmap

bmBitsPixel points to the number of adjacent color bits on each plane needed to define a pixel

bmBits points to the array containing the bit values for the bitmap

Return Value:

The CreateBitmapIndirect function returns the handle of the created bitmap. A NULL return value indicates that the function cannot create the bitmap.

CreateCompatibleBitmap

Syntax:

```
HBITMAP CreateCompatibleBitmap(hDC, nWidth, nHeight)
```

Parameter, Type, and Description:

hDC	HDC	Device context
nWidth	int	Width of the bitmap in bits
nHeight	int	Height of the bitmap in bits

Description:

The CreateCompatibleBitmap function creates a bitmap that is compatible with the device specified in hDC:

- When hDC specifies a device, the bitmap has the number of color planes and number of bits per pixel defined for the device.
- When hDC specifies a device context, the resulting bitmap has the same format as the current bitmap for the specified device context.

Return Value:

The CreateCompatibleBitmap function returns the handle of the created bitmap. A NULL return value indicates that the function cannot create the bitmap.

CreateDIBitmap

Syntax:

```
HBITMAP CreateDIBitmap(hDC, lpInfoHeader, dwUsage, lpInitBits,
                       lpInitInfo, wUsage)
```

Parameter, Type, and Description:

hDC	HDC	Device context
lpInfoHeader	LPBITMAPINFOHEADER	Pointer to BITMAPINFOHEADER structure containing size and format information for the bitmap
dwUsage	DWORD	Determines whether the bitmap will be initialized
lpInitBits	LPSTR	Pointer to byte array containing the initial bitmap values

lpInitInfo	LPBITMAPINFO	Pointer to BITMAPINFO structure containing dimensions and colors for lpInitBits
wUsage	WORD	Set to DIB_PAL_COLORS (the color table in lpInitInfo contains an array of 16-bit indexes for the currently realized logical palette) or DIB_RGB_COLORS (the color table in lpInitInfo contains RGB values)

Description:

The CreateDIBitmap function creates a device-specific memory bitmap from a device-independent bitmap. hDC (see following paragraphs) specifies the device context. lpInfoHeader points to a data structure of type BITMAPINFOHEADER, which contains information on the device-independent bitmap. The BITMAPINFOHEADER structure is:

```
typedef struct tagBITMAPINFOHEADER {
     DWORD biSize;
     DWORD biWidth;
     DWORD biHeight;
     WORD biPlanes;
     WORD biBitCount;
     DWORD biCompression;
     DWORD biSizeImage;
     DWORD biXPelsPerMeter;
     DWORD biYPelsPerMeter;
     DWORD biClrUsed;
     DWORD biClrImportant;
} BITMAPINFOHEADER;
```

where:

biSize is the number of bytes required for the structure

biWidth is the width of the bitmap in pixels

biHeight is the height of the bitmap in pixels

biPlanes is the number of planes; must be set to 1

biBitCount is the number of bits per pixel

biCompression is the type of compression and is selected from the following values:

Value	*Meaning*
BI_RGB	Bitmap is not compressed
BI_RLE8	Run-length encode format with 8 bits per pixel
BI_RLE4	Run-length encode format with 4 bits per pixel

biSizeImage is the size of the image in bytes

`biXPelsPerMeter` is the horizontal resolution in pixels per meter for the target device

`biYPelsPerMeter` is the vertical resolution in pixels per meter for the target device

`biClrUsed` is the number of color indexes in the color table the bitmap actually uses

`biClrImportant` is the number of color indexes considered important for the bitmap

`hDC` must specify a device context that supports color palettes. `wUsage` specifies the new use of the system palette:

- When `wUsage` is set to `SYSPAL_NOSTATIC`, the system palette will have no static colors—only black and white.
- When `wUsage` is set to `SYSPAL_STATIC`, the system palette will have static colors. The static colors will not change when the application realizes its logical palette. (See also `SetSystemPaletteUse` later in this chapter.)

`dwUsage` determines whether the resulting bitmap will be initialized. When `dwUsage` is set to `CBM_INIT`, `lpInitBits` and `lpInitInfo` are used to initialize the bitmap. `lpInitInfo` points to a data structure of type `BITMAPINFO`. The `BITMAPINFO` structure is:

```
typedef struct tagBITMAPINFO {
     BITMAPINFOHEADER bmiHeader;
     RGBQUAD bmiColors[1];
} BITMAPINFO;
```

where:

`bmiHeader` is the `BITMAPINFOHEADER` structure for the device-independent bitmap

`bmiColors` is an array of data structures of type `RGBQUAD` that defines the colors in the bitmap

Return Value:

The `CreateDIBitmap` function returns the handle of the created bitmap. A NULL return value indicates that the function cannot create the bitmap.

CreateDiscardableBitmap

Syntax:

```
HBITMAP CreateDiscardableBitmap(hDC, nWidth, nHeight)
```

Parameter, Type, and Description:

`hDC`	`HDC`	Device context
`nWidth`	`int`	Width of the bitmap in bits
`nHeight`	`int`	Height of the bitmap in bits

Description:

The `CreateDiscardableBitmap` function creates a discardable bitmap. The discardable bitmap is compatible with the device in `hDC`. The number of color planes and number of bits per pixel for the bitmap are set to the corresponding values for the specified device.

Return Value:

The `CreateDiscardableBitmap` function returns the handle of the created bitmap. A NULL return value indicates that the function cannot create the bitmap.

ExtFloodFill

Syntax:

```
BOOL ExtFloodFill(hDC, X, Y, crColor, wFillType)
```

Parameter, Type, and Description:

`hDC`	`HDC`	Device context
`X`	`int`	Logical x-coordinate of the fill point
`Y`	`int`	Logical y-coordinate of the fill point
`crColor`	`COLORREF`	Color of the boundary or area to fill
`wFillType`	`WORD`	Type of fill to perform

Description:

The `ExtFloodFill` function fills the specified area of the display by using the current brush. `X` and `Y` specify the points where the filling will begin. `crColor` specifies the color of the boundary or the color of the area to fill, depending on the setting of `wFillType`. `wFillType` is set to one of the following values:

Value	*Meaning*
`FLOODFILLBORDER`	`crColor` specifies the color of a boundary; everything within the boundary is filled
`FLOODFILLSURFACE`	`crColor` specifies the color of an area; everything in the area that is the specified color is filled

Return Value:

The `ExtFloodFill` function returns a nonzero value when the specified area is filled. A return value of zero indicates that the function cannot fill the area.

FloodFill

Syntax:

```
BOOL Floodfill(hDC, X, Y, crColor)
```

Parameter, Type, and Description:

hDC	HDC	Device context
X	int	Logical x-coordinate of the fill point
Y	int	Logical y-coordinate of the fill point
crColor	COLORREF	Color of boundary

Description:

The `FloodFill` function fills the boundary of a specified area of the display by using the current brush. `X` and `Y` specify the points where the filling will begin. `crColor` specifies the color of the boundary surrounding the area to fill.

Return Value:

The `FloodFill` function returns a nonzero value when the specified area is filled. A return value of zero indicates that the function cannot fill the area.

GetBitmapBits

Syntax:

```
DWORD GetBitmapBits(hBitmap, dwCount, lpBits)
```

Parameter, Type, and Description:

hBitmap	HBITMAP	Bitmap handle
dwCount	DWORD	Number of bytes to copy
lpBits	LPSTR	Pointer to the buffer to receive the bitmap

Description:

The `GetBitmapBits` function places the bits from the bitmap specified in `hBitmap` into the buffer pointed to by `lpBits`. `dwCount` specifies the number of bytes to copy. You can use the `GetObject` function to determine the value for `dwCount`. (See this chapter's description of the `GetObject` function for more information.)

Return Value:

The `GetBitmapBits` function returns the number of bytes in the bitmap. A return value of zero indicates that the function cannot place the bits into the buffer.

GetBitmapDimension

Syntax:

```
DWORD GetBitmapDimension(hBitmap)
```

Parameter, Type, and Description:

hBitmap	HBITMAP	Bitmap handle

Description:

The `GetBitmapDimension` function gets the dimensions of the bitmap specified in `hBitmap`.

Return Value:

The high-order word of the return value contains the height of the bitmap, in tenths of millimeters. The low-order word of the return value contains the width of the bitmap, in tenths of millimeters. A return value of zero indicates that the function cannot get the dimensions.

GetDIBits

Syntax:

```
int GetDIBits(hDC, hBitmap, nStartScan, nNumScans, lpBits,
              lpBitsInfo, wUsage)
```

Parameter, Type, and Description:

hDC	HDC	Device context
hBitmap	HBITMAP	Bitmap handle
nStartScan	WORD	First scan line of the destination bitmap
nNumScans	WORD	Number of lines to copy
lpBits	LPSTR	Pointer to the buffer to receive the bits for the bitmap in device-independent format

lpBitsInfo	LPBITMAPINFO	Pointer to a BITMAPINFO structure containing information for the device- independent bitmap
wUsage	WORD	Set to DIB_PAL_COLORS (the color table in lpBitsInfo contains an array of 16-bit indexes for the currently realized logical palette) or DIB_RGB_COLORS (the color table in lpBitsInfo contains RGB values)

Description:

The GetDIBits function retrieves the bits of a bitmap. The bits are then placed into the buffer pointed to by lpBits in device-independent format. hDC specifies the device context. hBitmap specifies the bitmap. lpBitsInfo points to a data structure of type BITMAPINFO. The BITMAPINFO structure is:

```
typedef struct tagBITMAPINFO {
     BITMAPINFOHEADER bmiHeader;
     RGBQUAD bmiColors[1];
} BITMAPINFO;
```

where:

bmiColors is an array of data structures of type RGBQUAD that defines the colors in the bitmap

bmiHeader is the BITMAPINFOHEADER structure for the device-independent bitmap. The BITMAPINFOHEADER structure is:

```
typedef struct BITMAPINFOHEADER {
     DWORD biSize;
     DWORD biWidth;
     DWORD biHeight;
     WORD biPlanes;
     WORD biBitCount;
     DWORD biCompression;
     DWORD biSizeImage;
     DWORD biXPelsPerMeter;
     DWORD biYPelsPerMeter;
     DWORD biClrUsed;
     DWORD biClrImportant;
} BITMAPINFOHEADER;
```

where:

biSize is the number of bytes required for the structure

biWidth is the width of the bitmap in pixels

biHeight is the height of the bitmap in pixels

biPlanes is the number of planes; must be set to 1

`biBitCount` is the number of bits per pixel

`biCompression` is the type of compression and is selected from the following values:

Value	*Meaning*
BI_RGB	Bitmap is not compressed
BI_RLE8	Run-length encode format with 8 bits per pixel
BI_RLE4	Run-length encode format with 4 bits per pixel

`biSizeImage` is the size of the image in bytes

`biXPelsPerMeter` is the horizontal resolution in pixels per meter for the target device

`biYPelsPerMeter` is the vertical resolution in pixels per meter for the target device

`biClrUsed` is the number of color indexes in the color table the bitmap actually uses

`biClrImportant` is the number of color indexes considered important for the bitmap

Return Value:

The `GetDIBits` function returns the number of scan lines copied from the bitmap. A return value of zero indicates that the function cannot retrieve the bits of the bitmap.

GetPixel

Syntax:

```
DWORD GetPixel(hDC, X, Y)
```

Parameter, Type, and Description:

hDC	HDC	Device context
X	int	Logical x-coordinate of pixel
Y	int	Logical y-coordinate of pixel

Description:

The `GetPixel` function determines the RGB color value for the pixel located at the position specified by the logical coordinates in `X` and `Y`. The specified point must lie within the clipping region. (See "Clipping Functions" in this chapter for more information on clipping regions.)

Return Value:

The `GetPixel` function returns the RGB color value for the specified position. A return value of –1 indicates that the point does not lie within the clipping region.

LoadBitmap

Syntax:

```
HBITMAP LoadBitmap(hInstance, lpBitmapName)
```

Parameter, Type, and Description:

`hInstance`	`HANDLE`	Instance of a module whose executable file contains the bitmap
`lpBitmapName`	`LPSTR`	Pointer to string that contains the name of the bitmap

Description:

The `LoadBitmap` function loads the bitmap resource specified in `lpBitmapName`. The bitmap is loaded from the executable file for the module specified in `hInstance`.

Return Value:

The `LoadBitmap` function returns the handle of the loaded bitmap resource. A NULL return value indicates that the function cannot load the bitmap resource.

PatBlt

Syntax:

```
BOOL PatBlt(hDC, X, Y, nWidth, nHeight, dwRop)
```

Parameter, Type, and Description:

`hDC`	`HDC`	Device context
`X`	`int`	Logical x-coordinate of the upper-left corner of the rectangle to receive the pattern
`Y`	`int`	Logical y-coordinate of the upper-left corner of the rectangle to receive the pattern
`nWidth`	`int`	Width of the receiving rectangle in logical units
`nHeight`	`int`	Height of the receiving rectangle in logical units
`dwRop`	`DWORD`	Raster operation to perform

Description:

The PatBlt function creates a bit pattern on the specified device that matches the specifications in the parameters. The resulting pattern is the combination of the selected brush and the existing pattern on the device. dwRop specifies the raster operation to perform. dwRop can be one of the following values:

Value	*Meaning*
BLACKNESS	Makes all output black
DSTINVERT	Inverts the destination bitmap
PATCOPY	Copies the pattern to the destination bitmap
PATINVERT	Uses Boolean OR to combine the destination bitmap and pattern
WHITENESS	Makes all output white

Return Value:

The PatBlt function returns a nonzero value when the bitmap is drawn. A return value of zero indicates that the function cannot draw the bitmap.

SetBitmapBits

Syntax:

```
LONG SetBitmapBits(hBitmap, dwCount, lpBits)
```

Parameter, Type, and Description:

hBitmap	HBITMAP	Bitmap to set
dwCount	DWORD	Number of bytes pointed to by lpBits
lpBits	LPSTR	Pointer to the array containing the bitmap bits

Description:

The SetBitmapBits function sets the bits for the bitmap specified in hBitmap to the bit values contained in the array pointed to by lpBits. dwCount specifies the number of bits in the array pointed to by lpBits.

Return Value:

The SetBitmapBits function returns the number of bytes used to set the bitmap bits. A return value of zero indicates that the function cannot set the bits for the bitmap.

SetBitmapDimension

Syntax:

```
DWORD SetBitmapDimension(hBitmap, X, Y)
```

Parameter, Type, and Description:

hBitmap	HANDLE	Bitmap handle
X	int	Width of the bitmap in tenths of millimeters
Y	int	Height of the bitmap in tenths of millimeters

Description:

The `SetBitmapDimension` function sets the width and height dimensions for the bitmap in `hBitmap` to the values expressed in `X` and `Y`, respectively. These values are not used internally by the GDI.

Return Value:

The high-order word of the return value contains the previous height of the bitmap. The low-order word of the return value contains the previous width of the bitmap.

SetDIBits

Syntax:

```
int SetDIBits(hDC, hBitmap, nStartScan, nNumScans, lpBits,
              lpBitsInfo, wUsage)
```

Parameter, Type, and Description:

hDC	HDC	Device context
hBitmap	HBITMAP	Bitmap handle
nStartScan	WORD	First scan line in the `lpBits` buffer
nNumScans	WORD	Number of scan lines in the `lpBits` buffer
lpBits	LPSTR	Pointer to a buffer that stores the bitmap bits for the device-independent bitmap
lpBitsInfo	LPBITMAPINFO	Pointer to a `BITMAPINFO` structure containing information for the device-independent bitmap

wUsage	WORD	Set to DIB_PAL_COLORS (the color table in lpBitsInfo contains an array of 16-bit indexes for the currently realized logical palette) or DIB_RGB_COLORS (the color table in lpBitsInfo contains RGB values)

Description:

The SetDIBits function sets the bits of a bitmap. The bits are placed into the buffer pointed to by lpBits in device-independent format. hDC specifies the device context. hBitmap specifies the bitmap. lpBitsInfo points to a data structure of type BITMAPINFO. The BITMAPINFO structure is:

```
typedef struct tagBITMAPINFO {
     BITMAPINFOHEADER bmiHeader;
     RGBQUAD bmiColors[1];
} BITMAPINFO;
```

where:

bmiColors is an array of data structures of type RGBQUAD that defines the colors in the bitmap

bmiHeader is the BITMAPINFOHEADER structure for the device-independent bitmap. The BITMAPINFOHEADER structure is:

```
typedef struct tagBITMAPINFOHEADER {
     DWORD biSize;
     DWORD biWidth;
     DWORD biHeight;
     WORD biPlanes;
     WORD biBitCount;
     DWORD biCompression;
     DWORD biSizeImage;
     DWORD biXPelsPerMeter;
     DWORD biYPelsPerMeter;
     DWORD biClrUsed;
     DWORD biClrImportant;
} BITMAPINFOHEADER;
```

where:

biSize is the number of bytes required for the structure

biWidth is the width of the bitmap in pixels

biHeight is the height of the bitmap in pixels

biPlanes is the number of planes; must be set to 1

biBitCount is the number of bits per pixel

biCompression is the type of compression and is selected from the following values:

Value	Meaning
BI_RGB	Bitmap is not compressed
BI_RLE8	Run-length encode format with 8 bits per pixel
BI_RLE4	Run-length encode format with 4 bits per pixel

biSizeImage is the size of the image in bytes

biXPelsPerMeter is the horizontal resolution in pixels per meter for the target device

biYPelsPerMeter is the vertical resolution in pixels per meter for the target device

biClrUsed is the number of color indexes in the color table the bitmap actually uses

biClrImportant is the number of color indexes considered important for the bitmap

Return Value:

The SetDIBits function returns the number of copied scan lines. A return value of zero indicates that the function cannot set the bits of the bitmap.

SetDIBitsToDevice

Syntax:

```
WORD SetDIBitsToDevice(hDC, DestX, DestY, nWidth, nHeight, SrcX,
                       SrcY, nStartScan, nNumScans, lpBits,
                       lpBitsInfo, wUsage)
```

Parameter, Type, and Description:

hDC	HDC	Device context
DestX	WORD	X-coordinate of origin for destination rectangle
DestY	WORD	Y-coordinate of origin for destination rectangle
nWidth	WORD	Width of the rectangle in the device-independent bitmap
nHeight	WORD	Height of the rectangle in the device-independent bitmap
SrcX	WORD	X-coordinate of the source in the device-independent bitmap

SrcY	WORD	Y-coordinate of the source in the device-independent bitmap
nStartScan	WORD	First scan line in the lpBits buffer
nNumScans	WORD	Number of scan lines contained in the lpBits buffer
lpBits	LPSTR	Pointer to the buffer that stores the bitmap bits for the device-independent bitmap
lpBitsInfo	LPBITMAPINFO	Pointer to a BITMAPINFO structure containing information for the device-independent bitmap
wUsage	WORD	Set to DIB_PAL_COLORS (the color table in lpBitsInfo contains an array of 16-bit indexes for the currently realized logical palette) or DIB_RGB_COLORS (the color table in lpBitsInfo contains RGB values)

Description:

The SetDIBitsToDevice function sets the bits from a device-independent bitmap onto the device surface of the output device specified by hDC. DestX and DestY specify the location of the destination rectangle. nWidth, nHeight, SrcX, and SrcY define the source rectangle in the device-independent bitmap. lpBitsInfo points to a data structure of type BITMAPINFO. The BITMAPINFO structure is:

```
typedef struct tagBITMAPINFO {
    BITMAPINFOHEADER bmiHeader;
    RGBQUAD bmiColors[1];
} BITMAPINFO;
```

where:

bmiColors is an array of data structures of type RGBQUAD that defines the colors in the bitmap

bmiHeader is the BITMAPINFOHEADER structure for the device-independent bitmap. The BITMAPINFOHEADER structure is:

```
typedef struct tagBITMAPINFOHEADER {
     DWORD biSize;
     DWORD biWidth;
     DWORD biHeight;
     WORD biPlanes;
     WORD biBitCount;
     DWORD biCompression;
     DWORD biSizeImage;
     DWORD biXPelsPerMeter;
     DWORD biYPelsPerMeter;
     DWORD biClrUsed;
     DWORD biClrImportant;
} BITMAPINFOHEADER;
```

where:

`biSize` is the number of bytes required for the structure

`biWidth` is the width of the bitmap in pixels

`biHeight` is the height of the bitmap in pixels

`biPlanes` is the number of planes, which must be set to 1

`biBitCount` is the number of bits per pixel

`biCompression` is the type of compression and is selected from the following values:

Value	*Meaning*
BI_RGB	Bitmap is not compressed
BI_RLE8	Run-length encode format with 8 bits per pixel
BI_RLE4	Run-length encode format with 4 bits per pixel

`biSizeImage` is the size of the image in bytes

`biXPelsPerMeter` is the horizontal resolution in pixels per meter for the target device

`biYPelsPerMeter` is the vertical resolution in pixels per meter for the target device

`biClrUsed` is the number of color indexes in the color table the bitmap actually uses

`biClrImportant` is the number of color indexes considered important for the bitmap

Return Value:

The `SetDIBitsToDevice` function returns the number of scan lines set. A return value of zero indicates that the function cannot set the bits.

SetPixel

Syntax:

```
DWORD SetPixel(hDC, X, Y, crColor)
```

Parameter, Type, and Description:

hDC	HDC	Device context
X	int	Logical x-coordinate of the point

Y	int	Logical y-coordinate of the point
crColor	COLORREF	Color to paint the point

Description:

The `SetPixel` function paints the pixel at the point specified by `X` and `Y` with the color closest to that specified in `crColor`. The specified point must lie within the clipping region. (See "Clipping Functions" in this chapter for more information on clipping regions.)

Return Value:

The `SetPixel` function returns the actual RGB color value with which the point is painted. This value may differ from the color specified in `crColor`. A return value of –1 indicates that the function cannot paint the point.

StretchBlt

Syntax:

```
BOOL StretchBlt(hDestDC, X, Y, nWidth, nHeight, hSrcDC, XSrc,
                YSrc, nSrcWidth, nSrcHeight, dwRop)
```

Parameter, Type, and Description:

hDestDC	HDC	Device context receiving the bitmap
X	int	Logical x-coordinate of the upper-left corner of the destination rectangle
Y	int	Logical y-coordinate of the upper-left corner of the destination rectangle
nWidth	int	Width of the destination rectangle in logical units
nHeight	int	Height of the destination rectangle in logical units
hSrcDC	HDC	Device context to the source bitmap
XSrc	int	Logical x-coordinate of the upper-left corner of the source rectangle
YSrc	int	Logical y-coordinate of the upper-left corner of the source rectangle
nSrcWidth	int	Width of the source rectangle in logical units
nSrcHeight	int	Height of the source rectangle in logical units
dwRop	DWORD	Raster operation to perform

Description:

The `StretchBlt` function places the device-independent bitmap from the source rectangle into the specified destination rectangle. The bitmap is stretched or compressed to fit the destination rectangle. `hDestDC`, `X`, `Y`, `nWidth`, and `nHeight` provide information on the destination rectangle and bitmap. `hSrcDC`, `XSrc`, `YSrc`, `nSrcWidth`, and `nSrcHeight` provide information on the source rectangle and bitmap. `dwRop` specifies the raster operation to perform and can be any of the following:

Value	*Meaning*
BLACKNESS	Makes all output black
DSTINVERT	Inverts the destination bitmap
MERGECOPY	Uses Boolean AND to combine the pattern and source bitmap
MERGEPAINT	Uses Boolean OR to combine the inverted source bitmap with the destination bitmap
NOTSRCCOPY	Copies the inverted source bitmap to the destination
NOTSRCERASE	Uses Boolean OR to combine the destination and source, then inverts the combination
PATCOPY	Copies the pattern to the destination bitmap
PATINVERT	Uses Boolean XOR to combine the destination bitmap with the pattern
PATPAINT	Uses Boolean OR to combine the inverted source with the pattern, then uses Boolean OR to combine the result of the previous operation with the destination
SRCAND	Uses Boolean AND to combine the source and destination bitmaps
SRCCOPY	Copies the source bitmap to the destination
SRCERASE	Uses Boolean AND to combine the inverted destination bitmap with the source bitmap
SRCINVERT	Uses Boolean XOR to combine the source and destination bitmaps
SRCPAINT	Uses Boolean OR to combine the source and destination bitmaps
WHITENESS	Makes all output white

Return Value:

The `StretchBlt` function returns a nonzero value when the bitmap is drawn. A return value of zero indicates that the function cannot draw the bitmap.

StretchDIBits

Syntax:

```
WORD StretchDIBits(hDC, DestX, DestY, wDestWidth, wDestHeight,
                   SrcX, SrcY, wSrcWidth, wSrcHeight, lpBits,
                   lpBitsInfo, wUsage, dwRop)
```

Parameter, Type, and Description:

hDC	HDC	Device context receiving the bitmap
DestX	WORD	Logical x-coordinate of the upper-left corner of the destination rectangle
DestY	WORD	Logical y-coordinate of the upper-left corner of the destination rectangle
wDestWidth	WORD	Width of the destination rectangle in logical units
wDestHeight	WORD	Height of the destination rectangle in logical units
SrcX	WORD	Logical x-coordinate of the upper-left corner of the source rectangle
SrcY	WORD	Logical y-coordinate of the upper-left corner of the source rectangle
wSrcWidth	WORD	Width of the source rectangle in logical units
wSrcHeight	WORD	Height of the source rectangle in logical units
lpBits	LPSTR	Pointer to an array of device-independent bitmap bits
lpBitsInfo	LPBITMAPINFO	Pointer to a BITMAPINFO data structure containing information on the device-independent bitmap
wUsage	WORD	Set to DIB_PAL_COLORS (the color table in lpBitsInfo contains an array of 16-bit indexes for the currently realized logical palette) or DIB_RGB_COLORS (the color table in lpBitsInfo contains RGB values)
dwRop	DWORD	Raster operation to perform

Description:

The StretchDIBits function places the device-independent bitmap in the source rectangle into the specified destination rectangle. The bitmap is stretched or compressed to fit the destination rectangle. lpBits, lpBitsInfo, and wUsage specify the device-independent bitmap. SrcX, SrcY, wSrcWidth, and wSrcHeight specify the source rectangle. DestX, DestY, wDestWidth, and wDestHeight specify the destination rectangle. dwRop specifies the raster operation to perform and can be any of the following:

Value	*Meaning*
BLACKNESS	Makes all output black
DSTINVERT	Inverts the destination bitmap
MERGECOPY	Uses Boolean AND to combine the pattern and source bitmap
MERGEPAINT	Uses Boolean OR to combine the inverted source bitmap with the destination bitmap
NOTSRCCOPY	Copies the inverted source bitmap to the destination
NOTSRCERASE	Uses Boolean OR to combine the destination and source, then inverts the combination
PATCOPY	Copies the pattern to the destination bitmap
PATINVERT	Uses Boolean XOR to combine the destination bitmap with the pattern
PATPAINT	Uses Boolean OR to combine the inverted source with the pattern, then uses Boolean OR to combine the result of the previous operation with the destination
SRCAND	Uses Boolean AND to combine the source and destination bitmaps
SRCCOPY	Copies the source bitmap to the destination
SRCERASE	Uses Boolean AND to combine the inverted destination bitmap with the source bitmap
SRCINVERT	Uses Boolean XOR to combine the source and destination bitmaps
SRCPAINT	Uses Boolean OR to combine the source and destination bitmaps
WHITENESS	Makes all output white

lpBitsInfo points to a data structure of type BITMAPINFO. The BITMAPINFO structure is:

```
typedef struct tagBITMAPINFO {
    BITMAPINFOHEADER bmiHeader;
    RGBQUAD bmiColors[1];
} BITMAPINFO;
```

where:

> bmiColors is an array of data structures of type RGBQUAD that defines the colors in the bitmap
>
> bmiHeader is the BITMAPINFOHEADER structure for the device-independent bitmap. The BITMAPINFOHEADER structure is:

```
typedef struct tagBITMAPINFOHEADER {
     DWORD biSize;
     DWORD biWidth;
     DWORD biHeight;
     WORD biPlanes;
     WORD biBitCount;
     DWORD biCompression;
     DWORD biSizeImage;
     DWORD biXPelsPerMeter;
     DWORD biYPelsPerMeter;
     DWORD biClrUsed;
     DWORD biClrImportant;
} BITMAPINFOHEADER;
```

where:

`biSize` is the number of bytes required for the structure

`biWidth` is the width of the bitmap in pixels

`biHeight` is the height of the bitmap in pixels

`biPlanes` is the number of planes; must be set to 1

`biBitCount` is the number of bits per pixel

`biCompression` is the type of compression and is selected from the following values:

Value	*Meaning*
`BI_RGB`	Bitmap is not compressed
`BI_RLE8`	Run-length encode format with 8 bits per pixel
`BI_RLE4`	Run-length encode format with 4 bits per pixel

`biSizeImage` is the size of the image in bytes

`biXPelsPerMeter` is the horizontal resolution in pixels per meter for the target device

`biYPelsPerMeter` is the vertical resolution in pixels per meter for the target device

`biClrUsed` is the number of color indexes in the color table the bitmap actually uses

`biClrImportant` is the number of color indexes considered important for the bitmap

Return Value:

The `StretchDIBits` function returns the number of copied scan lines.

Clipping Functions

A clipping region is a portion of a window's client area that restricts all graphics output. Any graphics output that extends beyond the boundaries of the clipping region is not displayed. The Clipping functions create, monitor, and alter clipping regions. The following functions are categorized as Clipping functions for the Graphics Device Interface:

Function	*Meaning*
`ExcludeClipRect`	Excludes the specified rectangle from the clipping region
`GetClipBox`	Gets the dimensions of the bounding rectangle for the clipping region
`IntersectClipRect`	Creates a new clipping region from the intersection of the clipping region and a rectangle
`OffsetClipRgn`	Moves the clipping region
`PtVisible`	Determines whether the point lies in the region
`RectVisible`	Determines whether part of the specified rectangle lies within the clipping region
`SelectClipRgn`	Selects a clipping region

The rest of this section provides detailed information on each of the functions in this list.

ExcludeClipRect

Syntax:

```
int ExcludeClipRect(hDC, X1, Y1, X2, Y2)
```

Parameter, Type, and Description:

`hDC`	`HDC`	Device context
`X1`	`int`	Logical x-coordinate of the upper-left corner of a rectangle
`Y1`	`int`	Logical y-coordinate of the upper-left corner of a rectangle
`X2`	`int`	Logical x-coordinate of the lower-right corner of a rectangle
`Y2`	`int`	Logical y-coordinate of the lower-right corner of a rectangle

Description:

The `ExcludeClipRect` function excludes the rectangle defined by `X1`, `Y1`, `X2`, and `Y2` from the current clipping region.

Return Value:

The `ExcludeClipRect` function returns one of the following values to describe the resulting clipping region:

Value	*Meaning*
COMPLEXREGION	Region has overlapping borders
ERROR	No region was created
NULLREGION	Region is empty
SIMPLEREGION	Region has no overlapping borders

GetClipBox

Syntax:

```
int GetClipBox(hDC, lpRect)
```

Parameter, Type, and Description:

hDC	HDC	Device context
lpRect	LPRECT	Pointer to a `RECT` data structure that receives the dimensions of the rectangle

Description:

The `GetClipBox` function gets the dimensions of the smallest rectangle that completely encloses the clipping region. The dimensions are placed into the data structure of type `RECT` pointed to by `lpRect`. The `RECT` data structure is:

```
typedef struct tagRECT{
     int left;
     int top;
     int right;
     int bottom;
} RECT;
```

where:

`left` is the x-coordinate of the upper-left corner

`top` is the y-coordinate of the upper-left corner

`right` is the x-coordinate of the lower-right corner

`bottom` is the y-coordinate of the lower-right corner

Return Value:

The `GetClipBox` function returns one of the following values to describe the clipping region:

Value	*Meaning*
`COMPLEXREGION`	Region has overlapping borders
`ERROR`	Device context is invalid
`NULLREGION`	Region is empty
`SIMPLEREGION`	Region has no overlapping borders

IntersectClipRect

Syntax:

```
int IntersectClipRect(hDC, X1, Y1, X2, Y2)
```

Parameter, Type, and Description:

`hDC`	`HDC`	Device context
`X1`	`int`	Logical x-coordinate of the upper-left corner of a rectangle
`Y1`	`int`	Logical y-coordinate of the upper-left corner of a rectangle
`X2`	`int`	Logical x-coordinate of the lower-right corner of a rectangle
`Y2`	`int`	Logical y-coordinate of the lower-right corner of a rectangle

Description:

The `IntersectRect` function redefines the clipping region as the intersection of the current clipping region and the rectangle defined by `X1`, `Y1`, `X2`, and `Y2`. The intersection is the smallest rectangle that contains the common parts of both rectangles.

Return Value:

The `IntersectRect` function returns one of the following values to describe the resulting clipping region:

Value	*Meaning*
`COMPLEXREGION`	Region has overlapping borders
`ERROR`	Device context is invalid
`NULLREGION`	Region is empty
`SIMPLEREGION`	Region has no overlapping borders

OffsetClipRgn

Syntax:

```
int OffsetClipRgn(hDC, X, Y)
```

Parameter, Type, and Description:

hDC	HDC	Device context
X	int	Number of logical units to move horizontally
Y	int	Number of logical units to move vertically

Description:

The `OffsetClipRgn` function moves the clipping region for the device specified in `hDC` by the amounts specified in `X` and `Y`. Positive values for `X` and `Y` move the clipping region to the right and down, respectively. Negative values for `X` and `Y` move the clipping region to the left and up, respectively.

Return Value:

The `OffsetClipRgn` function returns one of the following values to describe the clipping region:

Value	*Meaning*
COMPLEXREGION	Region has overlapping borders
ERROR	Device context is invalid
NULLREGION	Region is empty
SIMPLEREGION	Region has no overlapping borders

PtVisible

Syntax:

```
BOOL PtVisible(hDC, X, Y)
```

Parameter, Type, and Description:

hDC	HDC	Device context
X	int	Logical x-coordinate of a point
Y	int	Logical y-coordinate of a point

Description:

The `PtVisible` function determines whether the point specified by `X` and `Y` lies in the clipping region of the device context specified in `hDC`.

Return Value:

The PtVisible function returns a nonzero value if the point is within the clipping region. A return value of zero indicates that the point is not within the clipping region.

RectVisible

Syntax:

```
BOOL RectVisible(hDC, lpRect)
```

Parameter, Type, and Description:

hDC	HDC	Device context
lpRect	LPRECT	Pointer to a RECT data structure containing the coordinate of the rectangle

Description:

The RectVisible function determines whether any part of the rectangle specified in the data structure of type RECT, pointed to by lpRect, lies within the clipping region of the device context specified in hDC. The RECT data structure is:

```
typedef struct tagRECT{
      int left;
      int top;
      int right;
      int bottom;
} RECT;
```

where:

left is the x-coordinate of the upper-left corner

top is the y-coordinate of the upper-left corner

right is the x-coordinate of the lower-right corner

bottom is the y-coordinate of the lower-right corner

Return Value:

The RectVisible function returns a nonzero value if any part of the specified rectangle lies within the clipping region. A return value of zero indicates that no part of the specified rectangle lies within the clipping region.

SelectClipRgn

Syntax:

```
int SelectClipRgn(hDC, hRgn)
```

Parameter, Type, and Description:

`hDC`	`HDC`	Device context
`hRgn`	`HRGN`	Region to select

Description:

The `SelectClipRgn` function sets the region specified in `hRgn` as the clipping region for the device context specified in `hDC`.

Return Value:

The `SelectClipRgn` function returns one of the following values to describe the clipping region:

Value	*Meaning*
`COMPLEXREGION`	Region has overlapping borders
`ERROR`	Device context or region handle is invalid
`NULLREGION`	Region is empty
`SIMPLEREGION`	Region has no overlapping borders

Color Palette Functions

Color palettes are used to access the many colors that the system can generate. Most systems can generate thousands of colors but can display only up to 256 simultaneously. The color palette maintains a subset of the available system colors for an application to use.

Applications use logical palettes to maintain a list of colors. Each color in the palette has an appropriate palette index (the number of indexes available on the palette depends on the video mode and video hardware). By referencing the appropriate palette index, the corresponding color in the palette can be displayed. Color Palette functions create and manipulate logical and system palettes. The following functions are categorized as Color Palette functions for the Graphics Device Interface:

Function	*Meaning*
`AnimatePalette`	Replaces entries in a logical palette
`CreatePalette`	Creates a logical palette

Function	*Meaning*
`GetBValue`	Gets the blue value from an RGB color value
`GetGValue`	Gets the green value from an RGB color value
`GetNearestColor`	Gets the logical color that is the closest to a specified logical color
`GetNearestPaletteIndex`	Gets the index of a logical palette that is the closest match to the specified RGB value
`GetPaletteEntries`	Gets entries from a logical palette
`GetRValue`	Gets the red value from an RGB color value
`GetSystemPaletteEntries`	Gets palette entries from the system palette
`GetSystemPaletteUse`	Determines whether an application has access to the full system palette
`RealizePalette`	Maps entries from a logical palette to the system palette
`ResizePalette`	Changes the size of the logical palette
`SelectPalette`	Selects a logical palette
`SetPaletteEntries`	Sets the palette entries for a logical palette
`SetSystemPaletteUse`	Gives the application access to the full system palette
`UpdateColors`	Translates each pixel's current color to the system palette

The rest of this section provides detailed information on each of the functions in this list.

AnimatePalette

Syntax:

```
void AnimatePalette(hPalette, wStartIndex, wNumEntries, lpPaletteColors)
```

Parameter, Type, and Description:

`hPalette`	`HPALETTE`	Logical palette
`wStartIndex`	`WORD`	First palette entry to animate
`wNumEntries`	`WORD`	Number of entries to animate
`lpPaletteColors`	`LPPALETTEENTRY`	Pointer to the first member of an array of `PALETTEENTRY` data structures

Description:

The `AnimatePalette` function replaces palette entries in the logical palette specified in `hPalette`. `wStartIndex` and `wNumEntries` specify the palette entries to replace.

lpPaletteColors points to the first member of an array of PALETTEENTRY data structures used to replace the specified palette entries. The PALETTEENTRY data structure is:

```
typedef struct
     {
     BYTE peRed;
     BYTE peGreen;
     BYTE peBlue;
     BYTE peFlags;
     } PALETTEENTRY;
```

where:

peRed is the intensity of red for the palette entry

peGreen is the intensity of green for the palette entry

peBlue is the intensity of blue for the palette entry

peFlags is NULL or one of the following values:

Value	*Meaning*
PC_EXPLICIT	Low-order word of the palette entry contains a hardware palette index
PC_NOCOLLAPSE	Color is placed in an unused entry in the palette; color does not replace the existing entry
PC_RESERVED	Entry is used for palette animation; no color can be matched to this entry

Return Value:

There is no return value.

CreatePalette

Syntax:

```
HPALETTE CreatePalette(lpLogPalette)
```

Parameter, Type, and Description:

lpLogPalette	LPLOGPALETTE	Pointer to LOGPALETTE structure containing information on the colors in the logical palette

Description:

The CreatePalette function creates a logical palette using the information in the data structure of type LOGPALETTE, pointed to by lpLogPalette. The LOGPALETTE structure is:

```
typedef struct
     {
     WORD palVersion;
     WORD palNumEntries;
     PALETTEENTRY palPalEntry[];
     } LOGPALETTE;
```

where:

`palVersion` is the Windows version number

`palNumEntries` is the number of entries in the palette

`palPalEntry[]` is an array of `PALETTEENTRY` data structures defining the color and use of each palette entry. The `PALETTEENTRY` data structure is:

```
typedef struct
     {
     BYTE peRed;
     BYTE peGreen;
     BYTE peBlue;
     BYTE peFlags;
     } PALETTEENTRY;
```

where:

`peRed` is the intensity of red for the palette entry

`peGreen` is the intensity of green for the palette entry

`peBlue` is the intensity of blue for the palette entry

`peFlags` is NULL or one of the following values:

Value	*Meaning*
PC_EXPLICIT	Low-order word of the palette entry contains a hardware palette index
PC_NOCOLLAPSE	Color is placed in an unused entry in the palette; color does not replace the existing entry
PC_RESERVED	Entry is used for palette animation; no color can be matched to this entry

Return Value:

The `CreatePalette` function returns the handle of the logical palette when successful. A NULL return value indicates that the function cannot create the palette.

GetBValue

Syntax:

```
BYTE GetBValue(rgbColor)
```

Parameter, Type, and Description:

rgbColor	DWORD	RGB color field

Description:

The `GetBValue` macro gets the blue value from the RGB color value specified in `rgbColor`.

Return Value:

The `GetBValue` macro returns the blue value from the RGB color field.

GetGValue

Syntax:

```
BYTE GetGValue(rgbColor)
```

Parameter, Type, and Description:

rgbColor	DWORD	RGB color field

Description:

The `GetGValue` macro gets the green value from the RGB color value specified in `rgbColor`.

Return Value:

The `GetGValue` macro returns the green value from the RGB color field.

GetNearestColor

Syntax:

```
DWORD GetNearestColor(hDC, crColor)
```

Parameter, Type, and Description:

hDC	HDC	Device context
crColor	COLORREF	Color to match

Description:

The `GetNearestColor` function gets the logical color that is the closest match to the logical color specified in `crColor`.

Return Value:

The `GetNearestColor` function returns an RGB value representing the closest matching color from those colors that the specified device can represent.

GetNearestPaletteIndex

Syntax:

```
WORD GetNearestPaletteIndex(hPalette, crColor)
```

Parameter, Type, and Description:

`hPalette`	`HPALETTE`	Logical palette
`crColor`	`COLORREF`	Color to match

Description:

The `GetNearestPaletteIndex` function gets the palette entry index that is most like the color value specified in `crColor` from the logical palette in `hPalette`.

Return Value:

The `GetNearestPaletteIndex` function returns the palette entry index representing the closest matching color from those colors that the specified device can represent.

GetPaletteEntries

Syntax:

```
WORD GetPaletteEntries(hPalette, wStartIndex, wNumEntries,
                       lpPaletteEntries)
```

Parameter, Type, and Description:

`hPalette`	`HPALETTE`	Logical palette
`wStartIndex`	`WORD`	First entry of the logical palette to retrieve
`wNumEntries`	`WORD`	Number of palette entries to retrieve
`lpPaletteEntries`	`LPPALETTEENTRY`	Pointer to an array of `PALETTEENTRY` data structures receiving the palette entries

Description:

The `GetPaletteEntries` function gets a range of palette entries specified by `wStartIndex` and `wNumEntries` from the palette in `hPalette` and places the entries in the array of data structures of type `PALETTEENTRY`, pointed to by `lpPaletteEntries`. The `PALETTEENTRY` structure is:

```
typedef struct
     {
     BYTE peRed;
     BYTE peGreen;
     BYTE peBlue;
     BYTE peFlags;
     } PALETTEENTRY;
```

where:

`peRed` is the intensity of red for the palette entry

`peGreen` is the intensity of green for the palette entry

`peBlue` is the intensity of blue for the palette entry

`peFlags` is NULL or one of the following values:

Value	*Meaning*
`PC_EXPLICIT`	Low-order word of the palette entry contains a hardware palette index
`PC_NOCOLLAPSE`	Color is placed in an unused entry in the palette; color does not replace existing entry
`PC_RESERVED`	Entry is used for palette animation; no color can be matched to this entry

Return Value:

The `GetPaletteEntries` function returns the number of entries retrieved from the logical palette. Zero is returned when the function cannot retrieve the specified palette entries.

GetRValue

Syntax:

```
BYTE GetRValue(rgbColor)
```

Parameter, Type, and Description:

`rgbColor`	`DWORD`	RGB color field

Description:

The `GetRValue` function gets the red value from the RGB color value specified in `rgbColor`.

Return Value:

The `GetRValue` macro returns the red value from the RGB color field.

GetSystemPaletteEntries

Syntax:

```
WORD GetSystemPaletteEntries(hDC, wStartIndex, wNumEntries,
                             lpPaletteEntries)
```

Parameter, Type, and Description:

`hDC`	`HDC`	Device context
`wStartIndex`	`WORD`	First entry of the system palette to retrieve
`wNumEntries`	`WORD`	Number of system palette entries to retrieve
`lpPaletteEntries`	`LPPALETTEENTRY`	Pointer to an array of `PALETTEENTRY` data structures receiving the palette entries

Description:

The `GetSystemPaletteEntries` function gets the palette entries specified by `wStartIndex` and `wNumEntries` from the system palette and places the entries in the array of data structures of type `PALETTEENTRY`, pointed to by `lpPaletteEntries`. The `PALETTEENTRY` structure is:

```
typedef struct
     {
     BYTE peRed;
     BYTE peGreen;
     BYTE peBlue;
     BYTE peFlags;
     } PALETTEENTRY;
```

where:

> `peRed` is the intensity of red for the palette entry
>
> `peGreen` is the intensity of green for the palette entry
>
> `peBlue` is the intensity of blue for the palette entry
>
> `peFlags` is NULL or one of the following values:

Value	*Meaning*
PC_EXPLICIT	Low-order word of the palette entry contains a hardware palette index
PC_NOCOLLAPSE	Color is placed in an unused entry in the palette; color does not replace existing entry
PC_RESERVED	Entry is used for palette animation; no color can be matched to this entry

Return Value:

The `GetSystemPaletteEntries` function returns the number of palette entries retrieved from the system palette.

GetSystemPaletteUse

Syntax:

```
WORD GetSystemPaletteUse(hDC)
```

Parameter, Type, and Description:

hDC	HDC	Device context

Description:

The `GetSystemPaletteUse` function determines whether an application has access to the full system palette.

Return Value:

The `GetSystemPaletteUse` function returns one of the following values to indicate the current use of the system palette:

Value	*Meaning*
SYSPAL_NOSTATIC	System palette has no static colors, only black and white
SYSPAL_STATIC	System palette has static colors that will not change when the application realizes its logical palette

RealizePalette

Syntax:

```
int RealizePalette(hDC)
```

Parameter, Type, and Description:

hDC	HDC	Device context

Description:

The `RealizePalette` function maps entries in the logical palette for the device context specified in `hDC` to the system palette.

Return Value:

The `RealizePalette` function returns the number of logical palette entries mapped to the system palette.

ResizePalette

Syntax:

```
BOOL ResizePalette(hPalette, nNumEntries)
```

Parameter, Type, and Description:

hPalette	HPALETTE	Palette to modify
nNumEntries	int	New number of palette entries

Description:

The `ResizePalette` function modifies the size of the logical palette specified in `hPalette`. `nNumEntries` specifies the number of palette entries in the resized palette. New palette entries are set to black.

Return Value:

The `ResizePalette` function returns TRUE when the palette is modified. A return value of FALSE indicates that the function cannot modify the palette.

SelectPalette

Syntax:

```
HPALETTE SelectPalette(hDC, hPalette, bForceBackground)
```

Parameter, Type, and Description:

hDC	HDC	Device context
hPalette	HPALETTE	Logical palette

bForceBackground	BOOL	Determines whether the logical palette is a background or foreground palette

Description:

The SelectPalette function selects the logical palette in hPalette for the palette object of the device context in hDC. The Graphics Device Interface uses the selected palette to control colors displayed in the device context. bForceBackground determines whether the logical palette is a background or foreground palette:

- Set bForceBackground to a nonzero value if the logical palette is a background palette.
- Set bForceBackground to zero if the logical palette is a foreground palette when the window has the input focus.

Return Value:

The SelectPalette function returns the handle of the previous logical palette used by the Graphics Device Interface. A NULL return value indicates that the function cannot select the logical palette.

SetPaletteEntries

Syntax:

```
WORD SetPaletteEntries(hPalette, wStartIndex, wNumEntries,
                      lpPaletteEntries)
```

Parameter, Type, and Description:

hPalette	HPALETTE	Logical palette
wStartIndex	WORD	First entry of the logical palette to set
wNumEntries	WORD	Number of palette entries to set
lpPaletteEntries	LPPALETTEENTRY	Pointer to an array of PALETTEENTRY data structures containing the RGB values and flags

Description:

The SetPaletteEntries function defines the palette entries specified by wStartIndex and wNumEntries for the palette in hPalette. The palette entries are defined according to the array of data structures of type PALETTEENTRY, pointed to by lpPaletteEntries. The PALETTEENTRY structure is:

```
typedef struct
     {
     BYTE peRed;
     BYTE peGreen;
     BYTE peBlue;
     BYTE peFlags;
     } PALETTEENTRY;
```

where:

`peRed` is the intensity of red for the palette entry

`peGreen` is the intensity of green for the palette entry

`peBlue` is the intensity of blue for the palette entry

`peFlags` is NULL or one of the following values:

Value	*Meaning*
`PC_EXPLICIT`	Low-order word of the palette entry contains a hardware palette index
`PC_NOCOLLAPSE`	Color is placed in an unused entry in the palette; color does not replace the existing entry
`PC_RESERVED`	Entry is used for palette animation; no color can be matched to this entry

Return Value:

The `SetPaletteEntries` function returns the number of entries defined for the logical palette. Zero is returned when `SetPaletteEntries` is unsuccessful.

SetSystemPaletteUse

Syntax:

```
WORD SetSystemPaletteUse(hDC, wUsage)
```

Parameter, Type, and Description:

`hDC`	`HDC`	Device context
`wUsage`	`WORD`	New use of the system palette

Description:

The `SetSystemPaletteUse` function provides an application with full access to the system palette. `hDC` must specify a device context that supports color palettes. `wUsage` specifies the new use of the system palette:

- When `wUsage` is set to `SYSPAL_NOSTATIC`, the system palette will have no static colors—only black and white.

- When wUsage is set to SYSPAL_STATIC, the system palette will have static colors. The static colors will not change when the application realizes its logical palette.

Return Value:

The SetSystemPaletteUse function returns one of the following values representing the previous use of the system palette:

Value	*Meaning*
SYSPAL_NOSTATIC	System palette has no static colors, only black and white
SYSPAL_STATIC	System palette has static colors that do not change when the application realizes its logical palette

UpdateColors

Syntax:

```
int UpdateColors(hDC)
```

Parameter, Type, and Description:

hDC	HDC	Device context

Description:

The UpdateColors function updates the client area of the device context in hDC. Colors in the client area are matched to the system palette pixel by pixel.

Return Value:

The return value has no significance and is not used.

Coordinate Functions

Coordinate functions convert the various coordinate systems and points. Client coordinates are converted to and from screen coordinates. Device points are converted to and from logical points. The following functions are categorized as Coordinate functions for the Graphics Device Interface:

Function	*Meaning*
ChildWindowFromPoint	Finds the child window that contains a specified point
ClientToScreen	Converts client coordinates to screen coordinates

Function	Meaning
DPtoLP	Converts device points to logical points
GetCurrentPosition	Gets the logical coordinates of the current position
LPtoDP	Converts logical points to device points
ScreenToClient	Converts screen coordinates to client coordinates
WindowFromPoint	Finds the window that contains a specified point

The rest of this section provides detailed information on each of the functions in this list.

ChildWindowFromPoint

Syntax:

```
HWND ChildWindowFromPoint(hWndParent, Point)
```

Parameter, Type, and Description:

hWndParent	HWND	Parent window
Point	POINT	Client coordinates of the point

Description:

The `ChildWindowFromPoint` function finds the child window that contains the point specified in `Point`. `hWndParent` specifies the child window's parent window.

Return Value:

The `ChildWindowFromPoint` function returns the handle of the child window when a child window contains the point. If the point lies within the parent window, but not a child window, the function returns the handle of the parent window. A NULL return value indicates that the point lies outside the parent window.

ClientToScreen

Syntax:

```
void ClientToScreen(hWnd, lpPoint)
```

Parameter, Type, and Description:

hWnd	HWND	Window containing the client area used for conversion
lpPoint	LPPOINT	Pointer to a `POINT` data structure containing the client coordinates to convert

Description:

The `ClientToScreen` function converts the client coordinates in the data structure of type `POINT`, pointed to by `lpPoint`, to screen coordinates. The resulting screen coordinates are placed into the `POINT` data structure pointed to by `lpPoint`. The `POINT` data structure is:

```
typedef struct tagPOINT {
     int x;
     int y;
} POINT;
```

where:

`x` specifies the horizontal coordinate of the point

`y` specifies the vertical coordinate of the point

Return Value:

There is no return value.

DPtoLP

Syntax:

```
BOOL DPtoLP(hDC, lpPoints, nCount)
```

Parameter, Type, and Description:

`hDC`	`HDC`	Device context
`lpPoints`	`LPPOINT`	Pointer to an array of points defined with the `POINT` data structure
`nCount`	`int`	Number of points in `lpPoints`

Description:

The `DPtoLP` function converts each point defined in the array pointed to by `lpPoints`. The points are converted from device points to logical points. Each point in the array specified by `lpPoints` is defined with a data structure of type `POINT`. The `POINT` data structure is:

```
typedef struct tagPOINT {
     int x;
     int y;
} POINT;
```

where:

x specifies the horizontal coordinate of the point

y specifies the vertical coordinate of the point

Return Value:

The DPtoLP function returns a nonzero value when all the points are converted. A return value of zero indicates that the function cannot convert all or any of the points.

GetCurrentPosition

Syntax:

```
DWORD GetCurrentPosition(hDC)
```

Parameter, Type, and Description:

hDC	HDC	Device context

Description:

The GetCurrentPosition function gets the logical coordinates of the current position.

Return Value:

The low-order word of the return value contains the x-coordinate of the current position. The high-order word of the return value contains the y-coordinate of the current position.

LPtoDP

Syntax:

```
BOOL LPtoDP(hDC, lpPoints, nCount)
```

Parameter, Type, and Description:

hDC	HDC	Device context
lpPoints	LPPOINT	Pointer to an array of points defined with the POINT data structure
nCount	int	Number of points in lpPoints

Description:

The LPtoDP function converts each point defined in the array pointed to by lpPoints. The points are converted from logical points to device points. Each point in the array specified by `lpPoints` is defined with a data structure of type `POINT`. The `POINT` data structure is:

```
typedef struct tagPOINT {
     int x;
     int y;
} POINT;
```

where:

`x` specifies the horizontal coordinate of the point

`y` specifies the vertical coordinate of the point

Return Value:

The `LPtoDP` function returns a nonzero value if all the points are converted. A return value of zero indicates that the function cannot convert all or any of the points.

ScreenToClient

Syntax:

```
void ScreenToClient(hWnd, lpPoint)
```

Parameter, Type, and Description:

`hWnd`	`HWND`	Window containing the client area used for conversion
`lpPoint`	`LPPOINT`	Pointer to a `POINT` data structure containing the screen coordinates to convert

Description:

The `ScreenToClient` function converts the screen coordinates in the data structure of type `POINT`, pointed to by `lpPoint`, to client coordinates. The resulting client coordinates are placed into the `POINT` data structure pointed to by `lpPoint`. The `POINT` data structure is:

```
typedef struct tagPOINT {
     int x;
     int y;
} POINT;
```

where:

`x` specifies the horizontal coordinate of the point

`y` specifies the vertical coordinate of the point

Return Value:

There is no return value.

WindowFromPoint

Syntax:

```
HWND WindowFromPoint(Point)
```

Parameter, Type, and Description:

`Point`	`POINT`	Pointer to a `POINT` data structure containing the coordinates of the point

Description:

The `WindowFromPoint` function finds the window that contains the point specified by `Point`. `Point` identifies the data structure of type `POINT` that contains the screen coordinates of the point used to find the window. The `POINT` data structure is:

```
typedef struct tagPOINT {
     int x;
     int y;
} POINT;
```

where:

`x` specifies the horizontal coordinate of the point

`y` specifies the vertical coordinate of the point

Return Value:

The `WindowFromPoint` function returns the handle of that window containing the point, if such a window is found. A NULL return value indicates that no window contains the point.

Device Context Functions

A device context links Windows applications to device drivers and output devices. Through the device context link, a Windows application can pass device-independent information to the device driver. The device driver then creates the device-dependent operations required by the output device. The following functions are categorized as Device Context functions for the Graphics Device Interface:

Function	*Meaning*
`CreateCompatibleDC`	Creates a memory device context
`CreateDC`	Creates a device context
`CreateIC`	Creates an information context
`DeleteDC`	Deletes a device context
`GetDCOrg`	Gets the origin of a device context
`GetDeviceCaps`	Gets information on the specified device
`RestoreDC`	Restores a device context
`SaveDC`	Saves the state of a device context

The rest of this section provides detailed information on each of the functions in this list.

CreateCompatibleDC

Syntax:

```
HDC CreateCompatibleDC(hDC)
```

Parameter, Type, and Description:

`hDC`	`HDC`	Device context; can be set to NULL to create a memory device context that is compatible with the system display

Description:

The `CreateCompatibleDC` function creates a memory device context. The memory device context is compatible with the device specified in `hDC` and represents the display surface in memory. This function supports raster operations only.

Return Value:

The `CreateCompatibleDC` function returns the handle of the created memory device context. A NULL return value indicates that the function cannot create the memory device context.

CreateDC

Syntax:

```
HDC CreateDC(lpDriverName, lpDeviceName, lpOutput, lpInitData)
```

Parameter, Type, and Description:

lpDriverName	LPSTR	Pointer to a null-terminated string containing the DOS file name of the device driver
lpDeviceName	LPSTR	Pointer to a string containing the name of the device
lpOutput	LPSTR	Pointer to a null-terminated string containing the DOS file name or device name for output
lpInitData	LPDEVMODE	Pointer to a DEVMODE data structure containing the initialization date for the device driver

Description:

The CreateDC function creates a device context for the device specified by lpDriverName, lpDeviceName, and lpOutput. The ExtDeviceMode function is used to retrieve this structure and the information for a specified device. lpInitData points to a data structure of type DEVMODE that contains initialization data for the device driver. The DEVMODE structure is:

```
typedef struct _devicemode {
     char dmDeviceName[32];
     WORD dmSpecVersion;
     WORD dmDriverVersion;
     WORD dmSize;
     WORD dmDriverExtra;
     DWORD dmFields;
     short dmOrientation;
     short dmPaperSize;
     short dmPaperLength;
     short dmPaperWidth;
     short dmScale;
     short dmCopies;
     short dmDefaultSource;
     short dmPrintQuality;
     short dmColor;
     short dmDuplex;
     BYTE dmDriverData[dmDriverExtra];
} DEVMODE;
```

where:

dmDeviceName is the name of the device the driver supports

dmSpecVersion is version number of the initialization date specification (0x300 for Windows 3.0)

dmDriverVersion is the printer driver version

dmSize is the size in bytes of the DEVMODE structure

`dmDriverExtra` is the size of the `dmDriverData` field and the length of the data in the `DEVMODE` structure

`dmFields` specifies the remaining fields in `DEVMODE` that have been initialized

`dmOrientation` is the paper orientation—either `DMORIENT_PORTRAIT` or `DMORIENT_LANDSCAPE`

`dmPaperSize` is the paper size and is one of the following values:

Value	*Meaning*
DMPAPER_LETTER	8.5 by 11 inch
DMPAPER_LEGAL	8.5 by 14 inch
DMPAPER_A4	210 by 297 millimeter
DMPAPER_CSHEET	17 by 22 inch
DMPAPER_DSHEET	22 by 34 inch
DMPAPER_ESHEET	34 by 44 inch
DMPAPER_ENV_9	#9 envelope
DMPAPER_ENV_10	#10 envelope
DMPAPER_ENV_11	#11 envelope
DMPAPER_ENV_12	#12 envelope
DMPAPER_ENV_14	#14 envelope

`dmPaperLength` overrides the paper length in `dmPaperSize`

`dmPaperWidth` overrides the paper width in `dmPaperSize`

`dmScale` scales the output

`dmCopies` is the number of copies to print

`dmDefaultSource` is the default paper bin and is set to one of the following values:

Value	*Meaning*
DMBIN_DEFAULT	Default paper bin
DMBIN_UPPER	Upper paper bin
DMBIN_LOWER	Lower paper bin
DMBIN_MANUAL	Manual feed
DMBIN_TRACTOR	Tractor feed
DMBIN_ENVELOPE	Envelope feed

`dmPrintQuality` defines the printer resolution and is set to one of the following values:

Value	*Meaning*
`DMRES_HIGH`	High resolution
`DMRES_MEDIUM`	Medium resolution
`DMRES_LOW`	Low resolution
`DMRES_DRAFT`	Draft quality resolution

`dmColor` switches between color and monochrome and can be either `DMCOLOR_COLOR` or `DMCOLOR_MONOCHROME`

`dmDuplex` indicates double-sided (duplex) or single-sided (simplex) printing and is one of the following values:

`DMDUP_SIMPLEX`

`DMDUP_HORIZONTAL`

`DMDUP_VERTICAL`

`dmDriverData[]` is data defined by the device driver

Return Value:

The `CreateDC` function returns the device context for the specified device. A NULL return value indicates that the function cannot create the device context.

CreateIC

Syntax:

```
HDC CreateIC(lpDriverName, lpDeviceName, lpOutput, lpInitData)
```

Parameter, Type, and Description:

`lpDriverName`	`LPSTR`	Pointer to a null-terminated string containing the DOS file name of the device driver
`lpDeviceName`	`LPSTR`	Pointer to a null-terminated string containing the name of the device
`lpOutput`	`LPSTR`	Pointer to a null-terminated string containing the DOS file name or device name for output
`lpInitData`	`LPSTR`	Pointer to the initialization data for the device driver

Description:

The `CreateIC` function creates an information context for the device specified in `lpDriverName`, `lpDeviceName`, and `lpOutput`. `lpInitData` points to the initialization data for the device driver.

Return Value:

The `CreateIC` function returns the handle of the created information context. A NULL return value indicates that the function cannot create the information context for the device.

DeleteDC

Syntax:

```
BOOL DeleteDC(hDC)
```

Parameter, Type, and Description:

`hDC`	`HDC`	Device context

Description:

The `DeleteDC` function deletes the device context specified in `hDC`. The handle of the device context must be retrieved with the `ReleaseDC` function.

Return Value:

The `DeleteDC` function returns a nonzero value when the device context is deleted. A return value of zero indicates that the function cannot delete the device context.

GetDCOrg

Syntax:

```
DWORD GetDCOrg(hDC)
```

Parameter, Type, and Description:

`hDC`	`HDC`	Device context

Description:

The `GetDCOrg` function gets the final translation origin for the device context specified in `hDC`. The final translation origin is the offset that Windows uses to translate device coordinates into client coordinates. The offset is relative to the physical origin of the screen.

Return Value:

The low-order word of the return value specifies the x-coordinate of the final translation origin, in device coordinates. The high-order word of the return value specifies the y-coordinate of the final translation origin, in device coordinates.

GetDeviceCaps

Syntax:

```
int GetDeviceCaps(hDC, nIndex)
```

Parameter, Type, and Description:

hDC	HDC	Device context
nIndex	int	Value to return

Description:

The GetDeviceCaps function gets information on the display device specified in hDC. nIndex specifies the type of information to retrieve and can be any of the following values:

Value	*Meaning*
DRIVERVERSION	Version number
TECHNOLOGY	Device technology; can be any of the following: DT_PLOTTER is the vector plotter DT_RASDISPLAY is the raster display DT_RASPRINTER is the raster printer DT_RASCAMERA is the raster camera DT_CHARSTREAM is the character stream DT_METAFILE is the metafile DT_DISPFILE is the display file
HORZSIZE	Width of the display in millimeters
VERTSIZE	Height of the display in millimeters
HORZRES	Width of the display in pixels
VERTRES	Height of the display in pixels
LOGPIXELSX	Pixels per logical inch along the display width
LOGPIXELSY	Pixels per logical inch along the display height
BITSPIXEL	Color bits for each pixel
PLANES	Number of color planes
NUMBRUSHES	Number of device-specific brushes
NUMPENS	Number of device-specific pens
NUMFONTS	Number of device-specific fonts
NUMCOLORS	Number of entries in the device color table
ASPECTX	Width of pixel for line drawing
ASPECTY	Height of pixel for line drawing

Value	*Meaning*
ASPECTXY	Diagonal width of pixel for line drawing
PDEVICESIZE	Size of PDEVICE internal data structure
CLIPCAPS	Clipping capabilities: 1 if the device can clip to rectangle 2 if the device cannot clip to rectangle
SIZEPALETTE	Number of entries in the system palette
NUMRESERVED	Number of reserved entries in the system palette
COLORRES	Color resolution in bits per pixel
RASTERCAPS	Raster capabilities; can be any of the following: RC_BANDING requires banding support RC_BITBLT can transfer bitmaps RC_BITMAP64 supports bitmaps greater than 64K RC_DI_BITMAP supports SetDIBits and GetDIBits RC_DIBTODEV supports SetDIBitsToDevice RC_FLOODFILL can floodfill RC_GDI20_OUTPUT supports Windows 2.0 RC_PALETTE is a palette-based device RC_SCALING supports scaling RC_STRETCHBLT supports StretchBlt RC_STRETCHDIB supports StretchDIBits
CURVECAPS	Curve capabilities bitmask; possible bits are: 0, which creates circles 1, which creates pie wedges 2, which creates chord arcs 3, which creates ellipses 4, which creates wide borders 5, which creates styled borders 6, which creates wide, styled borders 7, which creates interiors
LINECAPS	Line capabilities bitmask; possible bits are: 0, which is reserved 1, which does polyline 2, which is reserved 3, which is reserved 4, which creates wide lines 5, which creates styled lines

Value	Meaning
	6, which creates wide, styled lines
	7, which does interiors
`POLYGONALCAPS`	Polygonal capabilities bitmask; possible bits are:
	0, which creates alternate fill polygon
	1, which creates a rectangle
	2, which creates winding number fill polygon
	3, which creates a scanline
	4, which creates wide borders
	5, which creates styled borders
	6, which creates wide, styled borders
	7, which creates interiors
`TEXTCAPS`	Text capabilities bitmask; possible bits are:
	0, which does character output precision
	1, which does stroke output precision
	2, which does stroke clip precision
	3, which does 90 degree character rotation
	4, which does any character rotation
	5, which does independent scaling
	6, which does doubled character for scaling
	7, which does integer multiples for scaling
	8, which does any multiples for scaling
	9, which does double-weight characters
	10, which italicizes
	11, which underlines
	12, which does strikeouts
	13, which does raster fonts
	14, which does vector fonts
	15, which is reserved and set to zero

Return Value:

The `GetDeviceCaps` function returns the value of the specified item.

RestoreDC

Syntax:

```
BOOL RestoreDC(hDC, nSavedDC)
```

Parameter, Type, and Description:

`hDC`	`HDC`	Device context
`nSavedDC`	`int`	Device context to restore

Description:

The `RestoreDC` function restores the device context in `hDC` to the state specified in `nSavedDC`:

- If `nSavedDC` is set to –1, the most recently saved device context is restored.
- Otherwise, `nSavedDC` is set to a value returned by a previous call to `SaveDC`.

The state information is saved in the context stack by a previous call to the `SaveDC` function.

Return Value:

The `RestoreDC` function returns TRUE when the device context is restored. A return value of FALSE indicates that the function cannot restore the device context to the state.

SaveDC

Syntax:

```
int SaveDC(hDC)
```

Parameter, Type, and Description:

`hDC`	`HDC`	Device context to save

Description:

The `SaveDC` function saves the state of the device context specified in `hDC`. The state information is copied onto the context stack.

Return Value:

The `SaveDC` function returns the saved device context. A return value of zero indicates that the function cannot save the device context.

Drawing Attribute Functions

Drawing Attribute functions control the appearance of line, brush, text, and bitmap output. The following functions are categorized as Drawing Attribute functions for the Graphics Device Interface:

Function	*Meaning*
`GetBkColor`	Gets the background color
`GetBkMode`	Gets the background mode
`GetPolyFillMode`	Gets the mode for filling polygons
`GetROP2`	Gets the drawing mode
`GetStretchBltMode`	Gets the stretching mode
`GetTextColor`	Gets the text color
`SetBkColor`	Sets the background color
`SetBkMode`	Sets the background mode
`SetPolyFillMode`	Sets the mode for filling polygons
`SetROP2`	Sets the drawing mode
`SetStretchBltMode`	Sets the stretching mode
`SetTextColor`	Sets the text color

The rest of this section provides detailed information on each of the functions in this list.

GetBkColor

Syntax:

```
DWORD GetBkColor(hDC)
```

Parameter, Type, and Description:

`hDC`	`HDC`	Device context

Description:

The `GetBkColor` function gets the background color for the device context specified in `hDC`.

Return Value:

The `GetBkColor` function returns the RGB color value of the background color.

GetBkMode

Syntax:

```
int GetBkMode(hDC)
```

Parameter, Type, and Description:

`hDC`	`HDC`	Device context

Description:

The `GetBkMode` function gets the background mode for the device context specified in `hDC`. The background mode can be either of the following values:

Value	*Meaning*
`OPAQUE`	Background is filled with the background color before any drawing takes place
`TRANSPARENT`	Background is not changed before drawing takes place

Return Value:

The `GetBkMode` function returns the background mode.

GetPolyFillMode

Syntax:

```
int GetPolyFillMode(hDC)
```

Parameter, Type, and Description:

`hDC`	`HDC`	Device context

Description:

The `GetPolyFillMode` function gets the mode used to fill polygons. The mode can be either of the following:

Mode	*Meaning*
`ALTERNATE`	Alternate mode
`WINDING`	Winding number mode

Return Value:

The `GetPolyFillMode` function returns the mode used to fill polygons—either `ALTERNATE` or `WINDING`.

GetROP2

Syntax:

```
int GetROP2(hDC)
```

Parameter, Type, and Description:

`hDC`	`HDC`	Device context

Description:

The `GetROP2` function gets the drawing mode for the device context specified in `hDC`.

Return Value:

The `GetROP2` function returns one of the following values representing the drawing mode:

Value	*Color of Pixel*
`R2_BLACK`	Black
`R2_COPYPEN`	The pen color
`R2_MASKNOTPEN`	The combination of the common colors of the display and the inverse of the pen
`R2_MASKPEN`	The combination of the common colors of the pen and the display
`R2_MASKPENNOT`	The combination of the common colors of the pen and the inverse of the display color
`R2_MERGENOTPEN`	The combination of the display color and the inverse of the pen color
`R2_MERGEPEN`	The combination of the pen and display colors
`R2_MERGEPENNOT`	The combination of pen color and inverse of display color
`R2_NOP`	Not changed
`R2_NOT`	The inverse of display color
`R2_NOTCOPYPEN`	The inverse of pen color
`R2_NOTMASKPEN`	The inverse of `R2_MASKPEN`
`R2_NOTMERGEPEN`	The inverse of `R2_MERGEPEN`
`R2_NOTXORPEN`	The inverse of the `R2_XORPEN` color
`R2_WHITE`	White
`R2_XORPEN`	The combination of the colors in the pen and in the display, but not both

GetStretchBltMode

Syntax:

```
int GetStretchBltMode(hDC)
```

Parameter, Type, and Description:

`hDC` `HDC` Device context

Description:

The `GetStretchBltMode` function gets the stretching mode for the device context in `hDC`, which can be one of the following:

Value	*Meaning*
BLACKONWHITE	Preserve black pixels by using the AND operator on all the eliminated and remaining lines
COLORONCOLOR	Delete all eliminated lines
WHITEONBLACK	Preserve white pixels by using the OR operator on all eliminated and remaining lines

Return Value:

The `GetStretchBltMode` function returns the stretching mode—either `BLACKONWHITE`, `COLORONCOLOR`, or `WHITEONBLACK`.

GetTextColor

Syntax:

```
DWORD GetTextColor(hDC)
```

Parameter, Type, and Description:

`hDC` `HDC` Device context

Description:

The `GetTextColor` function gets the text color for the device context in `hDC`. The `TextOut` and `ExtTextOut` functions use the text color for drawing text.

Return Value:

The `GetTextColor` function returns the RGB color value that represents the text color.

SetBkColor

Syntax:

```
DWORD SetBkColor(hDC, crColor)
```

Parameter, Type, and Description:

`hDC`	`HDC`	Device context
`crColor`	`COLORREF`	New background color

Description:

The `SetBkColor` function sets the background color for the device context in `hDC` to the color specified in `crColor`. `SetBkColor` uses the nearest physical color to `crColor` if the device cannot use the RGB value specified in `crColor`.

Return Value:

The `SetBkColor` function returns the previous background color as an RGB value. A return value of 0x80000000 indicates that the function cannot set the background color.

SetBkMode

Syntax:

```
int SetBkMode(hDC, nBkMode)
```

Parameter, Type, and Description:

`hDC`	`HDC`	Device context
`nBkMode`	`int`	Background mode

Description:

The `SetBkMode` function sets the background mode for the device context in `hDC`. The background mode is defined in `nBkMode` and can be either of the following values:

Value	*Meaning*
`OPAQUE`	Fill the background with the background color before any drawing takes place
`TRANSPARENT`	Do not change the background before drawing takes place

Return Value:

The `SetBkMode` function returns the previous background mode—either `OPAQUE` or `TRANSPARENT`.

SetPolyFillMode

Syntax:

```
int SetPolyFillMode(hDC, nPolyFillMode)
```

Parameter, Type, and Description:

`hDC`	`HDC`	Device context
`nPolyFillMode`	`int`	Filling mode

Description:

The `SetPolyFillMode` function sets the polygon filling mode for the device context in `hDC`. The polygon filling mode is used by Graphics Device Interface functions that must compute interior points by using the polygon algorithm. The filling mode is specified in `nPolyFillMode` and can be either of the following:

Mode	*Meaning*
`ALTERNATE`	Alternate mode
`WINDING`	Winding number mode

Return Value:

The `SetPolyFillMode` function returns the previous filling mode—either `ALTERNATE` or `WINDING`. A return value of zero indicates that the function cannot return the previous filling mode.

SetROP2

Syntax:

```
int SetROP2(hDC, nDrawMode)
```

Parameter, Type, and Description:

`hDC`	`HDC`	Device context
`nDrawMode`	`int`	Drawing mode

Description:

The `SetROP2` function sets the drawing mode for the device context specified in `hDC`. The drawing mode is specified in `nDrawMode` and can be any of the following values:

Value	Color of Pixel
R2_BLACK	Black
R2_COPYPEN	The pen color
R2_MASKNOTPEN	The combination of the common colors of the display and the inverse of the pen
R2_MASKPEN	The combination of the common colors of the pen and the display
R2_MASKPENNOT	The combination of the common colors of the pen and the inverse of the display color
R2_MERGENOTPEN	The combination of the display color and the inverse of the pen color
R2_MERGEPEN	The combination of the pen and display colors
R2_MERGEPENNOT	The combination of the pen color and inverse of the display color
R2_NOP	Not changed
R2_NOT	The inverse of the display color
R2_NOTCOPYPEN	The inverse of the pen color
R2_NOTMASKPEN	The inverse of R2_MASKPEN
R2_NOTMERGEPEN	The inverse of R2_MERGEPEN
R2_NOTXORPEN	The inverse of the R2_XORPEN color
R2_WHITE	White
R2_XORPEN	The combination of the colors in the pen and in the display, but not both

Return Value:

The SetROP2 function returns the previous drawing mode.

SetStretchBltMode

Syntax:

```
int SetStretchBltMode(hDC, nStretchMode)
```

Parameter, Type, and Description:

hDC	HDC	Device context
nStretchMode	int	Stretching mode

Description:

The SetStretchBltMode function sets the stretching mode for the device context specified in hDC. The stretching mode determines the scan lines and columns that are eliminated when a bitmap is contracted. nStretchMode specifies the stretching mode and can be any of the following values:

Value	*Meaning*
BLACKONWHITE	Preserve black pixels by using the AND operator on all eliminated and remaining lines
COLORONCOLOR	Delete all eliminated lines
WHITEONBLACK	Preserve white pixels by using the OR operator on all eliminated and remaining lines

Return Value:

The SetStretchBltMode function returns the previous stretching mode—either BLACKONWHITE, COLORONCOLOR, or WHITEONBLACK.

SetTextColor

Syntax:

```
DWORD SetTextColor(hDC, crColor)
```

Parameter, Type, and Description:

hDC	HDC	Device context
crColor	COLORREF	Text color

Description:

The SetTextColor function sets the text color for the device context in hDC to the text color specified in crColor. SetTextColor sets the text color to the closest physical color if the specified device cannot represent the specified color.

Return Value:

The SetTextColor function returns the RGB color value for the previous text color.

Drawing Tool Functions

The Graphics Device Interface uses drawing tools to create its output. The three drawing tools are the bitmap, brush, and pen. Drawing Tool functions create, control, and delete the drawing tools. The following functions are categorized as Drawing Tool functions for the Graphics Device Interface:

Function	*Meaning*
`CreateBrushIndirect`	Creates a logical brush
`CreateDIBPatternBrush`	Creates a logical brush that uses a device-independent bitmap
`CreateHatchBrush`	Creates a logical brush with a hatched pattern
`CreatePatternBrush`	Creates a logical brush with the specified pattern
`CreatePen`	Creates a logical pen
`CreatePenIndirect`	Creates a logical pen that uses a `LOGPEN` data structure
`CreateSolidBrush`	Creates a logical brush with a solid color
`DeleteObject`	Deletes a pen, brush, font, bitmap, or region
`EnumObjects`	Enumerates all pens and brushes
`GetBrushOrg`	Gets the current brush origin
`GetObject`	Gets the bytes of data that define an object
`GetStockObject`	Gets the handle to a predefined stock pen, brush, font, or color palette
`SelectObject`	Selects an object
`SetBrushOrg`	Sets the origin for the selected brushes
`UnrealizeObject`	Resets the origin of a brush

The rest of this section provides detailed information on each of the functions in this list.

CreateBrushIndirect

Syntax:

```
HBRUSH CreateBrushIndirect(lpLogBrush)
```

Parameter, Type, and Description:

`lpLogBrush`	`LOGBRUSH FAR *`	Pointer to the `LOGBRUSH` data structure that contains information on the brush

Description:

The `CreateBrushIndirect` function creates a logical brush. `lpLogBrush` points to the data structure of type `LOGBRUSH` that contains the style, color, and pattern for the brush. The `LOGBRUSH` data structure is:

```
typedef struct tagLOGBRUSH {
     WORD lbStyle;
     COLORREF lbColor;
     short int lbHatch;
} LOGBRUSH;
```

where:

lbStyle is the brush style and is set to one of the following values:

Value	Meaning
BS_DIBPATTERN	Pattern brush defined with a device-independent bitmap
BS_HATCHED	Hatched brush
BS_HOLLOW	Hollow brush
BS_PATTERN	Pattern brush defined with a memory bitmap
BS_SOLID	Solid brush

lbColor is the color for the brush and is one of the following values:

Value	Meaning
DIB_PAL_COLORS	Color table is an array of 16-bit indexes to the logical palette
DIB_RGB_COLORS	Color table contains literal RGB values

lbHatch is the hatch style and is interpreted as follows:

- If lbStyle is BS_DIBPATTERN, lbHatch contains the handle to a packed device-independent bitmap.
- If lbStyle is BS_HATCHED, lbHatch contains one of the following values, which specify the line orientation of the hatch:

Value	Meaning
HS_BDIAGONAL	45 degree upward hatch
HS_CROSS	Crosshatch with vertical and horizontal lines
HS_DIAGCROSS	45 degree crosshatch
HS_FDIAGONAL	45 degree downward hatch
HS_HORIZONTAL	Horizontal hatch
HS_VERTICAL	Vertical hatch

- If lbStyle is BS_PATTERN, lbHatch contains the handle to the bitmap for the pattern.
- If lbStyle is BS_SOLID or BS_HOLLOW, lbHatch is ignored.

Return Value:

The CreateBrushIndirect function returns the handle of the created brush. A NULL return value indicates that the function cannot create the brush.

CreateDIBPatternBrush

Syntax:

```
HBRUSH CreateDIBPatternBrush(hPackedDIB, wUsage)
```

Parameter, Type, and Description:

`hPackedDIB`	`GLOBALHANDLE`	Global memory object containing the packed, device- independent bitmap
`wUsage`	`WORD`	Indicates whether the `bmiColors[]` fields of the `BITMAPINFO` data structure contains RGB color values or indexes to the logical palette

Description:

The `CreateDIBPatternBrush` function creates a logical brush that uses the pattern from a device-independent bitmap. `hPackedDIB` specifies the global memory object that contains the packed, device-independent bitmap. The handle of this global object is defined when the `GlobalAlloc` function is called to allocate global memory. The application fills the global memory with a packed, device-independent bitmap that contains a `BITMAPINFO` data structure and array defining the pixels of the bitmap. `wUsage` indicates whether the `bmiColors[]` fields of the `BITMAPINFO` data structure contain RGB color values or indexes to the currently realized logical palette. `wUsage` is set to one of the following values:

Value	*Meaning*
`DIB_PAL_COLORS`	Color table contains 16-bit indexes into the currently realized logical palette
`DIB_RGB_COLORS`	Color table contains literal RGB values

Return Value:

The `CreateDIBPatternBrush` function returns the handle of the created brush. A NULL return value indicates that the function cannot create the brush.

CreateHatchBrush

Syntax:

```
HBRUSH CreateHatchBrush(nIndex, crColor)
```

Parameter, Type, and Description:

`nIndex`	`int`	Hatch style
`crColor`	`COLORREF`	Foreground color for the brush

Description:

The `CreateHatchBrush` function creates a logical brush that uses the hatch style specified in `nIndex` and the color specified in `crColor`. `nIndex` can be any of the following values:

Value	*Meaning*
HS_BDIAGONAL	45 degree downward hatch
HS_CROSS	Crosshatch with vertical and horizontal lines
HS_DIAGCROSS	45 degree crosshatch
HS_FDIAGONAL	45 degree upward hatch
HS_HORIZONTAL	Horizontal hatch
HS_VERTICAL	Vertical hatch

Return Value:

The `CreateHatchBrush` function returns the handle of the created brush. A NULL return value indicates that the function cannot create the brush.

CreatePatternBrush

Syntax:

```
HBRUSH CreatePatternBrush(hBitmap)
```

Parameter, Type, and Description:

hBitmap	HBITMAP	Bitmap used for the brush pattern

Description:

The `CreatePatternBrush` function creates a logical brush that uses the pattern specified in `hBitmap`.

Return Value:

The `CreatePatternBrush` function returns the handle of the created brush. A NULL return value indicates that the function cannot create the brush.

CreatePen

Syntax:

```
HPEN CreatePen(nPenStyle, nWidth, crColor)
```

Parameter, Type, and Description:

nPenStyle	int	Pen style
nWidth	int	Width of the pen in logical units
crColor	COLORREF	Color of the pen

Description:

The CreatePen function creates a logical pen. nWidth specifies the width, in logical units, of the pen. crColor specifies the pen color. nPenStyle specifies the style of the pen and can be any of the following constants:

Constant	*Value*	*Style*
PS_SOLID	0	Solid line
PS_DASH	1	Dashed line
PS_DOT	2	Dotted line
PS_DASHDOT	3	Dash-dot pattern line
PS_DASHDOTDOT	4	Dash-dot-dot pattern line
PS_NULL	5	No line drawn
PS_INSIDEFRAME	6	When pen width is greater than 1, the line is drawn inside the frame of the figure; when the pen width is less than or equal to 1, PS_INSIDEFRAME is equal to PS_SOLID

Return Value:

The CreatePen function returns the handle of the created pen. A NULL return value indicates that the function cannot create the pen.

CreatePenIndirect

Syntax:

```
HPEN CreatePenIndirect(lpLogPen)
```

Parameter, Type, and Description:

lpLogPen	LOGPEN FAR *	Pointer to the LOGPEN data structure containing information on the logical pen

Description:

The CreatePenIndirect function creates a logical pen that uses the information in the data structure of type LOGPEN, pointed to by lpLogPen. The LOGPEN structure is:

```
typedef struct tagLOGPEN {
    WORD lopnStyle;
    POINT lopnWidth;
    COLORREF lopnColor;
} LOGPEN;
```

where:

`lopnStyle` is the pen style and is chosen from one of the following constants:

Constant	*Value*	*Style*
PS_SOLID	0	Solid line
PS_DASH	1	Dashed line
PS_DOT	2	Dotted line
PS_DASHDOT	3	Dash-dot pattern line
PS_DASHDOTDOT	4	Dash-dot-dot pattern line
PS_NULL	5	No line drawn
PS_INSIDEFRAME	6	When pen width is greater than 1, the line is drawn inside the frame of the figure; when the pen width is less than or equal to 1, PS_INSIDEFRAME is equal to PS_SOLID

`lopnWidth` is the pen width in logical units

`lopnColor` is the pen color

Return Value:

The `CreatePenIndirect` function returns the handle of the created logical pen. A NULL return value indicates that the function cannot create the pen.

CreateSolidBrush

Syntax:

```
HBRUSH CreateSolidBrush(crColor)
```

Parameter, Type, and Description:

`crColor` `COLORREF` Color of brush

Description:

The `CreateSolidBrush` function creates a logical brush that uses the solid color specified in `crColor`.

Return Value:

The `CreateSolidBrush` function returns the handle of the created logical brush. A NULL return value indicates that the function cannot create the brush.

DeleteObject

Syntax:

```
BOOL DeleteObject(hObject)
```

Parameter, Type, and Description:

`hObject`	`HANDLE`	Handle of a logical pen, brush, font, bitmap, region, or palette

Description:

The `DeleteObject` function deletes the object specified in `hObject`. All system storage associated with the specified object is freed.

Return Value:

The `DeleteObject` function returns a nonzero value when the object is successfully deleted. A return value of zero indicates that the function cannot delete the object.

EnumObjects

Syntax:

```
int EnumObjects(hDC, nObjectType, lpObjectFunc, lpData)
```

Parameter, Type, and Description:

`hDC`	`HDC`	Device context
`nObjectType`	`int`	Object type; either `OBJ_BRUSH` or `OBJ_PEN`
`lpObjectFunc`	`FARPROC`	Procedure instance address of the application-supplied callback function
`lpData`	`LPSRT`	Pointer to data passed to the callback function

Description:

The `EnumObjects` function enumerates the pens and brushes available for the device context specified in `hDC`. `nObjectType` specifies the object type—either `OBJ_BRUSH` or

OBJ_PEN. lpObjectFunc specifies the procedure instance address of the application-supplied callback function. The address for lpObjectFunc is created with the MakeProcInstance function. The callback function is called for each object and must follow these conventions and formats:

Syntax:

```
int FAR PASCAL ObjectFunc(lpLogObject, lpData)
```

Parameter, Type, and Description:

lpLogObject	char FAR *	Pointer to LOGPEN or LOGBRUSH data structure containing information on the object
lpData	char FAR *	Pointer to data supplied by the application that is passed to EnumObjects

Description:

ObjectFunc is a placeholder for the function name supplied by the application. Use EXPORTS to include the application-supplied function name in the module definition file of the application.

Return Value:

The callback function returns zero to end enumeration.

Return Value:

The EnumObjects function returns the return value of the callback function.

GetBrushOrg

Syntax:

```
DWORD GetBrushOrg(hDC)
```

Parameter, Type, and Description:

hDC	HDC	Device context

Description:

The GetBrushOrg function gets the brush origin for the device context specified in hDC.

Return Value:

The low-order word of the return value contains the x-coordinate of the brush origin, in device units. The high-order word of the return value contains the y-coordinate of the brush origin, in device units.

GetObject

Syntax:

```
int GetObject(hObject, nCount, lpObject)
```

Parameter, Type, and Description:

`hObject`	`HANDLE`	Logical pen, brush, font, bitmap, or palette
`nCount`	`int`	Number of bytes to copy to the buffer
`lpObject`	`LPSTR`	Pointer to the buffer receiving the information

Description:

The `GetObject` function gets information on the object specified in `hObject`:

- For a pen, `GetObject` retrieves a `LOGPEN` data structure.
- For a brush, `GetObject` retrieves a `LOGBRUSH` data structure.
- For a font, `GetObject` retrieves a `LOGFONT` data structure.
- For a bitmap, `GetObject` retrieves the width, height, and color information from a `BITMAP` data structure.
- For a palette, `GetObject` retrieves a two-byte value specifying the number of entries in the palette.

The object information is placed in the buffer pointed to by `lpObject`. `nCount` specifies the number of bytes of information that should be placed in `lpObject`.

Return Value:

The `GetObject` function returns the number of bytes copied to the buffer. A return value of zero indicates that the function cannot get information on the object.

GetStockObject

Syntax:

```
HANDLE GetStockObject(nIndex)
```

Parameter, Type, and Description:

`nIndex`	`int`	Type of stock object

Description:

The `GetStockObject` function gets the handle of the stock pen, brush, or font specified in `nIndex`. The following values are used for `nIndex`:

Value	Meaning
Brushes	
BLACK_BRUSH	Black brush
DKGRAY_BRUSH	Dark gray brush
GRAY_BRUSH	Gray brush
HOLLOW_BRUSH	Hollow brush
LTGRAY_BRUSH	Light gray brush
NULL_BRUSH	Null brush
WHITE_BRUSH	White brush
Pens	
BLACK_PEN	Black
NULL_PEN	Null
WHITE_PEN	White
Fonts	
ANSI_FIXED_FONT	ANSI fixed system
ANSI_VAR_FONT	ANSI variable system
DEVICE_DEFAULT_FONT	Device-dependent
OEM_FIXED_FONT	OEM-dependent
SYSTEM_FONT	System
SYSTEM_FIXED_FONT	Fixed-width system
Palettes	
DEFAULT_PALETTE	Default color

Return Value:

The `GetStockObject` function returns the handle of the object. A NULL return value indicates that the function cannot get the handle of the object.

SelectObject

Syntax:

```
HANDLE SelectObject(hDC, hObject)
```

Parameter, Type, and Description:

hDC	HDC	Device context
hObject	HANDLE	Bitmap, brush, font, pen, or region to select

Description:

The `SelectObject` function selects the object specified in `hObject` as the current object selected for the device context in `hDC`.

Return Value:

The `SelectObject` function returns the handle of the previously selected object. A NULL return value indicates that the function cannot get the handle of the object.

SetBrushOrg

Syntax:

```
DWORD SetBrushOrg(hDC, X, Y)
```

Parameter, Type, and Description:

`hDC`	`HDC`	Device context
`X`	`int`	X-coordinate of new origin, in device units
`Y`	`int`	Y-coordinate of new origin, in device units

Description:

The `SetBrushOrg` function sets the origin of the currently selected brush for the device context in `hDC` to the point specified in `X` and `Y`. `X` and `Y` are the horizontal and vertical device coordinates, respectively, for the new origin and must be in the range of 0 to 7.

Return Value:

The low-order word of the return value contains the x-coordinate of the previous origin. The high-order word of the return value contains the y-coordinate of the previous origin.

UnrealizeObject

Syntax:

```
BOOL UnrealizeObject(hObject)
```

Parameter, Type, and Description:

`hObject`	`HANDLE`	Object to reset

Description:

The `UnrealizeObject` function resets the origin of a brush or realizes a palette, depending on the contents of `hObject`:

- When `hObject` specifies a brush, the Graphics Device Interface resets the origin of the brush.
- When `hObject` specifies a logical palette, the Graphics Device Interface realizes the palette as if it had not been previously realized.

Return Value:

The `UnrealizeObject` function returns a nonzero value when the origin of a brush is reset or the palette is realized. A return value of zero indicates that the function cannot reset the origin of the specified brush or realize the palette.

Ellipse and Polygon Functions

The Ellipse and Polygon functions provide fundamental drawing capabilities. You can include these functions in applications to create graphics images such as bar charts, pie charts, or engineering drawings. The following functions are categorized as Ellipse and Polygon functions for the Graphics Device Interface:

Function	*Shape Drawn*
`Chord`	A chord
`DrawFocusRect`	A rectangle that indicates focus
`Ellipse`	An ellipse
`Pie`	A pie
`Polygon`	A polygon
`PolyPolygon`	A series of closed polygons
`Rectangle`	A rectangle
`RoundRect`	A rounded rectangle

The rest of this section provides detailed information on each of the functions in this list.

Chord

Syntax:

```
BOOL Chord(hDC, X1, Y1, X2, Y2, X3, Y3, X4, Y4)
```

Parameter, Type, and Description:

hDC	HDC	Device context
X1	int	X-coordinate of the upper-left corner of a bounding rectangle
Y1	int	Y-coordinate of the upper-left corner of a bounding rectangle
X2	int	X-coordinate of the lower-right corner of a bounding rectangle
Y2	int	Y-coordinate of the lower-right corner of a bounding rectangle
X3	int	X-coordinate of the starting point of a line segment
Y3	int	Y-coordinate of the starting point of a line segment
X4	int	X-coordinate of the ending point of a line segment
Y4	int	Y-coordinate of the ending point of a line segment

Description:

The `Chord` function creates a chord. A chord is an ellipse that is cut at the intersections of a line segment. The ellipse is drawn inside the bounding rectangle specified by `X1`, `Y1` and `X2`, `Y2`. The line segment specified by `X3`, `Y3`, and `X4`, `Y4` intersects the ellipse. The part of the ellipse that is not cut off by the line segment is the chord. The chord is drawn with the selected pen and filled with the selected brush.

Return Value:

The `Chord` function returns a nonzero value when the chord is created. A return value of zero indicates that the function cannot create the chord.

DrawFocusRect

Syntax:

```
void DrawFocusRect(hDC, lpRect)
```

Parameter, Type, and Description:

hDC	HDC	Device context
lpRect	LPRECT	Pointer to a `RECT` data structure containing the coordinates of the rectangle to draw

Description:

The `DrawFocusRect` function creates a rectangle that is used to indicate focus. The function creates the rectangle by using the coordinates specified in the data structure of type `RECT` pointed to by `lpRect`. The `RECT` data structure is:

```
typedef struct tagRECT{
     int left;
     int top;
     int right;
     int bottom;
} RECT;
```

where:

`left` is the x-coordinate of the upper-left corner

`top` is the y-coordinate of the upper-left corner

`right` is the x-coordinate of the lower-right corner

`bottom` is the y-coordinate of the lower-right corner

Return Value:

There is no return value.

Ellipse

Syntax:

`BOOL Ellipse(hDC, X1, Y1, X2, Y2)`

Parameter, Type, and Description:

`hDC`	`HDC`	Device context
`X1`	`int`	X-coordinate of the upper-left corner of a bounding rectangle
`Y1`	`int`	Y-coordinate of the upper-left corner of a bounding rectangle
`X2`	`int`	X-coordinate of the lower-right corner of a bounding rectangle
`Y2`	`int`	Y-coordinate of the lower-right corner of a bounding rectangle

Description:

The `Ellipse` function draws an ellipse inside the rectangle specified by `X1`, `Y1` and `X2`, `Y2`. The current pen is used to draw the ellipse. The current brush is used to fill the ellipse.

Return Value:

The `Ellipse` function returns a nonzero value when the ellipse is drawn. A return value of zero indicates that the function cannot draw the ellipse.

Pie

Syntax:

```
BOOL Pie(hDC, X1, Y1, X2, Y2, X3, Y3, X4, Y4)
```

Parameter, Type, and Description:

`hDC`	`HDC`	Device context
`X1`	`int`	X-coordinate of the upper-left corner of a bounding rectangle
`Y1`	`int`	Y-coordinate of the upper-left corner of a bounding rectangle
`X2`	`int`	X-coordinate of the lower-right corner of a bounding rectangle
`Y2`	`int`	Y-coordinate of the lower-right corner of a bounding rectangle
`X3`	`int`	X-coordinate of the starting point for the arc
`Y3`	`int`	Y-coordinate of the starting point for the arc
`X4`	`int`	X-coordinate of the ending point for the arc
`Y4`	`int`	Y-coordinate of the ending point for the arc

Description:

The `Pie` function draws a pie-shaped wedge by using the current pen and brush. The pie-shaped wedge is specified with four sets of coordinates. The first and second set, `X1:Y1` and `X2:Y2`, specify the upper-left and lower-right corners, respectively, of the ellipse used to create the pie-shaped wedge. The third set of coordinates, `X3:Y3`, specifies the point used to determine where the arc for the pie-shaped wedge will begin. A line is projected from the center of the ellipse to the point specified in `X3:Y3`. The arc for the pie-shaped wedge begins where this projected line intercepts the ellipse. `X4:Y4` is used similarly to determine the ending point of the arc. The arc of the pie-shaped wedge begins at the point where the line segment between the center of the ellipse and `X3:Y3` intercepts the ellipse. The arc extends in a counterclockwise direction and ends at the point where the line segment between the center of the ellipse and `X4:Y4` intercepts the ellipse.

Return Value:

The `Pie` function returns a nonzero value when the wedge is drawn. A return value of zero indicates that the function cannot draw the wedge.

Polygon

Syntax:

```
BOOL Polygon(hDC, lpPoints, nCount)
```

Parameter, Type, and Description:

hDC	HDC	Device context
lpPoints	LPPOINT	Pointer to an array of POINT data structures
nCount	int	Number of points in lpPoints

Description:

The Polygon function creates an automatically closed polygon consisting of the points specified in lpPoints. lpPoints is a pointer to an array of data structures of type POINT. Each POINT data structure specifies a point in the polygon. The POINT structure is:

```
typedef struct tagPOINT {
     int x;
     int y;
} POINT;
```

where:

x specifies the horizontal coordinate of the point

y specifies the vertical coordinate of the point

nCount specifies the number of points in lpPoints. The function fills the resulting polygon by using the polygon-filling mode.

Return Value:

The Polygon function returns a nonzero value when the polygon is created. A return value of zero indicates that the function cannot create the polygon.

PolyPolygon

Syntax:

```
BOOL PolyPolygon(hDC, lpPoints, lpPolyCounts, nCount)
```

Parameter, Type, and Description:

hDC	HDC	Device context
lpPoints	LPPOINT	Pointer to an array of POINT data structures

`lpPolyCounts`	`LPINT`	Pointer to an array of integers
`nCount`	`int`	Number of integers in `lpPolyCounts`

Description:

The `PolyPolygon` function draws a series of closed polygons. The number of closed polygons is specified in `nCount`. The points for all of the polygons are contained in the array pointed to by `lpPoints`. Each point is specified in a `POINT` data structure. The `POINT` data structure is:

```
typedef struct tagPOINT {
     int x;
     int y;
} POINT;
```

where:

> `x` specifies the horizontal coordinate of the point
>
> `y` specifies the vertical coordinate of the point

`lpPolyCounts` points to an array of integers. Each integer represents the number of points from `lpPoints` used to create the closed polygon. The function fills each polygon by using the current polygon-filling mode. The polygons are not closed automatically.

Return Value:

The `PolyPolygon` function returns a nonzero value when the series of closed polygons is drawn. A return value of zero indicates that the function cannot draw the polygon series.

Rectangle

Syntax:

```
BOOL Rectangle(hDC, X1, Y1, X2, Y2)
```

Parameter, Type, and Description:

`hDC`	`HDC`	Device context
`X1`	`int`	X-coordinate of the upper-left corner of a rectangle
`Y1`	`int`	Y-coordinate of the upper-left corner of a rectangle
`X2`	`int`	X-coordinate of the lower-right corner of a rectangle
`Y2`	`int`	Y-coordinate of the lower-right corner of a rectangle

Description:

The `Rectangle` function creates a rectangle by using the logical coordinates in `X1`, `Y1`, `X2`, and `Y2`. The rectangle's border is drawn with the current pen. The function fills the rectangle by using the current brush.

Return Value:

The `Rectangle` function returns a nonzero value when it creates the rectangle. A return value of zero indicates that the function cannot create the rectangle.

RoundRect

Syntax:

```
BOOL RoundRect(hDC, X1, Y1, X2, Y2, X3, Y3)
```

Parameter, Type, and Description:

hDC	HDC	Device context
X1	int	X-coordinate of the upper-left corner of a rectangle
Y1	int	Y-coordinate of the upper-left corner of a rectangle
X2	int	X-coordinate of the lower-right corner of a rectangle
Y2	int	Y-coordinate of the lower-right corner of a rectangle
X3	int	Width of ellipse used to draw the rounded corners of a rectangle
Y3	int	Height of a ellipse used to draw the rounded corners of a rectangle

Description:

The `RoundRect` function creates a rounded rectangle. `X1`, `Y1` and `X2`, `Y2` specify the size of the rectangle. `X3` and `Y3` describe the shape and size of the rounded corners. The rectangle's border is drawn with the current pen. The function fills the rectangle by using the current brush.

Return Value:

The `RoundRect` function returns a nonzero value when the rounded rectangle is created. A return value of zero indicates that the function cannot create the rectangle.

Environment Functions

Environment functions either modify or retrieve information on the environment associated with an output device. The following functions are categorized as Environment functions for the Graphics Device Interface:

Function	*Meaning*
`GetEnvironment`	Places environment information in a buffer
`SetEnvironment`	Sets the environment associated with a device attached to a system port

The rest of this section provides detailed information on both of these functions.

GetEnvironment

Syntax:

```
int GetEnvironment(lpPortName, lpEnviron, nMaxCount)
```

Parameter, Type, and Description:

`lpPortName`	`LPSTR`	Pointer to the null-terminated string containing the name of the port
`lpEnviron`	`LPSTR`	Pointer to the buffer to receive environment information
`nMaxCount`	`WORD`	Maximum number of bytes to copy to the buffer

Description:

The `GetEnvironment` function places the environment associated with a device into the buffer pointed to by `lpEnviron`. The specified device is attached to the system port in `lpPortName`. `nMaxCount` specifies the maximum number of bytes to copy to the buffer.

Return Value:

The `GetEnvironment` function returns the number of bytes copied to `lpEnviron`. When `lpEnviron` is NULL, this function returns the size of the buffer required to store the environment. A return value of zero indicates that the function cannot place the environment into the buffer.

SetEnvironment

Syntax:

```
int SetEnvironment(lpPortName, lpEnviron, nCount)
```

Parameter, Type, and Description:

`lpPortName`	`LPSTR`	Pointer to the null-terminated string containing the name of the port
`lpEnviron`	`LPSTR`	Pointer to the buffer containing the new environment
`nCount`	`WORD`	Number of bytes to copy from the buffer

Description:

The `SetEnvironment` function copies the environment associated with a device into the contents of the buffer pointed to by `lpEnviron`. The device is attached to the system port specified in `lpPortName`. `nCount` specifies the number of bytes to copy from the buffer.

Return Value:

The `SetEnvironment` function returns the number of bytes copied from the buffer to the environment. A return value of zero indicates that the function cannot set the environment into the buffer. A return value of –1 indicates that the function deleted the environment.

Font Functions

A font is a set of characters that have the same basic typeface. A font family is a set of typefaces with similar characteristics. The Graphics Device Interface uses these six categories to distinguish typefaces and fonts:

Font Family	*Meaning*
`Dontcare`	Generic family name
`Decorative`	Novelty fonts
`Modern`	Constant stroke width, with or without serifs
`Roman`	Variable stroke width, with serifs
`Script`	Designed to appear as handwriting
`Swiss`	Variable stroke width, without serifs

The following functions are categorized as Font functions for the Graphics Device Interface:

Function	*Meaning*
`AddFontResource`	Adds a font resource to the system font table
`CreateFont`	Creates a logical font
`CreateFontIndirect`	Creates a logical font using information from a `LOGFONT` data structure
`EnumFonts`	Enumerates the available fonts
`GetAspectRatioFilter`	Gets the setting for the current aspect ratio filter
`GetCharWidth`	Gets the width of a character
`RemoveFontResource`	Removes a font resource from the font table
`SetMapperFlags`	Modifies the algorithm used by the font mapper

The rest of this section provides detailed information on each of the functions in this list.

AddFontResource

Syntax:

```
int AddFontResource(lpFilename)
```

Parameter, Type, and Description:

`lpFilename`	`LPSTR`	Specifies either a pointer to a character string containing the file name of the font resource file or the handle to a loaded module in the low-order word

Description:

The `AddFontResource` function adds the font resource from the file specified in `lpFilename` to the font table. Anytime a font is added or removed from the font table, all windows should be notified of the change. The `SendMessage` function is used to notify all top-level windows (set `hWnd` to –1 and send the `WM_FONTCHANGE` message).

Return Value:

The `AddFontResource` function returns the number of fonts added to the font table. Zero is returned if no fonts were loaded.

CreateFont

Syntax:

```
HFONT CreateFont(nHeight, nWidth, nEscapement, nOrientation, nWeight, cItalic,
                 cUnderline, cStrikeOut, cCharSet, cOutputPrecision,
                 cClipPrecision, cQuality, cPitchAndFamily, lpFacename)
```

Parameter, Type, and Description:

nHeight	int	Desired height of the font in logical units
nWidth	int	Average width of the characters in logical units
nEscapement	int	Angle of each line (measured in tenths of degrees) of text written in the font with respect to the bottom of the page
nOrientation	int	Angle of each character's baseline (in tenths of degrees) with respect to the bottom of the page
nWeight	int	Weight of the font, ranging from 0 to 1000
cItalic	BYTE	Indicates whether the font is italic
cUnderline	BYTE	Indicates whether the font is underlined
cStrikeOut	BYTE	Indicates whether the font uses strike out characters
cCharSet	BYTE	Specifies the character set
cOutputPrecision	BYTE	Specifies output precision
cClipPrecision	BYTE	Specifies the clipping precision
cQuality	BYTE	Specifies the output quality
cPitchAndFamily	BYTE	Specifies the pitch and family of the font
lpFacename	LPSTR	Pointer to a null-terminated character string containing the typeface name of the font

Description:

The `CreateFont` function creates a logical font with the characteristics specified in the various arguments. `nWeight` specifies the thickness, or weight, and must be in the range of 0 to 1000. `cCharSet` specifies the character set and can be any of the following:

ANSI_CHARSET

OEM_CHARSET

SYMBOL_CHARSET

cOutputPrecision specifies output precision and can be any of the following:

OUT_CHARACTER_PRECIS

OUT_DEFAULT_PRECIS

OUT_STRING_PRECIS

OUT_STROKE_PRECIS

cClipPrecision specifies the clipping precision and can be any of the following:

CLIP_CHARACTER_PRECIS

CLIP_DEFAULT_PRECIS

CLIP_STROKE_PRECIS

cQuality specifies the output quality and can be any of the following:

DEFAULT_QUALITY

DRAFT_QUALITY

PROOF_QUALITY

cPitchAndFamily specifies the pitch and family of the font. The two low-order bits define the pitch of the font and can be any of the following:

DEFAULT_PITCH

FIXED_PITCH

VARIABLE_PITCH

The four high-order bits define the font family and can be any of the following:

FF_DECORATIVE

FF_DONTCARE

FF_MODERN

FF_ROMAN

FF_SCRIPT

FF_SWISS

See “Text and Fonts” in Chapter 3, “The Graphic Device Interface,” for more details and examples.

Return Value:

The CreateFont function returns the handle of the created font. A NULL return value indicates that the function cannot create the font.

CreateFontIndirect

Syntax:

```
HFONT CreateFontIndirect(lpLogFont)
```

Parameter, Type, and Description:

`lpLogFont`	`LOGFONT FAR *`	Pointer to `LOGFONT` data structure containing the characteristics of the logical font

Description:

The `CreateFontIndirect` function creates a logical font that uses the font characteristics specified in the data structure of type `LOGFONT`, pointed to by `lpLogFont`. The `LOGFONT` structure is:

```
typedef struct tagLOGFONT {
     short int lfHeight;
     short int lfWidth;
     short int lfEscapement;
     short int lfOrientation;
     short int lfWeight;
     BYTE lfItalic;
     BYTE lfUnderline;
     BYTE lfStrikeOut;
     BYTE lfCharSet;
     BYTE lfOutPrecision;
     BYTE lfClipPrecision;
     BYTE lfQuality;
     BYTE lfPitchAndFamily;
     BYTE lfFaceName[LF_FACESIZE];
} LOGFONT;
```

where:

`lfHeight` is the average height of the font in user units

`lfWidth` is the average width of the characters in the font

`lfEscapement` is the angle between the escapement vector and the horizontal axis of the display, expressed in tenths of degrees

`lfOrientation` is the angle between the baseline of a character and the horizontal axis, expressed in tenths of degrees

`lfWeight` is the font weight and ranges from 0 to 1000

`lfItalic` indicates whether the font is italic (nonzero for italic)

`lfUnderline` indicates whether the font is underlined (nonzero for underline)

`lfStrikeOut` indicates whether the font is a strikeout font (nonzero for strikeout)

`lfCharSet` is the character set and can be any of the following:

ANSI_CHARSET

OEM_CHARSET

SYMBOL_CHARSET

`lfOutPrecision` is the output precision and can be any of the following:

OUT_CHARACTER_PRECIS

OUT_DEFAULT_PRECIS

OUT_STRING_PRECIS

OUT_STROKE_PRECIS

`lfClipPrecision` is the clipping precision and can be any of the following:

CLIP_CHARACTER_PRECIS

CLIP_DEFAULT_PRECIS

CLIP_STROKE_PRECIS

`lfQuality` is the output quality and can be any of the following:

DEFAULT_QUALITY

DRAFT_QUALITY

PROOF_QUALITY

`lfPitchAndFamily` is the font pitch and family. The two low-order bits define the pitch of the font and can be any of the following:

DEFAULT_PITCH

FIXED_PITCH

VARIABLE_PITCH

The four high-order bits define the font family and can be any of the following:

FF_DECORATIVE

FF_DONTCARE

FF_MODERN

FF_ROMAN

FF_SCRIPT

FF_SWISS

lpFaceName is a null-terminated character string containing the typeface

Return Value:

The CreateFontIndirect function returns the handle of the created font. A NULL return value indicates that the function cannot create the font.

EnumFonts

Syntax:

```
int EnumFonts(hDC, lpFacename, lpFontFunc, lpData)
```

Parameter, Type, and Description:

hDC	HDC	Device context
lpFacename	LPSTR	Pointer to a null-terminated character string containing the typeface name of the fonts
lpFontFunc	FARPROC	Procedure instance address of the callback function
lpData	LPSTR	Pointer to application-supplied data

Description:

The EnumFonts function enumerates the available fonts for the device specified in hDC. lpFacename contains the typeface name of the font. Information is retrieved for each font that has the specified typeface name. This retrieved information is passed to the callback function specified in lpFontFunc. The address specified in lpFontFunc is created with the MakeProcInstance function. The callback function must follow these conventions and formats:

Syntax:

```
int FAR PASCAL FontFunc(lpLogFont, lpTextMetrics, nFontType, lpData)
```

Parameter, Type, and Description:

lpLogFont	LPLOGFONT	Pointer to LOGFONT data structure that contains information on the logical font attributes
lpTestMetrics	LPTEXTMETRICS	Pointer to TEXTMETRIC data structure that contains information on the physical font attributes

`nFontType`	`short`	Font type
`lpData`	`LPSTR`	Pointer to the data supplied by the application

Description:

`FontFunc` is a placeholder for the function name supplied by the application. Use `EXPORTS` to include a `TEXTMETRIC` data structure containing the physical attributes of the font. `nFontType` is the font type. `lpData` is the pointer to the data passed by `EnumFonts`

Return Value:

The callback function returns an integer value.

Return Value:

The `EnumFonts` function returns the last value returned by the callback function.

GetAspectRatioFilter

Syntax:

```
DWORD GetAspectRatioFilter(hDC)
```

Parameter, Type, and Description:

`hDC`	`HDC`	Device context

Description:

The `GetAspectRatioFilter` function gets the setting of the current aspect ratio filter for the device specified in `hDC`.

Return Value:

The high-order word of the return value contains the x-coordinate of the aspect ratio used by the aspect ratio filter. The low-order word of the return value contains the y-coordinate.

GetCharWidth

Syntax:

```
BOOL GetCharWidth(hDC, wFirstChar, wLastChar, lpBuffer)
```

hDC	HDC	Device context
wFirstChar	WORD	First character
wLastChar	WORD	Last character
lpBuffer	LPINT	Pointer to the buffer to receive the widths of the characters

Description:

The GetCharWidth function determines the width of each of the characters from the group of consecutive characters specified by wFirstChar and wLastChar. The widths of each of the characters are stored in the buffer pointed to by lpBuffer.

Return Value:

The GetCharWidth function returns a nonzero value when the character widths are retrieved. A return value of zero indicates that the function cannot determine the width of the characters.

RemoveFontResource

Syntax:

```
BOOL RemoveFontResource(lpFilename)
```

Parameter, Type, and Description:

lpFilename	LPSTR	Specifies either a pointer to a character string containing the file name of the font resource file or the handle to a loaded module in the low-order word

Description:

The RemoveFontResource function removes the font resource specified by lpFilename from the font table. Anytime a font is added or removed from the font table, all windows should be notified of the change. The SendMessage function is used to notify all top-level windows (set hWnd to –1 and send the WM_FONTCHANGE message).

Return Value:

The RemoveFontResource function returns a nonzero value when the font resource is removed. A return value of zero indicates that the function cannot remove the font resource. Zero is returned if no fonts were loaded.

SetMapperFlags

Syntax:

```
DWORD SetMapperFlags(hDC, dwFlag)
```

Parameter, Type, and Description:

`hDC`	`HDC`	Device context containing the font-mapper flag
`dwFlag`	`DWORD`	Indicates whether the font mapper will try to match the aspect, height, and width for the font to the specified device

Description:

The `SetMapperFlags` function modifies the algorithm used by the font mapper. The algorithm is used to map logical fonts to physical fonts. `dwFlag` indicates whether the font mapper will try to match the aspect height and width for the font to the specified device:

- If the first bit of `dwFlag` is set to 1, only fonts with x-aspects and y-aspects that match the specified device are selected.
- If the first bit of `dwFlag` is set to 0, the font mapper does not attempt to match the aspect height and width for the font to the device.

Return Value:

The `SetMapperFlags` function returns the previous value of the font-mapper flag.

Line Output Functions

The Line Output functions provide fundamental line drawing capabilities. You can use these functions in applications to create graphics images such as bar charts, pie charts, or engineering drawings. The following functions are categorized as Line Output functions for the Graphics Device Interface:

Function	*Meaning*
`Arc`	Draws an arc
`LineDDA`	Calculates each point on a line
`LineTo`	Draws a line
`MoveTo`	Moves the current position to the specified point
`Polyline`	Draws a series of line segments

The rest of this section provides detailed information on each of the functions in this list.

Arc

Syntax:

```
BOOL Arc(hDC, X1, Y1, X2, Y2, X3, Y3, X4, Y4)
```

Parameter, Type, and Description:

`hDC`	`HDC`	Device context
`X1`	`int`	Logical x-coordinate of the upper-left corner of the bounding rectangle
`Y1`	`int`	Logical y-coordinate of the upper-left corner of the bounding rectangle
`X2`	`int`	Logical x-coordinate of the lower-right corner of the bounding rectangle
`Y2`	`int`	Logical y-coordinate of the lower-right corner of the bounding rectangle
`X3`	`int`	Logical x-coordinate of the starting point of the arc
`Y3`	`int`	Logical y-coordinate of the starting point of the arc
`X4`	`int`	Logical x-coordinate of the ending point of the arc
`Y4`	`int`	Logical y-coordinate of the ending point of the arc

Description:

The `Arc` function uses the current pen to draw an elliptical arc. The ellipse from which the arc is derived is defined by the bounding rectangle specified in `X1:Y1` and `X2:Y2`. The arc begins where the line segment that projects from the center of the ellipse to the point specified in `X3:Y3` intersects the ellipse. The arc then is drawn in a counterclockwise direction until it intercepts the line segment projected from the center of the ellipse to the point specified in `X4:Y4`.

Return Value:

The `Arc` function returns a nonzero value when the arc is drawn. A return value of zero indicates that the function cannot draw the arc.

LineDDA

Syntax:

```
void LineDDA(X1, Y1, X2, Y2, lpLineFunc, lpData)
```

Parameter, Type, and Description:

`X1`	`int`	Logical x-coordinate of the first endpoint of a line
`Y1`	`int`	Logical y-coordinate of the first endpoint of a line
`X2`	`int`	Logical x-coordinate of the second endpoint of a line
`Y2`	`int`	Logical y-coordinate of the second endpoint of a line
`lpLineFunc`	`FARPROC`	Procedure instance address of the callback function
`lpData`	`LPSTR`	Pointer to data supplied by the application

Description:

The `LineDDA` function calculates the points that make up the line between the specified endpoints `X1:Y1` and `X2:Y2`. `lpLineFunc` specifies the procedure instance address of the callback function supplied by the application. This address is created with the `MakeProcInstance` function. Each point on the line, except the end point, is passed to the callback function. `lpData` also is passed to the callback function. The callback function must follow these conventions and formats:

Syntax:

```
void FAR PASCAL LineFunc(X,Y,lpData)
```

Parameter, Type, and Description:

`X`	`int`	Logical x-coordinate of a point on the line
`Y`	`int`	Logical y-coordinate of a point on the line
`lpData`	`LPSTR`	Pointer to data supplied by the application

Description:

The callback function receives each point on the line, where `X` is the x-coordinate of the point and `Y` is the y-coordinate of the point. The callback function also receives any data supplied by the application; `lpData` points to the data.

Return Value:

There is no return value.

Return Value:

There is no return value.

LineTo

Syntax:

```
BOOL LineTo(hDC, X, Y)
```

Parameter, Type, and Description:

hDC	HDC	Device context
X	int	Logical x-coordinate of the endpoint
Y	int	Logical y-coordinate of the endpoint

Description:

The `LineTo` function draws a line from the current position to the point specified in `X:Y`. The point `X:Y` is not drawn. The current pen is used to draw the line. The current position is updated to the point specified in `X:Y` when the line is successfully drawn.

Return Value:

The `LineTo` function returns a nonzero value when the line is drawn. A return value of zero indicates that the function cannot draw the line.

MoveTo

Syntax:

```
DWORD MoveTo(hDC, X, Y)
```

Parameter, Type, and Description:

hDC	HDC	Device context
X	int	Logical x-coordinate of the point to move to
Y	int	Logical y-coordinate of the point to move to

Description:

The `MoveTo` function updates the current position to the point specified by `X:Y`. No drawing takes place as the current position is updated.

Return Value:

The low-order word of the return value contains the x-coordinate of the previous position. The high-order word of the return value contains the y-coordinate of the previous position.

Polyline

Syntax:

```
BOOL Polyline(hDC, lpPoints, nCount)
```

Parameter, Type, and Description:

hDC	HDC	Device context
lpPoints	LPPOINT	Pointer to an array of points to be connected by lines where each end point is a POINT data structure
nCount	int	Number of points in lpPoints

Description:

The Polyline function connects the points in the array pointed to by lpPoints with line segments. Each point in the array pointed to by lpPoints is defined with a data structure of type POINT. The POINT data structure is:

```
typedef struct tagPOINT {
     int x;
     int y;
} POINT;
```

where:

x specifies the horizontal coordinate of the point

y specifies the vertical coordinate of the point

The current pen is used to draw the line segments. The current position is not updated.

Return Value:

The Polyline function returns a nonzero value when it connects the points. A return value of zero indicates that function cannot connect the points.

Mapping Functions

The mapping mode specifies the relationship between units in logical space and the units for the device. The Graphics Device Interface operates with units in logical space. The use of logical space provides device independence. To create device-dependent coordinates, output to logical space is mapped to the device. Mapping functions control the Graphics Device Interface mapping modes. The following functions are categorized as Mapping functions for the Graphics Device Interface:

Function	*Meaning*
`GetMapMode`	Gets the current mapping mode
`GetViewportExt`	Gets the viewport extents for a device context
`GetViewportOrg`	Gets the viewport origin for a device context
`GetWindowExt`	Gets the window extents for a device context
`GetWindowOrg`	Gets the window origin for a device context
`OffsetViewportOrg`	Moves the viewport origin
`OffWindowOrg`	Moves the window origin
`ScaleViewportExt`	Alters the viewport extents
`ScaleWindowExt`	Alters the window extents
`SetMapMode`	Sets the mapping mode
`SetViewportExt`	Sets the viewport extents for a device context
`SetViewportOrg`	Sets the viewport origin for a device context
`SetWindowExt`	Sets the window extents for a device context
`SetWindowOrg`	Sets the window origin for a device context

The rest of this section provides detailed information on each of the functions in this list.

GetMapMode

Syntax:

```
int GetMapMode(hDC)
```

Parameter, Type, and Description:

`hDC` `HDC` Device context

Description:

The `GetMapMode` function gets the current mapping mode.

Return Value:

The `GetMapMode` function returns one of the following values representing the mapping mode:

Value	*Meaning*
`MM_ANISOTROPIC`	Logical units are mapped to arbitrary units with arbitrarily scaled axes
`MM_HIENGLISH`	Each logical unit is mapped to .001 inch; positive x is right, positive y is up

Value	*Meaning*
`MM_HIMETRIC`	Each logical unit is mapped to .01 millimeter; positive x is right, positive y is up
`MM_ISOTROPIC`	Logical units are mapped to arbitrary units with equally scaled axes
`MM_LOENGLISH`	Each logical unit is mapped to .01 inch; positive x is right, positive y is up
`MM_LOMETRIC`	Each logical unit is mapped to .1 millimeter; positive x is right, positive y is up
`MM_TEXT`	Each logical unit is mapped to one device pixel; positive x is right, positive y is down
`MM_TWIPS`	Each logical unit is mapped to one twentieth of a printer's point; positive x is right, positive y is up

GetViewportExt

Syntax:

```
DWORD GetViewportExt(hDC)
```

Parameter, Type, and Description:

`hDC`	`HDC`	Device context

Description:

The `GetViewportExt` function gets the width (x-extent) and height (y-extent) of the viewport for the device context specified in `hDC`. The retrieved extents are expressed in device units.

Return Value:

The low-order word of the return value contains the width (x-extent) of the viewport. The high-order word of the return value contains the height (y-extent) of the viewport.

GetViewportOrg

Syntax:

```
DWORD GetViewportOrg(hDC)
```

Parameter, Type, and Description:

`hDC`	`HDC`	Device context

Description:

The `GetViewportOrg` function gets the coordinates of the origin of the viewport for the device context specified in `hDC`.

Return Value:

The low-order word of the return value contains the x-coordinate of the viewport origin. The high-order word of the return value contains the y-coordinate of the viewport origin. The retrieved coordinates are expressed in device coordinates.

GetWindowExt

Syntax:

```
DWORD GetWindowExt(hDC)
```

Parameter, Type, and Description:

`hDC`	`HDC`	Device context

Description:

The `GetWindowExt` function gets the width (x-extent) and height (y-extent) of the window for the device context specified in `hDC`.

Return Value:

The low-order word of the return value contains the width (x-extent) of the window. The high-order word of the return value contains the height (y-extent) of the window. The retrieved extents are expressed in logical units.

GetWindowOrg

Syntax:

```
DWORD GetWindowOrg(hDC)
```

Parameter, Type, and Description:

`hDC`	`HDC`	Device context

Description:

The `GetWindowOrg` function gets the coordinates of the origin of the window for the device context specified in `hDC`.

Return Value:

The low-order word of the return value contains the x-coordinate of the window origin. The high-order word of the return value contains the y-coordinate of the window origin. The retrieved coordinates are expressed in logical coordinates.

OffsetViewportOrg

Syntax:

```
DWORD OffsetViewportOrg(hDC, X, Y)
```

Parameter, Type, and Description:

`hDC`	`HDC`	Device context
`X`	`int`	Offset in horizontal direction
`Y`	`int`	Offset in vertical direction

Description:

The `OffsetViewportOrg` function moves the origin of the viewport the amount specified by `X` and `Y`. The values in `X` and `Y` are added to the current viewport origin coordinates resulting in the new viewport origin position.

Return Value:

The low-order word of the return value contains the x-coordinate of the previous viewport origin. The high-order word of the return value contains the y-coordinate of the previous viewport origin. The retrieved coordinates are expressed in device units.

OffsetWindowOrg

Syntax:

```
DWORD OffsetWindowOrg(hDC, X, Y)
```

Parameter, Type, and Description:

`hDC`	`HDC`	Device context
`X`	`int`	Offset in horizontal direction
`Y`	`int`	Offset in vertical direction

Description:

The `OffsetWindowOrg` function moves the origin for the window of the device context specified in `hDC`. `X` and `Y` indicate the number of logical units that the origin will be moved. The values in `X` and `Y` are added to the coordinates of the current window origin, resulting in the new origin.

Return Value:

The low-order word of the return value specifies the x-coordinate of the previous window origin. The high-order word of the return value specifies the y-coordinate of the previous window origin.

ScaleViewportExt

Syntax:

```
DWORD ScaleViewportExt(hDC, Xnum, Xdenom, Ynum, Ydenom)
```

Parameter, Type, and Description:

`hDC`	`HDC`	Device context
`Xnum`	`int`	Numerator of the amount to scale the width (x-extent) of the viewport
`Xdenom`	`int`	Denominator of the amount to scale the width (x-extent) of the viewport
`Ynum`	`int`	Numerator of the amount to scale the height (y-extent) of the viewport
`Ydenom`	`int`	Denominator of the amount to scale the height (y-extent) of the viewport

Description:

The `ScaleViewportExt` function scales the width (x-extent) and height (y-extent) of the viewport for the device context specified in `hDC`. The width (x-extent) is multiplied by the fraction specified by `Xnum/Xdenom`. The height is multiplied by the fraction specified by `Ynum/Ydenom`.

Return Value:

The low-order word of the return value specifies the previous width (x-extent) of the viewport in device units. The high-order word of the return value specifies the previous height (y-extent) of the viewport in device units.

ScaleWindowExt

Syntax:

```
DWORD ScaleWindowExt(hDC, Xnum, Xdenom, Ynum, Ydenom)
```

Parameter, Type, and Description:

hDC	HDC	Device context
Xnum	int	Numerator of the amount to scale the width (x-extent) of the window
Xdenom	int	Denominator of the amount to scale the width (x-extent) of the window
Ynum	int	Numerator of the amount to scale the height (y-extent) of the window
Ydenom	int	Denominator of the amount to scale the height (y-extent) of the window

Description:

The `ScaleWindowExt` function scales the width (x-extent) and height (y-extent) of the window for the device context specified in `hDC`. The width (x-extent) is multiplied by the fraction specified by `Xnum/Xdenom`. The height is multiplied by the fraction specified by `Ynum/Ydenom`.

Return Value:

The low-order word of the return value specifies the previous width (x-extent) of the window in logical units. The high-order word of the return value specifies the previous height (y-extent) of the window in logical units.

SetMapMode

Syntax:

```
int SetMapMode(hDC, nMapMode)
```

Parameter, Type, and Description:

hDC	HDC	Device context
nMapMode	int	Mapping mode

Description:

The `SetMapMode` function defines the mapping mode for the device context specified in `hDC`. `nMapMode` specifies the mapping mode to set. The mapping mode is used to convert logical coordinates into device coordinates. The following values are used for the `nMapMode` function:

Value	*Meaning*
`MM_ANISOTROPIC`	Logical units are mapped to arbitrary units with arbitrarily scaled axes
`MM_HIENGLISH`	Each logical unit is mapped to .001 inch; positive x is right, positive y is up
`MM_HIMETRIC`	Each logical unit is mapped to .01 millimeter; positive x is right, positive y is up
`MM_ISOTROPIC`	Logical units are mapped to arbitrary units with equally scaled axes
`MM_LOENGLISH`	Each logical unit is mapped to .01 inch; positive x is right, positive y is up
`MM_LOMETRIC`	Each logical unit is mapped to .1 millimeter; positive x is right, positive y is up
`MM_TEXT`	Each logical unit is mapped to one device pixel; positive x is right, positive y is down
`MM_TWIPS`	Each logical unit is mapped to one twentieth of a printer's point; positive x is right, positive y is up

Return Value:

The `SetMapMode` function returns the previous mapping mode.

SetViewportExt

Syntax:

```
DWORD SetViewportExt(hDC, X, Y)
```

Parameter, Type, and Description:

`hDC`	`HDC`	Device context
`X`	`int`	Width (x-extent) of the viewport in device units
`Y`	`int`	Height (y-extent) of the viewport in device units

Description:

The `SetViewportExt` function defines the width (x-extent) and height (y-extent) of the viewport for the device context specified in `hDC`. `X` and `Y` specify the width

(x-extent) and height (y-extent) of the viewport, respectively. The call to the `SetViewportExt` function is ignored if any of the following mapping modes are set:

```
MM_HIENGLISH
MM_HIMETRIC
MM_LOENGLISH
MM_LOMETRIC
MM_TEXT
MM_TWIPS
```

See `SetMapMode` for a description of these mapping modes.

Return Value:

The low-order word of the return value contains the previous width (x-extent) of the viewport. The high-order word of the return value contains the previous height (y-extent) of the viewport. A return value of zero indicates that the function is unsuccessful.

SetViewportOrg

Syntax:

```
DWORD SetViewportOrg(hDC, X, Y)
```

Parameter, Type, and Description:

`hDC`	`HDC`	Device context
`X`	`int`	x-coordinate of the origin of the viewport in device coordinates
`Y`	`int`	y-coordinate of the origin of the viewport in device coordinates

Description:

The `SetViewportOrg` function sets the origin of the viewport for the device context specified in `hDC`. `X` and `Y` specify the horizontal and vertical device coordinates of the viewport origin, respectively.

Return Value:

The low-order word of the return value specifies the x device coordinate of the previous viewport origin. The high-order word of the return value specifies the y device coordinate of the previous viewport origin.

SetWindowExt

Syntax:

```
DWORD SetWindowExt(hDC, X, Y)
```

Parameter, Type, and Description:

hDC	HDC	Device context
X	int	Width (x-extent) of the window in logical units
Y	int	Height (y-extent) of the window in logical units

Description:

The SetWindowExt function defines the width (x-extent) and height (y-extent) of the window for the device context specified in hDC. X and Y specify the width (x-extent) and height (y-extent) of the window, respectively. If any of the following mapping modes are set, the call to the SetWindowExt function is ignored:

MM_HIENGLISH

MM_HIMETRIC

MM_LOENGLISH

MM_LOMETRIC

MM_TEXT

MM_TWIPS

See SetMapMode for a description of these mapping modes.

Return Value:

The low-order word of the return value contains the previous width (x-extent) of the window. The high-order word of the return value contains the previous height (y-extent) of the window. The return value is zero when the function is unsuccessful.

SetWindowOrg

Syntax:

```
DWORD SetWindowOrg(hDC, X, Y)
```

Parameter, Type, and Description:

hDC	HDC	Device context

`X`	`int`	X-coordinate of the origin of the window in logical coordinates
`Y`	`int`	Y-coordinate of the origin of the window in logical coordinates

Description:

The `SetWindowOrg` function sets the origin of the window for the device context specified in `hDC`. `X` and `Y` specify the horizontal and vertical logical coordinates of the window origin, respectively.

Return Value:

The low-order word of the return value specifies the logical x-coordinate of the previous window origin. The high-order word of the return value specifies the logical y-coordinate of the previous window origin.

Metafile Functions

A metafile is a series of Graphics Device Interface commands that create text or images. Because Graphics Device Interface commands are used to create the metafile, a metafile is device independent. Metafile functions create, delete, play, and manipulate metafiles. The following functions are categorized as Metafile functions for the Graphics Device Interface:

Function	*Meaning*
`CloseMetaFile`	Closes a metafile and creates a metafile handle
`CopyMetaFile`	Copies a metafile to a file
`CreateMetaFile`	Creates a metafile
`DeleteMetaFile`	Deletes a metafile
`EnumMetaFile`	Enumerates the Graphics Device Interface calls within the metafile
`GetMetaFile`	Creates a handle for a metafile
`GetMetaFileBits`	Retrieves and stores the bits of a metafile
`PlayMetaFile`	Plays the contents of a metafile
`PlayMetaFileRecord`	Plays a metafile record
`SetMetaFileBits`	Creates a memory metafile

The rest of this section provides detailed information on each of the functions in this list.

CloseMetaFile

Syntax:

```
HANDLE CloseMetaFile(hDC)
```

Parameter, Type, and Description:

`hDC`	`HANDLE`	Metafile device context to close

Description:

The `CloseMetaFile` function closes the metafile device context specified in `hDC` and creates a metafile handle. The metafile handle can be used to play the metafile.

Return Value:

The `CloseMetaFile` function returns the handle of the metafile. A NULL return value indicates that the function cannot close the metafile device context and create the metafile handle.

CopyMetaFile

Syntax:

```
HANDLE CopyMetaFile(hSrcMetaFile, lpFilename)
```

Parameter, Type, and Description:

`hSrcMetaFile`	`HANDLE`	Source metafile
`lpFilename`	`LPSTR`	Pointer to a null-terminated string that defines the file to receive the metafile

Description:

The `CopyMetaFile` function copies the metafile specified in `hSrcMetaFile` to the file specified in `lpFilename`. `lpFilename` can be set to NULL to indicate that the source metafile should be copied to a memory metafile.

Return Value:

The `CopyMetaFile` function returns the handle for the new metafile.

CreateMetaFile

Syntax:

```
HANDLE CreateMetaFile(lpFilename)
```

Parameter, Type, and Description:

`lpFilename`	`LPSTR`	Pointer to a null-terminated string that defines the name of the metafile

Description:

The `CreateMetaFile` function creates a metafile device context. `lpFilename` points to the string that defines the name of the metafile. `lpFilename` can be set to NULL to create a memory metafile.

Return Value:

The `CreateMetaFile` function returns the handle to the created metafile device context. A NULL return value indicates that the function cannot create the metafile device context.

DeleteMetaFile

Syntax:

```
BOOL DeleteMetaFile(hMF)
```

Parameter, Type, and Description:

`hMF`	`HANDLE`	Metafile to delete

Description:

The `DeleteMetaFile` function denies access to the metafile specified in `hMF`. The metafile is not destroyed; however, the handle to the metafile is no longer valid.

Return Value:

The `DeleteMetaFile` function returns a nonzero value when the metafile handle is no longer valid. A return value of zero indicates that the function cannot invalidate the handle.

EnumMetaFile

Syntax:

```
BOOL EnumMetaFile(hDC, hMF, lpCallbackFunc, lpClientData)
```

Parameter, Type, and Description:

hDC	HDC	Device context
hMF	LOCALHANDLE	Metafile
lpCallbackFunc	FARPROC	Procedure instance callback function
lpClientData	BYTE FAR *	Pointer to data passed to the callback function

Description:

The `EnumMetaFile` function enumerates the Graphics Device Interface calls within the metafile specified by `hMF`. Each Graphics Device Interface call is passed to the application-supplied callback function pointed to by `lpCallbackFunc`. The callback function must follow these conventions and formats:

Syntax:

```
int FAR PASCAL EnumFunc(hDC, lpHTable, lpMFR, nObj, lpClientData)
```

Parameter, Type, and Description:

hDC	HDC	Device context containing the metafile
lpHTable	LPHANDLETABLE	Pointer to the handle table associated with objects on the metafile
lpMFR	LPMETARECORD	Pointer to the metafile record contained in the metafile
nObj	int	Number of handles in the handle table
lpClientData	BYTE FAR *	Pointer to data supplied by the application

Description:

Each Graphics Device Interface call is passed to the application-supplied callback function. `hDC` is the device context containing the metafile. `lpHTable` is the table of handles associated with objects in the metafile. `lpMFR` points to a metafile record contained in the metafile. `nObj` is number of objects with handles in the handle table. `lpClientData` points to the data supplied by the application. `EnumFunc` is a placeholder for the function name supplied by the application. Use `EXPORTS` to include the actual name in the module definition file of the application.

Return Value:

The callback function returns a nonzero integer value to continue enumeration or a zero to stop enumeration.

Return Value:

The `EnumMetaFile` function returns a nonzero value if all the metafile's GDI calls are enumerated. Zero is returned if all the GDI calls could not be enumerated.

GetMetaFile

Syntax:

```
HANDLE GetMetaFile(lpFilename)
```

Parameter, Type, and Description:

`lpFilename`	`LPSTR`	Pointer to a null-terminated string containing the DOS filename of the metafile

Description:

The `GetMetaFile` function creates a handle for the metafile specified in `lpFilename`.

Return Value:

The `GetMetaFile` function returns the created handle of the metafile. A NULL return value indicates that the function cannot create a handle for the metafile.

GetMetaFileBits

Syntax:

```
HANDLE GetMetaFileBits(hMF)
```

Parameter, Type, and Description:

`hMF`	`HANDLE`	Memory metafile

Description:

The `GetMetaFileBits` function gets the handle of the global memory block containing the bits of the metafile specified in `hMF`.

Return Value:

The `GetMetaFileBits` function returns the handle to the global memory block. A NULL return value indicates that the function cannot get the handle of the global memory block.

PlayMetaFile

Syntax:

```
BOOL PlayMetaFile(hDC, hMF)
```

Parameter, Type, and Description:

`hDC`	`HDC`	Device context
`hMF`	`HANDLE`	Metafile

Description:

The `PlayMetaFile` function plays the metafile specified in `hMF` on the device specified in `hDC`.

Return Value:

The `PlayMetaFile` function returns a nonzero value when the metafile is played. A return value of zero indicates that the function cannot play the metafile.

PlayMetaFileRecord

Syntax:

```
void PlayMetaFileRecord(hDC, lpHandletable, lpMetaRecord, nHandles)
```

Parameter, Type, and Description:

`hDC`	`HDC`	Device context
`lpHandletable`	`LPHANDLETABLE`	Pointer to the handle table used for metafile playback
`lpMetaRecord`	`LPMETARECORD`	Pointer to the metafile to play
`nHandles`	`WORD`	Number of handles in the handle table

Description:

The `PlayMetaFileRecord` function plays the metafile record specified in `lpMetaRecord`. A metafile record contains a series of GDI function calls.

Return Value:

There is no return value.

SetMetaFileBits

Syntax:

```
HANDLE SetMetaFileBits(hMem)
```

Parameter, Type, and Description:

`hMem`	`HANDLE`	Global memory block containing the metafile data

Description:

The `SetMetaFileBits` function creates a memory metafile from the data in the global memory block specified in `hMem`.

Return Value:

The `SetMetaFileBits` function returns the handle of the created memory metafile. A NULL return value indicates that the function cannot create the memory metafile.

Printer Control Functions

Printer Control functions provide information on a printer and the printer device driver and modify the initialization state of the printer. The following functions are categorized as Printer Control functions for the Graphics Device Interface:

Function	*Meaning*
`DeviceCapabilities`	Gets the printer device driver capabilities
`DeviceMode`	Sets the printing modes
`Escape`	Enables an application to access a device that is not available through the Graphics Device Interface
`ExtDeviceMode`	Provides access to driver configurations and device initialization information

The rest of this section provides detailed information on each of the functions in this list.

DeviceCapabilities

Syntax:

```
DWORD DeviceCapabilities(lpDeviceName, lpPort, nIndex, lpOutput,
                         lpDevMode)
```

Parameter, Type, and Description:

lpDeviceName	LPSTR	Pointer to a null-terminated string containing the name of the printer device
lpPort	LPSTR	Pointer to a null-terminated string containing the name of the port where the device is connected
nIndex	WORD	Capabilities to query
lpOutput	LPSTR	Pointer to an array of bytes
lpDevMode	DEVMODE FAR *	Pointer to a DEVMODE data structure

Description:

The DeviceCapabilities function gets the capabilities of the printer device driver for the device specified in lpDeviceName. nIndex specifies the capabilities to query and is set to one of the following values:

Value	*Meaning*
DC_BINNAMES	Copies a structure identical to that returned by the ENUMPAPERBINS escape
DC_BINS	Gets a list of the available bins; the list of bins is copied into the array pointed to by lpOutput
DC_DRIVER	Gets the version of the printer driver
DC_DUPLEX	Returns 1 if the printer supports duplex printing, 0 if duplex printing is not supported
DC_EXTRA	Gets the number of bytes required for the device-specific part of the DEVMODE data structure for the printer driver
DC_FIELDS	Gets the dmFields field of the DEVMODE data structure for the printer driver
DC_MAXEXTENT	Returns the POINT data structure that contains the maximum paper size specified by the dmPaperLength and dmPaperWidth fields of the DEVMODE data structure for the printer driver
DC_MINEXTENT	Returns the POINT data structure that contains the mimimum paper size specified by the dmPaperLength and dmPaperWidth fields of the DEVMODE data structure for the printer driver

Value	Meaning
DC_PAPERS	Places a list of supported paper sizes in lpOutput
DC_PAPERSIZE	Places the dimensions of supported paper sizes (in tenths of a millimeter) into lpOutput; the dimensions are stored in POINT data structures
DC_SIZE	Gets the dmSize field of the DEVMODE data structure
DC_VERSION	Gets the specification version to which the printer driver conforms

The DEVMODE structure is used extensively with this function. The DEVMODE structure is:

```
typedef struct _devicemode {
    char dmDeviceName[32];
    WORD dmSpecVersion;
    WORD dmDriverVersion;
    WORD dmSize;
    WORD dmDriverExtra;
    DWORD dmFields;
    short dmOrientation;
    short dmPaperSize;
    short dmPaperLength;
    short dmPaperWidth;
    short dmScale;
    short dmCopies;
    short dmDefaultSource;
    short dmPrintQuality;
    short dmColor;
    short dmDuplex;
    BYTE dmDriverData[dmDriverExtra];
} DEVMODE;
```

where:

dmDeviceName is the name of the device the driver supports

dmSpecVersion is version number of the initialization date specificaton (0x300 for Windows 3.0)

dmDriverVersion is the printer driver version

dmSize is the size in bytes of the DEVMODE structure

dmDriverExtra is the size of the dmDriverData field and the length of the data in the DEVMODE structure

dmFields specifies the remaining fields in DEVMODE that have been initialized

dmOrientation is the paper orientation—either DMORIENT_PORTRAIT or DMORIENT_LANDSCAPE

dmPaperSize is the paper size and is one of the following values:

Value	*Meaning*
DMPAPER_LETTER	8.5 by 11 inch
DMPAPER_LEGAL	8.5 by 14 inch
DMPAPER_A4	210 by 297 millimeter
DMPAPER_CSHEET	17 by 22 inch
DMPAPER_DSHEET	22 by 34 inch
DMPAPER_ESHEET	34 by 44 inch
DMPAPER_ENV_9	#9 envelope
DMPAPER_ENV_10	#10 envelope
DMPAPER_ENV_11	#11 envelope
DMPAPER_ENV_12	#12 envelope
DMPAPER_ENV_14	#14 envelope

`dmPaperLength` overrides the paper length in `dmPaperSize`

`dmPaperWidth` overrides the paper width in `dmPaperSize`

`dmScale` scales the output

`dmCopies` is the number of copies to print

`dmDefaultSource` is the default paper bin and is selected from one of the following values:

Value	*Meaning*
DMBIN_DEFAULT	Default bin
DMBIN_UPPER	Upper bin
DMBIN_LOWER	Lower bin
DMBIN_MANUAL	Manual bin
DMBIN_TRACTOR	Tractor bin
DMBIN_ENVELOPE	Envelope bin

`dmPrintQuality` defines the printer resolution and is set to one of the following:

Value	*Meaning*
DMRES_HIGH	High resolution
DMRES_MEDIUM	Medium resolution
DMRES_LOW	Low resolution
DMRES_DRAFT	Draft resolution

`dmColor` switches between color and monochrome and is one of the following:

Value	*Meaning*
DMCOLOR_COLOR	Color printing
DMCOLOR_MONOCHROME	Monochrome printing

dmDuplex indicates double-sided (duplex) or single-sided (simplex) printing and is one of the following values:

Constant	*Value*
DMDUP_SIMPLEX	1
DMDUP_HORIZONTAL	2
DMDUP_VERTICAL	3

dmDriverData[] is data defined by the device driver

Return Value:

The return value depends on the setting of nIndex.

DeviceMode

Syntax:

```
void DeviceMode(hWnd, hModule, lpDeviceName, lpOutput)
```

Parameter, Type, and Description:

hWnd	HWND	Window to own the dialog box
hModule	HANDLE	Specifies the printer-driver module
lpDeviceName	LPSTR	Pointer to a null-terminated string containing the device name
lpOutput	LPSTR	Pointer to a null-terminated string containing the DOS file name or device name used for output

Description:

The DeviceMode function prompts the user to select a printing mode for the device specified in lpDeviceName. The selected mode is copied to the environment block associated with the device. This function is part of the printer's device driver. Use LoadLibrary to load the printer device driver, and GetProcAddress to retrieve the address of the function.

Return Value:

There is no return value.

Escape

Syntax:

```
int Escape(hDC, nEscape, nCount, lpInData, lpOutData)
```

Parameter, Type, and Description:

hDC	HDC	Device context
nEscape	int	Escape function
nCount	int	Number of bytes of data pointed to by lpInData
lpInData	LPSTR	Pointer to the input data structure required for the escape
lpOutData	LPSTR	Points to the data structure that receives output from the escape

Description:

The Escape function provides access to the facilities of the specified device that cannot be accessed through the Graphics Device Interface. nEscape specifies the escape function to generate. The escape functions are documented in *Microsoft Windows Programmer's Reference* by Microsoft Press.

Return Value:

The Escape function returns a positive value when the escape is implemented. A return value of zero indicates that the escape was not implemented. A negative return value indicates an error. Some possible error values are:

Value	*Meaning*
SP_ERROR	General error
SP_OUTOFDISK	Insufficient disk space
SP_OUTOFMEMORY	Insufficient memory
SP_USERABORT	Job terminated by user

ExtDeviceMode

Syntax:

```
int ExtDeviceMode(hWnd, hDriver, lpDevModeOutput, lpDeviceName,
                  lpPort, lpDevModeInput, lpProfile, wMode)
```

Parameter, Type, and Description:

hWnd	HWND	Window handle
hDriver	HANDLE	Device driver module
lpDevModeOutput	DEVMODE FAR *	Pointer to a DEVMODE data structure where the driver writes initialization information from lpDevModeInput
lpDeviceName	LPSTR	Pointer to a null-terminated string containing the printer device name
lpPort	LPSTR	Pointer to a null-terminated string containing the name of the port where the device is connected, such as LPT2:
lpDevModeInput	DEVMODE FAR *	Pointer to a DEVMODE data structure supplying initialization data to the printer driver
lpProfile	LPSTR	Pointer to a null-terminated string containing the name of the file holding initialization data
wMode	WORD	Mask of the values that specify the operations of the function

Description:

The ExtDeviceMode function does one of the following:

- Retrieves device initialization information for the printer driver
- Modifies device initialization information for the printer driver
- Displays a driver-supplied dialog box used for configuring the printer driver

wMode masks the values that specify the operations of the function and can be any combination of the following:

DM_COPY	Writes driver settings to DEVMODE structure pointed to by lpDevModeInput
DM_MODIFY	Modifies driver settings to initialization data in DEVMODE structure pointed to by lpDevModeInput
DM_PROMPT	Displays printer setup dialog box and enables the user to modify driver settings
DM_UPDATE	Writes driver settings to the printer and WIN.INI

This function is actually part of the printer's device driver. Before you can use this function, you must load the driver and use GetProcAddress to retrieve the address of the function. (See this chapter's description of GetProcAddress for more information.)

Return Value:

When the `ExtDeviceMode` function is successful the return value will be one of the following, depending on the stated condition:

- When `wMode` is zero, the return value is the size of the `DEVMODE` structure containing the driver initialization data.
- When the initialization dialog box is displayed, the return value is IDOK or IDCANCEL to indicate the button selected.
- When the dialog box is not displayed but is successful, the return value is IDOK.

A return value of less than zero is indicates that `ExtDeviceMode` was unsuccessful.

Region Functions

A region is an area used for output within a window. Region functions create and modify regions. These functions can be used with the Clipping functions, described earlier in this chapter, to create clipping regions. The following functions are categorized as Region functions for the Graphics Device Interface:

Function	*Meaning*
`CombineRgn`	Creates a new region by combining two regions
`CreateEllipticRgn`	Creates an elliptical region
`CreateEllipticRgnIndirect`	Creates an elliptical region by using a `RECT` data structure
`CreatePolygonRgn`	Creates a polygonal region
`CreatePolyPolygonRgn`	Creates a region made up of a series of closed, filled polygons
`CreateRectRgn`	Creates a rectangular region
`CreateRectRgnIndirect`	Creates a rectangular region by using a `RECT` data structure
`CreateRoundRectRegion`	Creates a rounded rectangular region
`EqualRgn`	Determines whether two regions are the same
`FillRgn`	Fills a region
`FrameRgn`	Draws a border around a region
`GetRgnBox`	Gets the coordinates of the rectangle bounding the region

Function	*Meaning*
`InvertRgn`	Inverts the colors in the region
`OffsetRgn`	Moves the region
`PaintRgn`	Fills the region by using the specified brush pattern
`PtInRegion`	Determines whether a point is in the region
`RecRegion`	Determines whether any part of the rectangle is in the region
`SetRectRgn`	Creates a rectangular region

The rest of this section provides detailed information on each of the functions in this list.

CombineRgn

Syntax:

```
int CombineRgn(hDestRgn, hSrcRgn1, hSrcRgn2, nCombineMode)
```

Parameter, Type, and Description:

`hDestRgn`	`HRGN`	Specifies the region to be replaced by the new region
`hSrcRgn1`	`HRGN`	Region to combine
`hSrcRgn2`	`HRGN`	Region to combine
`nCombineMode`	`int`	Method to use to combine the regions

Description:

The `CombineRgn` function combines the regions specified in `hSrcRgn1` and `hSrcRgn2` to form a new region. `hDestRgn` specifies the new region. `nCombinemode` specifies the method used to combine the regions and can be any one the following values:

Value	*Meaning*
`RGN_AND`	Uses the intersection of the regions
`RGN_COPY`	Creates a copy of `hSrcRgn1`
`RGN_DIFF`	Saves the areas of `hSrcRgn1` that are not part of `hSrcRgn2`
`RGN_OR`	Creates a union of both regions
`RGN_XOR`	Combines the regions but removes any overlapping areas

Return Value:

The `CombineRgn` function returns one of the following values representing the type of region created:

Value	*Meaning*
COMPLEXREGION	New region has overlapping borders
ERROR	No region was created
NULLREGION	New region is empty
SIMPLEREGION	New region has no overlapping borders

CreateEllipticRgn

Syntax:

```
HRGN CreateEllipticRgn(X1, Y1, X2, Y2)
```

Parameter, Type, and Description:

X1	int	X-coordinate of the upper-left corner of the bounding rectangle
Y1	int	Y-coordinate of the upper-left corner of the bounding rectangle
X2	int	X-coordinate of the lower-right corner of the bounding rectangle
Y2	int	Y-coordinate of the lower- right corner of the bounding rectangle

Description:

The `CreateEllipticRgn` function creates an elliptical region within the bounding rectangle specified by `X1`, `Y1`, `X2`, and `Y2`.

Return Value:

The `CreateEllipticRgn` function returns the handle of the created region. A NULL return value indicates that the function cannot create the region.

CreateEllipticRgnIndirect

Syntax:

```
HRGN CreateEllipticRgnIndirect(lpRect)
```

Parameter, Type, and Description:

lpRect	LPRECT	Pointer to a `RECT` data structure containing the coordinates of the bounding rectangle

Description:

The `CreateEllipticRgnIndirect` function creates an elliptical region within the bounding rectangle specified by the coordinates in the data structure of type `RECT` pointed to by `lpRect`. The `RECT` data structure is:

```
typedef struct tagRECT{
     int left;
     int top;
     int right;
     int bottom;
} RECT;
```

where:

`left` is the x-coordinate of the upper-left corner

`top` is the y-coordinate of the upper-left corner

`right` is the x-coordinate of the lower-right corner

`bottom` is the y-coordinate of the lower-right corner

Return Value:

The `CreateEllipticRgnIndirect` function returns the handle to the created region. A NULL return value indicates that the function cannot create the region.

CreatePolygonRgn

Syntax:

```
HRGN CreatePolygonRgn(lpPoints, nCount, nPolyFillMode)
```

Parameter, Type, and Description:

`lpPoints`	`LPPOINT`	Pointer to an array of `POINT` data structures where each data structure specifies a point on the polygon
`nCount`	`int`	Number of points in the array
`nPolyFillMode`	`int`	Polygon-filling mode

Description:

The `CreatePolygonRgn` function creates a polygonal region by using the points specified in `lpPoints`. Each point in `lpPoints` is specified with a data structure of type `POINT`. The `POINT` data structure is:

```
typedef struct tagPOINT {
     int x;
     int y;
} POINT;
```

where

`x` specifies the horizontal coordinate of the point

`y` specifies the vertical coordinate of the point

`nPolyFillMode` is the polygon-filling mode and can be either of the following:

Mode	*Meaning*
`ALTERNATE`	Alternate mode
`WINDING`	Winding number mode

Return Value:

The `CreatePolygonRgn` function returns the handle to the created region. A NULL return value indicates that the function cannot create the region.

CreatePolyPolygonRgn

Syntax:

```
HRGN CreatePolyPolygonRgn(lpPoints, lpPolyCounts, nCount,
                          nPolyFillMode)
```

Parameter, Type, and Description:

`lpPoints`	`LPPOINT`	Pointer to an array of `POINT` data structures that define the points in the polygons
`lpPolyCounts`	`LPINT`	Pointer to an array of integers that define the number of points from `lpPoints` used for each of the polygons
`nCount`	`int`	Total number of integer values in the `lpPolyCounts` array
`nPolyFillMode`	`int`	Polygon-filling mode

Description:

The `CreatePolyPolygonRgn` function creates a region that is made up of a series of closed, filled polygons. `lpPoints` is a pointer to an array of `POINT` data structures. These `POINT` data structures contain the individual points for the polygons. The `POINT` data structure is:

```
typedef struct tagPOINT {
     int x;
     int y;
} POINT;
```

where:

`x` specifies the horizontal coordinate of the point

`y` specifies the vertical coordinate of the point

The number of points from `lpPoints` required to create each polygon is contained in the array pointed to by `lpPolyCounts`. The number of polygons to draw is specified in `nCount`. `nPolyFillMode` is the polygon-filling mode and can be either of the following:

Mode	*Meaning*
`ALTERNATE`	Alternate mode
`WINDING`	Winding number mode

Return Value:

The `CreatePolyPolygonRgn` function returns the handle to the created region. A NULL return value indicates that the function cannot create the region.

CreateRectRgn

Syntax:

```
HRGN CreateRectRgn(X1, Y1, X2, Y2)
```

Parameter, Type, and Description:

`X1`	`int`	X-coordinate of the upper-left corner of the region
`Y1`	`int`	Y-coordinate of the upper-left corner of the region
`X2`	`int`	X-coordinate of the lower-right corner of the region
`Y2`	`int`	Y-coordinate of the lower-right corner of the region

Description:

The `CreateRectRgn` function creates a rectangular region by using the coordinates specified in `X1`, `Y1`, `X2`, and `Y2`. Both the width and height of the region are limited to 32,767 words.

Return Value:

The `CreateRectRgn` function returns the handle to the created region. A NULL return value indicates that the function cannot create the region.

CreateRectRgnIndirect

Syntax:

```
HRGN CreateRectRgnIndirect(lpRect)
```

Parameter, Type, and Description:

lpRect	LPRECT	Pointer to a RECT data structure containing the coordinates of the rectangular region

Description:

The CreateRectRgnIndirect function creates a rectangular region by using the coordinates in the data structure of type RECT pointed to by lpRect. The RECT data structure is:

```
typedef struct tagRECT{
     int left;
     int top;
     int right;
     int bottom;
} RECT;
```

where:

left is the x-coordinate of the upper-left corner

top is the y-coordinate of the upper-left corner

right is the x-coordinate of the lower-right corner

bottom is the y-coordinate of the lower-right corner

Both the width and height of the region are limited to 32,767 words.

Return Value:

The CreateRectRgnIndirect function returns the handle to the created region. A NULL return value indicates that the function cannot create the region.

CreateRoundRectRgn

Syntax:

```
HRGN CreateRoundRectRgn(X1, Y1, X2, Y2, X3, Y3)
```

Parameter, Type, and Description:

X1	int	X-coordinate of the upper-left corner of a rectangular region
Y1	int	Y-coordinate of the upper-left corner of a rectangular region

X2	int	X-coordinate of the lower-right corner of a rectangular region
Y2	int	Y-coordinate of the lower-right corner of a rectangular region
X3	int	Width of an ellipse used to create the rounded corners
Y3	int	Height of an ellipse used to create the rounded corners

Description:

The `CreateRoundRectRgn` function creates a rounded, rectangular region. `X1:Y1` specify the coordinates of the upper-left corner of the rectangular region. `X2:Y2` specify the coordinates of the lower-right corner of the rectangular region. `X3:Y3` specify the shape of the rounded corners of the rounded, rectangular region. Both the width and height of the region are limited to 32,767 words.

Return Value:

The `CreateRoundRectRgn` function returns the handle to the created region. A NULL return value indicates that the function cannot create the region.

EqualRgn

Syntax:

```
BOOL EqualRgn(hSrcRgn1, hSrcRgn2)
```

Parameter, Type, and Description:

hSrcRgn1	HRGN	First region
hSrcRgn2	HRGN	Second region

Description:

The `EqualRgn` function determines whether the regions specified in `hSrcRgn1` and `hSrcRgn2` are identical.

Return Value:

The `EqualRgn` function returns a nonzero value when the regions are identical. A return value of zero indicates that the regions are not identical.

FillRgn

Syntax:

```
BOOL FillRgn(hDC, hRgn, hBrush)
```

Parameter, Type, and Description:

`hDC`	`HDC`	Device context
`hRgn`	`HRGN`	Region to fill
`hBrush`	`HBRUSH`	Brush to use for filling the region

Description:

The `FillRgn` function fills the region in `hRgn` by using the brush specified in `hBrush`. The coordinates for the region in `hRgn` are device coordinates.

Return Value:

The `FillRgn` function returns a nonzero value when the region is filled. A return value of zero indicates that the function cannot fill the region as specifed.

FrameRgn

Syntax:

```
BOOL FrameRgn(hDC, hRgn, hBrush, nWidth, nHeight)
```

Parameter, Type, and Description:

`hDC`	`HDC`	Device context
`hRgn`	`HANDLE`	Specifies the region to frame
`hBrush`	`HBRUSH`	Brush to use to draw the border
`nWidth`	`int`	Width of the border in vertical brush strokes (logical units)
`nHeight`	`int`	Height of the border in horizontal brush strokes (logical units)

Description:

The `FrameRgn` function frames the region in `hRgn` with a border. The border is drawn with the brush specified in `hBrush`. `nWidth` and `nHeight` specify the width and height of the border, respectively.

Return Value:

The `FrameRgn` function returns a nonzero value when the region is framed. A return value of zero indicates that the function cannot frame the region.

GetRgnBox

Syntax:

```
int GetRgnBox(hRgn, lpRect)
```

Parameter, Type, and Description:

hRgn	HRGN	Region
lpRect	LPRECT	Pointer to a RECT data structure that stores the coordinates of the bounding rectangle of the region

Description:

The GetRgnBox function gets the coordinates of the rectangle that bounds the region specified in hRgn. The coordinates of the bounding rectangle are placed in the data structure of type RECT pointed to by lpRect. The RECT data structure is:

```
typedef struct tagRECT{
     int left;
     int top;
     int right;
     int bottom;
} RECT;
```

where:

left is the x-coordinate of the upper-left corner

top is the y-coordinate of the upper-left corner

right is the x-coordinate of the lower-right corner

bottom is the y-coordinate of the lower-right corner

Return Value:

The GetRgnBox function returns one of the following values representing the region's type:

Value	*Meaning*
COMPLEXREGION	New region has overlapping borders
NULLREGION	New region is empty
SIMPLEREGION	New region has no overlapping borders

InvertRgn

Syntax:

```
BOOL InvertRgn(hDC, hRgn)
```

Parameter, Type, and Description:

hDC	HDC	Device context
hRgn	HRGN	Region to fill

Description:

The `InvertRgn` function inverts all the colors inside the region specified by `hRgn`.

Return Value:

The `InvertRgn` function returns a nonzero value when the colors are inverted. A return value of zero indicates that the function cannot invert the colors.

OffsetRgn

Syntax:

```
int OffsetRgn(hRgn, X, Y)
```

Parameter, Type, and Description:

hRgn	HRGN	Region to move
X	int	Amount to move in the horizontal direction
Y	int	Amount to move in the vertical direction

Description:

The `OffsetRgn` function moves the region specified in `hRgn` the amounts specified in `X` and `Y`.

Return Value:

The `OffsetRgn` function returns one of the following values representing the region's type:

Value	*Meaning*
COMPLEXREGION	New region has overlapping borders
ERROR	No region was created
NULLREGION	New region is empty
SIMPLEREGION	New region has no overlapping borders

PaintRgn

Syntax:

```
BOOL PaintRgn(hDC, hRgn)
```

Parameter, Type, and Description:

`hDC`	`HDC`	Device context
`hRgn`	`HRGN`	Region to paint

Description:

The `PaintRgn` function paints the region specified in `hRgn`. The selected brush is used to fill the region.

Return Value:

The `PaintRgn` function returns a nonzero value when the region is painted. A return value of zero indicates that the function cannot paint the region.

PtInRegion

Syntax:

```
BOOL PtInRegion(hRgn, X, Y)
```

Parameter, Type, and Description:

`hRgn`	`HRGN`	Region
`X`	`int`	Logical x-coordinate of the point to check
`Y`	`int`	Logical y-coordinate of the point to check

Description:

The `PtInRegion` function determines whether the point specified by `X:Y` lies within the region specified in `hRgn`.

Return Value:

The `PtInRegion` function returns a nonzero value if the point lies within the specified region. A return value of zero indicates that the point does not lie within the specified region.

RectInRegion

Syntax:

```
BOOL RectInRegion(hRegion, lpRect)
```

Parameter, Type, and Description:

`hRegion`	`HRGN`	Region
`lpRect`	`LPRECT`	Pointer to a data structure of type `RECT` containing the coordinates of the rectangle to check

Description:

The `RectInRegion` function determines whether any part of the rectangle specified in `lpRect` lies within the region specified in `hRegion`. `lpRect` points to a data structure of type `RECT` that contains the coordinates of the rectangle. The `RECT` data structure is:

```
typedef struct tagRECT{
     int left;
     int top;
     int right;
     int bottom;
} RECT;
```

where:

`left` is the x-coordinate of the upper-left corner

`top` is the y-coordinate of the upper-left corner

`right` is the x-coordinate of the lower-right corner

`bottom` is the y-coordinate of the lower-right corner

Return Value:

The `RectInRegion` function returns TRUE if any part of the rectangle lies within the region. A return value of FALSE indicates that no part of the rectangle lies within the region.

SetRectRgn

Syntax:

```
void SetRectRgn(hRgn, X1, Y1, X2, Y2)
```

Parameter, Type, and Description:

hRgn	HANDLE	Region
X1	int	X-coordinate of the upper-left corner of a rectangular region
Y1	int	Y-coordinate of the upper-left corner of a rectangular region
X2	int	X-coordinate of the lower-right corner of a rectangular region
Y2	int	Y-coordinate of the lower-right corner of rectangular region

Description:

The `SetRectRgn` function creates a rectangular region but does not call the local memory manager, as the `CreateRectRegion` function does. The space allocated to the region specified by `hRgn` is used by the `SetRectRgn` function.

Return Value:

There is no return value.

Text Functions

The Graphics Device Interface uses the Text functions for text output and manipulation. The selected font also is used by the Graphics Device Interface for text output. The following functions are categorized as Text functions for the Graphics Device Interface:

Function	*Meaning*
`ExtTextOut`	Writes a character string, using the specified font, inside a rectangular region
`GetTabbedTextExtent`	Determines the width and height of a line of text that contains tab characters
`GetTextAlign`	Gets a mask of text alignment flags
`GetTextCharacterExtra`	Gets the current intercharacter spacing
`GetTextExtent`	Determines the width and height of text while considering the current font
`GetTextFace`	Copies the font name to a buffer
`GetTextMetrics`	Copies the metrics for a font to a buffer
`SetTextAlign`	Positions text on the display or device
`SetTextCharacterExtra`	Sets intercharacter spacing
`SetTextJustification`	Sets the text line justification

Function	*Meaning*
`TabbedTextOut`	Writes a string, using the specified font, with expanded tabs
`TextOut`	Writes a character string using the current font

The rest of this section provides detailed information on each of the functions in this list.

ExtTextOut

Syntax:

```
BOOL ExtTextOut(hDC, X, Y, wOptions, lpRect, lpString, nCount, lpDx)
```

Parameter, Type, and Description:

`hDC`	`HDC`	Device context
`X`	`int`	Logical x-coordinate of the character cell for the first character in the string
`Y`	`int`	Logical y-coordinate of the character cell for the first character in the string
`wOptions`	`WORD`	Specifies the rectangle type
`lpRect`	`LPRECT`	Pointer to a `RECT` data structure containing the coordinates that define the rectangle
`lpString`	`LPSTR`	Pointer to the character string
`nCount`	`int`	Number of characters in the string
`lpDx`	`LPINT`	Pointer to an array of values specifying the distance between character cells

Description:

The `ExtTextOut` function displays the character string specified in `lpString`, using the current font, inside the rectangle specified by `lpRect`. `wOptions` specifies the rectangle type and can be either or both of the following values:

Function	*Meaning*
`ETO_CLIPPED`	Clip the text at the rectangle's border
`ETO_OPAQUE`	Fill the rectangle with the background color

`X`, `Y`, and `lpDx` provide information used to display the text string.

Return Value:

The `ExtTextOut` function returns a nonzero value when the string is drawn successfully. A return value of zero indicates that the function cannot draw the string.

GetTabbedTextExtent

Syntax:

```
DWORD GetTabbedTextExtent(hDC, lpString, nCount, nTabPositions,
                          lpnTabStopPositions)
```

Parameter, Type, and Description:

`hDC`	`HDC`	Device context
`lpString`	`LPSTR`	Pointer to the text string
`nCount`	`int`	Number of characters in `lpString`
`nTabPositions`	`int`	Number of tab positions in the array specified in `lpnTabStopPositions`
`lpnTabStopPositions`	`LPINT`	Pointer to an array of integers specifying the tab stop positions in pixels

Description:

The `GetTabbedTextExtent` function determines the width and height (in logical units) of the text string specified in `lpString`. The current font is used when calculating the width and height of the string.

Return Value:

The low-order word of the return value contains the calculated width. The high-order word of the return value contains the calculated height.

GetTextAlign

Syntax:

```
WORD GetTextAlign(hDC)
```

Parameter, Type, and Description:

`hDC`	`HDC`	Device context

Description:

The `GetTextAlign` function gets the status of the text alignment flags for the device context specified in `hDC`.

Return Value:

The `GetTextAlign` function returns a combination of one or more of the following values representing the status of the text alignment flags:

Value	*Meaning*
TA_BASELINE	Alignment of x-axis and baseline of font within the bounding rectangle
TA_BOTTOM	Alignment of x-axis and bottom of bounding rectangle
TA_CENTER	Alignment of y-axis and center of bounding rectangle
TA_LEFT	Alignment of y-axis and left side of bounding rectangle
TA_NOUPDATECP	Current position is not updated
TA_RIGHT	Alignment of y-axis and right side of bounding rectangle
TA_TOP	Alignment of x-axis and top of bounding rectangle
TA_UPDATECP	Current position is updated

GetTextCharacterExtra

Syntax:

```
int GetTextCharacterExtra(hDC)
```

Parameter, Type, and Description:

hDC	HDC	Device context

Description:

The `GetTextCharacterExtra` function gets the intercharacter spacing used by the `TextOut` or `ExtTextOut` functions.

Return Value:

The `GetTextCharacterExtra` function returns the current intercharacter spacing.

GetTextExtent

Syntax:

```
DWORD GetTextExtent(hDC, lpString, nCount)
```

Parameter, Type, and Description:

`hDC`	`HDC`	Device context
`lpString`	`LPSTR`	Pointer to the text string
`nCount`	`int`	Number of characters in the string

Description:

The `GetTextExtent` function determines the width and height (in logical units) of the string specified by `lpString`. The current font is used when calculating the width and height of the string.

Return Value:

The low-order word of the return value contains the width of the string. The high-order word of the return value contains the height of the string.

GetTextFace

Syntax:

```
int GetTextFace(hDC, nCount, lpFacename)
```

Parameter, Type, and Description:

`hDC`	`HDC`	Device context
`nCount`	`int`	Size of buffer in bytes
`lpFacename`	`LPSTR`	Pointer to the buffer to receive the typeface name

Description:

The `GetTextFace` function gets the typeface name of the current font and places the name into the buffer pointed to by `lpFacename`. `nCount` specifies the maximum number of bytes to copy to the buffer.

Return Value:

The `GetTextFace` function returns the number of bytes copied to the buffer. A return value of zero indicates that the function cannot place the typeface name into the buffer.

GetTextMetrics

Syntax:

```
BOOL GetTextMetrics(hDC, lpMetrics)
```

Parameter, Type, and Description:

hDC	HDC	Device context
lpMetrics	LPTEXTMETRIC	Pointer to a TEXTMETRIC data structure that receives the text metrics

Description:

The `GetTextMetrics` function retrieves the metrics for the selected font and places these metrics in the data structure of type `TEXTMETRIC`, pointed to by `lpMetrics`. The `TEXTMETRIC` structure is:

```
typedef struct tagTEXTMETRIC {
     short int tmHeight;
     short int tmAscent;
     short int tmDescent;
     short int tmInternalLeading;
     short int tmExternalLeading;
     short int tmAveCharWidth;
     short int tmMaxCharWidth;
     short int tmWeight
     BYTE tmItalic;
     BYTE tmUnderlined;
     BYTE tmStruckOut;
     BYTE tmFirstChar;
     BYTE tmLastChar;
     BYTE tmDefaultChar;
     BYTE tmBreakChar;
     BYTE tmPitchAndFamily;
     BYTE tmCharSet;
     short int tmOverhang;
     short int tmDigitizedAspectX;
     short int tmDigitizedAspectY;
} TEXTMETRIC;
```

where:

`tmHeight` is the character height

`tmAscent` is the character ascent (units above baseline)

`tmDescent` is the character descent (units below baseline)

`tmInternalLeading` is the amount of space at the top of the character height specified by `tmHeight`

`tmExternalLeading` is the amount of space added between rows

`tmAveCharWidth` is the average character width

`mMaxCharWidth` is the width of the widest character

`tmWeight` is the font weight

`tmItalic` is nonzero if the font is italic

`tmUnderlined` is nonzero if the font is underlined

`tmStruckOut` is nonzero if the font is struck out

`tmFirstChar` is first character defined for the font

`tmLastChar` is the last character defined for the font

`tmDefaultChar` is the character substituted for characters not in the font

`tmBreakChar` is the character used for word breaks

`tmPitchAndFamily` is the pitch (low-order bit) and family (four high-order bits) of the font

`tmCharSet` is the character set for the font

`tmOverhang` is the extra width added to some synthesized fonts

`tmDigitizedAspectX` is the horizontal aspect of the device the font was designed for

`tmDigitizedAspectY` is the vertical aspect of the device the font was designed for

Return Value:

The `GetTextMetrics` function returns a nonzero value when the metrics are placed in the data structure. A return value of zero indicates that the function cannot place the metrics in the data structure.

SetTextAlign

Syntax:

```
WORD SetTextAlign(hDC, wFlags)
```

Parameter, Type, and Description:

`hDC`	`HDC`	Device context
`wFlags`	`WORD`	Specifies the text alignment

Description:

The `SetTextAlign` function sets the text alignment flags for the device context specified in `hDC` to the mask of values specified in `wFlags`. `wFlags` is a combination of the following values:

Value	*Meaning*
TA_BASELINE	Alignment of x-axis and baseline of font within the bounding rectangle
TA_BOTTOM	Alignment of x-axis and bottom of bounding rectangle
TA_CENTER	Alignment of y-axis and center of bounding rectangle
TA_LEFT	Alignment of y-axis and left side of bounding rectangle
TA_NOUPDATECP	Current position is not updated
TA_RIGHT	Alignment of y-axis and right side of bounding rectangle
TA_TOP	Alignment of x-axis and top of bounding rectangle
TA_UPDATECP	Current position is updated

Return Value:

The low-order word of the return value specifies the previous horizontal alignment. The high-order word of the return value specifies the previous vertical alignment.

SetTextCharacterExtra

Syntax:

```
int SetTextCharacterExtra(hDC, nCharExtra)
```

Parameter, Type, and Description:

hDC	HDC	Device context
nCharExtra	int	Extra space added to each character in logical units

Description:

The `SetTextCharacterExtra` function sets the amount of intercharacter spacing for the device in `hDC` to the amount specified in `nCharExtra`.

Return Value:

The `SetTextCharacterExtra` function returns the previous amount of intercharacter spacing.

SetTextJustification

Syntax:

```
int SetTextJustification(hDC, nBreakExtra, nBreakCount)
```

Parameter, Type, and Description:

hDC	HDC	Device context
nBreakExtra	int	Total extra space in logical units
nBreakCount	int	Number of break characters in the line

Description:

The `SetTextJustification` function tells the Graphics Device Interface how to justify a line a text. `nBreakExtra` and `nBreakCount` specify the justification parameters. The `SetTextJustification` function is used with the `GetTextExtent` function. The text width calculated with `GetTextExtent` is needed to determine the `nBreakExtra` value.

Return Value:

The `SetTextJustification` function returns a 1 when the text line justification is set. A return value of zero indicates that the function cannot set justification.

TabbedTextOut

Syntax:

```
long TabbedTextOut(hDC, X, Y, lpString, nCount, nTabPositions,
                   lpnTabStopPositions, nTabOrigin)
```

Parameter, Type, and Description:

hDC	HDC	Device context
X	int	Logical x-coordinate of the starting point for the string
Y	int	Logical y-coordinate of the starting point for the string
lpString	LPSTR	Pointer to the character string
nCount	int	Number of characters in `lpString`
nTabPositions	int	Number of tab stop positions in `lpnTabStopPositions`

`lpnTabStopPositions`	`LPINT`	Pointer to an array of integers that specify the tab stop positions in pixels
`nTabOrigin`	`int`	Logical x-coordinate of the starting position where tabs are expanded

Description:

The `TabbedTextOut` function displays the character string specified in `lpString` by using the current font and expanding tabs to columns as specified in `lpnTabStopPositions`.

Return Value:

The low-order word of the return value specifies the width of the displayed string. The high-order word of the return value specifies the height of the displayed string.

TextOut

Syntax:

```
BOOL TextOut(hDC, X, Y, lpString, nCount)
```

Parameter, Type, and Description:

`hDC`	`HDC`	Device context
`X`	`int`	Logical x-coordinate of the text starting point
`Y`	`int`	Logical y-coordinate of the text starting point
`lpString`	`LPSTR`	Pointer to the character string to draw
`nCount`	`int`	Number of characters in `lpString`

Description:

The `TextOut` function displays the character string specified in `lpString` using the current font. `X` and `Y` specify the logical coordinates of the starting point for the text.

Return Value:

The `TextOut` function returns a nonzero value when the string is drawn successfully. A return value of zero indicates that the function cannot draw the string.

System Services Interface Functions

The System Services Interface Functions provide a wide range of capabilities, including memory, module, resource, atom, and segment management. These functions also perform communications, sound, file input/output, operating system, and debugging operations. The System Services Interface functions are divided into the following subcategories:

Application Execution functions
Atom Management functions
Communication functions
Debugging functions
File I/O functions
Initialization functions
Memory Management functions
Module Management functions
Operating System Interrupt functions
Optimization Tool functions
Resource Management functions
Segment functions
Sound functions
String Manipulation functions
Task functions
Utility macros and functions

Application Execution Functions

Windows provides Application Execution functions so that one application can execute another application. The following functions are categorized as Application Execution functions for the System Services Interface:

Function	*Meaning*
`LoadModule`	Executes a Windows application and uses a DOS function 4BH, Code 00H, parameter block
`WinExec`	Executes a Windows or DOS application and specifies command parameters and the initial state of the application window
`WinHelp`	Executes the Windows Help application

The rest of this section provides detailed information on each of the functions in this list.

LoadModule

Syntax:

```
HANDLE LoadModule(lpModuleName, lpParameterBlock)
```

Parameter, Type, and Description:

lpModuleName	LPSTR	Pointer to a null-terminated string containing the file name of the application to execute
lpParameterBlock	LPVOID	Pointer to a data structure containing four fields (described below)

Description:

The LoadModule function executes the Windows application specified in lpModuleName or creates a new instance for the Windows application. lpModuleName specifies the name of the application to execute. If lpModuleName does not give a directory path, Windows searches the current directory, the Windows directory, the system directory, the directories of the PATH environment variable, and the directories mapped in a network, in that order. lpParameterBlock points to a data structure containing four fields. These fields are:

Field, Type, and Description

wEnvSeg	WORD	Segment address of the environment where the module will be run (0 for Windows)
lpCmdLine	LPSTR	Pointer to a null-terminated character string containing the command line
lpCmdShow	LPVOID	Pointer to a data structure containing two WORD values. The first value is set to 2. The second value is set to one of the values used for the nCmdShow parameter of the ShowWindow function.
dwReserved	DWORD	Set to NULL

Return Value:

The LoadModule function returns the instance of the loaded or created module. The function returns one of the following values when an error occurs:

Value	*Meaning*
0	Out of memory
2	File not found
3	Path not found
5	Attempt to dynamically link to a task

6	Library requires separate data segments for each task
10	Incorrect Windows version
11	Invalid .EXE file
12	OS/2 application
13	DOS 4.0 application
14	Unknown .EXE type
15	Attempt in protected mode to load an .EXE created for an earlier version of Windows
16	Attempt to load a second instance of an .EXE containing multiple, writable data segments
17	Attempt in large-frame EMS mode to load a second instance of an application that links to certain nonshareable DLLs already in use
18	Attempt in real mode to load an application marked for protected mode only

WinExec

Syntax:

```
WORD WinExec(lpCmdLine, nCmdShow)
```

Parameter, Type, and Description:

`lpCmdLine`	`LPSTR`	Pointer to null-terminated character string containing the command line for the application
`nCmdShow`	`int`	Indicates how the application window will be shown

Description:

The `WinExec` function executes a Windows or non-Windows application. `lpCmdLine` specifies the name of the application to execute. If `lpCmdLine` does not give a directory path, Windows searches the current directory, the Windows directory, the system directory, the directories of the `PATH` environment variable, and the directories mapped in a network, in that order. `nCmdShow` specifies the state of the application window and can be any of the following constants:

Constant	*Meaning*
`SW_HIDE`	Hides the window and another window becomes active
`SW_MINIMIZE`	Minimizes the window and the top level window becomes active
`SW_RESTORE`	Activates and displays the window

Constant	*Meaning*
`SW_SHOW`	Activates and displays the window in its current size and position
`SW_SHOWMAXIMIZED`	Activates, displays, and maximizes the window
`SW_SHOWMINIMIZED`	Activates and displays the window as minimized
`SW_SHOWMINNOACTIVE`	Displays the window as minimized
`SW_SHOWNA`	Displays the window in its current state
`SW_SHOWNOACTIVE`	Displays the window in its most recent size and position
`SW_SHOWNORMAL`	Activates and displays the window

Return Value:

The `WinExec` function returns a value greater than 32. A return value of less than 32 indicates one of the following error values:

Value	*Meaning*
0	Out of memory
2	File not found
3	Path not found
5	Attempt to dynamically link to a task
6	Library requires separate data segments for each task
10	Incorrect Windows version
11	Invalid .EXE file
12	OS/2 application
13	DOS 4.0 application
14	Unknown .EXE type
15	Attempt in protected mode to load an .EXE created for an earlier version of Windows
16	Attempt to load a second instance of an .EXE containing multiple, writeable data segments
17	Attempt in large-frame EMS mode to load a second instance of an application that links to certain nonshareable DLLs already in use
18	Attempt in real mode to load an application marked for protected mode only

WinHelp

Syntax:

```
BOOL WinHelp(hWnd, lpHelpFile, wCommand, dwData)
```

Parameter, Type, and Description:

hWnd	HWND	Window requesting help
lpHelpFile	LPSTR	Pointer to a null-terminated string containing the directory and file name of the help file to display
wCommand	WORD	Type of help requested
dwData	DWORD	Context or key word of help requested

Description:

The WinHelp function launches the Windows Help application. hWnd specifies the window requesting help. lpHelpFile contains the directory and file name of the Help file to display. wCommand specifies the type of help requested and can be any of the following values:

Value	*Meaning*
HELP_CONTEXT	Displays help for the context in dwData
HELP_HELPONHELP	Displays help on using the Help application
HELP_INDEX	Displays the index of a Help file
HELP_KEY	Displays help for the key word in dwData
HELP_MULTIKEY	Displays help for a key word in an alternate keyword table
HELP_QUIT	Tells the Help application that the help file is not being used
HELP_SETINDEX	Sets the context in dwData as the current index for the Help file specified by lpHelpFile

Depending on the setting of wCommand, dwData specifies the context or key word of the help requested. When wCommand is HELP_CONTEXT, dwData contains a 32-bit unsigned integer containing a context-identifier number. When wCommand is HELP_KEY, dwData is a long pointer to a null-terminated string containing the key word that identifies the Help topic. When wCommand is HELP_MULTIKEY, dwData is a long pointer to a data structure of type MULTIKEYHELP.

Return Value:

The WinHelp function returns TRUE when it successfully launches the Windows Help application. A return value of FALSE indicates that the function cannot launch Windows Help.

Atom Management Functions

An atom is an integer value that uniquely identifies a character string. Atoms are stored in atom tables. Atom tables can either be local or global. A global atom table is accessible by all applications. A local atom table can only be accessed by one application. The following functions are categorized as Atom Management functions for the System Service Interface:

Function	*Meaning*
`AddAtom`	Creates an atom for a character string
`DeleteAtom`	Deletes an atom when the reference count is zero
`FindAtom`	Finds the atom associated with a character string
`GetAtomHandle`	Gets the handle of the string that corresponds to an atom
`GetAtomName`	Gets the character string associated with an atom
`GlobalAddAtom`	Creates a global atom for a character string
`GlobalDeleteAtom`	Deletes a global atom when the reference count is zero
`GlobalFindAtom`	Gets the global atom associated with a character string
`GlobalGetAtomName`	Gets the character string associated with a global atom
`InitAtomTable`	Initializes an atom hash table
`MAKEINTATOM`	Casts an integer for use as a function argument

The rest of this section provides detailed information on each of the functions in this list.

AddAtom

Syntax:

```
ATOM AddAtom(lpString)
```

Parameter, Type, and Description:

`lpString`	`LPSTR`	Pointer to the null-terminated string to add to the table

Description:

The `AddAtom` function adds the string in `lpString` to the atom table.

Return Value:

The `AddAtom` function returns the atom identifying the added string. A NULL return value indicates that the function cannot add the string.

DeleteAtom

Syntax:

```
ATOM DeleteAtom(nAtom)
```

Parameter, Type, and Description:

`nAtom` `ATOM` Atom and character string to delete

Description:

The `DeleteAtom` function decreases the reference count for the atom in `nAtom`. If the reference count for the atom is zero, the string associated with the atom is removed.

Return Value:

The `DeleteAtom` function returns NULL when the reference count is decreased or the associated string removed. A return value of `nAtom` indicates that the function cannot decrease the reference count, or remove the string, of the atom.

FindAtom

Syntax:

```
ATOM FindAtom(lpString)
```

Parameter, Type, and Description:

`lpString` `LPSTR` Pointer to the null-terminated string to search for

Description:

The `FindAtom` function searches an atom table for the string in `lpString`.

Return Value:

The `FindAtom` function returns the atom associated with the specified string. A NULL return value indicates that the function cannot find the string.

GetAtomHandle

Syntax:

```
HMEM GetAtomHandle(wAtom)
```

Parameter, Type, and Description:

`wAtom` `WORD` Unsigned integer identifying the atom

Description:

The `GetAtomHandle` function gets the handle of the string associated with the atom in `wAtom`.

Return Value:

The `GetAtomHandle` function returns the handle of the string. A return value of zero indicates that the function cannot get the handle of the string.

GetAtomName

Syntax:

```
WORD  GetAtomName(nAtom, lpBuffer, nSize)
```

Parameter, Type, and Description:

`nAtom`	`ATOM`	Character string to retrieve
`lpBuffer`	`LPSTR`	Pointer to the buffer to receive the string
`nSize`	`int`	Maximum number of bytes in the buffer

Description:

The `GetAtomName` function puts a copy of the string associated with `nAtom` in `lpBuffer`. `nSize` specifies the maximum number of bytes in the buffer.

Return Value:

The `GetAtomName` function returns the number of bytes copied to the buffer. Zero is returned when the atom specified in `nAtom` is invalid.

GlobalAddAtom

Syntax:

```
ATOM GlobalAddAtom(lpString)
```

Parameter, Type, and Description:

`lpString`	`LPSTR`	Pointer to the null-terminated character string to be added to the table

Description:

The `GlobalAddAtom` function adds the string in `lpString` to the atom table and returns a global atom that identifies the string. The string is available to all applications referencing the global atom.

Return Value:

The `GlobalAddAtom` function returns the global atom. A NULL return value indicates that the function cannot add the string.

GlobalDeleteAtom

Syntax:

```
ATOM GlobalDeleteAtom(nAtom)
```

Parameter, Type, and Description:

`nAtom`	`ATOM`	Atom and character string to delete

Description:

The `GlobalDeleteAtom` function decreases the reference count for the atom in `nAtom`. If the reference count is zero, the string associated with the atom is removed.

Return Value:

The `GlobalDeleteAtom` function returns NULL when the reference count for the atom is decreased. A return value of `nAtom` indicates that the function cannot decrease the reference count or remove the associated string.

GlobalFindAtom

Syntax:

```
ATOM GlobalFindAtom(lpString)
```

Parameter, Type, and Description:

`lpString`	`LPSTR`	Pointer to the null-terminated character string to search for

Description:

The `GlobalFindAtom` function searches the atom table for the string in `lpString`.

Return Value:

The `GlobalFindAtom` function returns the global atom associated with the specified string. A NULL return value indicates that the function cannot find the string.

GlobalGetAtomName

Syntax:

```
WORD GlobalGetAtomName(nAtom, lpBuffer, nSize)
```

Parameter, Type, and Description:

nAtom	ATOM	Character string to retrieve
lpBuffer	LPSTR	Pointer to the buffer receiving the string
nSize	int	Maximum number of bytes in the string

Description:

The `GlobalGetAtomName` function puts a copy of the string associated with `nAtom` into `lpBuffer`. `nSize` specifies the maximum number of bytes in the string.

Return Value:

The `GlobalGetAtomName` function returns the number of bytes copied to the buffer. Zero is returned when the specified atom is invalid.

InitAtomTable

Syntax:

```
BOOL InitAtomTable(nSize)
```

Parameter, Type, and Description:

nSize	int	Number of entries for the atom hash table (should be a prime number)

Description:

The `InitAtomTable` function initializes an atom hash table. The number of entries in the table is set to the value in `nSize`. `nSize` must be a prime number. The default size of the atom hash table is 37. You should call this function before calling any of the atom management functions.

Return Value:

The `InitAtomTable` function returns a nonzero value when the atom hash table is initialized. A return value of zero indicates that the function cannot initialize the atom hash table.

MAKEINTATOM

Syntax:

```
LPSTR MAKEINTATOM(wInteger)
```

Parameter, Type, and Description:

`wInteger`	`WORD`	Value of the atom's character string

Description:

The `MAKEINTATOM` macro creates an integer atom representing a character string of decimal digits.

Return Value:

The `MAKEINTATOM` macro returns the pointer to the created atom.

Communication Functions

Windows provides the Communication functions for communications that use the serial and parallel ports of the system. The following functions are categorized as Communication functions for the System Services Interface:

Function	*Meaning*
`BuildCommDCB`	Loads a device control block with control codes
`ClearCommBreak`	Clears the communication break state for a communication device
`CloseComm`	Closes a communication device
`EscapeCommFunction`	Specifies that the device is to carry out an extended function
`FlushComm`	Flushes the characters from a communication device
`GetCommError`	Gets the communication status
`GetCommEventMask`	Gets and clears an event mask
`GetCommState`	Loads a buffer with a device control block
`OpenComm`	Opens a communication device
`ReadComm`	Reads from a communication device
`SetCommBreak`	Sets the break state for a communication device
`SetCommEventMask`	Gets and sets an event mask
`SetCommState`	Sets the state of the communication device to the state in the device control block

Function	Meaning
TransmitCommChar	Puts a character at the top of the transmit queue
UngetCommChar	Specifies the next character to read
WriteComm	Writes from a buffer to a communication device

The rest of this section provides detailed information on each of the functions in this list.

BuildCommDCB

Syntax:

```
int BuildCommDCB(lpDef, lpDCB)
```

Parameter, Type, and Description:

lpDef LPSTR	Pointer to a null-terminated string containing the device control information in DOS MODE command-line format
lpDCB DCB FAR *	Pointer to a DCB data structure receiving the translated string

Description:

The BuildCommDCB function translates the string in lpDef into device control block codes. These codes then are placed into the data structure of type DCB pointed to by lpDCB. The DCB structure is:

```
typedef struct tagDCB {
     BYTE Id;
     WORD BaudRate;
     BYTE ByteSize;
     BYTE Parity;
     BYTE StopBits;
     WORD RlsTimeout;
     WORD CtsTimeout;
     WORD DsrTimeout;

     BYTE fBinary: 1;
     BYTE fRtsDisable: 1;
     BYTE fParity: 1;
     BYTE fOutxCtsFlow: 1;
     BYTE fOutxDsrFlow: 1;
     BYTE fDummy: 2;
     BYTE fDtrDisable: 1;

     BYTE fOutX: 1;
     BYTE fInX: 1;
```

```
    BYTE fPeChar: 1;
    BYTE fNull: 1;
    BYTE fChEvt: 1;
    BYTE fDtrFlow: 1;
    BYTE fRtsFlow: 1;
    BYTE fDummy2: 1;

    char XonChar;
    char XoffChar;
    WORD XonLim;
    WORD XoffLim;
    char PeChar;
    char EofChar;
    char EvtChar;
    WORD TxDelay;
} DCB;
```

where:

`Id` identifies the communication device

`BaudRate` is the baud rate

`ByteSize` is the number of bits in a character (four to eight)

`Parity` is the parity scheme—either `EVENPARITY`, `MARKPARITY`, `NOPARITY`, `ODDPARITY`, or `SPACEPARITY`

`StopBits` is the number of stop bits to used—either `ONESTOPBIT`, `ONE5STOPBITS`, or `TWOSTOPBITS`

`RlsTimeout` is the maximum number of milliseconds the device should wait for the receive-line-signal-detect signal

`CtsTimeout` is the maximum number of milliseconds the device should wait for the clear-to-send signal

`DsrTimeout` is the maximum number of milliseconds the device should wait for the data-set-ready signal

`fBinary: 1` specifies binary mode

`fRtsDisable: 1` indicates whether the request-to-send signal is disabled

`fParity: 1` indicates whether parity checking is enabled

`fOutxCtsFlow: 1` specifies that the clear-to-send signal is monitored for output flow control

`fOutxDsrFlow: 1` specifies that the data-set-ready signal is monitored for output flow control

`fDummy: 2` is reserved

`fDtrDisable: 1` specifies whether the data-terminal-ready signal is disabled

`fOutX: 1` specifies that `XON/XOFF` flow control is used during transmission

`fInX: 1` specifies that `XON/XOFF` flow control is used while receiving

`fPeChar: 1` specifies that characters received with parity errors are to be replaced with the character in the `fPeChar` field

`fNull: 1` specifies that null characters are discarded

`fChEvt: 1` specifies that reception of the `EvtChar` character is to be flagged

`fDtrFlow: 1` specifies the data-terminal-ready signal is used for receive flow control

`fRtsFlow: 1` specifies the ready-to-send signal is used for receive flow control

`fDummy2: 1` is reserved

`XonChar` specifies the value of the `XON` character

`XoffChar` specifies the value of the `XOFF` character

`XonLim` is the minimum number of characters allowed in the receive queue before the `XON` character is sent

`XoffLim` specifies the maximum number of characters allowed in the receive queue before the `XOFF` character is sent

`PeChar` specifies the value of the character used to replace characters received with parity errors

`EofChar` specifies the character used to signal the end of data

`EvtChar` specifies the character used to signal an event

`TxDelay` is not used

Return Value:

The `BuildCommDCB` function returns zero when the string is translated into device control block codes. A negative return value indicates that the function cannot translate the string.

ClearCommBreak

Syntax:

```
int ClearCommBreak(nCid)
```

Parameter, Type, and Description:

`nCid`	`int`	Communication device to restore; the value is returned by `OpenComm`

Description:

The `ClearCommBreak` function restores character transmission for the device specified in `nCid`. The transmission line is placed in a nonbreak state.

Return Value:

The `ClearCommBreak` function returns zero when character transmission is restored. A negative value indicates that the `nCid` is invalid.

CloseComm

Syntax:

```
int CloseComm(nCid)
```

Parameter, Type, and Description:

`nCid`	`int`	Device to close

Description:

The `CloseComm` function closes the communication device specified in `nCid`. All memory allocated for the device queues is freed. The function transmits characters in the output queue before closing the device.

Return Value:

The `CloseComm` function returns zero when the communication device is closed. A negative return value indicates that the function cannot close the communication device.

EscapeCommFunction

Syntax:

```
int EscapeCommFunction(nCid, nFunc)
```

Parameter, Type, and Description:

`nCid`	`int`	Communication device
`nFunc`	`int`	Function code of the extended function

Description:

The `EscapeCommFunction` instructs the communication device in `nCid` to perform the extended function in `nFunc`. `nFunc` is one of the following values:

Value	*Meaning*
`CLRDTR`	Clears the data-terminal-ready (DTR) signal
`CLRRTS`	Clears the request-to-send (RTS) signal
`RESETDEV`	Resets the device
`SETDTR`	Sends the data-terminal-ready (DTR) signal
`SETRTS`	Sends the request-to-send (RTS) signal
`SETXOFF`	Forces transmission to respond as though an `XOFF` character was received
`SETXON`	Forces transmission to respond as though an `XON` character was received

Return Value:

The `EscapeCommFunction` function returns zero when successful. A negative return value is returned when `nFunc` is an invalid function code.

FlushComm

Syntax:

```
int FlushComm(nCid, nQueue)
```

Parameter, Type, and Description:

`nCid`	`int`	Communication device
`nQueue`	`int`	Queue to flush

Description:

The `FlushComm` function flushes the characters from the queue specified in `nQueue` for the communication device in `nCid`. `nQueue` is set to 0 to flush the transmission queue or to 1 to flush the receive queue.

Return Value:

The `FlushComm` function returns zero when the queue is flushed. A negative return value indicates that the function cannot flush the queue or that `nQueue` is invalid.

GetCommError

Syntax:

```
int GetCommError(nCid, lpStat)
```

Parameter, Type, and Description:

nCid	int	Communication device
lpStat	COMSTAT FAR *	Pointer to COMSTAT data structure to receive the device status

Description:

The GetCommError function clears the communication port in nCid when Windows locks the port as a result of a communications error. The status of the communication device is placed in the data structure of type COMSTAT, pointed to by lpStat. The COMSTAT structure is:

```
typedef struct tagCOMSTAT {
     BYTE fCtsHold: 1;
     BYTE fDsrHold: 1;
     BYTE fRlsdHold: 1;
     BYTE fXoffHold: 1;
     BYTE fXoffSent: 1;
     BYTE fEof: 1;
     BYTE fTxim: 1;
     WORD cbInQue;
     WORD cbOutQue;
} COMSTAT;
```

where:

fCtsHold: 1 indicates whether transmission is waiting for the clear-to-send (CTS) signal to be sent

fDsrHold: 1 indicates whether transmission is waiting for the data-set-ready (DSR) signal to be sent

fRlsdHold: 1 indicates whether transmission is waiting for the receive-line-signal-detect (RLSD) signal to be sent

fXoffHold: 1 indicates whether transmission is waiting as a result of the XoffChar character being received

fXoffSent: 1 indicates whether transmission is waiting as a result of the XoffChar character being transmitted `fEof: 1` indicates whether the `EofChar` character has been received

`fTxim: 1` indicates whether a character is waiting to be transmitted

`cbInQue` indicates the number of characters in the receive queue

`cbOutQue` indicates the number of characters in the transmit queue

When `lpStat` is set to NULL, the function returns only the error code. The status is not retrieved.

Return Value:

The `GetCommError` function returns a combination of one or more of the error codes returned by the most recent communications function. The possible error codes are:

Value	*Meaning*
CE_BREAK	Break condition detected
CE_CTSTO	Clear-to-send timeout
CE_DNS	Parallel device not selected
CE_DSRTO	Data-set-ready timeout
CE_FRAME	Framing error detected
CE_IOE	I/O error with parallel device
CE_MODE	Mode not supported or `nCid` is invalid
CE_OOP	Out-of-paper signal from parallel device
CE_OVERRUN	Character lost
CE_PTO	Timeout while attempting communication with the parallel port
CE_RLSDTO	Receive-line-signal-detect (RLSD) timeout
CE_RXOVER	Receive queue overflow
CE_RXPARITY	Parity error detected
CE_TXFULL	Transmit queue is full

GetCommEventMask

Syntax:

```
WORD GetCommEventMask(nCid, nEvtMask)
```

Parameter, Type, and Description:

`nCid`	`int`	Communication device
`nEvtMask`	`int`	Events to enable

Description:

The `GetCommEventMask` function gets the current event mask for the communication device in `nCid`. The mask is cleared after the event mask is retrieved. `nEvtMask` specifies the events to enable and can be any of the following event values:

Value	*Meaning*
EV_BREAK	Sets when a break is detected on input
EV_CTS	Sets when the clear-to-send signal changes state
EV_DSR	Sets when the data-set-ready signal changes state
EV_ERR	Sets when a line status error occurs
EV_PERR	Sets when a printer error is detected on a parallel device
EV_RING	Sets when a ring indicator is detected
EV_RSLD	Sets when the receive-line-signal-detect signal changes state
EV_RXCHAR	Sets when a character is received and placed in the receive queue
EV_RXFLAG	Sets when the event character is received and placed in the receive queue
EV_TXEMPTY	Sets when the last character in the transmit queue is sent

Return Value:

The `GetCommEventMask` function returns the current event mask value.

GetCommState

Syntax:

```
int GetCommState(nCid, lpDCB)
```

Parameter, Type, and Description:

nCid	int	Communication device
lpDCB	DCB FAR *	Pointer to the DCB data structure to receive the device control block

Description:

The `GetCommState` function gets the device control block for the communication device in `nCid` and places it in the data structure of type `DCB`, pointed to by `lpDCB`. The `DCB` data structure is:

```
typedef struct tagDCB {
     BYTE Id;
     WORD BaudRate;
     BYTE ByteSize;
     BYTE Parity;
     BYTE StopBits;
     WORD RlsTimeout;
     WORD CtsTimeout;
     WORD DsrTimeout;

     BYTE fBinary: 1;
     BYTE fRtsDisable: 1;
     BYTE fParity: 1;
     BYTE fOutxCtsFlow: 1;
     BYTE fOutxDsrFlow: 1;
     BYTE fDummy: 2;
     BYTE fDtrDisable: 1;

     BYTE fOutX: 1;
     BYTE fInX: 1;
     BYTE fPeChar: 1;
     BYTE fNull: 1;
     BYTE fChEvt: 1;
     BYTE fDtrFlow: 1;
     BYTE fRtsFlow: 1;
     BYTE fDummy2: 1;

     char XonChar;
     char XoffChar;
     WORD XonLim;
     WORD XoffLim;
     char PeChar;
     char EofChar;
     char EvtChar;
     WORD TxDelay;
} DCB;
```

where:

`Id` identifies the communication device

`BaudRate` is the baud rate

`ByteSize` is the number of bits in a character (four to eight)

`Parity` is the parity scheme—either `EVENPARITY`, `MARKPARITY`, `NOPARITY`, `ODDPARITY`, or `SPACEPARITY`

`StopBits` is the number of stop bits to use—either `ONESTOPBIT`, `ONE5STOPBITS`, or `TWOSTOPBITS`

`RlsTimeout` is the maximum number of milliseconds the device waits for the receive-line-signal-detect signal

`CtsTimeout` is the maximum number of milliseconds the device waits for the clear-to-send signal

`DsrTimeout` is the maximum number of milliseconds the device waits for the data-set-ready signal

`fBinary: 1` specifies binary mode

`fRtsDisable: 1` indicates whether the request-to-send signal is disabled

`fParity: 1` indicates whether parity checking is enabled

`fOutxCtsFlow: 1` specifies that the clear-to-send signal is monitored for output flow control

`fOutxDsrFlow: 1` specifies that the data-set-ready signal is monitored for output flow control

`fDummy: 2` is reserved

`fDtrDisable: 1` specifies whether the data-terminal-ready signal is disabled

`fOutX: 1` specifies that `XON/XOFF` flow control is used during transmission

`fInX: 1` specifies that `XON/XOFF` flow control is used while receiving

`fPeChar: 1` specifies that characters received with parity errors are to be replaced with the character in the `fPeChar` field

`fNull: 1` specifies that null characters are discarded

`fChEvt: 1` specifies that reception of the `EvtChar` character is to be flagged

`fDtrFlow: 1` specifies that the data-terminal-ready signal is used for receive flow control

`fRtsFlow: 1` specifies that the ready-to-send signal is used for receive flow control

`fDummy2: 1` is reserved

`XonChar` specifies the value of the `XON` character

`XoffChar` specifies the value of the `XOFF` character

`XonLim` is the minimum number of characters allowed in the receive queue before the `XON` character is sent

`XoffLim` specifies the maximum number of characters allowed in the receive queue before the `XOFF` character is sent

`PeChar` specifies the value of the character used to replace characters received with parity errors

`EofChar` specifies the character used to signal the end of data

`EvtChar` specifies the character used to signal an event

`TxDelay` is not used

Return Value:

The `GetCommState` function returns zero when it places the device control block in the data structure. A negative return value indicates that the function cannot place the device control block.

OpenComm

Syntax:

```
int OpenComm(lpComName, wInQueue, wOutQueue)
```

Parameter, Type, and Description:

`lpComName`	`LPSTR`	Pointer to a string containing the name of the communication device
`wInQueue`	`WORD`	Size of the receive queue
`wOutQueue`	`WORD`	Size of the transmit queue

Description:

The `OpenComm` function opens the communication device specified in `lpComName` and assigns a handle to the device. The handle can be used in other communication functions to identify the communication device. `lpComName` points to a string containing the name of the communication device. `lpComName` contains LPT1 for parallel port 1, LPT2 for parallel port 2, COM1 for serial port 1, and so forth. `wInQueue` and `wOutQueue` specify the size of the receive and transmit queues, respectively.

Return Value:

The `OpenComm` function returns a value identifying the communication device. One of the following values is returned when an error occurs:

Value	*Meaning*
`IE_BADID`	Invalid ID
`IE_BAUDRATE`	Unsupported baud rate
`IE_BYTESIZE`	Invalid byte size

Value	*Meaning*
`IE_DEFAULT`	Error in default parameters
`IE_HARDWARE`	Hardware not present
`IE_MEMORY`	Cannot allocate queues
`IE_NOPEN`	Device not open
`IE_OPEN`	Device already open

ReadComm

Syntax:

```
int ReadComm(nCid, lpBuf, nSize)
```

Parameter, Type, and Description:

`nCid`	`int`	Communcation device
`lpBuf`	`LPSTR`	Pointer to the buffer to receive characters
`nSize`	`int`	Number of characters to read

Description:

The `ReadComm` function reads from the communication device specified in `nCid`. The characters read are copied into the buffer pointed to by `lpBuf`. `nSize` specifies the number of characters to read.

Return Value:

The `ReadComm` function returns the number of characters read from the device. For parallel ports, the return value is zero. A negative value indicates an error.

SetCommBreak

Syntax:

```
int SetCommBreak(nCid)
```

Parameter, Type, and Description:

`nCid`	`int`	Communication device

Description:

The `SetCommBreak` function suspends character transmission for the device in `nCid`. The transmission line is placed in a break state.

Return Value:

The `SetCommBreak` function returns zero when character transmission is suspended for the device. A negative return value indicates that `nCid` is invalid.

SetCommEventMask

Syntax:

```
WORD FAR * SetCommEventMask(nCid, nEvtMask)
```

Parameter, Type, and Description:

`nCid`	`int`	Communication device
`nEvtMask`	`int`	Events to enable

Description:

The `SetCommEventMask` function sets the event mask for the communication device in `nCid`. `nEvtMask` specifies the events to enable and can be any of the following event values:

Value	*Meaning*
`EV_BREAK`	Sets when a break is detected on input
`EV_CTS`	Sets when the clear-to-send signal changes state
`EV_DSR`	Sets when the data-set-ready signal changes state
`EV_ERR`	Sets when a line status error occurs
`EV_PERR`	Sets when a printer error is detected on a parallel device
`EV_RING`	Sets when a ring indicator is detected
`EV_RLSD`	Sets when the receive-line-signal-detect signal changes state
`EV_RXCHAR`	Sets when a character is received and placed in the receive queue
`EV_RXFLAG`	Sets when the event character is received and placed in the receive queue
`EV_TXEMPTY`	Sets when the last character in the transmit queue is sent

Return Value:

The `SetCommEventMask` function returns the pointer to the event mask.

SetCommState

Syntax:

```
int SetCommState(lpDCB)
```

Parameter, Type, and Description:

`lpDCB`	`DCB FAR *`	Pointer to a `DCB` data structure containing the settings for the device

Description:

The `SetCommState` function sets the state of a communication device to the settings specified in the data structure of type `DCB`, pointed to by `lpDCB`. The `DCB` data structure is:

```
typedef struct tagDCB {
     BYTE Id;
     WORD BaudRate;
     BYTE ByteSize;
     BYTE Parity;
     BYTE StopBits;
     WORD RlsTimeout;
     WORD CtsTimeout;
     WORD DsrTimeout;

     BYTE fBinary: 1;
     BYTE fRtsDisable: 1;
     BYTE fParity: 1;
     BYTE fOutxCtsFlow: 1;
     BYTE fOutxDsrFlow: 1;
     BYTE fDummy: 2;
     BYTE fDtrDisable: 1;

     BYTE fOutX: 1;
     BYTE fInX: 1;
     BYTE fPeChar: 1;
     BYTE fNull: 1;
     BYTE fChEvt: 1;
     BYTE fDtrFlow: 1;
     BYTE fRtsFlow: 1;
     BYTE fDummy2: 1;

     char XonChar;
     char XoffChar;
     WORD XonLim;
     WORD XoffLim;
     char PeChar;
```

```
    char EofChar;
    char EvtChar;
    WORD TxDelay;
} DCB;
```

where:

`Id` identifies the communication device

`BaudRate` is the baud rate

`ByteSize` is the number of bits in a character (four to eight)

`Parity` is the parity scheme—either `EVENPARITY`, `MARKPARITY`, `NOPARITY`, `ODDPARITY`, or `SPACEPARITY`

`StopBits` is the number of stop bits to be used—either `ONESTOPBIT`, `ONE5STOPBITS`, or `TWOSTOPBITS`

`RlsTimeout` is the maximum number of milliseconds the device waits for the receive-line-signal-detect signal

`CtsTimeout` is the maximum number of milliseconds the device waits for the clear-to-send signal

`DsrTimeout` is the maximum number of milliseconds the device waits for the data-set-ready signal

`fBinary: 1` specifies binary mode

`fRtsDisable: 1` indicates whether the request-to-send signal is disabled

`fParity: 1` indicates whether parity checking is enabled

`fOutxCtsFlow:1` specifies that the clear-to-send signal is monitored for output flow control

`fOutxDsrFlow: 1` specifies that the data-set-ready signal is monitored for output flow control

`fDummy: 2` is reserved

`fDtrDisable: 1` specifies whether the data-terminal-ready signal is disabled

`fOutX: 1` specifies that `XON/XOFF` flow control is used during transmission

`fInX: 1` specifies that `XON/XOFF` flow control is used while receiving

`fPeChar: 1` specifies that characters received with parity errors are to be replaced with the character in the `fPeChar` field

`fNull: 1` specifies that null characters are discarded

`fChEvt: 1` specifies that reception of the `EvtChar` character is to be flagged

`fDtrFlow: 1` specifies that the data-terminal-ready signal is used for receive flow control

`fRtsFlow: 1` specifies that the ready-to-send signal is used for receive flow control

`fDummy2: 1` is reserved

`XonChar` specifies the value of the `XON` character

`XoffChar` specifies the value of the `XOFF` character

`XonLim` is the minimum number of characters allowed in the receive queue before the `XON` character is sent

`XoffLim` specifies the maximum number of characters allowed in the receive queue before the `XOFF` character is sent

`PeChar` specifies the value of the character used to replace characters received with parity errors

`EofChar` specifies the character used to signal the end of data

`EvtChar` specifies the character used to signal an event

`TxDelay` is not used

Return Value:

The `SetCommState` function returns zero when the state of the communication device is set. A negative return value indicates that the function cannot set the state of the communication device.

TransmitCommChar

Syntax:

```
int TransmitCommChar(nCid, cChar)
```

Parameter, Type, and Description:

`nCid`	`int`	Communication device; the value is returned by `OpenComm`
`cChar`	`char`	Character to transmit

Description:

The `TransmitCommChar` function places the character in `cChar` at the head of the transmit queue for the device in `nCid`.

Return Value:

The `TransmitCommChar` function returns zero when the character is placed at the head of the transmit queue. A negative return value indicates that the function cannot transmit the character.

UngetCommChar

Syntax:

```
int Unget\CommChar(nCid, cChar)
```

Parameter, Type, and Description:

`nCid`	`int`	Communication device
`cChar`	`char`	Character to place in the receive queue

Description:

The `UngetCommChar` function puts the character in `cChar` at the head of the receive queue for the device in `nCid`. The character placed in the receive queue is the next character read from the queue.

Return Value:

The `UngetCommChar` function returns zero when it puts the character at the head of the receive queue. A negative return value indicates that the function cannot put the character at the head of the receive queue.

WriteComm

Syntax:

```
int WriteComm(nCid, lpBuf, nSize)
```

Parameter, Type, and Description:

`nCid`	`int`	Communication device; the value is returned by `OpenComm`
`lpBuf`	`LPSTR`	Pointer to the buffer containing the characters to write
`nSize`	`int`	Number of characters to write

Description:

The `WriteComm` function writes the characters in the buffer pointed to by `lpBuf` to the communication device specified in `nCid`. `nSize` specifies the number of characters to write.

Return Value:

The `WriteComm` function returns the number of characters written. A negative value indicates an error. A negative value indicates an error.

Debugging Functions

Windows provides Debugging functions to enable you to locate and isolate programming errors. The following functions are categorized as Debugging functions for the System Services Interface:

Function	*Meaning*
`DebugBreak`	Forces a break to the debugger
`FatalAppExit`	Displays a message box and terminates the application
`FatalExit`	Displays the current state of Windows and prompts the user for information to proceed
`OutputDebugString`	Sends a debugging message
`ValidateCodeSegments`	Checks whether any code segments were modified by random memory overwrites
`ValidateFreeSpaces`	Checks free segments in memory for valid contents

The rest of this section provides detailed information on each of the functions in this list.

DebugBreak

Syntax:

```
void DebugBreak()
```

Description:

The `DebugBreak` function forces a break to the debugger.

Return Value:

There is no return value.

FatalAppExit

Syntax:

```
void FatalAppExit(wAction, lpMessageText)
```

Parameter, Type, and Description:

`wAction`	`WORD`	Must be set to zero (reserved)
`lpMessageText`	`LPSTR`	Pointer to the string to display in the message box

Description:

The `FatalAppExit` function displays the message in the string pointed to by `lpMessageText` inside a message box. When the message box is closed, the application is terminated.

Return Value:

There is no return value.

FatalExit

Syntax:

```
void FatalExit(Code)
```

Parameter, Type, and Description:

`Code`	`int`	Error code to display

Description:

The `FatalExit` function is used for debugging only and displays the current state of Windows, including the error code in `Code` and a symbolic stack trace.

Return Value:

There is no return value.

OutputDebugString

Syntax:

```
void OutputDebugString(lpOutputString)
```

Parameter, Type, and Description:

`lpOutputString`	`LPSTR`	Pointer to a null-terminated string containing the message to display

Description:

The `OutputDebugString` function sends the message in `lpOutputString` to the debugger when the debugger is present. The message is sent to an auxiliary device when the debugger is not present.

Return Value:

There is no return value.

ValidateCodeSegments

Syntax:

```
void ValidateCodeSegments()
```

Description:

The `ValidateCodeSegments` function sends debugging information whenever random memory overwrites modify a code segment. This function is available only in the debugging version of Windows.

Return Value:

There is no return value.

ValidateFreeSpaces

Syntax:

```
LPSTR ValidateFreeSpaces()
```

Description:

The `ValidateFreeSpaces` function checks free segments in memory for valid contents. When an invalid byte is encountered, debugging information is displayed and a fatal exit is initiated. This function is available only in the debugging version of Windows.

Return Value:

There is no return value.

File I/O Functions

Windows provides the File I/O functions for creating, opening, reading, writing, and closing files from inside the Windows environment. The following functions are categorized as File I/O functions for the System Services Interface:

Function	*Meaning*
`GetDriveType`	Determines the drive type: fixed, removable, or remote
`GetSystemDirectory`	Gets the path name for the subdirectory for the Windows system
`GetTempDrive`	Gets the drive letter for the best drive to use for temporary file storage
`GetTempFileName`	Creates a temporary file name
`GetWindowsDirectory`	Gets the path name for the Windows directory
`_lclose`	Closes a file
`_lcreat`	Creates a new file or opens an existing file
`_llseek`	Sets the pointer to a file
`_lopen`	Opens an existing file
`_lread`	Reads from a file
`_lwrite`	Writes to a file
`OpenFile`	Creates, opens, or deletes a file
`SetHandleCount`	Sets the number of file handles available for a task

The rest of this section provides detailed information on each of the functions in this list.

GetDriveType

Syntax:

```
WORD GetDriveType(nDrive)
```

Parameter, Type, and Description:

nDrive	int	Drive number

Description:

The GetDriveType function determines the drive type for the drive number specified in nDrive: fixed, remote, or removable. nDrive is 0 for Drive A, 1 for Drive B, and so forth.

Return Value:

The GetDriveType function returns the type of drive, represented by one of the following values:

Value	*Meaning*
DRIVE_FIXED	Disk cannot be removed from the drive
DRIVE_REMOTE	Drive is a remote drive (networked)
DRIVE_REMOVABLE	Disk can be removed from the drive

GetSystemDirectory

Syntax:

```
WORD GetSystemDirectory(lpBuffer, nSize)
```

Parameter, Type, and Description:

lpBuffer	LPSTR	Pointer to the null-terminated string to receive the path name
nSize	int	Maximum number of bytes in the buffer

Description:

The GetSystemDirectory function gets the path of the Windows system subdirectory. The retrieved path is placed in the buffer pointed to by lpBuffer. nSize specifies the maximum number of bytes in the buffer.

Return Value:

The GetSystemDirectory function returns the length of the string copied to lpBuffer. Zero is returned when the function cannot retrieve the path.

GetTempDrive

Syntax:

```
BYTE GetTempDrive(cDriveLetter)
```

Parameter, Type, and Description:

`cDriveLetter`	`BYTE`	Drive letter of disk

Description:

The `GetTempDrive` function gets the best drive to use for temporary file storage. The best drive is considered to be the drive that has the fastest access time. `cDriveLetter` is set to a drive letter or to zero.

Return Value:

When `cDriveLetter` is set to zero, the drive letter of the current disk is returned. When `cDriveLetter` is set to a drive letter, the drive letter of the best disk to use for temporary file storage is returned.

GetTempFileName

Syntax:

```
int GetTempFileName(cDriveLetter, lpPrefixString, wUnique,
                    lpTempFileName)
```

Parameter, Type, and Description:

`cDriveLetter`	`BYTE`	Drive for temporary file
`lpPrefixString`	`LPSTR`	Pointer to the null-terminated string containing the file name prefix for the temporary file; characters in the string must be from the OEM character set
`wUnique`	`WORD`	Unsigned short integer
`lpTempFileName`	`LPSTR`	Pointer to the buffer that receives the temporary file name

Description:

The `GetTempFileName` function creates a temporary file name. `cDriveLetter` specifies the drive letter for the file name. `lpPrefixstring` specifies the prefix of the file name.

wUnique is an unsigned short integer, converted to hexadecimal for use in the file name. lpTempFileName stores the resulting file name in the form of

```
drive:\path\prefixuuuu.tmp
```

where:

drive is specified in cDriveLetter

path is the path name for the temporary file specified in the TEMP environment variable

prefix is specified in lpPrefixString

uuuu is the hexadecimal equivalent to the value in wUnique

tmp is the file extension

Return Value:

The GetTempFileName function returns a unique numeric value used in the temporary file name.

GetWindowsDirectory

Syntax:

```
WORD GetWindowsDirectory(lpBuffer, nSize)
```

Parameter, Type, and Description:

lpBuffer	LPSTR	Pointer to the buffer to receive the string containing the path name
nSize	int	Maximum number of bytes in the buffer

Description:

The GetWindowsDirectory function gets the path name for the Windows directory. The path name is placed in the buffer pointed to by lpBuffer. nSize specifies the maximum number of bytes in the buffer.

Return Value:

The GetWindowsDirectory function returns the length of the string placed in the buffer. Zero is returned when the function cannot retrieve the Windows directory.

_lclose

Syntax:

```
int _lclose(hFile)
```

Parameter, Type, and Description:

`hFile`	`int`	DOS file handle of file to close

Description:

The `_lclose` function closes the file specified in `hFile`.

Return Value:

The `_lclose` function returns zero when the file is closed. A return value of –1 indicates that the function cannot close the file.

_lcreat

Syntax:

```
int _lcreat(lpPathName, iAttribute)
```

Parameter, Type, and Description:

`lpPathName`	`LPSTR`	Pointer to a null-terminated string naming the file to open; string must contain characters from the ANSI character set
`iAttribute`	`int`	Specifies the file attributes

Description:

The `_lcreate` function opens a file with the name specified in `lpPathName`. The file name string must contain characters from the ANSI character set. If the specified file does not exist, a new file is created and opened. If the file exists, the file is truncated to zero and opened. `iAttribute` specifies the attributes for the file and can be any of the following values:

Value	*Meaning*
0	Read and write
1	Read-only
2	Hidden
3	System

Return Value:

The `_lcreate` function returns the DOS file handle to the created file. A return value of –1 indicates that the function cannot create the file.

_llseek

Syntax:

```
LONG _llseek(hFile, lOffset, iOrigin)
```

Parameter, Type, and Description:

`hFile`	`int`	DOS file handle of file
`lOffset`	`LONG`	Number of bytes to move the pointer
`iOrigin`	`int`	Starting position and direction of the pointer

Description:

The `_llseek` function repositions the pointer in the opened file specified in `hFile`. `lOffset` specifies the number of bytes to move the pointer relative to the starting point and direction specified in `iOrigin`. The following values are used for `iOrigin`:

Value	*Meaning*
0	Moves the file pointer from the beginning of the file
1	Moves the file pointer from the current pointer position
2	Moves the file pointer from the end of the file

Return Value:

The `_llseek` function returns the new offset of the pointer, in bytes. A return value of –1 indicates that the function cannot reposition the pointer.

_lopen

Syntax:

```
int _lopen(lpPathName, iReadWrite)
```

Parameter, Type, and Description:

`lpPathName`	`LPSTR`	Pointer to a null-terminated string containing the name of the file to open; the string must contain characters from the ANSI character set
`iReadWrite`	`int`	Indicates the accessibility of the file

Description:

The `_lopen` function opens a file with the name specified in `lpPathName`. The file name string must contain characters from the ANSI character set. If the file already exists, the file is truncated to zero. `iReadWrite` specifies the accessibility of the file and can be any of the following values:

Value	*Meaning*
`OF_READ`	Read only
`OF_READWRITE`	Read and write
`OF_SHARE_COMPAT`	Open file with compatibility mode
`OF_SHARE_DENY_NONE`	Open file without denying other processes read or write access
`OF_SHARE_DENY_READ`	Open file and deny other processes read access
`OF_SHARE_DENY_WRITE`	Open file and deny other processes write access
`OF_SHARE_EXCLUSIVE`	Open file with exclusive mode and deny other processes read and write access
`OF_WRITE`	Write only

Return Value:

The `_lopen` function returns the DOS file handle. A return value of –1 indicates that the function cannot open the file.

_lread

Syntax:

```
int _lread(hFile, lpBuffer, wBytes)
```

Parameter, Type, and Description:

`hFile`	`int`	DOS file handle of the file to read
`lpBuffer`	`LPSTR`	Pointer to the buffer to receive the data read from the file
`wBytes`	`WORD`	Number of bytes to read from the file

Description:

The `_lread` function reads data from the file associated with the file handle in `hFile`. The data read from the file is placed in the buffer pointed to by `lpBuffer`. `wBytes` specifies the number of bytes to read from the file.

Return Value:

The `_lread` function returns the number of bytes read from the file. A return value of –1 indicates that the function cannot read from the file.

_lwrite

Syntax:

```
int _lwrite(hFile, lpBuffer, wBytes)
```

Parameter, Type, and Description:

`hFile`	`int`	DOS file handle of the file to read
`lpBuffer`	`LPSTR`	Pointer to the buffer containing the data to write to the file
`wBytes`	`WORD`	Number of bytes to write to the file

Description:

The `_lwrite` function writes the data in the buffer pointed to by `lpBuffer` to the file specified by the DOS file handle in `hFile`. `wBytes` specifies the number of bytes to write to the file.

Return Value:

The `_lwrite` function returns the number of bytes written to the file. A return value of –1 indicates that the function cannot write the data to the file.

OpenFile

Syntax:

```
int OpenFile(lpFileName, lpReOpenBuff, wStyle)
```

Parameter, Type, and Description:

`lpFileName`	`LPSTR`	Pointer to a null-terminated string containing the name of the file to open; the string must contain characters from the ANSI character set
`lpReOpenBuff`	`LPOFSTRUCT`	Pointer to a `OFSTRUCT` data structure receiving information about the file when the file is opened
`wStyle`	`WORD`	Action to take

Description:

The `OpenFile` function opens, creates, reopens, or deletes the file with the name specified in `lpFileName`. The file name string must contain characters from the ANSI character set. `lpReOpenBuff` points to a data structure of type `OFSTRUCT` containing information on the file when it is first opened. The `OFSTRUCT` structure is:

```
typedef struct tagOFSTRUCT {
     BYTE cBytes;
     BYTE fFixedDisk;
     WORD nErrCode;
     BYTE reserved[4];
     BYTE szPathName[120];
} OFSTRUCT;
```

where:

`cBytes` is the length of the `OFSTRUCT` structure in bytes

`fFixedDisk` indicates whether the file is on a fixed disk (0 means that the file is *not* on a fixed disk)

`nErrCode` is the DOS error code if `OpenFile` returns –1

`reserved[4]` is reserved

`szPathName` is the path name of the file

`wStyle` specifies the action to take and can be any combination of the following values:

Value	*Meaning*
OF_CANCEL	Add a Cancel button to the OF_PROMPT dialog box
OF_CREATE	Create a new file
OF_DELETE	Delete the file
OF_EXIST	Open, then close, the file
OF_PARSE	Fill the OFSTRUCT data structure
OF_PROMPT	Display a dialog box if the file does not exist
OF_READ	Open for read only
OF_READWRITE	Open for read and write
OF_REOPEN	Open file with information in the reopen buffer
OF_SHARE_COMPAT	Open file with compatibility mode
OF_SHARE_DENY_NONE	Open file without denying other processes read and write access

Value	*Meaning*
`OF_SHARE_DENY_READ`	Open file and deny other processes read access
`OF_SHARE_DENY_WRITE`	Open file and deny other processes write access
`OF_SHARE_EXCLUSIVE`	Open file and deny other processes read and write access
`OF_VERIFY`	Verify date and time
`OF_WRITE`	Write only

Combine constants by using the bitwise OR operator.

Return Value:

The `OpenFile` function returns the DOS file handle of the function. A return value of –1 indicates that the function cannot open, create, reopen, or delete the file.

SetHandleCount

Syntax:

```
WORD SetHandleCount(wNumber)
```

Parameter, Type, and Description:

`wNumber`	`WORD`	Number of file handles for the application; must be 255 or less

Description:

The `SetHandleCount` function defines the number of file handles available for the application. `wNumber` specifies the number of file handles that the application needs. The default number of file handles is 20. `wNumber` cannot exceed 255.

Return Value:

The `SetHandleCount` function returns the number of file handles available to the application.

Initialization File Functions

An initialization file contains run-time options for Windows applications. The Windows initialization file, WIN.INI, contains information that affects the Windows environment and all applications. Private initialization files contain information for a particular application. Windows provides a set of functions for retrieving and setting information for initialization files. The following functions are categorized as Initialization File functions for the System Services Interface:

Function	*Meaning*
`GetPrivateProfileInt`	Gets an integer value in a section from a private initialization file
`GetPrivateProfileString`	Gets a string in a section from a private initialization file
`GetProfileInt`	Gets an integer value in a section from WIN.INI
`GetProfileString`	Gets a string in a section from WIN.INI
`WritePrivateProfileString`	Either writes a string to a private initialization file or deletes lines from a private initialization file
`WriteProfileString`	Either writes a string to WIN.INI or deletes lines from WIN.INI

The rest of this section provides detailed information on each of the functions in this list.

GetPrivateProfileInt

Syntax:

```
WORD GetPrivateProfileInt(lpApplicationName, lpKeyName, nDefault,
                          lpFileName)
```

Parameter, Type, and Description:

`lpApplicationName`	`LPSTR`	Pointer to the name of a Windows application that appears in the initialization file
`lpKeyName`	`LPSTR`	Pointer to the key name that appears in the initialization file
`nDefault`	`int`	Default value for the key
`lpFileName`	`LPSTR`	Pointer to the string that contains the name of the initialization file

Description:

The `GetPrivateProfileInt` function gets the value of the key specified in `lpKeyName` from the initialization file specified in `lpFileName`. `lpApplicationName` specifies the application heading that the key name appears under.

Return Value:

The value of the digits in the key name is returned. The `GetPrivateProfileInt` function returns a zero if the value associated with the specified key is not an integer or a negative integer.

GetPrivateProfileString

Syntax:

```
int GetPrivateProfileString(lpApplicationName, lpKeyName,
     lpDefault, lpReturnedString, nSize, lpFileName)
```

Parameter, Type, and Description:

`lpApplicationName`	`LPSTR`	Pointer to the name of a Windows application that appears in the initialization file
`lpKeyName`	`LPSTR`	Pointer to a key name that appears in the initialization file
`lpDefault`	`LPSTR`	Default value for the key
`lpReturnedString`	`LPSTR`	Pointer to the buffer that receives the character string
`nSize`	`int`	Maximum number of characters to copy to the buffer
`lpFileName`	`LPSTR`	Pointer to the name of the initialization file

Description:

The `GetPrivateProfileString` function copies the string associated with the key name in `lpKeyName` from the initialization file specified in `lpFileName` into the buffer pointed to by `lpReturnedString`. `nSize` specifies the maximum number of characters to copy to the buffer. When the specified key name is not found, the value specified by `lpDefault` is copied to the buffer. If `lpKeyName` is NULL, the location pointed to by `lpReturnedString` is filled with a list of enumerated key names.

Return Value:

The `GetPrivateProfileString` function returns the number of characters copied to the buffer excluding the null terminator.

GetProfileInt

Syntax:

```
WORD GetPrivateProfileInt(lpAppName, lpKeyName, nDefault)
```

Parameter, Type, and Description:

lpAppName	LPSTR	Pointer to the name of a Windows application that appears in the Windows initialization file
lpKeyName	LPSTR	Pointer to the key name that appears in the Windows initialization file
nDefault	int	Default value for the key

Description:

The `GetProfileInt` function gets the value of the key specified in `lpKeyName` from the Windows initialization file. `lpAppName` specifies the application heading that the key name appears under.

Return Value:

The `GetProfileInt` function returns a zero if the value associated with the specified key is not an integer or a negative integer. If the associated value contains non-numeric characters followed by digits, the return value is the value of the digits. A return value of `nDefault` indicates that the function cannot find the specified key.

GetProfileString

Syntax:

```
int GetProfileString(lpAppName, lpKeyName, lpDefault,
     lpReturnedString, nSize)
```

Parameter, Type, and Description:

lpAppName	LPSTR	Pointer to the name of a Windows application that appears in the Windows initialization file
lpKeyName	LPSTR	Pointer to a key name that appears in the Windows initialization file
lpDefault	LPSTR	Default value for the key

`lpReturnedString`	`LPSTR`	Pointer to the buffer that receives the character string
`nSize`	`int`	Maximum number of characters to copy to the buffer

Description:

The `GetProfileString` function copies the string associated with the key name in `lpKeyName` from the Windows initialization file into the buffer pointed to by `lpReturnedString`. `nSize` specifies the maximum number of characters to copy to the buffer.

Return Value:

The `GetProfileString` function returns the number of characters copied to the buffer.

WritePrivateProfileString

Syntax:

```
BOOL WritePrivateProfileString(lpApplicationName, lpKeyName,
    lpString, lpFileName)
```

Parameter, Type, and Description:

`lpApplicationName`	`LPSTR`	Pointer to the name of a Windows application appearing in the initialization file
`lpKeyName`	`LPSTR`	Pointer to a key name that appears in the initialization file
`lpString`	`LPSTR`	Pointer to the string containing the new key value
`lpFileName`	`LPSTR`	Pointer to the string containing the name of the initialization file

Description:

The `WritePrivateProfileString` function writes the string pointed to by `lpString` to the initialization file specified in `lpFileName`. The string is assigned to the key specified in `lpKeyName`. `lpApplicationName` specifies the application heading that the key name appears under.

Return Value:

The `WritePrivateProfileString` function returns a nonzero value when the string is written. A return value of zero indicates that the function cannot write the string.

WriteProfileString

Syntax:

```
BOOL WriteProfileString(lpApplicationName, lpKeyName, lpString)
```

Parameter, Type, and Description:

`lpApplicationName`	`LPSTR`	Pointer to the name of a Windows application appearing in the Windows initialization file
`lpKeyName`	`LPSTR`	Pointer to a key name that appears in the Windows initialization file
`lpString`	`LPSTR`	Pointer to the string containing the new key value

Description:

The `WriteProfileString` function writes the string pointed to by `lpString` to the Windows initialization file. The string is assigned to the key specified in `lpKeyName`. `lpApplicationName` specifies the application heading under which the key name appears.

Return Value:

The `WriteProfileString` function returns a nonzero value when the string is written. A return value of zero indicates that the function cannot write the string.

Memory Management Functions

Windows provides Memory Management functions to manage both local and global memory. Global memory is system memory that has not been allocated by an application or reserved for the system. Local memory is the memory in the data segment of a Windows application. The following functions are categorized as Memory Management functions for the System Services Interface:

Function	*Meaning*
`DefineHandleTable`	Creates a private handle table in an application's data segment
`GetFreeSpace`	Determines the number of available bytes in the global heap
`GetWinFlags`	Gets information on the system memory configuration
`GlobalAlloc`	Allocates memory from the global heap
`GlobalCompact`	Compacts global memory
`GlobalDiscard`	Discards a global memory block
`GlobalDosAlloc`	Allocates global memory
`GlobalDosFree`	Frees global memory allocated with `GlobalDosAlloc`

Function	*Meaning*
GlobalFlags	Gets the flags and lock count of a global memory block
GlobalFree	Removes a global block and invalidates the handle
GlobalHandle	Gets the handle of a global memory object
GlobalLock	Gets the pointer for a handle to a global memory block
GlobalLRUNewest	Moves a global memory object to the newest least-recently-used (LRU) position
GlobalLRUOldest	Moves a global memory object to the oldest least-recently-used (LRU) position
GlobalNotify	Installs a notification procedure for the current task
GlobalReAlloc	Reallocates a global memory block
GlobalSize	Gets the number of bytes in a global memory block
GlobalUnlock	Invalidates the pointer to a global memory block
GlobalUnwire	Decreases the lock count and unlocks the memory block when the count is zero
GlobalWire	Moves an object to low memory and increases the lock count
LimitEMSPages	Sets the limits for the amount of expanded memory that Windows assigns to an application
LocalAlloc	Allocates memory from the local heap
LocalCompact	Compacts local memory
LocalDiscard	Discards local memory when the lock count is zero
LocalFlags	Gets the memory type of a local memory block
LocalFree	Frees a local memory block when the lock count is zero
LocalHandle	Gets the handle of a local memory block
LocalInit	Initializes a local heap
LocalLock	Locks a local memory block
LocalReAlloc	Reallocates a local memory block
LocalShrink	Shrinks the local heap
LocalSize	Gets the number of bytes in a local memory block
LocalUnlock	Unlocks a local memory block
LockData	Locks the current data segment
LockSegment	Locks the specified data segment
SetSwapAreaSize	Sets the amount of memory reserved for code segments of an application
SwitchStackBack	Returns the stack of the current task to the task's data segment
SwitchStackTo	Changes the stack of the current task to the specified data segment
UnlockData	Unlocks the current data segment
UnlockSegment	Unlocks the specified data segment

The rest of this section provides detailed information on each of the functions in this list.

DefineHandleTable

Syntax:

```
BOOL DefineHandleTable(wOffset)
```

Parameter, Type, and Description:

wOffset	WORD	Offset from the beginning of the data segment to the beginning of the private handle table

Description:

The `DefineHandleTable` function creates a private handle table in a Windows application's default data segment. This table is used to store the segment addresses of global memory objects. `wOffset` specifies the offset for the table from the beginning of the data segment to the beginning of the private handle table. The format of the private handle table is as follows:

```
Count
Clear_Number
Entry[0]
.
.
.
Entry[Count-1]
```

Return Value:

The `DefineHandleTable` function returns a nonzero value when the table is created. A return value of zero indicates that the function cannot create the table.

GetFreeSpace

Syntax:

```
DWORD GetFreeSpace(wFlags)
```

Parameter, Type, and Description:

wFlags	WORD	Indicates whether the heap is scanned above or below the EMS bank line in large- and small-frame EMS systems

Description:

The `GetFreeSpace` function determines the number of bytes of available memory by scanning the global heap. `wFlags` specifies whether the heap is to be scanned above or below the EMS bank line.

Return Value:

The `GetFreeSpace` function returns the number of available bytes of memory:

- When `wFlags` is set to `GMEM_NOT_BANKED`, the amount of available memory below the EMS bank line is returned.
- When `wFlags` is zero, the amount of available memory above the EMS bank line is returned.
- For non-EMS systems, `wFlags` is ignored.

GetWinFlags

Syntax:

```
DWORD GetWinFlags()
```

Description:

The `GetWinFlags` function gets a value representing the memory configuration of the system where Windows is running.

Return Value:

The `GetWinFlags` function returns a 32-bit value containing one or more flags that define the memory configuration:

Value	*Meaning*
`WF_80x87`	Intel math coprocessor present
`WF_CPU086`	8086 CPU present
`WF_CPU186`	80186 CPU present
`WF_CPU286`	80286 CPU present
`WF_CPU386`	80386 CPU present
`WF_CPU486`	80486 CPU present
`WF_ENHANCED`	Windows running in 386 enhanced mode
`WF_LARGEFRAME`	Windows running in EMS large frame memory configuration
`WF_PMODE`	Windows running in protected mode
`WF_SMALLFRAME`	Windows running in EMS small frame memory configuration
`WF_STANDARD`	Windows running in standard mode

Note: Windows is running in real mode when neither `WF_ENHANCED` nor `WF_STANDARD` is set.

GlobalAlloc

Syntax:

```
HANDLE GlobalAlloc(wFlags, dwBytes)
```

Parameter, Type, and Description:

`wFlags`	`WORD`	Flags to specify how to allocate memory
`dwBytes`	`int`	Number of bytes to allocate

Description:

The `GlobalAlloc` function allocates memory from the global heap. `dwBytes` specifies the number of bytes to allocate from the global heap. `wFlags` specifies one or more flags that indicate how the memory is to be allocated. `wFlags` can be any combination of the following:

Value	*Meaning*
`GMEM_DDESHARE`	Shared memory is allocated
`GMEM_DISCARDABLE`	Discardable memory is allocated
`GMEM_FIXED`	Fixed memory is allocated
`GMEM_MOVEABLE`	Moveable memory is allocated
`GMEM_NOCOMPACT`	Compacting or discarding does not occur to meet the memory allocation requirements
`GMEM_NODISCARD`	Discarding does not occur to meet the memory allocation requirements
`GMEM_NOT_BANKED`	Nonbanked memory allocated
`GMEM_NOTIFY`	Notification routine is called if the memory object is discarded
`GMEM_ZEROINT`	Contents of memory are initialized to zero

Combine flags by using the bitwise OR operator.

Return Value:

The `GlobalAlloc` function returns the handle to the allocated memory. A NULL return value indicates that the function cannot allocate memory.

GlobalCompact

Syntax:

```
DWORD GlobalCompact(dwMinFree)
```

Parameter, Type, and Description:

`dwMinFree` `DWORD` Number of bytes to free

Description:

The `GlobalCompact` function frees the number of bytes specified in `dwMinFree` by compacting the global heap. If necessary, unlocked discardable blocks are discarded to free the number of bytes requested.

Return Value:

The `GlobalCompact` function returns the number of bytes in the largest block of free global memory.

GlobalDiscard

Syntax:

```
HANDLE GlobalDiscard(hMem)
```

Parameter, Type, and Description:

`hMem` `HANDLE` Global memory block to discard

Description:

The `GlobalDiscard` function discards the global memory block specified in `hMem`. The lock count of the block must be zero. The handle to the memory block remains valid.

Return Value:

The `GlobalDiscard` function returns the handle to the discarded block. A return value of zero indicates that the function cannot discard the block.

GlobalDosAlloc

Syntax:

```
DWORD GlobalDosAlloc(dwBytes)
```

Parameter, Type, and Description:

`dwBytes` `DWORD` Number of bytes to allocate

Description:

The `GlobalDosAlloc` function allocates the number of bytes of global memory specified in `dwBytes` from the first megabyte of linear address space. DOS can access this memory in real mode.

Return Value:

The high-order word of the return value contains a paragraph-segment value. This value can be used to access the memory in real mode. The low-order word of the return value contains a selector. This selector can be used to access the memory in protected mode. A NULL return value indicates that the function cannot allocate the memory.

GlobalDosFree

Syntax:

```
WORD GlobalDosFree(wSelector)
```

Parameter, Type, and Description:

`wSelector` `WORD` Memory to free

Description:

The `GlobalDosFree` function frees the block of memory specified in `wSelector`. The block of memory must have been allocated with `GlobalDosAlloc`.

Return Value:

The `GlobalDosFree` function returns NULL when the block of memory is freed. A return value of `wSelector` indicates that the function cannot free the memory.

GlobalFlags

Syntax:

```
WORD GlobalFlags(hMem)
```

Parameter, Type, and Description:

`hMem` `HANDLE` Handle to global memory block

Description:

The `GlobalFlags` function gets information about the global memory block in `hMem`.

Return Value:

The high-order byte of the return value specifies the memory allocation flag, which will be one of the following values:

Value	*Meaning*
GMEM_DDESHARE	Shared block
GMEM_DISCARDABLE	Discardable block
GMEM_DISCARDED	Discarded block
GMEM_NOT_BANKED	Block cannot be banked

The low-order byte of the return value contains the lock count of the block. The `GMEM_LOCKCOUNT` mask is used to retrieve the lock-count value from the return value.

GlobalFree

Syntax:

```
HANDLE GlobalFree(hMem)
```

Parameter, Type, and Description:

`hMem` `HANDLE` Global block to free

Description:

The `GlobalFree` function frees the global memory block specified in `hMem`. The handle to the memory block becomes invalid.

Return Value:

The `GlobalFree` function returns NULL when the memory block is freed. A return value of `hMem` indicates that the function cannot free the memory block.

GlobalHandle

Syntax:

```
DWORD GlobalHandle(wMem)
```

Parameter, Type, and Description:

`wMem`	`WORD`	Segment address or selector of the global memory object

Description:

The `GlobalHandle` function gets the handle of the global memory object specified by the segment address or selector in `wMem`.

Return Value:

The low-order word of the return value contains the handle of the memory object. The high-order word of the return value contains the segment address or selector of the memory object. NULL is returned when there is no handle for the memory object.

GlobalLock

Syntax:

```
LPSTR GlobalLock(hMem)
```

Parameter, Type, and Description:

`hMem`	`HANDLE`	Global memory block to lock

Description:

The `GlobalLock` function gets the pointer to the global memory block specified in `hMem`. The lock count of the memory object is incremented.

Return Value:

The `GlobalLock` function returns the pointer to the first byte of memory in the memory block. A NULL return value indicates that the function cannot get the pointer to the memory block.

GlobalLRUNewest

Syntax:

```
HANDLE GlobalLRUNewest(hMem)
```

Parameter, Type, and Description:

`hMem`	`HANDLE`	Global memory object to move

Description:

The GlobalLRUNewest function moves the global memory object specified in hMem to the newest least-recently-used (LRU) position. The block in hMem must be discardable.

Return Value:

A NULL return value indicates that hMem is invalid.

GlobalLRUOldest

Syntax:

```
HANDLE GlobalLRUOldest(hMem)
```

Parameter, Type, and Description:

hMem	HANDLE	Global memory object to move

Description:

The GlobalLRUOldest function moves the global memory object specified in hMem to the oldest least-recently-used (LRU) position. The block in hMem must be discardable.

Return Value:

A NULL return value indicates that hMem is invalid.

GlobalNotify

Syntax:

```
void GlobalNotify(lpNotifyProc)
```

Parameter, Type, and Description:

lpNotifyProc	FARPROC	Procedure instance address of the current task's notification procedure

Description:

The GlobalNotify function defines the notification procedure for the current task. lpNotifyProc contains the procedure instance address of the current task's notification procedure. The notification procedure is called whenever a global memory block allocated with the GMEM_NOTIFY flag is about to be discarded. The conventions for the notification procedure follow.

Syntax:

```
BOOL FAR PASCAL NotifyProc(hMem)
HANDLE hMem;
```

Parameter, Type, and Description:

`hMem`	`HANDLE`	Handle to the global memory block to evaluate

Description:

`NotifyProc` is a placeholder for the function name supplied by the application. Use `EXPORTS` to include the application-supplied name in the module definition statement for the DLL.

Return Value:

The notification procedure will return either zero, indicating that Windows should not discard the memory object, or a nonzero value, indicating that the memory object can be discarded.

Return Value:

There is no return value.

GlobalReAlloc

Syntax:

```
HANDLE GlobalReAlloc(hMem, dwBytes, wFlags)
```

Parameter, Type, and Description:

`hMem`	`HANDLE`	Global memory block to reallocate
`dwBytes`	`DWORD`	New size for the memory block
`wFlags`	`WORD`	Combination of new allocation flags

Description:

The `GlobalReAlloc` function reallocates the global memory block in `hMem`. `dwBytes` specifies the new size for the memory block. `wFlags` indicates how the global block should be reallocated and can be any combination of the following:

Value	*Meaning*
`GMEM_DISCARDABLE`	Memory can be discarded
`GMEM_MODIFY`	Memory flags are modified

Value	*Meaning*
GMEM_MOVEABLE	Memory is moveable
GMEM_NOCOMPACT	Memory is not compacted or discarded to meet the allocation requirements
GMEM_NODISCARD	Memory is not discarded to meet the allocation requirements
GMEM_ZEROINT	If the block size is increased, any additional memory is initialized to zero

Combine values by using the bitwise OR operator.

Return Value:

The `GlobalReAlloc` function returns the handle to the reallocated block. A NULL return value indicates that the function cannot reallocate the block.

GlobalSize

Syntax:

```
DWORD GlobalSize(hMem)
```

Parameter, Type, and Description:

hMem	HANDLE	Handle to global memory block

Description:

The `GlobalSize` function gets the number of bytes in the global memory block specified in `hMem`.

Return Value:

The `GlobalSize` function returns the number of bytes in the block. A return value of zero indicates that the handle is invalid or the object has been discarded.

GlobalUnlock

Syntax:

```
BOOL GlobalUnlock(hMem)
```

Parameter, Type, and Description:

hMem	HANDLE	Handle to the global memory block to unlock

Description:

The `GlobalUnlock` function unlocks the global memory block specified in `hMem`. The lock count for the block is decremented.

Return Value:

The `GlobalUnlock` function returns zero if the lock count is decremented to zero. A nonzero value indicates that the lock count is not decremented to zero.

GlobalUnwire

Syntax:

```
BOOL GlobalUnwire(hMem)
```

Parameter, Type, and Description:

`hMem`	`HANDLE`	Segment to unlock

Description:

The `GlobalUnwire` function unlocks the memory segment specified in `hMem`. The lock count for the segment is decremented. The memory segment must have been locked with `GlobalWire`.

Return Value:

The `GlobalUnwire` function returns TRUE when the segment lock count is decremented to zero. A return value of FALSE indicates that the decremented lock count is not zero.

GlobalWire

Syntax:

```
LPSTR GlobalWire(hMem)
```

Parameter, Type, and Description:

`hMem`	`HANDLE`	Segment to lock

Description:

The `GlobalWire` function moves the segment specified in `hMem` to low memory and locks it.

Return Value:

The `GlobalWire` function returns the pointer to the new segment location. A NULL return value indicates that the function cannot move the segment.

LimitEmsPages

Syntax:

```
void LimitEmsPages(dwKbytes)
```

Parameter, Type, and Description:

`dwKbytes`	`DWORD`	Kilobytes of expanded memory

Description:

The `LimitEmsPages` function limits the amount of expanded memory assigned to an application to the number of kilobytes specified in `dwKbytes`. The application can obtain additional expanded memory through INT 67H.

Return Value:

There is no return value.

LocalAlloc

Syntax:

```
HANDLE LocalAlloc(wFlags, wBytes)
```

Parameter, Type, and Description:

`wFlags`	`WORD`	Indicates how the memory is to be allocated
`wBytes`	`WORD`	Number of bytes to allocate

Description:

The `LocalAlloc` function allocates memory from the local heap. The number of bytes of memory to allocate is specified in `wBytes`. `wFlags` specifies how the memory is to be allocated and can be any combination of the following values:

Value	*Meaning*
`LMEM_DISCARDABLE`	Discardable memory is allocated
`LMEM_FIXED`	Fixed memory is allocated

Value	*Meaning*
LMEM_MODIFY	The LMEM_DISCARDABLE flag is modified
LMEM_MOVEABLE	Moveable memory is allocated
LMEM_NOCOMPACT	Memory is not compacted or discarded to meet the memory requirements
LMEM_NODISCARD	Memory is not discarded to meet the memory requirements
LMEM_ZEROINT	The contents of the allocated memory is initialized to zero

Combine values by using the bitwise OR operator. You cannot use LMEM_FIXED and LMEM_MOVEABLE together.

Return Value:

The LocalAlloc function returns the handle to the allocated local memory block. A NULL return value indicates that the function cannot allocate the memory block.

LocalCompact

Syntax:

```
WORD LocalCompact(wMinFree)
```

Parameter, Type, and Description:

wMinFree	WORD	Number of bytes to free

Description:

The LocalCompact function finds the number of bytes specified in wMinFree by compacting the local heap. If necessary, unlocked discardable blocks are discarded to free the number of bytes requested.

Return Value:

The LocalCompact function returns the number of bytes in the largest block of free local memory.

LocalDiscard

Syntax:

```
HANDLE LocalDiscard(hMem)
```

Parameter, Type, and Description:

`hMem` `HANDLE` Local memory block to discard

Description:

The `LocalDiscard` function discards the local memory block specified in `hMem` if the lock count for the memory block is zero. The handle to the memory block remains valid. If the memory block is other nonzero, the function is ignored.

Return Value:

The `LocalDiscard` function returns NULL when the memory block is discarded. A return value of `hMem` indicates that the function cannot discard the memory block.

LocalFlags

Syntax:

```
WORD LocalFlags(hMem)
```

Parameter, Type, and Description:

`hMem` `HANDLE` Local memory block

Description:

The `LocalFlags` function returns information on the local memory block specified in `hMem`.

Return Value:

The high-order byte of the return value contains one of the following:

Value	*Meaning*
LMEM_DISCARDABLE	Block is discardable
LMEM_DISCARDED	Block has been discarded

The low-order byte of the return value contains the reference count for the memory block. Use the `LMEM_LOCKCOUNT` mask to get the lock count value from the return value.

LocalFree

Syntax:

```
HANDLE LocalFree(hMem)
```

Parameter, Type, and Description:

`hMem`	`HANDLE`	Local memory block to free

Description:

The `LocalFree` function frees the local memory block specified in `hMem`. The handle of the block becomes invalid.

Return Value:

The `LocalFree` function returns NULL when the memory block is freed. A return value of `hMem` indicates that the function cannot free the memory block.

LocalHandle

Syntax:

```
HANDLE LocalHandle(wMem)
```

Parameter, Type, and Description:

`wMem`	`WORD`	Address of local memory object

Description:

The `LocalHandle` function gets the handle of the local memory object that has the address specified in `wMem`.

Return Value:

The `LocalHandle` function returns the handle to the local memory object.

LocalInit

Syntax:

```
BOOL LocalInit(wSegment, pStart, pEnd)
```

Parameter, Type, and Description:

`wSegment`	`WORD`	Segment address
`pStart`	`PSTR`	Address of the start of the local heap
`pEnd`	`PSTR`	Address of the end of the local heap

Description:

The `LocalInit` function initializes a local heap. `wSegment` specifies the segment where the local heap is initialized. `pStart` specifies the starting address of the local heap. `pEnd` specifies the ending address of the local heap.

Return Value:

The `LocalInit` function returns a Boolean nonzero value when the heap is successfully initialized. A return value of zero indicates that the function cannot initialize the heap.

LocalLock

Syntax:

```
PSTR LocalLock(hMem)
```

Parameter, Type, and Description:

`hMem`	`HANDLE`	Local memory block to lock

Description:

The `LocalLock` function locks the local memory block in `hMem` at the given address. The reference count of the block is incremented. Use `LocalUnlock` to unlock the memory block.

Return Value:

The `LocalLock` function returns the pointer to the first byte in the local memory block. A NULL return value indicates that the function cannot lock the memory block.

LocalReAlloc

Syntax:

```
HANDLE LocalReAlloc(hMem, wBytes, wFlags)
```

Parameter, Type, and Description:

`hMem`	`HANDLE`	Local memory block to reallocate
`wBytes`	`WORD`	New size of memory block
`wFlags`	`WORD`	Indicates how the memory block is to be reallocated

Description:

The `LocalReAlloc` function modifies the size of the local memory block in `hMem`. `wBytes` specifies the new size of the local memory block. `wFlags` specifies how the memory block is to be reallocated and can be one or more of the following values:

Value	*Meaning*
LMEM_DISCARDABLE	Memory is discardable
LMEM_MODIFY	Memory flags are modified
LMEM_MOVEABLE	Memory is moveable
LMEM_NOCOMPACT	Memory is not compacted or discarded to meet the memory requirements
LMEM_NODISCARD	Memory is not discarded to meet the memory requirements
LMEM_ZEROINT	Any additional memory allocated to the block is initialized to zero

Return Value:

The `LocalReAlloc` function returns the handle to the reallocated local memory. A NULL return value indicates that the function cannot reallocate the memory.

LocalShrink

Syntax:

```
WORD LocalShrink(hSeg, wSize)
```

Parameter, Type, and Description:

hSeg	HANDLE	Segment that contains the local heap
wSize	WORD	Number of bytes in the heap after it has been sized

Description:

The `LocalShrink` function shrinks the local heap contained in the segment specified in `hSeg`. `wSize` specifies the size of the local heap after it has been sized. The function will not shrink the local head below the size specified in the module definition file for the application.

Return Value:

The `LocalShrink` function returns the final size of the heap.

LocalSize

Syntax:

```
WORD LocalSize(hMem)
```

Parameter, Type, and Description:

`hMem` `HANDLE` Local memory block handle

Description:

The `LocalSize` function gets the number of bytes in the local memory block specified in `hMem`.

Return Value:

The `LocalSize` function returns the number of bytes in the local memory block. A NULL return value indicates that the function cannot get the bytes in the local memory block.

LocalUnlock

Syntax:

```
BOOL LocalUnlock(hMem)
```

Parameter, Type, and Description:

`hMem` `HANDLE` Local memory block to unlock

Description:

The `LocalUnlock` function decrements the reference count for the local memory block in `hMem` and unlocks the memory block.

Return Value:

The `LocalUnlock` function returns zero if the block's reference count is decremented to zero. A nonzero return value indicates that the resulting reference count is not zero.

LockData

Syntax:

```
HANDLE LockData(Dummy)
```

Parameter, Type, and Description:

`Dummy` `int` Should be set to zero and is not used

Description:

The `LockData` function locks the current data segment in memory. You should use this function only with modules that have moveable data segments.

Return Value:

The `LockData` function returns the handle to the locked data segment. A NULL return value indicates that the function cannot lock the data segment.

LockSegment

Syntax:

```
HANDLE LockSegment(wSegment)
```

Parameter, Type, and Description:

`wSegment` `WORD` Segment address of segment to lock

Description:

The `LockSegment` function locks the segment with the segment address specified in `wSegment`. The segment lock count is incremented. When `wSegment` is –1, the current data segment is locked.

Return Value:

The `LockSegment` function returns the handle to the data segment. A NULL return value indicates that the function cannot lock the segment.

SetSwapAreaSize

Syntax:

```
LONG SetSwapAreaSize(rsSize)
```

Parameter, Type, and Description:

`rsSize` `WORD` Number of 16-byte paragraphs requested by the application

Description:

The `SetSwapAreaSize` function defines the amount of memory available for an application to use for code segments. `rsSize` specifies the number of 16-byte paragraphs to be used for code segments. Only one-half the memory available after Windows is loaded can be used.

Return Value:

The low-order word of the return value contains the number of paragraphs that can be used for code segments. The high-order word of the return value specifies the maximum size available.

SwitchStackBack

Syntax:

```
void SwitchStackBack()
```

Description:

The `SwitchStackBack` function returns the stack of the current task to the data segment of the task.

Return Value:

There is no return value.

SwitchStackTo

Syntax:

```
void SwitchStackTo(wStackSegment, wStackPointer, wStackTop)
```

Parameter, Type, and Description:

`wStackSegment`	`WORD`	Data segment to contain the stack
`wStackPointer`	`WORD`	Offset of the beginning of the stack
`wStackTop`	`WORD`	Offset of the top of the stack

Description:

The `SwitchStackTo` function changes the stack of the current task to the segment in `wStackSegment`. `wStackPointer` and `wStackTop` specify the beginning and top of the stack, respectively.

Return Value:

There is no return value.

UnlockData

Syntax:

```
HANDLE UnlockData(Dummy)
```

Parameter, Type, and Description:

`Dummy`	`int`	Should be set to zero and not used

Description:

The `UnlockData` macro unlocks the current data segment.

Return Value:

There is no return value.

UnlockSegment

Syntax:

```
BOOL UnlockSegment(wSegment)
```

Parameter, Type, and Description:

`wSegment`	`WORD`	Segment address of segment to unlock

Description:

The `UnlockSegment` function unlocks the segment specified by the segment address in `wSegment`. The lock count of the segment is decremented. When `wSegment` is –1, the current data segment is unlocked.

Return Value:

The `UnlockSegment` function returns zero if the lock count of the segment is decremented to zero. A nonzero return value indicates that the lock count of the segment is not decremented to zero.

Module Management Functions

Modules are executable units of code and data. Windows provides a set of functions for modifying and retrieving information for Windows modules. The following functions are categorized as Module Management functions for the System Services Interface:

Function	*Meaning*
`FreeLibrary`	Decreases the reference count of a library
`FreeModule`	Decreases the reference count of a module
`FreeProcInstance`	Removes a function instance entry at an address
`GetCodeHandle`	Finds the code segment that contains the specified function
`GetInstanceData`	Moves the data from the offset in an instance to the offset in another instance
`GetModuleFileName`	Gets the file name of a module
`GetModuleHandle`	Gets the handle of a module
`GetModuleUsage`	Gets the reference count of a module
`GetProcAddress`	Gets the address of a function in a module
`GetVersion`	Gets the Windows version number
`LoadLibrary`	Loads a library module
`MakeProcInstance`	Gets a function instance address

The rest of this section provides detailed information on each of the functions in this list.

FreeLibrary

Syntax:

```
void FreeLibrary(hLibModule)
```

Parameter, Type, and Description:

`hLibModule` `HANDLE` Loaded library module

Description:

The `FreeLibrary` function frees the memory associated with the loaded library module in `hLibModule` when the reference count of the module is zero. Each time the `FreeLibrary` function is called, the reference count for the specified module is decremented.

Return Value:

There is no return value.

FreeModule

Syntax:

```
void FreeModule(hModule)
```

Parameter, Type, and Description:

`hModule`	`HANDLE`	Loaded module

Description:

The `FreeModule` function frees the memory associated with the loaded module in `hModule` when the reference count of the module is zero. Each time the `FreeModule` function is called, the reference count for the specified module is decremented.

Return Value:

There is no return value.

FreeProcInstance

Syntax:

```
void FreeProcInstance(lpProc)
```

Parameter, Type, and Description:

`lpProc`	`FARPROC`	Procedure instance address of the function to free

Description:

The `FreeProcInstance` function frees the function specified by the procedure instance address in `lpProc`. The address in `lpProc` must be created with the `MakeProcInstance` function.

Return Value:

There is no return value.

GetCodeHandle

Syntax:

```
HANDLE GetCodeHandle(lpProc)
```

Parameter, Type, and Description:

`lpProc`	`FARPROC`	Procedure instance address

Description:

The `GetCodeHandle` function returns the handle of the code segment that contains the function with the procedure instance address in `lpProc`.

Return Value:

The `GetCodeHandle` function returns the handle of the code segment that contains the specified function.

GetInstanceData

Syntax:

```
int GetInstanceData(hInstance, pData, nCount)
```

Parameter, Type, and Description:

`hInstance`	`HANDLE`	Previous instance
`pData`	`NPSTR`	Pointer to a buffer in the current instance
`nCount`	`int`	Number of bytes to copy

Description:

The `GetInstanceData` function copies data from the previous instance specified in `hInstance` to the data area of the current instance specified in `pData`. `nCount` specifies the number of bytes to copy.

Return Value:

The `GetInstanceData` function returns the number of bytes copied.

GetModuleFileName

Syntax:

```
int GetModuleFileName(hModule, lpFilename, nSize)
```

Parameter, Type, and Description:

`hModule`	`HANDLE`	Module or instance of module
`lpFilename`	`LPSTR`	Pointer to the buffer to receive the file name
`nSize`	`int`	Maximum number of bytes to copy

Description:

The `GetModuleFileName` function gets the path name of an executable file for the module specified in `hModule`. The path name is copied into the buffer pointed to by `lpFilename`. `nSize` specifies the maximum number of bytes to copy to the buffer.

Return Value:

The `GetModuleFileName` function returns the length of the string copied to the buffer.

GetModuleHandle

Syntax:

```
HANDLE GetModuleHandle(lpModuleName)
```

Parameter, Type, and Description:

`lpModuleName`	`LPSTR`	Pointer to a null-terminated string that defines the module

Description:

The `GetModuleHandle` function gets the handle for the module specified by the string in `lpModuleName`.

Return Value:

The `GetModuleHandle` function returns the handle to the module. A NULL return value indicates that the function cannot get the handle for the module.

GetModuleUsage

Syntax:

```
int GetModuleUsage(hModule)
```

Parameter, Type, and Description:

`hModule`	`HANDLE`	Module or instance of module

Description:

The `GetModuleUsage` function gets the reference count for the module specified in `hModule`.

Return Value:

The `GetModuleUsage` function returns the reference count for the module.

GetProcAddress

Syntax:

```
FARPROC GetProcAddress(hModule, lpProcName)
```

Parameter, Type, and Description:

`hModule`	`HANDLE`	Library module that contains the function
`lpProcName`	`LPSTR`	Pointer to the function name

Description:

The `GetProcAddress` function gets the address of the function specified in `lpProcName`. `hModule` specifies the module that contains the function. If `hModule` is set to NULL, it is assumed that the current module contains the function.

Return Value:

The `GetProcAddress` function returns the pointer to the function's entry point. A NULL return value indicates that the function cannot get the address.

GetVersion

Syntax:

```
WORD GetVersion()
```

Description:

The `GetVersion` function determines and returns the Windows version number.

Return Value:

The low-order byte of the return value specifies the major Windows version number. The high-order byte of the return value specifies the minor Windows version number.

LoadLibrary

Syntax:

```
HANDLE LoadLibrary(lpLibFileName)
```

Parameter, Type, and Description:

`lpLibFileName`	`LPSTR`	Pointer to a null-terminated string that defines the library file

Description:

The `LoadLibrary` function loads the library module from the library file specified in `lpLibFilename`. The function also returns the handle of the loaded module instance.

Return Value:

The `LoadLibrary` function returns the handle of the loaded library module instance. The function returns one of the following error values instead when unable to load the library module:

Value	*Meaning*
0	Out of memory
2	File not found
3	Path not found
5	Attempt to dynamically link to a task
6	Library requires separate data segments for each task
10	Incorrect Windows version
11	Invalid .EXE file
12	OS/2 application
13	DOS 4.0 application
14	Unknown .EXE type
15	Attempt in protected mode to load an .EXE created for an earlier version of Windows

Value	*Meaning*
16	Attempt to load a second instance of an .EXE containing multiple, writable data segments
17	Attempt in large-frame EMS mode to load a second instance of an application that links to certain nonshareable DLLs already in use
18	Attempt in real mode to load an application marked for protected mode only

MakeProcInstance

Syntax:

```
FARPROC MakeProcInstance(lpProc, hInstance)
```

Parameter, Type, and Description:

`lpProc`	`FARPROC`	Procedure instance address
`hInstance`	`HANDLE`	Instance associated with the data segment

Description:

The `MakeProcInstance` function creates a procedure instance address and binds the data segment for the instance in `hInstance` to the function specified in `lpProc`.

Return Value:

The `MakeProcInstance` function returns the pointer to the function specified in `lpProc`. A NULL return value indicates that the function cannot create the procedure instance address.

Operating System Interrupt Functions

Windows provides the Operating System Interrupt functions to enable applications that use assembly language to generate DOS and NETBIOS interrupts without coding the interrupt. The following functions are categorized as Operating System Interrupt functions for the System Services Interface:

Function	*Interrupt Generated*
`DOS3Call`	DOS 21H
`NetBIOSCall`	NETBIOS 5CH

The rest of this section provides detailed information on each of the functions in this list.

DOS3Call

Syntax:

```
extrn DOS3Call     :far
```

Description:

The `DOS3Call` function issues a DOS function-request 21H. This function can only be called from an assembly language routine and is not defined in a Windows include file. All appropriate registers must be set before you call the `DOS3Call` function.

Return Value:

The `DOS3Call` function returns the registers of the DOS function.

NetBIOSCall

Syntax:

```
extrn NetBIOSCall      :far
```

Description:

The `NetBIOSCall` function generates the `NETBIOS` interrupt 5CH. This function can only be called from an assembly language routine and is not defined in a Windows include file. All appropriate registers must be set before you call the `NetBIOSCall` function.

Return Value:

There is no return value.

Optimization Tool Functions

Optimization Tool functions manipulate the Windows Profiler and Swap development tools. The following functions are categorized as Optimization Tool functions for the System Services Interface:

Function	*Meaning*
`ProfClear`	Discards the contents of the Profiler sampling buffer
`ProfFinish`	Stops Profiler sampling and flushes the buffer to disk

`ProfFlush`	Flushes the Profiler sampling buffer to disk
`ProfInsChk`	Determines whether Profiler is installed
`ProfSampRate`	Sets the Profiler sampling rate
`ProfSetup`	Sets the Profiler sampling buffer and recording rate
`ProfStart`	Begins Profiler sampling
`ProfStop`	Ends Profiler sampling
`SwapRecording`	Either starts or stops Swap analysis of the swapping behavior of the application

The rest of this section provides detailed information on each of the functions in this list.

ProfClear

Syntax:

```
void ProfClear()
```

Description:

The `ProfClear` function discards the samples in the sampling buffer. This function is used with the Windows Profiler.

Return Value:

There is no return value.

ProfFinish

Syntax:

```
void ProfFinish()
```

Description:

The `ProfFinish` function ends the sampling session and flushes the output buffer to disk. This function is used with the Windows Profiler.

Return Value:

There is no return value.

ProfFlush

Syntax:

```
void ProfFlush()
```

Description:

The `ProfFlush` function flushes the sampling buffer to disk. This function is used with the Windows Profiler.

Return Value:

There is no return value.

ProfInsChk

Syntax:

```
ProfInsCheck()
```

Description:

The `ProfInsCheck` function indicates whether the Windows Profiler is installed.

Return Value:

The `ProfInsCheck` function returns zero if the Profiler is not installed. A return value of 1 indicates that the Profiler is installed for any mode other than 386 enhanced mode. A return value of 2 indicates that the Profiler is installed for 386 enhanced mode.

ProfSampRate

Syntax:

```
void ProfSampRate(nRate286, nRate386)
```

Parameter, Type, and Description:

`nRate286`	`int`	Sampling rate if the application is not running with Windows in 386 enhanced mode
`nRate386`	`int`	Sampling rate if the application is running with Windows in 386 enhanced mode

Description:

The `ProfSampRate` function specifies the sampling rate for the Windows Profiler. For applications running with Windows in 386 enhanced mode, `nRate386` specifies a sampling rate ranging from 1 to 1000 milliseconds. For applications not running with Windows in 386 enhanced mode, `nRate286` specifies the sampling rate with one of the following values:

Value	*Sampling Rate*
1	122.070 microseconds
2	244.141 microseconds
3	488.281 microseconds
4	976.562 microseconds
5	1.953125 milliseconds (default rate)
6	3.90625 milliseconds
7	7.8125 milliseconds
8	15.625 milliseconds
9	31.25 milliseconds
10	62.5 milliseconds
11	125 milliseconds
12	250 milliseconds
13	500 milliseconds

Return Value:

There is no return value.

ProfSetup

Syntax:

```
void ProfSetup(nBufferSize, nSamples)
```

Parameter, Type, and Description:

`nBufferSize`	`int`	Number of kilobytes in the output buffer
`nSamples`	`int`	Amount of sampling data to write to disk

Description:

The `ProfSetup` function defines the size of the output buffer and the amount of sampling data to write to disk. `nBufferSize` specifies the number of kilobytes in the output buffer. `nBufferSize` can range between 1 and 1064 and has a default value of 64. nSamples specifies the amount of sampling data to write to the disk. When nSamples is zero—the default value—the amount of data written to the disk is unlimited. The ProfSetup function is used with the Windows Profiler. Windows must be running in 386 enhanced mode or the function has no effect.

Return Value:

There is no return value.

ProfStart

Syntax:

```
void ProfStart()
```

Description:

The ProfStart function initiates a sampling session. The ProfStart function is used with the Windows Profiler.

Return Value:

There is no return value.

ProfStop

Syntax:

```
void ProfStop()
```

Description:

The ProfStop function terminates a sampling session. The ProfStop function is used with the Windows Profiler.

Return Value:

There is no return value.

SwapRecording

Syntax:

```
void SwapRecording(wFlag)
```

Parameter, Type, and Description:

`wFlag`	`WORD`	Indicates whether Swap is to start or stop analyzing swapping behavior

Description:

The `SwapRecording` function specifies whether analysis of swapping behavior should begin or end. `wFlag` specifies whether to stop or to start analysis and can be any one of the following values:

Value	*Meaning*
0	Stop
1	Record swap calls, discard swap returns
2	Record swap calls and calls through thunks, discard swap returns

Return Value:

There is no return value.

Resource Management Functions

Windows provides the Resource Management functions for manipulating resources such as icons, bitmaps, cursors, fonts, and strings. The following functions are categorized as Resource Management functions for the System Services Interface:

Function	*Meaning*
`AccessResource`	Opens a resource
`AllocResource`	Allocates memory for a resource
`FindResource`	Gets the location of a resource
`FreeResource`	Removes a resource from memory
`LoadAccelerators`	Loads an accelerator table
`LoadBitmap`	Loads a bitmap resource
`LoadCursor`	Loads a cursor resource
`LoadIcon`	Loads an icon resource
`LoadMenu`	Loads a menu resource
`LoadResource`	Loads a resource
`LoadString`	Loads a string resource
`LockResource`	Gets the absolute memory address of a resource
`SetResourceHandler`	Defines a function to load resources
`SizeofResource`	Defines the size for a resource
`UnlockResource`	Unlocks a resource

The rest of this section provides detailed information on each of the functions in this list.

AccessResource

Syntax:

```
int AccessResource(hInstance, hResInfo)
```

Parameter, Type, and Description:

`hInstance`	`HANDLE`	Instance of a module whose executable file contains the resource
`hResInfo`	`HANDLE`	Resource

Description:

The `AccessResource` function reads the resource in `hResInfo` from the resource file specified in `hInstance`. The function opens the file, moves the file pointer to the beginning of the resource, and reads the resource. Close the resource file by using the `_lclose` function.

Return Value:

The `AccessResource` function returns the DOS handle to the resource file. A return value of –1 indicates that the function cannot read the resource.

AllocResource

Syntax:

```
HANDLE AllocResource(hInstance, hResInfo, dwSize)
```

Parameter, Type, and Description:

`hInstance`	`HANDLE`	Instance of module whose executable file contains the resource
`hResInfo`	`HANDLE`	Resource
`dwSize`	`DWORD`	Allocation override size in bytes

Description:

The `AllocResource` function allocates memory for the resource specified in `hResInfo`. `dwSize` specifies the override size to allocate for the resource.

Return Value:

The `AllocResource` function returns the handle to the allocated global memory block.

FindResource

Syntax:

```
HANDLE FindResource(hInstance, lpName, lpType)
```

Parameter, Type, and Description:

`hInstance`	`HANDLE`	Instance of a module whose executable file contains the resource
`lpName`	`LPSTR`	Pointer to a null-terminated string containing the name of the resource
`lpType`	`LPSTR`	Pointer to a null-terminated string containing the resource type

Description:

The `FindResource` function finds the resource specified by `lpName` and `lpType` in the resource file specified by `hInstance`. `lpName` specifies the name of the resource. `lpType` specifies the resource type. The following values are used for `lpType`:

Value	*Meaning*
`RT_ACCELERATOR`	Accelerator table
`RT_BITMAP`	Bitmap resource
`RT_DIALOG`	Dialog box
`RT_FONT`	Font resource
`RT_FONTDIR`	Font directory resource
`RT_MENU`	Menu resource
`RT_RCDATA`	User-defined resource

Return Value:

The `FindResource` function returns the handle of the specified resource. A NULL return value indicates that the function cannot find the resource.

FreeResource

Syntax:

```
BOOL FreeResource(hResData)
```

Parameter, Type, and Description:

hResData	HANDLE	Data associated with the resource

Description:

The FreeResource function removes the resource in hResData from memory and frees all associated memory if the reference count for the resource is zero.

Return Value:

The FreeResource function returns zero when the resource is removed. A nonzero return value indicates that the function cannot remove the resource.

LoadAccelerators

Syntax:

```
HANDLE  LoadAccelerators(hInstance,  lpTableName)
```

Parameter, Type, and Description:

hInstance	HANDLE	Instance of a module whose executable file contains the accelerator table
lpTableName	LPSTR	Pointer to a null-terminated string containing the name of the table

Description:

The LoadAccelerators function loads the accelerator table specified in lpTableName. hInstance specifies the module whose executable file contains the accelerator table to load.

Return Value:

The LoadAccelerators function returns the handle to the loaded accelerator table. A NULL return value indicates that the function cannot load the accelerator table.

LoadBitmap

Syntax:

```
HBITMAP LoadBitmap(hInstance, lpBitmapName)
```

Parameter, Type, and Description:

`hInstance`	`HANDLE`	Instance of a module whose executable file contains the bitmap
`lpBitmapName`	`LPSTR`	Pointer to the null-terminated string that contains the name of the bitmap

Description:

The `LoadBitmap` function loads the bitmap resource specified in `lpBitmapName`. The bitmap is loaded from the executable file for the module specified in `hInstance`. `LoadBitmap` can be used to load the following predefined Windows bitmaps:

```
OBM_BTNCORNERS      OBM_OLD_RESTORE
OBM_BTSIZE          OBM_OLD_RGARROW
OBM_CHECK           OBM_OLD_UPARROW
OBM_CHECKBOXES      OBM_OLD_ZOOM
OBM_CLOSE           OBM_REDUCE
OBM_COMBO           OBM_REDUCED
OBM_DNARROW         OBM_RESTORE
OBM_DNARROWD        OBM_RESTORED
OBM_LFARROW         OBM_RGARROW
OBM_LFARROWD        OBM_RGARROWD
OBM_MNARROW         OBM_SIZE
OBM_OLD_CLOSE       OBM_UPARROW
OBM_OLD_DNARROW     OBM_UPARROWD
OBM_OLD_LFARROW     OBM_ZOOM
OBM_OLD_REDUCE      OBM_ZOOMD
```

Return Value:

The `LoadBitmap` function returns the handle of the loaded bitmap. A NULL return value indicates that the function cannot load the bitmap resource.

LoadCursor

Syntax:

```
HCURSOR LoadCursor(hInstance, lpCursorName)
```

Parameter, Type, and Description:

`hInstance`	`HANDLE`	Module containing the cursor
`lpCursorName`	`LPSTR`	Pointer to the null-terminated string that contains the name of the cursor resource

Description:

The `LoadCursor` function loads the cursor specified in `lpCursorName`. `lpCursorName` points to a null-terminated character string that holds the name of the cursor resource. `hInstance` specifies the module that has the executable file containing the cursor resource. You can access the predefined Windows cursors with the `LoadCursor` function by setting `hInstance` to NULL and `CursorName` to one of these values:

Constant	*Meaning*
`IDC_ARROW`	Arrow cursor
`IDC_CROSS`	Cross hair cursor
`IDC_IBEAM`	I-beam text cursor
`IDC_ICON`	Empty icon
`IDC_SIZE`	Square with small square in lower-right corner
`IDC_SIZENESW`	Cursor with arrows pointing northeast and southwest
`IDC_SIZENS`	Cursor with arrows pointing north and south
`IDC_SIZENWSE`	Cursor with arrows pointing northwest and southeast
`IDC_SIZEWE`	Cursor with arrows pointing west and east
`IDC_UPARROW`	Vertical arrow cursor
`IDC_WAIT`	Hourglass cursor

Return Value:

The `LoadCursor` function returns the handle of the loaded cursor. A NULL return value indicates that the function cannot load the cursor.

Note: If `lpCursorName` specifies a resource type other than a cursor resource, the return value will be an invalid cursor handle.

LoadIcon

Syntax:

```
HICON LoadIcon(hInstance, lpIconName)
```

Parameter, Type, and Description:

hInstance	HANDLE	Instance of a module whose executable file contains the icon
lpIconName	LPSTR	Pointer to a null-terminated string containing the name of the icon

Description:

The `LoadIcon` function loads the icon specified in `lpIconName`. `hInstance` specifies the module whose executable file contains the specified icon resource. `LoadIcon` can be used to access the following predefined Windows icons:

Value	*Meaning*
IDI_APPLICATION	Default application icon
IDI_ASTERISK	Asterisk (used in information messages)
IDI_EXCLAMATION	Exclamation point (used in warning messages)
IDI_HAND	Hand shape (used in serious warning messages)
IDI_QUESTION	Question mark (used in prompts)

Return Value:

The `LoadIcon` function returns the handle to the icon resource. A NULL return value indicates that the function cannot load the icon.

LoadMenu

Syntax:

```
HMENU LoadMenu(hInstance, lpMenuName)
```

Parameter, Type, and Description:

hInstance	HANDLE	Instance of a module whose executable file contains the menu
lpMenuName	LPSTR	Pointer to a null-terminated string containing the name of the menu

Description:

The `LoadMenu` function loads the menu resource specified in `lpMenuName`. `hInstance` specifies the module whose executable file contains the menu resource.

Return Value:

The `LoadMenu` function returns the handle to the menu resource. A NULL return value indicates that the function cannot load the menu resource.

LoadResource

Syntax:

```
HANDLE LoadResource(hInstance, hResInfo)
```

Parameter, Type, and Description:

`hInstance`	`HANDLE`	Instance of a module whose executable file contains the resource
`hResInfo`	`HANDLE`	Resource handle

Description:

The `LoadResource` function loads the resource specified in `hResInfo`. `hInstance` specifies the instance of the module whose executable file contains the specified resource.

Return Value:

The `LoadResource` function returns the handle to the loaded resource. A NULL return value indicates that the function cannot load the resource.

LoadString

Syntax:

```
int LoadString(hInstance, wID, lpBuffer, nBufferMax)
```

Parameter, Type, and Description:

`hInstance`	`HANDLE`	Instance of a module whose executable file contains the string resource
`wID`	`WORD`	Integer ID of the string to load

`lpBuffer`	`LPSTR`	Pointer to the buffer to receive the string
`nBufferMax`	`int`	Maximum number of characters to copy to the buffer

Description:

The `LoadString` function copies the string resource specified `wID` into the buffer pointed to by `lpBuffer`. `nBufferMax` specifies the maximum number of characters to copy to the buffer. `hInstance` specifies the instance of the module whose executable file contains the string resource.

Return Value:

The `LoadString` function returns the number of characters copied to the buffer. A return value of zero indicates that the function cannot copy the string resource into the buffer.

LockResource

Syntax:

```
LPSTR LockResource(hResData)
```

Parameter, Type, and Description:

`hResData`	`HANDLE`	Resource handle

Description:

The `LockResource` function locks the resource specified in `hResData`. The absolute memory address is retrieved and the lock count of the resource is incremented.

Return Value:

The `LockResource` function returns the pointer to the first byte of the resource. A NULL return value indicates that the function cannot lock the resource.

SetResourceHandler

Syntax:

```
FARPROC SetResourceHandler(hInstance, lpType, lpLoadFunc)
```

Parameter, Type, and Description:

hInstance	HANDLE	Instance of the module whose executable file contains the resource
lpType	LPSTR	Pointer to a resource type
lpLoadFunc	FARPROC	Procedure instance address of the callback function

Description:

The `SetResourceHandler` function installs the callback function specified in `lpLoadFunc`. The callback function is used to load the resource type specified in `lpType`. The callback function must follow these conventions and formats:

Syntax:

```
FARPROC FAR PASCAL LoadFunc(hMem, hInstance, hResInfo)
```

Parameter, Type, and Description:

hMem	HANDLE	A stored resource
hInstance	HANDLE	The instance of the module whose executable file contains the resource
hResInfo	HANDLE	The resource

Description:

`LoadFunc` is a placeholder for the function name supplied by the application. Use `EXPORTS` to include the application-supplied name in the module definition file for the application.

Return Value:

The return value depends on the application.

Return Value:

The `SetResourceHandler` function returns the pointer to the application-supplied callback function.

SizeofResource

Syntax:

```
WORD SizeofResource(hInstance, hResInfo)
```

Parameter, Type, and Description:

`hInstance`	`HANDLE`	Instance of a module whose executable file contains the resource
`hResInfo`	`HANDLE`	Resource handle

Description:

The `SizeofResource` function gets the number of bytes in the resource specified in `hResInfo`. `hInstance` specifies the instance of the module whose executable file contains the specified resource.

Return Value:

The `SizeofResource` function returns the number of bytes in the resource. A zero return value indicates that the function cannot get the number of bytes in the resource.

UnlockResource

Syntax:

```
BOOL UnlockResource(hResData)
```

Parameter, Type, and Description:

`hResData`	`HANDLE`	Global memory block to unlock

Description:

The `UnlockResource` macro unlocks the resource specified in `hResData`. The reference count for the specified resource is decremented.

Return Value:

The `UnlockResource` macro returns zero when the reference count for the resource is decremented to zero. A nonzero value indicates that the resource is not decremented to zero.

Segment Functions

Windows uses the Segment functions to manipulate selectors and the memory blocks they reference and retrieve information on segments. The following functions are categorized as Segment functions for the System Services Interface:

Function	*Meaning*
`AllocDStoCSAlias`	Returns a code segment selector from the specified data segment selector
`AllocSelector`	Allocates a new selector
`ChangeSelector`	Generates a code or data selector that corresponds to the specified selector
`DefineHandleTable`	Creates a private handle table
`FreeSelector`	Frees a selector
`GetCodeInfo`	Gets code segment information
`GlobalFix`	Keeps a global memory block from being moved in linear memory
`GlobalPageLock`	Page locks the memory associated with the specified global selector
`GlobalPageUnlock`	Decreases the page lock count for a block of memory
`GlobalUnfix`	Unlocks a global memory block
`LockSegment`	Locks a segment in memory
`UnlockSegment`	Unlocks a segment in memory

The rest of this section provides detailed information on each of the functions in this list.

AllocDStoCSAlias

Syntax:

```
WORD AllocDStoCSAlias(wSelector)
```

Parameter, Type, and Description:

`wSelector` `WORD` Data segment selector

Description:

The `AllocDStoCSAlias` function gets the code segment selector for the data segment selector specified in `wSelector`. The returned code segment selector can be used to execute code in the data segment. You must free the new selector by calling `FreeSelector`.

Return Value:

The `AllocDStoCSAlias` function returns the code segment selector for the specified data segment selector. A return value of zero indicates that the function cannot get the code segment selector for the specified data segment selector.

AllocSelector

Syntax:

```
WORD AllocSelector(wSelector)
```

Parameter, Type, and Description:

wSelector	WORD	Selector to copy

Description:

The AllocSelector function allocates a new selector either by copying the selector in wSelector when wSelector specifies a selector or by creating an uninitialized selector when wSelector is NULL.

Return Value:

The AllocSelector function returns the allocated selector. A return value of zero indicates that the function cannot allocate the new selector.

ChangeSelector

Syntax:

```
WORD ChangeSelector(wDestSelector, wSourceSelector)
```

Parameter, Type, and Description:

wDestSelector	WORD	Selector to receive the converted selector
wSourceSelector	WORD	Selector to be converted

Description:

The ChangeSelector function converts a code selector to a data selector or a data selector to a code selector. wSourceSelector specifies the selector that will be converted. wDestSelector specifies the selector that receives the converted selector.

Return Value:

The ChangeSelector function returns the resulting selector. A return value of zero indicates that the function cannot perform the conversion.

DefineHandleTable

Syntax:

```
BOOL DefineHandleTable(wOffset)
```

Parameter, Type, and Description:

`wOffset`	`WORD`	Offset from the beginning of a data segment to the beginning of the private handle table

Description:

The `DefineHandleTable` function creates a private handle table in a Windows application's default data segment. This table is used to store the segment addresses of global memory objects. `wOffset` specifies the offset for the table from the beginning of the data segment to the beginning of the private handle table.

For real mode, the corresponding address is updated in the private handle table when a global memory object is moved.

For standard or 386 enhanced mode, the addresses in the private handle table are not updated.

Return Value:

The `DefineHandleTable` function returns a nonzero value when the private handle table is created. A return value of zero indicates that the function cannot create the private handle table.

FreeSelector

Syntax:

```
WORD FreeSelector(wSelector)
```

Parameter, Type, and Description:

`wSelector`	`WORD`	Selector to free

Description:

The `FreeSelector` function frees the selector specified by `wSelector`.

Return Value:

The `FreeSelector` function returns NULL when the selector is freed. A return value of `wSelector` indicates that the function cannot free the selector.

GetCodeInfo

Syntax:

```
void GetCodeInfo(lpProc, lpSegInfo)
```

Parameter, Type, and Description:

`lpProc`	`FARPROC`	Function address
`lpSegInfo`	`LPVOID`	Pointer to an array of four 32-bit values to be filled with code segment information

Description:

The `GetCodeInfo` function gets the pointer to an array of values that contain code segment information. This information is for the code segment containing the function specified in `lpProc`. `lpSegInfo` points to an array of 32-bit values filled with code segment information.

Return Value:

There is no return value.

GlobalFix

Syntax:

```
void GlobalFix(hMem)
```

Parameter, Type, and Description:

`hMem`	`HANDLE`	Global memory block handle

Description:

The `GlobalFix` function locks the global memory block specified by `GlobalFix` into linear memory at its current address. The lock count for the global block is incremented. Use `GlobalUnfix` to unlock the memory block.

Return Value:

There is no return value.

GlobalPageLock

Syntax:

```
WORD GlobalPageLock(wSelector)
```

Parameter, Type, and Description:

`wSelector`	`WORD`	Selector to be locked

Description:

The `GlobalPageLock` function increments the page-lock count of the memory associated with the global selector specified in `wSelector`. As the page-lock count for the memory is greater than zero, the memory associated with the specified selector is not moved and remains paged-in as long.

Return Value:

The `GlobalPageLock` function returns the resulting page-lock count. A return value of zero indicates that the function cannot increment the lock count.

GlobalPageUnlock

Syntax:

```
WORD GlobalPageUnlock(wSelector)
```

Parameter, Type, and Description:

`wSelector`	`WORD`	Selector to be unlocked

Description:

The `GlobalPageUnlock` function decrements the page-lock count of the memory associated with `wSelector`. The block of memory associated with the selector can be moved or paged to disk when the page-lock count reaches zero.

Return Value:

The `GlobalPageUnlock` function returns the resulting page-lock count. A return value of zero indicates that the function cannot decrement the page-lock count.

GlobalUnfix

Syntax:

```
BOOL GlobalUnfix(hMem)
```

Parameter, Type, and Description:

`hMem`	`HANDLE`	Global memory block to unlock

Description:

The `GlobalUnfix` function decrements the lock count of the global memory block specified in `hMem`. The block can be moved or discarded if the resulting lock count is zero.

Return Value:

The `GlobalUnfix` function returns zero if the resulting lock count is zero. A nonzero value indicates that the resulting lock count is not zero.

LockSegment

Syntax:

```
HANDLE LockSegment(wSegment)
```

Parameter, Type, and Description:

`wSegment`	`WORD`	Segment address of the segment to lock

Description:

The `LockSegment` function locks the segment with the segment address specified in `wSegment`. The segment lock count is incremented. If `wSegment` is –1, the current data segment is locked.

Return Value:

The `LockSegment` function returns the handle to the locked data segment. A NULL return value indicates that the function cannot lock the segment.

UnlockSegment

Syntax:

```
BOOL UnlockSegment(wSegment)
```

Parameter, Type, and Description:

wSegment	WORD	Segment address of the segment to unlock

Description:

The UnlockSegment function unlocks the segment specified by the segment address in wSegment. The lock count of the segment is decremented. When wSegment is –1, the current data segment is unlocked.

Return Value:

The UnlockSegment function returns zero if the lock count of the segment is decremented to zero. A nonzero return value indicates that the lock count of the segment is not decremented to zero.

Sound Functions

Windows provides the Sound functions for generating sound. The following functions are categorized as Sound functions for the System Services Interface:

Function	*Meaning*
CloseSound	Closes the play device and flushes the voice queues
CountVoiceNotes	Gets the number of notes in the specified queue
GetThresholdEvent	Gets a long pointer to a threshold flag
GetThresholdStatus	Gets the threshold event status for each voice
OpenSound	Opens the play device
SetSoundNoise	Sets the source and duration for a noise
SetVoiceAccent	Puts an accent in the voice queue
SetVoiceEnvelope	Puts the voice envelope in the voice queue
SetVoiceNote	Puts a note in the specified voice queue
SetVoiceQueueSize	Sets the size of the voice queue
SetVoiceSound	Puts a sound frequency and duration in a voice queue
SetVoiceThreshold	Sets the threshold for a voice
StartSound	Begins playing each queue

Function	*Meaning*
`StopSound`	Stops the playing of each queue and flushes the contents of the queues
`SyncAllVoices`	Places a sync mark in each queue
`WaitSoundState`	Waits for the play driver to enter a specified state

The rest of this section provides detailed information on each of the functions in this list.

CloseSound

Syntax:

```
void CloseSound()
```

Description:

The `CloseSound` function flushes the voice queues and frees the buffers associated with these queues. The play device is closed to the application and freed for other applications to use.

Return Value:

There is no return value.

CountVoiceNotes

Syntax:

```
int CountVoiceNotes(nVoice)
```

Parameter, Type, and Description:

`nVoice`	`int`	Voice queue to count

Description:

The `CountVoiceNotes` function returns the number of notes in the queue specified in `nVoice`. Only notes created with `SetVoiceNote` are counted.

Return Value:

The `CountVoiceNotes` function returns the number of notes counted in the queue.

GetThresholdEvent

Syntax:

```
LPINT GetThresholdEvent()
```

Description:

The `GetThresholdEvent` function gets a flag that specifies a threshold event. A threshold event is a transition of a voice queue from *n* to *n*–1.

Note: *n* is the threshold level in notes.

Return Value:

The `GetThresholdEvent` function returns a pointer to the short integer specifying the threshold event.

GetThresholdStatus

Syntax:

```
int GetThresholdStatus()
```

Description:

The `GetThresholdStatus` function gets the threshold-event status for each voice and clears the threshold-event flag. The retrieved status specifies the voice-queue level for each voice. If the corresponding bit in the retrieved status is set, the voice-queue level is below threshold.

Return Value:

The `GetThresholdStatus` function returns status flag for the threshold-event status.

OpenSound

Syntax:

```
int OpenSound()
```

Description:

The `OpenSound` function gives the application access to the play device. Other applications cannot access the play device until the `CloseSound` function is called.

Return Value:

The `OpenSound` function returns the number of voices available. A return value of `S_SERDVNA` indicates that the play device is already in use. A return value of `S_SEROFM` indicates that there is not enough memory to open the play device.

SetSoundNoise

Syntax:

```
int SetSoundNoise(nSource, nDuration)
```

Parameter, Type, and Description:

`nSource`	`int`	Noise source
`nDuration`	`int`	Duration, in clock ticks, of the noise

Description:

The `SetSoundNoise` function defines a noise for the noise hardware of the play device. `nDuration` specifies the duration of the noise, in clock ticks. `nSource` specifies the source of the noise. The following values are used for `nSource`:

Note: *N* represents a value used in deriving the target frequency.

Value	*Meaning*
`S_PERIOD512`	Source frequency is *N*/512
`S_PERIOD1024`	Source frequency is *N*/1024
`S_PERIOD2048`	Source frequency is *N*/2048
`S_PERIODVOICE`	Source frequency from voice channel 3
`S_WHITE512`	Source frequency is *N*/512
`S_WHITE1024`	Source frequency is *N*/1024
`S_WHITE2048`	Source frequency is *N*/2048
`S_WHITEVOICE`	Source frequency from voice channel 3

Return Value:

The `SetSoundNoise` function returns zero when the noise is defined. A return value of `S_SERDSR` indicates that the function cannot define the noise.

SetVoiceAccent

Syntax:

```
int SetVoiceAccent(nVoice, nTempo, nVolume, nMode, nPitch)
```

Parameter, Type, and Description:

`nVoice`	`int`	Voice queue
`nTempo`	`int`	Number of quarter notes per minute
`nVolume`	`int`	Volume
`nMode`	`int`	How notes are to be played
`nPitch`	`int`	Pitch

Description:

The `SetVoiceAccent` function defines the accent for the voice queue specified in `nVoice`. `nTempo` specifies the number of quarter notes to play per minute and ranges from 32 to 255. `nVolume` specifies the volume level and ranges from 0 to 255. `nPitch` specifies the pitch of the notes played and ranges from 0 to 83. `nMode` specifies the method to use to play the notes and can be any one of the following values:

Value	*Meaning*
`S_LEGATO`	Note is held for the full duration and blends into the next note
`S_NORMAL`	Note is held for the full duration and comes to a complete stop before the next note begins
`S_STACCATO`	Note is held for part of the duration, leaving a break between notes

Return Value:

The `SetVoiceAccent` function returns zero when the accent is defined. One of the following values is returned when the function cannot define the accent:

Value	*Meaning*
`S_SERDMD`	Invalid mode
`S_SERDTP`	Invalid tempo
`S_SERDVL`	Invalid volume
`S_SERQFUL`	Queue full

SetVoiceEnvelope

Syntax:

```
int SetVoiceEnvelope(nVoice, nShape, nRepeat)
```

Parameter, Type, and Description:

nVoice	int	Voice queue
nShape	int	Index to OEM wave-shape table
nRepeat	int	Number of repetitions of one wave shape during the duration of a note

Description:

The SetVoiceEnvelope function sets the envelope for the voice queue specified in nVoice. nShape and nRepeat define the shape and the repeat count for the envelope, respectively.

Return Value:

The SetVoiceEnvelope function returns zero when the envelope is set. One of the following values is returned instead when the function cannot set the envelope:

Value	*Meaning*
S_SERDRC	Invalid repeat count
S_SERDSH	Invalid shape
S_SERQFUL	Queue full

SetVoiceNote

Syntax:

```
int SetVoiceNote(nVoice, nValue, nLength, nCdots)
```

Parameter, Type, and Description:

nVoice	int	Voice queue to receive note
nValue	int	Note
nLength	int	Indicates the reciprocal of the note duration
nCdots	int	Duration of the note, measured in dots

Description:

The `SetVoiceNote` function places a note in the voice queue specified by `nVoice`. `nValue` specifies the note to place in the queue and ranges from 1 to 84. `nLength` specifies the reciprocal of the duration of the note; for example, 4 for quarter note, 2 for half note, and so on. `nCdots` specifies the duration of the note in dots (duration = `nLength` * (`nCdots` * 3/2)).

Return Value:

The `SetVoiceNote` function returns zero when the note is placed in the voice queue. One of the following values is returned instead when the function cannot place the note in the voice queue:

Value	*Meaning*
S_SERDCC	Invalid dot count
S_SERDLN	Invalid note length
S_SERDNT	Invalid note
S_SERQFUL	Queue full

SetVoiceQueueSize

Syntax:

```
int SetVoiceQueueSize(nVoice, nBytes)
```

Parameter, Type, and Description:

nVoice	int	Voice queue
nBytes	int	Number of bytes in the voice queue

Description:

The `SetVoiceQueueSize` function sets the size of the queue specified in `nVoice`. `nBytes` specifies the number of bytes to allocate for the voice queue.

Return Value:

The `SetVoiceQueueSize` function returns zero when the queue size is set. One of the following values is returned instead when the function cannot set the queue size:

Value	*Meaning*
S_SERMACT	Music active
S_SEROFM	Out of memory

SetVoiceSound

Syntax:

```
int SetVoiceSound(nVoice, lFrequency, nDuration)
```

Parameter, Type, and Description:

`nVoice`	`int`	Voice queue
`lFrequency`	`long`	Frequency
`nDuration`	`int`	Duration of the sound, measured in clock ticks

Description:

The `SetVoiceSound` function sets the frequency and duration of the sound in the voice queue specified by `nVoice`. The frequency is specified in `lFrequency`. The high-order word of `lFrequency` specifies the frequency in hertz. The low-order word of `lFrequency` specifies the fractional frequency. `nDuration` specifies the duration of the sound in clock ticks.

Return Value:

The `SetVoiceSound` function returns zero when the frequency and sound are set. One of the following values is returned instead when the function cannot set the frequency and duration:

Value	*Meaning*
`S_SERDDR`	Invalid duration
`S_SERDFQ`	Invalid frequency
`S_SERDVL`	Invalid volume
`S_SERQFUL`	Queue full

SetVoiceThreshold

Syntax:

```
int SetVoiceThreshold(nVoice, nNotes)
```

Parameter, Type, and Description:

`nVoice`	`int`	Voice queue
`nNotes`	`int`	Number of notes in the threshold level

Description:

The `SetVoiceThreshold` function sets the threshold level for the voice queue specified in `nVoice`. `nNotes` specifies the number of notes in the threshold level.

Return Value:

The `SetVoiceThreshold` function returns zero when the threshold level is set. A return value of 1 indicates that the number specified in `nNotes` is out of range.

StartSound

Syntax:

```
int StartSound()
```

Description:

The `StartSound` function starts the playing of each voice queue.

Return Value:

The return value has no significance and is not used.

StopSound

Syntax:

```
int StopSound()
```

Description:

The `StopSound` function stops the playing of all the voice queues. The contents of each queue are flushed and the sound driver for each voice is switched off.

Return Value:

The return value has no significance and is not used.

SyncAllVoices

Syntax:

```
int SyncAllVoices()
```

Description:

The `SyncAllVoices` function places a sync mark in each voice queue. As each voice is played and a sync mark is encountered, the corresponding voice is switched off until all other queues have reached their respective sync marks. In this way the voices are synchronized.

Return Value:

The `SyncAllVoices` function returns zero when sync marks are placed in each queue. A return value of `S_SERQFUL` indicates that a voice queue is full.

WaitSoundState

Syntax:

```
int WaitSoundState(nState)
```

Parameter, Type, and Description:

`nState`	`int`	State of the voice queue

Description:

The `WaitSoundState` function waits for the play driver to enter the state specified in `nState`. The following values are used for `nState`:

Value	*Meaning*
`S_ALLTHRESHOLD`	All voices have reached threshold
`S_QUEUEEMPTY`	All voice queues are empty and the sound drivers are turned off
`S_THRESHOLD`	A voice queue has reached the threshold

Return Value:

The `WaitSoundState` function returns zero when the wait state is set. A return value of `S_SERDST` indicates that the state is not valid.

String Manipulation Functions

Windows provides the String Manipulation functions to manipulate and translate character strings. The following functions are categorized as String Manipulation functions for the System Services Interface:

Function	*Meaning*
`AnsiLower`	Converts a string to lowercase
`AnsiLowerBuff`	Converts a string in a buffer to lowercase
`AnsiNext`	Gets the long pointer to the next character in a string
`AnsiPrev`	Gets the long pointer to the previous character in a string
`AnsiToOem`	Converts an ANSI string to an OEM string
`AnsiToOemBuff`	Converts an ANSI string in a buffer to an OEM string
`AnsiUpper`	Converts a string to uppercase
`AnsiUpperBuff`	Converts a string in a buffer to uppercase
`IsCharAlpha`	Determines whether a character is alphabetical
`IsCharAlphaNumeric`	Determines whether a character is alphanumeric
`IsCharLower`	Determines whether a character is lowercase
`IsCharUpper`	Determines whether a character is uppercase
`lstrcat`	Concatenates two strings
`lstrcmp`	Compares two strings and is case-sensitive
`lstrcmpi`	Compares two strings and is not case-sensitive
`lstrcpy`	Copies one string to another
`lstrlen`	Gets the length of a string
`OemToAnsi`	Converts an OEM string to an ANSI string
`OemToAnsiBuff`	Converts an OEM string in a buffer to an ANSI string
`ToAscii`	Translates a virtual-key code to ANSI characters
`wsprintf`	Formats characters and values and places them in a buffer; format arguments are passed separately
`wvsprintf`	Formats characters and values and places them in a buffer; format arguments are passed in an array

The rest of this section provides detailed information on each of the functions in this list.

AnsiLower

Syntax:

```
LPSTR AnsiLower(lpString)
```

Parameter, Type, and Description:

`lpString`	`LPSTR`	Pointer to a null-terminated string

Description:

The `AnsiLower` function converts the characters in the character string pointed to by `lpString` to lowercase. `lpString` may also specify a single character. When `lpString` specifies a single character, the character must be in the low-order byte of the low-order word.

Return Value:

The `AnsiLower` function returns the pointer to the character string when `lpString` specifies a character string. When `lpString` specifies a single character, the low-order byte of the low-order word of the returned 32-bit value contains the converted character.

AnsiLowerBuff

Syntax:

```
WORD AnsiLowerBuff(lpString, nLength)
```

Parameter, Type, and Description:

`lpString`	`LPSTR`	Pointer to a buffer containing the character string
`nLength`	`WORD`	Number of characters in the buffer

Description:

The `AnsiLowerBuff` function converts the character string in the buffer pointed to by `lpString` to lowercase. `nLength` specifies the number of characters in the buffer. When `nLength` is set to zero, the length is assumed to be 65,536.

Return Value:

The `AnsiLowerBuff` function returns the length of the converted string.

AnsiNext

Syntax:

```
LPSTR AnsiNext(lpCurrentChar)
```

Parameter, Type, and Description:

`lpCurrentChar`	`LPSTR`	Pointer to a character in a null-terminated string

Description:

The `AnsiNext` function returns the pointer to the next character in the string after the character pointed to by `lpCurrentChar`.

Return Value:

The `AnsiNext` function returns the pointer to the next character. The pointer points to the null terminator when no more characters are in the string.

AnsiPrev

Syntax:

```
LPSTR AnsiPrev(lpStart, lpCurrentChar)
```

Parameter, Type, and Description:

`lpStart`	`LPSTR`	Pointer to the beginning of the null-terminated string
`lpCurrentChar`	`LPSTR`	Pointer to the current character in the null-terminated string

Description:

The `AnsiPrev` function gets the character from the string that appears just before the character specified in `lpCurrentChar`.

Return Value:

The `AnsiPrev` function returns the pointer to the previous character. If `lpCurrentChar` and `lpStart` point to the same character, `lpStart` is returned.

AnsiToOem

Syntax:

```
int AnsiToOem(lpAnsiStr, lpOemStr)
```

Parameter, Type, and Description:

`lpAnsiStr`	`LPSTR`	Pointer to the null-terminated string containing ANSI characters
`lpOemStr`	`LPSTR`	Pointer to the string to receive the converted characters

Description:

The `AnsiToOem` function converts the ANSI characters in the string specified in `lpAnsiStr` to OEM characters and copies the coverted characters to the string specified in `lpOemStr`. `lpAnsiStr` and `lpOemStr` can point to the same string.

Return Value:

The `AnsiToOem` function always returns –1.

AnsiToOemBuff

Syntax:

```
void AnsiToOemBuff(lpAnsiStr, lpOemStr, nLength)
```

Parameter, Type, and Description:

`lpAnsiStr`	`LPSTR`	Pointer to a buffer containing ANSI characters
`lpOemStr`	`LPSTR`	Pointer to the buffer to receive the converted characters
`nLength`	`WORD`	Number of characters in `lpAnsiStr`

Description:

The `AnsiToOemBuff` function converts the ANSI characters in the buffer pointed to by `lpAnsiStr` and copies them to the buffer pointed to by `lpOemStr`. `nLength` specifies the number of characters in `lpAnsiStr`. `lpAnsiStr` and `lpOemStr` can specify the same buffer.

Return Value:

There is no return value.

AnsiUpper

Syntax:

```
LPSTR AnsiUpper(lpString)
```

Parameter, Type, and Description:

`lpString`	`LPSTR`	Pointer to a null-terminated string

Description:

The `AnsiUpper` function converts the characters in the character string pointed to by `lpString` to uppercase. `lpString` may also specify a single character. When `lpString` specifies a single character, the character must be in the low-order byte of the low-order word.

Return Value:

The `AnsiUpper` function returns the pointer to the character string when `lpString` specifies a character string. When `lpString` specifies a single character, the low-order byte of the low-order word of the returned 32-bit value contains the converted character.

AnsiUpperBuff

Syntax:

```
WORD AnsiUpperBuff(lpString, nLength)
```

Parameter, Type, and Description:

`lpString`	`LPSTR`	Pointer to a buffer containing the character string
`nLength`	`WORD`	Number of characters in the buffer

Description:

The `AnsiUpperBuff` function converts the character string in the buffer pointed to by `lpString` to uppercase. `nLength` specifies the number of characters in the buffer. When `nLength` is set to zero, the length is assumed to be 65,536.

Return Value:

The `AnsiUpperBuff` function returns the length of the converted string.

IsCharAlpha

Syntax:

```
BOOL IsCharAlpha(cChar)
```

Parameter, Type, and Description:

`cChar`	`char`	Character to test

Description:

The `IsCharAlpha` function determines whether the character specified in `cChar` is an alphabetical character.

Return Value:

The `IsCharAlpha` function returns TRUE when the character is alphabetical. A return value of FALSE indicates that the character is not alphabetical.

IsCharAlphaNumeric

Syntax:

```
BOOL IsCharAlphaNumeric(cChar)
```

Parameter, Type, and Description:

`cChar`	`char`	Character to test

Description:

The `IsCharAlphaNumeric` function determines whether the character specified in `cChar` is alphanumeric.

Return Value:

The `IsCharAlphaNumeric` function returns TRUE if the character is alphanumeric. A return value of FALSE indicates that the character is not alphanumeric.

IsCharLower

Syntax:

```
BOOL IsCharLower(cChar)
```

Parameter, Type, and Description:

`cChar`	`char`	Character to test

Description:

The `IsCharLower` function determines whether the character specified in `cChar` is a lowercase character.

Return Value:

The `IsCharLower` function returns TRUE if the character is lowercase. A return value of FALSE indicates that the character is not lowercase.

IsCharUpper

Syntax:

```
BOOL IsCharUpper(cChar)
```

Parameter, Type, and Description:

`cChar`	`char`	Character to test

Description:

The `IsCharUpper` function determines whether the character specified in `cChar` is an uppercase character.

Return Value:

The `IsCharUpper` function returns TRUE if the character is uppercase. A return value of FALSE indicates that the character is lowercase.

lstrcat

Syntax:

```
LPSTR lstrcat(lpString1, lpString2)
```

Parameter, Type, and Description:

`lpString1`	`LPSTR`	Pointer to the byte array containing a null-terminated string
`lpString2`	`LPSTR`	Pointer to a null-terminated string to be appended to `lpString1`

Description:

The `lstrcat` function appends the string specified in `lpString2` to the string specified in `lpString1` and returns the pointer to the resulting string.

Return Value:

The `lstrcat` function returns the pointer to the resulting string in `lpString1`. A return value of zero indicates that the function cannot append the string.

lstrcmp

Syntax:

```
int lstrcmp(lpString1, lpString2)
```

Parameter, Type, and Description:

lpString1	LPSTR	Pointer to a null-terminated string
lpString2	LPSTR	Pointer to a null-terminated string

Description:

The `lstrcmp` function performs a lexicographic comparison of the two strings specified in `lpString1` and `lpString2`. The comparison is case-sensitive.

Return Value:

The `lstrcmp` function returns a value less than zero when `lpString1` is less than `lpString2`. A return value of zero indicates that the strings are identical. A return value greater than zero indicates that `lpString1` is greater than `lpString2`.

lstrcmpi

Syntax:

```
int lstrcmpi(lpString1, lpString2)
```

Parameter, Type, and Description:

lpString1	LPSTR	Pointer to a null-terminated string
lpString2	LPSTR	Pointer to a null-terminated string

Description:

The `lstrcmpi` function performs a lexicographic comparison of the two strings specified in `lpString1` and `lpString2`. The comparison is case-sensitive.

Return Value:

The `lstrcmpi` function returns a value less than zero when `lpString1` is less than `lpString2`. A return value of zero indicates that the strings are identical. A return value greater than zero indicates that `lpString1` is greater than `lpString2`.

lstrcpy

Syntax:

```
LPSTR lstrcpy(lpString1, lpString2)
```

Parameter, Type, and Description:

`lpString1`	`LPSTR`	Pointer to the buffer to receive `lpString2`
`lpString2`	`LPSTR`	Pointer to the null-terminated string to copy to `lpString1`

Description:

The `lstrcpy` function copies the string pointed to by `lpString2` to the buffer pointed to by `lpString1`.

Return Value:

The `lstrcpy` function returns the pointer to `lpString1` when the string is copied. A return value of zero indicates that the function cannot copy the string.

lstrlen

Syntax:

```
int lstrlen(lpString)
```

Parameter, Type, and Description:

`lpString`	`LPSTR`	Pointer to a null-terminated string

Description:

The `lstrlen` function gets the number of bytes in the string pointed to by `lpString`. The null character is not included in the returned count.

Return Value:

The `lstrlen` function returns the number of bytes in the string.

OemToAnsi

Syntax:

```
int OemToAnsi(lpOemStr, lpAnsiStr)
```

Parameter, Type, and Description:

lpOemStr	LPSTR	Pointer to the null-terminated string containing OEM characters
lpAnsiStr	LPSTR	Pointer to the string to receive the converted characters

Description:

The `OemToAnsi` function converts the OEM characters in the string pointed to by `lpOemStr` to ANSI characters and copies the converted characters to the string pointed to by `lpAnsiStr`. `lpOemStr` and `lpAnsiStr` can point to the same string.

Return Value:

The `OemToAnsi` function always returns –1.

OemToAnsiBuff

Syntax:

```
void OemToAnsiBuff(lpOemStr, lpAnsiStr, nLength)
```

Parameter, Type, and Description:

lpOemStr	LPSTR	Pointer to the buffer containing OEM characters
lpAnsiStr	LPSTR	Pointer to the buffer to receive the converted characters
nLength	WORD	Number of characters in `lpOemStr`

Description:

The `OemToAnsiBuff` function converts the characters in the buffer pointed to by `lpOemStr` to ANSI characters and copies the converted characters into the buffer pointed to by `lpAnsiStr`. `nLength` specifies the number of characters in the buffer pointed to by `lpOemStr`. When `nLength` is set to zero, the buffer length is assumed to be 65,536.

Return Value:

There is no return value.

ToAscii

Syntax:

```
int ToAscii(wVirtKey, wScanCode, lpKeyState, lpChar, wFlags)
```

Parameter, Type, and Description:

wVirtKey	WORD	Virtual key code
wScanCode	WORD	Scan code of the key
lpKeyState	LPSTR	Pointer to an array of key states
lpChar	LPVOID	Pointer to the 32-bit buffer that receives the translated ANSI character
wFlags	WORD	Bit 0 flag's menu display

Description:

The ToAscii function converts the virtual key code specified in wVirtKey to the corresponding ANSI character or characters. wScanCode and lpKeyState are used in the conversion. The translated character or characters are copied to lpChar.

Return Value:

The ToAscii function returns the number of characters copied to lpChar. A return value of zero indicates that no translation is possible. A return value less than zero indicates that the virtual key code is converted.

wsprintf

Syntax:

```
int wsprintf(lpOutput, lpFormat[,argument]...)
```

Parameter, Type, and Description:

lpOutput	LPSTR	Pointer to string to receive the formatted output
lpFormat	LPSTR	Pointer to the format control string
argument	n/a	One or more arguments for the format control string

Description:

The `wsprintf` function formats a series of characters and stores the formatted values in the buffer pointed to by `lpOutput`. `lpFormat` specifies the format control string. The format control string contains format specifiers that control the format of the output. A format specifier follows this format:

```
%[-][#][0][width][.precision]type
```

where:

- indicates to pad the output for right and left justification

`#` indicates to precede hexadecimal values with 0x or 0X

`0` indicates that the output value should be padded with zeroes to fill the width of the field

`width` specifies the minimum number of characters to output

`.precision` specifies the maximum number of characters to output

`type` indicates the output type and is selected from the following:

Value	*Meaning*
`s`	String argument referenced by a long pointer
`c`	Single character argument
`d,i`	Signed decimal integer
`ld,li`	Long signed decimal integer
`u`	Unsigned integer argument
`lu`	Long unsigned integer argument
`x,X`	Unsigned hexadecimal integer
`lx, lX`	Long unsigned hexadecimal integer

`argument` refers to one or more arguments that correspond to the format specifiers in the format control string.

Return Value:

The `wsprintf` function returns the number of characters stored in `lpOutput`, excluding the null terminator.

wvsprintf

Syntax:

```
int wvsprintf(lpOutput, lpFormat, lpArglist)
```

Parameter, Type, and Description:

lpOutput	LPSTR	Pointer to a null-terminated string to receive the formatted output
lpFormat	LPSTR	Pointer to null-terminated string containing the format control string
lpArglist	LPSTR	Pointer to an array of arguments for the format control string

Description:

The `wvsprintf` function formats a series of characters and stores the formatted characters in the buffer pointed to by `lpOutput`. `lpFormat` points to the string containing the format control string. The format control string contains format specifiers that control the format of the output. A format specifier follows this format:

```
%[-][#][0][width][.precision]type
```

where:

- indicates to pad the output for right and left justification

`#` indicates to precede hexadecimal values with 0x or 0X

`0` indicates that the output value should be padded with zeroes to fill the width of the field

`width` specifies the minimum number of characters to output

`.precision` specifies the maximum number of characters to output

`type` indicates the output type and can be one of the following:

Value	*Meaning*
s	String argument referenced by a long pointer
c	Single character argument
d,i	Signed decimal integer
ld,li	Long signed decimal integer
u	Unsigned integer argument
lu	Long unsigned integer argument

Value	*Meaning*
`x,X`	Unsigned hexadecimal integer
`lx, lX`	Long unsigned hexadecimal integer

`lpArglist` points to an array that contains the arguments for the format control string.

Return Value:

The `wvsprintf` function returns the number of characters stored in `lpOutput`, excluding the null terminator.

Task Functions

A task is a Windows application call. Windows provides the Task functions to manipulate tasks. The following functions are categorized as Task functions for the System Services Interface:

Function	*Meaning*
`Catch`	Places the execution environment in a buffer
`ExitWindows`	Starts the Windows shutdown procedure
`GetCurrentPDB`	Gets the DOS Program Data Base (PDB); also called the Program Segment Prefix (PSP)
`GetCurrentTask`	Gets the handle of the current task
`GetDOSEnvironment`	Gets the environment string for the current task
`GetNumTasks`	Gets the number of executing tasks
`SetErrorMode`	Specifies whether Windows or the application handles DOS 24H errors
`Throw`	Restores the execution environment
`Yield`	Pauses the current task and begins a waiting task

The rest of this section provides detailed information on each of the functions in this list.

Catch

Syntax:

```
int Catch(lpCatchBuf)
```

Parameter, Type, and Description:

`lpCatchBuf`	`LPCATCHBUF`	Pointer to the `CATCHBUF` data structure to receive the execution environment

Description:

The `Catch` function captures the current execution environment and places it in the data structure of type `CATCHBUF` pointed to by `lpCatchBuf`.

Return Value:

The `Catch` function returns zero when the environment is successfully captured. A nonzero return value indicates that the function cannot capture the current environment.

ExitWindows

Syntax:

```
BOOL ExitWindows(dwReserved, wReturnCode)
```

Parameter, Type, and Description:

`dwReserved`	`DWORD`	Reserved and should be set to zero
`wReturnCode`	`WORD`	Return value to pass to DOS when Windows exits

Description:

The `ExitWindows` function attempts to shut down Windows. The `WM_QUERYENDSESSION` message is sent to all applications. If all applications okay the termination request, the `WM_ENDSESSION` is sent to all applications before exiting and control is returned to DOS.

Return Value:

The `ExitWindows` function returns FALSE if any one of the applications does not okay the termination request. If all applications okay the termination request, the function does not return.

GetCurrentPDB

Syntax:

```
WORD GetCurrentPDB()
```

Description:

The `GetCurrentPDB` function gets the paragraph address or selector for the DOS Program Data Base (PDB). The PDB is frequently called the Program Segment Prefix (PSP).

Return Value:

The `GetCurrentPDB` function returns the paragraph address or selector of the PDB.

GetCurrentTask

Syntax:

```
HANDLE GetCurrentTask()
```

Description:

The `GetCurrentTask` function gets the handle of the current task.

Return Value:

The `GetCurrentTask` function returns the handle to the current task. A NULL return value indicates that the function cannot get the handle of the current task.

GetDOSEnvironment

Syntax:

```
LPSTR GetDOSEnvironment()
```

Description:

The `GetDOSEnvironment` function gets the pointer to the environment string for the current task.

Return Value:

The `GetDOSEnvironment` function returns the far pointer to the environment string of the current task.

GetNumTasks

Syntax:

```
int GetNumTasks()
```

Description:

The `GetNumTasks` function determines the number of executing tasks.

Return Value:

The `GetNumTasks` function returns the number of executing tasks.

SetErrorMode

Syntax:

```
WORD SetErrorMode(wMode)
```

Parameter, Type, and Description:

`wMode`	`WORD`	Error mode flag

Description:

The `SetErrorMode` function defines the way DOS function 24H is handled. `wMode` specifies error mode flag:

- If `wMode` is set to zero, Windows displays an error message box whenever an INT 24H occurs.
- If `wMode` is set to one, Windows sends the original INT 21H call to the application whenever an INT 24H occurs.

Windows does not display a message box when `wMode` is set to one.

Return Value:

The `SetErrorMode` function returns the previous value of the error mode flag.

Throw

Syntax:

```
void Throw(lpCatchBuf, nThrowBack)
```

Parameter, Type, and Description:

`lpCatchBuf`	`LPCATCHBUF`	Pointer to an array that contains the execution environment
`nThrowBack`	`int`	Value to be returned to `Catch`

Description:

The `Throw` function sets the execution environment to the values stored in the buffer pointed to by `lpCatchBuf`. `nThrowback` specifies the return value to the `Catch` function.

Return Value:

There is no return value.

Yield

Syntax:

```
void Yield()
```

Description:

The `Yield` function halts the current task. Waiting tasks can be started.

Return Value:

There is no return value.

Utility Macros and Functions

Windows provides a variety of macros and functions that perform utility-type operations to make programming in Windows a little easier. The following functions and macros are categorized as Utility macros and functions for the System Services Interface:

Function	Meaning
HIBYTE	Gets the high-order byte of an integer
HIWORD	Gets the high-order word of a long integer
LOBYTE	Gets the low-order byte of an integer
LOWORD	Gets the low-order word of a long integer
MAKEINTATOM	Casts an integer for use as a function argument
MAKEINTRESOURCE	Converts an integer value to a long pointer to a string
MAKELONG	Creates an unsigned long integer
MAKEPOINT	Converts a long value that specifies the coordinates of a point into a POINT data structure
max	Determines the greater of two values
min	Determines the lesser of two values
MulDiv	Multiplies two values and divides the result by a third value
PALETTEINDEX	Converts an integer to a COLORREF value
PALETTERGB	Converts the red, green, and blue values into a palette-relative COLORREF value
RGB	Converts the red, green, and blue values into an explicit COLORREF value

The rest of this section provides detailed information on each of the functions in this list.

HIBYTE

Syntax:

```
BYTE HIBYTE(nInteger)
```

Parameter, Type, and Description:

nInteger	int	Value to convert

Description:

The HIBYTE macro returns the high-order byte of the value specified in nInteger.

Return Value:

The HIBYTE macro returns the high-order byte.

HIWORD

Syntax:

```
WORD HIWORD(dwInteger)
```

Parameter, Type, and Description:

`dwInteger` `DWORD` Value to convert

Description:

The `HIWORD` macro returns the high-order word of the 32-bit value specified in `dwInteger`.

Return Value:

The `HIWORD` macro returns the high-order word.

LOBYTE

Syntax:

```
BYTE LOBYTE(nInteger)
```

Parameter, Type, and Description:

`nInteger` `int` Value to convert

Description:

The `LOBYTE` macro returns the low-order byte of the value specified in `nInteger`.

Return Value:

The `LOBYTE` macro returns the low-order byte.

LOWORD

Syntax:

```
WORD LOWORD(dwInteger)
```

Parameter, Type, and Description:

`dwInteger` `DWORD` Value to be converted

Description:

The `LOWORD` macro returns the low-order word of the 32-bit value specified in `dwInteger`.

Return Value:

The `LOWORD` macro returns the low-order word.

MAKEINTATOM

Syntax:

```
LPSTR MAKEINTATOM(wInteger)
```

Parameter, Type, and Description:

`wInteger` `WORD` Numeric value of the atom's character string

Description:

The `MAKEINTATOM` macro creates an integer atom that represents a character string of decimal digits.

Return Value:

The `MAKEINTATOM` macro returns the pointer to the atom created for the specified integer.

MAKEINTRESOURCE

Syntax:

```
LPSTR MAKEINTRESOURCE(nInteger)
```

Parameter, Type, and Description:

`nInteger` `int` Value to convert

Description:

The `MAKEINTRESOURCE` function converts the value specified in `nInteger` to a long pointer to a string. The high-order word of the long pointer is set to zero.

Return Value:

The MAKEINTRESOURCE function returns the pointer to the string.

MAKELONG

Syntax:

```
DWORD MAKELONG(wLow, wHigh)
```

Parameter, Type, and Description:

wLow	WORD	Low-order word
wHigh	WORD	High-order word

Description:

The MAKELONG function gets an unsigned long integer created from wLow and wHigh.

Return Value:

The MAKELONG function returns the created unsigned long integer.

MAKEPOINT

Syntax:

```
POINT MAKEPOINT(dwInteger)
```

Parameter, Type, and Description:

dwInteger	DWORD	Coordinates of a point

Description:

The MAKEPOINT macro fills a POINT data structure by using the x- and y-coordinates contained in dwInteger. The POINT data structure is:

```
typedef struct tagPOINT {
     int x;
     int y;
} POINT;
```

where:

x is the horizontal coordinate of the point

y is the vertical coordinate of the point

Return Value:

The MAKEPOINT macro returns a value specifying the POINT data structure.

max

Syntax:

```
int max(value1, value2)
```

Parameter, Type, and Description:

value1	n/a	First value
value2	n/a	Second value

Description:

The max macro returns the greater of the values in value1 and value2. value1 and value2 can be any ordered type.

Return Value:

The max macro returns whichever is greater, value1 or value2.

min

Syntax:

```
int min(value1, value2)
```

Parameter, Type, and Description:

value1	n/a	First value
value2	n/a	Second value

Description:

The min macro returns the lesser of the values in value1 and value2. value1 and value2 can be any ordered type.

Return Value:

The min macro returns whichever is lesser, value1 or value2.

MulDiv

Syntax:

```
int MulDiv(nNumber, nNumerator, nDenominator)
```

Parameter, Type, and Description:

nNumber	int	Number multiplied by nNumerator
nNumerator	int	Number multiplied by nNumber
nDenominator	int	Number by which to divide the result of nNumber multiplied by nNumerator

Description:

The MulDiv function multiplies nNumber and nNumerator, divides the result of the multiplication by nDenominator, then returns the result of the division rounded to the nearest integer.

Return Value:

The MulDiv function returns the resulting integer. The function returns 32,767 or –32,767 when overflow occurs.

PALETTEINDEX

Syntax:

```
COLORREF PALETTEINDEX(nPaletteIndex)
```

Parameter, Type, and Description:

nPaletteIndex	int	Palette entry index containing the color to use

Description:

The PALETTEINDEX macro returns the palette entry specifier for the logical color palette entry index specified in nPaletteIndex. The palette entry specifier contains a 1 in the high-order byte and the palette entry index in the low-order bytes. The macro can pass a palette entry specifier to functions that require an RGB value rather than passing the RGB value.

Return Value:

The PALETTEINDEX macro returns the palette entry specifier.

PALETTERGB

Syntax:

```
COLORREF PALETTERGB(cRed, cGreen, cBlue)
```

Parameter, Type, and Description:

cRed	BYTE	Red intensity
cGreen	BYTE	Green intensity
cBlue	BYTE	Blue intensity

Description:

The PALETTERGB macro returns the palette-relative RGB specifier representing the red, green, and blue color intensities specified in cRed, cGreen, and cBlue respectively. The resulting RGB specifier contains 2 in the high-order byte and the RGB value in the three low-order bytes.

Return Value:

The PALETTERGB macro returns the palette-relative RGB specifier.

RGB

Syntax:

```
COLORREF RGB(cRed, cGreen, cBlue)
```

Parameter, Type, and Description:

cRed	BYTE	Red intensity
cGreen	BYTE	Green intensity
cBlue	BYTE	Blue intensity

Description:

The `RGB` macro selects an RGB color. The intensities specified in `cRed`, `cGreen`, and `cBlue` and the capabilities of the output device are considered before a color is selected.

Return Value:

The `RGB` macro returns the selected RGB color.

14

Windows Messages

This chapter provides reference information on the various Window messages. These messages are used by Windows applications to communicate with the Windows system and other Windows applications. The Windows messages are divided into the following categories:

Button Control

Clipboard

Combo Box

Control

Edit Control

Initialization

Input

List Box

Multiple Document Interface (MDI)

Non-Client Area

Notification codes:

- Button Notification
- Combo Box Notification
- Edit Control Notification
- List Box Notification

Owner Draw Control

Scroll Bar

System Information

System

Window Management

The messages that pertain to each category are documented under the category heading.

A message consists of three parts. The first part is the message number that is identified by the message name. The second part is a word parameter, referenced as `wParam`. The third part is a long parameter, referenced as `lParam`. The description of each message includes these three parts, along with the message's function and return value, in the following format:

MESSAGE_NAME

`wParam:`

Description of the word parameter.

`lParam:`

Description of the long parameter.

Description:

Information on the message.

Return Value:

Information on the return value.

The rest of this chapter provides the reference material, divided into appropriate categories, for the Windows messages.

Button Control Messages

Button control messages are sent by an application to a button control. The following messages are documented in this section:

BM_GETCHECK

BM_GETSTATE

BM_SETCHECK

BM_SETSTATE

BM_SETSTYLE

DM_GETDEFID

DM_SETDEFID

BM_GETCHECK

wParam:

wParam is not used.

lParam:

lParam is not used.

Description:

The BM_GETCHECK message determines whether a radio button or check box is checked.

Return Value:

BM_GETCHECK returns a nonzero value if the radio button or check box is checked. A return value of zero indicates that the radio button or check box is not checked.

BM_GETSTATE

wParam:

wParam is not used.

lParam:

lParam is not used.

Description:

The BM_GETSTATE message determines the button control state whenever the space bar or a mouse button is pressed.

Return Value:

BM_GETSTATE returns a nonzero value when any of the following conditions exist:

- A push-button is highlighted
- The mouse button or the space bar is pressed when a button has the input focus
- A button is selected

A return value of zero indicates that none of these conditions exist.

BM_SETCHECK

wParam:

In two-state buttons, wParam is set:

- To a nonzero value to place a check mark
- To zero to remove a check mark

In three-state buttons, wParam is set:

- To 1 to place a check mark
- To 2 to gray the button
- To zero to remove any check mark and the gray state, if grayed

lParam:

lParam is not used.

Description:

The BM_SETCHECK message either places or removes the check mark for a radio button or check box. The wParam parameter defines the state of the radio button or check box.

Return Value:

There is no meaningful return value.

BM_SETSTATE

wParam:

wParam is set to zero to display the button normally, or to a nonzero value to display the button in a highlighted state.

lParam:

lParam is not used.

Description:

The BM_SETSTATE message displays a button or check box. The wParam defines the state of the button or check box. Push-buttons cannot be highlighted.

Return Value:

There is no meaningful return value.

BM_SETSTYLE

wParam:

wParam defines the style for a button. The value for wParam is selected from one of the following:

Value	*Meaning*
BS_AUTOCHECKBOX	Box that may be checked; toggles between states when selected
BS_AUTORADIOBUTTON	Small circular button that may be checked; when this button is selected, all check marks on other buttons in the group are removed
BS_AUTO3STATE	Box that may be checked or grayed (three states); button state is toggled when selected
BS_CHECKBOX	Box that may be checked
BS_DEFPUSHBUTTON	Button with a bold border; the bold border designates this button as the default button
BS_GROUPBOX	Rectangle where other buttons are grouped; text is displayed in upper-left corner

Value	Meaning
BS_LEFTTEXT	Used with BS_CHECKBOX, BS_RADIOBUTTON, and BS_3STATE styles to make text appear on the left side of the radio button or check box (the default is for text to appear on the right side)
BS_OWNERDRAW	Owner-drawn button—parent window is told when the button is selected
BS_PUSHBUTTON	Button containing text; a message is sent to the parent window when the button is selected
BS_RADIOBUTTON	Small circular button that may be checked; often grouped with other radio buttons
BS_3STATE	Box that may be checked or grayed

lParam:

lParam is set to a nonzero value if the buttons are to be redrawn or to zero if the buttons are not to be redrawn.

Description:

The BM_SETSTYLE message modifies the button style. wParam specifies the new button style. lParam specifies if the buttons are to be redrawn.

Return Value:

There is no meaningful return value.

DM_GETDEFID

wParam:

wParam is not used.

lParam:

lParam is not used.

Description:

The DM_GETDEFID message gets the default push-button control ID for a dialog box.

Return Value:

DM_GETDEFID returns a 32-bit value. The high-order word of the return value contains DC_HASDEFID when the default button exists, and NULL if the default button does not exist. The low-order word of the return value contains the ID of the default button when the high-order word contains DC_HASDEFID.

DM_SETDEFID

wParam:

wParam specifies the ID of the default push-button.

lParam:

lParam is not used.

Description:

The DM_SETDEFID message changes the ID for the default push-button control for a dialog box.

Return Value:

There is no return value.

Clipboard Messages

Clipboard messages are sent to an application by the Windows system when another application attempts to use the window's clipboard. The following messages are documented in this section:

WM_ASKCBFORMATNAME

WM_CHANGECBCHAIN

WM_DESTROYCLIPBOARD

WM_DRAWCLIPBOARD

WM_HSCROLLCLIPBOARD

WM_PAINTCLIPBOARD

WM_RENDERALLFORMATS

WM_RENDERFORMAT

WM_SIZECLIPBOARD

WM_VSCROLLCLIPBOARD

WM_ASKCBFORMATNAME

wParam:

wParam specifies the maximum number of bytes to copy.

lParam:

lParam points to the buffer where the copied format name is to be placed.

Description:

The WM_ASKCBFORMATNAME message is sent when both of the following are true:

- The clipboard contains a data handle for the CF_OWNERDISPLAY format
- The clipboard requests a copy of the format name

wParam specifies the maximum number of bytes to copy into the buffer pointed to by lParam.

Return Value:

There is no return value.

WM_CHANGECBCHAIN

wParam:

wParam contains the window handle that is being removed from the clipboard viewer chain.

lParam:

The low-order word of lParam contains the window handle for the window that follows the window specified in wParam.

Description:

The WM_CHANGECBCHAIN message is sent to the first window in the clipboard-viewer chain whenever a window is removed from the chain. Each window that receives this message should send the message to the next window in the clipboard viewer chain. wParam contains the window handle of the window being removed from the chain. The low-order word of lParam contains the window handle of the window following the window in wParam.

Return Value:

There is no return value.

WM_DESTROYCLIPBOARD

wParam:

wParam is not used.

lParam:

lParam is not used.

Description:

The WM_DESTROYCLIPBOARD message is sent to the owner of the clipboard whenever the contents of the clipboard are emptied by a call to the EmptyClipboard function.

Return Value:

There is no meaningful return value.

WM_DRAWCLIPBOARD

wParam:

wParam is not used.

lParam:

lParam is not used.

Description:

The WM_DRAWCLIPBOARD message is sent to the first window of the clipboard viewer chain whenever the contents of the clipboard are modified. Each window that receives this message should pass the message to the next window in the clipboard viewer chain.

Return Value:

There is no meaningful return value.

WM_HSCROLLCLIPBOARD

wParam:

wParam contains the clipboard application window handle.

lParam:

The low-order word of `lParam` contains one of the following scroll-bar codes:

Value	Meaning
SB_BOTTOM	Scroll to lower right
SB_ENDSCROLL	End scroll
SB_LINEDOWN	Scroll down one line
SB_LINEUP	Scroll up one line
SB_PAGEDOWN	Scroll down one page
SB_PAGEUP	Scroll up one page
SB_THUMBPOSITION	Scroll to absolute position; when specified, the high-order word of `lParam` contains the thumb position of the scroll-bar code
SB_TOP	Scroll to upper left

Description:

The `WM_HSCROLLCLIPBOARD` message is sent when the following conditions exist:

- The clipboard contains the data handle for the `CF_OWNERDISPLAY` format
- A component of the clipboard application's horizontal scroll bar is selected

`wParam` contains the clipboard application window handle; `lParam` contains the scroll-bar code.

Return Value:

There is no meaningful return value.

WM_PAINTCLIPBOARD

wParam:

`wParam` contains the clipboard application window handle.

lParam:

The low-order word of `lParam` points to a data structure of type `PAINTSTRUCT`. The data structure defines the client area that is to be painted. The `PAINTSTRUCT` structure is:

```
typedef struct tagPAINTSTRUCT {
    HDC hdc;
    BOOL fErase;
    RECT rcPaint;
```

```
    BOOL fRestore;
    BOOL fIncUpdate;
    BYTE rgbReserved[16];
} PAINTSTRUCT;
```

where:

hdc is the display context used for painting

fErase specifies whether the background has been redrawn (nonzero if redrawn; otherwise, zero)

rcPaint identifies the upper-left and lower-right corners of the rectangle to paint

fRestore is reserved for use only by Windows

fIncUpdate is reserved for use only by Windows

rgbReserved[16] is reserved for use only by Windows

Description:

The WM_PAINTCLIPBOARD message is sent to the owner of the clipboard and requests that the clipboard application's client area be repainted. This message is sent only when both of the following conditions exist:

- The clipboard contains a data handle for the CF_OWNERDISPLAY format
- The clipboard application's client area needs to be repainted

Return Value:

There is no meaningful return value.

WM_RENDERALLFORMATS

wParam:

wParam is not used.

lParam:

lParam is not used.

Description:

The WM_RENDERALLFORMATS message is sent to the clipboard owner when the application is being destroyed. This allows the application to render the clipboard data in all available formats by passing the handle of each format to the SetClipboardData function.

Return Value:

There is no meaningful return value.

WM_RENDERFORMAT

wParam:

wParam defines the data format, which can be any one of the following:

Format	*Meaning*
CF_BITMAP	Handle to a bitmap
CF_DIB	Block containing a BITMAPINFO data structure and the bitmap
CF_DIF	Software Art's Data Interchange Format
CF_DSPBITMAP	Bitmap format which corresponds to a private format
CF_DSPMETAFILEPICT	Metafile format which corresponds to a private format
CF_DSPTEXT	Text display format which corresponds to a private format
CF_METAFILEPICT	Metafile defined by the METAFILEPICT structure
CF_OEMTEXT	Text format using the OEM character set
CF_OWNERDISPLAY	Owner display format
CF_PALETTE	Color palette handle
CF_PRIVATEFIRST to CF_PRIVATELAST	Used for private formats (ranges from CF_PRIVATEFIRST to CF_PRIVATELAST)
CF_SYLK	Microsoft Symbolic Link Format
CF_TEXT	Text format
CF_TIFF	Tag Image File Format

lParam:

lParam is not used.

Description:

The WM_RENDERFORMAT message is sent to the cliboard owner. The clipboard owner should format the data in the clipboard to the format in wParam and pass the handle of the formatted data to the clipboard.

Return Value:

There is no meaningful return value.

WM_SIZECLIPBOARD

wParam:

wParam contains the clipboard application window ID.

lParam:

The low-order word of lParam contains the reference to the data structure of type RECT that defines the area to paint. The RECT structure is:

```
typedef struct tagRECT {
     int left;
     int top;
     int right;
     int bottom;
} RECT;
```

where:

> left is the horizontal coordinate of the upper-left corner of the rectangular region
>
> top is the vertical coordinate of the upper-left corner of the rectangular region
>
> right is the horizontal coordinate of the lower-right corner of the rectangular region
>
> bottom is the vertical coordinate of the lower-right corner of the rectangular region

Description:

The WM_SIZECLIPBOARD message is sent when the following conditions exist:

- The clipboard contains a data handle for the CF_OWNERDISPLAY format
- The clipboard-application window's size has been modified

Return Value:

There is no meaningful return value.

WM_VSCROLLCLIPBOARD

wParam:

wParam specifies the clipboard application window handle.

lParam:

The low-order word of lParam specifies one of the following scroll-bar codes:

Value	*Meaning*
SB_BOTTOM	Scroll to lower right
SB_ENDSCROLL	End scroll
SB_LINEDOWN	Scroll down one line
SB_LINEUP	Scroll up one line
SB_PAGEDOWN	Scroll down one page
SB_PAGEUP	Scroll up one page
SB_THUMBPOSITION	Scroll to absolute position—when specified, the high-order word of lParam contains the thumb position of the scroll-bar code
SB_TOP	Scroll to upper left

Description:

The WM_VSCROLLCLIPBOARD message is sent when both of the following conditions exist:

- The clipboard contains the data handle for the CF_OWNERDISPLAY format
- A component of the clipboard application's vertical scroll bar is selected

wParam contains the clipboard application window handle; lParam contains the scroll-bar code.

Return Value:

There is no meaningful return value.

Combo Box Messages

Combo box messages are sent to a combo box from an application. The following messages are documented in this section:

CB_ADDSTRING
CB_DELETESTRING
CB_DIR
CB_FINDSTRING
CB_GETCOUNT
CB_GETCURSEL
CB_GETEDITSEL
CB_GETITEMDATA
CB_GETLBTEXT
CB_GETLBTEXTLEN
CB_INSERTSTRING
CB_LIMITTEXT
CB_RESETCONTENT
CB_SELECTSTRING
CB_SETCURSEL
CB_SETEDITSEL
CB_SETITEMDATA
CB_SHOWDROPDOWN

CB_ADDSTRING

wParam:

wParam is not used.

lParam:

lParam points to the string that will be added to the list box of the combo box.

Description:

The CB_ADDSTRING message adds the string in lParam to the list box of a combo box. If the list box is a sorted list box, the string is sorted and placed in the appropriate position. If the list box is not sorted, the string is added to the end of the list.

Return Value:

CB_ADDSTRING returns the index to the added string. A return value of CB_ERRSPACE indicates that there is not enough space to store the new string. A return value of CB_ERR indicates an error.

CB_DELETESTRING

wParam

wParam specifies the index of the string that is to be deleted from the list.

lParam:

lParam is not used.

Description:

The CB_DELETESTRING message deletes the string specified in wParam from the list box.

Return Value:

CB_DELETESTRING returns the number of strings left in the list. A return value of CB_ERR indicates that wParam contains an invalid index.

CB_DIR

wParam:

wParam specifies the DOS attribute and can be any of the following:

Value	*Meaning*
0x0000	Read/write—no additional attributes
0x0001	Read only
0x0002	Hidden file
0x0004	System file
0x0010	Subdirectory
0x0020	Archive
0x2000	LB_DIR flag
0x4000	Drive
0x8000	Exclusive bit

lParam:

lParam points to the file specification string.

Description:

The CB_DIR message puts a list of the files from the current directory into the list box. The files that are added to the list must match the DOS attributes specified in wParam and the file specification string in lParam.

Return Value:

CB_DIR returns the number of items in the list. A return value of CB_ERRSPACE indicates that there is not enough memory available. A return value of CB_ERR indicates an error.

CB_FINDSTRING

wParam:

wParam specifies the item just prior to the first item to search. When wParam is –1, the list box is searched starting from the top.

lParam:

lParam points to the string containing the prefix text.

Description:

The CB_FINDSTRING message searches the list box of a combo box for the first occurrence of the prefix string specified in lParam. The value in wParam specifies the index of the item just prior to the item where the search begins. The search begins with the item after the item specified in wParam and continues to the end of the list, begins again at the top, and (when no match is found) terminates on the item in wParam. lParam points to the null-terminated string that contains the prefix text.

Return Value:

CB_FINDSTRING returns the index of the matching item when a match is found. A return value of CB_ERR indicates that the search is unsuccessful.

CB_GETCOUNT

wParam:

wParam is not used.

lParam:

lParam is not used.

Description:

The CB_GETCOUNT message gets the number of items in a list box of a combo box.

Return Value:

CB_GETCOUNT returns the number of items in the list box.

CB_GETCURSEL

wParam:

wParam is not used.

lParam:

lParam is not used.

Description:

The CB_GETCURSEL message gets the index of the selected item from a list box of a combo box.

Return Value:

CB_GETCURSEL returns the index of the selected item. A return value of CB_ERR indicates that no item is currently selected.

CB_GETEDITSEL

wParam:

wParam is not used.

lParam:

lParam is not used.

Description:

The CB_GETEDITSEL message gets the beginning and ending position of the selected text. This message is used with the edit control of a combo box.

Return Value:

The low-order word of the returned value contains the starting position of the selected text. The high-order word of the return value contains the ending position. A return value of CB_ERR indicates that the message is sent to a combo box without an edit control.

CB_GETITEMDATA

wParam:

wParam contains the index to an item in a combo box.

lParam:

lParam is not used.

Description:

The CB_GETITEMDATA message gets the value associated with the combo box item specified in wParam. The retrieved value is a 32-bit value provided by the application.

Return Value:

CB_GETITEMDATA returns the 32-bit value associated with the item. A return value of CB_ERR indicates an error.

CB_GETLBTEXT

wParam:

wParam contains the index of the string to copy.

lParam:

lParam points to the buffer where the string will be stored.

Description:

The CB_GETLBTEXT message places the string from a list box of a combo box into the buffer pointed to by lParam. wParam specifies the index of the string to copy.

Return Value:

CB_GETLBTEXT returns the number of bytes in the string, excluding the null character. A return value of CB_ERR indicates that the message is unable to place the string into the buffer.

CB_GETLBTEXTLEN

wParam:

wParam specifies the index of the string to evaluate.

lParam:

lParam is not used.

Description:

The CB_GETLBTEXTLEN message determines the length of the string specified in wParam. The string is contained in the list box of a combo box.

Return Value:

CB_GETLBTEXTLEN returns the number of bytes in the string, not counting the null character. A return value of CB_ERR indicates that an invalid index is specified in wParam.

CB_INSERTSTRING

wParam:

wParam specifies the position index where the string will be inserted. If wParam is set to –1, the string is put at the bottom of the list.

lParam:

lParam points to the string to be inserted into the list.

Description:

The CB_INSERTSTRING message inserts the string pointed to by lParam into the list box of a combo box. wParam specifies the position where the string will be inserted.

Return Value:

CB_INSERTSTRING returns the position index of the inserted string. A return value of CB_ERRSPACE indicates that there is insufficient memory to store the string. A return value of CB_ERR indicates an error.

CB_LIMITTEXT

wParam:

wParam defines the maximum number of bytes you can enter into the edit control of a combo box.

lParam:

lParam is not used.

Description:

The CB_LIMITTEXT message restricts the number of bytes you can enter into the edit control of a combo box to the value specified in wParam.

Return Value:

CB_LIMITTEXT returns TRUE when the number of bytes is restricted. A return value of FALSE indicates that the number of bytes is not affected by CB_LIMITTEXT. A return value of CB_ERR indicates that the message is sent to a combo box with no edit control.

CB_RESETCONTENT

wParam:

wParam is not used.

lParam:

lParam is not used.

Description:

The CB_RESETCONTENT message removes all the strings from the list box of a combo box. All memory associated with the removed strings is freed.

Return Value:

There is no meaningful return value.

CB_SELECTSTRING

wParam:

wParam specifies the index of the item just prior to the first item to search. This item is the last item to search. If wParam is set to –1, the search begins at the top of the list.

lParam:

lParam points to the null terminated prefix string.

Description:

The CB_SELECTSTRING message selects the item from the list box of a combo box that matches the string pointed to by lParam. The search begins with the next item after the item specified in wParam. The search continues down the list and begins again at the top if no match is found by the time the bottom of the list is reached. The last item searched is the item specified in wParam. The edit control text of the combo box displays the selected text.

Return Value:

CB_SELECTSTRING returns the index of the selected item. A return value of CB_ERR indicates that the message is unable to select the item.

CB_SETCURSEL

wParam:

wParam specifies the index of the selected string. When wParam is –1, nothing in the list box is selected.

lParam:

lParam is not used.

Description:

The CB_SETCURSEL message selects the string specified in wParam. The combo box edit control text displays the selected string.

Return Value:

CB_SETCURSEL returns CB_ERR when an invalid index is specified.

CB_SETEDITSEL

wParam:

wParam is not used.

lParam:

lParam defines the position of the selected text. The beginning position is specified in the low-order word; the ending position is specified in the high-order word.

Description:

The CB_SETEDITSEL message selects a block of text in the edit control of a combo box. The starting position of the block is specified in the low-order word of lParam. The ending position of the block is specified in the high-order word of lParam.

Return Value:

CB_SETEDITSEL returns TRUE when the block of text is selected. A return value of FALSE indicates that the message is unable to select the block of text. A return value of CB_ERR indicates that the message is sent to a combo box with no edit control.

CB_SETITEMDATA

wParam:

wParam specifies the index to the item in the combo box.

lParam:

lParam specifies the value to be associated with the item in the combo box.

Description:

The CB_SETITEMDATA message defines the 32-bit value associated with the combo box item specified in wParam. The new value to associate with the item is specified in lParam.

Return Value:

CB_SETITEMDATA returns CB_ERR on error.

CB_SHOWDROPDOWN

wParam:

wParam specifies whether to show or hide the drop-down list box on a combo box. wParam is set to TRUE to show the list box or to FALSE to hide the list box.

lParam:

lParam is not used.

Description:

The CB_SHOWDROPDOWN message either shows or hides the drop-down list box of a combo box. wParam specifies whether the list box is shown or hidden. The drop-down list box must be created with the CBS_DROPDOWN or CBS_DROPDOWNLIST style.

Return Value:

There is no meaningful return value.

Control Messages

Control messages instruct controls to perform certain tasks and are sent by the SendMessage function. The following messages are documented in this section and apply to all types of controls including button controls, edit controls, list boxes, and combo boxes:

WM_GETFONT

WM_NEXTDLGCTL

WM_SETFONT

WM_GETFONT

wParam:

wParam is not used.

`lParam`:

`lParam` is not used.

Description:

The `WM_GETFONT` message gets the current font used by a control.

Return Value:

`WM_GETFONT` returns the handle for the retrieved font. A return value of NULL indicates that the control uses the system font.

WM_NEXTDLGCTL

`wParam`:

`wParam` specifies the control that will receive the control focus.

`lParam`:

`lParam` is used to determine how to interpret the value in `wParam`.

Description:

The `WM_NEXTDLGCTL` message, which is sent to the window function for a dialog box, gives the control focus to the control specified in `wParam`. `lParam` specifies how the value in `wParam` is interpreted:

- When `lParam` is nonzero, `wParam` contains the handle for the control which will receive the control focus.
- When `lParam` is zero, `wParam` is a flag to indicate if the previous or next control with the tab-stop style is given the control focus.
- When `wParam` is zero, the next control is given the control focus.
- When `wParam` is nonzero, the previous control is given the control focus.

Return Value:

There is no meaningful return value.

WM_SETFONT

`wParam`:

`wParam` specifies the handle of the font to use. If `wParam` is NULL, the system font is used.

lParam:

lParam specifies if the control should be redrawn. If lParam is TRUE, the control is redrawn. If lParam is FALSE, the control is not redrawn.

Description:

The WM_SETFONT message sets the font used by the dialog box control to the font specified in wParam.

Return Value:

There is no meaningful return value.

Edit Control Messages

Edit control messages are sent to an edit control from an application. Control messages instruct controls to perform certain tasks and are sent by the SendMessage function. The following messages are documented in this section:

EM_CANUNDO
EM_EMPTYUNDOBUFFER
EM_FMTLINES
EM_GETHANDLE
EM_GETLINE
EM_GETLINECOUNT
EM_GETMODIFY
EM_GETRECT
EM_GETSEL
EM_LIMITTEXT
EM_LINEFROMCHAR
EM_LINEINDEX
EM_LINELENGTH
EM_LINESCROLL
EM_REPLACESEL
EM_SETHANDLE
EM_SETMODIFY
EM_SETPASSWORDCHAR
EM_SETRECT
EM_SETRECTNP
EM_SETSEL
EM_SETTABSTOPS
EM_SETWORDBREAK
EM_UNDO
WM_CLEAR
WM_COPY
WM_CUT
WM_PASTE
WM_UNDO

EM_CANUNDO

wParam:

wParam is not used.

lParam:

lParam is not used.

Description:

The EM_CANUNDO message indicates if an edit control has the ability to respond to an EM_UNDO message.

Return Value:

EM_CANUNDO returns a nonzero value when the edit control is able to process the EM_UNDO message. A return value of zero indicates that the edit control is unable to process the EM_UNDO message.

EM_EMPTYUNDOBUFFER

wParam:

wParam is not used.

lParam:

lParam is not used.

Description:

The EM_EMPTYUNDOBUFFER message clears the undo buffer of an edit control.

Return Value:

There is no meaningful return value.

EM_FMTLINES

wParam:

wParam specifies how end-of-line characters are handled:

- When wParam is set to a nonzero value, end-of-line characters are placed to the end of wordwrapped lines.
- When wParam is zero, end-of-line characters are removed.

lParam:

lParam is not used.

Description:

The EM_FMTLINES message determines whether a multiline edit control adds or removes end-of-line characters from wordwrapped text. wParam specifies how the end-of-line characters are handled.

Return Value:

EM_FMTLINES returns a nonzero value when formatting occurs. A return value of zero indicates that no formatting is accomplished.

EM_GETHANDLE

wParam:

wParam is not used.

lParam:

lParam is not used.

Description:

The EM_GETHANDLE message gets the data handle of the buffer that stores the contents of the control window.

Return Value:

EM_GETHANDLE returns the retrieved data handle.

EM_GETLINE

wParam:

wParam defines the line number in the edit control. The first line of the control is numbered 0.

lParam:

lParam points to the buffer where the line will be placed. The maximum number of bytes to copy to the buffer is defined in the first word of the buffer.

Description:

The EM_GETLINE message gets the line specified in wParam from the edit control, and places the line in the buffer pointed to by lParam. This message is not processed by single-line edit controls.

Return Value:

EM_GETLINE returns the number of bytes copied to the buffer.

EM_GETLINECOUNT

wParam:

wParam is not used.

lParam:

lParam is not used.

Description:

The EM_GETLINECOUNT message gets the number of text lines in the edit control. This message is not processed by single-line edit controls.

Return Value:

EM_GETLINECOUNT returns the number of text lines in the edit control.

EM_GETMODIFY

wParam:

wParam is not used.

lParam:

lParam is not used.

Description:

The EM_GETMODIFY message gets the value of the modify flag for an edit control. The modify flag is set whenever text is modified in the control.

Return Value:

EM_GETMODIFY returns the value of the modify flag.

EM_GETRECT

wParam:

wParam is not used.

lParam:

lParam points to the data structure of type RECT that holds the dimensions for the control. The RECT structure is:

```
typedef struct tagRECT {
     int left;
     int top;
     int right;
     int bottom;
} RECT;
```

where

left is the horizontal coordinate of the upper-left corner of the rectangular region

top is the vertical coordinate of the upper-left corner of the rectangular region

right is the horizontal coordinate of the lower-right corner of the rectangular region

bottom is the vertical coordinate of the lower-right corner of the rectangular region

Description:

The EM_GETRECT message gets the dimensions of the formatting rectangle for the control.

Return Value:

There is no meaningful return value.

EM_GETSEL

wParam:

wParam is not used.

lParam:

lParam is not used.

Description:

The EM_GETSEL message gets the starting and ending positions for the selected text.

Return Value:

The low-order word of the return value contains the starting position of the selected text. The high-order word of the return value contains the ending position of the selected text.

EM_LIMITTEXT

wParam:

wParam defines the maximum number of bytes you can enter. When wParam is zero, the maximum number of bytes is limited by the amount of memory available.

lParam:

lParam is not used.

Description:

The EM_LIMITTEXT message limits the maximum number of bytes you can enter to the value specified in wParam. Text set by the WM_SETTEXT message and the buffer set by the EM_SETHANDLE message are not affected by this message.

Return Value:

There is no meaningful return value.

EM_LINEFROMCHAR

wParam:

wParam specifies the index value of the character when not set to –1. When wParam is set to –1, EM_LINEFROMCHAR gets the line number containing the first character of the selection.

lParam:

lParam is not used.

Description:

The EM_LINEFROMCHAR message gets the line number of the line that contains the character at the index value specified in wParam (when wParam is not –1). When wParam is –1, the EM_LINEFROMCHAR message gets the line number that contains the first character of the selection.

Return Value:

When wParam is –1, EM_LINEFROMCHAR returns the line number that contains the first character of the selection. When wParam is not –1, EM_LINEFROMCHAR returns the line number containing the character at the specified index value.

EM_LINEINDEX

wParam:

wParam defines the line number used for evaluation. When wParam is –1, the line number for the line that contains the caret is used.

lParam:

lParam is not used.

Description:

The EM_LINEINDEX message determines the number of character positions that precede the line number specified in wParam. This message is not processed by single-line edit controls.

Return Value:

EM_LINEINDEX returns the number of character positions that precede the line number specified in wParam.

EM_LINELENGTH

wParam:

wParam specifies the index of the character in the specified line. When wParam is –1, the line that contains the caret is evaluated.

lParam:

lParam is not used.

Description:

The EM_LINELENGTH message determines the number of bytes in a line from the text buffer of the edit control. The line number to evaluate is specified in wParam.

Return Value:

LINELENGTH returns the number of bytes in a line from the text buffer of the edit control.

EM_LINESCROLL

wParam:

wParam is not used.

lParam:

The low-order word of lParam contains the number of lines to scroll in the vertical direction. The high-order word of lParam contains the number of character positions to scroll in the horizontal direction.

Description:

The EM_LINESCROLL message scrolls the contents of the control the number of lines and character positions specified in lParam.

Return Value:

There is no meaningful return value.

EM_REPLACESEL

wParam:

wParam is not used.

lParam:

lParam points to the string that contains the replacement text.

Description:

The EM_REPLACESEL message replaces the selected text with the text string pointed to by lParam.

Return Value:

There is no meaningful return value.

EM_SETHANDLE

wParam:

wParam specifies the handle for the buffer used to store the contents of the control window.

lParam:

lParam is not used.

Description:

The `EM_SETHANDLE` function specifies the text buffer that stores the contents of the control window. Single-line edit controls do not process this message.

Return Value:

There is no meaningful return value.

EM_SETMODIFY

`wParam:`

`wParam` defines the setting for the modify flag.

`lParam:`

`lParam` is not used.

Description:

The `EM_SETMODIFY` message sets the value of the modify flag for an edit control to the value in `wParam`.

Return Value:

There is no meaningful return value.

EM_SETPASSWORDCHAR

`wParam:`

The `wParam` defines the character that is displayed whenever you press a key during password entry. When `wParam` is NULL, the actual character entered is displayed.

`lParam:`

`lParam` is not used.

Description:

The `EM_SETPASSWORDCHAR` message specifies the character that is displayed by an edit control with style `ES_PASSWORD`. `wParam` defines the character that is displayed. The default character is an asterisk (*).

Return Value:

There is no meaningful return value.

EM_SETRECT

wParam:

wParam is not used.

lParam:

lParam points to the data structure of type RECT that contains the rectangle's new dimensions. The RECT structure is:

```
typedef struct tagRECT {
     int left;
     int top;
     int right;
     int bottom;
} RECT;
```

where:

left is the horizontal coordinate of the upper-left corner of the rectangular region

top is the vertical coordinate of the upper-left corner of the rectangular region

right is the horizontal coordinate of the lower-right corner of the rectangular region

bottom is the vertical coordinate of the lower-right corner of the rectangular region

Description:

The EM_SETRECT message sets the formatting rectangle for a control to the dimensions stored in the data structure pointed to by lParam. Single-line edit controls do not process this message.

Return Value:

There is no meaningful return value.

EM_SETRECTNP

wParam:

wParam is not used.

lParam:

lParam points to the data structure of type RECT that contains the rectangle's new dimensions. The RECT structure is:

```
typedef struct tagRECT {
     int left;
     int top;
     int right;
     int bottom;
} RECT;
```

where:

> left is the horizontal coordinate of the upper-left corner of the rectangular region
>
> top is the vertical coordinate of the upper-left corner of the rectangular region
>
> right is the horizontal coordinate of the lower-right corner of the rectangular region
>
> bottom is the vertical coordinate of the lower-right corner of the rectangular region

Description:

The EM_SETRECTNP message sets the formatting rectangle for a control to the dimensions stored in the data structure pointed to by lParam. This message is similar to the EM_SETRECT message with the exception that the control is not repainted. Single-line edit controls do not process this message.

Return Value:

There is no meaningful return value.

EM_SETSEL

wParam:

wParam is not used.

lParam:

The low-order word of lParam contains the starting character position of the text to select. The high-order word of lParam contains the ending character position of the text to select. Setting the low- and high-order words to 0 and 32,767, respectively, selects the entire string.

Description:

The EM_SETSEL message selects the characters specified by the values in lParam from the current text.

Return Value:

There is no meaningful return value.

EM_SETTABSTOPS

wParam:

wParam defines the number of tab stops in the edit control.

lParam:

lParam points to the first member of the array that contains the tab stop positions. Tab stop positions are measured in dialog units.

Description:

The EM_SETTABSTOPS message positions the tab stops for a multiline edit control. wParam defines the number of tab stops. lParam points to the first member of the array that contains the tab stop positions. The relationship between wParam and lParam is as follows:

- When wParam is zero and lParam is NULL, the tab stops are set every 32 dialog units.
- When wParam is 1, lParam specifies the distance between tab stops. When lParam points to more than one value, a tab stop is set for each value of lParam.

Return Value:

SETTABSTOPS returns TRUE when tab stops are set. A return value of FALSE indicates that tab stops are unchanged.

EM_SETWORDBREAK

wParam:

wParam is not used.

lParam:

lParam specifies the procedure instance address for the callback function.

Description:

The EM_SETWORDBREAK message is sent to inform a multiline edit control that a new word break function has been installed by the application. A word break function determines where a line of text should be broken and the remainder of the text is carried to the next line. lParam specifies the procedure instance address of the callback function. The structure of the application-defined word break function is:

```
LPSTR FAR PASCAL WordBreakFunc(lpchEditText, ichCurrentWord,
                               cchEditText)

LPSTR lpchEditText;
short ichCurrentWord;
short cchEditText;
```

WordBreakFunc is a placeholder for the actual function name, which is supplied by the application and must be exported using EXPORTS.

Return Value:

EM_SETWORDBREAK returns the pointer to the first byte of the next word in the edit control text.

EM_UNDO

wParam:

wParam is not used.

lParam:

lParam is not used.

Description:

The EM_UNDO message performs an "undo" on the last edit using the edit control.

Return Value:

EM_UNDO returns a nonzero value when the "undo" operation is performed. A return value of zero indicates that EM_UNDO cannot perform the "undo" operation.

WM_CLEAR

wParam:

wParam is not used.

lParam:

lParam is not used.

Description:

The WM_CLEAR message deletes the current selection.

Return Value:

There is no meaningful return value.

WM_COPY

wParam:

wParam is not used.

lParam:

lParam is not used.

Description:

The WM_COPY message copies the current selection onto the clipboard using the CF_TEXT format.

Return Value:

There is no return value.

WM_CUT

wParam:

wParam is not used.

lParam:

lParam is not used.

Description:

The `WM_CUT` messages copies the current selection onto the clipboard in `CF_TEXT` format. The selection is then deleted from the control window.

Return Value:

There is no meaningful return value.

WM_PASTE

`wParam:`

`wParam` is not used.

`lParam:`

`lParam` is not used.

Description:

The `WM_PASTE` message pastes the contents of the clipboard into the control window at the current position of the cursor. The contents must be in `CF_TEXT` format.

Return Value:

There is no meaningful return value.

WM_UNDO

`wParam:`

`wParam` is not used.

`lParam:`

`lParam` is not used.

Description:

The `WM_UNDO` message performs an "undo" on the last operation.

Return Value:

There is no meaningful return value.

Initialization Messages

Windows sends initialization messages whenever a menu or dialog box is created by an application. The following messages are documented in this section:

WM_INITDIALOG

WM_INITMENU

WM_INITMENUPOPUP

WM_INITDIALOG

wParam:

wParam specifies the first item from the dialog box that is able to receive the input focus.

lParam:

lParam contains the value passed as the parameter dwInitParam of the function when the dialog box was created with any of the following functions:

- CreateDialogIndirectParam
- CreateDialogParam
- DialogBoxIndirectParam
- DialogBoxParam

When the dialog box was not created with any of these functions, lParam is not used.

Description:

The WM_INITDIALOG message is sent prior to the display of a dialog box. This allows the application to initialize the dialog box before the box is displayed. If the application returns a nonzero value when responding to this message, the input focus is given to the control item specified in wParam. If the application returns FALSE, the application must set the input focus.

Return Value:

There is no meaningful return value.

WM_INITMENU

wParam:

wParam holds the menu handle of the menu to initialize.

lParam:

lParam is not used.

Description:

The WM_INITMENU message is sent just before a menu is displayed. The application, therefore, has the opportunity to initialize the menu.

Return Value:

There is no meaningful return value.

WM_INITMENUPOPUP

wParam:

wParam specifies the menu handle of the pop-up menu.

lParam:

The low-order word of lParam specifies the index of the pop-up menu in the main menu. The high-order word of lParam contains a nonzero value when the pop-up menu is the system menu. The high-order word contains zero when the pop-up menu is not the system menu.

Description:

The WM_INITMENUPOPUP message is sent before a pop-up menu is displayed. This gives the application the opportunity to initialize the menu before the menu is displayed.

Return Value:

There is no meaningful return value.

Input Messages

Windows sends input messages when an application receives input from the mouse, keyboard, scroll bars, or system timer. The following messages are documented in this section:

WM_CHAR	WM_MBUTTONDOWN
WM_CHARTOITEM	WM_MBUTTONUP
WM_COMMAND	WM_MOUSEACTIVATE
WM_DEADCHAR	WM_MOUSEMOVE
WM_HSCROLL	WM_RBUTTONDBLCLK
WM_KEYDOWN	WM_RBUTTONDOWN
WM_KEYUP	WM_RBUTTONUP
WM_LBUTTONDBLCLK	WM_SETCURSOR
WM_LBUTTONDOWN	WM_TIMER
WM_LBUTTONUP	WM_VKEYTOITEM
WM_MBUTTONDBLCLK	WM_VSCROLL

WM_CHAR

wParam:

wParam contains the value of the key.

lParam:

lParam contains a 32-bit value. This value represents the repeat count, key-transition code, previous key state, and context code as follows:

Bit(s)	*Value*
0-15	The number of times the keystroke is repeated
16-23	Scan code
24	Set to 1 if extended key
25-26	Not used
27-28	Used only by Windows
29	Context code—set to 1 if Alt key is pressed
30	Previous state—1 if key is down before message is sent
31	Transition state—1 if key is being released

Description:

The WM_CHAR message is sent whenever a WM_KEYUP and WM_KEYDOWN message are translated. wParam and lParam contain information about the key being pressed or released.

Return Value:

There is no meaningful return value.

WM_CHARTOITEM

wParam:

wParam contains the value of the pressed key.

lParam:

The low-order word of lParam contains the current caret position. The high-order word of lParam contains the window handle of the list box.

Description:

The WM_CHARTOITEM message is sent in response to a WM_CHAR message. A list box with style LBS_WANTKEYBOARDINPUT sends this message to its owner.

Return Value:

WM_CHARTOITEM returns one of the following:

- A return value of –2 indicates that the application needs no further action from the list box.
- A return value of –1 indicates that the list box should perform the default action.
- A return value of zero or greater represents the index to an item in the list box, and indicates that the list box should perform the action for the list box item corresponding to the returned index number.

WM_COMMAND

wParam:

wParam contains a menu item, a control ID, or an accelerator ID, depending on the value of lParam.

lParam:

The high-order word of lParam contains the notification code. The high-order word of lParam contains 1 when the message is an accelerator message. The value of the low-order word affects wParam as follows:

- When the low-order word of `lParam` is zero, `wParam` contains a menu item.
- When the high-order word of `lParam` is 1, `wParam` contains an accelerator ID.
- When the low-order word of `lParam` contains the window handle of the control, `wParam` contains a control ID.

Description:

The `WM_COMMAND` message is sent when a menu item is selected, a control passes a message to its parent window, or an accelerator keystroke is translated.

Return Value:

There is no meaningful return value.

WM_DEADCHAR

`wParam:`

`wParam` holds the character value of the dead key.

`lParam:`

The value in `lParam` represents the repeat count, the scan code, the previous key state, and context code. The bits of this value are interpreted as follows:

Bit(s)	*Meaning*
0-15	Repeat count—the number of times the keystroke is repeated
16-23	Scan code
24	1 if dead key is an extended key
25-26	Not used
27-28	Used only by Windows
29	Context code—1 if Alt key is pressed
30	Previous key state—1 if key is down before the message is sent
31	Transition state—1 if key is being released

Description:

The `WM_DEADCHAR` message is sent when a `WM_KEYUP` and a `WM_KEYDOWN` message are translated. `wParam` specifies the character value of the dead key. A dead key character value is one that combines with other character values to form a distinct character.

Return Value:

There is no meaningful return value.

WM_HSCROLL

wParam:

wParam specifies the scroll bar code and can be any one of the following values:

Value	*Meaning*
SB_BOTTOM	Scroll to lower right
SB_ENDSCROLL	End scroll
SB_LINEDOWN	Scroll down one line
SB_LINEUP	Scroll up one line
SB_PAGEDOWN	Scroll down one page
SB_PAGEUP	Scroll up one page
SB_THUMBPOSITION	Scroll to absolute position—when specified, the low-order word of lParam contains the thumb position of the scroll-bar
SB_THUMBTRACK	Move thumb position to a specified position
SB_TOP	Scroll to upper left

lParam:

When the WM_HSCROLL message is sent by a scroll bar control, the high-order word of lParam specifies the window handle for the control. The low-order word of lParam specifies the thumb position of the scroll bar.

Description:

The WM_HSCROLL message is sent when the horizontal scroll bar is clicked and active.

Return Value:

There is no meaningful return value.

WM_KEYDOWN

wParam:

wParam specifies the virtual key code.

lParam:

lParam specifies the repeat count, the scan code, the previous key state, and the context code. The bits in lParam are interpreted as follows:

Bit(s)	*Meaning*
`0-15`	Repeat count—the number of times the keystroke is repeated
`16-23`	Scan code
`24`	1 if the key is an extended key
`25-26`	Not used
`27-28`	Used only by Windows
`29`	Context code—0 for `WM_KEYDOWN`
`30`	Previous key state—1 if key is down before the message is sent
`31`	Transition state—0 for `WM_KEYDOWN`

Description:

The `WM_KEYDOWN` message is sent when a nonsystem key is pressed. Nonsystem keys are either:

- Keys that are pressed without holding the Alt key down
- Keys that are pressed while a window has the input focus

Return Value:

There is no meaningful return value.

WM_KEYUP

`wParam:`

`wParam` specifies the virtual key code.

`lParam:`

`lParam` specifies the repeat count, the scan code, the previous key state, and the context code. The bits in `lParam` are interpreted as follows:

Bit(s)	*Meaning*
`0-15`	Repeat count—the number of times the keystroke is repeated
`16-23`	Scan code
`24`	1 if the key is an extended key
`25-26`	Not used
`27-28`	Used only by Windows
`29`	Context code—0 for `WM_KEYUP`
`30`	Previous key state—1 if key is down before the message is sent
`31`	Transition state—1 for `WM_KEYUP`

Description:

The `WM_KEYUP` message is sent when a nonsystem key is released. Nonsystem keys are either:

- Keys that are pressed without holding the Alt key down
- Keys that are pressed while a window has the input focus

Return Value:

There is no meaningful return value.

WM_LBUTTONDBLCLK

`wParam:`

`wParam` indicates which virtual keys are down. The following values, in any combination, indicate the virtual keys that are down:

Value	*Meaning*
`MK_CONTROL`	Ctrl key is down
`MK_LBUTTON`	Left button is down
`MK_MBUTTON`	Middle button is down
`MK_RBUTTON`	Right button is down
`MK_SHIFT`	Shift key is down

`lParam:`

The low-order word of `lParam` contains the horizontal coordinate of the cursor. The high-order word of `lParam` contains the vertical coordinate of the cursor. These coordinates are expressed relative to the upper-left corner of the window.

Description:

The `WM_LBUTTONDBLCLICK` message is sent when the left mouse button is double clicked.

Return Value:

There is no meaningful return value.

WM_LBUTTONDOWN

wParam:

wParam indicates which virtual keys are down. The following values, in any combination, indicate the virtual keys that are down:

Value	*Meaning*
MK_CONTROL	Ctrl key is down
MK_MBUTTON	Middle button is down
MK_RBUTTON	Right button is down
MK_SHIFT	Shift key is down

lParam:

The low-order word of lParam contains the horizontal coordinate of the cursor. The high-order word of lParam contains the vertical coordinate of the cursor. These coordinates are expressed relative to the upper-left corner of the window.

Description:

The WM_LBUTTONDOWN message is sent when the left mouse button is pressed.

Return Value:

There is no meaningful return value.

WM_LBUTTONUP

wParam:

wParam indicates which virtual keys are down. The following values, in any combination, indicate the virtual keys that are down:

Value	*Meaning*
MK_CONTROL	Ctrl key is down
MK_MBUTTON	Middle button is down
MK_RBUTTON	Right button is down
MK_SHIFT	Shift key is down

lParam:

The low-order word of lParam contains the horizontal coordinate of the cursor. The high-order word of lParam contains the vertical coordinate of the cursor. These coordinates are expressed relative to the upper-left corner of the window.

Description:

The `WM_LBUTTONUP` message is sent when the left mouse button is released.

Return Value:

There is no meaningful return value.

WM_MBUTTONDBLCLK

`wParam:`

`wParam` indicates which virtual keys are down. The following values, in any combination, indicate the virtual keys that are down:

Value	*Meaning*
`MK_CONTROL`	Ctrl key is down
`MK_LBUTTON`	Left button is down
`MK_MBUTTON`	Middle button is down
`MK_RBUTTON`	Right button is down
`MK_SHIFT`	Shift key is down

`lParam:`

The low-order word of `lParam` contains the horizontal coordinate of the cursor. The high-order word of `lParam` contains the vertical coordinate of the cursor. These coordinates are expressed relative to the upper-left corner of the window.

Description:

The `WM_MBUTTONDBLCLK` message is sent when the middle mouse button is double clicked.

Return Value:

There is no meaningful return value.

WM_MBUTTONDOWN

`wParam:`

`wParam` indicates which virtual keys are down. The following values, in any combination, indicate the virtual keys that are down:

Value	Meaning
MK_CONTROL	Ctrl key is down
MK_LBUTTON	Left button is down
MK_RBUTTON	Right button is down
MK_SHIFT	Shift key is down

lParam:

The low-order word of lParam contains the horizontal coordinate of the cursor. The high-order word of lParam contains the vertical coordinate of the cursor. These coordinates are expressed relative to the upper-left corner of the window.

Description:

The WM_BUTTONDOWN message is sent when the middle mouse button is pressed.

Return Value:

There is no meaningful return value.

WM_MBUTTONUP

wParam:

wParam indicates which virtual keys are down. The following values, in any combination, indicate the virtual keys that are down:

Value	Meaning
MK_CONTROL	Ctrl key is down
MK_LBUTTON	Left button is down
MK_RBUTTON	Right button is down
MK_SHIFT	Shift key is down

lParam:

The low-order word of lParam contains the horizontal coordinate of the cursor. The high-order word of lParam contains the vertical coordinate of the cursor. These coordinates are expressed relative to the upper-left corner of the window.

Description:

The WM_MBUTTONUP message is sent when the middle button is released.

Return Value:

There is no meaningful return value.

WM_MOUSEACTIVATE

wParam:

wParam specifies the window handle of the topmost parent window for the activated window.

lParam:

The low-order word of lParam contains the hit test code. A hit test checks the location of the mouse. The hit test codes used for the low-order word of lParam are:

Hit Test Code	*Meaning*
HTBOTTOM	Lower horizontal window border
HTBOTTOMLEFT	Lower-left corner of window border
HTBOTTOMRIGHT	Lower-right corner of window border
HTCAPTION	Caption area
HTCLIENT	Client area
HTERROR	Screen background or window dividing line; produces a beep on error
HTGROWBOX	Size box
HTHSCROLL	Horizontal scroll bar
HTLEFT	Left window border
HTMENU	Menu area
HTNOWHERE	Screen background or window dividing line
HTREDUCE	Minimize box
HTRIGHT	Right window border
HTSIZE	Size box
HTSYSMENU	Control menu box
HTTOP	Upper horizontal window border
HTTOPLEFT	Upper-left corner of window border
HTTOPRIGHT	Upper-right corner of window border
HTTRANSPARENT	Window covered by another window
HTVSCROLL	Vertical scroll bar
HTZOOM	Maximize box

The high-order word of lParam contains the mouse message number.

Description:

The WM_MOUSEACTIVATE message is sent when the cursor is moved to an inactive window and a mouse button is pressed. The DefWindowProc function should be used by the child window to pass this message to the parent window.

Return Value:

There is no meaningful return value.

WM_MOUSEMOVE

wParam:

wParam indicates which virtual keys are down. The following values, in any combination, indicate the virtual keys that are down:

Value	*Meaning*
MK_CONTROL	Ctrl key is down
MK_LBUTTON	Left button is down
MK_MBUTTON	Middle button is down
MK_RBUTTON	Right button is down
MK_SHIFT	Shift key is down

lParam:

The low-order word of lParam contains the horizontal coordinate of the cursor. The high-order word of lParam contains the vertical coordinate of the cursor. These coordinates are expressed relative to the upper-left corner of the window.

Description:

The WM_MOUSEMOVE message is sent whenever the mouse is moved. You can use the MAKEPOINT macro to convert the value in lParam to a structure of type POINT.

Return Value:

There is no return value.

WM_RBUTTONDBLCLK

wParam:

wParam indicates which virtual keys are down. The following values, in any combination, indicate the virtual keys that are down:

Value	*Meaning*
MK_CONTROL	Ctrl key is down
MK_LBUTTON	Left button is down
MK_MBUTTON	Middle button is down
MK_RBUTTON	Right button is down
MK_SHIFT	Shift key is down

lParam:

The low-order word of `lParam` contains the horizontal coordinate of the cursor. The high-order word of `lParam` contains the vertical coordinate of the cursor. These coordinates are expressed relative to the upper-left corner of the window.

Description:

The `WM_RBUTTONDBLCLK` message is sent when the right mouse button is double clicked.

Return Value:

There is no meaningful return value.

WM_RBUTTONDOWN

wParam:

`wParam` indicates which virtual keys are down. The following values, in any combination, indicate the virtual keys that are down:

Value	*Meaning*
`MK_CONTROL`	Ctrl key is down
`MK_LBUTTON`	Left button is down
`MK_MBUTTON`	Middle button is down
`MK_SHIFT`	Shift key is down

lParam:

The low-order word of `lParam` contains the horizontal coordinate of the cursor. The high-order word of `lParam` contains the vertical coordinate of the cursor. These coordinates are expressed relative to the upper-left corner of the window.

Description:

The `WM_RBUTTONDOWN` message is sent when the right mouse button is pressed.

Return Value:

There is no meaningful return value.

WM_RBUTTONUP

wParam:

`wParam` indicates which virtual keys are down. The following values, in any combination, indicate the virtual keys that are down:

Value	*Meaning*
MK_CONTROL	Ctrl key is down
MK_LBUTTON	Left button is down
MK_MBUTTON	Middle button is down
MK_SHIFT	Shift key is down

lParam:

The low-order word of `lParam` contains the horizontal coordinate of the cursor. The high-order word of `lParam` contains the vertical coordinate of the cursor. These coordinates are expressed relative to the upper-left corner of the window.

Description:

The `WM_RBUTTONUP` message is sent when the right mouse button is released.

Return Value:

There is no meaningful return value.

WM_SETCURSOR

wParam:

`wParam` specifies the window handle for the window that contains the cursor.

lParam:

The low-order word of `lParam` contains the hit test code. A hit test checks the location of the mouse. The hit test codes used for the low-order word of `lParam` are:

Hit Test Code	*Meaning*
HTBOTTOM	Lower horizontal window border
HTBOTTOMLEFT	Lower-left corner of window border
HTBOTTOMRIGHT	Lower-right corner of window border
HTCAPTION	Caption area
HTCLIENT	Client area
HTERROR	Screen background or window dividing line; produces a beep on error
HTGROWBOX	Size box
HTHSCROLL	Horizontal scroll bar

Hit Test Code	*Meaning*
HTLEFT	Left window border
HTMENU	Menu area
HTNOWHERE	Screen background or window dividing line
HTREDUCE	Minimize box
HTRIGHT	Right window border
HTSIZE	Size box
HTSYSMENU	Control menu box
HTTOP	Upper horizontal window border
HTTOPLEFT	Upper-left corner of window border
HTTOPRIGHT	Upper-right corner of window border
HTTRANSPARENT	Window covered by another window
HTVSCROLL	Vertical scroll bar
HTZOOM	Maximize box

The high-order word of `lParam` contains the mouse message number.

Description:

The `WM_SETCURSOR` message is sent when the cursor is moved due to mouse movement and the input is not captured.

Return Value:

There is no meaningful return value.

WM_TIMER

`wParam:`

`wParam` contains the timer ID.

`lParam:`

`lParam` points to the function specified when the `SetTimer` function is called and the `WM_TIMER` message is sent to this function. When `lParameter` is NULL, the `WM_TIMER` message is sent to the window function.

Description:

The `WM_TIMER` message is sent when the time limit for the timer specified in `wParam` has expired.

Return Value:

There is no meaningful return value.

WM_VKEYTOITEM

wParam:

wParam contains the virtual key code of the pressed key.

lParam:

The high-order word of lParam contains the position of the caret. The low-order word of lParam contains the window handle for the list box.

Description:

The WM_VKEYTOITEM message is sent in response to a WM_KEYDOWN message. A list box with style LBS_WANTKEYBOARDINPUT sends this message to its owner.

Return Value:

WM_VKEYTOITEM returns one of the following:

- A return value of –2 indicates that the application needs no further action from the list box.
- A return value of –1 indicates that the list box should perform the default action.
- A return value of zero or greater represents the index of the list box item that should perform the default action for the key stroke.

WM_VSCROLL

wParam

wParam contains the scroll-bar code and can be any one of the following values:

Value	*Meaning*
SB_BOTTOM	Scroll to bottom
SB_ENDSCROLL	End scroll
SB_LINEDOWN	Scroll down one line
SB_LINEUP	Scroll up one line
SB_PAGEDOWN	Scroll down one page
SB_PAGEUP	Scroll up one page
SB_THUMBPOSITION	Scroll to absolute position; when specified, the low-order word of lParam contains the thumb position of the scroll bar
SB_THUMBTRACK	Move thumb position to a specified position
SB_TOP	Scroll to top

lParam:

The high-order word of `lParam` contains the control ID when the message is sent by a scroll-bar control. The low-order word of `lParam` contains the current thumb position.

Description:

The `WM_VSCROLL` message is sent when the vertical scroll bar is selected and active.

Return Value:

There is no meaningful return value.

List Box Messages

List box messages are sent to a list box from an application. The following messages are documented in this section:

LB_ADDSTRING	LB_GETTEXTLEN
LB_DELETESTRING	LB_GETTOPINDEX
LB_DIR	LB_INSERTSTRING
LB_FINDSTRING	LB_RESETCONTENT
LB_GETCOUNT	LB_SELECTSTRING
LB_GETCURSEL	LB_SELITEMRANGE
LB_GETHORIZONTALEXTENT	LB_SETCOLUMNWIDTH
LB_GETITEMDATA	LB_SETCURSEL
LB_GETITEMRECT	LB_SETHORIZONTALEXTENT
LB_GETSEL	LB_SETITEMDATA
LB_GETSELCOUNT	LB_SETSEL
LB_GETSELITEMS	LB_SETTABSTOPS
LB_GETTEXT	LB_SETTOPINDEX

LB_ADDSTRING

wParam:

`wParam` is not used.

lParam:

lParam points to the null-terminated text string that should be added.

Description:

The LB_ADDSTRING message adds the string pointed to by lParam to a list box. The string is added to the bottom of the list if the list box is not sorted. If the list box is sorted, the string is added at the appropriate place.

Return Value:

LB_ADDSTRING returns the index to the added string. A return value of LB_ERR indicates an error.

LB_DELETESTRING

wParam:

wParam specifies the index of the string to delete.

lParam:

lParam is not used.

Description:

The LB_DELETESTRING message removes the string specified by the index value in wParam from the list box.

Return Value:

LB_DELETESTRING returns the number of strings left in the list when the string is successfully deleted. A return value of LB_ERR indicates that an error has occurred.

LB_DIR

wParam:

wParam specifies the DOS attribute value. The DOS attribute values that can be used for wParam are:

Value	Meaning
0x0000	Read/write—no additional attributes
0x0001	Read only
0x0002	Hidden file
0x0004	System file
0x0010	Subdirectory
0x0020	Archive
0x2000	LB_DIR flag
0x4000	Drive
0x8000	Exclusive bit

lParam:

`lParam` points to the file specification string.

Description:

The `LB_DIR` message builds a list of files for the list box. The files added to the list must be from the current directory, contain the DOS attribute specified in `wParam`, and match the file specification in `lParam`.

Return Value:

`LB_DIR` returns the number of items in the list. `LB_ERR` is returned when an error is generated. `LB_ERRSPACE` is returned when there is not enough memory available to store the list.

LB_FINDSTRING

wParam:

`wParam` specifies the item index just prior to the first item to search. When `wParam` is –1, the list box is searched starting from the top.

lParam:

`lParam` points to the string containing the prefix text.

Description:

The `LB_FINDSTRING` message searches the list box for the first occurrence of the prefix string specified in `lParam`. The value in `wParam` specifies the index of the item just prior to the item where the search begins. The search begins with the item after the item specified in `wParam` and continues to the end of the list, begins again at the top, and terminates on either the found text or the item in `wParam`. `lParam` points to the null terminated string that contains the prefix text.

Return Value:

LB_FINDSTRING returns the index of the matching item when a match is found. A return value of LB_ERR indicates that the search is unsuccessful.

LB_GETCOUNT

wParam:

wParam is not used.

lParam:

lParam is not used.

Description:

The LB_GETCOUNT message determines the number of items in the list box.

Return Value:

LB_GETCOUNT returns the number of items in the list box. A return value of LB_ERR indicates that the message is unable to determine the number of items in the list box.

LB_GETCURSEL

wParam:

wParam is not used.

lParam:

lParam is not used.

Description:

The LB_GETCURSEL message gets the item index of the selected item.

Return Value:

LB_GETCURSEL returns the item index of the selected item. A return value of LB_ERR indicates that no item is selected or more than one item is selected.

LB_GETHORIZONTALEXTENT

wParam

wParam is not used.

lParam:

lParam is not used.

Description:

The LB_GETHORIZONTALEXTENT message determines the scrollable width, in pixels, of the list box. The list box must have style WS_HSCROLL.

Return Value:

LB_GETHORIZONTALEXTENT returns the scrollable width of the list box, in pixels.

LB_GETITEMDATA

wParam:

wParam specifies the item index for the list box item.

lParam:

lParam is not used.

Description:

The LB_GETITEMDATA message gets the 32-bit value, supplied by the application, that is associated with the list box item specified in wParam.

Return Value:

LB_GETITEMDATA returns the retrieved 32-bit value. A return value of LB_ERR indicates that the message is unable to get the value.

LB_GETITEMRECT

wParam:

wParam specifies the item index for the list box item.

lParam:

lParam points to the data structure of type RECT that stores the client coordinates of the list box item. The RECT structure is:

```
typedef struct tagRECT {
     int left;
     int top;
     int right;
     int bottom;
} RECT;
```

where:

`left` is the horizontal coordinate of the upper-left corner of the rectangular region

`top` is the vertical coordinate of the upper-left corner of the rectangular region

`right` is the horizontal coordinate of the lower-right corner of the rectangular region

`bottom` is the vertical coordinate of the lower-right corner of the rectangular region

Description:

The `LB_GETITEMRECT` message gets the dimensions of the rectangle surrounding the list box item specified in `wParam`. The dimensions of the rectangle are stored in the data structure pointed to by `lParam`.

Return Value:

A return value of `LB_ERR` indicates an error.

LB_GETSEL

`wParam`:

`wParam` contains the item index.

`lParam`:

`lParam` is not used.

Description:

The `LB_GETSEL` message gets the selection state of the item specified in `wParam`.

Return Value:

`LB_GETSEL` returns a positive value when the specified item is selected. A return value of zero indicates that the item is not selected. A return value of `LB_ERR` indicates an error.

LB_GETSELCOUNT

`wParam`:

`wParam` is not used.

lParam:

lParam is not used.

Description:

The LB_GETSELCOUNT message gets the number of items selected from a multiselection list box.

Return Value:

LB_GETSELCOUNT returns the number of items selected from the mulitselection list box. A return value of LB_ERR indicates that the message is unable to get the number of items.

LB_GETSELITEMS

wParam:

wParam specifies the maximum number of selected items to place in the buffer pointed to by lParam.

lParam:

lParam points to the buffer that stores the item numbers of the selected items specified in wParam.

Description:

The LB_GETSELITEMS message places the item numbers of the selected items from a multiselection list box in the buffer pointed to by lParam. The wParam specifies the maximum number of item numbers to place into the buffer.

Return Value:

LB_GETSELITEMS returns the number of items placed in the buffer. A return value of LB_ERR indicates that the message is unable to place the items in the buffer.

LB_GETTEXT

wParam:

wParam specifies the index of the string to copy.

lParam:

lParam points to the buffer where the string will be placed.

Description:

The LB_GETTEXT message copies the string identified by the index in wParam into the buffer pointed to by lParam.

Return Value:

LB_GETTEXT returns the number of bytes in the string, not counting the null terminator. A return value of LB_ERR indicates that the message is unable to copy the string into the buffer.

LB_GETTEXTLEN

wParam:

wParam specifies the index to the string to examine.

lParam:

lParam is not used.

Description:

The LB_GETTEXTLEN message determines the length of the list box string specified in wParam.

Return Value:

LB_GETTEXTLEN returns the number of bytes in the string, not counting the null terminator. A return value of LB_ERR indicates that the message cannot determine the number of bytes.

LB_GETTOPINDEX

wParam:

wParam is not used.

lParam:

lParam is not used.

Description:

The LB_GETTOPINDEX message gets the item index for the first visible item in the list box.

Return Value:

LB_GETTOPINDEX returns the index for the first visible item in the list box.

LB_INSERTSTRING

wParam:

wParam specifies the index where the string will be inserted into the list box. When wParam is –1, the string is added to the end of the list.

lParam:

lParam points to the string to insert into the list box. The string is null-terminated.

Description:

The LB_INSERTSTRING message inserts the string pointed to by lParam into the list box at the position specified in wParam.

Return Value:

LB_INSERTSTRING returns the index of the position at which the string was inserted. A return value of LB_ERR indicates that the message cannot insert the string. A return value of LB_ERRSPACE indicates that there is not enough memory to store the string.

LB_RESETCONTENT

wParam:

wParam is not used.

lParam:

lParam is not used.

Description:

The LB_RESETCONTENT message deletes all the strings from the list box. All memory allocated for the strings is freed.

Return Value:

There is no meaningful return value.

LB_SELECTSTRING

wParam:

wParam specifies the index of the item just prior to the first item to search. This item is the last item to search. If wParam is set to –1, the search begins at the top of the list.

lParam:

lParam points to the null-terminated prefix string.

Description:

The LB_SELECTSTRING message selects the item from the list box of a combo box that matches the string pointed to by lParam. The search begins with the next item after the item specified in wParam. The search continues down the list and begins again at the top if no match is found by the time the bottom of the list is reached. The last item searched is the item specified in wParam.

Return Value:

LB_SELECTSTRING returns the index of the selected item. A return value of LB_ERR indicates that the message is unable to select the item.

LB_SELITEMRANGE

wParam:

wParam specifies the selection setting. When wParam is a nonzero value, the specified items are selected and highlighted. When wParam is zero, the items are not selected and not highlighted.

lParam:

The low-order word of lParam contains the item index of the first item. The high-order word of lParam contains the item index of the last item.

Description:

The LB_SELITEMRANGE sets the selection settings for a range of items in a multiselection list box. The first item to set is specified in the low-order word of lParam. The high-order word of lParam specifies the last item.

Return Value:

LB_ERR is returned when unsuccessful.

LB_SETCOLUMNWIDTH

wParam:

wParam specifies the column width in pixels.

lParam:

lParam is not used.

Description:

The LB_SETCOLUMNWIDTH message defines the column width, in pixels, for a multi-column list box with style LBS_MULTICOLUMN. The column width is specified in wParam.

Return Value:

There is no meaningful return value.

LB_SETCURSEL

wParam:

wParam specifies the index of the string to select. When wParam is –1, the list box will have no selection.

lParam:

lParam is not used.

Description:

The LB_SETCURSEL message selects the string specified in wParam. If the selected string is not visible in the list box, the string is scrolled into view. This message is used with single selection list boxes.

Return Value:

LB_ERR is returned when unsuccessful.

LB_SETHORIZONTALEXTENT

wParam:

wParam specifies the horizontal scroll width in pixels.

lParam:

lParam is not used.

Description:

The LB_SETHORIZONTALEXTENT message sets the horizontal scroll width of a list box to the value specified in wParam. The list box must have style WS_HSCROLL.

Return Value:

There is no meaningful return value.

LB_SETITEMDATA

wParam:

wParam specifies the item index of the item from the list box.

lParam:

lParam specifies the value to associate with the item in wParam.

Description:

The LB_SETITEMDATA message associates the 32-bit value in lParam with the item index specified in wParam.

Return Value:

LB_ERR is returned when unsuccessful.

LB_SETSEL

wParam:

wParam specifies the selection setting. When wParam is a nonzero value, the specified items are selected and highlighted. When wParam is zero, the items are not selected and not highlighted.

lParam:

The low-order word of lParam specifies the index of the string to set. When lParam is –1, all items are either selected or deselected depending upon wParam.

Description:

The LB_SETSEL message either selects a string or removes the highlighting from a string in a multiselection list box. The string is specified in lParam. wParam specifies whether the string will be selected or deselected. This message is for use with multiselection list boxes.

Return Value:

A return value of LB_ERR indicates that the message is unable to alter the state of the string.

LB_SETTABSTOPS

wParam:

wParam defines the number of tab stops in the list box.

lParam:

lParam points to the first member of the array that contains the tab stop positions. Tab stop positions are measured in dialog units.

Description:

The LB_SETTABSTOPS message positions the tab stops for a list box. wParam defines the number of tab stops; lParam points to the first member of the array containing the tab stop positions. The list box must have style LBS_USETABSTOPS. The relationship between wParam and lParam is as follows:

- When wParam is zero and lParam is NULL, the tab stops are set every two dialog units.
- When wParam is 1, lParam specifies the distance between tab stops. When lParam points to more than one value, a tab stop is set for each value of lParam.

Return Value:

LB_SETTABSTOPS returns TRUE when successful. A return value of FALSE indicates that the message is unable to set the tab stops.

LB_SETTOPINDEX

wParam:

wParam specifies the item index of the list box item.

lParam:

lParam is not used.

Description:

The LB_SETTOPINDEX message makes the list box item specified in wParam the first visible item in the list box.

Return Value:

LB_ERR is returned when unsuccessful.

Multiple Document Interface (MDI) Messages

MDI messages are used by MDI applications to control child windows. The following messages are documented in this section:

WM_MDIACTIVATE

WM_MDICASCADE

WM_MDICREATE

WM_MDIDESTROY

WM_MDIGETACTIVE

WM_MDIICONARRANGE

WM_MDIMAXIMIZE

WM_MDINEXT

WM_MDIRESTORE

WM_MDISETMENU

WM_MDITILE

WM_MDIACTIVATE

wParam:

wParam contains the window handle of the MDI child window to activate when the application sends the message to the MDI client window. When the client window sends the message to a child window, wParam contains TRUE if the child is to be activated or FALSE if the child is to be deactivated.

lParam:

The high-order word of lParam contains the window handle of the child window being deactivated. The low-order word of lParam contains the window handle of the child window being activated when the message is sent to an MDI child window. lParam is NULL when the message is sent to the client window.

Description:

The WM_MDIACTIVATE message is sent by an application to a multiple document interface (MDI) client window. When the client window receives the message, the WM_MDIACTIVATE message is sent to the child window to be activated and to the child window to be deactivated.

Return Value:

There is no meaningful return value.

WM_MDICASCADE

wParam:

wParam is not used.

lParam:

lParam is not used.

Description:

The WM_MDICASCADE message places the child windows of a multiple document interface (MDI) client window in a cascade fashion.

Return Value:

There is no meaningful return value.

WM_MDICREATE

wParam:

wParam is not used.

lParam:

lParam points to the data structure of type MDICREATESTRUCT. The MDICREATESTRUCT structure is as follows:

```
typedef struct tagMDICREATESTRUCT
  {
     LPSTR szClass;
     LPSTR szTitle;
     HANDLE hOwner;
     int x;
     int y;
     int cx;
     int cy;
     LONG style;
     LONG lParam;
  } MDICREATESTRUCT;
```

where:

> `szClass` is a long pointer to the application defined class of the MDI child window
>
> `szTitle` is a long pointer to the title of the MDI child window
>
> `hOwner` is the instance handle of the application
>
> `x` is the position of the left side of the MDI child window
>
> `y` is the position of the top edge of the MDI child window
>
> `cx` is the width of the MDI child window
>
> `cy` is the height of the MDI child window
>
> `style` is chosen from one or more of the following styles:

Style	*Meaning*
WS_MINIMIZE	MDI child window is minimized when created
WS_MAXIMIZE	MDI child window is maximized when created
WS_HSCROLL	MDI child window contains a horizontal scroll bar when created
WS_VSCROLL	MDI child window contains a vertical scroll bar when created

> `lParam` is a 32-bit value defined by the application

Description:

The `WM_MDICREATE` message is sent to the multiple document interface (MDI) client window. A child window is then created with the style bits

> `WS_CHILD`
>
> `WS_CLIPSIBLINGS`

WS_CLIPCHILDREN

WS_SYSMENU

WS_CAPTION

WS_THICKFRAME

WS_MINIMIZEBOX

WS_MAXIMIZEBOX

The child window may also have additional style bits as defined in the MDICREATESTRUCT structure pointed to by lParam.

Return Value:

The low-order word of the return value contains the ID of the new window. The high-order word contains zero.

WM_MDIDESTROY

wParam:

wParam specifies the handle of the child window to close.

lParam:

lParam is not used.

Description:

The WM_MDIDESTROY message is sent to a multiple document interface (MDI) client window. The child window specified in wParam is then closed.

Return Value:

There is no meaningful return value.

WM_MDIGETACTIVE

wParam:

wParam is not used.

lParam:

lParam is not used.

Description:

The WM_MDIGETACTIVE message gets the handle for the active multiple document interface (MDI) child window. In addition, the flag that indicates whether or not the child window is maximized is also retrieved.

Return Value:

The low-order word of the return value contains the handle of the active child window. The high-order word of the return value contains 1 when the child window is maximized or 0 when the child window is not maximized.

WM_MDIICONARRANGE

wParam:

wParam is not used.

lParam:

lParam is not used.

Description:

The WM_MDIICONARRANGE message arranges the minimized child windows for a multiple document interface (MDI) client window.

Return Value:

There is no meaningful return value.

WM_MDIMAXIMIZE

wParam:

wParam specifies the window handle of the child window.

lParam:

lParam is not used.

Description:

The WM_MDIMAXIMIZE message is sent to a multiple document interface (MDI) client window and causes the child window specified in wParam to be maximized.

Return Value:

There is no meaningful return value.

WM_MDINEXT

wParam:

wParam is not used.

lParam:

lParam is not used.

Description:

The WM_MDINEXT message is sent to the multiple document interface (MDI) client window. The message activates the MDI child window that is directly behind the active child window. The previously active window is then pushed behind all other child windows.

Return Value:

There is no meaningful return value.

WM_MDIRESTORE

wParam:

wParam specifies the window handle of the child window to restore.

lParam:

lParam is not used.

Description:

The WM_MDIRESTORE message restores the multiple document interface (MDI) child window specified in wParam from a maximized or minimized state.

Return Value:

There is no meaningful return value.

WM_MDISETMENU

wParam:

wParam is not used.

lParam:

The low-order word of lParam contains the menu handle of the new frame window menu. The high-order word of lParam contains the menu handle of the new pop-up menu. The corresponding menu is not changed if the appropriate word is set to zero.

Description:

The WM_MDISETMENU message replaces either the menu of the MDI frame window, the Window pop-up menu, or both, as specified by the high- and low-order words in lParam.

Return Value:

WM_MDISETMENU returns the handle of the frame window menu that was replaced.

WM_MDITILE

wParam:

wParam is not used.

lParam:

lParam is not used.

Description:

The WM_MDITILE message arranges the child windows of an multiple document interface (MDI) client area in a tiled format.

Return Value:

There is no meaningful return value.

Non-Client Area Messages

Windows sends non-client area messages to create and maintain the non-client area of an application window. The following messages are documented in this section:

WM_NCACTIVATE	WM_NCLBUTTONDOWN	WM_NCMOUSEMOVE
WM_NCCALCSIZE	WM_NCLBUTTONUP	WM_NCPAINT
WM_NCCREATE	WM_NCMBUTTONDBLCLK	WM_NCRBUTTONDBLCLK
WM_NCDESTROY	WM_NCMBUTTONDOWN	WM_NCRBUTTONDOWN
WM_NCHITTEST	WM_NCMBUTTONUP	WM_NCRBUTTONUP
WM_NCLBUTTONDBLCLK		

WM_NCACTIVATE

wParam:

wParam is nonzero when an active caption or icon is to be drawn, or zero for inactive captions or icons.

lParam:

lParam is not used.

Description:

The WM_NCACTIVATE message is sent to a window when its non-client area needs updating to reflect an active or inactive state.

Return Value:

There is no meaningful return value.

WM_NCCALCSIZE

wParam:

wParam is not used.

lParam:

lParam points to the data structure of type RECT that contains the screen coordinates of the window. The RECT structure is:

```
typedef struct tagRECT {
     int left;
     int top;
     int right;
     int bottom;
} RECT;
```

where:

> left is the horizontal coordinate of the upper-left corner of the rectangular region
>
> top is the vertical coordinate of the upper-left corner of the rectangular region
>
> right is the horizontal coordinate of the lower-right corner of the rectangular region
>
> bottom is the vertical coordinate of the lower-right corner of the rectangular region

Description:

The WM_NCCALCSIZE message is sent to determine the size of the window's client area.

Return Value:

There is no meaningful return value.

WM_NCCREATE

wParam:

wParam specifies the window handle of the window being created.

lParam:

lParam points to a data structure of type CREATESTRUCT. The CREATESTRUCT data structure is as follows:

```
typedef struct tagCREATESTRUCT {
     LPSTR lpCreateParams;
     HANDLE hInstance;
     HANDLE hMenu;
     HWND hwndParent;
     int cy;
     int cx;
     int y;
     int x;
     long style;
     LPSTR lpszName;
     LPSTR lpszClass;
     long ExStyle;
} CREATESTRUCT;
```

where:

lpCreateParams points to data to create the window

hInstance is the module instance handle of the module that owns the new window

hMenu is the menu that the new window will use

hwndParent is the window that owns the created window

cy is the height of the created window

cx is the width of the created window

`y` is the vertical coordinate of the upper-left corner of the created window

`x` is the horizontal coordinate of the upper-left corner of the created window

`style` is the style for the created window

`lpszName` is a pointer to the null-terminated string that contains the name for the created window

`lpszClass` is a pointer to the null-terminated string that contains the string that specifies the class name of the created window

`ExStyle` is the extended style for the created window

Description:

The `WM_NCCREATE` message creates a non-client area for a new window. `WM_NCCREATE` is sent before the `WM_CREATE` message, whenever a window is created.

Return Value:

`WM_NCCREATE` returns a nonzero value when the non-client area is created. A return value of zero indicates that the message is unable to create the non-client area.

WM_NCDESTROY

`wParam`:

`wParam` is not used.

`lParam`:

`lParam` is not used.

Description:

The `WM_NCDESTROY` message is sent to a window when the window's non-client area is being destroyed. This message is sent after the `WM_DESTROY` message.

Return Value:

There is no meaningful return value.

WM_NCHITTEST

wParam:

wParam is not used.

lParam:

The low-order word of lParam contains the horizontal screen coordinate of the current cursor position. The high-order word of lParam contains the vertical screen coordinate of the current cursor position.

Description:

The WM_NCHITTEST message is sent to the window that contains the cursor, whenever the mouse is moved.

Return Value:

The return value indicates the cursor position and is one of the following values:

Hit Test Code	*Meaning*
HTBOTTOM	Lower horizontal window border
HTBOTTOMLEFT	Lower-left corner of window border
HTBOTTOMRIGHT	Lower-right corner of window border
HTCAPTION	Caption area
HTCLIENT	Client area
HTERROR	Screen background or window dividing line; produces a beep on error
HTGROWBOX	Size box
HTHSCROLL	Horizontal scroll bar
HTLEFT	Left window border
HTMENU	Menu area
HTNOWHERE	Screen background or window dividing line
HTREDUCE	Minimize box
HTRIGHT	Right window border
HTSIZE	Size box
HTSYSMENU	Control menu box
HTTOP	Upper horizontal window border
HTTOPLEFT	Upper-left corner of window border
HTTOPRIGHT	Upper-right corner of window border
HTTRANSPARENT	Window covered by another window
HTVSCROLL	Vertical scroll bar
HTZOOM	Maximize box

WM_NCLBUTTONDBLCLK

wParam:

The wParam contains the hit test code returned by WM_NCHITTEST. The code can be any of the following values:

Hit Test Code	*Meaning*
HTBOTTOM	Lower horizontal window border
HTBOTTOMLEFT	Lower-left corner of window border
HTBOTTOMRIGHT	Lower-right corner of window border
HTCAPTION	Caption area
HTCLIENT	Client area
HTERROR	Screen background or window dividing line; produces a beep on error
HTGROWBOX	Size box
HTHSCROLL	Horizontal scroll bar
HTLEFT	Left window border
HTMENU	Menu area
HTNOWHERE	Screen background or window dividing line
HTREDUCE	Minimize box
HTRIGHT	Right window border
HTSIZE	Size box
HTSYSMENU	Control menu box
HTTOP	Upper horizontal window border
HTTOPLEFT	Upper-left corner of window border
HTTOPRIGHT	Upper-right corner of window border
HTTRANSPARENT	Window covered by another window
HTVSCROLL	Vertical scroll bar
HTZOOM	Maximize box

lParam:

lParam contains a data structure of type POINT. This data structure—described as follows—contains the horizontal and vertical screen coordinates of the cursor:

```
typedef struct tagPOINT {
     int x;
     int y;
} POINT;
```

where:

`x` is the horizontal coordinate of a point

`y` is the vertical coordinate of a point

Description:

The `WM_NCLBUTTONDBLCLK` message is sent to a window when the left mouse button is double clicked while the cursor is in a non-client area of the window.

Return Value:

There is no meaningful return value.

WM_NCLBUTTONDOWN

`wParam:`

`wParam` contains the hit test code returned by `WM_NCHITTEST`. The code can be any of the following values:

Hit Test Code	*Meaning*
HTBOTTOM	Lower horizontal window border
HTBOTTOMLEFT	Lower-left corner of window border
HTBOTTOMRIGHT	Lower-right corner of window border
HTCAPTION	Caption area
HTCLIENT	Client area
HTERROR	Screen background or window dividing line; produces a beep on error
HTGROWBOX	Size box
HTHSCROLL	Horizontal scroll bar
HTLEFT	Left window border
HTMENU	Menu area
HTNOWHERE	Screen background or window dividing line
HTREDUCE	Minimize box
HTRIGHT	Right window border
HTSIZE	Size box
HTSYSMENU	Control menu box
HTTOP	Upper horizontal window border
HTTOPLEFT	Upper-left corner of window border

Hit Test Code	*Meaning*
HTTOPRIGHT	Upper-right corner of window border
HTTRANSPARENT	Window covered by another window
HTVSCROLL	Vertical scroll bar
HTZOOM	Maximize box

lParam:

lParam contains a data structure of type POINT. The data structure contains the horizontal and vertical screen coordinates of the cursor. The POINT structure is:

```
typedef struct tagPOINT {
     int x;
     int y;
} POINT;
```

where:

x is the horizontal coordinate of a point

y is the vertical coordinate of a point

Description:

The WM_NCLBUTTONDOWN message is sent to a window when the left mouse button is pressed while the cursor is in a non-client area of the window.

Return Value:

There is no meaningful return value.

WM_NCLBUTTONUP

wParam:

wParam contains the hit test code returned by WM_NCHITTEST. The code can be any of the following values:

Hit Test Code	*Meaning*
HTBOTTOM	Lower horizontal window border
HTBOTTOMLEFT	Lower-left corner of window border
HTBOTTOMRIGHT	Lower-right corner of window border
HTCAPTION	Caption area
HTCLIENT	Client area
HTERROR	Screen background or window dividing line; produces a beep on error

Hit Test Code	*Meaning*
HTGROWBOX	Size box
HTHSCROLL	Horizontal scroll bar
HTLEFT	Left window border
HTMENU	Menu area
HTNOWHERE	Screen background or window dividing line
HTREDUCE	Minimize box
HTRIGHT	Right window border
HTSIZE	Size box
HTSYSMENU	Control menu box
HTTOP	Upper horizontal window border
HTTOPLEFT	Upper-left corner of window border
HTTOPRIGHT	Upper-right corner of window border
HTTRANSPARENT	Window covered by another window
HTVSCROLL	Vertical scroll bar
HTZOOM	Maximize box

lParam:

lParam contains a data structure of type POINT. The data structure contains the horizontal and vertical screen coordinates of the cursor. The POINT structure is:

```
typedef struct tagPOINT {
     int x;
     int y;
} POINT;
```

where:

x is the horizontal coordinate of a point

y is the vertical coordinate of a point

Description:

The WM_NCLBUTTONUP message is sent to a window when the left mouse button is released while the cursor is in a non-client area of the window.

Return Value:

There is no meaningful return value.

WM_NCMBUTTONDBLCLK

wParam:

wParam contains the hit test code returned by WM_NCHITTEST. The code can be any of the following values:

Hit Test Code	*Meaning*
HTBOTTOM	Lower horizontal window border
HTBOTTOMLEFT	Lower-left corner of window border
HTBOTTOMRIGHT	Lower-right corner of window border
HTCAPTION	Caption area
HTCLIENT	Client area
HTERROR	Screen background or window dividing line; produces a beep on error
HTGROWBOX	Size box
HTHSCROLL	Horizontal scroll bar
HTLEFT	Left window border
HTMENU	Menu area
HTNOWHERE	Screen background or window dividing line
HTREDUCE	Minimize box
HTRIGHT	Right window border
HTSIZE	Size box
HTSYSMENU	Control menu box
HTTOP	Upper horizontal window border
HTTOPLEFT	Upper-left corner of window border
HTTOPRIGHT	Upper-right corner of window border
HTTRANSPARENT	Window covered by another window
HTVSCROLL	Vertical scroll bar
HTZOOM	Maximize box

lParam:

lParam contains a data structure of type POINT. The data structure contains the horizontal and vertical screen coordinates of the cursor. The POINT structure is:

```
typedef struct tagPOINT {
     int x;
     int y;
} POINT;
```

where:

`x` is the horizontal coordinate of a point

`y` is the vertical coordinate of a point

Description:

The `WM_NCMBUTTONDBLCLK` message is sent to a window when the middle mouse button is double clicked while the cursor is in a non-client area of the window.

Return Value:

There is no meaningful return value.

WM_NCMBUTTONDOWN

`wParam:`

`wParam` contains the hit test code returned by `WM_NCHITTEST`. The code can be any of the following values:

Hit Test Code	*Meaning*
HTBOTTOM	Lower horizontal window border
HTBOTTOMLEFT	Lower-left corner of window border
HTBOTTOMRIGHT	Lower-right corner of window border
HTCAPTION	Caption area
HTCLIENT	Client area
HTERROR	Screen background or window dividing line; produces a beep on error
HTGROWBOX	Size box
HTHSCROLL	Horizontal scroll bar
HTLEFT	Left window border
HTMENU	Menu area
HTNOWHERE	Screen background or window dividing line
HTREDUCE	Minimize box
HTRIGHT	Right window border
HTSIZE	Size box
HTSYSMENU	Control menu box
HTTOP	Upper horizontal window border
HTTOPLEFT	Upper-left corner of window border

Hit Test Code	Meaning
HTTOPRIGHT	Upper-right corner of window border
HTTRANSPARENT	Window covered by another window
HTVSCROLL	Vertical scroll bar
HTZOOM	Maximize box

lParam:

lParam contains a data structure of type POINT. The data structure contains the horizontal and vertical screen coordinates of the cursor. The POINT structure is:

```
typedef struct tagPOINT {
     int x;
     int y;
} POINT;
```

where:

x is the horizontal coordinate of a point

y is the vertical coordinate of a point

Description:

The WM_NCMBUTTONDOWN message is sent to a window when the middle mouse button is pressed while the cursor is in a non-client area of the window.

Return Value:

There is no meaningful return value.

WM_NCMBUTTONUP

wParam:

wParam contains the hit test code returned by WM_NCHITTEST. The code can be any of the following values:

Hit Test Code	Meaning
HTBOTTOM	Lower horizontal window border
HTBOTTOMLEFT	Lower-left corner of window border
HTBOTTOMRIGHT	Lower-right corner of window border
HTCAPTION	Caption area
HTCLIENT	Client area
HTERROR	Screen background or window dividing line; produces a beep on error

Hit Test Code	*Meaning*
HTGROWBOX	Size box
HTHSCROLL	Horizontal scroll bar
HTLEFT	Left window border
HTMENU	Menu area
HTNOWHERE	Screen background or window dividing line
HTREDUCE	Minimize box
HTRIGHT	Right window border
HTSIZE	Size box
HTSYSMENU	Control menu box
HTTOP	Upper horizontal window border
HTTOPLEFT	Upper-left corner of window border
HTTOPRIGHT	Upper-right corner of window border
HTTRANSPARENT	Window covered by another window
HTVSCROLL	Vertical scroll bar
HTZOOM	Maximize box

lParam:

lParam contains a data structure of type POINT. The data structure contains the horizontal and vertical screen coordinates of the cursor. The POINT structure is:

```
typedef struct tagPOINT {
     int x;
     int y;
} POINT;
```

where:

x is the horizontal coordinate of a point

y is the vertical coordinate of a point

Description:

The WM_NCMBUTTONUP message is sent to a window when the middle mouse button is released while the cursor is in a non-client area of the window.

Return Value:

There is no meaningful return value.

WM_NCMOUSEMOVE

wParam:

wParam contains the hit test code returned by WM_NCHITTEST. The code can be any of the following values:

Hit Test Code	*Meaning*
HTBOTTOM	Lower horizontal window border
HTBOTTOMLEFT	Lower-left corner of window border
HTBOTTOMRIGHT	Lower-right corner of window border
HTCAPTION	Caption area
HTCLIENT	Client area
HTERROR	Screen background or window dividing line; produces a beep on error
HTGROWBOX	Size box
HTHSCROLL	Horizontal scroll bar
HTLEFT	Left window border
HTMENU	Menu area
HTNOWHERE	Screen background or window dividing line
HTREDUCE	Minimize box
HTRIGHT	Right window border
HTSIZE	Size box
HTSYSMENU	Control menu box
HTTOP	Upper horizontal window border
HTTOPLEFT	Upper-left corner of window border
HTTOPRIGHT	Upper-right corner of window border
HTTRANSPARENT	Window covered by another window
HTVSCROLL	Vertical scroll bar
HTZOOM	Maximize box

lParam:

lParam contains a data structure of type POINT. The data structure contains the horizontal and vertical screen coordinates of the cursor. The POINT structure is:

```
typedef struct tagPOINT {
     int x;
     int y;
} POINT;
```

where:

`x` is the horizontal coordinate of a point

`y` is the vertical coordinate of a point

Description:

The `WM_NCMOUSEMOVE` message is sent to a window when the cursor is moved in a non-client area of the window.

Return Value:

There is no meaningful return value.

WM_NCPAINT

wParam:

`wParam` is not used.

lParam:

`lParam` is not used.

Description:

The `WM_NCPAINT` message is sent to a window when the window frame needs to be painted. This function enables the application to paint custom window frames. The `DefWindowProc` function is used to paint the window frame.

Return Value:

There is no meaningful return value.

WM_NCRBUTTONDBLCLK

wParam:

`wParam` contains the hit test code returned by `WM_NCHITTEST`. The code can be any of the following values:

Hit Test Code	*Meaning*
HTBOTTOM	Lower horizontal window border
HTBOTTOMLEFT	Lower-left corner of window border
HTBOTTOMRIGHT	Lower-right corner of window border

Hit Test Code	Meaning
HTCAPTION	Caption area
HTCLIENT	Client area
HTERROR	Screen background or window dividing line; produces a beep on error
HTGROWBOX	Size box
HTHSCROLL	Horizontal scroll bar
HTLEFT	Left window border
HTMENU	Menu area
HTNOWHERE	Screen background or window dividing line
HTREDUCE	Minimize box
HTRIGHT	Right window border
HTSIZE	Size box
HTSYSMENU	Control menu box
HTTOP	Upper horizontal window border
HTTOPLEFT	Upper-left corner of window border
HTTOPRIGHT	Upper-right corner of window border
HTTRANSPARENT	Window covered by another window
HTVSCROLL	Vertical scroll bar
HTZOOM	Maximize box

lParam:

lParam contains a data structure of type POINT. The data structure contains the horizontal and vertical screen coordinates of the cursor. The POINT structure is:

```
typedef struct tagPOINT {
     int x;
     int y;
} POINT;
```

where:

x is the horizontal coordinate of a point

y is the vertical coordinate of a point

Description:

The WM_NCRBUTTONDBLCLK message is sent to a window when the right mouse button is double clicked while the cursor is in a non-client area of the window.

Return Value:

There is no meaningful return value.

WM_NCRBUTTONDOWN

wParam:

wParam contains the hit test code returned by WM_NCHITTEST. The code can be any of the following values:

Hit Test Code	*Meaning*
HTBOTTOM	Lower horizontal window border
HTBOTTOMLEFT	Lower-left corner of window border
HTBOTTOMRIGHT	Lower-right corner of window border
HTCAPTION	Caption area
HTCLIENT	Client area
HTERROR	Screen background or window dividing line; produces a beep on error
HTGROWBOX	Size box
HTHSCROLL	Horizontal scroll bar
HTLEFT	Left window border
HTMENU	Menu area
HTNOWHERE	Screen background or window dividing line
HTREDUCE	Minimize box
HTRIGHT	Right window border
HTSIZE	Size box
HTSYSMENU	Control menu box
HTTOP	Upper horizontal window border
HTTOPLEFT	Upper-left corner of window border
HTTOPRIGHT	Upper-right corner of window border
HTTRANSPARENT	Window covered by another window
HTVSCROLL	Vertical scroll bar
HTZOOM	Maximize box

lParam:

lParam contains a data structure of type POINT. The data structure contains the horizontal and vertical screen coordinates of the cursor. The POINT structure is:

```
typedef struct tagPOINT {
     int x;
     int y;
} POINT;
```

where:

`x` is the horizontal coordinate of a point

`y` is the vertical coordinate of a point

Description:

The `WM_NCRBUTTONDOWN` message is sent to a window when the right mouse button is pressed while the cursor is in a non-client area of the window.

Return Value:

There is no meaningful return value.

WM_NCRBUTTONUP

`wParam:`

`wParam` contains the hit test code returned by `WM_NCHITTEST`. The code can be any of the following values:

Hit Test Code	*Meaning*
HTBOTTOM	Lower horizontal window border
HTBOTTOMLEFT	Lower-left corner of window border
HTBOTTOMRIGHT	Lower-right corner of window border
HTCAPTION	Caption area
HTCLIENT	Client area
HTERROR	Screen background or window dividing line; produces a beep on error
HTGROWBOX	Size box
HTHSCROLL	Horizontal scroll bar
HTLEFT	Left window border
HTMENU	Menu area
HTNOWHERE	Screen background or window dividing line
HTREDUCE	Minimize box
HTRIGHT	Right window border
HTSIZE	Size box
HTSYSMENU	Control menu box
HTTOP	Upper horizontal window border
HTTOPLEFT	Upper-left corner of window border

Hit Test Code	*Meaning*
HTTOPRIGHT	Upper-right corner of window border
HTTRANSPARENT	Window covered by another window
HTVSCROLL	Vertical scroll bar
HTZOOM	Maximize box

lParam:

lParam contains a data structure of type POINT. The data structure contains the horizontal and vertical screen coordinates of the cursor. The POINT structure is:

```
typedef struct tagPOINT {
    int x;
    int y;
} POINT;
```

where:

x is the horizontal coordinate of a point

y is the vertical coordinate of a point

Description:

The WM_NCRBUTTONUP message is sent to a window when the right mouse button is released while the cursor is in a non-client area of the window.

Return Value:

There is no meaningful return value.

Notification Codes

Notification codes are sent to the parent window of a control as notification that certain actions have occurred. There are four basic types of notification codes: button notification codes, combo box notification codes, edit control notification codes, and list box notification codes.

Button Notification Codes

Button notification codes are for use with button controls. The following messages are documented in this section:

`BN_CLICKED`

`BN_DOUBLECLICKED`

BN_CLICKED

wParam:

wParam specifies the control ID.

lParam:

The low-order word of lParam specifies the handle for the button control. The high-order word of lParam specifies the BN_CLICKED notification code.

Description:

The BN_CLICKED code is sent through a WM_COMMAND message from a button control to the parent window when a button has been clicked.

Return Value:

There is no meaningful return value.

BN_DOUBLECLICKED

wParam:

wParam specifies the control ID.

lParam:

The low-order word of lParam contains the handle of the button control. The high-order word of lParam contains the BN_DOUBLECLICKED notification code.

Description:

The BN_DOUBLECLICKED code is sent through a WM_COMMAND message from a button control to the parent window when a button has been double clicked. The button must have style BS_RADIOBUTTON or BS_OWNERDRAW.

Return Value:

There is no meaningful return value.

Combo Box Notification Codes

Combo box notification codes are used with combo boxes. The following messages are documented in this section:

CBN_DBLCLK

CBN_DROPDOWN

CBN_EDITCHANGE

CBN_EDITUPDATE

CBN_ERRSPACE

CBN_KILLFOCUS

CBN_SELCHANGE

CBN_SETFOCUS

CBN_DBLCLK

wParam:

wParam contains the control ID for the combo box.

lParam:

The low-order word of lParam contains the handle of the combo box. The high-order word of lParam contains the CBN_DBLCLK notification code.

Description:

The CBN_DBLCLK code is sent through a WM_COMMAND message from a control to the parent window when a string in the list box of a combo box has been double clicked.

Return Value:

There is no meaningful return value.

CBN_DROPDOWN

wParam:

wParam specifies the control ID for the combo box.

lParam:

The low-order word of lParam contains the handle of the combo box. The high-order word of lParam contains the CBN_DROPDOWN code.

Description:

The CBN_DROPDOWN code is sent through a WM_COMMAND message from a control to the parent window when a list box of a combo box is to be dropped down. This code is sent prior to the list box becoming visible.

Return Value:

There is no meaningful return value.

CBN_EDITCHANGE

wParam:

wParam specifies the control ID for the combo box.

lParam:

The low-order word of lParam contains the handle of the combo box. The high-order word of lParam contains the CBN_EDITCHANGE code.

Description:

The CBN_EDITCHANGE code is sent through a WM_COMMAND message from a control to the parent window when the user modifies the text in an edit control of a combo box. This code is sent after Windows updates the display.

Return Value:

There is no meaningful return value.

CBN_EDITUPDATE

wParam:

wParam contains the control ID for the combo box.

lParam

The low-order word of lParam contains the handle of the combo box. The high-order word of lParam contains the CBN_EDITUPDATE code.

Description:

The CBN_EDITUPDATE code is sent through a WM_COMMAND message from a control to the parent window when the edit control of a combo box will display altered text. This code is sent before Windows updates the display.

Return Value:

There is no meaningful return value.

CBN_ERRSPACE

wParam:

wParam contains the control ID for the combo box.

lParam:

The low-order word of lParam contains the handle of the combo box. The high-order word of lParam contains the CBN_ERRSPACE code.

Description:

The CBN_ERRSPACE code is sent through a WM_COMMAND message from a control to the parent window when the list box of a combo box cannot allocate the needed memory.

Return Value:

There is no meaningful return value.

CBN_KILLFOCUS

wParam:

wParam contains the control ID for the combo box.

lParam:

The low-order word of lParam contains the handle of the combo box. The high-order word of lParam contains the CBN_KILLFOCUS code.

Description:

The CBN_KILLFOCUS code is sent through a WM_COMMAND message from a control to the parent window when the combo box loses the input focus.

Return Value:

There is no meaningful return value.

CBN_SELCHANGE

wParam:

wParam contains the control ID of the combo box.

lParam:

The low-order word of lParam contains the handle of the combo box. The high-order word of lParam contains the CBN_SELCHANGE code.

Description:

The CBN_SELCHANGE code is sent through a WM_COMMAND message from a control to the parent window when the user modifies a selection of the list box of a combo box.

Return Value:

There is no meaningful return value.

CBN_SETFOCUS

wParam:

wParam contains the control ID of the combo box.

lParam:

The low-order word of lParam contains the handle of the combo box. The high-order word of lParam contains the CBN_SETFOCUS code.

Description:

The CBN_SETFOCUS code is sent through a WM_COMMAND message from a control to the parent window when the combo box receives the input focus.

Return Value:

There is no meaningful return value.

Edit Control Notification Codes

Edit control notification codes are used with edit controls. The following messages are documented in this section:

EN_CHANGE

EN_ERRSPACE

EN_HSCROLL

EN_KILLFOCUS

EN_MAXTEXT

EN_SETFOCUS

EN_UPDATE

EN_VSCROLL

EN_CHANGE

wParam:

wParam specifies the control ID and contains the value of wParam from the WM_COMMAND message.

lParam:

The low-order word of lParam contains the edit control window handle. The high-order word of lParam contains the EN_CHANGE code.

Description:

The EN_CHANGE code is sent through a WM_COMMAND message from a control to the parent window when the user alters the text. This code is sent after Windows updates the display.

Return Value:

There is no meaningful return value.

EN_ERRSPACE

wParam:

wParam specifies the control ID and contains the value of wParam from the WM_COMMAND message.

lParam:

The low-order word of lParam contains the edit control window handle. The high-order word of lParam contains the EN_ERRSPACE code.

Description:

The EN_ERRSPACE code is sent through a WM_COMMAND message from a control to the parent window when the edit control cannot allocate the needed memory.

Return Value:

There is no meaningful return value.

EN_HSCROLL

wParam:

wParam specifies the control ID and contains the value of wParam from the WM_COMMAND message.

lParam:

The low-order word of lParam contains the edit control window handle. The high-order word of lParam contains the EN_HSCROLL code.

Description:

The EN_HSCROLL code is sent through a WM_COMMAND message from a control to the parent window when the horizontal scroll bar for the edit control has been clicked. This code is sent before Windows updates the display.

Return Value:

There is no meaningful return value.

EN_KILLFOCUS

wParam:

wParam specifies the control ID and contains the value of wParam from the WM_COMMAND message.

lParam:

The low-order word of lParam contains the edit control window handle. The high-order word of lParam contains the EN_KILLFOCUS code.

Description:

The EN_KILLFOCUS code is sent through a WM_COMMAND message from a control to the parent window when the edit control has lost the input focus.

Return Value:

There is no meaningful return value.

EN_MAXTEXT

wParam:

wParam specifies the control ID and contains the value of wParam from the WM_COMMAND message.

lParam:

The low-order word of lParam contains the edit control window handle. The high-order word of lParam contains the EN_MAXTEXT code.

Description:

The EN_MAXTEXT code is sent through a WM_COMMAND message from a control to the parent window when the current insertion of text exceeds the specified limits for the edit control.

Return Value:

There is no meaningful return value.

EN_SETFOCUS

wParam:

wParam specifies the control ID and contains the value of wParam from the WM_COMMAND message.

lParam:

The low-order word of lParam contains the edit control window handle. The high-order word of lParam contains the EN_SETFOCUS code.

Description:

The EN_SETFOCUS code is sent through a WM_COMMAND message from a control to the parent window when the edit control receives the input focus.

Return Value:

There is no meaningful return value.

EN_UPDATE

wParam:

wParam specifies the control ID and contains the value of wParam from the WM_COMMAND message.

lParam:

The low-order word of lParam contains the edit control window handle. The high-order word of lParam contains the EN_UPDATE code.

Description:

The EN_UPDATE code is sent through a WM_COMMAND message from a control to the parent window when the user alters text and the edit control will therefore display altered text. This code is sent before Windows updates the display.

Return Value:

There is no meaningful return value.

EN_VSCROLL

wParam:

wParam specifies the control ID and contains the value of wParam from the WM_COMMAND message.

lParam:

The low-order word of lParam contains the edit control window handle. The high-order word of lParam contains the EN_VSCROLL code.

Description:

The EN_VSCROLL code is sent through a WM_COMMAND message from a control to the parent window when the vertical scroll bar for the edit control has been clicked. This code is sent before Windows updates the display.

Return Value:

There is no meaningful return value.

List Box Notification Codes

List box notification codes are used with list boxes. The following messages are documented in this section:

LBN_DBLCLK

LBN_ERRSPACE

LBN_KILLFOCUS

LBN_SELCHANGE

LBN_SETFOCUS

LBN_DBLCLK

wParam:

wParam specifies the control ID and contains the value of wParam from the WM_COMMAND message.

lParam:

The low-order word of lParam contains the edit control window handle. The high-order word of lParam contains the LBN_DBLCLK code. The list box control must have style LBS_NOTIFY.

Description:

The LBN_DBLCLK code is sent through a WM_COMMAND message from a control to the parent window when a string from the list box has been double clicked.

Return Value:

There is no meaningful return value.

LBN_ERRSPACE

wParam:

The wParam specifies the control ID and contains the value of wParam from the WM_COMMAND message.

lParam:

The low-order word of lParam contains the edit control window handle. The high-order word of lParam contains the LBN_ERRSPACE code.

Description:

The LBN_ERRSPACE code is sent through a WM_COMMAND message from a control to the parent window when the list box control is unable to allocate the needed memory.

The list box control must have style LBS_NOTIFY.

Return Value:

There is no meaningful return value.

LBN_KILLFOCUS

wParam:

wParam specifies the control ID and contains the value of wParam from the WM_COMMAND message.

lParam:

The low-order word of lParam contains the edit control window handle. The high-order word of lParam contains the LBN_KILLFOCUS code.

Description:

The LBN_KILLFOCUS code is sent through a WM_COMMAND message from a control to the parent window when the list box loses the input focus.

Return Value:

There is no meaningful return value.

LBN_SELCHANGE

wParam:

wParam specifies the control ID and contains the value of wParam from the WM_COMMAND message.

lParam:

The low-order word of lParam contains the edit control window handle. The high-order word of lParam contains the LBN_SELCHANGE code.

Description:

The LBN_SELCHANGE code is sent through a WM_COMMAND message from a control to the parent window when the selection in a list box has changed. The list box must have style LBS_NOTIFY.

Return Value:

There is no meaningful return value.

LBN_SETFOCUS

wParam:

wParam specifies the control ID and contains the value of wParam from the WM_COMMAND message.

lParam:

The low-order word of lParam contains the edit control window handle. The high-order word of lParam contains the LBN_SETFOCUS code.

Description:

The LBN_SETFOCUS code is sent through a WM_COMMAND message from a control to the parent window when the list box receives the input focus.

Return Value:

There is no meaningful return value.

Owner Draw Control Messages

Owner draw control messages indicate to the owner of a control that the control needs to be drawn and needs to furnish drawing information. The following messages are documented in this section:

WM_COMPAREITEM

WM_DELETEITEM

WM_DRAWITEM

WM_MEASUREITEM

WM_COMPAREITEM

wParam:

wParam is not used.

lParam:

lParam points to a structure of type COMPAREITEMSTRUCT that contains the identifiers and data for two items of the combo or list box. The COMPAREITEMSTRUCT structure is:

```
typedef struct COMPAREITEMSTRUCT {
     WORD CtlType;
     WORD CtlID;
     HWND hwndItem;
     WORD itemID1;
     DWORD itemData1;
     WORD itemID2;
     DWORD itemData2;
} COMPAREITEMSTRUCT;
```

where:

CtlType is ODT_LISTBOX for owner draw list box or ODT_COMBOBOX for owner draw combo box

CtlID is the control ID for the list or combo box

hwndItem is the window handle of the control

itemID1 is the first item index to compare from the list or combo box

itemData1 is the application supplied data for the first item to compare

itemID2 is the second item index to compare from the list or combo box

itemData2 is the application supplied data for the second item to compare

Description:

The WM_COMPAREITEM message determines the position of a new item for a sorted owner draw combo box or list box. This message is often sent several times to determine the position of the new item.

Return Value:

The return value indicates the position of one item relative to the other, as follows:

Value	*Meaning*
–1	Item 1 before Item 2
0	Items are the same
1	Item 2 before Item 1

WM_DELETEITEM

wParam:

wParam is not used.

lParam:

lParam points to a data structure of type DELETEITEMSTRUCT that contains information on the deleted item. The DELETEITEMSTRUCT structure is:

```
typedef struct DELETEITEMSTRUCT
  {
     WORD CtlType;
     WORD CtlID;
     WORD itemID;
     HWND hwndItem;
     DWORD itemData;
  } DELETEITEMSTRUCT;
```

where:

> CtlType is ODT_LISTBOX for owner draw list box or ODT_COMBOBOX for owner draw combo box
>
> CtlID is the control ID for the list or combo box
>
> itemID is the item index for the deleted item
>
> hwndItem is the window handle of the control
>
> itemData is the value passed to the control in lParam from LB_INSERTSTRING, LB_ADDSTRING, CB_INSERTSTRING, or CB_ADDSTRING when the item was originally added to the list box

Description:

The WM_DELETEITEM message is sent to the owner of an owner draw list or combo box when the list or combo box is destroyed, or an item is removed using LB_DELETESTRING, LB_RESETCONTENT, CB_DELETESTRING, or CB_RESETCONTENT.

Return Value:

There is no meaningful return value.

WM_DRAWITEM

wParam:

wParam is not used.

lParam:

lParam points to a structure of type DRAWITEMSTRUCT that contains information about the item to draw. The DRAWITEMSTRUCT structure is:

```
typedef struct tagDRAWITEMSTRUCT
```

```
{
    WORD CtlType;
    WORD CtlID;
    WORD itemID;
    WORD itemAction;
    WORD itemState;
    HWND hwndItem;
    HDC hDC;
    RECT rcItem;
    DWORD itemData;
} DRAWITEMSTRUCT;
```

where:

`CtlType` is the control type:

- `ODT_BUTTON` for owner draw button
- `ODT_COMBOBOX` for owner draw combo box
- `ODT_LISTBOX` for owner draw list box
- `ODT_MENU` for owner draw menu

`CtlID` is the control ID for the combo box, list box, or button

`itemID` is the menu item ID (for a menu) or the item index (for a list box or combo box)

`itemAction` is the drawing action: `ODA_DRAWENTIRE` when the entire control need redrawn, `ODA_FOCUS` when the control gets or loses the input focus, `ODA_SELECT` when the selection status changes

`itemState` is the state of the item after drawing:

- `ODS_CHECKED` when the menu item is to be checked
- `ODS_DISABLED` to disable the item
- `ODS_FOCUS` when the item has the input focus
- `ODS_GRAYED` when the item is grayed
- `ODS_SELECTED` when the item is selected

`hwndItem` is the window handle of the control

`hDC` is the device context

`rcItem` is a rectangle in the device context that defines the boundaries of the control

`itemData` is the value passed in `lParam` from `CB_ADDSTRING`, `CB_INSERTSTRING`, `LB_ADDSTRING`, or `LB_INSERTSTRING`

Description:

The WM_DRAWITEM message is sent to an owner draw button, a combo box, a list box, or a menu when the control has visually changed.

Return Value:

There is no meaningful return value.

WM_MEASUREITEM

wParam:

wParam is not used.

lParam:

lParam points to a data structure of type MEASUREITEMSTRUCT that contains the dimensions of an owner draw control. The MEASUREITEMSTRUCT structure is:

```
typedef struct tagMEASUREITEMSTRUCT
  {
     WORD CtlType;
     WORD CtlID;
     WORD itemID;
     WORD itemWidth;
     WORD itemHeight;
     DWORD itemData;
  } MEASUREITEMSTRUCT;
```

where:

CtlType is the control type:

- ODT_BUTTON for owner draw button
- ODT_COMBOBOX for owner draw combo box
- ODT_LISTBOX for owner draw list box
- ODT_MENU for owner draw menu

CtlID is the control ID for a combo box, list box, or button

itemID is the either a menu ID or a list box item ID

itemWidth is the width of a menu item

itemHeight is the height of an item in a menu or list box

itemData is the value passed to the control in lParam from CB_ADDSTRING, CB_INSERTSTRING, LB_ADDSTRING, or LB_INSERTSTRING

Description:

The WM_MEASUREITEM message is sent to the owner of an owner draw button, list box, combo box, or menu item when the control is created. The MEASUREITEM data structure is then filled by the owner.

Return Value:

There is no meaningful return value.

Scroll Bar Messages

Scroll bar messages are sent by the scroll bar control to the scroll bar owner when the scroll bar control is clicked. The following messages are documented in this section:

WM_HSCROLL

WM_VSCROLL

WM_HSCROLL

wParam:

The wParam specifies the scroll bar code. The scroll bar code is selected from the following values:

Value	*Meaning*
SB_BOTTOM	Scroll to lower right
SB_ENDSCROLL	End scroll
SB_LINEDOWN	Scroll down one line
SB_LINEUP	Scroll up one line
SB_PAGEDOWN	Scroll down one page
SB_PAGEUP	Scroll up one page
SB_THUMBPOSITION	Scroll to absolute position; when specified, the low-order word of lParam contains the thumb position of the scroll-bar
SB_THUMBTRACK	Move thumb position to a specified position.
SB_TOP	Scroll to upper left

lParam:

When the WM_HSCROLL message is sent by a scroll bar control, the high-order word of lParam specifies the window handle for the control. The low-order word of lParam specifies the thumb position of the scroll bar.

Description:

The WM_HSCROLL message is sent when the horizontal scroll bar is clicked and active.

Return Value:

There is no meaningful return value.

WM_VSCROLL

wParam:

wParam contains the scroll bar code and can be any one of the following values:

Value	*Meaning*
SB_BOTTOM	Scroll to bottom
SB_ENDSCROLL	End scroll
SB_LINEDOWN	Scroll down one line
SB_LINEUP	Scroll up one line
SB_PAGEDOWN	Scroll down one page
SB_PAGEUP	Scroll up one page
SB_THUMBPOSITION	Scroll to absolute position; when specified, the low-order word of lParam contains the thumb position of the scroll bar
SB_THUMBTRACK	Move thumb position to a specified position
SB_TOP	Scroll to top

lParam:

The high-order word of lParam contains the control ID when the message is sent by a scroll bar control. The low-order word of lParam contains the thumb position of the scroll bar.

Description:

The WM_VSCROLL message is sent when the vertical scroll bar is selected and active.

Return Value:

There is no meaningful return value.

System Information Messages

Windows sends system information messages whenever an application makes a change that affects other applications. The following messages are documented in this section:

WM_COMPACTING

WM_DEVMODECHANGE

WM_FONTCHANGE

WM_PALETTECHANGED

WM_SPOOLERSTATUS

WM_SYSCOLORCHANGE

WM_TIMECHANGE

WM_WININICHANGE

WM_COMPACTING

wParam:

wParam specifies the ratio of CPU time Windows spends compacting memory.

lParam:

lParam is not used.

Description:

The WM_COMPACTING message is sent to all top-level windows when Windows is spending more that 12.5% of its CPU time compacting memory. This message is usually an indicator that memory is running low and the application should free as much memory as possible.

Return Value:

There is no meaningful return value.

WM_DEVMODECHANGE

wParam:

wParam is not used.

`lParam:`

`lParam` points to the specified device name in WIN.INI.

Description:

The `WM_DEVMODECHANGE` message is sent to all top level windows when device mode settings are modified.

Return Value:

There is no meaningful return value.

WM_FONTCHANGE

`wParam:`

`wParam` is not used.

`lParam:`

`lParam` is not used.

Description:

The `WM_FONTCHANGE` message should be sent to all top level windows whenever a font resource is added or removed.

Return Value:

There is no meaningful return value.

WM_PALETTECHANGED

`wParam:`

`wParam` specifies the handle of the window causing the change to the system palette.

`lParam:`

`lParam` is not used.

Description:

The `WM_PALETTECHANGED` message is sent to all windows when the window with the input focus realizes its logical palette. When the window realizes its logical palette, the system palette is changed. At that point windows that do not have the input focus and use a color palette should realize their logical palette and update their client area.

Return Value:

There is no meaningful return value.

WM_SPOOLERSTATUS

wParam:

wParam contains SP_JOBSTATUS.

lParam:

The low-order word of lParam contains the number of jobs left in the Print Manager queue. The high-order word of lParam is not used.

Description:

The WM_SPOOLERSTATUS message is sent whenever the Print Manager queue is modified by adding or removing a print job.

Return Value:

There is no meaningful return value.

WM_SYSCOLORCHANGE

wParam:

wParam is not used.

lParam:

lParam is not used.

Description:

The WM_SYSCOLORCHANGE message is sent to all top level windows when the system color setting has been modified. The WM_PAINT message is sent by Windows to all the windows affected by the change.

Return Value:

There is no meaningful return value.

WM_TIMECHANGE

wParam:

wParam is not used.

lParam:

lParam is not used.

Description:

The WM_TIMECHANGE message indicates that the system time has been changed. This message should be sent to all top level windows by the application that makes the modification.

Return Value:

There is no meaningful return value.

WM_WININICHANGE

wParam:

wParam is not used.

lParam:

lParam points to the string that contains the name of the modified section.

Description:

The WM_WININICHANGE message indicates that WIN.INI, the Windows initialization file, is modified. The application that modifies WIN.INI should send this message to all top level windows.

Return Value:

There is no meaningful return value.

System Messages

Windows sends system messages whenever the window's System menu, scroll bars, or size box are accessed. The following messages are documented in this section:

WM_SYSCHAR

WM_SYSCOMMAND

WM_SYSDEADCHAR

WM_SYSKEYDOWN

WM_SYSKEYUP

WM_SYSCHAR

wParam:

wParam contains the ASCII key code of a System-menu key.

lParam:

lParam specifies the repeat count, scan code, key transition code, previous key state, and context code. The value in lParam is interpreted as follows:

Bit(s)	*Meaning*
0–15	Repeat count—the number of times the key is repeated
16–23	Scan code
24	1 if extended key
25–26	Not used
27–28	Used by Windows
29	Context code—1 if Alt key is down
30	Previous key state—1 if key is down before the message is sent
31	Transition state—1 if key is being released

Description:

The WM_SYSCHAR message specifies the virtual key code of the System menu key and is sent when a WM_SYSKEYUP and WM_SYSKEYDOWN message are translated.

Return Value:

There is no meaningful return value.

WM_SYSCOMMAND

wParam:

wParam specifies the system command. The following values are used for wParam:

Value	*Meaning*
SC_CLOSE	Close window
SC_HSCROLL	Horizontal scroll
SC_ICON	Minimize window
SC_KEYMENU	Get menu with keystroke
SC_MAXIMIZE	Maximize window
SC_MINIMIZE	Minimize window
SC_MOUSEMENU	Get menu with keystroke
SC_MOVE	Move window
SC_NEXTWINDOW	Go to next window
SC_PREVWINDOW	Go to previous window
SC_RESTORE	Checkpoint
SC_SIZE	Size window
SC_VSCROLL	Vertical scroll
SC_ZOOM	Maximize window

lParam:

When the mouse is used to choose a System menu command, the low-order word of lParam contains the horizontal coordinate of the cursor position; the high-order word of lParam contains the vertical coordinate.

Description:

The WM_SYSCOMMAND message is sent when a System menu command is selected or the minimize or maximize box is selected.

Return Value:

There is no meaningful return value.

WM_SYSDEADCHAR

wParam:

wParam specifies the dead-key character value.

lParam:

The low-order word of lParam contains the repeat count. The high-order word of lParam contains the auto-repeat count.

Description:

The WM_SYSDEADCHAR message specifies the dead-key character value and is sent when a WM_SYSKEYUP and a WM_SYSKEYDOWN message are translated.

Return Value:

There is no meaningful return value.

WM_SYSKEYDOWN

wParam:

wParam contains the virtual-key code of the pressed key.

lParam:

lParam specifies the repeat count, scan code, key transition code, previous key state, and context code. The value in lParam is interpreted as follows:

Bit(s)	*Meaning*
0–15	Repeat count—the number of times the key is repeated
16–23	Scan code
24	1 if extended key
25–26	Not used
27–28	Used by Windows
29	Context code—1 if Alt key is down
30	Previous key state—1 if key is down before the message is sent
31	Transition state—0 for WM_KEYDOWN

Description:

The WM_SYSKEYDOWN message is sent either when an Alt key sequence is pressed or there is not a window that has the input focus. The message is sent to the active window when no window has the input focus.

Return Value:

There is no meaningful return value.

WM_SYSKEYUP

wParam:

wParam contains the virtual-key code of the released key.

`lParam`:

`lParam` specifies the repeat count, scan code, key transition code, previous key state, and context code. The value in `lParam` is interpreted as follows:

Bit(s)	*Meaning*
0–15	Repeat count—the number of times the key is repeated
16–23	Scan code
24	1 if extended key
25–26	Not used
27–28	Used by Windows
29	Context code—1 if Alt key is down
30	Previous key state—1 if key is down before the message is sent
31	Transition state—1 for `WM_SYSKEYUP`

Description:

The `WM_SYSKEYUP` message is sent when an Alt key sequence is released or when there is not a window that contains the input focus. When no window has the input focus, the `WM_SYSKEYUP` message is sent to the active window.

Return Value:

There is no meaningful return value.

Window Management Messages

Windows sends window management messages to an application when the window state changes. The following messages are documented in this section:

WM_ACTIVATE	WM_ENDSESSION	WM_MENUCHAR	WM_QUERYOPEN
WM_ACTIVATEAPP	WM_ENTERIDLE	WM_MENUSELECT	WM_QUIT
WM_CANCELMODE	WM_ERASEBKGND	WM_MOVE	WM_SETFOCUS
WM_CHILDACTIVATE	WM_GETDLGCODE	WM_PAINT	WM_SETFONT
WM_CLOSE	WM_GETMINMAXINFO	WM_PAINTICON	WM_SETREDRAW
WM_CREATE	WM_GETTEXT	WM_PARENTNOTIFY	WM_SETTEXT
WM_CTLCOLOR	WM_GETTEXTLENGTH	WM_QUERYDRAGICON	WM_SHOWWINDOW
WM_DESTROY	WM_ICONERASEBKGND	WM_QUERYENDSESSION	WM_SIZE
WM_ENABLE	WM_KILLFOCUS	WM_QUERYNEWPALETTE	

WM_ACTIVATE

wParam:

wParam specifies the state of the window and can be any one of the following values:

Value	Meaning
0	Window is not active
1	Window is being activated without a mouse click
2	Window is being activated with a mouse click

lParam:

lParam is set as follows:

When the window is minimized, the high-order word of lParam is nonzero. When the window is not minimized, the high-order word of lParam is zero.

When wParam is zero, the low-order word of lParam contains a handle to the window being activated. When wParam is a nonzero value, the low-order word of lParam contains the handle to the window being deactivated.

Description:

The WM_ACTIVATE message is sent whenever a window is activated or deactivated.

Return Value:

There is no meaningful return value.

WM_ACTIVATEAPP

wParam:

wParam is a nonzero value when a window is to be activated or zero when a window is to be deactivated.

lParam:

When wParam is zero, the low-order word of lParam specifies the task handle of the application that owns the window to deactivate. When wParam is a nonzero value, the low-order word of lParam specifies the task handle of the application that owns the window to activate. The high-order word of lParam is not used.

Description:

The WM_ACTIVATEAPP message is sent to the applications whose windows are being activated and deactivated whenever the window being activated belongs to a different application than the active window.

Return Value:

There is no meaningful return value.

WM_CANCELMODE

wParam:

wParam is not used.

lParam:

lParam is not used.

Description:

The WM_CANCELMODE message cancels the current system mode.

Return Value:

There is no meaningful return value.

WM_CHILDACTIVATE

wParam:

wParam is not used.

lParam:

lParam is not used.

Description:

The WM_CHILDACTIVATE message is sent to the parent window of the child window moved by the SetWindowPos function.

Return Value:

There is no meaningful return value.

WM_CLOSE

wParam:

wParam is not used.

lParam:

lParam is not used.

Description:

The WM_CLOSE message is sent whenever a window is closed.

Return Value:

There is no meaningful return value.

WM_CREATE

wParam:

wParam is not used.

lParam:

lParam points to data structure of type CREATESTRUCT that contains the parameters passed to the CreateWindow function. The CREATESTRUCT structure is:

```
typedef struct tagCREATESTRUCT {
     LPSTR lpCreateParams;
     HANDLE hInstance;
     HANDLE hMenu;
     HWND hwndParent;
     int cy;
     int cx;
     int y;
     int x;
     long style;
     LPSTR lpszName;
     LPSTR lpszClass;
     long ExStyle;
} CREATESTRUCT;
```

where:

`lpCreateParams` points to data to create the window

`hInstance` is the module instance handle of the module that owns the new window

`hMenu` is the menu the new window will use

`hwndParent` is the window that owns the created window

`cy` is the height of the created window

`cx` is the width of the created window

`y` is the vertical coordinate of the upper-left corner of the created window

`x` is the horizontal coordinate of the upper-left corner of the created window

`style` is the style for the created window

`lpszName` is a pointer to the null-terminated string containing the name for the created window

`lpszClass` is the null-terminated string that specifies the class name of the created window

`ExStyle` is the extended style for the created window

Description:

The `WM_CREATE` message is sent by the `CreateWindow` function to allow the window procedure to perform initialization.

Return Value:

There is no meaningful return value.

WM_CTLCOLOR

`wParam:`

`wParam` specifies the handle for the display context for the child window.

`lParam:`

The low-order word of `lParam` contains the handle for the child window. The high-order word of `lParam` specifies the type of control and can be any one of the following:

Value	*Meaning*
`CTLCOLOR_BTN`	Button control
`CTLCOLOR_DLG`	Dialog box
`CTLCOLOR_EDIT`	Edit control
`CTLCOLOR_LISTBOX`	List box control
`CTLCOLOR_MSGBOX`	Message box
`CTLCOLOR_SCROLLBAR`	Scroll bar control
`CTLCOLOR_STATIC`	Static control

Description:

The `WM_CTLCOLOR` message is sent to the parent window of the control or message box to be drawn. The parent window is then able to set the background and text colors for the child window.

Return Value:

There is no meaningful return value.

WM_DESTROY

wParam:

`wParam` is not used.

lParam:

`lParam` is not used.

Description:

The `DestroyWindow` function sends the `WM_DESTROY` message to the window being destroyed, telling it that it is being destroyed.

Return Value:

There is no meaningful return value.

WM_ENABLE

wParam:

`wParam` is a nonzero value when the window has been enabled or zero when the window has been disabled.

lParam:

lParam is not used.

Description:

The WM_ENABLE message is sent whenever a window has been enabled or disabled. wParam specifies whether the window was enabled or disabled.

Return Value:

There is no meaningful return value.

WM_ENDSESSION

wParam:

wParam is a nonzero value when the session is ending or zero when the session is not ending.

lParam:

lParam is not used.

Description:

The WM_ENDSESSION message is sent to an application that returns a nonzero value in response to the WM_QUERYENDSESSION message. The value in wParam indicates whether the session is actually ending.

Return Value:

There is no meaningful return value.

WM_ENTERIDLE

wParam:

wParam indicates whether the message resulted from the displaying of a dialog box or menu and can be either of the following values:

Value	Meaning
MSGF_DIALOGBOX	Dialog box is being displayed
MSGF_MENU	Menu is being displayed

lParam:

The low-order word of lParam contains the handle of the dialog box, when wParam is MSGF_DIALOGBOX, or the handle of the window that contains the menu, when wParam is MSGFMENU. The high-order word of lParam is not used.

Description:

The WM_ENTERIDLE message is sent to an application's main window procedure when a modal dialog box or menu is going into an idle state.

Return Value:

There is no meaningful return value.

WM_ERASEBKGND

wParam:

wParam contains the device context handle.

lParam:

lParam is not used.

Description:

The WM_ERASEBKGND message is sent when the background of a window needs repainting. The class background brush specified in the hbrbackground field of the class structure is used to erase the background.

Return Value:

WM_ERASEBKGND returns a nonzero value when the background is successfully erased. A return value of zero indicates that the message is unable to erase the background.

WM_GETDLGCODE

wParam:

wParam is not used.

lParam:

lParam is not used.

Description:

The WM_GETDLGCODE message is sent to the input procedure for a control. Windows sends this message to an application so that the application can process certain types of inputs generally handled by Windows.

Return Value:

WM_GETDLGCODE returns the types of input that the application processed, indicated by one or more of the following values:

Value	*Meaning*
DLGC_DEFPUSHBUTTON	Default push-button
DLGC_HASSETSEL	EM_SETSEL messages
DLGC_PUSHBUTTON	Push-button
DLGC_RADIOBUTTON	Radio button
DLGC_WANTALLKEYS	All keys
DLGC_WANTARROWS	Direction keys
DLGC_WANTCHARS	WM_CHAR messages
DLGC_WANTMESSAGE	All keys; message is passed to control
DLGC_WANTTAB	Tab key

WM_GETMINMAXINFO

wParam:

wParam is not used.

lParam:

lParam points to an array containing five points, interpreted as follows:

Point	*Interpretation*
rgpt[0]	Used only by Windows.
rgpt[1]	The maximized size. Width is (SM_CXSCREEN + (2 * SM_CXFRAME)); height is (SM_CYSCREEN + (2 * SM_CYFRAME)).
rgpt[2]	The position of the upper-left corner of the maximized window. This position is SM_CXFRAME, SM_CYFRAME by default.
rgpt[3]	The minimum tracking size: width is SM_CXMINTRACK, height is CY_MINTRACK.
rgpt[4]	The maximum tracking size: width is (SM_CXSCREEN + (2 * SM_CXFRAME)), height is (SM_CYSCREEN + (2 * SM_CYFRAME)).

Description:

The WM_GETMINMAXINFO message is sent by Windows to a window to retrieve the maximized window size, the minimum and maximum tracking size, and the maximized window position.

Return Value:

There is no meaningful return value.

WM_GETTEXT

wParam:

wParam contains the maximum number of bytes to copy and includes the null terminator.

lParam:

lParam points to the buffer where the text is placed.

Description:

The WM_GETTEXT message copies text to a buffer. The contents of the edit control are copied for edit controls including combo box edit controls. The button name is copied for buttons. The selected item is copied from list boxes. The window caption is copied for windows.

Return Value:

WM_GETTEXT returns the number of bytes copied. A return value of LB_ERR indicates that no item is selected from a list box. A return value of CB_ERR indicates that the combo box does not have an edit control.

WM_GETTEXTLENGTH

wParam:

wParam is not used.

lParam:

lParam is not used.

Description:

The WM_GETTEXTLENGTH message determines the length, in bytes and not including the null terminator, for the specified text. The text in the edit control is evaluated for edit controls and combo box edit controls. The selected item is evaluated for list boxes. The button name is evaluated for button controls. The window caption is evaluated for windows.

Return Value:

WM_GETTEXTLENGTH returns the number of bytes in the text, not including the null terminator.

WM_ICONERASEBKGND

wParam:

wParam contains the device context handle of the icon.

lParam:

lParam is not used.

Description:

The WM_ICONERASEBKGND message is. sent to a minimized window when the icon's background has to be filled before the icon is painted.

Return Value:

There is no meaningful return value.

WM_KILLFOCUS

wParam:

wParam specifies the handle of the window receiving the input focus.

lParam:

lParam is not used.

Description:

The WM_KILLFOCUS message is sent just before a window loses the input focus.

Return Value:

There is no meaningful return value.

WM_MENUCHAR

wParam:

wParam specifies the ASCII character entered.

lParam:

The low-order word of lParam contains MF_POPUP if the menu is a pop-up menu or MF_SYSMENU if the menu is a System menu. The high-order word of lParam contains the handle for the menu.

Description:

The WM_MENUCHAR message is sent to the owner of the menu when a mnemonic character is entered that doesn't match the mnemonic characters defined for the current menu.

Return Value:

The high-order byte of the return value contains one of the following command codes:

Value	*Meaning*
0	The entered character is discarded and the system speaker is beeped; the low-order word of the return value is ignored
1	The current menu should be closed; the low-order word of the return value is ignored
2	The low-order word of the return value contains the menu item number for an item

WM_MENUSELECT

wParam:

The wParam contains a menu item ID when a menu item is selected. The wParam contains the handle to a pop-up menu when the selected item contains a pop-up menu.

lParam:

The low-order word of lParam contains the one or more of the following menu flags. The high-order word of lParam is not used except when the low-order word contains MF_SYSMENU.

Value	*Meaning*
MF_BITMAP	Bitmap item
MF_CHECKED	Checked item
MF_DISABLED	Disabled item
MF_GRAYED	Grayed item
MF_MOUSESELECT	Item selected with a mouse
MF_OWNERDRAW	Owner draw item
MF_POPUP	Contains a pop-up menu
MF_SYSMENU	Item is in System menu—the high-order word of lParam specifies the menu associated with the message

Description:

The WM_MENUSELECT message indicates that a menu item has been selected.

Return Value:

There is no meaningful return value.

WM_MOVE

wParam:

wParam is not used.

lParam:

The low-order word of lParam specifies the horizontal screen coordinate for the new location of the upper-left corner of the client area. The high-order word of lParam specifies the vertical screen coordinate for the new location of the upper-left corner of the client area.

Description:

The `WM_MOVE` message is sent when a window has been moved.

Return Value:

There is no meaningful return value.

WM_PAINT

`wParam:`

`wParam` is not used.

`lParam:`

`lParam` is not used.

Description:

The `WM_PAINT` message is sent when a request is made to repaint an application's window.

Return Value:

There is no meaningful return value.

WM_PAINTICON

`wParam:`

`wParam` is not used.

`lParam:`

`lParam` is not used.

Description:

The `WM_PAINTICON` message is sent to a minimized window when its icon needs to be painted

Return Value:

There is no meaningful return value.

WM_PARENTNOTIFY

wParam:

wParam defines the reason the parent window is being notified and can be any one of the following values:

Value	*Meaning*
WM_CREATE	Creating child window
WM_DESTROY	Destroying child window
WM_LBUTTONDOWN	Left button clicked on a child window
WM_MBUTTONDOWN	Middle button clicked on a child window
WM_RBUTTONDOWN	Right button clicked on a child window

lParam:

The low-order word of lParam contains the window handle for the child window. The high-order word of lParam specifies the ID of the child window.

Description:

The WM_PARENTNOTIFY message is sent to the child window's parent and ancestor windows when the child window is created, destroyed, or clicked.

Return Value:

There is no meaningful return value.

WM_QUERYDRAGICON

wParam:

wParam is not used.

lParam:

lParam is not used.

Description:

The WM_QUERYDRAGICON message is sent to a minimized window when the window is about to be dragged yet has no icon defined for its class. When this happens, Windows replaces the icon with the default icon cursor.

Return Value:

The low-order word of the return value contains the handle of the cursor displayed while the icon is moved. NULL is returned when Windows displays the default icon cursor.

WM_QUERYENDSESSION

wParam:

wParam is not used.

lParam:

lParam is not used.

Description:

The WM_QUERYENDSESSION message is sent when the End Session command is chosen. The session is not ended if any of the applications return zero.

Return Value:

WM_QUERYENDSESSION returns a nonzero value when able to shut down. A return value of zero indicates that the session cannot shut down.

WM_QUERYNEWPALETTE

wParam:

wParam is not used.

lParam:

lParam is not used.

Description:

The WM_QUERYNEWPALETTE message is sent to a window when the window receives the input focus. The window should return an indication of whether or not it can realize its logical palette when it receives the input focus.

Return Value:

WM_QUERYNEWPALETTE returns TRUE when the logical palette is realized. A return value of FALSE indicates that the message is unable to realize the logical palette.

WM_QUERYOPEN

wParam:

wParam is not used.

lParam:

lParam is not used.

Description:

The WM_QUERYOPEN message is sent to an icon when a request has been made to open the icon into a window.

Return Value:

WM_QUERYOPEN returns zero when the application does not allow the icon to be opened. A nonzero return value indicates that the icon can be opened.

WM_QUIT

wParam:

wParam specifies the exit code from the call to PostQuitMessage.

lParam:

lParam is not used.

Description:

The WM_QUIT message is sent when the PostQuitMessage function is called by the application (indicating a termination request) and causes the GetMessage function to return zero.

Return Value:

There is no meaningful return value.

WM_SETFOCUS

wParam:

wParam specifies the handle of the window that loses the input focus.

lParam:

lParam is not used.

Description:

The WM_SETFOCUS message is sent when a window receives the input focus.

Return Value:

There is no meaningful return value.

WM_SETFONT

wParam:

wParam specifies the handle of the font to use. The default system font is used when wParam is NULL.

lParam:

When lParam is TRUE, the control is redrawn. When lParam is FALSE, the control is not redrawn.

Description:

The WM_SETFONT messages specifies the font used by a dialog box for text output.

Return Value:

There is no meaningful return value.

WM_SETREDRAW

wParam:

wParam is nonzero to set the redraw flag or zero to clear the redraw flag.

lParam:

lParam is not used.

Description:

The WM_SETREDRAW message sets or clears the redraw flag and is sent by a application to a window. The redraw flag indicates whether or not changes made in the window can be redrawn. When the redraw flag is set, the control can be redrawn to reflect changes. When the redraw flag is cleared, the control cannot be redrawn.

Return Value:

There is no meaningful return value.

WM_SETTEXT

wParam:

wParam is not used.

lParam:

lParam points to a null-terminated string containing the window text.

Description:

The WM_SETTEXT message defines the text for a window. The text of the edit control is set for edit controls and combo box edit controls. The button name is set for buttons. The window caption is set for windows.

Return Value:

WM_SETTEXT returns LB_ERRSPACE for a list box or CB_ERRSPACE for a combo box when there is not enough memory for the text. A return value of CB_ERR indicates that the combo box receiving the message has an edit control.

WM_SHOWWINDOW

wParam:

wParam is nonzero when the window is visible or shown, or zero if the window is hidden.

lParam:

lParam is zero if the message is sent as a result of a call to the ShowWindow function. lParam is SW_PARENTCLOSING when the parent window is closing or a pop-up window is being hidden. lParam is SW_PARENTOPENING when the parent window is opening or a pop-up window is shown.

Description:

The WM_SHOWWINDOW message is sent when a window is being shown or hidden.

Return Value:

There is no meaningful return value.

WM_SIZE

wParam:

wParam specifies the type of sizing and is selected from the following values:

Value	*Meaning*
SIZEFULLSCREEN	Maximized
SIZEICONIC	Minimized
SIZENORMAL	Resized
SIZEZOOMHIDE	Pop-up windows notified when other window is maximized
SIZEZOOMSHOW	Pop-up windows notified when other window is minimized

lParam:

The low-order word of lParam contains the new width of the client area. The high-order word of lParam contains the new height of the client area.

Description:

The WM_SIZE message is sent whenever a window is sized.

Return Value:

There is no meaningful return value.

15

Windows Printer Escapes

This chapter provides reference information for the Microsoft Windows printer escapes used with the Microsoft Windows function `Escape`. Printer escapes provide more direct control over the output device and enhance the capabilities of the Graphics Device Interface (GDI). Chapter 13, "Windows Functions," provides reference information on the use of the `Escape` function.

ABORTDOC

Syntax:

```
short Escape(hDC, ABORTDOC, NULL, NULL, NULL)
```

Parameter, Type, and Description:

hDC	HDC	Device context

Description:

The ABORTDOC escape aborts the current job. When the job is terminated, all data sent to the device since the previous ENDDOC escape is erased.

Return Value:

ABORTDOC returns a positive value when the job is aborted. A negative return value indicates that this escape cannot abort the job.

BANDINFO

Syntax:

```
short Escape(hDC, BANDINFO, sizeof(BANDINFOSTRUCT), lpInData, lpOutData)
```

Parameter, Type, and Description:

hDC	HDC	Device context
lpInData	BANDINFOSTRUCT FAR *	Pointer to a data structure of type BANDINFOSTRUCT containing information for the driver
lpOutData	BANDINFOSTRUCT FAR *	Pointer to a data structure of type BANDINFOSTRUCT containing information from the driver

Description:

The BANDINFO escape retrieves information about devices with banding capabilities. Banding refers to the capability to store a page of output in a metafile that is divided into bands. The lpInData parameter points to a data structure of type BANDINFOSTRUCT and contains information that is sent to the device driver from the application. The lpOutData parameter points to a data structure of type BANDINFOSTRUCT and stores information about the device. The BANDINFOSTRUCT data structure is:

```
typedef struct {
     BOOL fGraphicsFlag;
     BOOL fTextFlag;
     BOOL GraphicsRect;
} BANDINFOSTRUCT;
```

For lpInData, the fields of the BANDINFOSTRUCT data structure are interpreted as follows:

- fGraphicsFlag is TRUE when the application is sending graphics on the page
- fTextFlag is TRUE when the application is sending text on the page
- GraphicsRect defines the rectangle that binds the graphics for the page using a data structure of type RECT

For lpOutData, the fields of the BANDINFOSTRUCT data structure are interpreted as follows:

- fGraphicsFlag is TRUE when the device is expecting graphics on the page
- fTextFlag is TRUE when the device is expecting text on the page
- GraphicsRect contains no valid data

Return Value:

BANDINFO returns a value of 1 when information is retrieved. A return value of zero indicates that the escape cannot retrieve information.

BEGIN_PATH

Syntax:

```
short Escape(hDC, BEGIN_PATH, NULL, NULL, NULL)
```

Parameter, Type, and Description:

hDC	HDC	Device context

Description:

The BEGIN_PATH escape, with the END_PATH escape, creates a path. *Paths* consist of a series of primitives drawn in succession, and these paths can be used to create complex shapes and images on a device. The END_PATH escape specifies the path.

Return Value:

BEGIN_PATH returns the number of BEGIN_PATH escape calls that do not have corresponding END_PATH escape calls. A return value of zero indicates that the escape cannot create a path.

CLIP_TO_PATH

Syntax:

```
short Escape(hDC, CLIP_TO_PATH, sizeof(int), lpClipMode, NULL)
```

Parameter, Type, and Description:

hDC	HDC	Device context
lpClipMode	LPINT	Pointer to clipping mode

Description:

The CLIP_TO_PATH escape specifies a clipping region bound by the open path. The lpClipMode specifies the clipping mode and is selected from one of the following values:

Constant	*Value*	*Meaning*
CLIP_SAVE	0	Saves the clipping region
CLIP_RESTORE	1	Restores the clipping region
CLIP_INCLUSIVE	2	Defines an inclusive clipping region; primitives that extend beyond the borders of the clipping region are clipped
CLIP_EXCLUSIVE	3	Defines an exclusive clipping region; primitives that are inside the clipping region are clipped

Use the following steps to define and implement a clipping region using a path:

1. Use CLIP_TO_PATH to save the current clipping region
2. Use BEGIN_PATH to begin a path
3. Draw the primitives bounding the clipping region
4. Use CLIP_TO_PATH to define the clipping region
5. Use END_PATH to end the path
6. Draw the primitives (which will be clipped)
7. Use CLIP_TO_PATH to restore the original clipping region

Return Value:

CLIP_TO_PATH returns a nonzero value when the clipping region is specified. A return value of zero indicates that the escape cannot specify a clipping region.

DEVICEDATA

Syntax:

```
short Escape(hDC, DEVICEDATA, nCount, lpInData, lpOutData)
```

Parameter, Type, and Description:

hDC	HDC	Device context
nCount	short	Number of bytes that lpInData points to
lpInData	LPSTR	Pointer to data structure of input data

Description:

The DEVICEDATA escape sends data to the printer while bypassing the print-driver code. The nCount specifies the number of bytes pointed to by lpInData, and lpInData points to a data structure containing the input data. The first word of the data structure contains the number of bytes of input data. This escape is equivalent to the PASSTHROUGH escape. (See PASSTHROUGH in this chapter for more information.)

Return Value:

DEVICEDATA returns the number of bytes sent to the device when successful. A return value of zero or less indicates that the escape cannot send data to the printer.

DRAFTMODE

Syntax:

```
short Escape(hDC, DRAFTMODE, sizeof(int), lpDraftMode, NULL)
```

Parameter, Type, and Description:

hDC	HDC	Device context
lpDraftMode	LPINT	Specifies the draft mode

Description:

The DRAFTMODE escape specifies the draft mode of the device. The lpDraftMode parameter points to the value specifying the draft mode, which can be either of the following:

Value	Meaning
0	Draft mode off
1	Draft mode on

The draft mode is off by default.

Return Value:

DRAFTMODE returns a positive value when the draft mode is specified. A negative return value indicates that the escape cannot specify the draft mode.

DRAWPATTERNRECT

Syntax:

```
short Escape(hDC, DRAWPATTERNRECT, sizeof(PRECTSTRUCT), lpInData, NULL)
```

Parameter, Type, and Description:

hDC	HDC	Device context
lpInData	PRECT_STRUCT FAR *	Pointer to a data structure of type PRECT_STRUCT that specifies the rectangle

Description:

The DRAWPATTERNRECT escape draws a rectangle on Hewlett-Packard LaserJet or compatible printers. You can generate a patterned, gray-scaled, or filled rectangle using the Hewlett-Packard Page Control Language (PCL). The lpInData points to a data structure of type PRECT_STRUCT that specifies the rectangle to draw. The PRECT_STRUCT data structure is:

```
typedef struct{
     POINT prPosition;
     POINT prSize;
     WORD prStyle;
     WORD prPattern;
} PRECT_STRUCT;
```

where:

prPosition is the upper-left corner of the rectangle

prSize is the lower-right corner of the rectangle

prStyle is the type of pattern. The following values are used for prStyle:

Value	*Meaning*
0	Black rule
1	White rule—HP LaserJet IIP only
2	Gray scale
3	HP-defined

`prPattern` is the pattern:

- When `prStyle` is 0, `prPattern` is ignored
- When `prStyle` is 2, `prPattern` specifies a percentage of gray for the gray scale
- When `prStyle` is 3, `prPattern` is one of six HP-defined patterns

Return Value:

`DRAWPATTERNRECT` returns a value of 1 when the rectangle is drawn. A return value of zero indicates that the escape cannot draw the specified rectangle.

ENABLEDUPLEX

Syntax:

```
short Escape(hDC, ENABLEDUPLEX, sizeof(WORD), lpInData, NULL)
```

Parameter, Type, and Description:

`hDC`	`HDC`	Device context
`lpInData`	`WORD FAR *`	Pointer to value that specifies either duplex or simplex printing

Description:

The `ENABLEDUPLEX` escape selects either duplex or simplex printing for devices capable of printing on both sides of the paper. The `lpInData` parameter points to a value that specifies either duplex or simplex printing and can be any of the following values:

Value	*Meaning*
0	Simplex printing
1	Duplex printing with vertical binding
2	Duplex printing with horizontal binding

Return Value:

`ENABLEDUPLEX` returns a value of 1 when successful. A return value of zero indicates that the escape cannot select duplex or simplex as specified.

ENABLEPAIRKERNING

Syntax:

```
short Escape(hDC, ENABLEPAIRKERNING, sizeof(int), lpNewKernFlag,
          lpOldKernFlag)
```

Parameter, Type, and Description:

`hDC`	`HDC`	Device context
`lpNewKernFlag`	`LPINT`	Pointer to value specifying whether automatic pair kerning is enabled or disabled
`lpOldKernFlag`	`LPINT`	Pointer to value to receive the previous automatic pair kerning setting

Description:

The `ENABLEPAIRKERNING` escape either enables or disables automatic pair kerning. The device driver automatically modifies the space between characters in text strings, according to the font's character pair kerning table, when automatic pair kerning is enabled. The `lpNewKernFlag` points to a value that specifies the new setting for automatic pair kerning:

- When `lpNewKernFlag` is 1, automatic pair kerning is enabled
- When `lpNewKernFlag` is 0, automatic pair kerning is disabled

Automatic pair kerning is the default.

The previous automatic pair kerning setting is stored in the value pointed to by `lpOldKernFlag`.

Return Value:

`ENABLEPAIRKERNING` returns a value of 1 when automatic pair kerning is either enabled or disabled. A return value of zero indicates that the escape cannot enable or disable automatic pair kerning.

ENABLERELATIVEWIDTHS

Syntax:

```
short Escape(hDC, ENABLERELATIVEWIDTHS, sizeof(int),
             lpNewWidthFlag, lpOldWidthFlag)
```

Parameter, Type, and Description:

hDC	HDC	Device context
lpNewWidthFlag	LPINT	Pointer to value that indicates whether to enable or disable relative widths
lpOldWidthFlag	LPINT	Pointer to value to receive the previous relative width setting

Description:

The ENABLERELATIVEWIDTHS escape either enables or disables relative character widths, depending on the value pointed to by lpNewWidthFlag:

- When lpNewWidthFlag is 0, relative widths are disabled and the width of each character is the same number of device units
- When lpNewWidthFlag is 1, relative widths are enabled and the width of each character is defined by the font's extent table

Relative character widths are disabled by default.

Return Value:

ENABLERELATIVEWIDTHS returns a value of 1 when relative character widths are enabled or disabled. A return value of zero indicates that the escape cannot enable or disable relative character widths.

ENDDOC

Syntax:

```
short Escape(hDC, ENDDOC, NULL, NULL, NULL)
```

Parameter, Type, and Description:

hDC	HDC	Device context

Description:

The ENDDOC escape ends the print job initiated by a STARTDOC escape.

Return Value:

ENDDOC returns a positive value when successful. A negative return value indicates that the escape cannot end the print job.

END_PATH

Syntax:

```
short Escape(hDC, END_PATH, sizeof(PATH_INFO), lpInData, NULL)
```

Parameter, Type, and Description:

hDC	HDC	Device context
lpInData	PATH_INFO FAR *	Pointer to a PATH_INFO data structure that specifies the path to create

Description:

The END_PATH escape ends a path initiated with a BEGIN_PATH escape. Paths consist of a series of primitives drawn in succession and can be used to create complex shapes and images on a device. A path is defined in the data structure of type PATH_INFO pointed to by lpInData. The PATH_INFO data structure is:

```
typedef struct {
     short RenderMode;
     BYTE FillMode;
     BYTE BkMode;
     LOGPEN Pen;
     LOGBRUSH Brush;
     DWORD BkColor;
} PATH_INFO;
```

where:

RenderMode specifies how the path is to be created and can be any of the following values:

Constant	*Value*	*Meaning*
NO_DISPLAY	0	Path is not drawn
OPEN	1	Path is open polygon
CLOSED	2	Path is closed polygon

`FillMode` specifies how the path is to be filled and can be either of the following values:

Constant	*Value*	*Meaning*
`ALTERNATE`	1	Fill uses alternate fill algorithm
`WINDING`	2	Fill uses winding fill algorithm

`BkMode` specifies the background mode used to fill the path and can be either of the following values:

Constant	*Meaning*
`OPAQUE`	Background is filled with the background color before the brush is drawn
`TRANSPARENT`	Background is not modified

`Pen` specifies the pen used to draw the path

`Brush` specifies the brush used to fill the path

`BkColor` specifies the color used to fill the path

Return Value:

`END_PATH` returns the number of `BEGIN_PATH` escapes that do not have matching `END_PATH` escapes. A return value of –1 indicates that the escape cannot end the path.

ENUMPAPERBINS

Syntax:

```
short Escape(hDC, ENUMPAPERBINS, sizeof(int), lpNumBins, lpOutData)
```

Parameter, Type, and Description:

`hDC`	`HDC`	Device context
`lpNumBins`	`LPINT`	Pointer to value specifying the number of bins
`lpOutData`	`LPSTR`	Pointer to a data structure where paper bin information will be stored

Description:

The `ENUMPAPERBINS` escape gathers information about the paper bins of the device. The number of paper bins about which to retrieve information is specified in `lpNumBins`. Information about the paper bins is copied to the data structure pointed to by `lpOutData`. This data structure contains two arrays. The first array contains the paper bin identification numbers, as follows:

```
short BinList[cBinMax]
```

where:

`cBinMax` is equal to `lpNumBins`

The second array is an array of characters as follows:

```
char PaperNames[cBinMax][cchBinName]
```

where:

`cBinMax` is equal to `lpNumBins`

`cchBinName` is the length of each string (24)

Return Value:

`ENUMPAPERBINS` returns a value of 1 when successful. A return value of zero indicates that the escape cannot gather paper bin information.

ENUMPAPERMETRICS

Syntax:

```
short Escape(hDC, ENUMPAPERMETRICS, sizeof(int), lpMode, lpOutData)
```

Parameter, Type, and Description:

`hDC`	`HDC`	Device context
`lpMode`	`LPINT`	Pointer to value specifying the escape mode
`lpOutData`	`LPRECT`	Pointer to array of `RECT` data structures

Description:

The `ENUMPAPERMETRICS` escape works in two ways, depending on the setting of `lpMode`:

- When `lpMode` is set to 0, the `ENUMPAPERMETRICS` escape returns the number of paper types supported by the device. The returned value is then used to allocate an array of data structures of type `RECT`.
- When `lpMode` is set to 1, the `ENUMPAPERMETRICS` escape returns one or more data structures of type `RECT` defining the page regions able to receive an image. The array of `RECT` data structures receiving the page region information is pointed to by `lpOutData`.

Return Value:

`ENUMPAPERMETRICS` returns a positive value when successful. A negative return value indicates that the escape is unsuccessful. A return value of zero indicates that the escape is not implemented.

EPSPRINTING

Syntax:

```
short Escape(hDC, EPSPRINTING, sizeof(BOOL), lpBool, NULL)
```

Parameter, Type, and Description:

hDC	HDC	Device context
lpBool	BOOL FAR *	Pointer to value specifying whether to enable or disable downloading

Description:

The EPSPRINTING escape enables or disables the output of the Windows PostScript header control section. GDI calls cannot be used by applications generating this escape. The lpBool parameter points to a value that specifies whether to enable or disable downloading:

- When lpBool is TRUE, downloading is enabled
- When lpBool is FALSE, downloading is disabled

Return Value:

EPSPRINTING returns a positive value when output is enabled or disabled. A negative return value indicates that the escape cannot enable or disable the output. A return value of zero indicates that the escape is not implemented.

EXT_DEVICE_CAPS

Syntax:

```
short Escape(hDC, EXT_DEVICE_CAPS, sizeof(int), lpIndex, lpCaps)
```

Parameter, Type, and Description:

hDC	HDC	Device context
lpIndex	LPINT	Pointer to value indicating the capability to retrieve
lpCaps	DWORD FAR *	Pointer to value to receive capability information

Description:

The EXT_DEVICE_CAPS escape determines the capabilities of a device. The lpCaps parameter points to the value where the retrieved capability information is stored; lpIndex points to a value that specifies the capability to examine, and it can be any of the following:

Constant	*Value*	*Meaning*
R2_CAPS	1	The value returned in lpCaps indicates which of the 16 binary raster operations are supported by the device driver.
PATTERN_CAPS	2	The low-order word of lpCaps contains the maximum width of a pattern brush bitmap. The high-order word of lpCaps contains the maximum height of a pattern brush bitmap.
PATH_CAPS	3	You can use the logical OR operation with the lpCaps value to determine whether paths can use alternate or winding interiors or whether the device supports inclusive and exclusive clipping. The following values are used with logical OR to determine the capabilities: PATH_ALTERNATE(1), PATH_WINDING(2), PATH_INCLUSIVE(4), and PATH_EXCLUSIVE(8).
POLYGON_CAPS	4	The value in lpCaps indicates the maximum number of polygon points the device supports.
PATTERN_COLOR_CAPS	5	The value in lpCaps indicates whether monochrome pattern bitmaps can be converted to color: 1 if conversions are supported, 0 if not supported.
R2_TEXT_CAPS	6	The low-order word of lpCaps indicates the raster operations the device supports for text. The high-order word of the lpCaps indicates the type of text for the raster operations. The following values can be used with the logical OR operation to determine the text type: RASTER_TEXT, DEVICE_TEXT, and VECTOR_TEXT.

Return Value:

`EXT_DEVICE_CAPS` returns a nonzero value when the specified capability is supported. A return value of zero indicates that the specified capability is not supported.

EXTTEXTOUT

Syntax:

```
short Escape(hDC, EXTTEXTOUT, sizeof(EXTTEXT_STRUCT, lpInData, NULL)
```

Parameter, Type, and Description:

`hDC`	`HDC`	Device context
`lpInData`	`EXTTEXT_STRUCT FAR *`	Pointer to data structure of type `EXTTEXT_STRUCT`

Description:

The `EXTTEXTOUT` escape enables the application to call the GDI `TextOut` function while specifying string characteristics. This function is provided for compatibility with earlier versions of Windows. The `lpInData` points to a data structure of type `EXTTEXT_STRUCT`. This data structure contains information on the characteristics of the character string. The `EXTTEXT_STRUCT` data structure is:

```
typedef struct {
     WORD X;
     WORD Y;
     WORD FAR *lpText;
     WORD FAR *lpWidths;
} EXTTEXT_STRUCT;
```

where:

> `X` is the x-coordinate of the upper-left corner of the starting point for the string
>
> `Y` is the y-coordinate of the upper-left corner of the starting point for the string
>
> `lpText` is a pointer to an array of CCH character codes
>
> `lpWidths` is a pointer to an array of CCH character widths used to print the string

Return Value:

`EXTTEXTOUT` returns a value of 1 when successful. A return value of zero indicates that the escape cannot let the application call the `TextOut` function.

FLUSHOUTPUT

Syntax:

```
short Escape(hDC, FLUSHOUTPUT, NULL, NULL, NULL)
```

Parameter, Type, and Description:

`hDC`	`HDC`	Device context

Description:

The `FLUSHOUTPUT` escape flushes output from the device buffer.

Return Value:

`FLUSHOUTPUT` returns a positive value when the output is flushed. A negative return value indicates that the escape cannot flush the output.

GETCOLORTABLE

Syntax:

```
short Escape(hDC, GETCOLORTABLE, sizeof(int), lpIndex, lpColor)
```

Parameter, Type, and Description:

`hDC`	`HDC`	Device context
`lpIndex`	`LPINT`	Pointer to value specifying the the color index
`lpColor`	`DWORD FAR *`	Pointer to value where RGB value is stored

Description:

The `GETCOLORTABLE` escape copies the RGB value for the color table index specified in `lpIndex` to the value pointed to by `lpColor`.

Return Value:

`GETCOLORTABLE` returns a positive value when the RGB value is copied. A negative return value indicates that the escape cannot copy the RGB value.

GETEXTENDEDTEXTMETRICS

Syntax:

```
short Escape(hDC, GETEXTENDEDTEXTMETRICS, sizeof(WORD), lpInData,
          lpOutData)
```

Parameter, Type, and Description:

hDC	HDC	Device context
lpInData	WORD FAR *	Pointer to value specifying the number of bytes pointed to by lpOutData
lpOutData	EXTTEXTMETRIC FAR *	Pointer to data structure of type EXTTEXTMETRIC

Description:

The GETEXTENDEDTEXTMETRICS escape retrieves extended text metrics for the selected font. The text metrics are placed in the data structure of type EXTTEXTMETRIC pointed to by lpOutData. The EXTTEXTMETRIC structure is:

```
typedef struct {
     short etmSize;
     short etmPointSize;
     short etmOrientation;
     short etmMasterHeight;
     short etmMinScale;
     short etmMaxScale;
     short etmMasterUnits;
     short etmCapHeight;
     short etmXHeight;
     short etmLowerCaseAscent;
     short etmLowerCaseDescent;
     short etmSlant;
     short etmSuperScript;
     short etmSubScript;
     short etmSuperScriptSize;
     short etmSubScriptSize;
     short etmUnderlineOffset;
     short etmUnderlineWidth;
     short etmDoubleUpperUnderlineOffset;
     short etmDoubleLowerUnderlineOffset;
     short etmDoubleUpperUnderlineWidth;
     short etmDoubleLowerUnderlineWidth;
     short etmStrikeOutOffset;
     short etmStrikeOutWidth;
     WORD etmKernPairs;
     WORD etmKernTracks;
} EXTTEXTMETRIC;
```

where:

`etmSize` is the number of bytes in the structure

`etmPointSize` is the point size in twips (twentieths of a point, or 1/1440 inches)

`etmOrientation` is the font orientation:

Value	Meaning
0	Either
1	Portrait
2	Landscape

`etmMasterHeight` is the font size in device units

`etmMinScale` is the minimum size for the font

`etmMaxScale` is the maximum size for the font

`etmMasterUnits` is `etmMasterHeight`, expressed in font units

`etmCapHeight` is the height of upper case letters in font units

`etmXHeight` is the height of lower case letters in font units

`etmLowerCaseAscent` is the number of font units that the ascender of lowercase letters extends above the baseline

`etmLowerCaseDescent` is the number of font units that the descender of lowercase letters extends below the baseline

`etmSlant` is the angle of slant for the font; this angle is measured in tenths of degrees clockwise from the vertical font

`etmSuperScript` is the number of font units used to offset superscript characters from the baseline

`etmSubScript` is the number of font units used to offset subscript characters from the baseline

`etmSuperScriptSize` is the number of font units used for superscript characters

`etmSubScriptSize` is the number of font units used for subscript characters

`etmUnderlineOffset` is the number of font units from the baseline where the top of an underline bar is to be located

`etmUnderlineWidth` is the thickness (font units) of the underline bar

`etmDoubleUpperUnderlineOffset` is the number of font units from the baseline where the top of a upper double underline bar is to be located `etmDoubleLowerUnderlineOffset` is the number of font units from the baseline where the top of a lower double underline bar is to be located

`etmDoubleUpperUnderlineWidth` is the thickness of the upper underline bar in font units

`etmDoubleLowerUnderlineWidth` is the thickness of the lower underline bar in font units

`etmStrikeOutOffset` is the number of font units from the baseline where the top of the strike out bar is to be located

`etmStrikeOutWidth` is the thickness of the strike out bar in font units

`etmKernPairs` is the number of kerning pairs defined for the font

`etmKernTracks` is the number of kerning tracks defined for the font

Return Value:

`GETEXTENDEDTEXTMETRICS` returns the number of bytes copied to the data structure. A return value of zero indicates that the escape cannot retrieve the extended text metrics.

GETEXTENTTABLE

Syntax:

```
short Escape(hDC, GETEXTENTTABLE, sizeof(CHAR_RANGE_STRUCT),
            lpInData, lpOutData)
```

Parameter, Type, and Description:

`hDC`	`HDC`	Device context
`lpInData`	`LPSTR`	Pointer to data structure of type `CHAR_RANGE_STRUCT` defining a range of characters
`lpOutData`	`LPINT`	Pointer to array that stores the retrieved character widths

Description:

The `GETEXTENTTABLE` escape determines the character width of each character in a specified range of characters. The `lpInData` parameter points to a data structure of type `CHAR_RANGE_STRUCT` that defines the range of characters. The `CHAR_RANGE_STRUCT` data structure is:

```
typedef struct {
     BYTE chFirst;
     BYTE chLast;
} CHAR_RANGE_STRUCT;
```

where:

chFirst is the character code of the first character in the character range

chLast is the character code of the last character in the character range

lpOutData points to array of characters that stores the widths of the specified characters. The size of the array is (chLast – chFirst + 1).

Return Value:

GETEXTENTTABLE returns a value of 1 when successful. A return value of zero indicates that the escape is unsuccessful.

GETFACENAME

Syntax:

```
short Escape(hDC, GETFACENAME, NULL, NULL, lpFaceName)
```

Parameter, Type, and Description:

hDC	HDC	Device context
lpFaceName	LPSTR	Pointer to buffer that is to receive the face name

Description:

The GETFACENAME escape retrieves the face name of the current physical font and stores it in the buffer pointed to by lpFaceName.

Return Value:

GETFACENAME returns a positive value when it retrieves the face name. A negative return value indicates that the escape cannot retrieve the face name. A return value of zero indicates that the escape is not implemented.

GETPAIRKERNTABLE

Syntax:

```
short Escape(hDC, GETPAIRKERNTABLE, NULL, NULL, lpOutData)
```

Parameter, Type, and Description:

hDC	HDC	Device context
lpOutData	KERNPAIR FAR *	Pointer to array of data structures of type KERNPAIR

Description:

The GETPAIRKERNTABLE escape retrieves the character pair kerning table for the font and places the table in the array pointed to by lpOutData. The lpOutData parameter points to an array of data structures of type KERNPAIR. The KERNPAIR data structure is:

```
typedef struct {
     union {
           BYTE each [2];
           WORD both;
           } kpPair;
     short kpKernAmount;
} KERNPAIR;
```

where:

kpPair.each[0] is the character code of the first character in the kerning pair

kpPair.each[1] is the character code of the second character in the kerning pair

kpPair.both contains the first character of the kerning pair in the low-order byte and the second character of the kerning pair in the high-order byte

kpKernAmount is the amount of kerning involved when the characters in the kerning pair are placed next to each other in the same font and size

Return Value:

GETPAIRKERNTABLE returns the number of data structures copied to the array. A return value of zero indicates that the escape is unsuccessful.

GETPHYSPAGESIZE

Syntax:

```
short Escape(hDC, GETPHYSPAGESIZE, NULL, NULL, lpDimensions)
```

Parameter, Type, and Description:

hDC	HDC	Device context
lpDimensions	LPPOINT	Pointer to the POINT data structure to store the page size

Description:

The GETPHYSPAGESIZE escape determines the page size and stores the page size in the data structure of type POINT pointed to by lpDimensions. The POINT data structure is:

```
typedef struct tagPOINT {
     int x;
     int y;
} POINT;
```

where:

x specifies the horizontal page size in device units

y specifies the vertical page size in device units

Return Value:

GETPHYSPAGESIZE returns a positive value when the page size is determined and stored. A negative return value indicates that the escape cannot determine or store the page size.

GETPRINTINGOFFSET

Syntax:

```
short Escape(hDC, GETPRINTINGOFFSET, NULL, NULL, lpOffset)
```

Parameter, Type, and Description:

hDC	HDC	Device context
lpOffset	LPPOINT	Pointer to POINT data structure that will store the offset

Description:

The GETPRINTINGOFFSET escape determines the printing offset of the page in device units. The offset is considered to be the upper-left corner of the page where printing begins. The offset is placed in the data structure of type POINT pointed to by lpOffset. The POINT data structure is:

```
typedef struct tagPOINT {
     int x;
     int y;
} POINT;
```

where:

x specifies the horizontal device coordinate of the offset

y specifies the vertical device coordinate of the offset

Return Value:

GETPRINTINGOFFSET returns a positive value when the offset is determined. A negative return value indicates that the escape cannot determine the offset.

GETSCALINGFACTOR

Syntax:

```
short Escape(hDC, GETSCALINGFACTOR, NULL, NULL, lpFactors)
```

Parameter, Type, and Description:

hDC	HDC	Device context
lpFactors	LPPOINT	Pointer to POINT data structure that will hold the scaling factor

Description:

The GETSCALINGFACTOR escape determines the scaling factors for the axes of the device. The scaling factors are copied to the data structure of type POINT pointed to by lpFactors and are exponents of 2 (for example, 3 indicates 2^3, or 8). The POINT data structure is:

```
typedef struct tagPOINT {
     int x;
     int y;
} POINT;
```

where:

`x` specifies the horizontal axis scaling factor

`y` specifies the vertical axis scaling factor

Return Value:

`GETSCALINGFACTOR` returns a positive value when the scaling factors are determined. A negative return value indicates that the escape cannot determine the scaling factors.

GETSETPAPERBINS

Syntax:

```
short Escape(hDC, GETSETPAPERBINS, nCount, lpInData, lpOutData)
```

Parameter, Type, and Description:

`hDC`	`HDC`	Device context
`nCount`	`int`	Number of bytes pointed to by `lpInData`
`lpInData`	`BinInfo FAR *`	Pointer to `BinInfo` data structure specifying new bin
`lpOutData`	`BinInfo FAR *`	Pointer to `BinInfo` data structure containing bin information

Description:

The `GETSETPAPERBINS` escape determines the number of paper bins for the device and specifies the bin to use. Both `lpInData` and `lpOutData` can either point to a data structure of type `BinInfo` or be set to NULL, with the following results:

- When `lpInData` is NULL and `lpOutData` points to a `BinInfo` data structure, the current bin number and the number of bins is retrieved
- When both `lpInData` and `lpOutData` point to a `BinInfo` data structure, `lpInData` specifies the new bin to use and `lpOutData` stores the previous bin number
- When `lpInData` points to a `BinInfo` data structure and `lpOutData` is NULL, `lpInData` specifies the new bin number

The `BinInfo` data structure is:

```
typedef struct {
     DWORD BinNumber;
     DWORD NbrofBins;
     DWORD Reserved;
     DWORD Reserved;
     DWORD Reserved;
     DWORD Reserved;
} BinInfo;
```

where:

`BinNumber` is the paper bin number

`NbrofBins` is the number of paper bins available

Return Value:

`GETSETPAPERBINS` returns a positive value when successful.

GETSETPAPERMETRICS

Syntax:

```
short Escape(hDC, GETSETPAPERMETRICS, sizeof(RECT), lpNewPaper,
          lpPrevPaper)
```

Parameter, Type, and Description:

`hDC`	`HDC`	Device context
`lpNewPaper`	`LPRECT`	Pointer to a `RECT` data structure specifying the new area
`lpPrevPaper`	`LPRECT`	Pointer to a `RECT` data structure where the previous area is stored

Description:

The `GETSETPAPERMETRICS` escape stores the previous paper metrics information and defines the paper type using the specified paper metrics information. The `lpNewPaper` parameter points to a data structure of type `RECT` that specifies the usable region of the page; `lpPrevPaper` points to a data structure of type `RECT` that stores the previous usable region.

Return Value:

`GETSETPAPERMETRICS` returns a positive value when successful. A negative return value indicates that the escape is unsuccessful. A return value of zero indicates that the escape is not implemented.

GETSETPAPERORIENT

Syntax:

```
short Escape(hDC, GETSETPAPERORIENT, nCount, lpInData, NULL)
```

Parameter, Type, and Description:

hDC	HDC	Device context
nCount	int	Number of bytes pointed to by lpInData
lpInData	ORIENT FAR *	Pointer to ORIENT data structure defining the paper orientation

Description:

The GETSETPAPERORIENT escape either determines or defines the paper orientation:

- When lpInData is NULL, the current paper orientation is returned
- When lpInData is not NULL, lpInData points to a data structure of type ORIENT that defines the new paper orientation

The ORIENT data structure is:

```
typedef struct {
    DWORD Orientation;
    DWORD Reserved;
    DWORD Reserved;
    DWORD Reserved;
    DWORD Reserved;
} ORIENT;
```

where:

Orientation is either 1 for portrait or 2 for landscape

Return Value:

GETSETPAPERORIENT returns the current orientation when lpInData is NULL. If lpInData is not NULL, the escape returns the previous orientation. A return value of –1 indicates that the escape is unsuccessful.

GETSETSCREENPARAMS

Syntax:

```
short Escape(hDC, GETSETSCREENPARAMS, sizeof(SCREENPARAMS),
             lpInData, lpOutData)
```

Parameter, Type, and Description:

hDC	HDC	Device context
lpInData	SCREENPARAMS FAR *	Pointer to a data structure of type SCREENPARAMS that specifies new screen information
lpOutData	SCREENPARAMS FAR *	Pointer to a data structure of type SCREENPARAMS where previous screen information is stored

Description:

The GETSETSCREENPARAMS escape either sets or determines screen information. Both lpInData and lpOutData will either point to a data structure of type SCREENPARAMS or be set to NULL. The behavior of the escape depends on the settings of lpInData and lpOutData. If you set lpInData or lpOutData to NULL, the corresponding action will not take place. The SCREENPARAMS data structure is:

```
typedef struct {
     int angle;
     int frequency;
     DWORD types;
} SCREENPARAMS;
```

where:

angle is the angle of the halftone screen in degrees

frequency is the screen frequency in dots per inch

types is a mask that contains bits that specify the type of screen cell; bit values include DIAMOND, DOT, ELLIPSE, and LINE

Return Value:

GETSETSCREENPARAMS returns a positive value when it sets or determines screen information. A negative return value indicates that the escape cannot set or determine screen information.

GETTECHNOLOGY

Syntax:

```
short Escape(hDC, GETTECHNOLOGY, NULL, NULL, lpTechnology)
```

Parameter, Type, and Description:

hDC	HDC	Device context
lpTechnology	LPSTR	Pointer to buffer where the string that describes the device technology is placed

Description:

The GETTECHNOLOGY escape determines the printer technology type, and copies a string that describes the technology type to the buffer pointed to by lpTechnology.

Return Value:

GETTECHNOLOGY returns a value of 1 when successful. A return value of zero indicates that the escape cannot determine the printer technology type or copy the string to the buffer.

GETTRACKKERNTABLE

Syntax:

```
short Escape(hDC, GETTRACKKERNTABLE, NULL, NULL, lpOutData)
```

Parameter, Type, and Description:

hDC	HDC	Device context
lpOutData	KERNTRACK FAR *	Pointer to array of data structures of type KERNSTACK

Description:

The GETTRACKKERNTABLE escape copies the track kerning table for the current font to the array pointed to by lpOutData. The lpOutData parameter points to an array of data structures of type KERNSTACK. The KERNSTACK data structure is:

```
typedef struct {
     short ktDegree;
     short ktMinSize;
```

```
    short ktMinAmount;
    short ktMaxSize;
    short ktMaxAmount;
} KERNTRACK;
```

where:

`ktDegree` is the amount of track kerning

`ktMinSize` is the minimum font size (device units) where linear track kerning applies

`ktMinAmount` is the amount of track kerning (font units) applied to fonts that are less than or equal to the size specified in `ktMinSize`

`ktMaxSize` is the maximum font size (device units) where linear track kerning applies

`ktMaxAmount` is the amount of track kerning (logical units) applied to fonts that are greater than or equal to the size specified in `ktMaxSize`

The array must contain enough structures to hold all the kerning tracks for the font. The `EXTTEXTMETRIC` structure returned by the `GETEXTENDEDTEXTMETRICS` escape can determine the number of kerning tracks for the font.

Return Value:

`GETTRACKKERNTABLE` returns the number of data structures copied when successful. A return value of zero indicates that the escape cannot copy the data structures to the array.

GETVECTORBRUSHSIZE

Syntax:

```
short Escape(hDC, GETVECTORBRUSHSIZE, sizeof(LOGBRUSH), lpInData,
          lpOutData)
```

Parameter, Type, and Description:

`hDC`	`HDC`	Device context
`lpInData`	`LOGBRUSH FAR *`	Pointer to a data structure of type `LOGBRUSH` specifying the brush
`lpOutData`	`LPPOINT`	Pointer to a data structure of `POINT` specifying the width of the pen

Description:

The `GETVECTORBRUSHSIZE` escape determines the size of the pen (in device units) used for filling figures. The `lpInData` parameter points to a data structure of type `LOGBRUSH` that defines the brush. The `LOGBRUSH` data structure is:

```
typedef struct tagLOGBRUSH {
    WORD lbStyle;
    COLORREF lbColor;
    short int lbHatch;
} LOGBRUSH;
```

where:

`lbStyle` is the brush style and is set to one of the following values:

Value	*Meaning*
`BS_DIBPATTERN`	Pattern brush defined with a device-independent bitmap
`BS_HATCHED`	Hatched brush
`BS_HOLLOW`	Hollow brush
`BS_PATTERN`	Pattern brush defined with a memory bitmap
`BS_SOLID`	Solid brush

`lbColor` is the color for the brush and is one of the following values:

Value	*Meaning*
`DIB_PAL_COLORS`	Color table is an array of 16-bit indexes to the logical palette
`DIB_RGB_COLORS`	Color table contains literal RGB values

`lbHatch` is the hatch style and is interpreted as follows:

- If `lbStyle` is `BS_DIBPATTERN`, `lbHatch` contains the handle to a packed device independent bitmap
- If `lbStyle` is `BS_HATCHED`, `lbHatch` contains one of the following values that specify the line orientation of the hatch:

Value	*Meaning*
`HS_BDIAGONAL`	45-degree upward hatch
`HS_CROSS`	Crosshatch with vertical/horizontal lines
`HS_DIAGCROSS`	45-degree crosshatch
`HS_FDIAGONAL`	45-degree downward hatch
`HS_HORIZONTAL`	Horizontal hatch
`HS_VERTICAL`	Vertical hatch

- If lbStyle is BS_PATTERN, lbHatch contains the handle to the bitmap for the pattern
- If lbStyle is BS_SOLID or BS_HOLLOW, lbHatch is ignored

lpOutData points to a data structure of type POINT that specifies the width of the pen. The second word of the POINT data structure contains the pen width in device units.

Return Value:

GETVECTORBRUSHSIZE returns a value of 1 when the size of the pen used to fill figures is determined. A return value of zero indicates that the escape cannot determine the pen size.

GETVECTORPENSIZE

Syntax:

```
short Escape(hDC, GETVECTORPENSIZE, sizeof(LOGPEN), lpInData, lpOutData)
```

Parameter, Type, and Description:

hDC	HDC	Device context
lpInData	LOGPEN FAR *	Pointer to a data structure of type LOGPEN specifying the pen
lpOutData	LPPOINT	Pointer to a data structure of type POINT specifying the pen width

Description:

The GETVECTORPENSIZE escape determines the size of the plotter pen (in device units) used for drawing. The lpInData points to a data structure of type LOGPEN that defines the pen. The LOGPEN data structure is:

```
typedef struct tagLOGPEN {
     WORD lopnStyle;
     POINT lopnWidth;
     COLORREF lopnColor;
} LOGPEN;
```

where:

lopnStyle is the pen style and is chosen from one of the following constants:

Constant	*Value*
PS_SOLID	0
PS_DASH	1
PS_DOT	2
PS_DASHDOT	3
PS_DASHDOTDOT	4
PS_NULL	5
PS_INSIDEFRAME	6

lopnWidth is the pen width in logical units

lopnColor is the pen color

lpOutData points to a data structure of type POINT that specifies the width of the pen. The second word of the POINT data structure contains the pen width in device units.

Return Value:

GETVECTORPENSIZE returns a value of 1 when the size of the pen used for drawing is determined. A return value of zero indicates that the escape cannot determine the size of the pen.

MFCOMMENT

Syntax:

```
BOOL Escape(hDC, MFCOMMENT, nCount, lpComment, NULL)
```

Parameter, Type, and Description:

hDC	HDC	Device context
nCount	short	Number of characters pointed to by lpComment
lpComment	LPSTR	Pointer to the string containing the comment to appear in the metafile

Description:

The MFCOMMENT escape adds the comment in the string pointed to by lpComment to a metafile. The nCount parameter specifies the number of characters in the buffer pointed to by lpComment.

Return Value:

MFCOMMENT returns a positive value when the comment is added to the metafile. A return value of –1 indicates that an error has occurred.

NEWFRAME

Syntax:

```
short Escape(hDC, NEWFRAME, NULL, NULL, NULL)
```

Parameter, Type, and Description:

`hDC`	`HDC`	Device context

Description:

The `NEWFRAME` escape indicates that the application is done writing to the page.

Return Value:

`NEWFRAME` returns a positive value when successful. When unsuccessful, one of the following values is returned:

Value	*Meaning*
`SP_APPABORT`	Job terminated due to a return value of zero from the application's abort function
`SP_ERROR`	Error
`SP_OUTOFDISK`	Insufficient disk space for spooling
`SP_OUTOFMEMORY`	Insufficient memory for spooling
`SP_USERABORT`	Job terminated by the user through Print Manager

NEXTBAND

Syntax:

```
short Escape(hDC, NEXTBAND, NULL, NULL, lpBandRect)
```

Parameter, Type, and Description:

`hDC`	`HDC`	Device context
`lpBandRect`	`LPRECT`	Pointer to a data structure of type `RECT` to receive next band coordinates

Description:

The `NEXTBAND` escape indicates that the application has completed the writing of a band. The device then sends the band to the Print Manager and returns the coordinates of the next band. The `lpBandRect` parameter points to the data structure or type `RECT` that receives the band coordinates. The `RECT` data structure is:

```
typedef struct tagRECT{
     int left;
     int top;
     int right;
     int bottom;
} RECT;
```

where:

`left` is the x-coordinate of the upper-left corner

`top` is the y-coordinate of the upper-left corner

`right` is the x-coordinate of the lower-right corner

`bottom` is the y-coordinate of the lower-right corner

Return Value:

`NEXTBAND` returns a positive value when successful. When unsuccessful, one of the following values is returned:

Value	*Meaning*
`SP_APPABORT`	Job terminated due to a return value of zero from the application's abort function
`SP_ERROR`	Error
`SP_OUTOFDISK`	Insufficient disk space for spooling
`SP_OUTOFMEMORY`	Insufficient memory for spooling
`SP_USERABORT`	Job terminated by the user through Print Manager

PASSTHROUGH

Syntax:

```
short Escape(hDC, PASSTHROUGH, nCount, lpInData, NULL)
```

Parameter, Type, and Description:

`hDC`	`HDC`	Device context
`nCount`	`short`	Number of bytes that `lpInData` points to
`lpInData`	`LPSTR`	Pointer to data structure of input data

Description:

The PASSTHROUGH escape sends data to the printer while bypassing the print-driver code. The nCount parameter specifies the number of bytes pointed to by lpInData; lpInData points to a data structure containing the input data. The first word of the data structure contains the number of bytes of input data.

Return Value:

PASSTHROUGH returns the number of bytes sent to the device when successful. A return value of zero or less indicates that the escape cannot send data to the printer.

QUERYESCSUPPORT

Syntax:

```
short Escape(hDC, QUERYESCSUPPORT, sizeof(int), lpEscNum, NULL)
```

Parameter, Type, and Description:

hDC	HDC	Device context
lpEscNum	LPINT	Pointer to value specifying the escape

Description:

The QUERYESCSUPPORT escape determines whether the device driver implements the escape specified in lpEscNum.

Return Value:

QUERYESCSUPPORT returns a nonzero value when the specified escape is implemented. A return value of zero indicates that the specified escape is not implemented. When lpEscNum is DRAWPATTERNRECT, one of the following values is returned:

Value	*Meaning*
0	DRAWPATTERNRECT not implemented
1	DRAWPATTERNRECT implemented for printer other than HP LaserJet IIP (white rules supported)
2	DRAWPATTERNRECT implemented for HP LaserJet IIP

RESTORE_CTM

Syntax:

```
short Escape(hDC, RESTORE_CTM, NULL, NULL, NULL)
```

Parameter, Type, and Description:

`hDC`	`HDC`	Device context

Description:

The `RESTORE_CTM` escape restores the transformation matrix to its previous state.

Return Value:

`RESTORE_CTM` returns the number of `SAVE_CTM` calls without corresponding `RESTORE_CTM` calls when successful. A return value of –1 indicates that the escape was unsuccessful.

SAVE_CTM

Syntax:

```
short Escape(hDC, SAVE_CTM, NULL, NULL, NULL)
```

Parameter, Type, and Description:

`hDC`	`HDC`	Device context

Description:

The `SAVE_CTM` escape saves the current transformation matrix. The transformation matrix determines how coordinates are translated, rotated, and scaled by the device.

Return Value:

`SAVE_CTM` returns the number of `SAVE_CTM` calls without corresponding `RESTORE_CTM` calls when successful. A return value of –1 indicates that the escape was unsuccessful.

SETABORTPROC

Syntax:

```
short Escape(hDC, SETABORTPROC, NULL, lpAbortFunc, NULL)
```

Parameter, Type, and Description:

`hDC`	`HDC`	Device context
`lpAbortFunc`	`FARPROC`	Pointer to abort function

Description:

The `SETABORTPROC` escape defines the abort function for the print job. The `lpAbortFunc` parameter points to the abort function supplied by the application. The abort function has the following conventions:

Syntax:

```
short FAR PASCAL AbortFunc(hPr, code)
```

Parameter, Type, and Description:

hPr	HDC	Device context
code	short	Indicates whether an error has occurred

Description:

AbortFunc is a placeholder for the function name supplied by the application. Use EXPORTS to include the function name in the module definition file for the application.

Return Value:

The abort function should return a nonzero value to continue the print job and a zero to cancel the print job.

Return Value:

SETABORTPROC returns a positive value when the escape is successful. A negative return value indicates that the escape is unsuccessful.

SETALLJUSTVALUES

Syntax:

```
short Escape(hDC, SETALLJUSTVALUES, sizeof(JUST_VALUE_STRUCT),
          lpInData, NULL)
```

Parameter, Type, and Description:

hDC	HDC	Device context
lpInData	JUST_VALUE_STRUCT FAR *	Pointer to a data structure of type JUST_VALUE_STRUCT defining the justification

Description:

The SETALLJUSTVALUES escape defines the justification values for text. The text justification values are defined in the data structure of type JUST_VALUE_STRUCT pointed to by lpInData. The JUST_VALUE_STRUCT data structure is:

```
typedef struct {
     short nCharExtra;
     WORD nCharCount;
     short nBreakExtra;
     WORD nBreakCount;
} JUST_VALUE_STRUCT;
```

where:

> `nCharExtra` is the extra space in font units to be allocated between the characters defined in `nCharCount`
>
> `nCharCount` is the number of characters over which the extra space in `nCharExtra` is distributed
>
> `nBreakExtra` is the extra space in font units to be allocated between the characters defined in `nBreakCount`
>
> `nBreakCount` is the number of characters over which the extra space in `nBreakExtra` is distributed

Return Value:

`SETALLJUSTVALUES` returns a value of 1 when justification values are defined. A return value of zero indicates that the escape cannot define justification values.

SET_ARC_DIRECTION

Syntax:

```
short Escape(hDC, SET_ARC_DIRECTION, sizeof(int), lpDirection, NULL)
```

Parameter, Type, and Description:

`hDC`	`HDC`	Device context
`lpDirection`	`LPINT`	Pointer to value indicating arc direction

Description:

The `SET_ARC_DIRECTION` escape defines the direction used by the Windows function `Arc` when drawing elliptical arcs. `lpDirection` points to the value that specifies the arc direction, which can be either of the following:

Constant	*Value*	*Meaning*
`COUNTERCLOCKWISE`	0	Arc drawn counterclockwise
`CLOCKWISE`	1	Arc drawn clockwise

Return Value:

SET_ARC_DIRECTION returns the previous arc direction.

SET_BACKGROUND_COLOR

Syntax:

```
short Escape(hDC, SET_BACKGROUND_COLOR, nCount, lpNewColor, lpOldColor)
```

Parameter, Type, and Description:

hDC	HDC	Device context
nCount	int	Number of bytes pointed to by lpNewColor
lpNewColor	DWORD FAR *	Pointer to new background color
lpOldColor	DWORD FAR *	Pointer to value that receives the previous background color

Description:

The SET_BACKGROUND_COLOR escape defines the background color for the device. The lpNewColor parameter points to a 32-bit value that specifies the new background color; lpOldColor points to the 32-bit value that receives the previous background color. The background color, by default, is white.

Return Value:

SET_BACKGROUND_COLOR returns TRUE when the background color is defined. A return value of FALSE indicates that the escape cannot define the background color.

SET_BOUNDS

Syntax:

```
short Escape(hDC, SET_BOUNDS, sizeof(RECT), lpInData, NULL)
```

Parameter, Type, and Description:

hDC	HDC	Device context
lpInData	LPRECT	Pointer to a data structure of type RECT that contains the coordinates of the image

Description:

The SET_BOUNDS escape defines a rectangle for an image produced by file formats such as Encapsulated Postscript or Hewlett-Packard Graphics Language. The lpInData parameter points to a data structure of type RECT that defines the rectangle that binds the image. The RECT data structure is:

```
typedef struct tagRECT{
     int left;
     int top;
     int right;
     int bottom;
} RECT;
```

where:

left is the x-coordinate of the upper-left corner

top is the y-coordinate of the upper-left corner

right is the x-coordinate of the lower-right corner

bottom is the y-coordinate of the lower-right corner

Return Value:

SET_BOUNDS returns TRUE when the rectangle is defined. A return value of FALSE indicates that the escape cannot define the rectangle.

SETCOLORTABLE

Syntax:

```
short Escape(hDC, SETCOLORTABLE, sizeof(COLORTABLE_STRUCT), lpInData,
             lpColor)
```

Parameter, Type, and Description:

hDC	HDC	Device context
lpInData	COLORTABLE_STRUCT FAR *	Pointer to data structure of type COLORTABLE_STRUCT defining the color table entry
lpColor	DWORD FAR *	Pointer to value to receive the RGB color value

Description:

The SETCOLORTABLE escape defines an RGB value for the color table. The lpInData parameter points to a data structure of type COLORTABLE_STRUCT that defines the index and RGB value of the color table entry. The COLORTABLE_STRUCT data structure is:

```
typedef struct {
     WORD Index;
     DWORD rgb;
} COLORTABLE_STRUCT;
```

where:

Index is the color table index (0 = first entry)

rgb is the RGB color value

Return Value:

SETCOLORTABLE returns a positive value when the RGB value is defined. A negative return value indicates that the escape cannot define the RGB value.

SETCOPYCOUNT

Syntax:

```
short Escape(hDC, SETCOPYCOUNT, sizeof(int), lpNumCopies, lpActualCopies)
```

Parameter, Type, and Description:

hDC	HDC	Device context
lpNumCopies	LPINT	Pointer to value that indicates the number of uncollated copies to print
lpActualCopies	LPINT	Pointer to value that will store the number of copies to print

Description:

The SETCOPYCOUNT escape defines the number of uncollated copies of each page that should be printed.

Return Value:

SETCOPYCOUNT returns a value of 1 if successful. A return value of zero indicates that the escape is unsuccessful.

SETKERNTRACK

Syntax:

```
short Escape(hDC, SETKERNTRACK, sizeof(int), lpNewTrack, lpOldTrack)
```

Parameter, Type, and Description:

hDC	HDC	Device context
lpNewTrack	LPINT	Pointer to value specifying the track to use
lpOldTrack	LPINT	Pointer to the value receiving the previous kerning track

Description:

The SETKERNTRACK escape defines the kerning track used by device drivers that support automatic track kerning. By default, automatic kerning is disabled. The lpNewTrack parameter points to the value that specifies the kerning track to be used by the device drivers. Set lpNewTrack to zero to disable this feature.

Return Value:

SETKERNTRACK returns a value of 1 when the kerning track is defined. A return value of zero indicates that the escape cannot define the kerning track.

SETLINECAP

Syntax:

```
short Escape(hDC, SETLINECAP, sizeof(int), lpNewCap, lpOldCap)
```

Parameter, Type, and Description:

hDC	HDC	Device context
lpNewCap	LPINT	Pointer to value that specifies the end-cap type
lpOldCap	LPINT	Pointer to value that specifies the previous end-cap type

Description:

The SETLINECAP escape sets the line end-cap, the portion of the line segment that appears on either end of the line segment. The lpNewCap parameter points to the value that specifies the new end-cap type. The following values are used for lpNewCap:

Value	*Meaning*
–1	Line segments are drawn with default GDI end caps
0	Line segments are drawn with squared end points; end points do not extend past the defined line segment
1	Line segments are drawn with rounded end points; the diameter of the rounded portion of the segment is equal to the line width
2	Line segments are drawn with squared end points; end points extend one-half the line width past the defined line segment

Return Value:

`SETLINECAP` returns a positive value when the line end-cap is set. A negative return value indicates that the escape cannot set the line end-cap.

SETLINEJOIN

Syntax:

```
short Escape(hDC, SETLINEJOIN, sizeof(int), lpNewJoin, lpOldJoin)
```

Parameter, Type, and Description:

`hDC`	`HDC`	Device context
`lpNewJoin`	`LPINT`	Pointer to the value specifying the intersection type
`lpOldJoin`	`LPINT`	Pointer to the value that receives the previous intersection type

Description:

The `SETLINEJOIN` escape defines the intersection type for intersecting line segments. The `lpNewJoin` parameter specifies the intersection type and can be any of the following:

Value	*Meaning*
–1	Default GDI intersection
0	Mitered corner (miter join)
1	Rounded corner (round join)
2	Squared end point (bevel join)

Return Value:

`SETLINEJOIN` returns a positive value when the intersection type is defined. A negative return value indicates that the escape cannot define the intersection type.

SETMITERLIMIT

Syntax:

```
short Escape(hDC, SETMITERLIMIT, sizeof(int), lpNewMiter, lpOldMiter)
```

Parameter, Type, and Description:

hDC	HDC	Device context
lpNewMiter	LPINT	Pointer to value specifying the new miter limit
lpOldMiter	LPINT	Pointer to value containing the previous miter limit

Description:

The SETMITERLIMIT escape defines the miter limit for the device. The lpNewMiter parameter points to the value that specifies the new miter limit. When the value pointed to by lpNewMiter is –1, the device driver will use the default GDI miter limit. The miter limit is used to define the angle where the device driver will replace a miter join with a bevel join.

Return Value:

SETMITERLIMIT returns a positive value when the miter limit is defined. A negative return value indicates that the escape cannot define the miter limit.

SET_POLY_MODE

Syntax:

```
short Escape(hDC, SET_POLY_MODE, sizeof(int), lpMode, NULL)
```

Parameter, Type, and Description:

hDC	HDC	Device context
lpMode	LPINT	Pointer to value specifying the poly mode

Description:

The SET_POLY_MODE escape defines the poly mode. The poly mode specifies the way calls to the Windows functions Polygon and Polyline are handled. The lpMode parameter points to the value that specifies the poly mode. The following values are used for the value pointed to by lpMode:

Value	*Meaning*
`PM_POLYLINE`	Points define standard polygon or polyline
`PM_BEZIER`	Points define a 4-point Bezier spline curve; the first and last points are endpoints, the second and third points are control points and are used to specify the shape and direction of the curve
`PM_POLYLINESEGMENT`	Points define a list of coordinate pairs; these pairs are connected with lines

Return Value:

`SET_POLY_MODE` returns the previous poly mode. A negative return value indicates that the escape was not successful.

SET_SCREEN_ANGLE

Syntax:

```
short Escape(hDC, SET_SCREEN_ANGLE, sizeof(int), lpAngle, NULL)
```

Parameter, Type, and Description:

`hDC`	`HDC`	Device context
`lpAngle`	`LPINT`	Pointer to value specifying the screen angle

Description:

The `SET_SCREEN_ANGLE` escape defines the screen angle. The `lpAngle` parameter points to the value that specifies the screen angle in tenths of a degree counterclockwise. The screen angle is used by an application for image color separation.

Return Value:

`SET_SCREEN_ANGLE` returns the previous screen angle.

SET_SPREAD

Syntax:

```
short Escape(hDC, SET_SPREAD, sizeof(int), lpSpread, NULL)
```

Parameter, Type, and Description:

`hDC`	`HDC`	Device context
`lpSpread`	`LPINT`	Pointer to value specifying the number of pixels that nonwhite primitives are to be expanded

Description:

The `SET_SPREAD` function defines the number of pixels that nonwhite primitives are expanded. The `lpSpread` parameter points to the value that specifies the amount of expansion. Expansion is often desired to correct for flaws during printing. By default, the spread is zero.

Return Value:

`SET_SPREAD` returns the previous spread value.

STARTDOC

Syntax:

```
short Escape(hDC, STARTDOC, nCount, lpDocName, NULL)
```

Parameter, Type, and Description:

`hDC`	`HDC`	Device context
`nCount`	`short`	Number of characters pointed to by `lpDocName`
`lpDocName`	`LPSTR`	Pointer to null-terminated string specifying the document name

Description:

The `STARTDOC` escape starts a new print job. All `NEWFRAME` escape calls that are generated after the `STARTDOC` escape and prior to an `ENDDOC` escape are spooled under the specified job name. The `lpDocName` parameter points to the string that contains the document name.

Return Value:

`STARTDOC` returns a positive value when the new print job is started. A return value of –1 indicates that the escape cannot start the new print job.

TRANSFORM_CTM

Syntax:

```
short Escape(hDC, TRANSFORM_CTM, 36, lpMatrix, NULL)
```

Parameter, Type, and Description:

hDC	HDC	Device context
lpMatrix	LPSTR	Pointer to array of values defining the new transformation matrix

Description:

The TRANSFORM_CTM escape modifies the current transformation matrix. The new current transformation matrix is the product of the current transformation matrix and the matrix pointed to by lpMatrix.

Return Value:

TRANSFORM_CTM returns TRUE when the current transformation matrix is modified. A return value of FALSE indicates that the escape cannot modify the current transformation matrix.

16

The Whitewater Resource Toolkit

Borland C++ is a sophisticated set of programming tools for the development of C and C++ programs using the American National Standards Institute (ANSI) C standard, the AT&T C++ version 2.0 definition, and the Kernighan and Ritchie definition. C and C++ programs can be compiled at the command line or inside the Integrated Development Environment (IDE). Borland C++ includes tools for the development of Microsoft Windows applications using C or C++. The features of Borland C++ enable you to develop Windows applications from within the IDE while creating and manipulating resources for the Windows application with the Whitewater Resource Toolkit. This chapter introduces the components of the Whitewater Resource Toolkit. Appendix D introduces the features of the IDE and the command-line compiler.

The Resource Toolkit contains a powerful set of tools for building and modifying resources used in Microsoft Windows applications. With this toolkit, you can create and manage the user interface of any target Windows application. The Resource Toolkit operates inside the Windows environment and provides a variety of editors for creating and modifying resources such as keyboard accelerators, bitmaps, cursors, icons, dialog boxes, menus, and strings.

Because the Resource Toolkit operates under Windows, you must have Windows Version 3.0, or a newer version, up and running on your system. Additional system requirements include 1MB of RAM, a graphics display and adapter, a pointing device, and at least 700K of available disk space.

You can start the Resource Toolkit from the DOS prompt, the Windows Program Manager, the Windows File Manager, or the Windows MS-DOS executive.

To start the Resource Toolkit from the DOS prompt, go to the Resource Toolkit's main directory and type the following:

```
WIN WRT <Enter>
```

To start the Resource Toolkit from the Windows Program Manager, you first must add the Resource Toolkit icon to the Program Manager. Then you can start the Resource Toolkit by double clicking the icon.

To add the Resource Toolkit, follow these steps:

1. Enter Windows and activate the Program Manager.
2. Activate the window to which you want to add the icon.
3. Select the `New` option of the `File` menu.
4. Click `OK` on the dialog box that appears. The `Program Item Properties` dialog box is then displayed.
5. Type the name you want to display under the icon in the `Description` field of the dialog box.
6. Type the path and filename `WRT.EXE` in the `Command Line` field.
7. Click the `Change Icon` button to select an icon for the toolkit. Click the `OK` button when done. Double clicking the resulting icon starts the resource toolkit.

To start the Resource Toolkit from the Windows File Manager or MS-DOS executive, open the directory that contains the file WRT.EXE and double click the file name.

Resources

Windows applications consist of several graphical elements. These elements range from dialog boxes to cursors. Under Windows, each of these elements is stored as a resource that can be loaded into the application. Resources are separated from the source code and thus offer several advantages in application development. One advantage is that by separating the resource, you can use a resource definition for several applications. This reduces development time for subsequent applications. Another advantage is that you can modify a resource without affecting the source code. This enables you to develop resources and source code simultaneously while shortening software modification phases.

It is very important to understand that resources do not define interface functionality. Resources are merely the visual representation of program elements. For example, you can define a dialog box resource that contains a series of buttons and that can be displayed by your application. The user can select the buttons of the dialog box; however, nothing happens when the buttons are selected unless the application defines the action for each button. The dialog box resource merely defines the location and appearance (the visual representation) of the buttons. The application must define the action of each button in the dialog box (the interface functionality). Table 16.1 lists the resources that the Resource Toolkit can edit.

Table 16.1. *Resources.*

Resource	*Meaning*
Accelerators	Keys or key sequences used as an alternative to menu selection
Bitmaps	Series of data that represent an element, or picture, on the screen
Cursors	Screen markers used to indicate position
Dialog boxes	Input screens that offer the user options for the application
Icons	Screen elements that can be selected to control the application
Menus	Lists of program options
Strings	The text displayed in the menus, dialog boxes, and so on

The Resource Toolkit can edit, create, copy, view, save, and delete a variety of file types. Table 16.2 lists the various file types and provides information on how the Resource Toolkit can manipulate each of these file types.

Table 16.2. *File types.*

Type	*Manipulation*	*Meaning*	*Description*
.BMP	Edit	Bitmap resource file	Contains a single bitmap resource in bitmap format. .BMP resources can be generated by the Resource Toolkit and included in .RC files.

continues

Table 16.2. continued

Type	Manipulation	Meaning	Description
.CUR	Edit	Cursor resource file	Contains a single cursor resource in bitmap format. .CUR resources can be generated in the Resource Toolkit and included in .RC files.
.DAT	Copy, rename, delete	Raw data sources	Contains raw data resources used by the application. .DAT files can be copied, renamed, or deleted.
.DLG	Generated by Resource Toolkit but must be compiled by Microsoft's Resource Compiler	Dialog box resource script file	Contains dialog box resources in text format. DLG files can be generated with a text editor.
.EXE	Edit	Executable file	Contains all the application's resources and compiled program code. The resources of the .EXE file can be modified and saved without recompiling the source code.
.FON	Copy, rename, delete	Font file	Contains fonts used by the application to display text.
.H	Edit	Header file	Contains symbolic names that are assigned to the numbers used to identify the action resulting from a menu selection.
.ICO	Edit	Icon resource file	Contains a single icon resource in bit-map format. .ICO resources can be generated by the Resource Toolkit and included in .RC files.
.RC	Generated by Resource Toolkit but must be compiled by Microsoft's Resource Compiler	Resource script file	Contains resources in binary format. .RC files identify resources by name or number and describe resource attributes, styles, and so on. These files can be generated by the Resource Toolkit or created with a text editor.

Type	Manipulation	Meaning	Description
.RES	Edit	Compiled Microsoft Resource Compiler file	Contains resources in binary format. .RES files can be edited and saved using the Resource Toolkit.

The Resource Manager

The Resource Manager is the main window of the Resource Toolkit. From this window, you can enter any of the resource editors, access existing resources, and create or close new files. As shown in Figure 16.1, the resource manager has three primary sets of options. These options include editor buttons, resource browsers, and the include button.

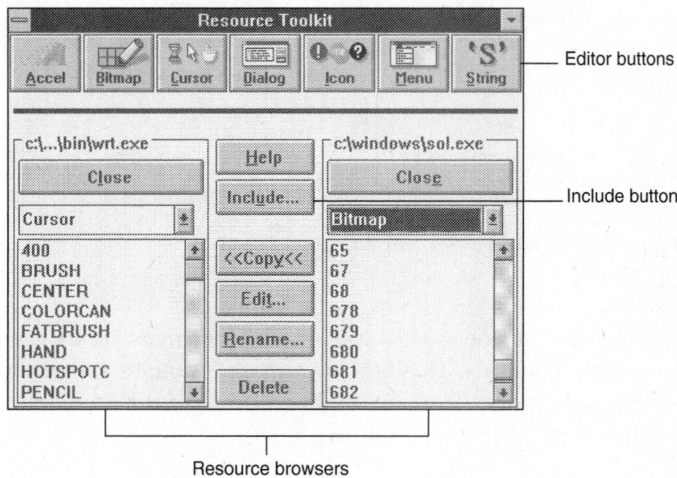

Figure 16.1. *The Resource Manager.*

The editor buttons are used to start the resource editors. To enter one of the editors, just click on the appropriate editor button. Once the editor is open, you can create new resources or edit existing resources.

The two resource browsers enable you to open files. You can use the two browsers to open two files simultaneously. Therefore, you can easily copy resources from one file to another.

The include button enables you to select the resource types to display. Clicking the `Include` button opens a dialog box that lists the resource types you can edit or copy.

The features of the Resource Manager are easy to use and operation is intuitive. The remainder of this chapter describes the editors included in the Resource Manager.

The Accelerator Editor

The Accelerator editor is used to create and edit accelerator resources. Accelerators are "hot keys" or "key sequences" that are used as alternatives to selecting menu options with the mouse. Figure 16.2 shows the Accelerator editor.

Accelerator: C:\BORLANDC\BIN\WRT.EXE WRT

File Edit Header Help

Type	Key	Code	Shift	Ctrl	Alt	Value	Invert
Virtkey	HOME	36	No	No	No	309	Yes
Virtkey	END	35	No	No	No	308	Yes
Virtkey	F3	114	No	No	No	114	Yes
Virtkey	DELETE	46	No	No	No	304	Yes
Virtkey	F1	112	No	No	No	699	Yes
Ascii	^O	15				999	Yes
Ascii	^L	12				641	Yes
Virtkey	BACK	8	No	No	Yes	300	Yes
Virtkey	ESCAPE	27	No	No	No	27	Yes

***Figure 16.2.** The Accelerator editor.*

The Accelerator editor stores accelerator resources in an accelerator table that contains eight columns. This accelerator table defines the use and function of the specified accelerators. There are eight columns in the accelerator table: Type, Key, Code, Shift, Ctrl, Alt, Value, and Invert.

The Type Column

The Type column defines the accelerator as a virtual key or ASCII code. To define the accelerator according to a virtual key definition, move to the Type column and then press the space bar to the desired type or press the V key. Virtual keys name accelerators according to a set of virtual key definitions defined for Windows. To define the accelerator according to an ASCII code, move to the Type column and then press the space bar to the desired type or press the A key.

The Key Column

The Key column defines the actual key or key sequence that represents the accelerator. To define the accelerator, first move to the Key column and then press the desired key or key sequence. For example, if you want Ctrl-G as an accelerator, move to the Key column and press Ctrl-G. The ASCII or virtual key representation, whichever is selected in the Type column, then appears in the Key column.

The Code Column

The Code column displays the keyboard scan code—the key ID number for the keyboard—for the accelerator key or key sequence defined in the Key column. This column is filled automatically when the Key column is filled. The displayed keyboard scan code varies depending on the ASCII or virtual key selection in the Type column.

The Shift Column

The Shift column is filled only when the Type column is set to virtual key. The Shift column is filled automatically and indicates whether the Shift key must be pressed to activate the specified accelerator. You can modify this field by first moving to the column and then pressing the space bar to the desired option, or by pressing the Y (yes) or N (no) keys.

The Ctrl Column

The Ctrl column is filled only when the Type Column is set to virtual key. This Ctrl column is filled automatically and indicates whether the Ctrl key must be pressed to activate the specified accelerator. You can modify this field by first moving to the column and then pressing the space bar to the desired option, or by pressing the Y (yes) or N (no) keys.

The Alt Column

The Alt column, which is similar to the Ctrl and Shift columns, indicates whether the Alt key must be pressed to activate the specified accelerator. You can modify this field by first moving to the column and then pressing the space bar to the desired option. You also can press the Y (yes) or N (no) keys to set the values in this column.

The Value Column

The Value column displays the integer ID number for the accelerator specified in the Key column. This ID number is used to load the accelerator into the application's source code.

The Invert Column

The Invert column specifies whether the main menu item associated with the specified accelerator should be highlighted when the accelerator is pressed. For most purposes, this column is set to Yes.

The Symbol Column

The Symbol column displays the symbol that has a matching ID number in the header file for the current accelerator. This symbol can be used to load the accelerator into the application. The Symbol column is displayed only when a header file has been opened. Header files and the Header editor are discussed in more detail later in this chapter.

Table 16.3 lists the keys used to move around inside the Accelerator editor. Ctrl-Enter is used to add another row to the accelerator table.

Table 16.3. Keys for moving around the Accelerator editor.

Key	*Meaning*
Up arrow	Moves up one row
Down arrow	Moves down one row
Tab	Moves to the right one column
Shift-Tab	Moves to the left one column
Right arrow	Moves to the right one space in the current field
Left arrow	Moves to the left one space in the current field
Home	Moves to the first position of the current field
End	Moves to the last position of the current field

The Bitmap Editor

The Bitmap editor is a graphics tool for creating and editing bitmap resources. Bitmap resources describe a picture and can be either 2-color or 16-color images. The maximum size for each bitmap is 200-by-200 pixels. The defaults for each bitmap are 72-by-72 pixels using 16 colors. The Bitmap Editor is shown in Figure 16.3. In Figure 16.3, one of the bitmaps used for the back of the cards in the Windows Solitaire game has been opened.

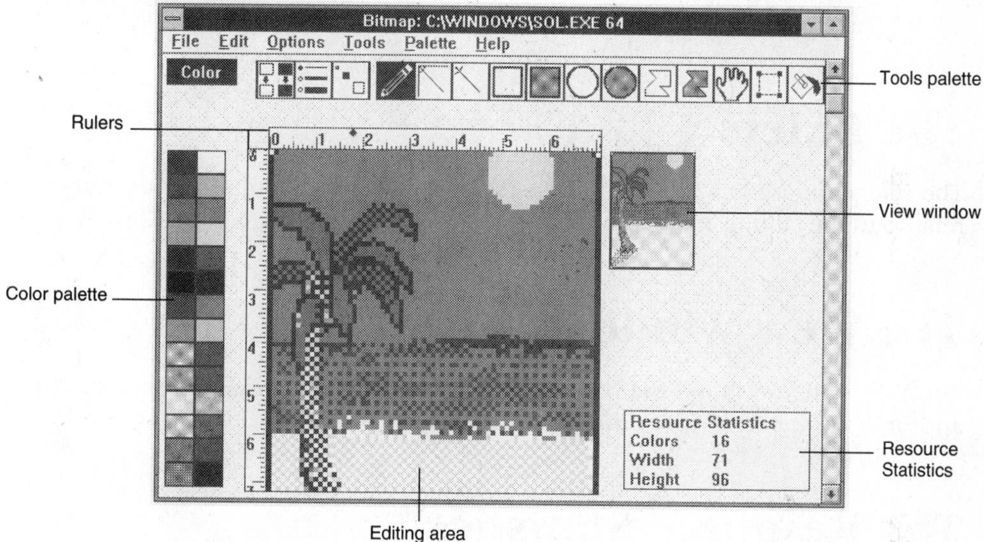

Figure 16.3. *The Bitmap editor.*

The Bitmap editor contains six basic parts. These are the Color palette, the Tools palette, the editing area, the rulers, the View window, and the Resource Statistics.

The Color Palette

The Color palette is on the left side of the screen. It displays all the available colors for creating the bitmap and the current drawing color. For the Bitmap editor, 28 colors are available for use. When a 16-color bitmap is specified, the first 16 colors are solid, true colors. The remainder of the colors are shades of some of the first 16 colors. When a 2-color bitmap is specified, black, white, and 26 shades of gray are

available. You can change the colors in the Bitmap editor Color palette by selecting the color and then selecting `Edit Color` option from the `Palette` menu. A dialog box then is displayed that allows you to modify the red, blue, and green fields of each color.

The Editing Area

The editing area is the area of the screen where the bitmaps are actually created and/or modified. This area can be actual size, four times actual size, or eight times actual size.

The Rulers

The rulers are used to provide precise information on the location of the cursor relative to the editing area.

The View Window

The View window shows the bitmap being created and/or modified as it would appear in the application. For the Bitmap editor, the bitmap is shown in actual size.

The Resource Statistics

The Resource Statistics appear in the bottom right corner of the editor. The statistics displayed include the number of colors available for creating and/or modifying the bitmap, the pixel height of the bitmap, and the pixel width of the bitmap.

The Tools Palette

The Bitmap editor provides a number of drawing tools similar to those in Paintbrush programs, and the Tools palette contains the drawing tools. The Tools palette for the Bitmap editor includes the following:

- Toggle tool
- Line Width tool
- Magnifying tool

- Pencil tool
- Line tool
- Constrained Line tool
- Rectangle tool
- Filled Rectangle tool
- Ellipse tool
- Filled Ellipse tool
- Polygon tool
- Filled Polygon tool
- Dragging tool
- Selecting tool
- Pouring tool

Let's look at each of these tools along with their respective icon symbols:

The *Toggle* tool draws with the inverse of a color when you use the Pencil tool. When the Toggle tool is off (the default setting), you can draw with the color selected from the Color palette. When the Toggle tool is on, you can draw with the inverse of the color of the pixel at the current cursor position.

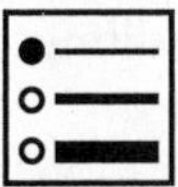

The *Line Width* tool is used to select the line width in pixels. Three line thicknesses are provided: 1 (the default), 3, and 5 pixels. All lines drawn by the editors use this line width.

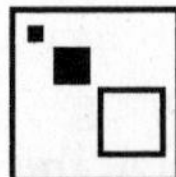

The *Magnifying* tool is used to select the scale of the editing area. Three options are provided: actual size, four times actual size (the default), and eight times actual size.

The *Pencil* tool creates free-hand lines. The pencil is moved by the mouse and lines are drawn the entire time you press the mouse button.

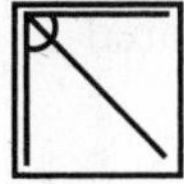

The *Line* tool draws a straight line between any two points at any angle.

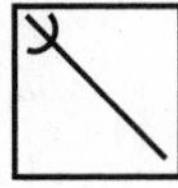

The *Constrained Line* tool draws a straight line that is a multiple of 45 degrees (0, 45, 90, 165, 180, 225, 270, 315, 360 degrees).

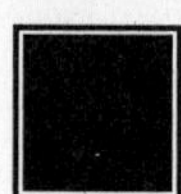

The *Rectangle* tool draws an unfilled rectangle.

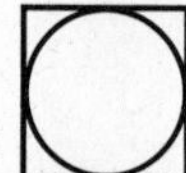

The *Filled Rectangle* tool draws a rectangle that is filled in with the current color.

The *Ellipse* tool draws an unfilled ellipse.

The *Filled Ellipse* tool draws an ellipse filled with the current color.

The *Polygon* tool draws an unfilled polygon. You define each side of the polygon by clicking at the starting point and dragging to the next point. The Polygon tool automatically closes the polygon.

The *Filled Polygon* tool draws a polygon filled with the current color. You define each side of the polygon by clicking at the starting point and dragging to the next point. The Filled Polygon tool automatically closes the polygon.

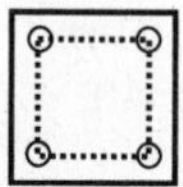

The *Dragging* tool drags a selected graphic around the editing area.

The *Selecting* tool is used to select an existing object in the editing area. By selecting an object, you can copy it onto the clipboard. From the clipboard, the object can be modified with the operations available in the `Edit` menu.

The *Pouring* tool fills an area with the current color. The Pouring tool fills an area by first evaluating the color value of the pixel at the current cursor position. The Pouring tool then converts that pixel to the current color and moves in all directions, changing each pixel that matches the pixel value evaluated at the starting cursor position. The Pouring tool stops filling the area when, in all directions, the tool finds a pixel value other than that of the evaluated pixel.

The Cursor Editor

The Cursor editor is a graphics tool for creating and editing cursor resources. Cursor resources are bitmaps that represent the current location of the mouse. You can use different cursor bitmaps to represent different cursor modes. Figure 16.4 shows the Cursor editor.

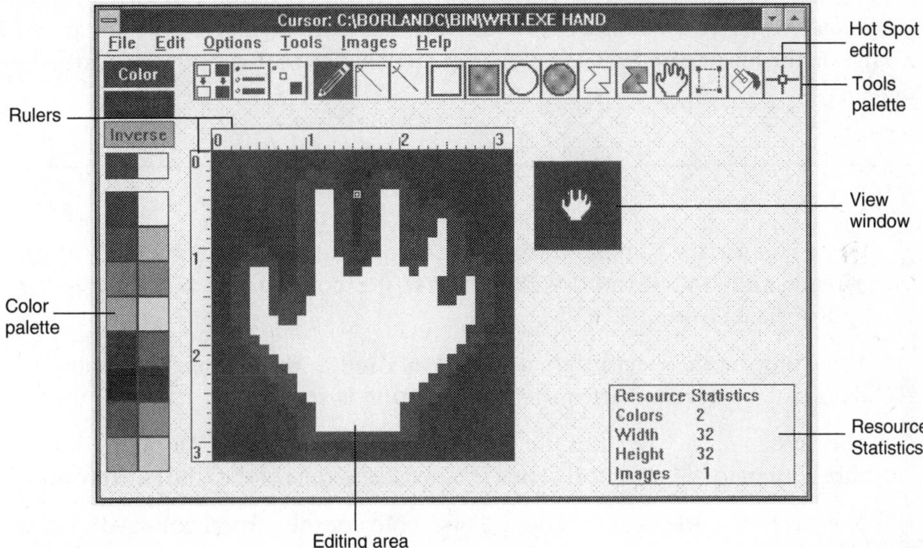

Figure 16.4. *The Cursor editor.*

When creating a cursor, you must define in the WRT.DAT file the dimensions and number of colors to use in the cursor bitmap. The WRT.DAT file stores resolution information in records for various device drivers. Each record in the file contains fields that describe a particular device. Table 16.4 describes the fields.

Table 16.4. *Record fields for cursor resources.*

Field	*Contents*
Name	The name that describes the device; maximum length is 10 characters
Number of colors	The number of colors available for the bitmap
Cursor width	The width, in pixels, of a cursor
Cursor height	The height, in pixels, of a cursor
Icon width	The width, in pixels, of an icon
Icon height	The height, in pixels, of an icon

The Cursor editor contains six basic parts: the Color palette, the Tools palette, the editing area, the rulers, the View window, and the Resource Statistics.

The Color Palette

The Color palette is on the left side of the screen. It displays all the available colors for creating the bitmap and the current drawing color. For the Cursor editor, only black and white are available. However, 16 screen and inverse colors are available for use on the lower palette. The following sidebar about color modes provides more details.

Color Modes

When you use the Cursor editor, three color modes are available: the Color, Screen, and Inverse modes. You select the color mode by clicking the appropriate button.

The Color mode specifies that the colors used in the bitmap will maintain their true colors no matter what background is specified.

The Screen mode specifies the screen's background color. All pixels drawn subsequent to the selection of this mode take on the color of the background.

The Inverse mode specifies the inverse color of the screen color. All pixels drawn after the selection of this mode will be drawn in the inverse of the screen color.

The Tools Palette

The Cursor editor provides a number of drawing tools similar to those in Paintbrush programs, and the Tools palette contains the drawing tools. The Tools palette for the Cursor editor includes the following:

- Toggle tool
- Line Width tool
- Magnifying tool
- Pencil tool
- Line tool

- Constrained Line tool
- Rectangle tool
- Filled Rectangle tool
- Ellipse tool
- Filled Ellipse tool
- Polygon tool
- Filled Polygon tool
- Dragging tool
- Selecting tool
- Pouring tool
- Hot Spot tool

Most of these tools are the same as described in our section on the Bitmap editor toolkit. However, the Cursor editor includes one additional tool:

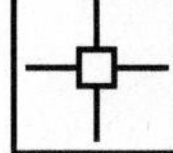

The *Hot Spot* tool is used with the Cursor editor to define a cursor hot spot. A hot spot is one point on the screen that identifies where a cursor operation will occur.

The Editing Area

The editing area is the area of the screen where the cursors are actually created and/or modified. This area can be actual size, four times actual size, or eight times actual size.

The Rulers

The rulers are used to provide precise information on the location of the cursor relative to the editing area.

The View Window

The View window shows the cursor being created and/or modified as it would appear in the application. For the Cursor editor, the cursor is shown in larger than actual size.

The Resource Statistics

The Resource Statistics appear in the bottom right corner of the editor. The statistics displayed include the number of colors available for creating and/or modifying the cursor, the pixel height of the cursor, and the pixel width of the cursor.

The Dialog Box Editor

The Dialog Box editor creates and edits dialog box resources. Dialog boxes are resources containing controls for specific tasks in the application's user interface. Figure 16.5 shows the Dialog Box editor.

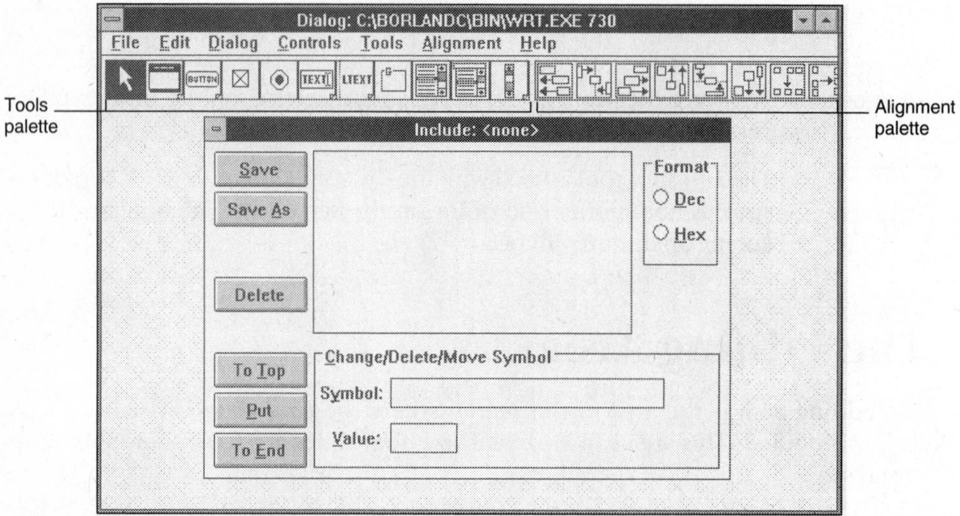

Figure 16.5. *The Dialog Box editor.*

The Dialog Box editor, which is similar to a paint program, has two palettes: the Tools palette and the Alignment palette.

The Tools Palette

The Tools palette provides a list of tools used to create the dialog box and its controls. The tools included with the Tools palette are the following:

The *Pointer* tool is automatically activated when you select a tool. The pointer then is displayed, and you can use it to draw with a selected tool, choose a dialog box, or modify existing controls.

The *Dialog Box* tools are used to create a standard dialog box or a captioned dialog box. A standard dialog box has no title bar and can't be moved within an application. A captioned dialog box has a title bar and can be moved within an application.

The *Button* tools are used to create standard or default push buttons. You must select a standard push button before it can be activated. A default push button is the button that is automatically selected when a dialog box is open. Only one default push button should be defined for each dialog box.

The *Check Box* tool is used to create options that can be checked on or off.

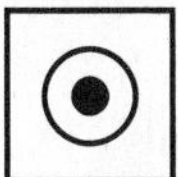

The *Radio Button* tool is used to create a series of options. From the options in this series, only one option can be selected at any time. A set of radio buttons must be defined as a logical group.

Edit Control tools are used for text entry. Single line edit, multiple line edit, multiple line edit with vertical scrolling, and multiple line edit with vertical and horizontal scrolling styles are provided.

Text tools display static text. Three formatting options are provided: left justified formatting, right justified formatting, and centered text.

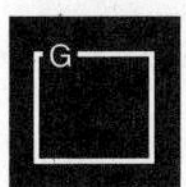

The *Group Box* tool is used to define groups of push buttons, check boxes, or radio buttons. Although the Group Box tool surrounds these buttons with a titled border, you must use the `Set Group` option under the `Dialog` menu to define the buttons as a logical group.

The *List Box* tool creates a list box, a list of text items. List boxes often are used to show a file list. Scroll bars are provided to permit vertical scrolling of the list. List boxes can be customized.

The *Combo Box* tool creates a combo box, a box that combines the features of an edit and a list box. Single combo box, drop-down combo box, and drop-down list combo box styles are provided. The simple combo box displays both the edit area and the list box. The drop-down combo box displays the combo box first. The list box is opened whenever you select the down arrow on the right.

The drop-down list combo box functions like the drop-down combo box. The difference between these two styles is that the drop-down combo box allows the user to enter text, and the drop-down list combo box limits text selections to those items in the list box.

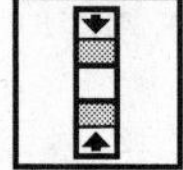

The *Scroll Bar, Icon, and Custom Control* tool is a multistyle tool. Double clicking this icon provides several tool options. The Standard Scroll Bar tool creates a scroll bar with standard width. The Scroll Bar tool creates a scroll bar with a specified width. The Icon tool creates a box in which you can place an icon. Windows automatically sizes the box. The Custom Control tool creates a box for placing a customized control. A custom control must have a dynamic-link library that fully defines the control's procedures and functionality.

The Alignment Palette

The Alignment palette is used to position and adjust the size of controls. The Alignment tools in the Alignment palette provide the power to make your controls perfectly spaced and aligned. The procedure for using each of the Alignment tools is the same. One control is first selected. By selecting this control, you designate it as the standard for sizing or alignment. You then can select other controls while pressing the Shift key; the selected controls then will be aligned or sized according to the standard control and the Alignment tool you chose.

The Alignment palette tools are the following:

The *Align Left* tool aligns all the selected controls with the standard control's left border. Vertical positioning is not changed.

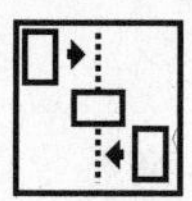

The *Center on Vertical* tool aligns the centers of the selected controls with the standard control's vertical axis. Vertical positioning is not changed.

The *Align Right* tool aligns all the selected controls with the standard control's right border. Vertical positioning is not changed.

The *Align Top* tool aligns all the selected controls with the standard control's top border. Horizontal positioning is not changed.

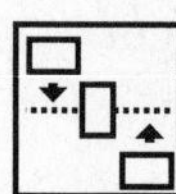

The *Center on Horizontal* tool aligns the centers of the selected controls with the standard control's horizontal axis. Horizontal positioning is not changed.

The *Align Bottom* tool aligns all the selected controls with the standard control's bottom border. Horizontal positioning is not changed.

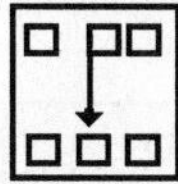

The *Spread Horizontally* tool evenly spaces the selected controls horizontally through the dialog box's width. The standard control does not affect this tool.

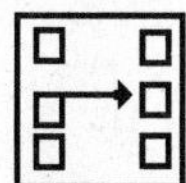

The *Spread Vertically* tool evenly spaces the selected controls vertically through the dialog box. The standard control does not affect this tool.

The *Make Same Size* tool makes all the selected controls the same size as the standard control. Positioning is not changed.

The Icon Editor

The Icon editor contains graphics tools for creating and editing icon resources. Icons are bitmaps that represent applications or actions within an application. Figure 16.6 shows the Icon editor. The icon that represents the minimized Windows Paintbrush accessory is open and ready for editing in Figure 16.6.

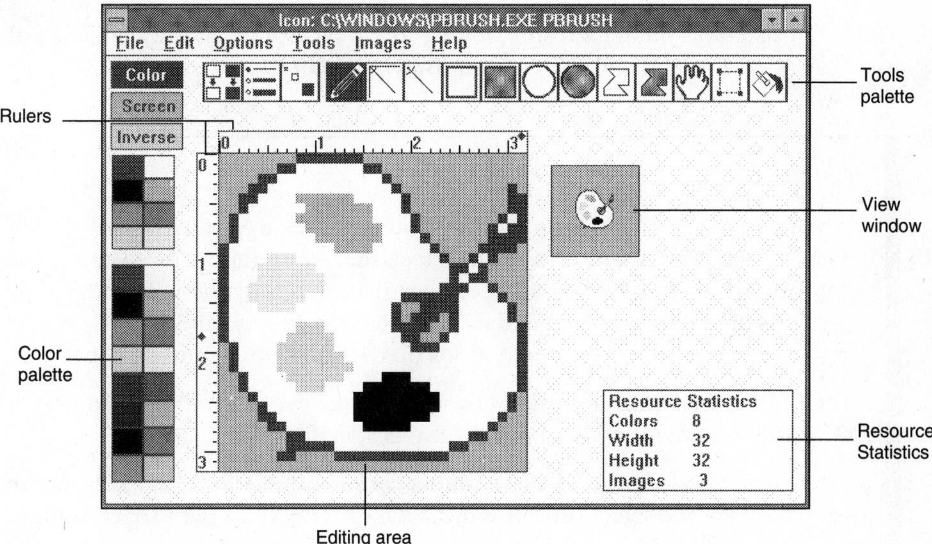

***Figure 16.6.** The Icon editor.*

When you create an icon, you need to define (in the WRT.DAT file) the dimensions and numbers of colors to use in the cursor bitmap. The WRT.DAT file stores resolution information in records for various device drivers. Each record in the file contains fields that describe a particular device. Table 16.5 describes the fields.

Table 16.5. *Record fields for icon resources.*

Field	*Contents*
Name	The name that describes the device; maximum length is 10 characters
Number of colors	The number of colors available for the bitmap
Cursor width	The width, in pixels, of a cursor
Cursor height	The height, in pixels, of a cursor
Icon width	The width, in pixels, of an icon
Icon height	The height, in pixels, of an icon

The Icon editor contains six basic parts: the Color palette, the Tools palette, the editing area, the rulers, the View window, and the Resource Statistics.

The Color Palette

The Color palette is on the left side of the screen. It displays all the available colors for creating the bitmap and the current drawing color.

Color Modes

When you use the Icon editor, three color modes are available: the Color, Screen, and Inverse modes. You select the color mode by clicking the appropriate button. For the Icon editor, the number of colors in the palette depends on the device specified in the WRT.DAT file. In addition, the colors available in the lower palette depends on the color mode and device in use.

The Color mode indicates that the colors used in the icon will maintain their true colors no matter what background is specified.

The Screen mode specifies the screen's background color. All pixels drawn subsequent to the selection of this mode take on the color of the background.

The Inverse mode specifies the inverse color of the screen color. All pixels drawn after the selection of this mode will be drawn in the inverse of the screen color.

The Tools Palette

The Icon editor provides a number of drawing tools similar to those in Paintbrush programs. The Tools palette for the Icon editor (shown in Figure 16.6) contains the drawing tools. The tools from left to right are the Toggle tool, the Line Width tool, the Magnifying tool, the Pencil tool, the Line tool, the Constrained Line tool, the Rectangle tool, the Filled Rectangle tool, the Ellipse tool, the Filled Ellipse tool, the Polygon tool, the Filled Polygon tool, the Dragging tool, the Selecting tool, and the Pouring tool. Each of these tools was discussed in the "Cursor Editor" section.

The Editing Area

The editing area is the area of the screen where the icons are actually created and/or modified. This area can be actual size, four times actual size, or eight times actual size.

The Rulers

The rulers provide precise information on the location of the icon relative to the editing area.

The View Window

The View window shows the icon being created and/or modified as it would appear in the application. The Icon editor shows the icon in larger than actual size.

The Resource Statistics

The Resource Statistics appear in the bottom right corner of the editor. The statistics displayed include the number of colors available for creating and/or modifying the icon, the pixel height of the icon, and the pixel width of the icon.

The Menu Editor

The Menu editor creates and edits menu resources. The editor, shown in Figure 16.7, features a menu table, movement buttons, style and attribute fields, and a test window.

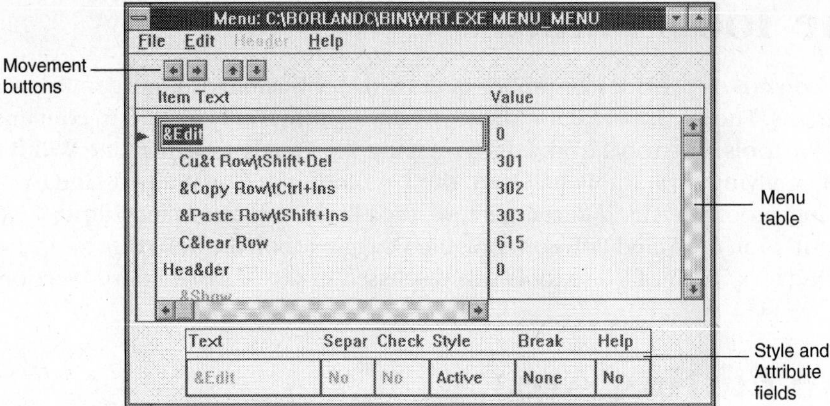

Figure 16.7. *The Menu editor.*

The Menu Table

When the Menu editor is opened, the menu table appears. This table contains an Item Text column and a Value column. In the Item Text column you enter and edit text for the menu items. In the Value column you enter or edit a value for the current item. An additional column, which shows the symbolic name for each menu item, is shown when a header file is open. Table 16.6 lists the keys used to move around the menu table.

Table 16.6. *Keys for moving around the Menu editor.*

Key	*Meaning*
Up arrow	Moves up one row
Down arrow	Moves down one row
Tab	Moves to the right one column
Shift-Tab	Moves to the left one column
Right arrow	Moves to the right one space in the current field
Left arrow	Moves to the left one space in the current field
Home	Moves to the first position of the current field
End	Moves to the last position of the current field

The Item Text Field

The `Item Text` field lists the text that will appear on the menu. This field can contain any alphanumeric character and has a maximum length of 255 characters. The ampersand (&) character defines an activation key. For example, the text field `&Remove` defines the character R as the activation key for the `Remove` menu item. Although the `Item Text` field appears as `&Remove`, the actual menu item appears on the menu as `Remove` with an underscored R. You also can insert a tab mark into the `Text` field by using `\t`. The tab mark is useful for lining up menu options.

The Value Field

The `Value` field contains the ID number for the menu item. The ID number is the unique integer value between 0 and 65,535 returned when you select the menu item. This value is used as a reference to the menu item when you develop the source code that describes the action resulting from a menu selection.

The Symbol Field

The `Symbol` field appears only when a header file is open. This field shows the symbol and ID number in the header file that matches the value for the current menu item. You can use the symbol rather than the ID in the `Value` field in the application's source code.

The Movement Buttons

Four movement buttons are provided above the menu table for moving through the information on a menu item. The Left and Right movement buttons are used to move through a menu item's hierarchy. The Up and Down movement buttons change the position of the menu item relative to other menu items.

The Left and Right movement buttons move an item up or down the menu hierarchy. Windows applications use a hierarchy of menus to represent levels. Each menu item in a top-level menu can offer other menu options in which each option, in turn, offers more options. At each level, the items of the pop-up menus are indented to represent the hierarchic level of the menu. To move the hierarchic level of a particular menu item, the Left and Right movement buttons are provided. The Left movement button moves the item up one level. The Right movement button moves the item down one level. All menus assigned to the moved item are also moved.

The Up and Down movement buttons change the position of menu items. The Up movement button moves the selected ménu item up on the menu. The Down movement button moves the selected menu item down on the menu. Menu items can only be moved up or down at current level in the menu hierarchy. The Up and Down movement buttons are used to change the menu item's hierarchy.

The Style and Attributes Fields

`Style` and `Attribute` fields are provided below the menu table. These fields define menu styles and attributes. Features include the ability to add separator lines, use checkmarks, define text styles, align columns, and assign help attributes.

Separator lines—lines that divide menu items—can be easily added to menus. Simply insert a blank line into the menu table (by pressing Ctrl-Enter) and type `YES` in the `Separator` field. For each blank line, a separator line can be inserted.

You can place checkmarks on menu items to indicate that they are turned on. Many menu items are merely switches that turn features on or off. For this type of menu item, checkmarks are good indicators of the menu item's status. To indicate that a checkmark should be used for the menu item, type `YES` in the menu item's check field.

The text style of the menu item is set by the `Style` field. The three options for the `Style` field are `Active`, `Inactive`, and `Gray`. When the `Active` style is specified, the text is displayed normally. The `Active` style also is used to indicate that the menu item is active. The `Inactive` style indicates that the menu item is initially inactive. Text is displayed normally with the `Inactive` style. The `Gray` style indicates that the menu item does not return a value when selected. Text is displayed as gray text indicating that the menu item cannot be selected.

You can define two types of breaks for menu item alignment: bar and column breaks. To define the breaks, type `None`, `Column`, or `Bar` in the Break field. `None` indicates that no break is defined. `Column` indicates that the menu item will begin a new column. All text subsequent to the setting of the column break is aligned with the new column. The `Bar` break is the same as the column break except that a vertical bar is inserted between the columns.

You can set the Help attribute for top-level menu items and for only one item in a menu. Set the Help attribute by typing `Yes` in the `Help` field of the menu item.

The Test Window

Above the menu table, a Test window is provided that tests the menu as it is developed. The menus displayed in the Test window function exactly as they will in the application. Each time the Test window is used, the menu reflects all current changes to the menu. Figure 16.8 shows the Test window.

Figure 16.8. *The Test window.*

The String Editor

The String editor creates and edits string resources. The application uses string resources to display text such as error messages or captions. Figure 16.9 shows the String editor.

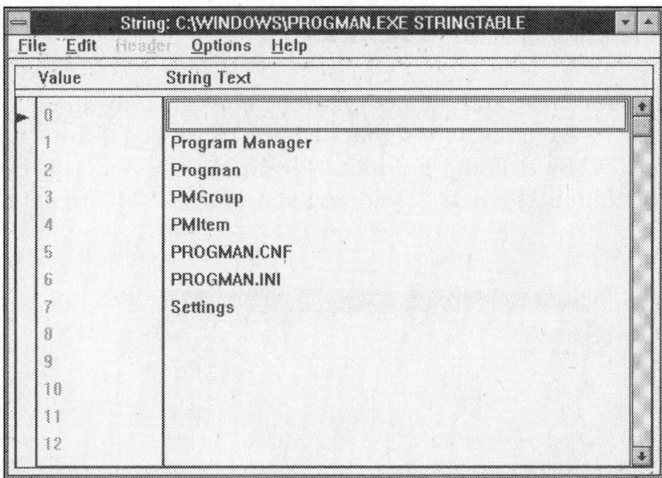

Figure 16.9. *The String editor.*

The String editor defines strings with a string table that contains two or three columns. The first column holds the integer value of the string ID. The second column contains the string as it will be displayed on the screen. The third column appears when a header file is open and shows the symbolic name for the string ID. Table 16.7 lists the keys you use to move around inside the string table.

Table 16.7. *Keys for moving around the String editor.*

Key	*Meaning*
Up arrow	Moves up one row
Down arrow	Moves down one row
Tab	Moves to the right one column
Shift-Tab	Moves to the left one column
Right arrow	Moves to the right one space in the current field
Left arrow	Moves to the left one space in the current field
Home	Moves to the first position of the current field
End	Moves to the last position of the current field

The Header Editor

The Header editor creates and edits symbolic constants. Symbolic constants, or symbols for short, are global constants that are set to equal the ID numbers for various resources. By defining a symbol for an ID number, you can substitute symbols for ID numbers when developing source code. Figure 16.10 shows the Header editor.

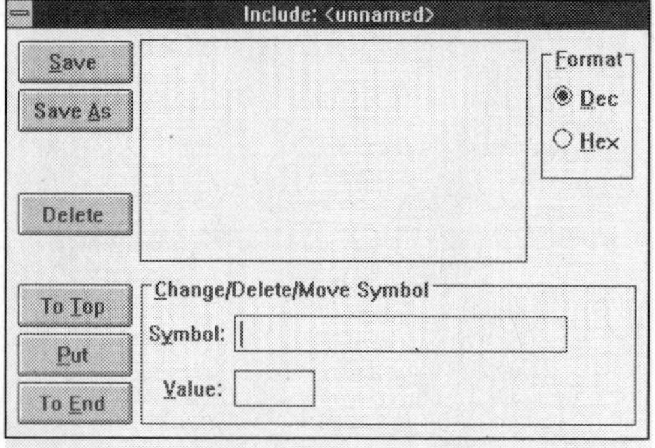

Figure 16.10. *The Header editor.*

17

The Resource Workshop

The Resource Workshop provides the editors and the resource compiler that you need to create your own Windows 3.0 compatible resources. The Resource Workshop includes an Accelerator editor, Dialog editor, Menu editor, Paint editor, String editor, and Text editor. With the Resource editor you can edit both binary files and resource scripts. You can create and edit the resources described in the following section using the Resource Workshop.

Resources

As described in Chapter 16, "The Whitewater Resource Toolkit," Windows applications generally contain numerous graphical elements ranging from dialog boxes to cursors. Under Windows, each of these elements is stored as a resource that can be loaded into the application. Resources are separated from the source code and thus offer several advantages in application development. One advantage is that by separating the resource, you can use a resource definition for several applications.

This reduces development time for subsequent applications. Another advantage is that you can modify a resource without affecting the source code. This enables you to develop resources and source codes simultaneously while shortening software modification phases.

You must understand that resources do not define interface functionality. Resources are merely the visual representation of program elements. For example, you can define a dialog box resource that contains a series of buttons that your application can display. The user can select the buttons of the dialog box; however, nothing happens when the buttons are selected unless the application defines the action for each button. The dialog box resource merely defines the location and appearance (the visual representation) of the buttons. The application must define the action of each button in the dialog box (the interface functionality). You can create and edit the following resources with the Resource Workshop:

- *Accelerators* are keyboard combinations that generate a response by the application. Accelerators are usually tied to menu item selections as alternatives to selecting the menu item with the mouse. Accelerators are created and edited with the Accelerator editor of the Resource Workshop.
- *Bitmaps* are binary representations of graphical images. Bitmaps frequently used in Windows applications include the scroll bars, the minimize arrow, and the maximize arrow. Bitmaps are created and edited with the Paint editor of the Resource Workshop.
- *Cursors* are 32-by-32 pixel bitmaps that indicate the current screen position of the mouse. The most common cursor used by Windows applications is the arrow. Cursors are created and edited with the Paint editor of the Resource Workshop.
- *Dialog boxes* are windows that contain controls, such as buttons and check boxes, that enable the user to select options. Dialog boxes are created and edited with the Dialog editor of the Resource Workshop.
- *Fonts* define the typeface, size, and style of text characters. The Paint editor is used to create and edit font resources.
- *Icons* are bitmaps that represent minimized windows. Icons are usually either 32-by-32 pixels or 16-by-32 pixels. The Paint editor of the Resource Workshop is used to create and edit icons.
- *Menus* provide the user with a hierarchy of choices for using the application. The Menu editor of the Resource Workshop is used to create and edit menu resources.
- *String tables* define a table of text strings that the application can display. For example, a string table may contain all the error messages that the

application can display. String tables can be created and edited with the String editor of the Resource Workshop.

- *User defined and rcdata resources* consist of data (generally read-only text) that you need to add to your executable file.

File Types

The Resource Workshop enables you to edit and create both binary and text files. The following standard Windows file formats are supported by the Resource Workshop:

- .BMP files contain a bitmap resource in binary format.
- .CUR files contain a cursor resource in binary format.
- .DLL files contain a dynamic link library (DLL). You can use the Resource Workshop to bind resources to DLLs. You can also use the Resource Workshop to decompile a .DLL file and edit the resources contained in that .DLL file.
- .EXE files are executable files. You can use the Resource Workshop to bind resources to .EXE files. You can also use the Resource Workshop to decompile a .EXE file and edit the resources contained in that .EXE file.
- .FNT files are binary font files that contain the definition of a font.
- .FON files are font library files that contain a font directory and one or more font definitions. You cannot create .FON files with the Resource Workshop; however, you can use the Resource Workshop to edit .FON files.
- .ICO files contain an icon resource in binary format.
- .RC files are resource compiler script files that contain the definitions of one of more resources.
- .RES files are resource files that contain one or more compiled resources.

The Resource Workshop uses projects to group the various resource types used by an application.

Projects

When you start the Resource Workshop, you will either create a new project or open an existing project. A project file is usually an .RC file that often contains references

to other resources. The .RC file can reference other .RC files, .DLG files, .BMP files, .ICO files, .CUR files, .FNT files, header files, include files, and .PAS (Pascal) files.

You are not limited to creating projects based on an .RC file. You can also create a project based on .RES, .CUR, .ICO, .BMP, or .FNT files. However, most projects are based on the .RC file because you can combine numerous types of resources into one file.

When a project has been created or an existing project has been opened, the Project window of the Resource Workshop is displayed. The Project window lists the files in the project, the types of resources in each file, and the identifiers associated with the resources (as long as the file is not an .EXE, .DLL, or .RES file). The project window for the Solitaire game of Windows (SOL.EXE) is shown in Figure 17.1.

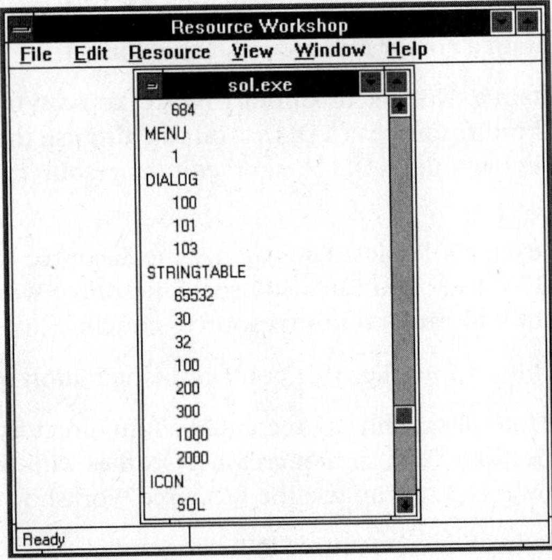

Figure 17.1. *The Project Window.*

The View menu of the Resource Workshop lets you define the way that the Project window displays the resource information. The following options are included in the View menu:

- `By type` groups resources according to the resource type.
- `By file` groups resources according to the files that they are in.
- `Show identifiers` shows any identifiers in the project.
- `Show resources` lists the name of each resource in the project.

- `Show items` displays items within each resource.
- `Show unused types` displays all types of resources, even if some are not included in the project. To use this option, you must check the `By type` option.

You can edit and add resources to the project by using the various editors of the Resource Workshop. The remainder of this chapter introduces the editors of the Resource Workshop.

The Accelerator Editor

The Accelerator editor of the Resource Workshop enables you to create and edit accelerators for your application. Accelerators are key combinations that are often used as substitutes for menu commands to initiate an action in the application. Accelerators are stored in an accelerator table. Each accelerator table entry defines a key combination—an accelerator.

The Accelerator editor is divided into two panes: the outline pane and the dialog box. Figure 17.2 illustrates the Accelerator editor and the Project window. The accelerator table that is loaded into the Accelerator editor in Figure 17.2 is the PBRUSH accelerator table from the Windows Paintbrush executable file.

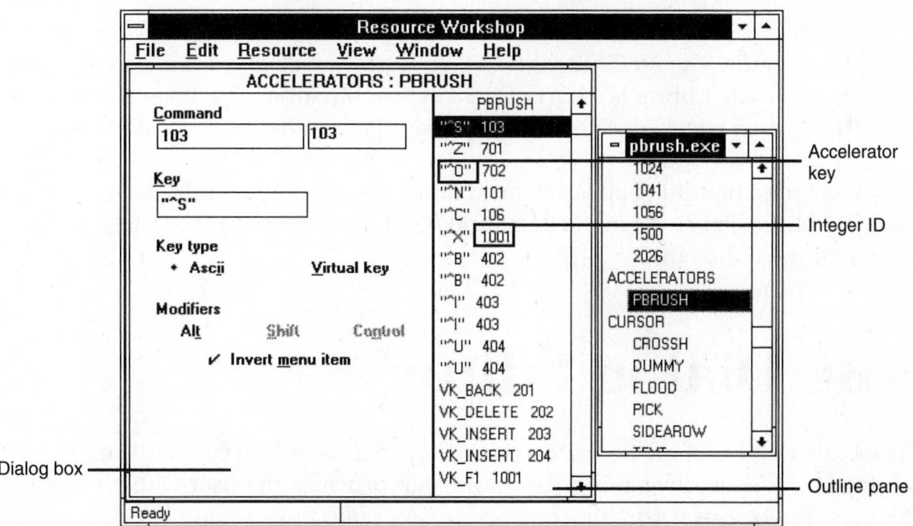

Figure 17.2. The Accelerator editor.

The outline pane of the Accelerator editor (shown on the right side of the editor in Figure 17.2) lists the accelerators, or key combinations, defined in the accelerator table PBRUSH. The lines that follow the accelerator table name PBRUSH are entries to the accelerator table.

An accelerator table entry has two parts. The first part is the accelerator key. The key can either be a virtual key or ASCII key. Virtual keys represent keys such as the function and arrow keys. ASCII keys represent the upper- and lowercase letters. You can join both virtual keys and ASCII keys with any combination of the Ctrl, Alt, or Shift keys. The second part of an accelerator key entry is the integer ID of the command that the accelerator invokes. This integer ID is usually the ID of a menu item.

The Dialog Box pane of the Accelerator editor (shown on the left side of the editor) reflects the settings of the currently selected accelerator. The selections of the dialog box are the following:

- `Command` is the item ID of the command that is invoked by the accelerator. Either an integer or an identifier can be added.
- `Key` is the accelerator key. Highlight this field and press the appropriate key sequence. The editor will automatically fill this field and select the appropriate key type (the appropriate radio button in the `Key Type` field is selected automatically).
- `Key Type` is the key type of the accelerator: either ASCII or virtual. This field is selected automatically when you enter the accelerator in the `Key` field.
- `Modifiers` are the check boxes that define the key combination used for the accelerator. The Alt, Shift, and Ctrl boxes, when checked, indicate that the appropriate button is a part of the key combination. The `Invert Menu Item` box, when checked, causes the associated menu bar command to flash.

When creating or editing an accelerator table, you should start the menu editor so that you can easily see the menu items and IDs that you need to accurately define the accelerators in the table.

The Dialog Editor

The Dialog editor of the Resource Workshop enables you to create dialog boxes. A dialog box is generally a pop-up window that provides the user with a number of choices. Dialog boxes contain controls such as radio buttons and check boxes that enable the user to specify settings and other types of information.

Figure 17.3 shows the Dialog editor. In this figure, the Options dialog box of the Windows Solitaire game is opened for editing. There are four basic parts to the Dialog Editor: the dialog box, the Caption control, the Tools palette, and the Alignment palette.

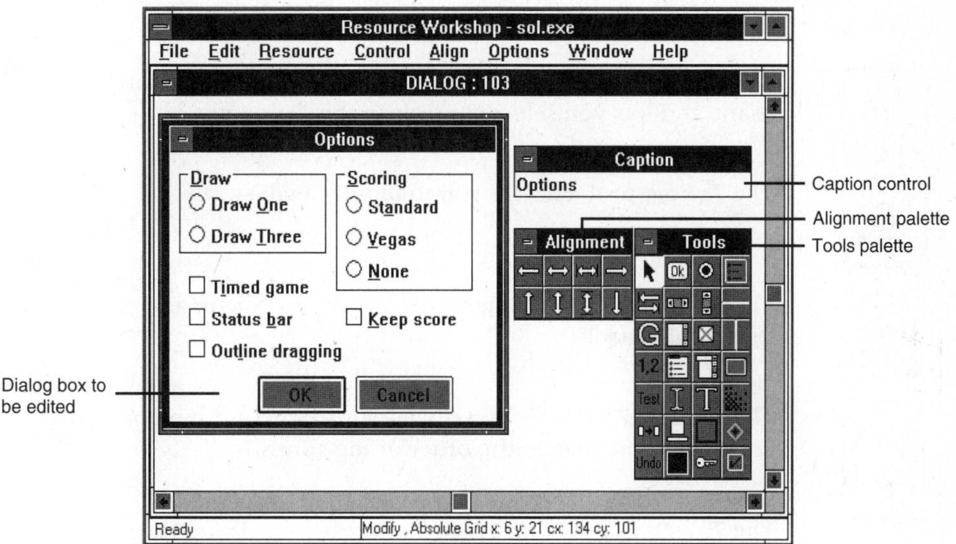

Figure 17.3. *The Dialog editor.*

The Dialog Box

The actual dialog box that you are creating or editing is displayed on the left side of the Dialog editor. The dialog box can be moved, sized, and edited. You can use the features of the Tools palette, the Caption control, and the Alignment palette to edit or create controls in the dialog box. In Figure 17.3, the Options dialog box of the Solitaire game is opened and appears on the left side of the dialog box.

The Caption Control

The Caption control enables you to add a caption to your dialog box. To add text to the control, and thus to your dialog box caption, simply select the field with the mouse and type the appropriate text. In Figure 17.3, the dialog box caption is Options. The Caption control appropriately contains the text Options.

The Tools Palette

The Tools palette of the Dialog editor enables you to add buttons, scroll bars, list boxes, edit controls, static controls, and combo boxes to the dialog box. In Figure 17.3, the Tools palette is shown on the right side of the Dialog editor. The following tools are provided in the Tools palette:

The *Pick Rectangle* tool returns the cursor to the standard arrow shape and lets you select controls in the dialog box.

The *Tab Set* tool \enables you to modify a tab stop.

The *Set Groups* tool changes the cursor to a G icon and enables you to group controls.

The *Set Order* tool changes the cursor to a Set Order icon and enables to you change the order of the controls.

The *Test Dialog* tool enables you to test your dialog box.

The *Duplicate* tool enables you to duplicate controls.

The *Undo* tool performs an "undo" on the last edit to the dialog box.

The *Push Button* tool creates a rectangular button that contains text and can be selected by the user.

The *Radio Button* tool creates a circular button with text on its left or right side that the user can select.

The *Horizontal Scroll Bar* tool creates a horizontal scroll bar.

The *Vertical Scroll Bar* tool creates a vertical scroll bar.

The *List Box* tool creates a rectangle that contains a list of text strings. The list box contains a vertical scroll bar.

The *Check Box* tool creates a rectangular button with text to the left or right. The user can toggle the check box on and off.

The *Group Box* tool creates a rectangular box that visually groups a series of controls. The group box may include a caption.

The *Combo Box* tool creates a combo box. A combo box is a combination of a list box and an edit control.

The *Edit Text Control* tool creates an edit control where a user can enter text.

The *Text Static Control* tool creates static text that appears in the dialog box.

The *Iconic Static Control* tool displays an icon.

The *White Frame Static Control* tool creates a rectangular, empty frame that is the color of the current background and therefore is invisible.

The *Black Rectangle* tool displays a static control icon—a black rectangle.

The *Custom Control* tool creates a control that doesn't match predefined Windows types and has a different window class.

The Alignment Palette

The Alignment palette enables you to align the controls in the dialog box. In Figure 17.3, the Alignment palette appears between the Tools palette and the dialog box. The Alignment palette includes the following tools:

This tool moves controls horizontally and aligns them along the left side of the sizing frame.

This tool moves controls horizontally and centers controls in the sizing frame.

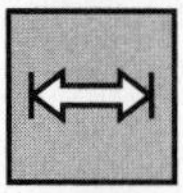

This tool moves the sizing frame and the controls horizontally and centers them in the dialog box.

This tool moves controls horizontally and aligns controls along the right side of the sizing frame.

This tool moves controls vertically and aligns them at the top of the sizing frame.

This tool moves controls vertically and centers the controls in the sizing frame.

This tool moves controls vertically and aligns them at the bottom of the sizing frame.

This tool moves the sizing frame and the controls vertically and centers them in the dialog box.

The Dialog editor is very flexible and enables you to quickly create dialog boxes.

The Menu Editor

A menu provides the user with a hierarchial choice of options for controlling the application. The Resource Workshop's Menu editor (shown in Figure 17.4) enables you to create and test menus. In Figure 17.4, one of the menus from the Windows Solitaire game has been opened for editing.

The Menu editor contains three panes: the outline pane, the test menu pane, and the dialog box pane.

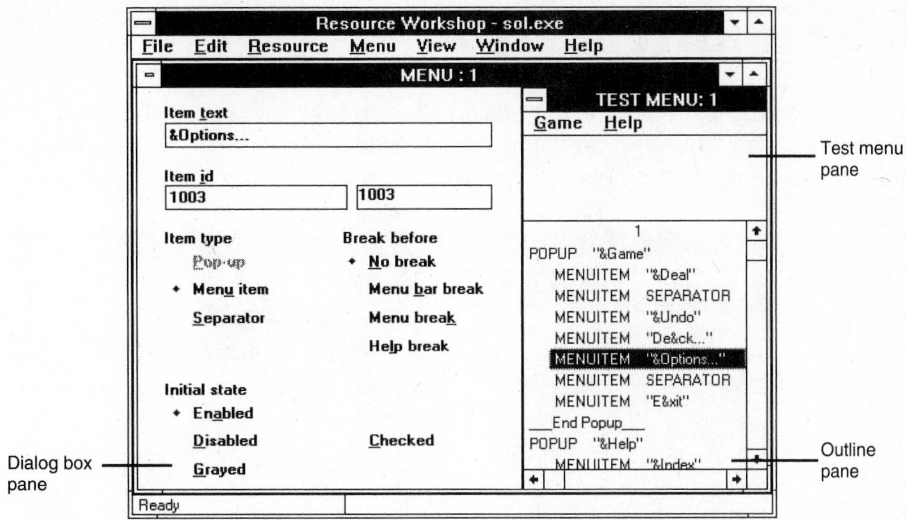

Figure 17.4. *The Menu editor.*

The outline pane is shown in the lower-right corner of the Menu editor in Figure 17.4. The outline pane contains the pseudocode of the menu. You can select lines from this pane to edit. In addition, any lines added to the menu are reflected in this pane.

The test menu pane displays your menu and enables you to test it. In Figure 17.4, the test menu pane is shown in the upper-right corner of the Menu editor.

The dialog box pane enables you to create and edit menu items and pop-up menus. In Figure 17.4, the dialog box pane is shown on the left side of the Menu editor. The selections of the dialog pane are the following:

- `Item Text` is the name of the menu or pop-up command.
- `Item ID` is the menu item ID. Pop-up commands and separators have no ID.
- `Item Type` is the type of item being created or edited: either pop-up, menu item, or separator.
- `Break Before` is the format of the menu commands: either `No Break` (no break before a command), `Menu Break` (new line or new column), `Menu Bar Break` (a new line or new column with a vertical line separator), or `Help Break` (move a menu item to the far right of the Menu bar).

The Menu editor is easy to use and enables you to quickly develop and test menu resources.

The Paint Editor

The Paint editor of the Resource Workshop is used to create and edit bitmap, cursor, font, and icon resources. The Paint editor, shown in Figure 17.5, contains three fundamental parts: the Tools palette, the Colors Palette, and the window pane.

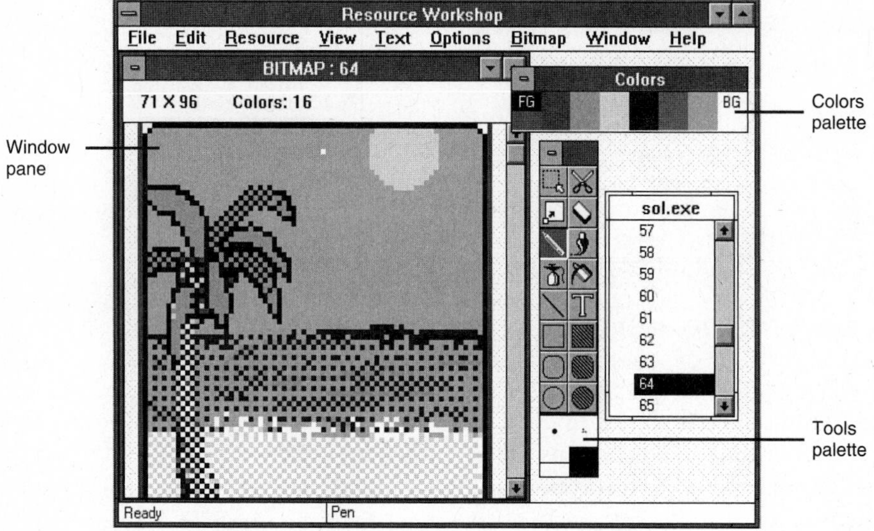

Figure 17.5. Bitmaps and the Paint editor.

The Tools Palette

The Tools palette provides a series of tools that enable you to create and edit a resource. The tools of the Tools palette are similar to the painting tools of most paintbrush programs, including Windows Paintbrush. The following tools are included in the Tools palette:

The *Pick Rectangle* tool enables you to select a rectangular area of the screen for moving, copying, or deleting.

The *Scissors* tool enables you to select a region of the screen for moving, copying, or deleting. The region does not have to be rectangular.

The *Zoom* tool enables you to zoom the image in or out by multiples of 400% (1600% maximum, 100% minimum).

The *Eraser* tool fills a small rectangular area with the current background.

The *Pen* tool draws freehand lines and shapes using either the current background color (press the right mouse button) or the current foreground color (press the left mouse button).

The *Paintbrush* tool paints free-form patterns using the current foreground color (press the left mouse button) or the current background color (press the right mouse button). The paintbrush uses the current brush shape and pattern.

The *Airbrush* tool paints free-form patterns like Paintbrush; however, Airbrush works more like a spray paint can—the faster you move the cursor, the thinner the painted pattern.

The *Paint Can* tool fills an area with the current color. Only a single color is filled.

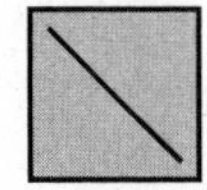

The *Line* tool draws a straight line using the current foreground color (press the left mouse button) or the current background color (press the right mouse button). The line is drawn using the current line width and style.

The *Text* tool enables you to add text to the image. The text is drawn using the current font and text alignment.

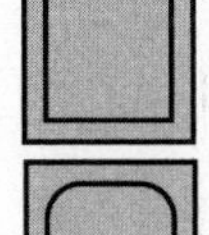

The *Empty Frames* tools enable you to create empty rectangles, rounded boxes, or ellipses. The foreground color (press the left mouse button) or the background color (press the right mouse button) is used to draw the frames. The current line style is used when the image is drawn.

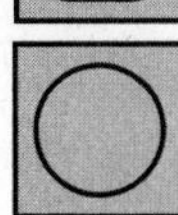

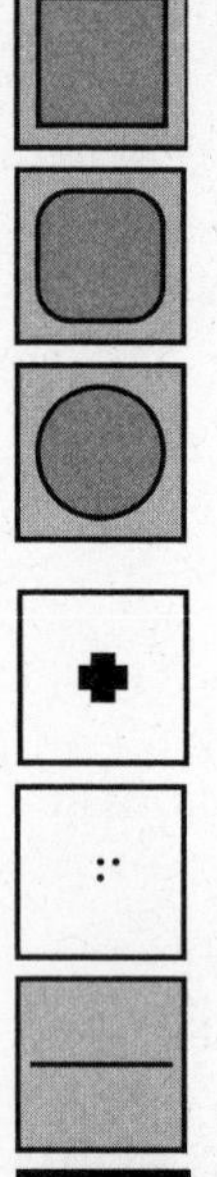

The *Filled-in Frames* tools enable you to create filled rectangles, rounded boxes, or ellipses. The foreground color (press the left mouse button) or the background color (press the right mouse button) is used to draw the figures. The current line style and fill pattern is used when the image is drawn.

The *Style Selections* tools indicate the paintbrush shape, the airbrush shape, the line style, and the patterns used by the other drawing tools.

The Colors Palette

The Colors palette, shown in Figure 17.6, enables you to select the color that you want to draw with. The Colors palette works generally in the same way for all the resources that can be edited by the Paint editor. With the Colors palette, you can select the foreground and background colors and the inverted and transparent areas:

- The *foreground (FG) color* is the color typically used to draw figures such as rectangles and ellipses.
- The *background (BG) color* is the color that appears to be behind the figure.
- The *Transparent area* (icons and cursors only) is the color of the area behind the transparent area that shows through the icon or cursor.
- The *Inverted area* is the color of the area behind the inverted area and shows through the icon or cursor.

The Window Pane

The window pane is where the actual creating and editing of the figure takes place. The window pane can be split into two sections, as shown in Figure 17.6, or can be one pane as shown in Figure 17.5. The window pane can be zoomed in and out so that you can easily edit the figure.

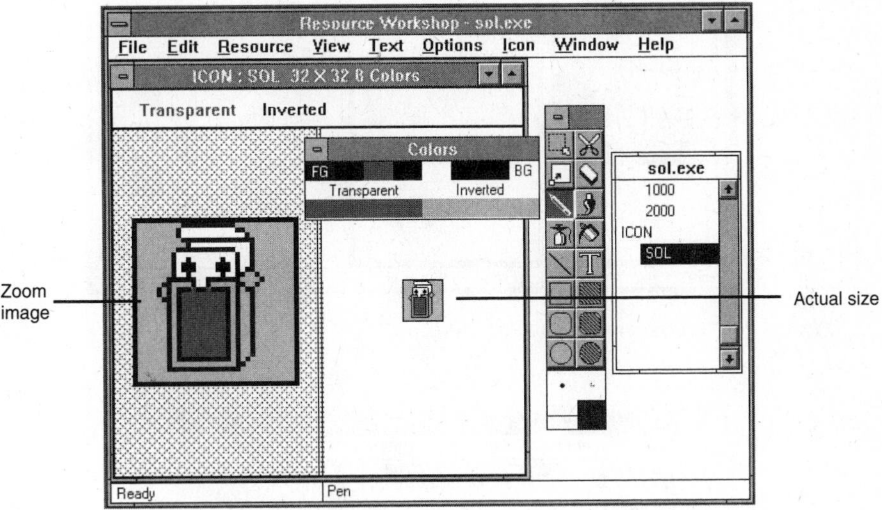

Figure 17.6. *Icons and the Paint editor.*

As was mentioned previously, the Paint editor is used to create and edit bitmaps. Figure 17.5 shows a bitmap being edited with the Paint editor. The bitmap that is being edited is one of the bitmaps used for the Windows Solitaire game.

The Paint editor also can be used to create and edit icons as shown in Figure 17.6. In Figure 17.6, the icon used for the Windows Solitaire game has been opened and is ready for editing.

The Paint editor can create and edit cursor resources. In Figure 17.7, the Paint editor is being used to edit the paintbrush cursor of the Windows Paintbrush program.

In addition to creating and editing icons, cursors, and bitmaps, you can use the Paint editor to create and edit font resources. In Figure 17.8, the Paint editor is being used to create a symbol for a font.

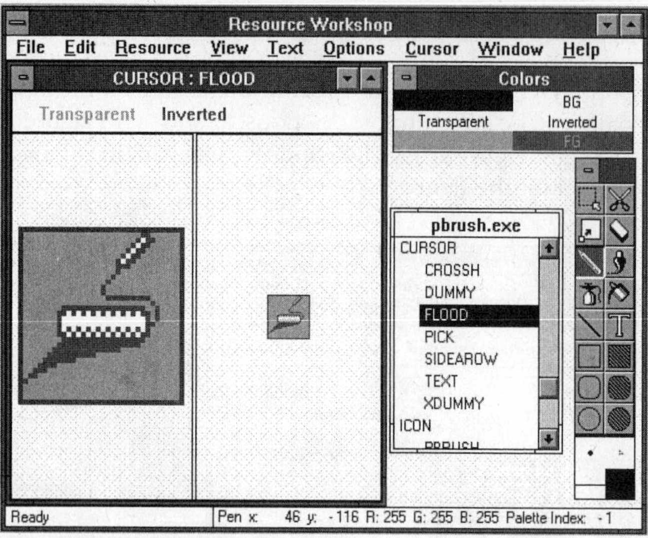

***Figure** 17.7. Cursors and the Paint editor.*

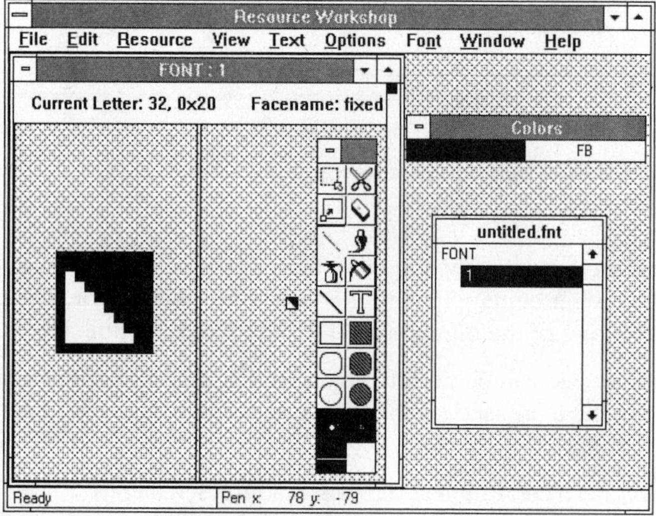

***Figure** 17.8. Fonts and the Paint editor.*

The String Editor

The String editor of the Resource Workshop enables you to create and edit string tables. A string table holds a list of text strings that the application can display.

As Figure 17.9 shows, the String editor contains three columns: the ID Source column, the ID Value column, and the String column.

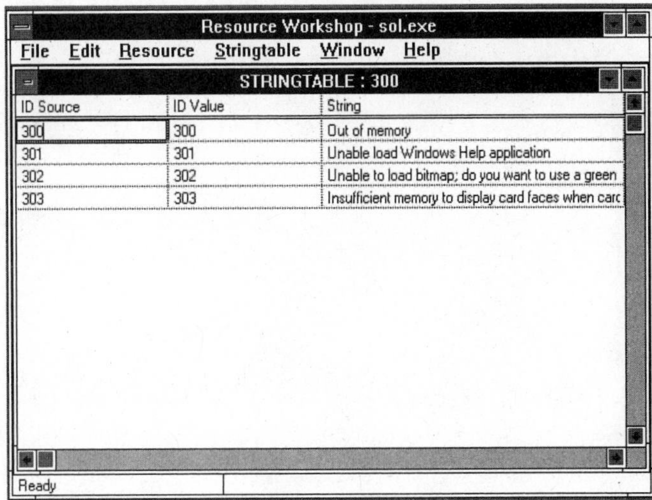

Figure 17.9. *The String editor.*

The ID Source column contains an integer for the string. In this column, you can assign an identifier for the string, such as `sth_FileNew`. However, if no identifier is specified, the integer ID of the string, as specified in the ID Value column, will appear in the ID Source column. In Figure 17.9, notice that the ID Source column and the ID Value column contain the same values.

The ID Value column always contains the integer ID for the string. If the ID Source column contains an identifier rather than the integer ID for the string, both the ID and the identifier can be used in the application to reference the string.

The String column contains the string that the application can display. The string in the String column can be referenced in the application by either the value in the ID Source column or the value in the ID Value column.

Although you can create string tables with a standard text editor, the String editor of the Resource Workshop provides a quick, easy, and efficient way to create string tables.

18

ObjectWindows Classes

This chapter introduces the ObjectWindows classes. The ObjectWindows classes follow:

`Object`	`TFileDialog`	`TRadioButton`
`TApplication`	`TFileWindow`	`TScrollBar`
`TButton`	`TGroupBox`	`TScroller`
`TCheckBox`	`TInputDialog`	`TSearchDialog`
`TComboBox`	`TListBox`	`TStatic`
`TControl`	`TMDIClient`	`TStreamable`
`TDialog`	`TMDIFrame`	`TWindow`
`TEdit`	`TModule`	`TWindowsObject`
`TEditWindow`		

As described previously in this reference section of the book, the ObjectWindows library consists of a hierarchy of classes. Figure 11.2 shows this hierarchy of ObjectWindows classes.

The descriptions for each class include the class header file, a description of the class, data members, constructors as well as the destructor and member functions. Each class is described in the following format:

Class Name:

This heading lists the name of the class.

Class Header File:

This section lists the class header file.

Description:

This section provides a brief description of the class.

Data Member(s):

This section lists the data members for the class and provides the syntax and a description of each data member. The member access for the data member follows the description and is enclosed in brackets. The format for the presentation of data member information is:

`Data Member Name` `Data Member Syntax`

Data Member Description [Member Access]

Constructor(s):

This section lists the constructors for the class. The member access for the constructor follows the description and is enclosed in brackets. The format for the presentation of constructor information is:

`Constructor Syntax` Constructor Description [Member Access]

Destructor:

This section provides the syntax and a description of the destructor. The member access for the destructor follows the description and is enclosed in brackets. The format for the presentation of destructor information is:

`Destructor Syntax` Destructor Description [Member Access]

Additional Member Function(s):

This section lists the member functions of the class, excluding constructors and destructors. The format provides the function name, syntax, and a description of the function. The member access for the member function follows the description and

Description:

The `TApplication` class provides the structure of, and defines the behavior for, ObjectWindows applications. All ObjectWindows applications contain a derived class of `TApplication`.

Data Member(s):

`HAccTable` `HANDLE HAccTable;`

`HAccTable` stores the handle to the current Windows accelerator table. [Public]

`hPrevInstance` `HANDLE hPrevInstance;`

`hPrevInstance` defines the handle of the previous instance of the application; `hPrevInstance` is 0 when there is no previous instance. [Public]

`KBHandlerWnd` `PTWindowsObject KBHandlerWnd;`

`KBHandlerWnd` points to the active window if the keyboard handler for the window is enabled. [Public]

`MainWindow` `PTWindowsObject MainWindow;`

`MainWindow` points to the main window of the application. [Public]

`nCmdShow` `int nCmdShow;`

`nCmdShow` specifies whether the application should be displayed as an icon or as an open window. [Public]

Constructor:

```
TApplication
    (LPSTR AName,
    HANDLE AnInstance,
    HANDLE APrevInstance,
    LPSTR ACmdLine,
    int ACmdShow);
```

Constructs the `TApplication` object [Public]

Destructor:

`~TApplication();` Destroys the `TApplication` object [Public]

Additional Member Function(s):

`CanClose` `virtual BOOL CanClose();`

The `CanClose` function determines whether the application can close. The function calls the `CanClose` member function of the main window and returns the value returned by that `CanClose` member function. TRUE is returned when the application can close. [Public]

`IdleAction` `virtual void IdleAction();`

The `IdleAction` function is invoked when the application is idle. This function can be redefined to perform special functions when the application is idle. [Protected]

`InitApplication` `virtual void InitApplication();`

The `InitApplication` function makes the initializations required for the first executing instance of the application. `InitApplication` can be redefined by derived classes for custom initializations. [Protected]

`InitInstance` `virtual void InitInstance();`

The `InitInstance` function makes the initializations required for all executing instances of the application. [Protected]

`InitMainWindow` `virtual void InitMainWindow();`

The `InitMainWindow` function constructs a generic `TWindow` object using the application name; `InitMainWindow` can be redefined to construct a main window object of a derived class. [Protected]

`isA` `virtual classType isA() const;`

The `isA` function redefines the pure virtual function in class `Object`. This function returns the class ID of `TApplication`. [Public]

`MessageLoop` `virtual void MessageLoop();`

The `MessageLoop` function manages the message loop of the application. [Protected]

`nameOf` `virtual Pchar nameOf() const;`

The `nameOf` function redefines the pure virtual function in class `Object`. This function returns "TApplication", the class ID string. [Public]

`ProcessAccels` `virtual BOOL ProcessAccels(LPMSG PMessage);`

The `ProcessAccels` function processes accelerator messages. [Protected]

`ProcessAppMsg` `virtual BOOL ProcessAppMsg(LPMSG PMessage);`

The `ProcessAppMsg` function calls `ProcessDlgMsg`, `ProcessMDIAccels`, and `ProcessAccels` for the processing of modeless dialog messages, MDI accelerator messages, and accelerator messages, respectively. This function returns TRUE when any modeless dialog message, MDI accelerator message, or accelerator message is encountered. [Protected]

`ProcessDlgMsg` `virtual BOOL ProcessDlgMsg(LPMSG PMessage);`

The `ProcessDlgMsg` function provides message processing of keyboard input for modeless dialog boxes and windows with controls. [Protected]

`ProcessMDIAccels` `virtual BOOL ProcessMDIAccels(LPMSG PMessage);`

The `ProcessMDIAccels` function processes accelerator messages for MDI applications. [Protected]

`Run` `virtual void Run();`

The `Run` function initializes the instance and executes the application. `InitApplication` is called if no other instances of the application are running. `MessageLoop` is called to begin the execution of the application if initialization is successful. [Public]

`SetKBHandler` `void SetKBHandler(PTWindowsObject AWindowsObject);`

The `SetKBHandler` function enables keyboard handling for the specified window. [Public]

Class Name: TButton

Class Header File:

button.h

Description:

The `TButton` class represents a Windows push-button interface. There are two primary types of push-buttons:

- Default buttons. The default button has a heavy, thick border. This button performs the default action of a window. Each window can have only one default button.
- Regular buttons. Regular buttons (buttons that are not the default button) appear with a thin border and can be programmed to perform various actions.

Data Member(s):

None.

Constructor(s):

`TButton(PTWindowsObject AParent, int AnId, LPSTR AText, int X, int Y, int W, int H, BOOL IsDefault, PTModule AModule = NULL);`	Constructs a button object with the specified parent window, control ID, associated text, position, width, and height [Public]

`TButton(PTWindowsObject AParent, int ResourceId, PTModule AModule = NULL);`	Constructs a `TButton` object to be associated with a button control of `TDialog` [Public]
`TButton(StreamableInit);`	`TButton` stream constructor [Protected]

Destructor:

None.

Additional Member Function(s):

`build` `static PTStreamable build();`

The `build` function constructs an object of type `TButton` before reading its data members from an input stream. [Public]

`GetClassName` `virtual LPSTR GetClassName();`

The `GetClassName` function returns "Button", the name of `TButton`'s Windows registration class. [Protected]

Class Name: TCheckBox

Class Header File:

checkbox.h

Description:

The `TCheckBox` class represents a Windows check box interface. There are two primary types of check boxes:

- Two-state boxes, which are either checked or unchecked
- Three-state boxes, which are checked, grayed, or unchecked

Data Member(s):

`Group` `PTGroupBox Group;`

`Group` is a pointer to the `TGroupBox` control object that groups the check box with other check boxes and radio buttons. `Group` is NULL if the check box is not grouped. [Public]

Constructor(s):

`TCheckBox(PTWindowsObject AParent, int AnId, LPSTR ATitle, int X, int Y, int W, int H, PTGroupBox AGroup, PTModule AModule = NULL);`	Constructs a check box object using the specified parent window, control ID, associated text, position, width, height, and group box. [Public]

`TCheckBox(PTWindowsObject AParent, int ResourceId, PTGroupBox AGroup, PTModule AModule = NULL);`	Constructs a `TCheckBox` object associated with a check box control of `TDialog` [Public]
`TCheckBox (StreamableInit)`	`TCheckBox` stream constructor [Protected]

Destructor:

None.

Additional Member Function(s):

```
BNClicked                virtual void BNClicked(RTMessage Msg)
                              = [NF_FIRST + BN_CLICKED];
```

The `BNClicked` function responds to notification messages indicating that the check box was clicked. When the check box is a part of a group, `TGroupBox` is notified of the change in the check box state. [Protected]

```
build                    static PTStreamable build();
```

The `build` function constructs an object of type `TCheckBox` before reading its data members from an input stream. [Public]

```
Check                    void Check();
```

The `Check` function places the check box into the checked state by calling `SetCheck`. [Public]

```
GetCheck                 WORD GetCheck();
```

The `GetCheck` function determines the check state of the check box. This function returns `BF_UNCHECKED` if the check box is unchecked, `BF_CHECKED` if the check box is checked, or `BF_GRAYED` if the check box is grayed. [Public]

```
read                     virtual Pvoid (Ripstream is);
```

The `read` function calls `TWindow::read` to read in the base `TWindow` object. [Protected]

```
SetCheck                 void SetCheck(WORD CheckFlag);
```

The `SetCheck` function sets the state of the check box to the state specified in `CheckFlag`—which can be `BF_UNCHECKED` (box is unchecked), `BF_CHECKED` (box is checked), or `BF_GRAYED` (box is grayed). [Public]

```
Toggle                   void Toggle();
```

The `Toggle` function toggles between the states of the check box. [Public]

```
Transfer                 virtual WORD Transfer(Pvoid DataPtr,
                              WORD TransferFlag);
```

The `Transfer` function transfers the state of the check box to or from the location pointed to by `DataPtr`. `TransferFlag` specifies whether data is transferred to or from the check box:

- When `TransferFlag` is `TF_GETDATA`, `Transfer` transfers the state of the check box to the memory location pointed to by `DataPtr`
- When `TransferFlag` is `TF_SETDATA`, `Transfer` sets the state of the check box to the state specified in the location pointed to by `DataPtr`
- When `TransferFlag` is `TF_SIZEDATA`, `Transfer` returns the size of the transfer data [Public]

`Uncheck` `void Uncheck();`

The `Uncheck` function places the check box in an unchecked state by calling `SetCheck`. [Public]

`write` `virtual void write (Ropstream os);`

The `write` function calls `TWindow::write` to write the base `TWindow` object. [Protected]

Class Name: TComboBox

Class Header File:

combobox.h

Description:

The `TComboBox` class represents a Windows combo box interface. There are three primary types of combo boxes:

- Simple. `CBS_SIMPLE` specifies a simple combo box.
- Drop-down. `CBS_DROPDOWN` specifies a drop-down combo box.
- Drop-down list. `CBS_DROPDOWNLIST` specifies a drop-down list combo box.

Data Member(s):

`TextLen` `WORD TextLen;`

`TextLen` specifies the length of the buffer used for the edit control of the combo box. The maximum length of the buffer is `TextLen` minus one. [Public]

Constructor(s):

`TComboBox(PTWindowsObject AParent, int AnId, int X, int Y, int W, int H, DWORD AStyle, WORD ATextLen, PTModule AModule = NULL);`	Constructs a combo box object with the given parent window, control ID, position, width, height, style, and text length [Public]

`TComboBox(PTWindowsObject AParent, int ResourceId, WORD ATextLen, PTModule AModule = NULL);`	Constructs a `TComboBox` object to be associated with a combo box control of `TDialog` [Public]
`TComboBox (StreamableInit);`	`TComboBox` stream constructor [Protected]

Destructor:

None.

Additional Member Function(s):

`build` `static PTStreamable build();`

The `build` function constructs an object of type `TComboBox` before reading its data members from a stream. [Public]

`GetClassName` `virtual LPSTR GetClassName();`

The `GetClassName` function returns "COMBOBOX", the `TComboBox` Windows registration class. [Protected]

`GetMsgID` `virtual WORD GetMsgID(WORD AnId);`

The `GetMsgID` function returns the message ID of the Windows combo box message that is associated with the ObjectWindows message ID. [Protected]

`HideList` `void HideList();`

The `HideList` function hides the list of a drop-down or drop-down list combo box. [Public]

`nameOf` `virtual Pchar nameOf()const;`

The `nameOf` function redefines the pure virtual function in class `Object`. This function returns "TComboBox", the class ID string for `TComboBox`. [Public]

`read` `virtual Pvoid read(Ripstream is);`

The `read` function calls `TListBox::read` to read in the base `TListBox` object. [Protected]

`SetupWindow` `virtual void SetupWindow();`

The `SetupWindow` function limits the length of the text in the edit control to `TextLen` minus 1 when setting up the combo box. [Protected]

`ShowList` `void ShowList();`

The `ShowList` function shows the list of a drop-down or drop-down list combo box. [Public]

```
Transfer                    virtual WORD Transfer(Pvoid DataPtr,
                                  WORD TransferFlag);
```

The `Transfer` function moves data to and from a transfer buffer pointed to by `DataPtr`. The transfer buffer should point to a `PTComboBoxData` object.

The `TransferFlag` parameter of the `Transfer` function can be set to `TF_SETDATA`, `TF_GETDATA`, or `TF_SIZEDATA` as follows:

- Set `TransferFlag` to `TF_SETDATA` to fill the list of the combo box from the data in the transfer buffer
- Set `TransferFlag` to `TF_GETDATA` to copy the current list selection to the transfer buffer
- Set `TransferFlag` to `TF_SIZEDATA` to return the size of the transfer data; no data is transferred in this case. [Public]

```
write                       virtual void write(Rostream os);
```

The `write` function calls `TListBox::write` to write out the base `TListBox` object. [Protected]

Class Name: TControl

Class Header File:

control.h

Description:

The `TControl` class is an abstract class that is an ancestor to the derived control classes. This class defines functions to create controls and process messages for the derived control classes.

Data Member(s):

None.

Constructor(s):

`TControl(PTWindowsObject AParent, int AnId, LPSTR ATitle, int X, int Y, int W, int H, PTModule AModule = NULL);`	Constructs a control object using the specified parent window, control ID, associated text, position, width, and height [Public]

`TControl(PTWindowsObject AParent, int ResourceId, PTModule AModule = NULL);`	Constructs a control object to be associated with a control of `TDialog` [Public]
`TControl (StreamableInit);`	`TControl` stream constructor [Protected]

Destructor:

None.

Additional Member Function(s):

`GetId` `virtual int GetId();`

The `GetId` function returns the window ID, `Attr.Id`. [Public]

`ODADrawEntire`
```
virtual void ODADrawEntire
     (DRAWITEMSTRUCT _FAR & DrawInfo);
```

The `ODADrawEntire` function responds when notified that a drawable control needs to be redrawn. [Protected]

`ODAFocus`
```
virtual void ODAFocus
     (DRAWITEMSTRUCT _FAR & DrawInfo);
```

The `ODAFocus` function responds when notified that the focus has been given to or taken from the drawable control. [Protected]

`ODASelect`
```
virtual void ODASelect
     (DRAWITEMSTRUCT _FAR & DrawInfo);
```

The `ODASelect` function responds when notified that the selection state of the drawable control has changed. [Protected]

`WMDrawItem`
```
virtual void WMDrawItem(RTMessage Msg) =
     [WM_FIRST + WM_DRAWITEM];
```

The `WMDrawItem` function responds to the `WM_DRAWITEM` message that is sent when the drawable control needs to be redrawn. [Public]

`WMPaint`
```
virtual void WMPaint(RTMessage Msg) =
     [WM_FIRST + WM_PAINT];
```

The `WMPaint` function calls `DefWndProc` for painting. [Public]

Class Name: TDialog

Class Header File:

dialog.h

Description:

The `TDialog` class is the base class for modal and modeless dialog interface elements. For each dialog box there exists a resource definition that describes its controls. The resource definition identifier must be provided to the `TDialog` constructor. The member functions of this class handle communications between the dialog box and its controls.

Data Member(s):

`Attr` `TDialogAttr Attr;`

`Attr` stores the attributes used to create the dialog box. [Public]

`IsModal` `BOOL IsModal;`

`IsModal` indicates whether the dialog box is modal or modeless. TRUE indicates that the dialog box is modal. FALSE indicates that the dialog box is modeless. [Public]

Constructor(s):

`TDialog (PTWindowsObject AParent, LPSTR AName, PTModule AModule = NULL)`	Invokes `TWindowsObject's` constructor [Public]
`TDialog (PTWindowsObject AParent, int ResourceId, PTModule AModule = NULL);`	Invokes a `TWindowsObject` constructor and calls `DisableAutoCreate` [Public]
`TDialog (StreamableInit)`	`TDialog` stream constructor [Protected]

Destructor:

`virtual ~TDialog();`	Frees the memory allocated to `TDialog` [Public]

Additional Member Function(s):

`build` `static PTStreamable build();`

The `build` function invokes the `TDialog` constructor and constructs an object of type `TDialog` before reading its data members from a stream. [Public]

`Cancel`
```
virtual void Cancel(RTMessage Msg) =
        [ID_FIRST + ID_CANCEL];
```

The `Cancel` function calls `CloseWindow` using IDCANCEL when the `Cancel` button for the dialog box is selected. [Protected]

`CloseWindow` `virtual void CloseWindow(int ARetValue);`

The `CloseWindow` function calls `TWindowsObject::CloseWindow` when `this` is a modeless dialog box or `CanClose` for a modal dialog box to determine whether the dialog box can be shut. If `CanClose` is called and returns TRUE, the function calls `TransferData` and then `ShutDownWindow` and passes `ARetValue`. [Public]

```
CloseWindow              virtual void CloseWindow();
```

The `CloseWindow` function calls `TWindowsObject::CloseWindow` when `this` is a modeless dialog box or `CloseWindow` for a modal dialog box to determine whether the dialog box can be shut. IDCANCEL is passed as the integer `ARetValue`. [Public]

```
Create                   virtual BOOL Create();
```

The `Create` function creates a modeless dialog box associated with the object. This function returns TRUE when successful or FALSE when unsuccessful. [Public]

```
Destroy                  virtual void Destroy(int ARetValue);
```

The `Destroy` function destroys the interface element associated with `TDialog`. `TWindowsObject::Destroy` is called for modeless dialog boxes. [Public]

```
Destroy                  virtual void Destroy();
```

The `Destroy` function destroys the interface element associated with `TDialog`. `TWindowsObject::Destroy` is called for modeless dialog boxes. `Destroy` is called, with IDCANCEL passed as `ARetValue`, for modal dialog boxes. [Public]

```
Execute                  virtual int Execute();
```

The `Execute` function executes the modal dialog box associated with `TDialog`. The function should not return until the dialog box is closed. [Public]

```
GetClassName             virtual LPSTR GetClassName();
```

The `GetClassName` function returns the name of the default Windows class for modal dialog boxes. The function returns "OWLDialog" for modeless dialog boxes. [Protected]

```
GetItemHandle            HWND GetItemHandle(int DlgItemID);
```

The `GetItemHandle` function returns the handle of the dialog control that has the ID specified in `DlgItemID`. [Public]

```
GetWindowClass           virtual void GetWindowClass(WNDCLASS
                                 FAR & AWndClass);
```

The `GetWindowClass` function fills `AWndClass` (a `WNDCLASS` structure) with the registration attributes for `TDialog`. This function can be redefined to change the default registration attributes. [Protected]

```
isA                      virtual classType isA() const;
```

The `isA` function redefines the pure virtual function in class `Object`. This function returns the class ID of `TDialog`. [Public]

```
nameOf                    virtual Pchar nameOf()const;
```

The `nameOf` function redefines the pure virtual function in class `Object`. This function returns "TDialog", the class ID string for `TDialog`. [Public]

```
Ok                        virtual void Ok(RTMessage Msg) =
                              [ID_FIRST + ID_OK];
```

The `Ok` function calls `CloseWindow` when the `Ok` button of the dialog box is selected, and passes IDOK. [Protected]

```
read                      virtual Pvoid read(Ripstream is);
```

The `read` function calls `TWindowsObject::read` to read in the base `TWindowsObject` object. [Protected]

```
SendDlgItemMsg            DWORD SendDlgItemMsg(int DlgItemID,
                              WORD AMsg, WORD WParam, DWORD
                              LParam);
```

The `SendDlgItemMsg` function sends the control message (`AMsg`) to the dialog box control that has the ID specified in `DlgItemID`. `WParam` and `LParam` are message parameters. `SendDlgItemMsg` returns the value returned by the control when successful. A return value of zero indicates that the specified ID is invalid. [Public]

```
SetCaption                void SetCaption(LPSTR ATitle);
```

The `SetCaption` function calls `TWindowsObject::SetCaption` unless `ATitle` is –1. [Public]

```
SetupWindow               virtual void SetupWindow();
```

The `SetupWindow` function calls `SetCaption` and `TWindowsObject::SetupWindow` to set up the dialog box. [Protected]

```
ShutDownWindow            virtual void ShutDownWindow();
```

The `ShutDownWindow` function calls `TWindowsObject::ShutDownWindow` for modeless dialog boxes or `Destroy` (passing IDCANCEL) for modal dialog boxes to shut down the dialog box. [Public]

```
ShutDownWindow            virtual void ShutDownWindow(int ARetValue);
```

The `ShutDownWindow` function calls `TWindowsObject::ShutDownWindow` for modeless dialog boxes or `Destroy` (passing `ARetValue`) for modal dialog boxes to shut down the dialog box. [Public]

```
WMClose                   virtual void WMClose(RTMessage Msg) =
                             [WM_FIRST + WM_CLOSE];
```

The `WMClose` function handles the `WM_CLOSE` message. [Protected]

`WMInitDialog`	`virtual void WMInitDialog(RTMessage Msg) = [WM_FIRST + WM_INITDIALOG];`

The `WMInitDialog` function calls `SetupWindow` and is automatically called before the dialog box is displayed. [Protected]

`WMQueryEndSession`	`virtual void WMQueryEndSession(RTMessage Msg) = [WM_FIRST + WM_QUERYENDSESSION];`

The `WMQueryEndSession` function responds when Windows attempts to shut down. [Protected]

`write`	`virtual void write(Ropstream os);`

The `write` function calls `TWindowsObject::write` to write out the base `TWindowsObject` object. [Protected]

Class Name: TEdit

Class Header File:

edit.h

Description:

The `TEdit` class is the Windows edit control interface and provides the features of a text editor. There are two basic types of edit controls:

- Single line edit controls. These controls contain only one line.
- Multiline edit controls. These contain more that one line of text and may contain vertical scroll bars.

Data Member(s):

None.

Constructor(s):

`TEdit(PTWindowsObject AParent, int AnId, LPSTR AText, int X, int Y, int W, int H, WORD ATextLen, BOOL Multiline, PTModule AModule = NULL);`	Constructs an edit control object with the specified parent window, text, position, width, height, and buffer length [Public]
`TEdit(PTWindowsObject AParent, int ResourceId, WORD ATextLen, PTModule AModule = NULL);`	Invokes `TStatic`'s constructor [Public]

`TEdit(StreamableInit);`   `TEdit` stream constructor [Protected]

Destructor:

None.

Additional Member Function(s):

`build`   `static PStreamable build();`

The `build` function invokes the `TEdit` constructor and constructs an object of type `TEdit` before reading its data members from a stream. [Public]

`CanUndo`   `BOOL CanUndo();`

The `CanUndo` function indicates whether it is possible to undo the last edit. This function returns TRUE when it is possible to undo the last edit. [Public]

`ClearModify`   `void ClearModify();`

The `ClearModify` function resets the edit control change flag. [Public]

`CMEditClear`

```
virtual void CMEditClear(RTMessage
     Msg) = [CM_FIRST + CM_EDITCLEAR];
```

The `CMEditClear` function calls `Clear` when a menu item with menu ID `CM_EDITCLEAR` is selected. [Protected]

`CMEditCopy`

```
virtual void CMEditCopy(RTMessage
     Msg) = [CM_FIRST + CM_EDITCOPY];
```

The `CMEditCopy` function calls `Copy` when a menu item with menu ID `CM_EDITCOPY` is selected. [Protected]

`CMEditCut`

```
virtual void CMEditCut(RTMessage Msg) =
     [CM_FIRST + CM_EDITCUT];
```

The `CMEditCut` function calls `Cut` when a menu item with the menu ID `CM_EDITCUT` is selected. [Protected]

`CMEditDelete`

```
virtual void CMEditDelete(RTMessage Msg)
     = [CM_FIRST + CM_EDITDELETE];
```

The `CMEditDelete` function calls `DeleteSelection` when a menu item with menu ID `CM_EDITDELETE` is selected. [Protected]

`CMEditPaste`

```
virtual void CMEditPaste(RTMessage Msg)
     = [CM_FIRST + CM_EDITPASTE];
```

The `CMEditPaste` function calls `Paste` when a menu item with menu ID `CM_EDITPASTE` is selected. [Protected]

`CMEditUndo`

```
virtual void CMEditUndo(RTMessage Msg)
     = [CM_FIRST + CM_EDITUNDO];
```

The `CMEditUndo` function calls `Undo` when a menu item with menu ID `CM_EDITUNDO` is selected. [Protected]

```
Copy                    void Copy();
```

The `Copy` function copies the selected text to the clipboard. [Public]

```
Cut                     void Cut();
```

The `Cut` function deletes the selected text and copies it to the clipboard. [Public]

```
DeleteLine              BOOL DeleteLine(int LineNumber);
```

The `DeleteLine` function deletes the line of text specified in `LineNumber`. This function returns TRUE when successful. [Public]

```
DeleteSelection         BOOL DeleteSelection();
```

The `DeleteSelection` function deletes the selected text. This function returns TRUE when successful. A return value of FALSE indicates that no text was selected. [Public]

```
DeleteSubText           BOOL DeleteSubText(int StartPos, int
                             EndPos);
```

The `DeleteSubText` function deletes the text between the text positions specified in `StartPos` and `EndPos`. This function returns TRUE when successful. [Public]

```
ENErrSpace              virtual void ENErrSpace(RTMessage Msg)
                             = [NF_FIRST + EN_ERRSPACE];
```

The `ENErrSpace` function sounds a beep when the edit control cannot allocate more memory. [Protected]

```
GetClassName            virtual LPSTR GetClassName();
```

The `GetClassName` function returns “EDIT”, the `TEdit` Windows registration class. [Public]

```
GetLine                 BOOL GetLine(LPSTR ATextString, int
                             StrSize, int LineNumber);
```

The `GetLine` function gets a line of text from the edit control. `LineNumber` specifies the line number to retrieve. `ATextString` specifies the location where the line of text is copied. `StrSize` specifies the number of characters to retrieve. [Public]

```
GetLineFromPos          int GetLineFromPos(int CharPos);
```

The `GetLineFromPos` function gets the line number from a multiline edit control of the line that contains the character position specified in `CharPos`. [Public]

```
GetLineIndex            int GetLineIndex(int LineNumber);
```

The `GetLineIndex` function returns the number of characters prior to the specified line number in a multiline edit control. [Public]

```
GetLineLength           int GetLineLength(int LineNumber);
```

The `GetLineLength` function gets the number of characters in a line of text from a multiline edit control. `LineNumber` specifies the line number. [Public]

`GetNumLines` `int GetNumLines();`

The `GetNumLines` function gets the number of lines in a multiline edit control. [Public]

```
GetSelection            void GetSelection(Rint StartPos,
                             Rint EndPos);
```

The `GetSelection` function returns the starting and ending positions of the selected text in `StartPos` and `EndPos`, respectively. [Public]

```
GetSubText              void GetSubText(LPSTR ATextString,
                             int StartPos, int EndPos);
```

The `GetSubText` function gets the text specified by `StartPos` and `EndPos` and returns the text to `ATextString`. [Public]

`Insert` `void Insert(LPSTR ATextString);`

The `Insert` function inserts the text in `ATextString` into the edit control at the current cursor position. [Public]

`IsModified` `BOOL IsModified();`

The `IsModified` function indicates whether the text in the edit control has been modified. This function returns TRUE when the text has been modified. [Public]

`Paste` `void Paste();`

The `Paste` function places the text in the clipboard into the edit control at the current cursor position. [Public]

```
Scroll                  void Scroll(int HorizontalUnit,
                             int VerticalUnit);
```

The `Scroll` function scrolls the multiline edit control horizontally or vertically. `HorizontalUnit` specifies the number of characters to scroll horizontally. `VerticalUnit` specifies the number of characters to scroll vertically. Positive values scroll right and down; negative values scroll left and up. [Public]

```
Search                  int Search(int StartPos, LPSTR AText,
                             BOOL CaseSensitive);
```

The `Search` function searches for the text specified in `AText`. `StartPos` specifies the starting point for the search. `CaseSensitive` indicates whether the text search is case-sensitive. [Public]

```
SetSelection            BOOL SetSelection(int StartPos,
                             int EndPos);
```

The `SetSelection` function defines the current text selection. `StartPos` specifies the first character in the selected text. `EndPos` marks the location immediately after the last character in the selected text. [Public]

`SetupWindow` `virtual void SetupWindow();`

The `SetupWindow` function defines the limit for the number of characters in the edit control as `TextLen` minus 1. [Protected]

`Undo` `void Undo();`

The `Undo` function performs an "undo" on the last edit. [Public]

Class Name: TEditWindow

Class Header File:

editwnd.h

Description:

The `TEditWindow` class defines an object for text editing. `TEditWindow` is derived from `TWindow`.

Data Member(s):

`Editor` `PTEdit Editor;`

`Editor` points to a multiline edit control that provides text editing for the edit window. [Public]

`IsReplaceOp` `BOOL IsReplaceOp;`

`IsReplaceOp` is TRUE when the next search will also perform a replace. [Public]

`SearchStruct` `TSearchStruct SearchStruct;`

`SearchStruct` is a transfer buffer used with `TSearchDialog`. [Public]

Constructor(s):

`TEditWindow (PTWindowsObject AParent, LPSTR ATitle, PTModule AModule = NULL);`	Initializes `Editor` and `SearchStruct` [Public]
`TEditWindow (StreamableInit)`	`TEditWindow` stream constructor [Protected]

Destructor:

None.

Additional Member Function(s):

`build` `static PTStreamable build();`

The `build` function invokes the `TEditWindow` constructor and constructs an object of type `TEditWindow` before reading its data members from a stream. [Public]

```
CMEditFind              virtual void CMEditFind(RTMessage Msg)
                             = [CM_FIRST + CM_EDITFIND];
```

The CMEditFind function initiates a text search and displays a search dialog box when a Find menu item is selected. After the user has made selections to the dialog box, SearchStruct is updated to reflect the user's selections, IsReplaceOp is set to FALSE, and DoSearch is called. [Protected]

```
CMEditFindNext          virtual void CMEditFindNext(RTMessage
                             Msg) = [CM_FIRST +
                             CM_EDITFINDNEXT];
```

The CMEditFindNext function initiates a text search when a Find Next menu item is selected. No dialog box is displayed since it is assumed that SearchStruct contains the proper settings. DoSearch is called by CMEditFindNext. [Protected]

```
CMEditReplace           virtual void CMEditReplace(RTMessage
                             MSG) = [CM_FIRST +
                             CM_EDITREPLACE];
```

The CMEditReplace function initiates a text search and replace operation and displays a search dialog box when a Replace menu item is selected. After the user has made selections to the dialog box, SearchStruct is updated to reflect the user's selections, IsReplaceOp is set to TRUE, and DoSearch is called. [Protected]

```
DoSearch                void DoSearch();
```

The DoSearch function offers search functions using the options and features in SearchStruct. [Public]

```
read                    virtual Pvoid read(Ripstream is);
```

The read function calls TWindow::read to read in the base TWindow object. [Protected]

```
WMSetFocus              virtual void WMSetFocus(RTMessage Msg) =
                             [WM_FIRST + WM_SETFOCUS];
```

The WMSetFocus function sets the focus to Editor edit control when the WM_SETFOCUS message is detected. [Protected]

```
WMSize                  virtual void WMSize(RTMessage Msg) =
                             [WM_FIRST + WM_SIZE];
```

The WMSize function sizes the Editor edit control to the TEditWindow's client area when the WM_SIZE message is detected. [Protected]

```
write                   virtual void  write(Ropstream os);
```

The write function calls TWindow::write to write out the base TWindow object and then PutChildPtr to write out the edit control child window. [Protected]

Class Name: TFileDialog

Class Header File:

filedial.h

Description:

The `TFileDialog` class creates a dialog box that enables the user to select a file for opening or saving. An open and save dialog box resource is provided in the FILEDIAL.DLG dialog box resource.

Data Member(s):

`Extension` `char Extension[MAXTEXT];`

`Extension` holds the file name extension. [Public]

`FilePath` `LPSTR FilePath;`

`FilePath` points to the buffer that returns the file name defined by the user. [Public]

`FileSpec` `char FileSpec[FILESPEC];`

`FileSpec` contains the current file name. [Public]

`PathName` `char PathName[MAXPATH];`

`PathName` contains the current file path. [Public]

Constructor(s):

`TFileDialog (PTWindowsObject AParent, int ResourceId, LPSTR AFilePath, PTModule AModule = NULL);`	Invokes the `TDialog` constructor [Public]
`TFileDialog(StreamableInit);`	`TFileDialog` stream constructor [Protected]

Destructor:

None.

Additional Member Function(s):

`build` `static PTStreamable build();`

The `build` function invokes the `TFileDialog` constructor and constructs an object of type `TFileDialog` before reading its data members from a stream. [Public]

`CanClose` `virtual BOOL CanClose();`

The `CanClose` function returns TRUE when the user entered a valid file name. A return value of FALSE indicates that the user did not enter a valid file name. [Public]

```
HandleDList              virtual void HandleDList(RTMessage Msg)
                               = [ID_FIRST + ID_DLIST];
```

The HandleDList function responds to messages from the directory list box. This function calls UpdateListBoxes when an entry is double clicked. Otherwise, UpdateFileName is called. [Protected]

```
HandleFList              virtual void HandleFList(RTMessage Msg)
                               = [ID_FIRST + ID_FLIST];
```

The HandleFList function responds to messages from the file list box and calls UpdateFileName when the list box selection changes. [Protected]

```
HandleFName              virtual void HandleFName(RTMessage Msg)
                               = [ID_FIRST + ID_FNAME];
```

The HandleFName function responds to messages from the edit control and enables the OK button when the edit control contains text. [Protected]

```
SelectFileName           void SelectFileName();
```

The SelectFileName function selects text from the edit control and sets the focus to the edit control. [Public]

```
SetupWindow              virtual void SetupWindow();
```

The SetupWindow function calls TDialog::SetupWindow to set up the dialog box. [Protected]

```
UpdateFileName           void UpdateFileName();
```

The UpdateFileName function sets the text of the edit control to PathName and selects the text. [Public]

```
UpdateListBoxes          BOOL UpdateListBoxes();
```

The UpdateListBoxes function updates the file and directory list boxes. TRUE is returned when updating is successful. [Public]

Class Name: TFileWindow

Class Header File:

filewnd.h

Description:

The TFileWindow class is derived from TEditWindow and provides the capability to open, read, write, and save files.

Data Member(s):

`FileName` `LPSTR FileName;`

`FileName` is the name of the file being edited. [Public]

`IsNewFile` `BOOL IsNewFile;`

`IsNewFile` indicates whether the file being edited is a new file or a previously opened file. TRUE indicates a new file. FALSE indicates a previously opened file. [Public]

Constructor(s):

```
TFileWindow
(PTWindowsObject AParent,
LPSTR ATitle, LPSTR
AFileName, PTModule AModule = NULL);
```

Invokes the `TEditWindow` constructor [Public]

```
TFileWindow
(StreamableInit);
```

`TFileWindow` stream constructor [Protected]

Destructor:

`virtual ~TFileWindow();` Frees memory associated with `TFileWindow` [Public]

Additional Member Function(s):

`build` `static PTStreamable build();`

The `build` function invokes the `TFileWindow` constructor and constructs an object of type `TFileWindow` before reading its data members from a stream. [Public]

`CanClear` `virtual BOOL CanClear();`

The `CanClear` function determines whether it is all right to clear the text in the editor. This function returns TRUE if the text has not been modified. A return value of FALSE indicates that the text has been modified. [Public]

`CanClose` `virtual BOOL CanClose();`

The `CanClose` function determines whether it is all right to close the file. This function calls `CanClear` and returns the value returned by `CanClear`. [Public]

`CMFileNew`

```
virtual void CMFileNew(RTMessage Msg)
        = [CM_FIRST + CM_FILENEW];
```

The `CMFileNew` function calls `NewFile` when a "FILE New" command with a `CM_FILENEW` ID is detected. [Protected]

`CMFileOpen`

```
virtual void CMFileOpen(RTMessage Msg)
        = [CM_FIRST + CM_FILEOPEN];
```

The `CMFileOpen` function calls `Open` when a "FILE Open" command with a `CM_FILEOPEN` ID is detected. [Protected]

```
CMFileSave                virtual void CMFileSave(TMessage& Msg)
                              = [CM_FIRST + CM_FILESAVE];
```

The `CMFileSave` function calls `Save` when a "FILE Save" command with a `CM_FILESAVE` ID is detected. [Protected]

```
CMFileSaveAs              virtual void CMFileSaveAs(RTMessage Msg)
                              = [CM_FIRST + CM_FILESAVEAS];
```

The `CMFileSaveAs` function calls `SaveAs` when a "FILE SaveAs" command with a `CM_FILESAVEAS` ID is detected. [Protected]

```
NewFile                   void NewFile();
```

The `NewFile` function calls `CanClear` to determine whether the current text in the editor can be cleared. If the existing text can be cleared, a new file is opened. [Public]

```
Open                      void Open();
```

The `Open` function calls `CanClear` to determine whether the current text in the editor can be cleared. If the existing text can be cleared, `Open` displays a file dialog box that enables the user to select a file. Once a file has been selected, `Open` calls `ReplaceWith` and passes the selected file name. [Public]

```
Read                      BOOL Read();
```

The `Read` function reads the contents of a file into the editor and sets `IsNewFile` to FALSE. [Public]

```
read                      virtual Pvoid read(Ripstream is);
```

The `read` function calls `TEditWindow::read` to read in the base `TEditWindow` object. [Protected]

```
ReplaceWith               void ReplaceWith(LPSTR AFileName);
```

The `ReplaceWith` function replaces the current file in the editor with the specified file. `ReplaceWith` calls `SetFileName` and `Read`. [Public]

```
Save                      BOOL Save();
```

The `Save` function saves the current file. When `IsNewFile` is TRUE, `Save` calls `SaveAs`. When `IsNewFile` is FALSE, `Save` calls `Write`. `Save` returns the result of the call to the appropriate function. [Public]

```
SaveAs                    BOOL SaveAs();
```

The `SaveAs` function saves the current file by using a file name retrieved from the user. A "Save" file dialog is displayed to prompt for the file name. Once a file name has been established, `SaveAs` calls `SetFileName` and `Write`. `SaveAs` returns TRUE when the file is successfully saved. [Public]

`SetFileName` `void SetFileName(LPSTR AFileName);`

The `SetFileName` function sets the `FileName` data member and modifies the window caption. [Public]

`SetupWindow` `virtual void SetupWindow();`

The `SetupWindow` function establishes the edit window's Editor edit control. [Protected]

`Write` `BOOL Write();`

The `Write` function saves the contents of the editor to the file specified in `FileName`. TRUE is returned when the file is successfully saved. [Public]

`write` `virtual void write(Ropstream os);`

The `write` function calls `TEditWindow::write` to write out the base `TEditWindow` object and then writes out `FileName`. [Protected]

Class Name: TGroupBox

Class Header File:

groupbox.h

Description:

The `TGroupBox` class is an interface object representing group box elements. Group boxes are used to group a series of check boxes and radio buttons that usually represent user options and application settings.

Data Member(s):

`NotifyParent` `BOOL NotifyParent;`

`NotifyParent` indicates whether the parent should be notified when one of the group box's selection boxes has changed state. [Public]

Constructor(s):

`TGroupBox(PTWindowsObject AParent, int AnId, LPSTR AText, int X, int Y, int W, int H, PTModule AModule = NULL);`	Constructs a group box object using the specified parent window, control ID, text, position, width, and height [Public]
`TGroupBox(PTWindowsObject AParent, int ResourceId, PTModule AModule = NULL);`	Constructs a `TGroupBox` object to be associated with `TDialog` group box control [Public]

`TGroupBox (StreamableInit);` — `TGroupBox` stream constructor [Protected]

Destructor:

None.

Additional Member Function(s):

`build` — `static PTStreamable build();`

The `build` function invokes the `TGroupBox` constructor and constructs an object of type `TGroupBox` before reading its data members from a stream. [Public]

`GetClassName` — `virtual LPSTR GetClassName();`

The `GetClassName` function returns "BUTTON", the `TGroupBox` Windows registration class. [Protected]

`read` — `virtual Pvoid read(Ripstream is);`

The `read` function calls `TWindow::read` to read in the base `TGroupBox` object. [Protected]

`SelectionChanged` — `virtual void SelectionChanged(int ControlId);`

The `SelectionChanged` function notifies the parent window of a group box that a change has been made in the group box *only* if `NotifyParent` is TRUE. [Public]

`write` — `virtual void write(Ropstream os);`

The `write` function calls `TWindow::write` to write out the base `TGroupBox` object. [Protected]

Class Name: TInputDialog

Class Header File:

inputdia.h

Description:

The `TInputDialog` class defines a dialog box that enables the user to input a single text item.

Data Member(s):

`Buffer` — `LPSTR Buffer;`

`Buffer` is a pointer to a buffer that returns the text entered by the user. [Public]

`BufferSize` `WORD BufferSize;`

`BufferSize` stores the size of `Buffer`. [Public]

`Prompt` `LPSTR Prompt;`

`Prompt` points the input dialog box prompt. [Public]

Constructor(s):

`TInputDialog (PTWindowsObject AParent, LPSTR ATitle, LPSTR APrompt, LPSTR ABuffer, WORD ABufferSize, PTModule AModule = NULL);`	Invokes the `TDialog` constructor [Public]
`TInputDialog(StreamableInit);`	`TInputDialog` stream constructor. [Protected]

Destructor:

None.

Additional Member Function(s):

`build` `static PTStreamable build();`

The `build` function invokes the `TInputDialog` constructor and constructs an object of type `TInputDialog` before reading its data members from a stream. [Public]

`read` `virtual Pvoid read(Ripstream is);`

The `read` function calls `TDialog::read` to read in the base `TDialog` object. [Protected]

`SetupWindow` `virtual void SetupWindow();`

The `SetupWindow` function calls `TDialog::SetupWindow` to set up the window and limit the number of characters that can be input to `BufferSize` minus 1. [Protected]

`TransferData` `void TransferData(WORD Direction);`

The `TransferData` function transfers input dialog data. `Direction` can be set to `TF_SETDATA` or `TF_GETDATA`. When `Direction` is `TF_SETDATA`, the text for the controls is set to the text in `Prompt` and `Buffer`. When `Direction` is set to `TF_GETDATA`, the current text in the editor is copied to `Buffer`. [Public]

`write` `virtual void write(Ropstream os);`

The `write` function calls `TDialog::write` to write out the base `TDialog` object. [Protected]

Class Name: TListBox

Class Header File:

listbox.h

Description:

The `TListBox` class is an interface object that represents a Windows list box. `TListBox` creates and manages list boxes.

Data Member(s):

None.

Constructor(s):

`TListBox(PTWindowsObject AParent, int AnId, int X, int Y, int W, int H, PTModule AModule = NULL);`	Constructs a list box object using the specified parent window,control ID, position, width, and height [Public]
`TListBox(PTWindowsObject AParent, int ResourceId, PTModule AModule = NULL);`	Constructs a `TListBox` object to be associated with a `TDialog` list box [Public]
`TListBox (StreamableInit);`	`TListBox` stream constructor [Protected]

Destructor:

None.

Additional Member Function(s):

`AddString` `int AddString(LPSTR AString);`

The `AddString` function adds the string specified in `AString` to the list box. This function returns the string's position in the list box when successful. A negative return value indicates that the function cannot add the string to the list box. [Public]

`build` `static PTStreamable build();`

The `build` function invokes the `TListBox` constructor and constructs an object of type `TListBox` before reading its data members from a stream. [Public]

`ClearList` `void ClearList();`

The `ClearList` function clears all list items. [Public]

`DeleteString` `int DeleteString(int Index);`

The `DeleteString` function deletes the list item at the location specified by `Index`. When successful, this function returns the number of list items remaining. A negative return value indicates that the function cannot delete the list item. [Public]

```
FindExactString          int FindExactString(LPSTR AString, int
SearchIndex);
```

The `FindExactString` function searches the list box for a string that exactly matches the string specified in `AString`. The search begins at the index specified in `SearchIndex`. The index of the matching string is returned. [Public]

```
FindString               int FindString(LPSTR AString, int SearchIndex);
```

The `FindString` function searches the list box for a string that begins with the string specified in `AString`. The search begins at the index specified in `SearchIndex`. The index of the matching string is returned. [Public]

```
GetClassName             virtual LPSTR GetClassName();
```

The `GetClassName` function returns "LISTBOX", the `TListBox` Windows registration class. [Protected]

```
GetCount                 int GetCount();
```

When successful, the `GetCount` function returns the number of list box items. A negative return value indicates that the function is unsuccessful. [Public]

```
GetMsgID                 virtual WORD GetMsgID(WORD AMsg);
```

The `GetMsgID` function returns the Windows list box message ID associated with the specified ObjectWindows message ID. [Protected]

```
GetSelIndex              int GetSelIndex();
```

When successful, the `GetSelIndex` function returns the position of the currently selected item. A negative return value indicates that the function is unsuccessful. [Public]

```
GetSelString             int GetSelString(LPSTR AString, int
                              MaxChars);
```

The `GetSelString` function places the currently selected list item in `AString`. `MaxChars` specifies the maximum number of characters to copy. When successful, this function returns the length of the copied string. A negative return value indicates that the function is unsuccessful. [Public]

```
GetString                int GetString(LPSTR AString, int Index);
```

The `GetString` function copies the item at the location specified in `Index` to `AString`. When successful, this function returns the length of the copied string. A negative return value indicates that the function is unsuccessful. [Public]

```
GetStringLen             int GetStringLen(int Index);
```

When successful, the `GetStringLen` function returns the length of the item at the location specified in `Index`. A negative return value indicates that the function is unsuccessful. [Public]

```
InsertString            int InsertString(LPSTR AString, int
                            Index);
```

The `InsertString` function inserts the string specified in `AString` at the list position specified in `Index`. When successful, this function returns the string's list position. A negative return value indicates that the function is unsuccessful. [Public]

```
SetSelIndex             int SetSelIndex(int Index);
```

When successful, the `SetSelIndex` function selects the item at the position specified in `Index`. This function returns a negative value when unsuccessful. `Index` can be set to –1 to clear all selections. [Public]

```
SetSelString            int SetSelString(LPSTR AString, int
                            AIndex);
```

The `SetSelString` function selects the list box item that matches `AString`. The search for a match begins at the position specified by `AIndex`. When successful, this function returns the position of the matching item. A negative return value indicates that the function is unsuccessful. [Public]

```
Transfer                virtual WORD Transfer(Pvoid DataPtr,
                            WORD TransferFlag);
```

The `Transfer` function uses the buffer pointed to by `DataPtr` to transfer data. The transfer buffer contains a pointer to a `PTListBoxData` object.

The `TransferFlag` parameter of the `Transfer` function can be set to `TF_SETDATA`, `TF_GETDATA`, or `TF_SIZEDATA` as follows:

- Set `TransferFlag` to `TF_SETDATA` to fill the list and select one or more items using the data in the buffer.
- Set `TransferFlag` to `TF_GETDATA` to fill the buffer using the current list and selection(s) from the list box.
- Set `TransferFlag` to `TF_SIZEDATA` to return the size of `PTListBoxData`. No data is transferred in this case. [Public]

Class Name: TMDIClient

Class Header File:

mdi.h

Description:

The `TMDIClient` class represents Multiple Document Interface (MDI) client windows and manages the MDI client area and the MDI child windows.

Data Member(s):

`ClientAttr`	`LPCLIENTCREATESTRUCT ClientAttr;`

`ClientAttr` stores the attributes of the MDI client window. [Public]

Constructor(s):

`TMDIClient(PTMDIFrame AParent, PTModule AModule = NULL);`	Constructs an MDI client window object [Public]
`TMDIClient(PTMDIFrame AParent, HWND AnHWindow);`	Constructs an MDI client object to be associated with the MDI client window [Public]
`TMDIClient (StreamableInit)`	`TMDIClient` stream constructor [Protected]

Destructor:

`~TMDIClient();`	Frees the `ClientAttr` structure [Public]

Additional Member Function(s):

`ArrangeIcons`	`virtual void ArrangeIcons();`

The `ArrangeIcons` function aligns MDI child window icons along the bottom of the MDI client window. [Public]

`build`	`static PTStreamable build();`

The `build` function invokes the `TMDIClient` constructor and constructs an object of type `TMDIClient` before reading its data members from a stream. [Public]

`CascadeChildren`	`virtual void CascadeChildren();`

The `CascadeChildren` function adjusts the size of all MDI child windows that are not minimized and arranges them in an overlapping style. [Public]

`GetClassName`	`virtual LPSTR GetClassName();`

The `GetClassName` function returns "MDICLIENT", the `TMDIClient` Windows registration class name. [Protected]

`read`	`virtual Pusid read(Ripstream is);`

The `read` function calls `TWindows::read` to read the base `TWindows` object. [Protected]

`TileChildren`	`virtual void TileChildren();`

The `TileChildren` function adjusts the size of all MDI child windows that are not minimized and arranges them in a nonoverlapping, tiled style. [Public]

`WMPaint`	`virtual void WMPaint(RTMessage Msg) = [WM_FIRST + WM_PAINT];`

The `WMPaint` function redefines `TWindow::WMPaint` to call `DefWndProc`. [Protected]

`write` `virtual void write (Ropstream os);`

The `write` function calls `TWindow::write` to write out the base `TWindow` object. [Protected]

Class Name: TMDIFrame

Class Header File:

mdi.h

Description:

The `TMDIFrame` class represents Multiple Document Interface (MDI) frame windows, the main windows for MDI applications. `TMDIFrame` can automatically create and manipulate MDI child windows.

Data Member(s):

`ChildMenuPos` `int ChildMenuPos;`

`ChildMenuPos` stores the top-level menu position for the MDI window. [Public]

`ClientWnd` `PTMDIClient ClientWnd;`

`ClientWnd` is a pointer to the `TMDIFrame` client window. [Public]

Constructor(s):

`TMDIFrame(LPSTR ATitle, int MenuId, PTModule AModule = NULL);`	Constructs an MDI frame window object using the specified caption and menu [Public]
`TMDIFrame(HWND AnHWindow, HWND ClientWnd);`	Constructs an MDI window object associated with the specified handle. [Public]
`TMDIFrame StreamableInit)`	`TMDIFrame` stream constructor [Protected]

Destructor:

`virtual ~TMDIFrame();`	Deletes the MDI client window object [Public]

Additional Member Function(s):

`ArrangeIcons` `virtual void ArrangeIcons();`

The `ArrangeIcons` function calls the `ArrangeIcons` member function of the client window to arrange the iconized MDI child windows along the bottom of the client window. [Public]

```
build                    static PTStreamable build();
```

The `build` function invokes the `TMDIFrame` constructor and constructs an object of type `TMDIFrame` before reading its data members from a stream. [Public]

```
CascadeChildren          virtual void CascadeChildren();
```

The `CascadeChildren` function calls the `CascadeChildren` member function of the client window to arrange the MDI child windows that are not iconized in an overlapping style. [Protected]

```
CloseChildren            virtual BOOL CloseChildren();
```

The `CloseChildren` function calls the `CanClose` member function of each MDI child window and closes all the child windows if possible. [Public]

```
CMArrangeIcons           virtual void CMArrangeIcons(RTMessage
                              Msg) = [CM_FIRST +
                              CM_ARRANGEICONS];
```

The `CMArrangeIcons` function calls `ArrangeIcons` when a menu item with a `CM_ARRANGEICONS` ID is selected. [Protected]

```
CMCascadeChildren        virtual void CMCascadeChildren(RTMessage
                              Msg) = [CM_FIRST +
                              CM_CASCADECHILDREN];
```

The `CMCascadeChildren` function calls `CascadeChildren` when a menu item with a `CM_CASCADECHILDREN` ID is selected. [Protected]

```
CMCloseChildren          virtual void CMCloseChildren(RTMessage
                              Msg) = [CM_FIRST +
                              CM_CLOSECHILDREN];
```

The `CMCloseChildren` function calls `CloseChildren` when a menu item with a `CM_CLOSECHILDREN` ID is selected. [Protected]

```
CMCreateChild            virtual void CMCreateChild(RTMessage
                              Msg) = [CM_FIRST + CM_CREATECHILD];
```

The `CMCreateChild` function calls `CreateChild` when a menu item with a `CM_CREATECHILD` ID is selected. [Protected]

```
CMTileChildren           virtual void CMTileChildren(RTMessage
                              Msg) = [CM_FIRST +
                              CM_TILECHILDREN];
```

The `CMTileChildren` function calls `TileChildren` when a menu item with a `CM_TILECHILDREN` ID is selected. [Protected]

```
CreateChild              virtual PTWindowsObject CreateChild();
```

The `CreateChild` function creates an MDI child window and returns a pointer to the created child window. [Public]

```
GetClassName            virtual LPSTR GetClassName();
```

The `GetClassName` function returns "OWLMDIFrame". [Protected]

```
GetClient               virtual PTMDIClient GetClient();
```

The `GetClient` function returns the pointer to the client window stored in `ClientWnd`. [Public]

```
GetWindowClass          virtual void GetWindowClass(WNDCLASS _FAR &
                              AWndClass);
```

The `GetWindowClass` function calls `TWindow::GetWindowClass` and sets `AWndClass.Style` to 0. [Protected]

```
InitChild               virtual PTWindowsObject InitChild();
```

The `InitChild` function constructs an instance of `TWindow` as an MDI child window. This function returns the pointer to the instance. You can redefine this member function in the derived window class to construct an instance of a derived MDI child class. [Public]

```
InitClientWindow        virtual void InitClientWindow();
```

The `InitClientWindow` function constructs the MDI client window as an instance of `TMDIClient`. The pointer to the client window is stored in `ClientWnd`. [Public]

```
read                    virtual Pvoid read (Ripstream is);
```

The `read` function calls `TWindow::read` to read in the base `TWindow` object. [Protected]

```
SetupWindow             virtual void SetupWindow();
```

The `SetupWindow` function calls `InitClientWindow` to construct an MDI client window and creates the interface element. [Protected]

```
TileChildren            virtual void TileChildren();
```

The `TileChildren` function calls the `TileChildren` member function of the client window to size and arrange the MDI child windows that are not iconized in a nonoverlapping style. [Protected]

```
write                   virtual void write(Ropstream os);
```

The `write` function calls `TWindow::write` to write out the base `TWindow` object. [Protected]

Class Name: TModule

Class Header File:

module.h

Description:

The `TModule` class defines behaviors shared by library and application modules. Instances of `TModule` act as stand-ins for library (DLL) modules.

Data Member(s):

`hInstance` `HANDLE hInstance;`

`hInstance` stores the handle of the currently executing instance of the application. [Public]

`lpCmdLine` `LPSTR lpCmdLine;`

`lpCmdLine` points to the command line string. [Public]

`Name` `LPSTR Name;`

`Name` is the application name or DLL module name. [Public]

`Status` `int Status;`

`Status` indicates whether an error has been generated that could keep the application from creating the main window or entering the message loop. [Public]

Constructor(s):

`TModule(LPSTR AName, HANDLE AnInstance, LPSTR ACmdLine);` Initializes the data members for the object [Public]

Destructor:

`virtual ~TModule();` Destroys a `TModule` object [Public]

Additional Member Function(s):

`Error` `virtual void Error(int ErrorCode);`

The `Error` function processes the error specified in `ErrorCode`. `ErrorCode` can be defined by the application or can be one of the following ObjectWindows errors:

```
EM_INVALIDWINDOW

EM_OUTOFMEMORY

EM_INVALIDCLIENT

EM_INVALIDCHILD

EM_INVALIDMAINWINDOW
```

The `Error` function displays a message box that lists the error code and asks the user to proceed. Depending on the input from the user, the program may continue or be terminated. [Public]

```
ExecDialog                virtual int ExecDialog(PTWindowsObject
                                 ADialog);
```

The `ExecDialog` function determines whether the specified dialog object is valid and, if so, executes the dialog object. This function returns IDCANCEL when the specified dialog object is not valid. [Public]

```
GetClientHandle           HWND GetClientHandle(HWND AnHWindow);
```

The `GetClientHandle` function returns the handle of the MDI client window for the specified window. This function returns zero when the window has no MDI client window. [Public]

```
GetParentObject           virtual PTWindowsObject
                          GetParentObject(HWND ParentHandle);
```

The `GetParentObject` function is called in a DLL to get a pointer to a parent window object. [Public]

```
hashValue                 virtual hashValueType hashValue() const;
```

The `hashValue` function must be redefined by all objects derived from the base class object. This function returns the hash value of `TModule`, `hInstance`. [Public]

```
isA                       virtual classType isA() const;
```

The `isA` function must be redefined by all objects derived from the base class object. This function returns the object ID of `TModule`, `moduleClass`. [Public]

```
isEqual                   virtual int isEqual(RCObject module)
                                 const;
```

The `isEqual` function redefines the pure virtual function in class `Object`. [Public]

```
LowMemory                 BOOL LowMemory();
```

The `LowMemory` function returns TRUE when the safety pool has been used up. [Public]

```
MakeWindow                virtual PTWindowsObject MakeWindow
                                 (PTWindowsObject AWindowsObject);
```

The `MakeWindow` function creates a window or modeless dialog element and associates it with the specified object as long as the specified object is valid. A return value of NULL indicates that the function is unsuccessful. [Public]

```
nameOf                    virtual Pchar nameOf() const;
```

The `nameOf` function redefines the pure virtual function in class `Object`. This function returns the class ID string of `TModule`, "TModule". [Public]

```
printOn                  virtual void printOn(Rostream
                              outputStream) const;
```

The `printOn` function redefines the pure virtual function in class `Object`. The hexadecimal value of the instance handle for the module is printed on the specified stream. [Public]

```
RestoreMemory            void RestoreMemory();
```

The `RestoreMemory` function allocates a safety pool. [Public]

```
ValidWindow              virtual PTWindowsObject ValidWindow
                              (PWindowsObject AWindowsObject);
```

The `ValidWindow` function determines whether the specified object is valid. This function returns the pointer to the object when the object is valid. The object is deleted and NULL is returned when the object is not valid. [Public]

Class Name: TRadioButton

Class Header File:

radiobut.h

Description:

The `TRadioButton` class is derived from `TCheckBox` and represents a Windows radio button. A radio button is a two-state button; it can either be checked or unchecked. `TRadioButton` creates and manages radio buttons.

Data Member(s):

None.

Constructor(s):

`TRadioButton (PTWindowsObject AParent, int AnId, LPSTR ATitle, int X, int Y, int W, int H, PTGroupBox AGroup, PTModule AModule = NULL);`	Constructs a radio button object using the specified parent, control ID, text, position, width, height, and group [Public]
`TRadioButton (PTWindowsObject AParent, int ResourceId, PTGroupBox AGroup, PTModule AModule = NULL);`	Constructs a `TRadioButton` object [Public]

`TRadioButton (StreamableInit);`	`TRadioButton` stream constructor [Protected]

Destructor:

None.

Additional Member Function(s):

`build`	`static PTStreamable build();`

The `build` function invokes the `TRadioButton` constructor and constructs an object of type `TRadioButton` before reading its data members from a stream. [Public]

Class Name: TScrollBar

Class Header File:

scrollba.h

Description:

The `TScrollBar` class represents and manages standalone horizontal and vertical scroll bars. Do not use `TScrollBar` objects with windows that contain the `WS_HSCROLL` or `WS_VSCROLL` style attributes.

Data Member(s):

`LineMagnitude`	`int LineMagnitude;`

`LineMagnitude` specifies the number of range units that the scroll bar is scrolled when one of the scroll bar arrows is clicked. By default, `LineMagnitude` is 1 and the scroll range is 0 to 100. [Public]

`PageMagnitude`	`int PageMagnitude;`

`PageMagnitude` specifies the number of range units that the scroll bar is scrolled when the scrolling area of the scroll bar is clicked. By default, `PageMagnitude` is 10 and the scroll range is 0 to 100. [Public]

Constructor(s):

`TScrollBar (PTWindowsObject AParent, int AnId, int X, int Y, int W, int H, BOOL IsHScrollBar, PTModule AModule = NULL);`	Constructs a scroll bar object using the specified parent, control ID, position, width, and height; set `IsHScrollBar` to TRUE to add `SBS_HORZ` to the styles in `Attr.Style` or `FALSE` to add `SBS_VERT` to the styles in `Attr.Style` [Public]

`TScrollBar (PTWindowsObject AParent, int ResourceId, PTModule AModule = NULL);`	Constructs a `TScrollBar` object [Public]
`TScrollBar (StreamableInit);`	`TScrollBar` stream constructor [Protected]

Destructor:

None.

Additional Member Function(s):

`build` `static PTStreamable build();`

The `build` function invokes the `TScrollBar` constructor and constructs an object of type `TScrollBar` before reading its data members from a stream. [Public]

`DeltaPos` `int DeltaPos(int Delta);`

The `DeltaPos` function changes the thumb position of the scroll bar by calling `SetPosition`. `Delta` specifies the amount to move the thumb position (negative for left or up, positive for right or down). `DeltaPos` returns the new thumb position. [Public]

`GetClassName` `virtual LPSTR GetClassName();`

The `GetClassName` function returns "SCROLLBAR", the `TScrollBar` Windows registration class name. [Protected]

`GetPosition` `int GetPosition();`

The `GetPosition` function returns the thumb position of the scroll bar. [Public]

`GetRange` `void GetRange(Rint LoVal, Rint HiVal);`

The `GetRange` function returns the scroll bar range in `LoVal` and `HiVal`. [Public]

`read` `virtual Pvoid read (Ripstream is);`

The `read` function calls `TWindow::read` to read in the base `TWindow` object. [Protected]

```
SBBottom        virtual void SBBottom(RTMessage Msg) =
                     [NF_FIRST + SB_BOTTOM];
```

The `SBBottom` function calls `SetPosition` to move the scroll thumb to the bottom of the scroll bar for vertical scroll bars or to the right for horizontal scroll bars. [Protected]

```
SBLineDown      virtual void SBLineDown(RTMessage Msg) =
                     [NF_FIRST + SB_LINEDOWN];
```

The `SBLineDown` function calls `SetPosition` to move the scroll thumb down for vertical scroll bars or right for horizontal scroll bars. `LineMagnitude` defines the number of range units the thumb is moved. [Protected]

SBLineUp

```
virtual void SBLineUp(RTMessage Msg) =
      [NF_FIRST + SB_LINEUP];
```

The `SBLineUp` function calls `SetPosition` to move the scroll thumb up for vertical scroll bars or left for horizontal scroll bars. `LineMagnitude` defines the number of range units the thumb is moved. [Protected]

SBPageDown

```
virtual void SBPageDown(RTMessage Msg) =
      [NF_FIRST + SB_PAGEDOWN];
```

The `SBPageDown` function calls `SetPosition` to move the scroll thumb down for vertical scroll bars or right for horizontal scroll bars. `PageMagnitude` defines the number of range units the thumb is moved. [Protected]

SBPageUp

```
virtual void SBPageUp(RTMessage Msg) =
      [NF_FIRST + SB_PAGEUP];
```

The `SBPageUp` function calls `SetPosition` to move the scroll thumb up for vertical scroll bars or left for horizontal scroll bars. `PageMagnitude` defines the number of range units the thumb is moved. [Protected]

SBThumbPosition

```
virtual void SBThumbPosition(RTMessage
      Msg) = [NF_FIRST +
      SB_THUMBPOSITION];
```

The `SBThumbPosition` function calls `SetPosition` to move the scroll thumb. [Protected]

SBThumbTrack

```
virtual void SBThumbTrack(RTMessage
      Msg) = [NF_FIRST + SB_THUMBTRACK];
```

The `SBThumbTrack` function calls `SetPosition` to move the scroll thumb to a new position as it is being dragged. [Protected]

SBTop

```
virtual void SBTop(RTMessage Msg) =
      [NF_FIRST + SB_TOP];
```

The `SBTop` function calls `SetPosition` to move the scroll thumb to the top for vertical scroll bars or the left for horizontal scroll bars. [Protected]

SetPosition

```
void SetPosition(int ThumbPos);
```

The `SetPosition` function moves the thumb position to the position specified in `ThumbPos`. The thumb position will not be moved outside the range of the scroll bar. [Public]

SetRange

```
void SetRange(int LoVal, int HiVal);
```

The `SetRange` function sets to scroll bar range to the values specified in `LoVal` and `HiVal`. [Public]

SetupWindow

```
virtual void SetupWindow();
```

The `SetupWindow` function defines the scroll bar range as 0 to 100. [Protected]

```
Transfer                virtual WORD Transfer(Pvoid DataPtr,
                             WORD TransferFlag);
```

The `Transfer` function uses the data buffer pointed to by `DataPtr` to transfer scroll bar information. `DataPtr` should point to a `TScrollBarData` structure, as follows:

```
struct TScrollBarData {
     int LowValue;
     int HighValue;
     int Position;
};
```

[Public]

```
write                   virtual void write(Ropstream os);
```

The `write` function calls `TWindow::write` to write out the base `TWindow` object. [Protected]

Class Name: TScroller

Class Header File:

scroller.h

Description:

The `TScroller` class provides automated scrolling for window displays. `TScroller` is usually associated with scroll bars; however, `TScroller` works with windows without scroll bars. Windows without scroll bars are automatically scrolled when the mouse is dragged from inside the client area to outside the client area.

Data Member(s):

```
AutoMode                BOOL AutoMode;
```

`AutoMode` indicates whether auto-scrolling is in effect. TRUE indicates auto-scrolling is in effect. FALSE indicates auto-scrolling is not in effect. By default, `AutoMode` is TRUE. [Public]

```
AutoOrg                 BOOL AutoOrg;
```

`AutoOrg` indicates whether the origin of the client area should automatically be offset when preparing the area for painting. TRUE indicates automatic offset. [Public]

```
ClassHashValue          static hashValueType ClassHashValue;
```

`ClassHashValue` contains the hash value of the last constructed instance of `TScroller`. [Protected]

```
HasHScrollBar           BOOL HasHScrollBar;
```

The `HasHScrollBar` function is TRUE when the owner window has a horizontal scroll bar. [Public]

`HasVScrollBar` `BOOL HasVScrollBar;`

The `HasVScrollBar` function is TRUE when the owner window has a vertical scroll bar. [Public]

`InstanceHashValue` `hashValueType InstanceHashValue;`

`InstanceHashValue` contains the hash value of `this`. [Protected]

`TrackMode` `BOOL TrackMode;`

The `TrackMode` function indicates whether the display should be scrolled as the scroll thumb is dragged. TRUE, the default, indicates that the display should be scrolled as the thumb is dragged. FALSE indicates that the display should not be scrolled as the thumb is dragged. [Public]

`Window` `PTWindow Window;`

`Window` points to the owner window.

`XLine` `int XLine;`

`XLine` specifies the number of horizontal scroll units to move when the scroll arrow is clicked. The default value for `XLine` is 1. [Public]

`XPage` `int XPage;`

`XPage` specifies the number of horizontal scroll units to move when the thumb area of the scroll bar is clicked. The default value for `XPage` is equal to the current window width. [Public]

`XPos` `long XPos;`

`XPos` is the horizontal position of the scroller in horizontal scroll units. [Public]

`XRange` `long XRange;`

`XRange` is the maximum number of horizontal scroll units for the window. [Public]

`XUnit` `int XUnit;`

`XUnit` is the horizontal logical scroll unit used by `TScroller`. `XUnit` is expressed in device units. [Public]

`YLine` `int YLine;`

`YLine` is the number of vertical units scrolled when the scroll arrow is clicked. The default is 1. [Public]

`YPage` `int YPage;`

`YPage` is the number of vertical units scrolled when the thumb area of the scroll bar is clicked. `YPage` is set to the number of vertical units in the window. [Public]

`YPos` `long YPos;`

`YPos` is the current vertical position of the scroller. [Public]

`YRange` `long YRange;`

`YRange` is the maximum number of vertical scroll units for the window. [Public]

`YUnit` `int YUnit;`

`YUnit` is the vertical logical scroll unit used by `TScroller`. `YUnit` is expressed in device units. [Public]

Constructor(s):

`TScroller(PTWindow TheWindow, int TheXUnit, int TheYUnit, long TheXRange, long TheYRange);`	Constructs a `TScroller` object using the specified owner window, x unit, y unit, x range, and y range [Public]
`TScroller (StreamableInit);`	`TScroller` stream constructor [Protected]

Destructor:

`~TScroller();`	Destroys a `TScroller` object [Public]

Additional Member Function(s):

`AutoScroll` `virtual void AutoScroll();`

The `AutoScroll` function scrolls the display of the owner window when the mouse is dragged from the inside of the window to the outside. [Public]

`BeginView`

```
virtual void BeginView(HDC PaintDC,
        PAINTSTRUCT _FAR & PaintInfo);
```

The `BeginView` function sets the origin of the owner window's paint display context relative to the current scroller position when `AutoOrg` is TRUE. [Public]

`build` `static PTStreamable build();`

The `build` function invokes the `TScroller` constructor and constructs an object of type `TScroller` before reading its data members from a stream. [Public]

`EndView` `virtual void EndView();`

The `EndView` function updates the scroll bar positions to correspond to the position of `TScroller`. [Public]

`hashValue`

```
virtual hashValueType hashValue()
        const;
```

The `hashValue` function redefines the pure virtual function in class `Object`. This function returns the unique ID of a `TScroller` instance. [Public]

HScroll `virtual void HScroll(WORD ScrollEvent, int ThumbPos);`

The `HScroll` function calls `ScrollTo` or `ScrollBy` to handle the specified horizontal scroll event. `ThumbPos` specifies the current thumb position. [Public]

isA `virtual classType isA() const;`

The `isA` function must be redefined by all objects derived from the base class object. This function returns the class ID of `TScroller`. [Public]

isEqual `virtual int isEqual(RCObject testobj) const;`

The `isEqual` function redefines the pure virtual function in class `Object`. This function returns TRUE when `this` points to `testobj`. [Public]

IsVisibleRect `BOOL IsVisibleRect(long X, long Y, int XExt, ing YExt);`

The `IsVisibleRect` function determines whether any part of the specified rectangle is visible in the owner window. This function returns TRUE if any part of the rectangle is visible. [Public]

nameOf `virtual Pchar nameOf() const;`

The `nameOf` function must be redefined by all objects derived from the base class object. This function returns "TScroller", the class ID string. [Public]

printOn `virtual void printOn(Rostream outputStream) const;`

The `printOn` function must be redefined by all objects derived from the base class object. [Public]

read `virtual Pvoid read(Ripstream is);`

The `read` function reads `AutoMode`, `AutoOrg`, `HasHScrollBar`, `HasVScrollBar`, `TrackMode`, `XLine`, `XPage`, `XPos`, `XRange`, `XUnit`, `YLine`, `YPage`, `YPos`, `YRange`, and `YUnit`. [Protected]

ScrollBy `void ScrollBy(long Dx, long Dy);`

The `ScrollBy` function calls `ScrollTo` to scroll the display the amount specified in `Dx` and `Dy`. [Public]

ScrollTo `virtual void ScrollTo(long X, long Y);`

The `ScrollTo` function scrolls the display to the specified position. [Public]

SetPageSize `virtual void SetPageSize();`

The `SetPageSize` function sets the page width and height to the size of the client area of the owner window. [Public]

SetRange `void SetRange(long TheXRange, long TheYRange);`

The `SetRange` function sets the scroll ranges of `TScroller` to those specified and calls `SetSBarRange` to coordinate the ranges of the owner window scroll bars. [Public]

SetSBarRange `virtual void SetSBarRange();`

The `SetSBarRange` function sets the range of the scroll bars for the owner window to fit within the range specified for `TScroller`. [Public]

SetUnits `void SetUnits(int TheXUnit, int TheYUnit);`

The `SetUnits` function defines the data members `XUnit` and `YUnit`. [Public]

VScroll `virtual void VScroll(WORD ScrollEvent, int ThumbPos);`

The `VScroll` function calls `ScrollTo` or `ScrollBy` to handle the specified vertical scroll event. `ThumbPos` specifies the current thumb position. [Public]

write `virtual void write(Ropstream os);`

The `write` function writes `AutoMode`, `AutoOrg`, `HasHScrollBar`, `HasVScrollBar`, `TrackMode`, `XLine`, `XPage`, `XPos`, `XRange`, `XUnit`, `YLine`, `YPage`, `YPos`, `YRange`, and `YUnit`. [Protected]

XRangeValue `long XRangeValue(int AScrollUnit);`

The `XRangeValue` function converts a horizontal scroll value to a horizontal range value. [Public]

XScrollValue `int XScrollValue(long ARangeUnit);`

The `XScrollValue` function converts a horizontal range value to a horizontal scroll value. [Public]

YRangeValue `long YRangeValue(int AScrollUnit);`

The `YRangeValue` function converts a vertical scroll value to a vertical range value. [Public]

YScrollValue `int YScrollValue(long ARangeUnit);`

The `YScrollValue` function converts a vertical range value to a vertical scroll value. [Public]

Class Name: TStatic

Class Header File:

static.h

Description:

The TStatic class represents a static text interface element and provides functions for the management of the element.

Data Member(s):

TextLen	`WORD TextLen;`

TextLen specifies the size of the text buffer for the static control. [Public]

Constructor(s):

`TStatic(PTWindowsObject AParent, int AnId, LPSTR ATitle, int X, int Y, int W, int H, WORD ATextLen, PTModule AModule = NULL);`	Constructs a static control object using the specified parent window, control ID, text, position, width, height, and text length [Public]
`TStatic(PTWindowsObject AParent, int ResourceId, WORD ATextLen, PTModule AModule = NULL);`	Constructs a TStatic object to be associated with TDialog [Public]
`TStatic (StreamableInit)`	TStatic stream constructor [Protected]

Destructor:

None.

Additional Member Function(s):

build	`static PTStreamable build();`

The build function invokes the TStatic constructor and constructs an object of type TStatic before reading its data members from a stream. [Public]

Clear	`void Clear();`

The Clear function clears the text of the static control. [Public]

GetClassName	`virtual LPSTR GetClassName();`

The GetClassName function returns "STATIC". [Protected]

GetText	`int GetText(LPSTR ATextString, int MaxChars);`

The GetText function returns the text of the static control in ATextString. MaxChars specifies the size of ATextString. [Public]

nameOf	`virtual Pchar nameOf() const;`

The nameOf function redefines the pure virtual function in class Object. This function returns "TStatic", the class ID string. [Public]

```
read                     virtual Pvoid read(Ripstream is);
```

The `read` function calls `TWindow::read` to read in the base `TWindow` object. [Protected]

```
SetText                  void SetText(LPSTR ATextString);
```

The `SetText` function sets the text of the static control to the string specified in `ATextString`. [Public]

```
Transfer                 virtual WORD Transfer(Pvoid DataPtr,
                              WORD TransferFlag);
```

The `Transfer` function transfers text to and from the buffer pointed to by `DataPtr`. The `TransferFlag` parameter of the `Transfer` function can be set to `TF_SETDATA`, `TF_GETDATA`, or `TF_SIZEDATA` as follows:

- Set `TransferFlag` to `TF_SETDATA` to copy the text from the buffer to the static control.
- Set `TransferFlag` to `TF_GETDATA` to copy the text of the static control to the transfer buffer.
- When `TransferFlag` is set to `TF_SIZEDATA`, this function returns `TextLen`. [Public]

```
write                    virtual void write(Ropstream os);
```

The `write` function calls `TWindow::write` to write out the base `TWindow` object. [Protected]

Class Name: TStreamable

Class Header File:

objstrm.h

Description:

`TStreamable` is an abstract class. Classes (known as streamable classes) can inherit from `TStreamable`; however, no object can be instantiated from this class. Objects of streamable classes can read from and write to streams. Classes that inherit from `TStreamable` must redefine the pure virtual member functions described in following sections.

Data Member(s):

None.

Constructor(s):

None.

Destructor:

None.

Additional Member Function(s):

`read` `virtual Pvoid read(Ripstream) = 0;`

The `read` function is a pure virtual function that must be redefined by all derived classes. The `read` function permits the application to read from the specified input stream. [Protected]

`streamableName` `virtual const Pchar streamableName() const = 0;`

The `streamableName` function is a pure virtual function that must be redefined by all derived classes. The name of the streamable class of the object is returned. [Private]

`write` `virtual void write(Ropstream) = 0;`

The `write` function is a pure virtual function that must be redeclared by all derived classes. The `write` function permits the application to write to the specified output stream. [Protected]

Class Name: TWindow

Class Header File:

window.h

Description:

The `TWindow` class is derived from `TWindowsObject` and offers the fundamental features for a window. `TWindow` objects are basic windows and can be used as application main windows or pop-up windows.

Data Member(s):

`Attr` `TWindowAttr Attr;`

`Attr` references a `TWindowAttr` structure that specifies the attributes used to create the window including the control ID, menu, text, and style. [Public]

`FocusChildHandle` `HANDLE FocusChildHandle;`

`FocusChildHandle` is the child window handle of the child window that had the focus when the window was last activated. [Public]

`Scroller` `PTScroller Scroller;`

`Scroller` points to the `TScroller` object used for display scrolling. [Public]

Constructor(s):

`TWindow(PTWindowsObject AParent, LPSTR ATitle, PTModule AModule = NULL);`	Constructs a window object using the specified parent window and text [Public]
`TWindow(HWND AnHWindow);`	Constructor for a `TWindow` that is to be used in a DLL as an alias for a non-ObjectWindows window [Public]
`TWindow(StreamableInit);`	`TWindow` stream constructor [Protected]

Destructor:

`virtual ~TWindow();`	Frees `Attr.Menu` and deletes `Scroller` [Public]

Additional Member Function(s):

`AssignMenu` `virtual BOOL AssignMenu(LPSTR MenuName);`

The `AssignMenu` function sets `Attr.Menu` to the specified menu name. [Public]

`AssignMenu` `virtual BOOL AssignMenu(int MenuId);`

The `AssignMenu` function passes the specified menu ID to the previous `AssignMenu` function. The other `AssignMenu` function assigns the corresponding menu to the window. [Public]

`build` `static PTStreamable build();`

The `build` function invokes the `TWindow` constructor and constructs an object of type `TWindow` before reading its data members from a stream. [Public]

`Create` `virtual BOOL Create();`

The `Create` function creates an interface object associated with the `TWindow` object. `Create` returns TRUE when successful. When unsuccessful, this function calls `Error` and returns FALSE. [Public]

`GetClassName` `virtual LPSTR GetClassName();`

The `GetClassName` function returns "OWLWindow", the default Windows registration class name for `TWindow`. [Protected]

`GetWindowClass` `virtual void GetWindowClass(WndClass _FAR & AWndClass);`

The `GetWindowClass` function places the default values for the registration attributes into the window class structure referenced by `AWndClass`. [Protected]

`isA` `virtual classType isA() const;`

The `isA` function redefines the pure virtual function in class `Object`. This function returns the class ID of `TWindow`. [Public]

```
nameOf                virtual Pchar nameOf() const;
```

The `nameOf` function redefines the pure virtual function in class `Object`. This function returns "TWindow", the class ID string of `TWindow`. [Public]

```
Paint                 virtual void Paint(HDC PaintDC,
                          PAINTSTRUCT _FAR & PaintInfo);
```

The `Paint` function stores derived types that define `Paint` member functions. `Paint` is called automatically when a `WM_PAINT` message is detected. [Protected]

```
read                  virtual Pvoid read(Pipstream is);
```

The `read` function uses `TWindowsObject::read` to read the base `TWindowsObject` object. [Protected]

```
SetupWindow           virtual void SetupWindow();
```

The `SetupWindow` function initializes the new window by calling `TWindowsObject::SetupWindow`. [Protected]

```
WMActivate            virtual void WMActivate(RTMessage Msg)
                          = [WM_FIRST + WM_ACTIVATE];
```

The `WMActivate` function gives a window a keyboard interface when it is being activated or deactivated. During deactivation, the handle of the child control that currently has the focus is stored in `FocusChildHandle`. On activation, the child that previously had the focus is, once again, given the focus. [Protected]

```
WMCreate              virtual void WMCreate(RTMessage Msg) =
                          [WM_FIRST + WM_CREATE];
```

The `WMCreate` function calls `SetupWindow` when the `WM_CREATE` message is detected. [Protected]

```
WMHScroll             virtual void WMHScroll(RTMessage Msg) =
                          [WM_FIRST + WM_HSCROLL];
```

The `WMHScroll` function handles horizontal scroll bar events. [Protected]

```
WMLButtonDown         virtual void WMLButtonDown(RTMessage
                          Msg) = [WM_FIRST + WM_LBUTTONDOWN];
```

The `WMLButtonDown` function responds to `WM_LBUTTONDOWN` messages. [Protected]

```
WMMove                virtual void WMMove(RTMessage Msg) =
                          [WM_FIRST + WM_MOVE];
```

The `WMMove` function saves the new window coordinates in the `X` and `Y` members of `Attr` when a `WM_MOVE` message is detected. [Protected]

```
WMPaint               virtual void WMPaint(RTMessage Msg) =
                          [WM_FIRST + WM_PAINT];
```

The `WMPaint` function calls `Paint` when a `WM_PAINT` message is detected. [Protected]

```
WMSize                    virtual void WMSize(RTMessage Msg) =
                               [WM_FIRST + WM_SIZE];
```

The `WMSize` function calls `SetPageSize` when a window with scrollers has been sized. [Protected]

```
WMVScroll                 virtual void WMVScroll(RTMessage Msg) =
                               [WM_FIRST + WM_VSCROLL];
```

The `WMVScroll` function calls `DispatchScroll` when the `WM_VSCROLL` message is detected from a scroll bar control. [Protected]

```
write                     virtual void write(Ropstream os);
```

The `write` function uses `TWindowsObject::write` to write the base `TWindowsObject` object. [Protected]

Class Name: TWindowsObject

Class Header File:

windobj.h

Description:

The `TWindowsObject` class is an abstract class and defines behaviors for ObjectWindows interface objects including windows, dialogs, and controls. The member functions of this class create window objects, handle message processing, and destroy window objects.

Data Member(s):

```
DefaultProc               FARPROC DefaultProc;
```

`DefaultProc` holds the address of the default window procedure. [Protected]

```
HWindow                   HWND HWindow;
```

`HWindow` specifies the handle of the interface element associated with the interface object. [Public]

```
Parent                    PTWindowsObject Parent;
```

`Parent` points to the interface object that acts as the parent window for the interface object. [Public]

```
Status                    int Status;
```

`Status` can indicate an error in the initialization of an interface object. [Public]

```
Title                     LPSTR Title;
```

`Title` points to the caption for the window. [Public]

`TransferBuffer`	`Pvoid TransferBuffer;`

`TransferBuffer` points to a buffer used to transfer data. [Protected]

Constructor(s):

`TWindowsObject (PTWindowsObject AParent, PTModule AModule = NULL);`	Sets the `Parent` data member to the value specified in `AParent` [Public]
`TWindowsObject (StreamableInit)`	`TWindowsObject` stream constructor [Protected]

Destructor:

`virtual ~TWindowsObject();`	Calls `Destroy` to destroy the interface element [Public]

Additional Member Function(s):

`AfterDispatchHandler`	`virtual void AfterDispatchHandler();`

The `AfterDispatchHandler` message is called by `DispatchAMessage` after responding to a message. This function should be redefined to perform postprocessing for incoming messages. [Public]

`BeforeDispatchHandler`	`virtual void BeforeDispatchHandler();`

The `BeforeDispatchHandler` function is called by `DispatchAMessage` before invoking a message response. This function should be redefined to process incoming messages. [Public]

`build`	`static PTStreamable build();`

The `build` function invokes the `TWindowsObject` constructor and constructs an object of type `TWindowsObject` before reading its data members from a stream. [Public]

`CanClose`	`virtual BOOL CanClose();`

The `CanClose` function determines whether the associated interface element can be closed by calling the `CanClose` member functions of each of the child windows. This function returns TRUE when the window can be closed or FALSE if any of the `CanClose` member functions of the child windows returned FALSE. [Public]

`ChildWithId`	`PTWindowsObject ChildWithId(int Id);`

The `ChildWithID` function returns the pointer to the child window from child window list that has the specified ID. A NULL return value indicates that no child window has the ID specified. [Public]

`CloseWindow`	`void CloseWindow();`

The `CloseWindow` function calls `ShutDownWindow` to close the window. [Public]

```
CMExit                  virtual void CMExit
                              (RTMessage Msg) = [CM_FIRST +
                              CM_EXIT];
```

The `CMExit` function is called when a menu item with an ID of `CM_EXIT` is selected. When `this` is the main window, `CloseWindow` is called. [Protected]

```
Create                  virtual BOOL Create() = 0;
```

The `Create` function is a pure virtual function. `Create` should be redefined in derived types to create the associated interface element. [Public]

```
CreateChildren          BOOL CreateChildren();
```

The `CreateChildren` function creates child windows from the child list. The child windows must contain the `WB_AUTOCREATE` mask. [Public]

```
DefChildProc            virtual void DefChildProc(RTMessage
                              Msg);
```

By default, the `DefChildProc` function handles incoming child-ID-based messages. [Protected]

```
DefCommandProc          virtual void DefCommandProc(RTMessage
                              Msg);
```

The `DefCommandProc` function, by default, handles command-based messages. [Protected]

```
DefNotificationProc     virtual void DefNotificationProc
                              (RTMessage Msg);
```

The `DefNotificationProc` function provides the default processing of notification messages and passes these notification messages to the parent as a child-ID-based message. [Protected]

```
DefWndProc              virtual void DefWndProc(RTMessage Msg);
```

The `DefWndProc` function handles default message processing. [Public]

```
Destroy                 virtual void Destroy();
```

The `Destroy` function destroys an associated interface element. [Public]

```
DisableAutoCreate       void DisableAutoCreate();
```

The `DisableAutoCreate` function disables the autocreate feature. The autocreate feature allows the interface object to be created and displayed as a child window. [Public]

```
DisableTransfer         void DisableTransfer();
```

The `DisableTransfer` function disables the transfer of state data to and from the transfer buffer. [Public]

DispatchAMessage

```
virtual void DispatchAMessage(WORD AMsg,
        RTMessage AMessage, void
        (TWindowsObject::*)(RTMessage));
```

The DispatchAMessage function dispatches Windows messages to the appropriate response member function. [Public]

DispatchScroll

```
void DispatchScroll(RTMessage Msg);
```

The DispatchScroll function dispatches messages from scroll bar controls. [Protected]

DrawItem

```
virtual void DrawItem(DRAWITEMSTRUCT _FAR &
        DrawInfo);
```

The DrawItem function is called when a control or menu item needs to be redrawn. [Public]

EnableAutoCreate

```
void EnableAutoCreate();
```

The EnableAutoCreate function enables the autocreate feature. The autocreate feature allows the interface object to be created and displayed as a child window. [Public]

EnableKBHandler

```
void EnableKBHandler();
```

The EnableKBHandler function enables windows and modeless dialog boxes to provide a keyboard interface to child controls. [Public]

EnableTransfer

```
void EnableTransfer();
```

The EnableTransfer function enables the transfer of state data to and from the transfer buffer. [Public]

FirstThat

```
PTWindowsObject FirstThat(TCondFunc
        Test, Pvoid PParamList);
```

The FirstThat function calls the specified test function for each child window in ChildList. When TRUE is returned by the test function, testing stops and FirstThat returns the child window object that was successfully tested. Otherwise, this function returns NULL and testing continues. [Public]

FirstThat

```
TWindowsObject FirstThat(TCondMemFunc Test,
        Pvoid PParamList);
```

The FirstThat function calls the specified test function for each child window in ChildList. When TRUE is returned by the test function, testing stops and FirstThat returns the child window object that was successfully tested. Otherwise, this function returns a value of NULL and testing continues. [Public]

ForEach

```
void ForEach(TActionFunc Action, Pvoid
        PParamList);
```

The ForEach function calls the specified function and passes each child window in ChildList as an argument. [Public]

```
ForEach                 void ForEach(TActionMemFunc Action, Pvoid
                             PParamList);
```

This `ForEach` function is like the previous `ForEach` function with the exception that this function takes a member function as a parameter. [Public]

```
GetApplication          PTApplication GetApplication();
```

The `GetApplication` function gets the pointer to the `TApplication` object that is associated with `this`. [Public]

```
GetChildPtr             void GetChildPtr(Ripstream is,
                             RPTWindowsObject P);
```

The `GetChildPtr` function reads a reference to a pointer to a child window from the specified stream. [Protected]

```
GetChildren             void GetChildren(Ripstream is);
```

The `GetChildren` function reads child windows from the specified stream into the child list. [Public]

```
GetClassName            virtual LPSTR GetClassName() = 0;
```

The `GetClassName` function returns the Windows registration class name and must be redefined for derived classes. [Protected]

```
GetClient               virtual PTMDIClient GetClient();
```

The `GetClient` function returns NULL for non-MDI interface objects. `TMDIFrame` redefines this function to return a pointer to the MDI client window. [Public]

```
GetFirstChild           PTWindowsObject GetFirstChild();
```

The `GetFirstChild` function returns the pointer to the first child window in the child list for the interface object. [Public]

```
GetId                   virtual int GetId();
```

The `GetId` function returns 0 by default. `TControl` redefines this function to return the control ID of the class. [Public]

```
GetInstance             FARPROC GetInstance();
```

The `GetInstance` function returns the instance thunk of the window. [Public]

```
GetLastChild            PTWindowsObject GetLastChild();
```

The `GetLastChild` function returns the pointer to the last child window in the child list for the interface object. [Public]

```
GetModule               PTModule GetModule();
```

The `GetModule` function returns the pointer to the `TModule` that owns the object. [Public]

```
GetSiblingPtr             void GetSiblingPtr(Ripstream is,
                              RPTWindowsObject P);
```

The `GetSiblingPtr` function is used only during a `read` operation to references written by a call to `PutSiblingPtr`. [Protected]

```
GetWindowClass            virtual void GetWindowClass(WNDCLASS _FAR &
                              AWndClass);
```

The `GetWindowClass` function fills the specified Windows registration class with attributes. [Protected]

```
hashValue                 virtual hashValueType hashValue() const;
```

The `hashValue` function must be redefined by all objects derived from the base class object. This function returns the hash value of `TWindowsObject`, `HWindow`. [Public]

```
isA                       virtual classType isA() const = 0;
```

The `isA` function redefines the pure virtual function in class `Object` and should be redefined to return a unique class ID. [Public]

```
isEqual                   virtal int isEqual(RCObject
                              testwin) const;
```

The `isEqual` function redefines the pure virtual function in class `Object`. This function returns TRUE when `this` points to `testwin`. [Public]

```
IsFlagSet                 BOOL IsFlagSet(WORD Mask);
```

The `IsFlagSet` function returns TRUE if the bit flag of the `Flags` data member with the specified mask is set. Otherwise, this function returns FALSE. [Public]

```
nameOf                    virtual Pchar nameOf() const = 0;
```

The `nameOf` function is a pure virtual function. This function should be redefined by derived classes to return a class ID string. [Public]

```
Next                      PTWindowsObject Next();
```

The `Next` function returns a pointer to the next window in the child window list. [Public]

```
printOn                   virtual void printOn(Rostream
                              outputStream) const;
```

The `printOn` function redefines the pure virtual function in class `Object`. [Public]

```
Previous                  PTWindowsObject Previous();
```

The `Previous` function returns a pointer to the previous window in the child window list. [Public]

```
PutChildPtr                 void PutChildPtr(Ropstream os,
                                 PTWindowsObject P);
```

The PutChildPtr function writes a child window to the specified output stream and should only be used during a write operation to write pointers that GetChildPtr can read. [Protected]

```
PutChildren                 void PutChildren(Ropstream os);
```

The PutChildren writes child windows to the specified stream. [Public]

```
PutSiblingPtr               void PutSiblingPtr(Ropstream os,
                                 PTWindowsObject P);
```

The PutSiblingPtr function writes the reference to a sibling window to the specified output stream and should only by used during a write operation to write a pointer that GetSiblingPtr can read. [Protected]

```
read                        virtual Pvoid read(Ripstream is);
```

The read function creates an object instance and calls GetChildren to read in the child windows. The child list, HWindow, Parent, and TransferBuffer are set to 0. Title, Status, flags, and CreateOrder are read in. [Protected]

```
Register                    virtual BOOL Register();
```

The Register function registers the Windows registration class of this. This function returns TRUE if the class is successfully registered. [Public]

```
RemoveClient                void RemoveClient();
```

The RemoveClient function removes the specified client window from the child list. [Protected]

```
SetCaption                  void SetCaption(LPSTR ATitle);
```

The SetCaption function defines the caption of the interface element as the value specified in ATitle. [Public]

```
SetFlags                    void SetFlags(WORD Mask, BOOL OnOff);
```

The SetFlags function sets the bit flag of the Flags data member with the specified mask according to the value specified in OnOff. [Public]

```
SetParent                 virtual void SetParent(PTWindowsObject NewParent);
```

The SetParent function sets Parent to the parent window specified in NewParent, removes this from the child list of the previous parent, and adds this to the child list of the new parent. [Public]

```
SetTransferBuffer         void SetTransferBuffer (Pvoid ATransferBuffer);
```

The SetTransferBuffer function sets TransferBuffer to the buffer specified in ATransferBuffer. [Public]

`SetupWindow` `virtual void SetupWindow();`

The `SetupWindow` function attempts to create an associated interface element for each child window in `ChildList` that has the autocreate feature enabled. [Protected]

`Show` `void Show(int ShowCmd);`

The `Show` function displays the interface element as specified in `ShowCmd`. `ShowCmd` can be any of the following values:

Value	*Meaning*
`SW_HIDE`	Hidden
`SW_SHOW`	Shown using window's current size and position
`SW_SHOWMAXIMIZED`	Shown maximized and active
`SW_SHOWMINIMIZED`	Shown minimized and active
`SW_SHOWNORMAL`	Shown restored and active

[Public]

`ShutDownWindow` `virtual void ShutdownWindow();`

The `ShutDownWindow` function destroys the associated interface element. [Public]

`Transfer`
```
virtual WORD Transfer(Pvoid DataPtr,
         WORD TransferFlag);
```

The `Transfer` function transfers data to and from the buffer referenced by `DataPtr`. `TransferFlag` specifies how the buffer is used:

- When `TransferFlag` is set to `TF_GETDATA`, information is copied to the buffer.
- When `TransferFlag` is set to `TF_SETDATA`, information is retrieved from the buffer.
- When TransferFlag is set to `TF_SIZEDATA`, the size of the transfer data is returned. [Public]

`TransferData` `virtual void TransferData(WORD Direction);`

The `TransferData` function transfers data between the buffer and the interface object's child windows that have the `WM_TRANSFER` flag set. `TranferData` calls `Transfer` for each child window and uses `Direction` to specify how data is transferred. `Direction` can be set to `TF_SETDATA`, `TF_GETDATA`, or `TF_SIZEDATA`:

- When `Direction` is set to `TF_SETDATA`, the list is filled and item(s) selected using the data in the buffer.
- When `Direction` is set to `TF_GETDATA`, the buffer is filled using the current list and selection(s) from the list box.

- When `Direction` is set to `TF_SIZEDATA`, the size of the transfer data is returned and no data is transferred. [Public]

```
WMActivate                 virtual void WMActivate(RTMessage Msg)
                                = [WM_FIRST + WM_ACTIVATE];
```

The `WMActivate` function enables keyboard handling if requested when a `WM_ACTIVATE` message is detected. [Protected]

```
WMClose                    virtual void WMClose(RTMessage Msg) =
                                [WM_FIRST + WM_CLOSE];
```

The `WMClose` function calls `CloseWindow` to close the window. [Protected]

```
WMCommand                  virtual void WMCommand(RTMessage Msg)
                                = [WM_FIRST + WM_COMMAND];
```

The `WMCommand` function calls the appropriate member functions when command-based, child-ID-based, or notify-based messages are detected. [Protected]

```
WMDestroy                  virtual void WMDestroy(RTMessage Msg)
                                = [WM_FIRST + WM_DESTROY];
```

The `WMDestroy` function handles the `WM_DESTROY` message. [Protected]

```
WMDrawItem                 virtual void WMDrawItem(RTMessage Msg)
                                = [WM_FIRST + WM_DRAWITEM];
```

The `WMDrawItem` function dispatches the `WM_DRAWITEM` message for drawable controls. [Protected]

```
WMHScroll                  virtual void WMHScroll(RTMessage Msg)
                                = [WM_FIRST + WM_HSCROLL];
```

The `WMHScroll` function calls `DispatchScroll` in response to a `WM_HSCROLL` message. [Protected]

```
WMNCDestroy                virtual void WMNCDestroy(RTMessage Msg)
                                = [WM_FIRST + WM_NCDESTROY];
```

The `WMNCDestroy` function handles the `WM_NCDESTROY` message. [Protected]

```
WMQueryEndSession          virtual void WMQueryEndSession(RTMessage Msg)
                              = [WM_FIRST + WM_QUERYENDSESSION];
```

The `WMQueryEndSession` function calls the appropriate `CanClose` function to determine whether the session can close. [Protected]

```
WMVScroll                  virtual void WMVScroll(RTMessage Msg)
                                = [WM_FIRST + WM_VScroll];
```

The `WMVScroll` function calls `DispatchScroll` in response to the detection of vertical scroll bar messages. [Protected]

```
write                        virtual void write(Ropstream os);
```

The `write` function writes `Title`, `Status`, flags, and `CreateOrder` and calls `PutChildren` to write out child windows. [Protected]

19

ObjectWindows Functions

This chapter provides information on each of the member functions for the various classes listed in Chapter 18. Member functions are listed in alphabetical order and explained in the following format:

Function Name

Member Access Control:

This section lists the member function's access.

Syntax:

This section lists the function syntax.

Class:

This section lists the class containing the member function being described.

Class Header File:

This section lists the header file for the member function and its class.

Description:

This section describes the function.

This chapter reviews the various features of the member functions. Member functions are listed in alphabetical order for quick reference. The remainder of this chapter consists of member function information.

AddString

Member Access Control:

Public

Syntax:

```
int AddString(LPSTR AString);
```

Class:

`TListBox`

Class Header File:

listbox.h

Description:

The `AddString` function adds the string specified in `AString` to the list box. This function returns the string's position in the list box when successful. A negative return value indicates that the function is unsuccessful.

AfterDispatchHandler

Member Access Control:

Public

Syntax:

```
virtual void AfterDispatchHandler();
```

Class:

`TWindowsObject`

Class Header File:

windobj.h

Description:

The `AfterDispatchHandler` message is called by `DispatchAMessage` after responding to a message. This function should be redefined to perform postprocessing for incoming messages.

ArrangeIcons

Member Access Control:

Public

Syntax:

```
virtual void ArrangeIcons();
```

Class:

`TMDIClient`

Class Header File:

mdi.h

Description:

The `ArrangeIcons` function aligns MDI child window icons along the bottom of the MDI client window.

ArrangeIcons

Member Access Control:

Public

Syntax:

```
virtual void ArrangeIcons();
```

Class:

`TMDIFrame`

Class Header File:

mdi.h

Description:

The `ArrangeIcons` function calls the `ArrangeIcons` member function of the client window to arrange the iconized MDI child windows along the bottom of the client window.

AssignMenu

Member Access Control:

Public

Syntax:

```
virtual BOOL AssignMenu(LPSTR MenuName);
```

Class:

`TWindow`

Class Header File:

window.h

Description:

The `AssignMenu` function defines the menu for the window to the menu in `MenuName`. `Attr.Menu` is set to `MenuName`.

AssignMenu

Member Access Control:

Public

Syntax:

```
virtual BOOL AssignMenu(int MenuId);
```

Class:

`TWindow`

Class Header File:

window.h

Description:

The `AssignMenu` function calls the previous `AssignMenu` function and passes the menu ID of the window specified in `MenuId`.

AutoScroll

Member Access Control:

Public

Syntax:

```
virtual void AutoScroll();
```

Class:

`TScroller`

Class Header File:

scroller.h

Description:

The `AutoScroll` function scrolls the display of the owner window when the mouse is dragged from the inside of the window to the outside.

BeforeDispatchHandler

Member Access Control:

Public

Syntax:

```
virtual void  BeforeDispatchHandler();
```

Class:

`TWindowsObject`

Class Header File:

windobj.h

Description:

`DispatchAMessage` calls the `BeforeDispatchHandler` function before invoking a message response. This function should be redefined to process incoming messages.

BeginView

Member Access Control:

Public

Syntax:

```
virtual void BeginView(HDC PaintDC, PAINTSTRUCT _FAR & PaintInfo);
```

Class:

`TScroller`

Class Header File:

scroller.h

Description:

The `BeginView` function sets the origin of the owner window's paint display context relative to the current scroller position when `AutoOrg` is TRUE. When `AutoOrg` is FALSE, the offset must be set manually.

BNClicked

Member Access Control:

Protected

Syntax:

```
virtual void BNClicked(RTMessage Msg) = [NF_FIRST + BN_CLICKED];
```

Class:

`TCheckBox`

Class Header File:

checkbox.h

Description:

The `BNClicked` function responds to the notification messages that indicate that the check box was clicked. When the check box is a part of a group, `TGroupBox` is notified of the change in the check box state.

build

Member Access Control:

Public

Syntax:

```
static PTStreamable build();
```

Class:

`TButton`

Class Header File:

button.h

Description:

The `build` function invokes the `TButton` constructor and constructs an object of type `TButton` before reading its data members from a stream.

build

Member Access Control:

Public

Syntax:

```
static PTStreamable build();
```

Class:

`TCheckBox`

Class Header File:

checkbox.h

Description:

The `build` function invokes the `TCheckBox` constructor and constructs an object of type `TCheckBox` before reading its data members from a stream.

build

Member Access Control:

Public

Syntax:

```
static PTStreamable build();
```

Class:

`TComboBox`

Class Header File:

combobox.h

Description:

The `build` function invokes the `TComboBox` constructor and constructs an object of type `TComboBox` before reading its data members from a stream.

build

Member Access Control:

Public

Syntax:

```
static PTStreamable build();
```

Class:

`TDialog`

Class Header File:

dialog.h

Description:

The `build` function invokes the `TDialog` constructor and constructs an object of type `TDialog` before reading its data members from a stream.

build

Member Access Control:

Public

Syntax:

```
static PTStreamable build();
```

Class:

`TEdit`

Class Header File:

edit.h

Description:

The `build` function invokes the `TEdit` constructor and constructs an object of type `TEdit` before reading its data members from a stream.

build

Member Access Control:

Public

Syntax:

```
static PTStreamable build();
```

Class:

`TEditWindow`

Class Header File:

editwnd.h

Description:

The `build` function invokes the `TEditWindow` constructor and constructs an object of type `TEditWindow` before reading its data members from a stream.

build

Member Access Control:

Public

Syntax:

```
static PTStreamable build();
```

Class:

`TFileDialog`

Class Header File:

filedial.h

Description:

The `build` function invokes the `TFileDialog` constructor and constructs an object of type `TFileDialog` before reading its data members from a stream.

build

Member Access Control:

Public

Syntax:

```
static PTStreamable build();
```

Class:

`TFileWindow`

Class Header File:

filewnd.h

Description:

The `build` function invokes the `TFileWindow` constructor and constructs an object of type `TFileWindow` before reading its data members from a stream.

build

Member Access Control:

Public

Syntax:

```
static PTStreamable build();
```

Class:

`TGroupBox`

Class Header File:

groupbox.h

Description:

The `build` function invokes the `TGroupBox` constructor and constructs an object of type `TGroupBox` before reading its data members from a stream.

build

Member Access Control:

Public

Syntax:

```
static PTStreamable build();
```

Class:

TInputDialog

Class Header File:

inputdia.h

Description:

The `build` function invokes the `TInputDialog` constructor and constructs an object of type `TInputDialog` before reading its data members from a stream.

build

Member Access Control:

Public

Syntax:

```
static PTStreamable build();
```

Class:

TListBox

Class Header File:

listbox.h

Description:

The `build` function invokes the `TListBox` constructor and constructs an object of type `TListBox` before reading its data members from a stream.

build

Member Access Control:

Public

Syntax:

```
static PTStreamable build();
```

Class:

`TMDIClient`

Class Header File:

mdi.h

Description:

The `build` function invokes the `TMDIClient` constructor and constructs an object of type `TMDIClient` before reading its data members from a stream.

build

Member Access Control:

Public

Syntax:

```
static PTStreamable build();
```

Class:

`TMDIFrame`

Class Header File:

mdi.h

Description:

The `build` function invokes the `TMDIFrame` constructor and constructs an object of type `TMDIFrame` before reading its data members from a stream.

build

Member Access Control:

Public

Syntax:

```
static PTStreamable build();
```

Class:

`TRadioButton`

Class Header File:

radiobut.h

Description:

The `build` function invokes the `TRadioButton` constructor and constructs an object of type `TRadioButton` before reading its data members from a stream.

build

Member Access Control:

Public

Syntax:

```
static PTStreamable build();
```

Class:

`TScrollBar`

Class Header File:

scrollba.h

Description:

The `build` function invokes the `TScrollBar` constructor and constructs an object of type `TScrollBar` before reading its data members from a stream.

build

Member Access Control:

Public

Syntax:

```
static PTStreamable build();
```

Class:

`TScroller`

Class Header File:

scroller.h

Description:

The `build` function invokes the `TScroller` constructor and constructs an object of type `TScroller` before reading its data members from a stream.

build

Member Access Control:

Public

Syntax:

```
static PTStreamable build();
```

Class:

`TStatic`

Class Header File:

static.h

Description:

The `build` function invokes the `TStatic` constructor and constructs an object of type `TStatic` before reading its data members from a stream.

build

Member Access Control:

Public

Syntax:

```
static PTStreamable build();
```

Class:

`TWindow`

Class Header File:

window.h

Description:

The `build` function invokes the `TWindow` constructor and constructs an object of type `TWindow` before reading its data members from a stream.

build

Member Access Control:

Public

Syntax:

```
static PTStreamable build();
```

Class:

`TWindowsObject`

Class Header File:

windobj.h

Description:

The `build` function invokes the `TWindowsObject` constructor and constructs an object of type `TWindowsObject` before reading its data members from a stream.

Cancel

Member Access Control:

Protected

Syntax:

```
virtual void Cancel(RTMessage Msg) = [ID_FIRST + ID_CANCEL];
```

Class:

`TDialog`

Class Header File:

dialog.h

Description:

The `Cancel` function calls `CloseWindow` by using IDCANCEL when the `Cancel` button for the dialog box is selected.

CanClear

Member Access Control:

Public

Syntax:

```
virtual BOOL CanClear();
```

Class:

`TFileWindow`

Class Header File:

filewnd.h

Description:

The `CanClear` function determines whether it is alright to clear the text in the Editor. This value returns TRUE if the text has not been modified. A prompt to the user is displayed when the text has been modified.

CanClose

Member Access Control:

Public

Syntax:

```
virtual BOOL CanClose();
```

Class:

`TApplication`

Class Header File:

applicat.h

Description:

The `CanClose` function determines whether the application can close. The function calls the `CanClose` member function of the main window and returns the value returned by that `CanClose` member function. TRUE is returned when the application can close.

CanClose

Member Access Control:

Public

Syntax:

```
virtual BOOL CanClose();
```

Class:

`TFileDialog`

Class Header File:

filedial.h

Description:

The `CanClose` function returns TRUE when the user entered a valid file name. A return value of FALSE indicates that the user did not enter a valid file name.

CanClose

Member Access Control:

Public

Syntax:

```
virtual BOOL CanClose();
```

Class:

`TFileWindow`

Class Header File:

filewnd.h

Description:

The `CanClose` function determines whether it is alright to close the `TFileWindow`. This functions calls `CanClear` and returns the value returned by `CanClear`.

CanClose

Member Access Control:

Public

Syntax:

```
virtual BOOL CanClose();
```

Class:

`TWindowsObject`

Class Header File:

windobj.h

Description:

The `CanClose` function determines whether the associated interface element can be closed by calling the `CanClose` member functions of each of the child windows. This function returns TRUE when the window can be closed. A return value of FALSE indicates that one or more of the `CanClose` member functions of the child windows returned FALSE.

CanUndo

Member Access Control:

Public

Syntax:

```
BOOL CanUndo();
```

Class:

`TEdit`

Class Header File:

edit.h

Description:

The `CanUndo` function indicates whether it is possible to undo the last edit. This function returns TRUE when it is possible to undo the last edit.

CascadeChildren

Member Access Control:

Public

Syntax:

```
virtual void CascadeChildren();
```

Class:

`TMDIClient`

Class Header File:

mdi.h

Description:

The `CascadeChildren` function adjusts the size of all MDI child windows that are not minimized and arranges them in an overlapping style.

CascadeChildren

Member Access Control:

Public

Syntax:

```
virtual void CascadeChildren();
```

Class:

`TMDIFrame`

Class Header File:

mdi.h

Description:

The `CascadeChildren` function calls the `CascadeChildren` member function of the client window to arrange the MDI child windows that are not iconized in an overlapping style.

Check

Member Access Control:

Public

Syntax:

```
void Check();
```

Class:

`TCheckBox`

Class Header File:

checkbox.h

Description:

The `Check` function places the check box into the checked state by calling `SetCheck`.

ChildWithId

Member Access Control:

Public

Syntax:

```
PTWindowsObject ChildWithId(int Id);
```

Class:

`TWindowsObject`

Class Header File:

windobj.h

Description:

The `ChildWithID` function returns the pointer to the child window from child window list that has the specified ID. A return value of NULL indicates that no child window has the ID specified.

Clear

Member Access Control:

Public

Syntax:

```
void Clear();
```

Class:

`TStatic`

Class Header File:

static.h

Description:

The `Clear` function clears the text of the static control.

ClearList

Member Access Control:

Public

Syntax:

```
void ClearList();
```

Class:

`TListBox`

Class Header File:

listbox.h

Description:

The `ClearList` function clears all list items.

ClearModify

Member Access Control:

Public

Syntax:

```
void ClearModify();
```

Class:

`TEdit`

Class Header File:

edit.h

Description:

The `ClearModify` function resets the edit control change flag.

CloseChildren

Member Access Control:

Public

Syntax:

```
virtual BOOL CloseChildren();
```

Class:

`TMDIFrame`

Class Header File:

mdi.h

Description:

The `CloseChildren` function calls the `CanClose` member function of each MDI child window and closes all the child windows if possible.

CloseWindow

Member Access Control:

Public

Syntax:

```
virtual void CloseWindow(int ARetValue);
```

Class:

`TDialog`

Class Header File:

dialog.h

Description:

The `CloseWindow` function calls `TWindowsObject::CloseWindow` when `this` is a modeless dialog box or `CanClose` for a modal dialog box to determine whether the dialog box can be shut. If `CanClose` is called and returns TRUE, the function calls `TransferData` and then `ShutDownWindow`, and passes `ARetValue`.

CloseWindow

Member Access Control:

Public

Syntax:

```
virtual void CloseWindow();
```

Class:

`TDialog`

Class Header File:

dialog.h

Description:

The `CloseWindow` function calls `TWindowsObject::CloseWindow` when `this` is a modeless dialog box or `CloseWindow` for a modal dialog box to determine whether the dialog box can be shut. IDCANCEL is passed as the integer `ARetValue`.

CloseWindow

Member Access Control:

Public

Syntax:

```
void CloseWindow();
```

Class:

`TWindowsObject`

Class Header File:

windobj.h

Description:

The `CloseWindow` function calls `ShutDownWindow` to close the window.

CMArrangeIcons

Member Access Control:

Protected

Syntax:

```
virtual void CMArrangeIcons(RTMessage Msg) = [CM_FIRST + CM_ARRANGEICONS];
```

Class:

`TMDIFrame`

Class Header File:

mdi.h

Description:

The `CMArrangeIcons` function calls `ArrangeIcons` when a menu item with a `CM_ARRANGEICONS` ID is selected.

CMCascadeChildren

Member Access Control:

Protected

Syntax:

```
virtual void CMCascadeChildren(RTMessage Msg) = [CM_FIRST +
    CM_CASCADECHILDREN];
```

Class:

`TMDIFrame`

Class Header File:

mdi.h

Description:

The `CMCascadeChildren` function calls `CascadeChildren` when a menu item with a `CM_CASCADECHILDREN` ID is selected.

CMCloseChildren

Member Access Control:

Protected

Syntax:

```
virtual void CMCloseChildren (RTMessage Msg) = [CM_FIRST +
     CM_CLOSECHILDREN];
```

Class:

`TMDIFrame`

Class Header File:

mdi.h

Description:

The `CMCloseChildren` function calls `CloseChildren` when a menu item with a `CM_CLOSECHILDREN` ID is selected.

CMCreateChild

Member Access Control:

Protected

Syntax:

```
virtual void CMCreateChild(RTMessage Msg) = [CM_FIRST + CM_CREATECHILD];
```

Class:

`TMDIFrame`

Class Header File:

mdi.h

Description:

The `CMCreateChild` function calls `CreateChild` when a menu item with a `CM_CREATECHILD` ID is selected.

CMEditClear

Member Access Control:

Protected

Syntax:

```
virtual void CMEditClear(RTMessage Msg) = [CM_FIRST + CM_EDITCLEAR];
```

Class:

`TEdit`

Class Header File:

edit.h

Description:

The `CMEditClear` function calls `Clear` when a menu item with menu ID `CM_EDITCLEAR` is selected.

CMEditCopy

Member Access Control:

Protected

Syntax:

```
virtual void CMEditCopy(RTMessage Msg) = [CM_FIRST + CM_EDITCOPY];
```

Class:

`TEdit`

Class Header File:

edit.h

Description:

The `CMEditCopy` function calls `Copy` when a menu item with menu ID `CM_EDITCOPY` is selected.

CMEditCut

Member Access Control:

Protected

Syntax:

```
virtual void CMEditCut(RTMessage Msg) = [CM_FIRST + CM_EDITCUT];
```

Class:

`TEdit`

Class Header File:

edit.h

Description:

The `CMEditCut` function calls `Cut` when a menu item with the menu ID `CM_EDITCUT` is selected.

CMEditDelete

Member Access Control:

Protected

Syntax:

```
virtual void CMEditDelete(RTMessage Msg) = [CM_FIRST + CM_EDITDELETE];
```

Class:

`TEdit`

Class Header File:

edit.h

Description:

The `CMEditDelete` function calls `DeleteSelection` when a menu item with menu ID `CM_EDITDELETE` is selected.

CMEditFind

Member Access Control:

Protected

Syntax:

```
virtual void CMEditFind(RTMessage Msg) = [CM_FIRST + CM_EDITFIND];
```

Class:

`TEditWindow`

Class Header File:

editwnd.h

Description:

The `CMEditFind` function initiates a text search and displays a search dialog box when a `Find` menu item is selected. After the user has made selections to the dialog box, `SearchStruct` is updated to reflect the user's selections, `IsReplaceOp` is set to FALSE, and `DoSearch` is called.

CMEditFindNext

Member Access Control:

Protected

Syntax:

```
virtual void CMEditFindNext(RTMessage Msg) = [CM_FIRST + CM_EDITFINDNEXT];
```

Class:

`TEditWindow`

Class Header File:

editwnd.h

Description:

The `CMEditFindNext` function initiates a text search when a `Find Next` menu item is selected. No dialog box is displayed because it is assumed that `SearchStruct` contains the proper settings. `CMEditFindNext` calls `DoSearch`.

CMEditPaste

Member Access Control:

Protected

Syntax:

```
virtual void CMEditPaste(RTMessage Msg) = [CM_FIRST + CM_EDITPASTE];
```

Class:

`TEdit`

Class Header File:

edit.h

Description:

The `CMEditPaste` function calls `Paste` when a menu item with menu ID `CM_EDITPASTE` is selected.

CMEditReplace

Member Access Control:

Protected

Syntax:

```
virtual void CMEditReplace(RTMessage Msg) = [CM_FIRST + CM_EDITREPLACE];
```

Class:

`TEditWindow`

Class Header File:

editwnd.h

Description:

The `CMEditReplace` function initiates a text search and replace operation and displays a search dialog box when a `Replace` menu item is selected. After the user has made selections to the dialog box, `SearchStruct` is updated to reflect the user's selections, `IsReplaceOp` is set to TRUE, and `DoSearch` is called.

CMEditUndo

Member Access Control:

Protected

Syntax:

```
virtual void CMEditUndo(RTMessage Msg) = [CM_FIRST + CM_EDITUNDO];
```

Class:

`TEdit`

Class Header File:

edit.h

Description:

The `CMEditUndo` function calls `Undo` when a menu item with menu ID `CM_EDITUNDO` is selected.

CMExit

Member Access Control:

Protected

Syntax:

```
virtual void CMExit(RTMessage Msg) = [CM_FIRST + CM_EXIT];
```

Class:

`TWindowsObject`

Class Header File:

windobj.h

Description:

The `CMExit` function is called when a menu item with an ID of `CM_EXIT` is selected. When `this` is the main window, `CloseWindow` is called.

CMFileNew

Member Access Control:

Protected

Syntax:

```
virtual void CMFileNew(RTMessage Msg) = [CM_FIRST + CM_FILENEW];
```

Class:

`TFileWindow`

Class Header File:

filewnd.h

Description:

The `CMFileNew` function calls `NewFile` when a `File New` command with a `CM_FILENEW` ID is detected.

CMFileOpen

Member Access Control:

Protected

Syntax:

```
virtual void CMFileOpen(RTMessage Msg) = [CM_FIRST + CM_FILEOPEN];
```

Class:

`TFileWindow`

Class Header File:

filewnd.h

Description:

The `CMFileOpen` function calls `Open` when a `File Open` command with a `CM_FILEOPEN` ID is detected.

CMFileSave

Member Access Control:

Protected

Syntax:

```
virtual void CMFileSave(RTMessage Msg) = [CM_FIRST + CM_FILESAVE];
```

Class:

`TFileWindow`

Class Header File:

filewnd.h

Description:

The `CMFileSave` function calls `Save` when a `File Save` command with a `CM_FILESAVE` ID is detected.

CMFileSaveAs

Member Access Control:

Protected

Syntax:

```
virtual void CMFileSaveAs(RTMessage Msg) = [CM_FIRST + CM_FILESAVEAS];
```

Class:

`TFileWindow`

Class Header File:

filewnd.h

Description:

The `CMFileSaveAs` function calls `SaveAs` when a `File Save As` command with a `CM_FILESAVEAS` ID is detected.

CMTileChildren

Member Access Control:

Protected

Syntax:

```
virtual void CMTileChildren(RTMessage Msg) = [CM_FIRST + CM_TILECHILDREN];
```

Class:

`TMDIFrame`

Class Header File:

mdi.h

Description:

The `CMTileChildren` function calls `TileChildren` when a menu item with a `CM_TILECHILDREN` ID is selected.

Copy

Member Access Control:

Public

Syntax:

```
void Copy();
```

Class:

`TEdit`

Class Header File:

edit.h

Description:

The `Copy` function copies the selected text to the clipboard.

Create

Member Access Control:

Public

Syntax:

```
virtual BOOL Create();
```

Class:

`TDialog`

Class Header File:

dialog.h

Description:

The `Create` function creates a modeless dialog box associated with the `TDialog` object. This function returns TRUE when successful. A return value of FALSE indicates that the function is unsuccessful.

Create

Member Access Control:

Public

Syntax:

```
virtual BOOL Create();
```

Class:

`TWindow`

Class Header File:

window.h

Description:

The `Create` function creates an interface object associated with the `TWindow` object. This function returns TRUE when successful. `Create` calls `Error` and returns FALSE when unsuccessful.

Create

Member Access Control:

Public

Syntax:

```
virtual BOOL Create() = 0;
```

Class:

`TWindowsObject`

Class Header File:

windobj.h

Description:

The `Create` function is a pure virtual function. `Create` should be redefined in derived types to create the associated interface element.

CreateChild

Member Access Control:

Public

Syntax:

```
virtual PTWindowsObject CreateChild();
```

Class:

`TMDIFrame`

Class Header File:

mdi.h

Description:

The `CreateChild` function uses `InitChild` and `MakeWindows` to create an MDI child window and returns a pointer to the created child window.

CreateChildren

Member Access Control:

Public

Syntax:

```
BOOL CreateChildren();
```

Class:

`TWindowsObject`

Class Header File:

windobj.h

Description:

The `CreateChildren` function creates child windows from the child list. The child windows must contain the `WB_AUTOCREATE` mask.

Cut

Member Access Control:

Public

Syntax:

```
void Cut();
```

Class:

`TEdit`

Class Header File:

edit.h

Description:

The `Cut` function deletes the selected text and copies it to the clipboard.

DefChildProc

Member Access Control:

Protected

Syntax:

```
virtual void DefChildProc(RTMessage Msg);
```

Class:

`TWindowsObject`

Class Header File:

windobj.h

Description:

By default, the `DefChildProc` function handles incoming child-ID-based messages.

DefCommandProc

Member Access Control:

Protected

Syntax:

```
virtual void DefCommandProc(RTMessage Msg);
```

Class:

`TWindowsObject`

Class Header File:

windobj.h

Description:

The `DefCommandProc` function, by default, handles command-based messages.

DefNotificationProc

Member Access Control:

Protected

Syntax:

```
virtual void DefNotificationProc(RTMessage Msg);
```

Class:

`TWindowsObject`

Class Header File:

windobj.h

Description:

The `DefNotificationProc` function provides the default processing of notification messages and passes these notification messages to the parent as a child-ID-based message.

DefWndProc

Member Access Control:

Public

Syntax:

```
virtual void DefWndProc(RTMessage Msg);
```

Class:

`TWindowsObject`

Class Header File:

windobj.h

Description:

The `DefWndProc` function handles default message processing.

DeleteLine

Member Access Control:

Public

Syntax:

```
BOOL DeleteLine(int LineNumber);
```

Class:

`TEdit`

Class Header File:

edit.h

Description:

The `DeleteLine` function deletes the line of text specified in `LineNumber` from a multiline edit control. This function returns TRUE when the line of text is deleted. A return value of FALSE indicates that the function cannot delete the line of text.

DeleteSelection

Member Access Control:

Public

Syntax:

```
BOOL DeleteSelection();
```

Class:

`TEdit`

Class Header File:

edit.h

Description:

The `DeleteSelection` function deletes the selected text. This function returns TRUE when the text is deleted. A return value of FALSE indicates that no text was selected.

DeleteString

Member Access Control:

Public

Syntax:

```
int DeleteString(int Index);
```

Class:

`TListBox`

Class Header File:

listbox.h

Description:

The `DeleteString` function deletes the list item at the location specified by `Index`. When successful, this function returns the number of list items remaining. A negative return value indicates that the function cannot delete the specified list item.

DeleteSubText

Member Access Control:

Public

Syntax:

```
BOOL DeleteSubText(int StartPos, int EndPos);
```

Class:

`TEdit`

Class Header File:

edit.h

Description:

The `DeleteSubText` function deletes the text between the text positions specified in `StartPos` and `EndPos`. This function returns TRUE when the text is deleted.

DeltaPos

Member Access Control:

Public

Syntax:

```
int DeltaPos(int Delta);
```

Class:

`TScrollBar`

Class Header File:

scrollba.h

Description:

The `DeltaPos` function changes the thumb position of the scroll bar by calling `SetPosition`. `Delta` specifies the amount to move the thumb position (negative for left or up, positive for right or down). `DeltaPos` returns the new thumb position.

Destroy

Member Access Control:

Public

Syntax:

```
virtual void Destroy(int ARetValue);
```

Class:

`TDialog`

Class Header File:

dialog.h

Description:

The `Destroy` function destroys the interface element associated with `TDialog`. `TWindowsObject::Destroy` is called for modeless dialog boxes. For modal dialog boxes, `EnableAutoCreate` is called for each window in the child list. `ARetValue` is passed to `EndDialog`.

Destroy

Member Access Control:

Public

Syntax:

```
virtual void Destroy();
```

Class:

`TDialog`

Class Header File:

dialog.h

Description:

The `Destroy` function destroys the interface element associated with `TDialog`. `TWindowsObject::Destroy` is called for modeless dialog boxes. `Destroy` is called, with IDCANCEL passed as `ARetValue`, for modal dialog boxes.

Destroy

Member Access Control:

Public

Syntax:

```
virtual void Destroy();
```

Class:

`TWindowsObject`

Class Header File:

windobj.h

Description:

The `Destroy` function destroys an associated interface element after calling `EnableAutoCreate` for each window in the child list.

DisableAutoCreate

Member Access Control:

Public

Syntax:

```
void DisableAutoCreate();
```

Class:

TWindowsObject

Class Header File:

windobj.h

Description:

The `DisableAutoCreate` function disables the autocreate feature. The autocreate feature lets you create and display the interface object as a child window.

DisableTransfer

Member Access Control:

Public

Syntax:

```
void DisableTransfer();
```

Class:

TWindowsObject

Class Header File:

windobj.h

Description:

The `DisableTransfer` function disables the transfer of state data to and from the transfer buffer.

DispatchAMessage

Member Access Control:

Public

Syntax:

```
virtual void DispatchAMessage(WORD AMsg, RTMessage AMessage,
     void (TWindowsObject::*)(RTMessage));
```

Class:

`TWindowsObject`

Class Header File:

windobj.h

Description:

The `DispatchAMessage` function dispatches Windows messages to the appropriate response member function.

DispatchScroll

Member Access Control:

Protected

Syntax:

```
void DispatchScroll(RTMessage Msg);
```

Class:

`TWindowsObject`

Class Header File:

windobj.h

Description:

The `DispatchScroll` function dispatches messages from scroll-bar controls by calling `WMHScroll` and `WMVScroll`.

DoSearch

Member Access Control:

Public

Syntax:

```
void DoSearch();
```

Class:

`TEditWindow`

Class Header File:

editwnd.h

Description:

The `DoSearch` function offers search functions that use the options and features in `SearchStruct`.

DrawItem

Member Access Control:

Public

Syntax:

```
virtual void DrawItem(DRAWITEMSTRUCT _FAR & DrawInfo);
```

Class:

`TWindowsObject`

Class Header File:

windobj.h

Description:

The `DrawItem` function is called when a control or menu item needs to be redrawn.

EnableAutoCreate

Member Access Control:

Public

Syntax:

```
void EnableAutoCreate();
```

Class:

TWindowsObject

Class Header File:

windobj.h

Description:

The `EnableAutoCreate` function enables the autocreate feature. The autocreate feature lets you create and display the interface object as a child window.

EnableKBHandler

Member Access Control:

Public

Syntax:

```
void EnableKBHandler();
```

Class:

TWindowsObject

Class Header File:

windobj.h

Description:

The `EnableKBHandler` function enables windows and modeless dialog boxes to provide a keyboard interface to child controls.

EnableTransfer

Member Access Control:

Public

Syntax:

```
void EnableTransfer();
```

Class:

`TWindowsObject`

Class Header File:

windobj.h

Description:

The `EnableTransfer` function enables the transfer of state data to and from the transfer buffer.

EndView

Member Access Control:

Public

Syntax:

```
virtual void EndView();
```

Class:

`TScroller`

Class Header File:

scroller.h

Description:

The `EndView` function updates the scroll bar positions to correspond to the position of `TScroller`.

ENErrSpace

Member Access Control:

Protected

Syntax:

```
virtual void ENErrSpace(RTMessage Msg) = [NF_FIRST + EN_ERRSPACE];
```

Class:

`TEdit`

Class Header File:

edit.h

Description:

The `ENErrSpace` function sounds a beep when the edit control cannot allocate more memory.

Error

Member Access Control:

Public

Syntax:

```
virtual void Error(int ErrorCode);
```

Class:

`TModule`

Class Header File:

module.h

Description:

The `Error` function processes the error specified in `ErrorCode`. `ErrorCode` can be defined by the application or can be one of the following ObjectWindows errors:

```
EM_INVALIDWINDOW
EM_OUTOFMEMORY
EM_INVALIDCLIENT
EM_INVALIDCHILD
EM_INVALIDMAINWINDOW
```

The `Error` function displays a message box that lists the error code and asks the user to proceed. Depending on the input from the user, the program may continue or be terminated.

ExecDialog

Member Access Control:

Public

Syntax:

```
virtual int ExecDialog(PTWindowsObject ADialog);
```

Class:

TModule

Class Header File:

module.h

Description:

The `ExecDialog` function determines whether the specified dialog object is valid and, if so, executes the dialog object. This function returns IDCANCEL when the specified dialog object is not valid.

Execute

Member Access Control:

Public

Syntax:

```
virtual int Execute();
```

Class:

TDialog

Class Header File:

dialog.h

Description:

The `Execute` function executes the modal dialog box associated with `TDialog`. The function should not return until the dialog box is closed.

FindExactString

Member Access Control:

Public

Syntax:

```
int FindExactString(LPSTR AString, int SearchIndex);
```

Class:

`TListBox`

Class Header File:

listbox.h

Description:

The `FindExactString` function searches the list box for a string that exactly matches the string specified in `AString`. The search begins at the index specified in `SearchIndex`. The index of the matching string is returned.

FindString

Member Access Control:

Public

Syntax:

```
int FindString(LPSTR AString, int SearchIndex);
```

Class:

`TListBox`

Class Header File:

listbox.h

Description:

The `FindString` function searches the list box for a string that begins with the string specified in `AString`. The search begins at the index specified in `SearchIndex`. The index of the matching string is returned.

FirstThat

Member Access Control:

Public

Syntax:

```
PTWindowsObject FirstThat(TCondFunc Test, Pvoid PParamList);
```

Class:

`TWindowsObject`

Class Header File:

windobj.h

Description:

The `FirstThat` function calls the specified test function for each child window in `ChildList`. When the test function returns TRUE, testing stops and `FirstThat` returns the child window object that was successfully tested. Otherwise, this function returns a value of NULL and testing continues.

FirstThat

Member Access Control:

Public

Syntax:

```
PTWindowsObject FirstThat(TCondMemFunc Test, Pvoid PParamList);
```

Class:

`TWindowsObject`

Class Header File:

windobj.h

Description:

This `FirstThat` function is like the previous `FirstThat` function except that this function takes a member function as a parameter.

firstThat

Member Access Control:

Public

Syntax:

```
virtual RCObject firstThat(condFuncType, Pvoid) const;
```

Class:

`Object`

Class Header File:

object.h

Description:

The `firstThat` function calls the specified test function for an object. This function returns the object when the specified test is successful. A return value of NOOBJECT indicates that the test is unsuccessful.

ForEach

Member Access Control:

Public

Syntax:

```
void ForEach(TActionFunc Action, Pvoid PParamList);
```

Class:

`TWindowsObject`

Class Header File:

windobj.h

Description:

The `ForEach` function calls the specified function and passes each child window in `ChildList` as an argument.

ForEach

Member Access Control:

Public

Syntax:

```
void ForEach(TActionMemFunc, Pvoid PParamList);
```

Class:

`TWindowsObject`

Class Header File:

windobj.h

Description:

This `ForEach` function is like the previous `ForEach` function except that this function takes a member function as a parameter.

forEach

Member Access Control:

Public

Syntax:

```
virtual void forEach(iterFuncType, Pvoid);
```

Class:

`Object`

Class Header File:

object.h

Description:

The `forEach` function calls the specified iterator for an object. This function iterates through each object in the container.

GetApplication

Member Access Control:

Public

Syntax:

```
PTApplication GetApplication();
```

Class:

`TWindowsObject`

Class Header File:

windobj.h

Description:

The `GetApplication` function gets the pointer to the `TApplication` object that is associated with `this`.

GetCheck

Member Access Control:

Public

Syntax:

```
WORD GetCheck();
```

Class:

`TCheckBox`

Class Header File:

checkbox.h

Description:

The `GetCheck` function determines the check state of the check box. This function returns `BF_UNCHECKED` if the check box is unchecked, `BF_CHECKED` if the check box is checked, or `BF_GRAYED` if the check box is grayed.

GetChildPtr

Member Access Control:

Protected

Syntax:

```
void GetChildPtr(Ripstream is, RPTWindowsObject P);
```

Class:

`TWindowsObject`

Class Header File:

windobj.h

Description:

The `GetChildPtr` function reads a reference to a pointer to a child window from the specified stream.

GetChildren

Member Access Control:

Public

Syntax:

```
void GetChildren(Ripstream is);
```

Class:

`TWindowsObject`

Class Header File:

windobj.h

Description:

The `GetChildren` function reads child windows from the specified stream into the child list.

GetClassName

Member Access Control:

Protected

Syntax:

```
virtual LPSTR GetClassName();
```

Class:

`TButton`

Class Header File:

button.h

Description:

The `GetClassName` function returns "BUTTON", the name of `TButton`'s Windows registration class.

GetClassName

Member Access Control:

Protected

Syntax:

```
virtual LPSTR GetClassName();
```

Class:

`TComboBox`

Class Header File:

combobox.h

Description:

The `GetClassName` function returns "COMBOBOX", the name of the `TComboBox` Windows registration class.

GetClassName

Member Access Control:

Protected

Syntax:

```
virtual LPSTR GetClassName();
```

Class:

`TDialog`

Class Header File:

dialog.h

Description:

The `GetClassName` function returns the name of the default Windows class for modal dialog boxes. The function returns "OWLDialog" for modeless dialog boxes.

GetClassName

Member Access Control:

Protected

Syntax:

```
virtual LPSTR GetClassName();
```

Class:

`TEdit`

Class Header File:

edit.h

Description:

The `GetClassName` function returns "EDIT", the name of the `TEdit` Windows registration class.

GetClassName

Member Access Control:

Protected

Syntax:

```
virtual LPSTR GetClassName();
```

Class:

`TGroupBox`

Class Header File:

groupbox.h

Description:

The `GetClassName` function returns "BUTTON", the `TGroupBox` Windows registration class name.

GetClassName

Member Access Control:

Protected

Syntax:

```
virtual LPSTR GetClassName();
```

Class:

`TListBox`

Class Header File:

listbox.h

Description:

The `GetClassName` function returns "LISTBOX", the `TListBox` Windows registration class name.

GetClassName

Member Access Control:

Protected

Syntax:

```
virtual LPSTR GetClassName();
```

Class:

`TMDIClient`

Class Header File:

mdi.h

Description:

The `GetClassName` function returns "MDICLIENT", the `TMDIClient` Windows registration class name.

GetClassName

Member Access Control:

Protected

Syntax:

```
virtual LPSTR GetClassName();
```

Class:

`TMDIFrame`

Class Header File:

mdi.h

Description:

The `GetClassName` function returns "OWLMDIFrame", the `TMDIFrame` Windows registration class name.

GetClassName

Member Access Control:

Protected

Syntax:

```
virtual LPSTR GetClassName();
```

Class:

`TScrollBar`

Class Header File:

scrollba.h

Description:

The `GetClassName` function returns "SCROLLBAR", the `TScrollBar` Windows registration class name.

GetClassName

Member Access Control:

Protected

Syntax:

```
virtual LPSTR GetClassName();
```

Class:

`TStatic`

Class Header File:

static.h

Description:

The `GetClassName` function returns "STATIC", the `TStatic` Windows registration class name.

GetClassName

Member Access Control:

Protected

Syntax:

```
virtual LPSTR GetClassName();
```

Class:

`TWindow`

Class Header File:

window.h

Description:

The `GetClassName` function returns "OWLWindow", the default Windows registration class name for `TWindow`.

GetClassName

Member Access Control:

Protected

Syntax:

```
virtual LPSTR GetClassName() = 0;
```

Class:

`TWindowsObject`

Class Header File:

windobj.h

Description:

The `GetClassName` function returns the Windows registration class name and must be redefined for derived classes.

GetClient

Member Access Control:

Public

Syntax:

```
virtual PTMDIClient GetClient();
```

Class:

`TMDIFrame`

Class Header File:

mdi.h

Description:

The `GetClient` function returns the pointer to the client window stored in `ClientWnd`.

GetClient

Member Access Control:

Public

Syntax:

```
virtual PTMDIClient GetClient();
```

Class:

`TWindowsObject`

Class Header File:

windobj.h

Description:

The `GetClient` function returns NULL for non-MDI interface objects without MDI client windows. `TMDIWindow` redefines this function to return a pointer to the MDI client window.

GetClientHandle

Member Access Control:

Public

Syntax:

```
HWND GetClientHandle (HWND AnHWindow);
```

Class:

`TModule`

Class Header File:

module.h

Description:

The `GetClientHandle` function returns the handle of the MDI client window for the specified window. This function returns zero when then window has no MDI client window.

GetCount

Member Access Control:

Public

Syntax:

```
int GetCount();
```

Class:

`TListBox`

Class Header File:

listbox.h

Description:

When successful, the `GetCount` function returns the number of list box items. A negative return value indicates that the function is unsuccessful.

GetFirstChild

Member Access Control:

Public

Syntax:

```
PTWindowsObject GetFirstChild();
```

Class:

`TWindowsObject`

Class Header File:

windobj.h

Description:

The `GetFirstChild` function returns the pointer to the first child window in the child list for the interface object.

GetId

Member Access Control:

Public

Syntax:

```
virtual int GetId();
```

Class:

`TControl`

Class Header File:

control.h

Description:

The `GetId` function returns the window ID, `Attr.Id`.

GetId

Member Access Control:

Public

Syntax:

```
virtual int GetId();
```

Class:

`TWindowsObject`

Class Header File:

windobj.h

Description:

The `GetId` function returns 0 by default. However, `TControl` redefines `GetId` to return the control ID of the class.

GetInstance

Member Access Control:

Public

Syntax:

```
FARPROC GetInstance();
```

Class:

TWindowsObject

Class Header File:

windobj.h

Description:

The `GetInstance` function returns the instance thunk of the window.

GetItemHandle

Member Access Control:

Public

Syntax:

```
HWND GetItemHandle(int DlgItemID);
```

Class:

`TDialog`

Class Header File:

dialog.h

Description:

The `GetItemHandle` function returns the handle of the dialog control that has the ID specified in `DlgItemID`.

GetLastChild

Member Access Control:

Public

Syntax:

```
PTWindowsObject GetLastChild();
```

Class:

TWindowsObject

Class Header File:

windobj.h

Description:

The `GetLastChild` function returns the pointer to the last child window in the child list for the interface object.

GetLine

Member Access Control:

Public

Syntax:

```
BOOL GetLine(LPSTR ATextString, int StrSize, int LineNumber);
```

Class:

`TEdit`

Class Header File:

edit.h

Description:

The `GetLine` function gets a line of text from the edit control. `LineNumber` specifies the line number to retrieve. `ATextString` specifies the location where the line of text is copied. `StrSize` specifies the number of characters to retrieve.

GetLineFromPos

Member Access Control:

Public

Syntax:

```
int GetLineFromPos(int CharPos);
```

Class:

`TEdit`

Class Header File:

edit.h

Description:

The `GetLineFromPos` function gets the line number from a multiline edit control of the line that contains the character position specified in `CharPos`.

GetLineIndex

Member Access Control:

Public

Syntax:

```
int GetLineIndex(int LineNumber);
```

Class:

`TEdit`

Class Header File:

edit.h

Description:

The `GetLineIndex` function returns the number of characters prior to the specified line number in a multiline edit control.

GetLineLength

Member Access Control:

Public

Syntax:

```
int GetLineLength(int LineNumber);
```

Class:

`TEdit`

Class Header File:

edit.h

Description:

The `GetLineLength` function gets the number of characters in a line of text from a multiline edit control. `LineNumber` specifies the line number.

GetModule

Member Access Control:

Public

Syntax:

```
PTModule GetModule();
```

Class:

TWindowsObject

Class Header File:

windobj.h

Description:

The `GetModule` function returns the pointer to the `TModule` that owns the object.

GetMsgID

Member Access Control:

Protected

Syntax:

```
virtual WORD GetMsgID(WORD AnId);
```

Class:

`TComboBox`

Class Header File:

combobox.h

Description:

The `GetMsgID` function returns the message ID of the Windows combo box message that is associated with the ObjectWindows message ID.

GetMsgID

Member Access Control:

Protected

Syntax:

```
virtual WORD GetMsgID(WORD AMsg);
```

Class:

`TListBox`

Class Header File:

listbox.h

Description:

The `GetMsgID` function returns the Windows list box message ID associated with the specified ObjectWindows message ID.

GetNumLines

Member Access Control:

Public

Syntax:

```
int GetNumLines();
```

Class:

`TEdit`

Class Header File:

edit.h

Description:

The `GetNumLines` function gets the number of lines in a multiline edit control.

GetParentObject

Member Access Control:

Public

Syntax:

```
virtual PTWindowsObject GetParentObject(HWND ParentHandle);
```

Class:

`TModule`

Class Header File:

module.h

Description:

The `GetParentObject` function is called in a DLL to get a pointer to a parent window object.

GetPosition

Member Access Control:

Public

Syntax:

```
int GetPosition();
```

Class:

`TScrollBar`

Class Header File:

scrollba.h

Description:

The `GetPosition` function returns the thumb position of the scroll bar.

GetRange

Member Access Control:

Public

Syntax:

```
void GetRange(Rint LoVal, Rint HiVal);
```

Class:

`TScrollBar`

Class Header File:

scrollba.h

Description:

The `GetRange` function returns the scroll bar range in `LoVal` and `HiVal`.

GetSelection

Member Access Control:

Public

Syntax:

```
void GetSelection(Rint StartPos, Rint EndPos);
```

Class:

`TEdit`

Class Header File:

edit.h

Description:

The `GetSelection` function returns the starting and ending positions of the selected text in `StartPos` and `EndPos`, respectively.

GetSelIndex

Member Access Control:

Public

Syntax:

```
int GetSelIndex();
```

Class:

`TListBox`

Class Header File:

listbox.h

Description:

When successful, the `GetSelIndex` function returns the position of the currently selected item. A negative return value indicates that the function is unsuccessful. This function is for use with single selection list boxes only.

GetSelString

Member Access Control:

Public

Syntax:

```
int GetSelString(LPSTR AString, int MaxChars);
```

Class:

`TListBox`

Class Header File:

listbox.h

Description:

The `GetSelString` function places the currently selected list item in `AString`. `MaxChars` specifies the maximum number of characters to copy. When successful, this function returns the length of the copied string. A negative return value indicates that the function is unsuccessful.

GetSiblingPtr

Member Access Control:

Protected

Syntax:

```
void GetSiblingPtr(Ripstream is, RPTWindowsObject P);
```

Class:

`TWindowsObject`

Class Header File:

windobj.h

Description:

The `GetSiblingPtr` function is used only during a `read` operation to references written by a call to `PutSiblingPtr`. `GetSiblingPtr` reads a reference to a sibling window from the specified stream.

GetString

Member Access Control:

Public

Syntax:

```
int GetString(LPSTR AString, int Index);
```

Class:

`TListBox`

Class Header File:

listbox.h

Description:

The `GetString` function copies the item at the location specified in `Index` to `AString`. When successful, this function returns the length of the copied string. A negative return value indicates that the function is unsuccessful.

GetStringLen

Member Access Control:

Public

Syntax:

```
int GetStringLen(int Index);
```

Class:

`TListBox`

Class Header File:

listbox.h

Description:

When successful, the `GetStringLen` function returns the length of the item at the location specified in `Index`. A negative return value indicates that the function is unsuccessful.

GetSubText

Member Access Control:

Public

Syntax:

```
void GetSubText(LPSTR ATextString, int StartPos, int EndPos);
```

Class:

`TEdit`

Class Header File:

edit.h

Description:

The `GetSubText` function gets the text specified by `StartPos` and `EndPos` and returns the text to `ATextString`.

GetText

Member Access Control:

Public

Syntax:

```
int GetText(LPSTR ATextString, int MaxChars);
```

Class:

TStatic

Class Header File:

static.h

Description:

The GetText function returns the text of the static control in ATextString. MaxChars specifies the size of ATextString.

GetWindowClass

Member Access Control:

Protected

Syntax:

```
virtual void GetWindowClass(WNDCLASS _FAR & AWndClass);
```

Class:

TDialog

Class Header File:

dialog.h

Description:

The GetWindowClass function fills AWndClass (a WNDCLASS structure) with the registration attributes for TDialog. This function can be redefined to change the default registration attributes.

GetWindowClass

Member Access Control:

Protected

Syntax:

```
virtual void GetWindowClass(WNDCLASS _FAR & AWndClass);
```

Class:

`TMDIFrame`

Class Header File:

mdi.h

Description:

The `GetWindowClass` function calls `TWindow::GetWindowClass` and sets `AWndClass.Style` to 0.

GetWindowClass

Member Access Control:

Protected

Syntax:

```
virtual void GetWindowClass(WndClass _FAR & AWndClass);
```

Class:

`TWindow`

Class Header File:

window.h

Description:

The `GetWindowClass` function places the default values for the registration attributes into the window class structure referenced by `AWndClass`.

GetWindowClass

Member Access Control:

Protected

Syntax:

```
virtual void GetWindowClass(WNDCLASS _FAR & AWndClass);
```

Class:

`TWindowsObject`

Class Header File:

windobj.h

Description:

The `GetWindowClass` function is a pure virtual function. Derived classes must redefine this function to copy the registration attributes to the specified window class structure.

HandleDList

Member Access Control:

Protected

Syntax:

```
virtual void HandleDList(RTMessage Msg) = [ID_FIRST + ID_DLIST];
```

Class:

`TFileDialog`

Class Header File:

filedial.h

Description:

The `HandleDList` function responds to messages from the directory list box. This function calls `UpdateListBoxes` when an entry is double-clicked. Otherwise, `UpdateFileName` is called.

HandleFList

Member Access Control:

Protected

Syntax:

```
virtual void HandleFList(RTMessage Msg) = [ID_FIRST + ID_FLIST];
```

Class:

`TFileDialog`

Class Header File:

filedial.h

Description:

The `HandleFList` function responds to messages from the file list box and calls `UpdateFileName` when the list box selection changes.

HandleFName

Member Access Control:

Protected

Syntax:

```
virtual void HandleFName(RTMessage Msg) = [ID_FIRST + ID_FNAME];
```

Class:

`TFileDialog`

Class Header File:

filedial.h

Description:

The `HandleFName` function responds to messages from the edit control and enables the `OK` button when the edit control contains text.

hashValue

Member Access Control:

Public

Syntax:

```
virtual hashValueType hashValue() const = 0;
```

Class:

`Object`

Class Header File:

object.h

Description:

The `hashValue` function is a pure virtual function for derived classes. The function returns a hash value.

hashValue

Member Access Control:

Public

Syntax:

```
virtual hashValueType hashValue() const;
```

Class:

`TModule`

Class Header File:

module.h

Description:

The `hashValue` function redefines the pure virtual function in class `Object`. This function returns the hash value of `TModule`, `hInstance`.

hashValue

Member Access Control:

Public

Syntax:

```
virtual hashValueType hashValue() const;
```

Class:

`TScroller`

Class Header File:

scroller.h

Description:

The `hashValue` function redefines the pure virtual function in class `Object`. This function returns the unique ID of a `TScroller` instance.

hashValue

Member Access Control:

Public

Syntax:

```
virtual hashValueType hashValue() const;
```

Class:

`TWindowsObject`

Class Header File:

windobj.h

Description:

The `hashValue` function redefines the pure virtual function in class `Object`. This function returns the hash value of `TWindowsObject`, `HWindow`.

HideList

Member Access Control:

Public

Syntax:

```
void HideList();
```

Class:

`TComboBox`

Class Header File:

combobox.h

Description:

The `HideList` function hides the list of a drop-down or drop-down list combo box.

HScroll

Member Access Control:

Public

Syntax:

```
virtual void HScroll(WORD ScrollEvent, int ThumbPos);
```

Class:

`TScroller`

Class Header File:

scroller.h

Description:

The `HScroll` function calls `ScrollTo` or `ScrollBy` to handle the specified horizontal scroll event. `ThumbPos` specifies the current thumb position.

IdleAction

Member Access Control:

Protected

Syntax:

```
virtual void IdleAction();
```

Class:

TApplication

Class Header File:

applicat.h

Description:

The `IdleAction` function is invoked when the application is idle. This function can be redefined to perform special functions when the application is idle.

InitApplication

Member Access Control:

Protected

Syntax:

```
virtual void InitApplication();
```

Class:

`TApplication`

Class Header File:

applicat.h

Description:

The `InitApplication` function makes the initializations required for the first executing instance of the application. `InitApplication` can be redefined by derived classes for custom initializations.

InitChild

Member Access Control:

Public

Syntax:

```
virtual PTWindowsObject InitChild();
```

Class:

`TMDIFrame`

Class Header File:

mdi.h

Description:

The `InitChild` function constructs an instance of `TWindow` as an MDI child window. This function returns the pointer to the instance. This member function can be redefined in the derived window class to construct an instance of a derived MDI child class.

InitClientWindow

Member Access Control:

Public

Syntax:

```
virtual void InitClientWindow();
```

Class:

`TMDIFrame`

Class Header File:

mdi.h

Description:

The `InitClientWindow` function constructs the MDI client window as an instance of `TMDIClient`. The pointer to the client window is stored in `ClientWnd`.

InitInstance

Member Access Control:

Protected

Syntax:

```
virtual void InitInstance();
```

Class:

`TApplication`

Class Header File:

applicat.h

Description:

The `InitInstance` function makes the initializations required for all executing instances of the application.

InitMainWindow

Member Access Control:

Protected

Syntax:

```
virtual void InitMainWindow();
```

Class:

`TApplication`

Class Header File:

applicat.h

Description:

The `InitMainWindow` function constructs a generic `TWindow` class that uses the application name for the caption. The `InitMainWindow` function can be redefined to construct a main window object of a derived class.

Insert

Member Access Control:

Public

Syntax:

```
void Insert(LPSTR ATextString);
```

Class:

`TEdit`

Class Header File:

edit.h

Description:

The `Insert` function inserts the text in `ATextString` into the edit control at the current cursor position.

InsertString

Member Access Control:

Public

Syntax:

```
int InsertString(LPSTR AString, int Index);
```

Class:

`TListBox`

Class Header File:

listbox.h

Description:

The `InsertString` function inserts the string specified in `AString` at the list position specified in `Index`. When successful, this function returns the string's list position. A negative return value indicates that the function is unsuccessful.

isA

Member Access Control:

Public

Syntax:

```
virtual classType isA() const = 0;
```

Class:

`Object`

Class Header File:

object.h

Description:

The `isA` function is a pure virtual function for derived classes. The function returns a unique class ID for the class.

isA

Member Access Control:

Public

Syntax:

```
virtual classType isA() const;
```

Class:

`TApplication`

Class Header File:

applicat.h

Description:

The `isA` function redefines the pure virtual function in class `Object`. This function returns the class ID of `TApplication`.

isA

Member Access Control:

Public

Syntax:

```
virtual classType isA() const;
```

Class:

`TDialog`

Class Header File:

dialog.h

Description:

The `isA` function redefines the pure virtual function in class `Object`. This function returns the class ID of `TDialog`.

isA

Member Access Control:

Public

Syntax:

```
virtual classType isA() const;
```

Class:

`TModule`

Class Header File:

module.h

Description:

The `isA` function redefines the pure virtual function in class `Object`. This function returns the object ID of `TModule`, `moduleClass`.

isA

Member Access Control:

Public

Syntax:

```
virtual classType isA() const;
```

Class:

`TScroller`

Class Header File:

scroller.h

Description:

The `isA` function redefines the pure virtual function in class `Object`. This function returns the class ID of `TScroller`.

isA

Member Access Control:

Public

Syntax:

```
virtual classType isA() const;
```

Class:

`TWindow`

Class Header File:

window.h

Description:

The `isA` function redefines the pure virtual function in class `Object`. This function returns the object ID of `TWindow`.

isA

Member Access Control:

Public

Syntax:

```
virtual classType isA() const = 0;
```

Class:

`TWindowsObject`

Class Header File:

windobj.h

Description:

The `isA` function redefines the pure virtual function in class `Object` and should be redefined to return a unique class ID.

isAssociation

Member Access Control:

Public

Syntax:

```
virtual int isAssociation() const;
```

Class:

`Object`

Class Header File:

object.h

Description:

The `isAssociation` function determines whether or not an object is derived from the class `Association`.

isEqual

Member Access Control:

Public

Syntax:

```
virtual int isEqual(RCObject) const = 0;
```

Class:

`Object`

Class Header File:

object.h

Description:

The `isEqual` function is a pure virtual function for derived classes.

isEqual

Member Access Control:

Public

Syntax:

```
virtual int isEqual(RCObject module) const;
```

Class:

`TModule`

Class Header File:

module.h

Description:

The `isEqual` function redefines the pure virtual function in class `Object`.

isEqual

Member Access Control:

Public

Syntax:

```
virtual int isEqual(RCObject testobj) const;
```

Class:

`TScroller`

Class Header File:

scroller.h

Description:

The `isEqual` function redefines the pure virtual function in class `Object`. This function returns TRUE when `this` points to `testobj`.

isEqual

Member Access Control:

Public

Syntax:

```
virtual int isEqual(RCObject testwin) const;
```

Class:

`TWindowsObject`

Class Header File:

windobj.h

Description:

The `isEqual` function redefines the pure virtual function in class `Object`. This function returns TRUE when `this` points to `testwin`.

IsFlagSet

Member Access Control:

Public

Syntax:

```
BOOL IsFlagSet(WORD Mask);
```

Class:

`TWindowsObject`

Class Header File:

windobj.h

Description:

The `IsFlagSet` function returns TRUE if the bit flag of the `Flags` data member with the specified mask is set. A return value of FALSE indicates that the bit flag is not set.

IsModified

Member Access Control:

Public

Syntax:

```
BOOL IsModified();
```

Class:

`TEdit`

Class Header File:

edit.h

Description:

The `IsModified` function indicates whether the text in the edit control has been modified. This function returns TRUE when the text has been modified.

isSortable

Member Access Control:

Public

Syntax:

```
virtual int isSortable() const;
```

Class:

`Object`

Class Header File:

object.h

Description:

The `isSortable` function determines whether or not an object is derived from the class `Sortable`.

isVisibleRect

Member Access Control:

Public

Syntax:

```
BOOL IsVisibleRect(long X, long Y, int XExt, int YExt);
```

Class:

`TScroller`

Class Header File:

scroller.h

Description:

The `IsVisibleRect` function determines whether any part of the specified rectangle is visible in the owner window. This function returns TRUE if any part of the rectangle is visible.

lastThat

Member Access Control:

Public

Syntax:

```
virtual RCObject lastThat(condFuncType, Pvoid) const;
```

Class:

`Object`

Class Header File:

object.h

Description:

The `lastThat` function is identical to `firstThat` for noncontainer objects.

LowMemory

Member Access Control:

Public

Syntax:

```
BOOL LowMemory();
```

Class:

`TModule`

Class Header File:

module.h

Description:

The `LowMemory` function returns TRUE when the safety pool has been used up.

MakeWindow

Member Access Control:

Public

Syntax:

```
virtual PTWindowsObject MakeWindow(PTWindowsObject AWindowsObject);
```

Class:

TModule

Class Header File:

module.h

Description:

The MakeWindow function creates and associates a window or modeless dialog element with the specified object as long as the specified object is valid. A return value of NULL indicates that the function is unsuccessful.

MessageLoop

Member Access Control:

Protected

Syntax:

```
virtual void MessageLoop();
```

Class:

TApplication

Class Header File:

applicat.h

Description:

The MessageLoop function manages the message loop of the application.

nameOf

Member Access Control:

Public

Syntax:

```
virtual Pchar nameOf() const = 0;
```

Class:

`Object`

Class Header File:

object.h

Description:

The `nameOf` function is a pure virtual function for derived classes. The function returns a class ID string.

nameOf

Member Access Control:

Public

Syntax:

```
virtual Pchar nameOf() const;
```

Class:

`TApplication`

Class Header File:

applicat.h

Description:

The `nameOf` function redefines the pure virtual function in class `Object`. This function returns “TApplication”, the class ID string.

nameOf

Member Access Control:

Public

Syntax:

```
virtual Pchar nameOf() const;
```

Class:

`TComboBox`

Class Header File:

combobox.h

Description:

The `nameOf` function redefines the pure virtual function in class `Object`. This function returns "TComboBox", the class ID string for `TComboBox`.

nameOf

Member Access Control:

Public

Syntax:

```
virtual Pchar nameOf() const;
```

Class:

`TDialog`

Class Header File:

dialog.h

Description:

The `nameOf` function redefines the pure virtual function in class `Object`. This function returns "TDialog", the class ID string for `TDialog`.

nameOf

Member Access Control:

Public

Syntax:

```
virtual Pchar nameOf() const;
```

Class:

`TModule`

Class Header File:

module.h

Description:

The `nameOf` function redefines the pure virtual function in class `Object`. This function returns the class ID string of `TModule`, "TModule".

nameOf

Member Access Control:

Public

Syntax:

```
virtual Pchar nameOf() const;
```

Class:

`TScroller`

Class Header File:

scroller.h

Description:

The `nameOf` function redefines the pure virtual function in class `Object`. This function returns "TScroller", the class ID string of `TScroller`.

nameOf

Member Access Control:

Public

Syntax:

```
virtual Pchar nameOf() const;
```

Class:

`TStatic`

Class Header File:

static.h

Description:

The `nameOf` function redefines the pure virtual function in class `Object`. This function returns "TStatic", the class ID string.

nameOf

Member Access Control:

Public

Syntax:

```
virtual Pchar nameOf() const;
```

Class:

`TWindow`

Class Header File:

window.h

Description:

The `nameOf` function redefines the pure virtual function in class `Object`. This function returns "TWindow", the class ID string of `TWindow`.

nameOf

Member Access Control:

Public

Syntax:

```
virtual Pchar nameOf() const = 0;
```

Class:

`TWindowsObject`

Class Header File:

windobj.h

Description:

The `nameOf` function is a pure virtual function. Derived classes should redefine this function to return a class ID string.

new

Member Access Control:

Public

Syntax:

```
Pvoid operator new(size_t);
```

Class:

`Object`

Class Header File:

object.h

Description:

The new function allocates the specified number of bytes for an object. ZERO is returned when the function cannot allocate the required space.

NewFile

Member Access Control:

Public

Syntax:

```
void NewFile();
```

Class:

`TFileWindow`

Class Header File:

filewnd.h

Description:

The `NewFile` function calls `CanClear` to determine whether the current text in the editor can be cleared. If the existing text can be cleared, a new file is opened.

Next

Member Access Control:

Public

Syntax:

```
PTWindowsObject Next();
```

Class:

`TWindowsObject`

Class Header File:

windobj.h

Description:

The `Next` function returns a pointer to the next window in the child window list.

ODADrawEntire

Member Access Control:

Protected

Syntax:

```
virtual void ODADrawEntire (DRAWITEMSTRUCT _FAR & DrawInfo);
```

Class:

`TControl`

Class Header File:

control.h

Description:

The `ODADrawEntire` function responds when notified that a drawable control needs to be redrawn.

ODAFocus

Member Access Control:

Protected

Syntax:

```
virtual void ODAFocus(DRAWITEMSTRUCT _FAR & DrawInfo);
```

Class:

`TControl`

Class Header File:

control.h

Description:

The `ODAFocus` function responds when notified that the focus has been given to or taken from the drawable control.

ODASelect

Member Access Control:

Public

Syntax:

```
virtual void ODASelect(DRAWITEMSTRUCT _FAR & DrawInfo);
```

Class:

`TControl`

Class Header File:

control.h

Description:

The `ODASelect` function responds when notified that the selection state of the drawable control has changed.

Ok

Member Access Control:

Protected

Syntax:

```
virtual void Ok(RTMessage Msg) = [ID_FIRST + ID_OK];
```

Class:

`TDialog`

Class Header File:

dialog.h

Description:

The `Ok` function calls `CloseWindow` when the `Ok` button of the dialog box is selected.

Open

Member Access Control:

Public

Syntax:

```
void Open();
```

Class:

`TFileWindow`

Class Header File:

filewnd.h

Description:

The `Open` function calls `CanClear` to determine whether the current text in the editor can be cleared. If the existing text can be cleared, `Open` displays a file dialog box that enables the user to select a file. Once a file has been selected, `Open` calls `ReplaceWith` and passes the selected file name.

Paint

Member Access Control:

Protected

Syntax:

```
virtual void Paint(HDC PaintDC, PAINTSTRUCT _FAR & PaintInfo);
```

Class:

`TWindow`

Class Header File:

window.h

Description:

The `Paint` function stores derived types that define `Paint` member functions. `Paint` is called automatically when a `WM_PAINT` message is detected.

Paste

Member Access Control:

Public

Syntax:

```
void Paste();
```

Class:

`TEdit`

Class Header File:

edit.h

Description:

The `Paste` function places the text in the clipboard into the edit control at the current cursor position.

Previous

Member Access Control:

Public

Syntax:

```
PTWindowsObject Previous();
```

Class:

`TWindowsObject`

Class Header File:

windobj.h

Description:

The `Previous` function returns a pointer to the previous window in the child window list.

printOn

Member Access Control:

Public

Syntax:

```
virtual void printOn(Rostream) const = 0;
```

Class:

`Object`

Class Header File:

object.h

Description:

The `printOn` function is a pure virtual function for derived classes. This function writes the printable representation of the object on a stream.

printOn

Member Access Control:

Public

Syntax:

```
virtual void printOn(Rostream outputStream) const;
```

Class:

`TModule`

Class Header File:

module.h

Description:

The `printOn` function redefines the pure virtual function in class `Object`. The hexadecimal value of the instance handle for the module is printed on the specified stream.

printOn

Member Access Control:

Public

Syntax:

```
virtual void printOn(Rostream outputStream) const;
```

Class:

TScroller

Class Header File:

scroller.h

Description:

The `printOn` function redefines the pure virtual function in class `Object`.

printOn

Member Access Control:

Public

Syntax:

```
virtual void printOn(Rostream outputStream) const;
```

Class:

TWindowsObject

Class Header File:

windobj.h

Description:

The `printOn` function redefines the pure virtual function in class `Object`. This function prints a hexadecimal representation of `HWindow` on the specified stream.

ProcessAccels

Member Access Control:

Protected

Syntax:

```
virtual BOOL ProcessAccels(LPMSG PMessage);
```

Class:

`TApplication`

Class Header File:

applicat.h

Description:

The `ProcessAccels` function processes accelerator messages.

ProcessAppMsg

Member Access Control:

Protected

Syntax:

```
virtual BOOL ProcessAppMsg(LPMSG PMessage);
```

Class:

`TApplication`

Class Header File:

applicat.h

Description:

The `ProcessAppMsg` function calls `ProcessDlgMsg`, `ProcessMDIAccels`, and `ProcessAccels` to process modeless dialog messages, MDI accelerator messages, and accelerator messages, respectively. This function returns TRUE when any modeless dialog message, MDI accelerator message, or accelerator message is encountered.

ProcessDlgMsg

Member Access Control:

Protected

Syntax:

```
virtual BOOL ProcessDlgMsg(LPMSG PMessage);
```

Class:

`TApplication`

Class Header File:

applicat.h

Description:

The `ProcessDlgMsg` function provides message processing of keyboard input for modeless dialog boxes and windows with controls.

ProcessMDIAccels

Member Access Control:

Protected

Syntax:

```
virtual BOOL ProcessMDIAccels(LPMSG PMessage);
```

Class:

`TApplication`

Class Header File:

applicat.h

Description:

The `ProcessMDIAccels` function processes accelerator messages for MDI applications.

PutChildPtr

Member Access Control:

Protected

Syntax:

```
void PutChildPtr(Ropstream os, PTWindowsObject P);
```

Class:

`TWindowsObject`

Class Header File:

windobj.h

Description:

The `PutChildPtr` function writes a child window to the specified output stream. This function should be used only during a `write` operation to write pointers that can be read by `GetChildPtr`.

PutChildren

Member Access Control:

Public

Syntax:

```
void PutChildren(Ropstream os);
```

Class:

`TWindowsObject`

Class Header File:

windobj.h

Description:

The `PutChildren` function writes child windows to the specified stream.

PutSiblingPtr

Member Access Control:

Protected

Syntax:

```
void PutSiblingPtr(Ropstream os, PTWindowsObject P);
```

Class:

`TWindowsObject`

Class Header File:

windobj.h

Description:

The `PutSiblingPtr` function writes the pointer to a sibling window to the specified output stream. This function should by used only during a `write` operation to write pointers that `GetSiblingPtr` can read.

Read

Member Access Control:

Public

Syntax:

```
BOOL Read();
```

Class:

`TFileWindow`

Class Header File:

filewnd.h

Description:

The `Read` function reads the contents of a file into the editor and sets `IsNewFile` to FALSE. TRUE is returned when the function is successful.

read

Member Access Control:

Protected

Syntax:

```
virtual Pvoid read(Ripstream is);
```

Class:

`TCheckBox`

Class Header File:

checkbox.h

Description:

The `read` function calls `TWindow::read` to read in the base `TWindow` object.

read

Member Access Control:

Protected

Syntax:

```
virtual Pvoid read(Ripstream is);
```

Class:

`TComboBox`

Class Header File:

combobox.h

Description:

The `read` function calls `TListBox::read` to read in the base `TListBox` object.

read

Member Access Control:

Protected

Syntax:

```
virtual Pvoid read(Ripstream is);
```

Class:

`TDialog`

Class Header File:

dialog.h

Description:

The `read` function calls `TWindowsObject::read` to read in the base `TWindowsObject` object.

read

Member Access Control:

Protected

Syntax:

```
virtual Pvoid read(Ripstream is);
```

Class:

`TEditWindow`

Class Header File:

editwnd.h

Description:

The `read` function calls `TWindow::read` to read in the base `TWindow` object.

read

Member Access Control:

Protected

Syntax:

```
virtual Pvoid read(Ripstream is);
```

Class:

`TFileWindow`

Class Header File:

filewnd.h

Description:

The `read` function calls `TEditWindow::read` to read in the base `TEditWindow` object.

read

Member Access Control:

Protected

Syntax:

```
virtual Pvoid read(Ripstream is);
```

Class:

`TGroupBox`

Class Header File:

groupbox.h

Description:

The `read` function calls `TWindow::read` to read in the base `TGroupBox` object.

read

Member Access Control:

Protected

Syntax:

```
virtual Pvoid read(Ripstream is);
```

Class:

`TInputDialog`

Class Header File:

inputdia.h

Description:

The `read` function calls `TDialog::read` to read in the base `TDialog` object.

read

Member Access Control:

Protected

Syntax:

```
virtual Pusid read(Ripstream is);
```

Class:

`TMDIClient`

Class Header File:

mdi.h

Description:

The `read` function calls `TWindow::read` to read the base `TWindow` object.

read

Member Access Control:

Protected

Syntax:

```
virtual Pvoid read(Ripstream is);
```

Class:

`TMDIFrame`

Class Header File:

mdi.h

Description:

The `read` function calls `TWindow::read` to read in the base `TWindow` object.

read

Member Access Control:

Protected

Syntax:

```
virtual Pvoid read(Ripstream is);
```

Class:

`TScrollBar`

Class Header File:

scrollba.h

Description:

The `read` function calls `TWindow::read` to read in the base `TWindow` object.

read

Member Access Control:

Protected

Syntax:

```
virtual Pvoid read(Ripstream is);
```

Class:

`TScroller`

Class Header File:

scroller.h

Description:

The `read` function reads `AutoMode`, `AutoOrg`, `HasHScrollBar`, `HasVScrollBar`, `TrackMode`, `XLine`, `XPage`, `XPos`, `XRange`, `XUnit`, `YLine`, `YPage`, `YPos`, `YRange`, and `YUnit`.

read

Member Access Control:

Protected

Syntax:

```
virtual Pvoid read(Ripstream is);
```

Class:

`TStatic`

Class Header File:

static.h

Description:

The `read` function calls `TWindow::read` to read in the base `TWindow` object.

read

Member Access Control:

Protected

Syntax:

```
virtual Pvoid read(Ripstream) = 0;
```

Class:

`TStreamable`

Class Header File:

objstrm.h

Description:

The `read` function is a pure virtual function that must be redefined by all derived classes. The `read` function permits the application to read from the specified input stream.

read

Member Access Control:

Protected

Syntax:

```
virtual Pvoid read(Pipstream is);
```

Class:

`TWindow`

Class Header File:

window.h

Description:

The `read` function uses `TWindowsObject::read` to read the base `TWindowsObject` object.

read

Member Access Control:

Protected

Syntax:

```
virtual Pvoid read(Ripstream is);
```

Class:

`TWindowsObject`

Class Header File:

windobj.h

Description:

The `read` function creates an object instance and calls `GetChildren` to read in the child windows. The child list, `HWindow`, `Parent`, and `TransferBuffer` are set to 0. `Title`, `Status`, flags, and `CreateOrder` are read in.

Register

Member Access Control:

Public

Syntax:

```
virtual BOOL Register();
```

Class:

`TWindowsObject`

Class Header File:

windobj.h

Description:

The `Register` function registers the Windows registration class of `this`. This function returns TRUE if the class is successfully registered.

RemoveClient

Member Access Control:

Public

Syntax:

```
void RemoveClient();
```

Class:

`TWindowsObject`

Class Header File:

windobj.h

Description:

The `RemoveClient` function removes the specified client window from the child list.

ReplaceWith

Member Access Control:

Public

Syntax:

```
void ReplaceWith(LPSTR AFileName);
```

Class:

`TFileWindow`

Class Header File:

filewnd.h

Description:

The `ReplaceWith` function replaces the current file in the editor with the specified file. `Replacewith` calls `SetFileName` and `Read`.

RestoreMemory

Member Access Control:

Public

Syntax:

```
void RestoreMemory();
```

Class:

`TModule`

Class Header File:

module.h

Description:

The `RestoreMemory` function allocates a safety pool if one has not already been allocated.

Run

Member Access Control:

Public

Syntax:

```
virtual void Run();
```

Class:

`TApplication`

Class Header File:

applicat.h

Description:

The `Run` function initializes the instance and executes the application. `InitApplication` is called if no other instances of the application are running. `MessageLoop` is called to begin the execution of the application if initialization is successful.

Save

Member Access Control:

Public

Syntax:

```
BOOL Save();
```

Class:

`TFileWindow`

Class Header File:

filewnd.h

Description:

The `Save` function saves the current file. When `IsNewFile` is TRUE, `Save` calls `SaveAs`. When `IsNewFile` is FALSE, `Save` calls `Write`. `Save` returns the result of the call to the appropriate function.

SaveAs

Member Access Control:

Public

Syntax:

```
BOOL SaveAs();
```

Class:

`TFileWindow`

Class Header File:

filewnd.h

Description:

The `SaveAs` function saves the current file by using a file name retrieved from the user. A `File Save` file dialog is displayed to prompt for the file name. Once a file name is established, `SaveAs` calls `SetFileName` and `Write`. `SaveAs` returns TRUE when the file is successfully saved.

SBBottom

Member Access Control:

Protected

Syntax:

```
virtual void SBBottom(RTMessage Msg) = [NF_FIRST + SB_BOTTOM];
```

Class:

TScrollBar

Class Header File:

scrollba.h

Description:

The `SBBottom` function calls `SetPosition` to move the scroll thumb to the bottom of the scroll bar for vertical scroll bars or to the right for horizontal scroll bars.

SBLineDown

Member Access Control:

Protected

Syntax:

```
virtual void SBLineDown(RTMessage Msg) = [NF_FIRST + SB_LINEDOWN];
```

Class:

TScrollBar

Class Header File:

scrollba.h

Description:

The `SBLineDown` function calls `SetPosition` to move the scroll thumb down for vertical scroll bars or right for horizontal scroll bars. `LineMagnitude` defines the number of range units the thumb is moved.

SBLineUp

Member Access Control:

Protected

Syntax:

```
virtual void SBLineUp(RTMessage Msg) = [NF_FIRST + SB_LINEUP];
```

Class:

`TScrollBar`

Class Header File:

scrollba.h

Description:

The `SBLineUp` function calls `SetPosition` to move the scroll thumb up for vertical scroll bars or left for horizontal scroll bars. `LineMagnitude` defines the number of range units the thumb is moved.

SBPageDown

Member Access Control:

Protected

Syntax:

```
virtual void SBPageDown(RTMessage Msg) = [NF_FIRST + SB_PAGEDOWN];
```

Class:

`TScrollBar`

Class Header File:

scrollba.h

Description:

The `SBPageDown` function calls `SetPosition` to move the scroll thumb down for vertical scroll bars or right for horizontal scroll bars. `PageMagnitude` defines the number of range units the thumb is moved.

SBPageUp

Member Access Control:

Protected

Syntax:

```
virtual void SBPageUp(RTMessage Msg) = [NF_FIRST + SB_PAGEUP];
```

Class:

`TScrollBar`

Class Header File:

scrollba.h

Description:

The `SBPageUp` function calls `SetPosition` to move the scroll thumb up for vertical scroll bars or left for horizontal scroll bars. `PageMagnitude` defines the number of range units the thumb is moved.

SBThumbPosition

Member Access Control:

Protected

Syntax:

```
virtual void SBThumbPosition(RTMessage Msg) = [NF_FIRST + SB_THUMBPOSITION];
```

Class:

`TScrollBar`

Class Header File:

scrollba.h

Description:

The `SBThumbPosition` function calls `SetPosition` to move the scroll thumb.

SBThumbTrack

Member Access Control:

Protected

Syntax:

```
virtual void SBThumbTrack(RTMessage Msg) = [NF_FIRST + SB_THUMBTRACK];
```

Class:

TScrollBar

Class Header File:

scrollba.h

Description:

The SBThumbTrack function calls SetPosition to move the scroll thumb to a new position as it is being dragged.

SBTop

Member Access Control:

Protected

Syntax:

```
virtual void SBTop(RTMessage Msg) = [NF_FIRST + SB_TOP];
```

Class:

TScrollBar

Class Header File:

scrollba.h

Description:

The SBTop function calls SetPosition to move the scroll thumb to the top for vertical scroll bars or the left for horizontal scroll bars.

Scroll

Member Access Control:

Public

Syntax:

```
void Scroll(int HorizontalUnit, int VerticalUnit);
```

Class:

`TEdit`

Class Header File:

edit.h

Description:

The `Scroll` function scrolls the multiline edit control horizontally or vertically. `HorizontalUnit` specifies the number of characters to scroll horizontally. `VerticalUnit` specifies the number of characters to scroll vertically. Positive values scroll right and down; negative values scroll left and up.

ScrollBy

Member Access Control:

Public

Syntax:

```
void ScrollBy(long Dx, long Dy);
```

Class:

`TScroller`

lass Header File:

scroller.h

Description:

The `ScrollBy` function calls `ScrollTo` to scroll the display the amount specified in `Dx` and `Dy`.

ScrollTo

Member Access Control:

Public

Syntax:

```
virtual void ScrollTo(long X, long Y);
```

Class:

`TScroller`

Class Header File:

scroller.h

Description:

The `ScrollTo` function scrolls the display to the specified position and forces a `WM_PAINT` message to be sent.

Search

Member Access Control:

Public

Syntax:

```
int Search(int StartPos, LPSTR AText, BOOL CaseSensitive);
```

Class:

`TEdit`

Class Header File:

edit.h

Description:

The `Search` function searches for the text specified in `AText`. `StartPos` specifies the starting point for the search. `CaseSensitive` indicates whether the text search is case-sensitive. The text is selected when found.

SendDlgItemMsg

Member Access Control:

Public

Syntax:

```
DWORD SendDlgItemMsg(int DlgItemID, WORD AMsg, WORD WParam, DWORD LParam);
```

Class:

`TDialog`

Class Header File:

dialog.h

Description:

The `SendDlgItemMsg` function sends the control message (`AMsg`) to the dialog box control that has the ID specified in `DlgItemID`. `WParam` and `LParam` are message parameters. The value returned by the control is returned by `SendDlgItemMsg` when the function is successful. A return value of zero indicates that the specified ID is invalid.

SelectFileName

Member Access Control:

Public

Syntax:

```
void SelectFileName();
```

Class:

`TFileDialog`

Class Header File:

filedial.h

Description:

The `SelectFileName` function selects text from the edit control and sets the focus to the edit control.

SelectionChanged

Member Access Control:

Public

Syntax:

```
virtual void SelectionChanged(int ControlId);
```

Class:

TGroupBox

Class Header File:

groupbox.h

Description:

The `SelectionChanged` function notifies the parent window of a group box that a change has been made in the group box if, and only if, `NotifyParent` is TRUE.

SetCaption

Member Access Control:

Public

Syntax:

```
void SetCaption(LPSTR ATitle);
```

Class:

TDialog

Class Header File:

dialog.h

Description:

The `SetCaption` function calls `TWindowsObject::SetCaption` unless `ATitle` is –1.

SetCaption

Member Access Control:

Public

Syntax:

```
void SetCaption(LPSTR ATitle);
```

Class:

`TWindowsObject`

Class Header File:

windobj.h

Description:

The `SetCaption` function defines the caption of the interface element as the value specified in `ATitle`.

SetCheck

Member Access Control:

Public

Syntax:

```
void SetCheck(WORD CheckFlag);
```

Class:

`TCheckBox`

Class Header File:

checkbox.h

Description:

The `SetCheck` function sets the state of the check box to the state specified in `CheckFlag`. `CheckFlag` can be `BF_UNCHECKED` (box is unchecked), `BF_CHECKED` (box is checked), or `BF_GRAYED` (box is grayed).

SetFileName

Member Access Control:

Public

Syntax:

```
void SetFileName(LPSTR AFileName);
```

Class:

`TFileWindow`

Class Header File:

filewnd.h

Description:

The `SetFileName` function sets the `FileName` data member and modifies the window caption. This function calls `TEditWindow::SetupWindow` to create the Editor edit control for the edit window.

SetFlags

Member Access Control:

Public

Syntax:

```
void SetFlags(WORD Mask, BOOL OnOff);
```

Class:

`TWindowsObject`

Class Header File:

windobj.h

Description:

The `SetFlags` function sets the bit flag of the `Flags` data member with the specified mask according to the value specified in `OnOff`.

SetKBHandler

Member Access Control:

Public

Syntax:

```
void SetKBHandler(PTWindowsObject, AWindowsObject);
```

Class:

`TApplication`

Class Header File:

applicat.h

Description:

The `SetKBHandler` function enables keyboard handling for the specified window.

SetPageSize

Member Access Control:

Public

Syntax:

```
virtual void SetPageSize();
```

Class:

`TScroller`

Class Header File:

scroller.h

Description:

The `SetPageSize` function sets the page width and height to the size of the client area of the owner window.

SetParent

Member Access Control:

Public

Syntax:

```
virtual void SetParent(PTWindowsObject NewParent);
```

Class:

`TWindowsObject`

Class Header File:

windobj.h

Description:

The `SetParent` function sets `Parent` to the parent window specified in `NewParent`, removes `this` from the child list of the previous parent, and adds `this` to the child list of the new parent.

SetPosition

Member Access Control:

Public

Syntax:

```
void SetPosition(int ThumbPos);
```

Class:

`TScrollBar`

Class Header File:

scrollba.h

Description:

The `SetPosition` function moves the thumb position to the position specified in `ThumbPos`. The thumb position will not be moved outside the range of the scroll bar.

SetRange

Member Access Control:

Public

Syntax:

```
void SetRange(int LoVal, int HiVal);
```

Class:

`TScrollBar`

Class Header File:

scrollba.h

Description:

The `SetRange` function sets the scroll bar range to the values specified in `LoVal` and `HiVal`.

SetRange

Member Access Control:

Public

Syntax:

```
void SetRange(long TheXRange, long TheYRange);
```

Class:

`TScroller`

Class Header File:

scroller.h

Description:

The `SetRange` function sets the scroll ranges of `TScroller` to those specified and calls `SetSBarRange` to coordinate the ranges of the owner window scroll bars.

SetSBarRange

Member Access Control:

Public

Syntax:

```
virtual void SetSBarRange();
```

Class:

`TScroller`

Class Header File:

scroller.h

Description:

The `SetSBarRange` function sets the range of the scroll bars for the owner window to fit within the range specified for `TScroller`.

SetSelection

Member Access Control:

Public

Syntax:

```
BOOL SetSelection(int StartPos, int EndPos);
```

Class:

`TEdit`

Class Header File:

edit.h

Description:

The `SetSelection` function defines the current text selection. `StartPos` specifies the first character in the selected text. `EndPos` marks the location immediately after the last character in the selected text.

SetSelIndex

Member Access Control:

Public

Syntax:

```
int SetSelIndex(int Index);
```

Class:

TListBox

Class Header File:

listbox.h

Description:

When successful, the `SetSelIndex` function selects the item at the position specified in `Index`. This function returns a negative value when unsuccessful. `Index` can be set to –1 to clear all selections.

SetSelString

Member Access Control:

Public

Syntax:

```
int SetSelString(LPSTR AString, int AIndex);
```

Class:

TListBox

Class Header File:

listbox.h

Description:

The `SetSelString` function selects the list box item that begins with the text in `AString`. The search for a match begins at the position specified by `AIndex`. When successful, this function returns the position of the matching item. A negative return value indicates that the function is unsuccessful.

SetText

Member Access Control:

Public

Syntax:

```
void SetText(LPSTR ATextString);
```

Class:

`TStatic`

Class Header File:

static.h

Description:

The `SetText` function sets the text of the static control to the string specified in `ATextString`.

SetTransferBuffer

Member Access Control:

Public

Syntax:

```
void SetTransferBuffer (Pvoid ATransferBuffer);
```

Class:

`TWindowsObject`

Class Header File:

windobj.h

Description:

The `SetTransferBuffer` function sets `TransferBuffer` to the buffer specified in `ATransferBuffer`.

SetUnits

Member Access Control:

Public

Syntax:

```
void SetUnits(int TheXUnit, int TheYUnit);
```

Class:

`TScroller`

Class Header File:

scroller.h

Description:

The `SetUnits` function defines the data members `XUnit` and `YUnit`.

SetupWindow

Member Access Control:

Protected

Syntax:

```
virtual void SetupWindow();
```

Class:

`TComboBox`

Class Header File:

combobox.h

Description:

The `SetupWindow` function limits the length of the text in the edit control to `TextLen` minus 1 when setting up the combo box.

SetupWindow

Member Access Control:

Protected

Syntax:

```
virtual void SetupWindow();
```

Class:

`TDialog`

Class Header File:

dialog.h

Description:

The `SetupWindow` function calls `SetCaption` and `TWindowsObject::SetupWindow` to set up the dialog box.

SetupWindow

Member Access Control:

Protected

Syntax:

```
virtual void SetupWindow();
```

Class:

`TEdit`

Class Header File:

edit.h

Description:

The `SetupWindow` function defines the limit for the number of characters in the edit control as `TextLen` minus 1.

SetupWindow

Member Access Control:

Protected

Syntax:

```
virtual void SetupWindow();
```

Class:

`TFileDialog`

Class Header File:

filedial.h

Description:

The `SetupWindow` function calls `TDialog::SetupWindow` to set up the file dialog box. The number of characters for the edit control is limited to `MAXPATH`. This function calls `UpdateListBoxes` and `SelectFileName`.

SetupWindow

Member Access Control:

Protected

Syntax:

```
virtual void SetupWindow();
```

Class:

`TFileWindow`

Class Header File:

filewnd.h

Description:

The `SetupWindow` function establishes the edit window's Editor edit control by calling `TEditWindow::SetupWindow`.

SetupWindow

Member Access Control:

Protected

Syntax:

```
virtual void SetupWindow();
```

Class:

`TInputDialog`

Class Header File:

inputdia.h

Description:

The `SetupWindow` function calls `TDialog::SetupWindow` to set up the window and limit the number of characters that can be input to `BufferSize` minus 1.

SetupWindow

Member Access Control:

Protected

Syntax:

```
virtual void SetupWindow();
```

Class:

`TMDIFrame`

Class Header File:

mdi.h

Description:

The `SetupWindow` function calls `InitClientWindow` to construct an MDI client window.

SetupWindow

Member Access Control:

Protected

Syntax:

```
virtual void SetupWindow();
```

Class:

`TScrollBar`

Class Header File:

scrollba.h

Description:

The `SetupWindow` function defines the scroll bar range as 0 to 100.

SetupWindow

Member Access Control:

Protected

Syntax:

```
virtual void SetupWindow();
```

Class:

`TWindow`

Class Header File:

window.h

Description:

The `SetupWindow` function calls `TWindowsObject::SetupWindow` to initialize the new window.

SetupWindow

Member Access Control:

Protected

Syntax:

```
virtual void SetupWindow();
```

Class:

`TWindowsObject`

lass Header File:

windobj.h

Description:

The `SetupWindow` function attempts to create an associated interface element for each child window in `ChildList` that has the autocreate feature enabled.

Show

Member Access Control:

Public

Syntax:

```
void Show(int ShowCmd);
```

Class:

`TWindowsObject`

Class Header File:

windobj.h

Description:

The `Show` function displays the interface element as specified in `ShowCmd`, which can be any of the following values:

Value	*Meaning*
`SW_HIDE`	Hidden
`SW_SHOW`	Shown using window's current size and position
`SW_SHOWMAXIMIZED`	Shown maximized and active
`SW_SHOWMINIMIZED`	Shown minimized and active
`SW_SHOWNORMAL`	Shown restored and active

ShowList

Member Access Control:

Public

Syntax:

```
void ShowList();
```

Class:

`TComboBox`

Class Header File:

combobox.h

Description:

The `ShowList` function shows the list of a drop-down or drop-down list combo box.

ShutDownWindow

Member Access Control:

Public

Syntax:

```
virtual void ShutDownWindow();
```

Class:

`TDialog`

Class Header File:

dialog.h

Description:

The `ShutDownWindow` function calls `TWindowsObject::ShutDownWindow` for modeless dialog boxes or `Destroy` (passing IDCANCEL) for modal dialog boxes to shut down the dialog box.

ShutDownWindow

Member Access Control:

Public

Syntax:

```
virtual void ShutDownWindow(int ARetValue);
```

Class:

`TDialog`

Class Header File:

dialog.h

Description:

The `ShutDownWindow` function calls `TWindowsObject::ShutDownWindow` for modeless dialog boxes or `Destroy` (passing `ARetValue`) for modal dialog boxes to shut down the dialog box.

ShutDownWindow

Member Access Control:

Public

Syntax:

```
virtual void ShutDownWindow();
```

Class:

`TWindowsObject`

Class Header File:

windobj.h

Description:

The `ShutDownWindow` function destroys the associated interface element.

streamableName

Member Access Control:

Private

Syntax:

```
virtual const Pchar streamableName() const = 0;
```

Class:

TStreamable

Class Header File:

objstrm.h

Description:

The `streamableName` function is a pure virtual function that must be redefined by all derived classes. This function returns the name of the streamable class of the object.

TileChildren

Member Access Control:

Public

Syntax:

```
virtual void TileChildren();
```

Class:

TMDIClient

Class Header File:

mdi.h

Description:

The `TileChildren` function adjusts the size of all MDI child windows that are not minimized and arranges them in a nonoverlapping, tiled style.

TileChildren

Member Access Control:

Protected

Syntax:

```
virtual void TileChildren();
```

Class:

`TMDIFrame`

Class Header File:

mdi.h

Description:

The `TileChildren` function calls the `TileChildren` member function of the client window to size and arrange the MDI child windows that are not iconized in a nonoverlapping style.

Toggle

Member Access Control:

Public

Syntax:

```
void Toggle();
```

Class:

`TCheckBox`

Class Header File:

checkbox.h

Description:

The `Toggle` function toggles between the states of the check box.

Transfer

Member Access Control:

Public

Syntax:

```
virtual WORD Transfer (Pvoid DataPtr, WORD TransferFlag);
```

Class:

`TCheckBox`

Class Header File:

checkbox.h

Description:

The `Transfer` function transfers the state of the check box to or from the location pointed to by `DataPtr`. `TransferFlag` can be set to `TF_SETDATA`, `TF_GETDATA`, or `TF_SIZEDATA` as follows:

- When `TransferFlag` is `TF_SETDATA`, the state of the check box is set to the state specified in the location pointed to by `DataPtr`.
- When `TransferFlag` is `TF_GETDATA`, the state of the check box is transferred to the memory location pointed to by `DataPtr`.
- When `TransferFlag` is `TF_SIZEDATA`, this function returns the size of the transfer data. No data is transferred in this case.

Transfer

Member Access Control:

Public

Syntax:

```
virtual WORD Transfer(LPSTR DataPtr, WORD TransferFlag);
```

Class:

`TComboBox`

Class Header File:

combobox.h

Description:

The `Transfer` function moves data to and from a transfer buffer pointed to by `DataPtr`. The transfer buffer should point to a `PTComboBoxData` object.

The `TransferFlag` parameter of the `Transfer` function can be set to `TF_SETDATA`, `TF_GETDATA`, or `TF_SIZEDATA` as follows:

- Set `TransferFlag` to `TF_SETDATA` to fill the list of the combo box from the data in the transfer buffer.
- Set `TransferFlag` to `TF_GETDATA` to copy the current list selection to the transfer buffer.
- Set `TransferFlag` to `TF_SIZEDATA` to return the size of the transfer data. No data is transferred in this case.

Transfer

Member Access Control:

Public

Syntax:

```
virtual WORD Transfer(Pvoid DataPtr, WORD TransferFlag);
```

Class:

`TListBox`

Class Header File:

listbox.h

Description:

The `Transfer` function uses the buffer pointed to by `DataPtr` to transfer data. The transfer buffer contains a pointer to a `PTListBoxData` object.

The `TransferFlag` parameter of the `Transfer` function can be set to `TF_SETDATA`, `TF_GETDATA`, or `TF_SIZEDATA` as follows:

- Set `TransferFlag` to `TF_SETDATA` to fill the list and select one or more items using the data in the buffer.
- Set `TransferFlag` to `TF_GETDATA` to fill the buffer by using the current list and selection(s) from the list box.
- Set `TransferFlag` to `TF_SIZEDATA` to return the size of `PTListBoxData`. No data is transferred in this case.

Transfer

Member Access Control:

Public

Syntax:

```
virtual WORD Transfer(Pvoid DataPtr, WORD TransferFlag);
```

Class:

TScrollBar

Class Header File:

scrollba.h

Description:

The `Transfer` function uses the data buffer pointed to by `DataPtr` to transfer scroll bar information. `DataPtr` should point to a `TScrollBarData` structure, as follows:

```
struct TScrollBarData {
     int LowValue;
     int HighValue;
     int Position;
};
```

The `TransferFlag` parameter of the `Transfer` function can be set to `TF_SETDATA`, `TF_GETDATA`, or `TF_SIZEDATA` as follows:

- Set `TransferFlag` to `TF_SETDATA` to retrieve data from the transfer buffer.
- Set `TransferFlag` to `TF_GETDATA` to send data to the transfer buffer.
- Set `TransferFlag` to `TF_SIZEDATA` to return the size of the transfer data. No data is transferred in this case.

Transfer

Member Access Control:

Public

Syntax:

```
virtual WORD Transfer(Pvoid DataPtr, WORD TransferFlag);
```

Class:

TStatic

Class Header File:

static.h

Description:

The `Transfer` function transfers text to and from the buffer pointed to by `DataPtr`. The `TransferFlag` parameter of the `Transfer` function can be set to `TF_SETDATA`, `TF_GETDATA`, or `TF_SIZEDATA` as follows:

- Set `TransferFlag` to `TF_SETDATA` to copy the text from the buffer to the static control.
- Set `TransferFlag` to `TF_GETDATA` to copy the text of the static control to the transfer buffer.
- When `TransferFlag` is set to `TF_SIZEDATA`, this function returns `TextLen`.

Transfer

Member Access Control:

Public

Syntax:

```
virtual WORD Transfer(Pvoid DataPtr, WORD TransferFlag);
```

Class:

`TWindowsObject`

Class Header File:

windobj.h

Description:

The `Transfer` function transfers data to and from the buffer referenced by `DataPtr`. The `TransferFlag` parameter of the `Transfer` function can be set to `TF_SETDATA`, `TF_GETDATA`, or `TF_SIZEDATA` as follows:

- Set `TransferFlag` to `TF_SETDATA` to retrieve the information from the buffer.
- Set `TransferFlag` to `TF_GETDATA` to copy the information to the buffer.
- When `TransferFlag` is set to `TF_SIZEDATA`, this function returns the size of the transfer data. No data is transferred in this case.

TransferData

Member Access Control:

Public

Syntax:

```
void TransferData(WORD Direction);
```

Class:

`TInputDialog`

Class Header File:

inputdia.h

Description:

The `TransferData` function transfers input dialog data. `Direction` can be set to `TF_SETDATA` or `TF_GETDATA`. When `Direction` is `TF_SETDATA`, the text for the controls is set to the text in `Prompt` and `Buffer`. When `Direction` is set to `TF_GETDATA`, the current text in the editor is copied to `Buffer`.

TransferData

Member Access Control:

Public

Syntax:

```
virtual void TransferData(WORD Direction);
```

Class:

`TWindowsObject`

Class Header File:

windobj.h

Description:

The `TransferData` function transfers data between the buffer and the interface object's child windows that have the `WB_TRANSFER` flag set. `TranferData` calls `Transfer` for each child window and uses `Direction` to specify how data is transferred. `Direction` can be set to `TF_SETDATA`, `TF_GETDATA`, or `TF_SIZEDATA`.

Uncheck

Member Access Control:

Public

Syntax:

```
void Uncheck();
```

Class:

`TCheckBox`

Class Header File:

checkbox.h

Description:

The `Uncheck` function places the check box in an unchecked state.

Undo

Member Access Control:

Public

Syntax:

```
void Undo();
```

Class:

`TEdit`

Class Header File:

edit.h

Description:

The `Undo` function performs an "undo" on the last edit.

UpdateFileName

Member Access Control:

Public

Syntax:

```
void UpdateFileName();
```

Class:

`TFileDialog`

Class Header File:

filedial.h

Description:

The `UpdateFileName` function sets the text of the edit control to `PathName` and selects the text.

UpdateListBoxes

Member Access Control:

Public

Syntax:

```
BOOL UpdateListBoxes();
```

Class:

`TFileDialog`

Class Header File:

filedial.h

Description:

The `UpdateListBoxes` function updates the file and directory list boxes. TRUE is returned when updating is successful.

ValidWindow

Member Access Control:

Public

Syntax:

```
virtual PTWindowsObject ValidWindow (PTWindowsObject AWindowsObject);
```

Class:

`TModule`

Class Header File:

module.h

Description:

The `ValidWindow` function determines whether the specified object is valid. This function returns the pointer to the object when the object is valid. When the object is not valid, this function deletes the object and returns a value of NULL.

VScroll

Member Access Control:

Public

Syntax:

```
virtual void VScroll(WORD ScrollEvent, int ThumbPos);
```

Class:

`TScroller`

Class Header File:

scroller.h

Description:

The `VScroll` function calls `ScrollTo` or `ScrollBy` to handle the specified vertical scroll event. `ThumbPos` specifies the current thumb position.

WMActivate

Member Access Control:

Protected

Syntax:

```
virtual void WMActivate(RTMessage Msg) = [WM_FIRST + WM_ACTIVATE];
```

Class:

`TWindow`

Class Header File:

window.h

Description:

The `WMActivate` function gives a window a keyboard interface when it is being activated or deactivated. During deactivation, the handle of the child control that currently has the focus is stored in `FocusChildHandle`. On activation, the child that previously had the focus is, once again, given the focus.

WMActivate

Member Access Control:

Protected

Syntax:

```
virtual void WMActivate(RTMessage Msg) = [WM_FIRST + WM_ACTIVATE];
```

Class:

`TWindowsObject`

Class Header File:

windobj.h

Description:

The `WMActivate` function enables keyboard handling, if requested, when a `WM_ACTIVATE` message is detected.

WMClose

Member Access Control:

Protected

Syntax:

```
virtual void WMClose(RTMessage Msg) = [WM_FIRST + WM_CLOSE];
```

Class:

`TDialog`

Class Header File:

dialog.h

Description:

The `WMClose` function handles the `WM_CLOSE` message.

WMClose

Member Access Control:

Protected

Syntax:

```
virtual void WMClose(RTMessage Msg) = [WM_FIRST + WM_CLOSE];
```

Class:

`TWindowsObject`

Class Header File:

windobj.h

Description:

The `WMClose` function calls `CloseWindow` to close the window.

WMCommand

Member Access Control:

Protected

Syntax:

```
virtual void WMCommand(RTMessage Msg) = [WM_FIRST + WM_COMMAND];
```

Class:

`TWindowsObject`

Class Header File:

windobj.h

Description:

The `WMCommand` function calls the appropriate member functions when command-based, child-ID-based, or notify-based messages are detected.

WMCreate

Member Access Control:

Protected

Syntax:

```
virtual void WMCreate(RTMessage Msg) = [WM_FIRST + WM_CREATE];
```

Class:

`TWindow`

Class Header File:

window.h

Description:

The `WMCreate` function calls `SetupWindow` when the `WM_CREATE` message is detected.

WMDestroy

Member Access Control:

Protected

Syntax:

```
virtual void WMDestroy(RTMessage Msg) = [WM_FIRST + WM_DESTROY];
```

Class:

`TWindowsObject`

Class Header File:

windobj.h

Description:

The `WMDestroy` function handles the `WM_DESTROY` message.

WMDrawItem

Member Access Control:

Public

Syntax:

```
virtual void WMDrawItem(RTMessage Msg) = [WM_FIRST + WM_DRAWITEM];
```

Class:

`TControl`

Class Header File:

control.h

Description:

The `WMDrawItem` function responds to the `WM_DRAWITEM` message that is sent when the drawable control needs to be redrawn.

WMDrawItem

Member Access Control:

Protected

Syntax:

```
virtual void WMDrawItem(RTMessage Msg) = [WM_FIRST + WM_DRAWITEM];
```

Class:

`TWindowsObject`

Class Header File:

windobj.h

Description:

The `WMDrawItem` function dispatches the `WM_DRAWITEM` message for drawable controls.

WMHScroll

Member Access Control:

Protected

Syntax:

```
virtual void WMHScroll(RTMessage Msg) = [WM_FIRST + WM_HSCROLL];
```

Class:

`TWindow`

Class Header File:

window.h

Description:

The `WMHScroll` function handles horizontal scroll bar events.

WMHScroll

Member Access Control:

Protected

Syntax:

```
virtual void WMHScrollR(TMessage Msg) = [WM_FIRST + WM_HSCROLL];
```

Class:

`TWindowsObject`

Class Header File:

windobj.h

Description:

The `WMHScroll` function calls `DispatchScroll` in response to a `WM_HSCROLL` message.

WMInitDialog

Member Access Control:

Protected

Syntax:

```
virtual void WMInitDialog(RTMessage Msg) = [WM_FIRST + WM_INITDIALOG];
```

Class:

`TDialog`

Class Header File:

dialog.h

Description:

The `WMInitDialog` function calls `SetupWindow` and is automatically called prior to displaying the dialog box.

WMLButtonDown

Member Access Control:

Protected

Syntax:

```
virtual void WMLButtonDown(RTMessage Msg) = [WM_FIRST + WM_LBUTTONDOWN];
```

Class:

`TWindow`

Class Header File:

window.h

Description:

The `WMLButtonDown` function responds to `WM_LBUTTONDOWN` messages.

WMMove

Member Access Control:

Protected

Syntax:

```
virtual void WMMove(RTMessage Msg) = [WM_FIRST + WM_MOVE];
```

Class:

`TWindow`

Class Header File:

window.h

Description:

The `WMMove` function saves the new window coordinates in the `X` and `Y` members of `Attr` when a `WM_MOVE` message is detected.

WMNCDestroy

Member Access Control:

Protected

Syntax:

```
virtual void WMNCDestroy(RTMessage Msg) = [WM_FIRST + WM_NCDESTROY];
```

Class:

`TWindowsObject`

Class Header File:

windobj.h

Description:

The `WMNCDestroy` function handles the `WM_NCDESTROY` message.

WMPaint

Member Access Control:

Public

Syntax:

```
virtual void WMPaint(RTMessage Msg) = [WM_FIRST + WM_PAINT];
```

Class:

`TControl`

Class Header File:

control.h

Description:

The `WMPaint` function calls `DefWndProc` for painting if the control has a predefined Windows class.

WMPaint

Member Access Control:

Protected

Syntax:

```
virtual void WMPaint(RTMessage Msg) = [WM_FIRST + WM_PAINT];
```

Class:

`TMDIClient`

Class Header File:

mdi.h

Description:

The `WMPaint` function redefines `TWindow::WMPaint` to call `DefWndProc`.

WMPaint

Member Access Control:

Protected

Syntax:

```
virtual void WMPaint(RTMessage Msg) = [WM_FIRST + WM_PAINT];
```

Class:

`TWindow`

Class Header File:

window.h

Description:

The `WMPaint` function calls `Paint` or `DefWndProc` when a `WM_PAINT` message is detected.

WMQueryEndSession

Member Access Control:

Protected

Syntax:

```
virtual void WMQueryEndSession(RTMessage Msg) = [WM_FIRST + WM_QUERYENDSESSION];
```

Class:

`TDialog`

Class Header File:

dialog.h

Description:

The `WMQueryEndSession` function responds when Windows attempts to shut down.

WMQueryEndSession

Member Access Control:

Protected

Syntax:

```
virtual void WMQueryEndSession(RTMessage Msg) = [WM_FIRST + WM_QUERYENDSESSION];
```

Class:

`TWindowsObject`

Class Header File:

windobj.h

Description:

The `WMQueryEndSession` function calls the appropriate `CanClose` function to determine whether the session can close.

WMSetFocus

Member Access Control:

Protected

Syntax:

```
virtual void WMSetFocus(RTMessage Msg) = [WM_FIRST + WM_SETFOCUS];
```

Class:

`TEditWindow`

Class Header File:

editwnd.h

Description:

The `WMSetFocus` function sets the focus to the Editor edit control when the `WM_SETFOCUS` message is detected.

WMSize

Member Access Control:

Protected

Syntax:

```
virtual void WMSize(RTMessage Msg) = [WM_FIRST + WM_SIZE];
```

Class:

`TEditWindow`

Class Header File:

editwnd.h

Description:

The `WMSize` function sizes the Editor edit control to the `TEditWindow`'s client area when the `WM_SIZE` message is detected.

WMSize

Member Access Control:

Protected

Syntax:

```
virtual void WMSize(RTMessage Msg) = [WM_FIRST + WM_SIZE];
```

Class:

`TWindow`

Class Header File:

window.h

Description:

The `WMSize` function calls `SetPageSize` when a window with scrollers has been sized.

WMVScroll

Member Access Control:

Protected

Syntax:

```
virtual void WMVScroll(RTMessage Msg) = [WM_FIRST + WM_VSCROLL];
```

Class:

`TWindow`

Class Header File:

window.h

Description:

The `WMVScroll` function calls `DispatchScroll` when the `WM_VSCROLL` message is detected from a scroll-bar control.

WMVScroll

Member Access Control:

Protected

Syntax:

```
virtual void WMVScroll(RTMessage Msg) = [WM_FIRST + WM_VScroll];
```

Class:

`TWindowsObject`

Class Header File:

windobj.h

Description:

The `WMVScroll` function calls `DispatchScroll` in response to the detection of vertical scroll-bar messages.

Write

Member Access Control:

Public

Syntax:

```
BOOL Write();
```

Class:

`TFileWindow`

Class Header File:

filewnd.h

Description:

The `Write` function saves the contents of the editor to the file specified in `FileName`. TRUE is returned when the file is successfully saved.

write

Member Access Control:

Protected

Syntax:

```
virtual void write(Ropstream os);
```

Class:

`TCheckBox`

Class Header File:

checkbox.h

Description:

The `write` function calls `TWindow::write` to write out the base `TWindow` object.

write

Member Access Control:

Protected

Syntax:

```
virtual void write(Ropstream os);
```

Class:

`TComboBox`

Class Header File:

combobox.h

Description:

The `write` function calls `TListBox::write` to write out the base `TListBox` object.

write

Member Access Control:

Protected

Syntax:

```
virtual void write(Ropstream os);
```

Class:

`TDialog`

Class Header File:

dialog.h

Description:

The `write` function calls `TWindowsObject::write` to write out the base `TWindowsObject` object.

write

Member Access Control:

Protected

Syntax:

```
virtual void write(Ropstream os);
```

Class:

`TEditWindow`

Class Header File:

editwnd.h

Description:

The `write` function calls `TWindow::write` to write out the base `TWindow` object and then calls `PutChildPtr` to write out the edit control child window.

write

Member Access Control:

Protected

Syntax:

```
virtual void write(Ropstream os);
```

Class:

`TFileWindow`

Class Header File:

filewnd.h

Description:

The `write` function calls `TEditWindow::write` to write out the base `TEditWindow` object and then writes out `FileName`.

write

Member Access Control:

Protected

Syntax:

```
virtual void write(Ropstream os);
```

Class:

`TGroupBox`

Class Header File:

groupbox.h

Description:

The `write` function calls `TWindow::write` to write out the base `TGroupBox` object.

write

Member Access Control:

Protected

Syntax:

```
virtual void write(Ropstream os);
```

Class:

`TInputDialog`

Class Header File:

inputdia.h

Description:

The `write` function calls `TDialog::write` to write out the base `TDialog` object.

write

Member Access Control:

Protected

Syntax:

```
virtual void write(Ropstream os);
```

Class:

`TMDIClient`

Class Header File:

mdi.h

Description:

The `write` function calls `TWindow::write` to write out the base `TWindow` object.

write

Member Access Control:

Protected

Syntax:

```
virtual void write(Ropstream os);
```

Class:

`TMDIFrame`

Class Header File:

mdi.h

Description:

The `write` function calls `TWindow::write` to write out the base `TWindow` object.

write

Member Access Control:

Protected

Syntax:

```
virtual void write(Ropstream os);
```

Class:

`TScrollBar`

Class Header File:

scrollba.h

Description:

The `write` function calls `TWindow::write` to write out the base `TWindow` object.

write

Member Access Control:

Protected

Syntax:

```
virtual void write(Ropstream os);
```

Class:

`TScroller`

Class Header File:

scroller.h

Description:

The `write` function writes `AutoMode`, `AutoOrg`, `HasHScrollBar`, `HasVScrollBar`, `TrackMode`, `XLine`, `XPage`, `XPos`, `XRange`, `XUnit`, `YLine`, `YPage`, `YPos`, `YRange`, and `YUnit`.

write

Member Access Control:

Protected

Syntax:

```
virtual void write(Ropstream os);
```

Class:

`TStatic`

Class Header File:

static.h

Description:

The `write` function calls `TWindow::write` to write out the base `TWindow` object.

write

Member Access Control:

Protected

Syntax:

```
virtual void write(Ropstream os);
```

Class:

`TWindow`

Class Header File:

window.h

Description:

The `write` function calls `TWindowsObject::write` to write out the base `TWindowsObject` object.

write

Member Access Control:

Protected

Syntax:

```
virtual void write(Ropstream os);
```

Class:

`TWindowsObject`

Class Header File:

windobj.h

Description:

The `write` function writes `Title`, `Status`, flags, and `CreateOrder` and calls `PutChildren` to write out child windows.

write

Member Access Control:

Protected

Syntax:

```
virtual void write(Ropstream) = 0;
```

Class:

`TStreamable`

Class Header File:

objstrm.h

Description:

The `write` function is a pure virtual function that must be redeclared by all derived classes. The `write` function permits the application to write to the specified output stream.

XRangeValue

Member Access Control:

Public

Syntax:

```
long XRangeValue(int AScrollUnit);
```

Class:

`TScroller`

Class Header File:

scroller.h

Description:

The `XRangeValue` function converts a horizontal scroll value to a horizontal range value.

XScrollValue

Member Access Control:

Public

Syntax:

```
int XScrollValue(long ARangeUnit);
```

Class:

`TScroller`

Class Header File:

scroller.h

Description:

The `XScrollValue` function converts a horizontal range value to a horizontal scroll value.

YRangeValue

Member Access Control:

Public

Syntax:

```
long YRangeValue(int AScrollUnit);
```

Class:

`TScroller`

Class Header File:

scroller.h

Description:

The `YRangeValue` function converts a vertical scroll value to a vertical range value.

YScrollValue

Member Access Control:

Public

Syntax:

```
int YScrollValue(long ARangeUnit);
```

Class:

`TScroller`

Class Header File:

scroller.h

Description:

The `YScrollValue` function converts a vertical range value to a vertical scroll value.

A

Windows Functions Quick Reference Guide

This appendix is a quick reference guide to the Windows functions. Two pieces of information are provided for each function. The first, the Interface/Category column, lists the interface and the category where the function is documented. The value for the interface is one of the following:

WMI	Window Manager Interface
GDI	Graphics Device Interface
SSI	System Services Interface

The category portion of the Interface/Category column represents the interface category where the function is documented. Chapter 13 provides the reference material for each function. Each function is described under the interface and category shown in the Interface/Category column. For example, the Access Resource function has the Interface category of SSI/resource management. To find the

complete reference material for this function, you would look in Chapter 13, first under the "System Services Interface Functions" section, and then in the "Resource Management Functions" section. The last piece of information provided for each function is in the Meaning column, which briefly describes the function.

Function	*Interface/Category*	*Meaning*
`AccessResource`	SSI/Resource Management	Opens a resource
`AddAtom`	SSI/Atom Management	Creates an atom for a character string
`AddFontResource`	GDI/Font	Adds a font resource to the system font table
`AdjustWindowRect`	WMI/Window Creation	Determines the window size for the specified client area
`AdjustWindowRectEx`	WMI/Window Creation	Determines the window size with extended style for the specified client area
`AllocDStoCSAlias`	SSI/Segment	Returns a code segment selector from the specified data segment selector
`AllocResource`	SSI/Resource Management	Allocates memory for a resource
`AllocSelector`	SSI/Segment	Allocates a new selector
`AnimatePalette`	GDI/Color Palette	Replaces entries in a logical palette
`AnsiLower`	SSI/String Manipulation	Converts a string to lowercase
`AnsiLowerBuff`	SSI/String Manipulation	Converts a string in a buffer to lowercase
`AnsiNext`	SSI/String Manipulation	Gets the long pointer to the next character in a string
`AnsiPrev`	SSI/String Manipulation	Gets the long pointer to the previous character in a string
`AnsiToOem`	SSI/String Manipulation	Converts an ANSI string to an OEM string
`AnsiToOemBuff`	SSI/String Manipulation	Converts an ANSI string in a buffer to an OEM string
`AnsiUpper`	SSI/String Manipulation	Converts a string to uppercase
`AnsiUpperBuff`	SSI/String Manipulation	Converts a string in a buffer to uppercase
`AnyPopup`	WMI/Information	Determines whether a pop-up window exists
`AppendMenu`	WMI/Menu	Appends a menu item to the menu

Function	*Interface/Category*	*Meaning*
`Arc`	GDI/Line Output	Draws an arc
`ArrangeIconicWindows`	WMI/Display and Movement	Arranges minimized child windows
`BeginDeferWindowPos`	WMI/Display and Movement	Allocates memory for `DeferWindowPos`
`BeginPaint`	WMI/Painting	Prepares a window for painting
`BitBlt`	GDI/Bitmap	Copies a bitmap from a source to the specified device
`BringWindowToTop`	WMI/Display and Movement	Brings a window to the top of the stack
`BuildCommDCB`	SSI/Communication	Loads a device control block with control codes
`CallMsgFilter`	WMI/Hook	Passes a message to the current filter function
`CallWindowProc`	WMI/Message	Sends message information to the specified function
`Catch`	SSI/Task	Places the execution environment in a buffer
`ChangeClipboardChain`	WMI/Clipboard	Removes a window from the clipboard viewer chain

`ChangeMenu`	WMI/Menu	This function was replaced in Windows 3.0 with the following five functions:
		`AppendMenu`
		`DeleteMenu`
		`InsertMenu`
		`ModifyMenu`
		`RemoveMenu`

`ChangeSelector`	SSI/Segment	Generates a code or data selector
`CheckDlgButton`	WMI/Dialog Box	Modifies the state of a button
`CheckMenuItem`	WMI/Menu	Either puts or removes a check mark beside a pop-up menu item
`CheckRadioButton`	WMI/Dialog Box	Puts a check beside a button while removing the check from all other buttons in a group

Function	*Interface/Category*	*Meaning*
`ChildWindowFromPoint`	GDI/Coordinate or WMI/Information	Finds the child window that contains a specified point
`Chord`	GDI/Ellipse and Polygon	Draws a chord
`ClearCommBreak`	SSI/Communication	Clears the communication break state or a communication device
`ClientToScreen`	GDI/Coordinate	Converts client coordinates to screen coordinates
`ClipCursor`	WMI/Cursor	Confines the cursor to a rectangular region
`CloseClipboard`	WMI/Clipboard	Closes the clipboard
`CloseComm`	SSI/Communication	Closes a communication device
`CloseMetafile`	GDI/Metafile	Closes a metafile and creates a metafile handle
`CloseSound`	SSI/Sound	Closes the play device and flushes the voice queues
`CloseWindow`	WMI/Display and Movement	Hides or minimizes a window
`CombineRgn`	GDI/Region	Creates a new region by combining two regions
`CopyMetaFile`	GDI/Metafile	Copies a metafile to a file
`CopyRect`	WMI/Rectangle	Copies a rectangle
`CountClipboardFormats`	WMI/Clipboard	Gets the number of formats the clipboard can render
`CountVoiceNotes`	SSI/Sound	Gets the number of notes in the specified queue
`CreateBitmap`	GDI/Bitmap	Creates a bitmap
`CreateBitmapIndirect`	GDI/Bitmap	Creates a bitmap using the data from a `BITMAP` structure
`CreateBrushIndirect`	GDI/Drawing Tool	Creates a logical brush
`CreateCaret`	WMI/Caret	Creates a caret
`CreateCompatibleBitmap`	GDI/Bitmap	Creates a bitmap compatible with the specified device
`CreateCompatibleDC`	GDI/Device Context	Creates a memory device context
`CreateCursor`	WMI/Cursor	Creates a cursor from two bit masks
`CreateDC`	GDI/Device Context	Creates a device context
`CreateDialog`	WMI/Dialog Box	Creates a modeless dialog box

Function	Interface/Category	Meaning
CreateDialogIndirect	WMI/Dialog Box	Creates a modeless dialog box from a template
CreateDialogIndirectParam	WMI/Dialog Box	Creates a modeless dialog box from a template and passes initialization data
CreateDialogParam	WMI/Dialog Box	Creates a modeless dialog box and passes initialization data
CreateDIBitmap	GDI/Bitmap	Creates a device specific memory bitmap
CreateDIBPatternBrush	GDI/Drawing Tool	Creates a logical brush using a device independent bitmap
CreateDiscardableBitmap	GDI/Bitmap	Creates a bitmap that is discardable and compatible with the specified device
CreateEllipticRgn	GDI/Region	Creates an elliptical region
CreateEllipticRgnIndirect	GDI/Region	Creates an elliptical region using a RECT data structure
CreateFont	GDI/Font	Creates a logical font
CreateFontIndirect	GDI/Font	Creates a logical font using information from a LOGFONT data structure
CreateHatchBrush	GDI/Drawing Tool	Creates a logical brush with a hatched pattern
CreateIC	GDI/Device Context	Creates an information context
CreateIcon	WMI/Painting	Creates an icon
CreateMenu	WMI/Menu	Creates an empty menu
CreateMetaFile	GDI/Metafile	Creates a metafile
CreatePalette	GDI/Color Palette	Creates a logical palette
CreatePatternBrush	GDI/Drawing Tool	Creates a logical brush with a specified pattern
CreatePen	GDI/Drawing Tool	Creates a logical pen
CreatePenIndirect	GDI/Drawing Tool	Creates a logical pen using a LOGPEN data structure
CreatePolygonRgn	GDI/Region	Creates a polygonal region
CreatePolyPolygonRgn	GDI/Region	Creates a polygonal region made up of a series of closed, filled polygons
CreatePopupMenu	WMI/Menu	Creates an empty pop-up menu

Function	*Interface/Category*	*Meaning*
`CreateRectRgn`	GDI/Region	Creates a rectangular region
`CreateRectRgnIndirect`	GDI/Region	Creates a rectangular region using a `RECT` data structure
`CreateRoundRectRgn`	GDI/Region	Creates a rounded rectangular region
`CreateSolidBrush`	GDI/Drawing Tool	Creates a logical brush using a solid color
`CreateWindow`	WMI/Window Creation	Creates a window
`CreateWindowEx`	WMI/Window Creation	Creates a window with extended style
`DebugBreak`	SSI/Debugging	Forces a break to the debugger
`DefDlgProc`	WMI/Dialog Box or WMI/Window Creation	Processes messages that a dialog box with a private window class cannot process
`DeferWindowPos`	WMI/Display and Movement	Stores window position information for `EndDeferWindowPos`
`DefFrameProc`	WMI/Window Creation	Provides default processing for multiple document interface (MDI) frame window messages
`DefHookProc`	WMI/Hook	Calls the next function in the filter function chain
`DefineHandleTable`	SSI/Memory Management or SSI/Segment	Creates a private handle table in an application's data segment
`DefMDIChildProc`	WMI/Window Creation	Provides default processing for MDI child window messages
`DefWindowProc`	WMI/Window Creation	Provides default processing for window messages
`DeleteAtom`	SSI/Atom Management	Deletes an atom when the reference count is zero
`DeleteDC`	GDI/Device Context	Deletes a device context
`DeleteMenu`	WMI/Menu	Deletes a menu item
`DeleteMetaFile`	GDI/Metafile	Deletes a metafile
`DeleteObject`	GDI/Drawing Tool	Deletes a pen, brush, font, bitmap, or region
`DestroyCaret`	WMI/Caret	Destroys a caret

Function	*Interface/Category*	*Meaning*
`DestroyCursor`	WMI/Cursor	Destroys a cursor
`DestroyIcon`	WMI/Painting	Destroys an icon
`DestroyMenu`	WMI/Menu	Destroys a menu
`DestroyWindow`	WMI/Window Creation	Destroys a window
`DeviceCapabilities`	GDI/Printer Control	Gets the printer device driver capabilities
`DeviceMode`	GDI/Printer Control	Sets the printing modes
`DialogBox`	WMI/Dialog Box	Creates a modal dialog box
`DialogBoxIndirect`	WMI/Dialog Box	Creates a modal dialog box from a template
`DialogBoxIndirectParam`	WMI/Dialog Box	Creates a modal dialog box from a template and passes initialization data
`DialogBoxParam`	WMI/Dialog Box	Creates a modal dialog box and passes initialization data
`DispatchMessage`	WMI/Message	Sends a message to the window function of the specified window
`DlgDirList`	WMI/Dialog Box	Fills the list box with file names that match the specified path
`DlgDirListComboBox`	WMI/Dialog Box	Fills a combo box with file names that match the specified path
`DlgDirSelect`	WMI/Dialog Box	Copies the current selection of a list box to a string
`DlgDirSelectComboBox`	WMI/Dialog Box	Copies the current selection of a combo box to a string
`DOS3Call`	SSI/Operating System Interrupt	Generates a DOS 21H interrupt
`DPtoLP`	GDI/Coordinate	Converts device points to logical points
`DrawFocusRect`	GDI/Ellipse and Polygon or WMI/Painting	Draws a rectangle that indicates focus
`DrawIcon`	WMI/Painting	Draws an icon
`DrawMenuBar`	WMI/Menu	Redraws the menu bar
`DrawText`	WMI/Text or WMI/Painting	Draws the specified string
`Ellipse`	GDI/Ellipse and Polygon	Draws an ellipse
`EmptyClipboard`	WMI/Clipboard	Empties the clipboard

Function	*Interface/Category*	*Meaning*
`EnableHardwareInput`	WMI/Hardware	Either enables or disables keyboard and mouse input
`EnableMenuItem`	WMI/Menu	Sets the state of a menu item
`EnableWindow`	WMI/Input	Either enables or disables mouse and keyboard input for the application
`EndDeferWindowPos`	WMI/Display and Movement	Used with `DeferWindowPos` to move or size one or more windows
`EndDialog`	WMI/Dialog Box	Terminates a modal dialog box
`EndPaint`	WMI/Painting	Ends window repainting
`EnumChildWindows`	WMI/Information	Enumerates the child windows that belong to the specified parent window
`EnumClipboardFormats`	WMI/Clipboard	Enumerates all the clipboard formats available
`EnumFonts`	GDI/Font	Enumerates the available fonts
`EnumMetaFile`	GDI/Metafile	Enumerates the GDI calls within the metafile
`EnumObjects`	GDI/Drawing Tool	Enumerates all pens and brushes
`EnumProps`	WMI/Property	Enumerates the window's properties
`EnumTaskWindows`	WMI/Information	Enumerates the windows associated with the specified task
`EnumWindows`	WMI/Information	Enumerates the windows currently displayed
`EqualRect`	WMI/Rectangle	Determines whether two rectangles are equal
`EqualRgn`	GDI/Region	Determines whether two regions are the same
`Escape`	GDI/Printer Control	Lets an application access a device that is not available through the GDI
`EscapeCommFunction`	SSI/Communication	Specifies that the device is to carry out an extended function

Function	*Interface/Category*	*Meaning*
`ExcludeClipRect`	GDI/Clipping	Excludes the specified rectangle from the clipping region
`ExcludeUpdateRgn`	WMI/Painting	Prevents drawing in invalid window areas
`ExitWindows`	SSI/Task	Starts the Windows shutdown procedure
`ExtDeviceMode`	GDI/Printer Control	Provides access to driver configurations and device initialization information
`ExtFloodFill`	GDI/Bitmap	Fills the specified display surface
`ExtTextOut`	GDI/Text	Writes a character string inside a rectangular region using the specified font
`FatalAppExit`	SSI/Debugging	Displays a message box and terminates the application
`FatalExit`	SSI/Debugging	Displays the current state of Windows and prompts the user for information to proceed
`FillRect`	WMI/Painting	Fills a rectangle
`FillRgn`	GDI/Region	Fills a region
`FindAtom`	SSI/Atom Management	Finds the atom associated with a character string
`FindResource`	SSI/Resource Management	Gets the location of a resource
`FindWindow`	WMI/Information	Gets the window handle for the specified class and caption
`FlashWindow`	WMI/Error	Flashes a window
`FloodFill`	GDI/Bitmap	Fills the display area surrounded by the specified border
`FlushComm`	SSI/Communication	Flushes the characters from a communication device
`FrameRect`	WMI/Painting	Draws a border on the specified rectangle
`FrameRgn`	GDI/Region	Draws a border around a region
`FreeLibrary`	SSI/Module Management	Decreases the reference count of a library

Function	*Interface/Category*	*Meaning*
`FreeModule`	SSI/Module Management	Decreases the reference count of a module
`FreeProcInstance`	SSI/Module Management	Removes a function instance entry to an address
`FreeResource`	SSI/Resource Management	Removes a resource from memory
`FreeSelector`	SSI/Segment	Frees a selector
`GetActiveWindow`	WMI/Input	Gets the handle of the active window
`GetAspectRatioFilter`	GDI/Font	Gets the setting for the aspect-ratio filter
`GetAsyncKeyState`	WMI/Hardware	Gets interrupt-level information on the key state
`GetAtomHandle`	SSI/Atom Management	Gets the handle of the string that corresponds to an atom
`GetAtomName`	SSI/Atom Management	Gets the character string associated with an atom
`GetBitmapBits`	GDI/Bitmap	Gets the bitmap bits for the specified bitmap
`GetBitmapDimension`	GDI/Bitmap	Gets the dimensions for the specified bitmap
`GetBkColor`	GDI/Drawing Attribute	Gets the background color
`GetBkMode`	GDI/Drawing Attribute	Gets the background mode
`GetBrushOrg`	GDI/Drawing Tool	Gets the current brush origin
`GetBValue`	GDI/Color Palette	Gets the blue value from an RGB color value
`GetCapture`	WMI/Input	Gets the handle of the window that has the mouse capture
`GetCaretBlinkTime`	WMI/Caret	Gets the caret blink time
`GetCaretPos`	WMI/Caret	Gets the caret position
`GetCharWidth`	GDI/Font	Gets the width of a character
`GetClassInfo`	WMI/Window Creation	Gets information on the specified class
`GetClassLong`	WMI/Window Creation	Gets a long integer from a `WNDCLASS` structure
`GetClassName`	WMI/Window Creation	Gets a class name
`GetClassWord`	WMI/Window Creation	Gets a word from a `WNDCLASS` structure

Function	Interface/Category	Meaning
GetClientRect	WMI/Display and Movement	Gets the coordinates of a window's client area
GetClipboardData	WMI/Clipboard	Gets data from the clipboard
GetClipboardFormatName	WMI/Clipboard	Gets the format for the clipboard
GetClipboardOwner	WMI/Clipboard	Gets the window handle associated with the clipboard owner
GetClipboardViewer	WMI/Clipboard	Gets the handle of the first window in the clipboard viewer chain
GetClipBox	GDI/Clipping	Gets the dimensions of the bounding rectangle for the clipping region
GetCodeHandle	SSI/Module Management	Finds the code segment that contains the specified function
GetCodeInfo	SSI/Segment	Gets code segment information
GetCommError	SSI/Communication	Gets the communication status
GetCommEventMask	SSI/Communication	Gets and clears an event mask
GetCommState	SSI/Communication	Loads a buffer with a device control block
GetCurrentPDB	SSI/Task	Gets the DOS Program Data Base (PDB); also called the Program Segment Prefix (PSP)
GetCurrentPosition	GDI/Coordinate	Gets the logical coordinates of the current position
GetCurrentTask	SSI/Task	Gets the handle of the current task
GetCurrentTime	WMI/Input or WMI/System	Gets the Windows time
GetCursorPos	WMI/Cursor	Gets the screen coordinates of the cursor position
GetDC	WMI/Painting	Gets the display context for a client area
GetDCOrg	GDI/Device Context	Deletes a device context
GetDesktopWindow	WMI/Information	Gets the window handle of the Windows desktop window
GetDeviceCaps	GDI/Device Context	Gets information on a display device

Function	Interface/Category	Meaning
GetDialogBaseUnits	WMI/Dialog Box	Gets the base dialog units
GetDIBits	GDI/Bitmap	Gets the bits for a device independent bitmap
GetDlgCtrlID	WMI/Dialog Box	Gets the ID value of a control window
GetDlgItem	WMI/Dialog Box	Gets the handle of an item from the specified dialog box
GetDlgItemInt	WMI/Dialog Box	Converts the item's control text to an integer
GetDlgItemText	WMI/Dialog Box	Copies an item's control text to a string
GetDOSEnvironment	SSI/Task	Gets the environment string for the current task
GetDoubleClickTime	WMI/Input	Gets the mouse double-click time
GetDriveType	SSI/File I/O	Determines the drive type (fixed, removable, or remote)
GetEnvironment	GDI/Environment	Places environment information in a buffer
GetFocus	WMI/Input	Gets the handle of the window that has the input focus
GetFreeSpace	SSI/Memory Management	Determines the number of bytes available in the global heap
GetGValue	GDI/Color Palette	Gets the green value from an RGB color value
GetInputState	WMI/Hardware	Determines whether there is any mouse or keyboard input
GetInstanceData	SSI/Memory Management	Moves the data from the offset in an instance to the offset in another instance
GetKBCodePage	WMI/Hardware	Indicates the OEM and ANSI tables that are loaded
GetKeyboardState	WMI/Hardware	Gets the state of the keyboard keys
GetKeyboardType	WMI/Hardware	Gets the system keyboard type
GetKeyNameText	WMI/Hardware	Gets the string that contains the name of a key
GetKeyState	WMI/Hardware	Gets the state of a virtual key

Function	*Interface/Category*	*Meaning*
`GetLastActivePopup`	WMI/Window Creation	Gets the most recently active pop-up window
`GetMapMode`	GDI/Mapping	Gets the current mapping mode
`GetMenu`	WMI/Menu	Gets the menu handle for a window
`GetMenuCheckMarkDimensions`	WMI/Menu	Gets the dimensions of the default menu check mark bitmap
`GetMenuItemCount`	WMI/Menu	Gets the number of items in a menu
`GetMenuItemID`	WMI/Menu	Gets the ID for a menu item
`GetMenuState`	WMI/Menu	Gets the status for a menu item
`GetMenuString`	WMI/Menu	Copies a menu label to a string
`GetMessage`	WMI/Message	Gets a message
`GetMessagePos`	WMI/Message	Gets the position of the mouse when the message was retrieved
`GetMessageTime`	WMI/Message	Gets the time when the message was retrieved
`GetMetaFile`	GDI/Metafile	Creates a handle for a metafile
`GetMetaFileBits`	GDI/Metafile	Retrieves and stores the bits of a metafile
`GetModuleFileName`	SSI/Module Management	Gets the file name of a module
`GetModuleHandle`	SSI/Module Management	Gets the handle of a module
`GetModuleUsage`	SSI/Module Management	Gets the reference count of a module
`GetNearestColor`	GDI/Color Palette	Gets the closest logical color to the specified color
`GetNearestPaletteIndex`	GDI/Color Palette	Gets the index of a logical palette that is the closest match to the specified RGB value
`GetNextDlgGroupItem`	WMI/Dialog Box	Gets the handle for the next item in the group
`GetNextDlgTabItem`	WMI/Dialog Box	Gets the handle of the next or previous item

Function	Interface/Category	Meaning
GetNextWindow	WMI/Information	Gets the handle for the next or previous window
GetNumTasks	SSI/Task	Gets the number of executing tasks
GetObject	GDI/Drawing Tool	Gets the bytes of data that define an object
GetPaletteEntries	GDI/Color Palette	Gets entries from a logical palette
GetParent	WMI/Information	Gets the window handle for the parent window of the specified window
GetPixel	GDI/Bitmap	Gets the RGB value for a pixel
GetPolyFillMode	GDI/Drawing Attribute	Gets the mode for filling polygons
GetPriorityClipboardFormat	WMI/Clipboard	Gets data in the first format from a prioritized format list
GetPrivateProfileInt	SSI/Initialization File	Gets an integer value in a section from a private initialization file
GetPrivateProfileString	SSI/Initialization File	Gets a string in a section from a private initialization file
GetProcAddress	SSI/Module Management	Gets the address of a function in a module
GetProfileInt	SSI/Initialization File	Gets an integer value in a section from WIN.INI
GetProfileString	SSI/Initialization File	Gets a string in a section from WIN.INI
GetProp	WMI/Property	Gets the handle for the specified string
GetRgnBox	GDI/Region	Gets the coordinates of the rectangle binding the region
GetROP2	GDI/Drawing Attribute	Gets the drawing mode
GetRValue	GDI/Color Palette	Gets the red value from an RGB color value
GetScrollPos	WMI/Scrolling	Gets the thumb position of a scroll bar
GetScrollRange	WMI/Scrolling	Gets the position range for a scroll bar
GetStockObject	GDI/Drawing Tool	Gets the handle to a predefined stock pen, brush, font, or color palette

Function	*Interface/Category*	*Meaning*
GetStretchBltMode	GDI/Drawing Attribute	Gets the stretching mode
GetSubMenu	WMI/Menu	Gets the menu handle for a pop-up menu
GetSysColor	WMI/System	Gets the system color
GetSysModalWindow	WMI/Input	Gets the handle of a system modal window
GetSystemDirectory	SSI/File I/O	Gets the pathname for the subdirectory for the Windows system
GetSystemMenu	WMI/Menu	Provides access to the System menu
GetSystemMetrics	WMI/System	Gets system metrics information
GetSystemPaletteEntries	GDI/Color Palette	Gets palette entries from system palette
GetSystemPaletteUse	GDI/Color Palette	Determines whether an application has access to the full system palette
GetTabbedTextExtent	GDI/Text	Determines the width and height of a line of text that contains tab characters
GetTempDrive	SSI/File I/O	Gets the drive letter for the best drive to use for temporary file storage
GetTempFileName	SSI/File I/O	Creates a temporary file name
GetTextAlign	GDI/Text	Gets a mask of text alignment flags
GetTextCharacterExtra	GDI/Text	Gets the current intercharacter spacing
GetTextColor	GDI/Drawing Attribute	Gets the text color
GetTextExtent	GDI/Text	Gets the width and height of text
GetTextFace	GDI/Text	Copies the font name to a buffer
GetTextMetrics	GDI/Text	Copies the metrics for a font to a buffer
GetThresholdEvent	SSI/Sound	Gets a long pointer to a threshold flag
GetThresholdStatus	SSI/Sound	Gets the threshold event status for each voice

Function	Interface/Category	Meaning
GetTickCount	WMI/Input	Gets the number of timer ticks that have occurred since the system was booted
GetTopWindow	WMI/Information	Gets the handle to the top-level child window
GetUpdateRect	WMI/Painting	Gets the dimensions of the rectangle around the update region
GetUpdateRgn	WMI/Painting	Copies the update region of a window
GetVersion	SSI/Module Management	Gets the Windows version number
GetViewportExt	GDI/Mapping	Gets the viewport extents for a device context
GetViewportOrg	GDI/Mapping	Gets the viewport origin for a device context
GetWindow	WMI/Information	Gets a window handle from the window manager's list
GetWindowDC	WMI/Painting	Gets the display context for a window
GetWindowExt	GDI/Mapping	Gets the window extents for a device context
GetWindowLong	WMI/Window Creation	Gets a long integer descriptor for the window
GetWindowOrg	GDI/Mapping	Gets the window origin for a device context
GetWindowRect	WMI/Display and Movement	Gets the coordinates of a window
GetWindowsDirectory	SSI/File I/O	Gets the path name for the Windows directory
GetWindowTask	WMI/Information	Gets a task handle for the task associated with the window
GetWindowText	WMI/Display and Movement	Copies the window caption to a buffer
GetWindowTextLength	WMI/Display and Movement	Gets the number of characters in the window caption or text
GetWindowWord	WMI/Window Creation	Gets a word descriptor for the window
GetWinFlags	SSI/Memory Management	Gets information on the system memory configuration

Function	*Interface/Category*	*Meaning*
`GlobalAddAtom`	SSI/Atom Management	Creates a global atom for a character string
`GlobalAlloc`	SSI/Memory Management	Allocates memory from global heap
`GlobalCompact`	SSI/Memory Management	Compacts global memory
`GlobalDeleteAtom`	SSI/Atom Management	Deletes a global atom when the reference count is zero
`GlobalDiscard`	SSI/Memory Management	Discards a global memory
`GlobalDosAlloc`	SSI/Memory Management	Allocates global memory
`GlobalDosFree`	SSI/Memory Management	Frees global memory allocated with `GlobalDosAlloc`
`GlobalFindAtom`	SSI/Atom Management	Gets the global atom associated with a character string
`GlobalFix`	SSI/Segment	Keeps a global memory block from being moved in linear memory
`GlobalFlags`	SSI/Memory Management	Gets the flags and lock count of a memory block
`GlobalFree`	SSI/Memory Management	Removes a global block and invalidates the handle
`GlobalGetAtomName`	SSI/Atom Management	Gets the character string associated with a global atom
`GlobalHandle`	SSI/Memory Management	Gets the handle of a global memory object
`GlobalLock`	SSI/Memory Management	Gets the pointer for a handle to a global memory block
`GlobalLRUNewest`	SSI/Memory Management	Moves a global memory object to the newest least-recently-used (LRU) position
`GlobalLRUOldest`	SSI/Memory Management	Moves a global memory object to the oldest least-recently-used (LRU) position
`GlobalNotify`	SSI/Memory Management	Installs a notification procedure
`GlobalPageLock`	SSI/Segment	Page locks the memory associated with the specified global selector

Function	*Interface/Category*	*Meaning*
`GlobalPageUnlock`	SSI/Segment	Decreases the page lock count for a block of memory
`GlobalReAlloc`	SSI/Memory Management	Reallocates a global memory block
`GlobalSize`	SSI/Memory Management	Gets the number of bytes in a global memory block
`GlobalUnfix`	SSI/Segment	Unlocks a global memory block
`GlobalUnlock`	SSI/Memory Management	Invalidates the pointer to a global memory block
`GlobalUnWire`	SSI/Memory Management	Decreases the lock count and unlocks the memory block when the count is zero
`GlobalWire`	SSI/Memory Management	Moves an object to low memory and increases the lock count
`GrayString`	WMI/Painting	Writes a string in gray text
`HIBYTE`	SSI/Utility	Gets the high-order byte of an integer
`HideCaret`	WMI/Caret	Removes the caret from a window
`HiliteMenuItem`	WMI/Menu	Either highlights or removes the highlight from a top-level menu item
`HIWORD`	SSI/Utility	Gets the high-order word of a long integer
`InflateRect`	WMI/Rectangle	Sizes the specified rectangle
`InitAtomTable`	SSI/Atom Management	Initializes an atom hash table
`InSendMessage`	WMI/Message	Determines whether the current window function is processing a message; passed by `SendMessage`
`InsertMnu`	WMI/Menu	Inserts a menu item into a menu
`IntersectClipRect`	GDI/Clipping	Creates a new clipping region from the intersection of the clipping region and a rectangle
`IntersectRect`	WMI/Rectangle	Determines the intersection of two rectangles

Function	*Interface/Category*	*Meaning*
InvalidateRect	WMI/Painting	Defines a rectangle for repainting
InvalidateRgn	WMI/Painting	Defines a region for repainting
InvertRect	WMI/Painting	Inverts the bits of the specified rectangle
InvertRgn	GDI/Region	Inverts the colors in the region
IsCharAlpha	SSI/String Manipulation	Determines whether a character is alphabetical
IsCharAlphaNumeric	SSI/String Manipulation	Determines whether a character is alphanumeric
IsCharLower	SSI/String Manipulation	Determines whether a character is lowercase
IsCharUpper	SSI/String Manipulation	Determines whether a character is uppercase
IsChild	WMI/Information	Determines whether a window is a descendent of the specified window
IsClipboardFormatAvailable	WMI/Clipboard	Determines whether data is available in the specified format
IsDialogMessage	WMI/Dialog Box	Determines whether a message is sent to the specified dialog box
IsDlgButtonChecked	WMI/Dialog Box	Determines whether a button is checked
IsIconic	WMI/Display and Movement	Determines whether a window is open or closed
IsRectEmpty	WMI/Rectangle	Determines whether a rectangle is empty
IsWindow	WMI/Information	Determines whether a window is valid
IsWindowEnabled	WMI/Input	Determines whether mouse and keyboard input is enabled for the specified window
IsWindowVisible	WMI/Display and Movement	Determines whether a window is visible
IsZoomed	WMI/Display and Movement	Determines whether a window is zoomed
KillTimer	WMI/Input	Kills the specified timer event

Function	*Interface/Category*	*Meaning*
`_lclose`	SSI/File I/O	Closes a file
`_lcreat`	SSI/File I/O	Creates a new file or opens an existing file
`LimitEmsPages`	SSI/Memory Management	Sets the limits for the amount of expanded memory that Windows assigns to an application
`LineDDA`	GDI/Line Output	Calculates each point on a line
`LineTo`	GDI/Line Output	Draws a line
`_llseek`	SSI/File I/O	Sets the pointer to a file
`LoadAccelerators`	SSI/Resource Management	Loads an accelerator table
`LoadBitmap`	GDI/Bitmap or SSI/Resource Management	Loads the specified bitmap
`LoadCursor`	SSI/Resource Management or WMI/Cursor	Loads a cursor resource
`LoadIcon`	SSI/Resource Management	Loads an icon resource
`LoadLibrary`	SSI/Module Management	Loads a library module
`LoadMenu`	SSI/Resource Management	Loads a menu resource
`LoadMenuIndirect`	WMI/Menu	Loads a menu resource defined by a template
`LoadModule`	SSI/Application Execution	Executes a Windows application and uses a DOS Function 4BH, Code 00H, parameter block
`LoadResource`	SSI/Resource Management	Loads a resource
`LoadString`	SSI/Resource Management	Loads a string resource
`LOBYTE`	SSI/Utility	Gets the low-order byte of an integer
`LocalAlloc`	SSI/Memory Management	Allocates memory from the local heap
`LocalCompact`	SSI/Memory Management	Compacts local memory
`LocalDiscard`	SSI/Memory Management	Discards local memory when the lock count is zero
`LocalFlags`	SSI/Memory Management	Gets the memory type of a local memory block
`LocalFree`	SSI/Memory Management	Frees a local memory block when the lock count is zero

Function	Interface/Category	Meaning
LocalHandle	SSI/Memory Management	Gets the handle of a local memory block
LocalInit	SSI/Memory Management	Initializes a local heap
LocalLock	SSI/Memory Management	Locks a local memory block
LocalReAlloc	SSI/Memory Management	Reallocates a local memory block
LocalShrink	SSI/Memory Management	Shrinks the local heap
LocalSize	SSI/Memory Management	Gets the number of bytes in a local memory block
LocalUnlock	SSI/Memory Management	Unlocks a local memory block
LockData	SSI/Memory Management	Locks the current data segment
LockResource	SSI/Resource Management	Gets the absolute memory address of a resource
LockSegment	SSI/Memory Management or SSI/Segment	Locks the specified data segment
_lopen	SSI/File I/O	Opens an existing file
LOWORD	SSI/Utility	Gets the low-order word of a long integer
LPtoDP	GDI/Coordinate	Converts logical points to device points
_lread	SSI/File I/O	Reads from a file
lstrcat	SSI/String Manipulation	Concatenates two strings
lstrcmp	SSI/String Manipulation	Compares two strings and is case-sensitive
lstrcmpi	SSI/String Manipulation	Compares two strings and is not case-sensitive
lstrcpy	SSI/String Manipulation	Copies one string to another
lstrlen	SSI/String Manipulation	Gets the length of a string
_lwrite	SSI/File I/O	Writes to a file
MAKEINTATOM	SSI/Atom Management or SSI/Utility	Casts an integer for use as a function argument
MAKEINTRESOURCE	SSI/Utility	Converts an integer value to a long pointer to a string
MAKELONG	SSI/Utility	Creates an unsigned long integer
MAKEPOINT	SSI/Utility	Converts a long value that specifies the coordinates of a point into a POINT data structure

Function	Interface/Category	Meaning
MakeProcInstance	SSI/Module Management	Gets a function instance address
MapDialogRect	WMI/Dialog Box	Converts dialog box coordinates to client coordinates
MapVirtualKey	WMI/Hardware	Gets the scan code, virtual key code, or ASCII value for the specified virtual key code or scan code
max	SSI/Utility	Determines the greater of two values
MessageBeep	WMI/Error	Sends a beep out the system speaker
MessageBox	WMI/Error	Creates a window containing the specified caption and text
min	SSI/Utility	Determines the lesser of two values
ModifyMenu	WMI/Menu	Modifies a menu item
MoveTo	GDI/Line Output	Moves the current position to the specified point
MoveWindow	WMI/Display and Movement	Changes the size and position of a window
MulDiv	SSI/Utility	Multiplies two values and divides the result by a third value
NetBIOSCall	SSI/Operating System Interrupt	Generates a NETBIOS 5CH interrupt
OemKeyScan	WMI/Hardware	Maps OEM ASCII codes 0 to 0x0FF into the OEM scan codes and shift states
OemToAnsi	SSI/String Manipulation	Converts an OEM string to an ANSI string
OemToAnsiBuff	SSI/String Manipulation	Converts an OEM string in a buffer to an ANSI string
OffsetClipRgn	GDI/Clipping	Moves the clipping region
OffsetRect	WMI/Rectangle	Moves a rectangle
OffsetRgn	GDI/Region	Moves the region
OffsetViewportOrg	GDI/Mapping	Moves the viewport origin
OffsetWindowOrg	GDI/Mapping	Moves the window origin

Function	*Interface/Category*	*Meaning*
`OpenClipboard`	WMI/Clipboard	Opens the clipboard
`OpenComm`	SSI/Communication	Opens a communication device
`OpenFile`	SSI/File I/O	Creates, opens, or deletes a file
`OpenIcon`	WMI/Display and Movement	Opens a window
`OpenSound`	SSI/Sound	Opens the play device
`OutputDebugString`	SSI/Debugging	Sends a debugging message
`PaintRgn`	GDI/Region	Fills the region using the specified brush pattern
`PALETTEINDEX`	SSI/Utility	Converts an integer to a `COLORREF` value
`PALETTERGB`	SSI/Utility	Converts the red, green, and blue values into a palette-relative `COLORREF` value
`PatBlt`	GDI/Bitmap	Creates a bit pattern
`PeekMessage`	WMI/Message	Checks the application queue
`Pie`	GDI/Ellipse and Polygon	Draws a pie
`PlayMetaFile`	GDI/Metafile	Plays the contents of a metafile
`PlayMetaFileRecord`	GDI/Metafile	Plays a metafile record
`Polygon`	GDI/Ellipse and Polygon	Draws a polygon
`Polyline`	GDI/Line Output	Draws a series of line segments
`PolyPolygon`	GDI/Ellipse and Polygon	Draws a series of closed polygons
`PostAppMessage`	WMI/Message	Sends a message to the application
`PostMessage`	WMI/Message	Puts a message in the application queue
`PostQuitMessage`	WMI/Message	Sends `WM_QUIT` to the application
`ProfClear`	SSI/Optimization Tool	Discards the contents of the Profiler sampling buffer
`ProfFinish`	SSI/Optimization Tool	Stops Profiler sampling and flushes the buffer to disk
`ProfFlush`	SSI/Optimization Tool	Flushes the sampling buffer for the Profiler to disk
`ProfInsChk`	SSI/Optimization Tool	Determines whether Profiler is installed

Function	Interface/Category	Meaning
ProfSampRate	SSI/Optimization Tool	Sets the Profiler sampling rate
ProfSetup	SSI/Optimization Tool	Sets the Profiler sampling buffer and recording rate
ProfStart	SSI/Optimization Tool	Begins Profiler sampling
ProfStop	SSI/Optimization Tool	Ends Profiler sampling
PtInRect	WMI/Rectangle	Determines whether the specified point is within the rectangle
PtInRegion	GDI/Region	Determines whether a point is in the region
PtVisible	GDI/Clipping	Determines whether the point lies in the region
ReadComm	SSI/Communication	Reads from a communication device
RealizePalette	GDI/Color Palette	Maps entries from a logical palette to the system palette
Rectangle	GDI/Ellipse and Polygon	Draws a rectangle
RectInRegion	GDI/Region	Determines whether any part of the rectangle is in the region
RectVisible	GDI/Clipping	Determines whether part of the specified rectangle lies within the clipping region
RegisterClass	WMI/Window Creation	Registers the window class
RegisterClipboardFormat	WMI/Clipboard	Registers a new clipboard format
RegisterWindowMessage	WMI/Message	Defines a new, unique message
ReleaseCapture	WMI/Input	Releases the mouse capture
ReleaseDC	WMI/Painting	Releases the display context
RemoveFontResource	GDI/Font	Removes a font resource from the font table
RemoveMenu	WMI/Input	Removes an item from a menu
RemoveProp	WMI/Property	Removes the specified string from the property list
ReplyMessage	WMI/Message	Replies to a message
ResizePalette	GDI/Color Palette	Changes the size of the color palette
RestoreDC	GDI/Device Context	Restores a device context

Function	*Interface/Category*	*Meaning*
`RGB`	SSI/Utility	Converts the red, green, and blue values into an explicit `COLORREF` value
`RoundRect`	GDI/Ellipse and Polygon	Draws a rounded rectangle
`SaveDC`	GDI/Device Context	Saves the state of a device context
`ScaleViewportExt`	GDI/Mapping	Alters the viewport extents
`ScaleWindowExt`	GDI/Mapping	Alters the window extents
`ScreenToClient`	GDI/Coordinate	Converts screen coordinates to client coordinates
`ScrollDC`	WMI/Scrolling	Scrolls a rectangle vertically and horizontally
`ScrollWindow`	WMI/Scrolling	Moves the contents of the client area
`SelectClipRgn`	GDI/Clipping	Selects a clipping region
`SelectObject`	GDI/Drawing Tool	Selects an object
`SelectPalette`	GDI/Color Palette	Selects a logical palette
`SendDlgItemMessage`	WMI/Dialog Box	Sends a message to a dialog box
`SendMessage`	WMI/Message	Sends a message
`SetActiveWindow`	WMI/Input	Makes a window the active window
`SetBitmapBits`	GDI/Bitmap	Sets the bits for a bitmap
`SetBitmapDimension`	GDI/Bitmap	Defines the dimensions of a bitmap
`SetBkColor`	GDI/Drawing Attribute	Sets the background color
`SetBkMode`	GDI/Drawing Attribute	Sets the background mode
`SetBrushOrg`	GDI/Drawing Tool	Sets the origin for the selected brushes
`SetCapture`	WMI/Input	Gives the mouse capture to the specified window
`SetCaretBlinkTime`	WMI/Caret	Sets the caret blink time
`SetCaretPos`	WMI/Caret	Moves the caret to the specified position
`SetClassLong`	WMI/Window Creation	Replaces a long integer in a WNDCLASS structure
`SetClassWord`	WMI/Window Creation	Replaces a word in a WNDCLASS structure
`SetClipboardData`	WMI/Clipboard	Copies a handle for data

Function	Interface/Category	Meaning
`SetClipboardViewer`	WMI/Clipboard	Adds a handle to the clipboard viewer chain
`SetCommBreak`	SSI/Communication	Sets the break state for a communication device
`SetCommEventMask`	SSI/Communication	Gets and sets an event mask
`SetCommState`	SSI/Communication	Sets the state of the communication device to the state in the device control block
`SetCursor`	WMI/Cursor	Sets the shape of the cursor
`SetCursorPos`	WMI/Cursor	Moves the cursor to the specified position
`SetDIBits`	GDI/Bitmap	Sets the bits for a device independent bitmap
`SetDIBitsToDevice`	GDI/Bitmap	Sets bits on a device directly from a device independent bitmap
`SetDlgItemInt`	WMI/Dialog Box	Sets the caption or text for an item to a string representing an integer
`SetDlgItemText`	WMI/Dialog Box	Sets the caption or text for an item to a string
`SetDoubleClickTime`	WMI/Input	Sets the mouse double-click time
`SetEnvironment`	GDI/Environment	Sets the environment associated with a device attached to a system port
`SetErrorMode`	SSI/Task	Specifies whether Windows or the application handles DOS 24H errors
`SetFocus`	WMI/Input	Gives the input focus to the specified window
`SetHandleCount`	SSI/File I/O	Sets the number of file handles available for a task
`SetKeyboardState`	WMI/Hardware	Sets the state of keyboard keys
`SetMapMode`	GDI/Mapping	Sets the mapping mode
`SetMapperFlags`	GDI/Font	Modifies the algorithm used by the font mapper
`SetMenu`	WMI/Menu	Defines a new menu for the window

Function	*Interface/Category*	*Meaning*
SetMenuItemBitmaps	WMI/Menu	Defines bitmaps for a menu item
SetMessageQueue	WMI/Message	Creates a new message queue
SetMetaFileBits	GDI/Metafile	Creates a memory metafile
SetPaletteEntries	GDI/Color Palette	Sets the palette entries for a logical palette
SetParent	WMI/Information	Sets the parent window for a child window
SetPixel	GDI/Bitmap	Defines the RGB value for a pixel
SetPolyFillMode	GDI/Drawing Attribute	Sets the mode for filling polygons
SetProp	WMI/Property	Adds an entry to the property list
SetRect	WMI/Rect	Creates a new rectangle
SetRectEmpty	WMI/Rectangle	Creates an empty rectangle
SetRectRgn	GDI/Region	Creates a rectangular region
SetResourceHandler	SSI/Resource Management	Defines a function to load resources
SetROP2	GDI/Drawing Attribute	Sets the drawing mode
SetScrollPos	WMI/Scrolling	Sets the thumb position of the scroll bar
SetScrollRange	WMI/Scrolling	Sets the position range for a scroll bar
SetSoundNoise	SSI/Sound	Sets the source and duration for a noise
SetStretchBltMode	GDI/Drawing Attribute	Sets the stretching mode
SetSwapAreaSize	SSI/Memory Management	Sets the amount of memory reserved for code segments of an application
SetSysColors	WMI/System	Modifies system colors
SetSysModalWindow	WMI/Input	Defines the specified window as a system modal window
SetSystemPaletteUse	GDI/Color Palette	Gives the application access to the full system palette
SetTextAlign	GDI/Text	Positions text on the display or device
SetTextCharacterExtra	GDI/Text	Sets intercharacter spacing
SetTextColor	GDI/Drawing Attribute	Sets the text color

Function	*Interface/Category*	*Meaning*
`SetTextJustification`	GDI/Text	Sets the text line justification
`SetTimer`	WMI/Input	Creates a system timer event
`SetViewportExt`	GDI/Mapping	Sets the viewport extents for a device context
`SetViewportOrg`	GDI/Mapping	Sets the viewport origin for a device context
`SetVoiceAccent`	SSI/Sound	Puts an accent in the voice queue
`SetVoiceEnvelope`	SSI/Sound	Puts the voice envelope in the voice queue
`SetVoiceNote`	SSI/Sound	Puts a note in the specified voice queue
`SetVoiceQueueSize`	SSI/Sound	Sets the size of the voice queue
`SetVoiceSound`	SSI/Sound	Puts a sound frequency and duration in a voice queue
`SetVoiceThreshold`	SSI/Sound	Sets the threshold for a voice
`SetWindowExt`	GDI/Mapping	Sets the window extents for a device context
`SetWindowLong`	WMI/Window Creation	Modifies an integer attribute
`SetWindowOrg`	GDI/Mapping	Sets the window origin for a device context
`SetWindowPos`	WMI/Display and Movement	Modifies a child or pop-up window's size, position, and ordering
`SetWindowsHook`	WMI/Hook	Specifies a system and/or application filter function
`SetWindowText`	WMI/Display and Movement	Defines the caption or text for a window
`SetWindowWord`	WMI/Window Creation	Modifies a word attribute
`ShowCaret`	WMI/Caret	Displays a new caret or redisplays a hidden caret
`ShowCursor`	WMI/Cursor	Either increases or decreases the cursor display count
`ShowOwnedPopups`	WMI/Display and Movement	Either shows or hides all pop-up windows
`ShowScrollBar`	WMI/Scrolling	Either hides or displays a scroll bar
`ShowWindow`	WMI/Display and Movement	Either displays or removes the window

Function	*Interface/Category*	*Meaning*
`SizeofResource`	SSI/Resource Management	Defines the size for a resource
`StartSound`	SSI/Sound	Begins playing each queue
`StopSound`	SSI/Sound	Stops the playing of each queue and flushes the contents of the queues
`StretchBlt`	GDI/Bitmap	Copies the bitmap to a destination device
`StretchDIBits`	GDI/Bitmap	Copies the device-independent bitmap to a destination device
`SwapMouseButton`	WMI/Input	Switches the left and right mouse buttons
`SwapRecording`	SSI/Optimization Tool	Either starts or stops Swap analysis of the swapping behavior of the application
`SwitchStackBack`	SSI/Memory Management	Returns the stack of the current task to the task's data segment
`SwitchStackTo`	SSI/Memory Management	Changes the stack of the current task to the specified data segment
`SyncAllVoices`	SSI/Sound	Places a sync mark in each queue
`TabbedTextOut`	GDI/Text	Writes a string, using the specified font, with expanded tabs
`TextOut`	GDI/Text	Writes a character string using the current font
`Throw`	SSI/Task	Restores the execution environment
`ToAscii`	SSI/String Manipulation	Translates a virtual-key code to ANSI characters
`TrackPopupMenu`	WMI/Menu	Displays a pop-up menu at the specified position
`TranslateAccelerator`	WMI/Message	Translates keyboard accelerators
`TranslateMDISysAccel`	WMI/Message	Translates MDI child window command accelerators
`TranslateMessage`	WMI/Message	Translates virtual keystroke messages to character messages

Function	*Interface/Category*	*Meaning*
`TransmitCommChar`	SSI/Communication	Puts a character at the top of the transmit queue
`UngetCommChar`	SSI/Communication	Specifies the next character to read
`UnhookWindowsHook`	WMI/Hook	Removes a filter function from the filter function chain
`UnionRect`	WMI/Rectangle	Determines the union of two rectangles
`UnlockData`	SSI/Memory Management	Unlocks the current data segment
`UnlockResource`	SSI/Resource Management	Unlocks a resource
`UnlockSegment`	SSI/Memory Management or SSI/Segment	Unlocks the specified data segment
`UnrealizeObject`	GDI/Drawing Tool	Resets the origin of a brush
`UnregisterClass`	WMI/Window Creation	Removes a window class
`UpdateColors`	GDI/Color Palette	Translates each pixel's current color to the system palette
`UpdateWindow`	WMI/Painting	Tells the application that the window needs repainting
`ValidateCodeSegments`	SSI/Debugging	Checks whether any code segments were modified by random memory overwrites
`ValidateFreeSpaces`	SSI/Debugging	Checks free segments in memory for valid contents
`ValidateRect`	WMI/Painting	Validates the specified rectangle
`ValidateRgn`	WMI/Painting	Validates the specified region
`VkKeyScan`	WMI/Hardware	Converts the ANSI character to its corresponding virtual key code and shift state
`WaitMessage`	WMI/Message	Yields control to other applications
`WaitSoundState`	SSI/Sound	Waits for the play driver to enter a specified state
`WindowFromPoint`	GDI/Coordinate or WMI/Information	Finds the window that contains a specified point
`WinExec`	SSI/Application Execution	Executes a Windows or DOS application and specifies command parameters and the initial state of the application window

Function	*Interface/Category*	*Meaning*
`WinHelp`	SSI/Application Execution	Executes the Windows Help application
`WriteComm`	SSI/Communication	Writes from a buffer to a communication device
`WritePrivateProfileString`	SSI/Initialization File	Either writes a string to a private initialization file or deletes lines from a private initialization file
`WriteProfileString`	SSI/Initialization File	Either writes a string to WIN.INI or deletes lines from WIN.INI
`wsprintf`	SSI/String Manipulation	Formats characters and values and places them in a buffer; format arguments are passed separately
`wvsprintf`	SSI/String Manipulation	Formats characters and values and places them in a buffer; format arguments are passed in an array
`Yield`	SSI/Task	Pauses the current task and begins a waiting task

B

Windows Messages Quick Reference Guide

This appendix is a quick reference guide to the Windows messages. Two pieces of information are provided for each of the Windows messages. The first piece of information is the category. Windows messages can be divided into the following categories:

- Button Control messages
- Clipboard messages
- Combo Box messages
- Control messages
- Edit Control messages

- Initialization messages
- Input messages
- List Box messages
- Multiple Document Interface (MDI) messages
- Non-Client Area messages
- Notification codes

  Button notification codes

  Combo Box notification codes

  Edit Control notification codes

  List Box notification codes

- Owner Draw Control messages
- Scroll Bar messages
- System Information messages
- System messages
- Window Management messages

The category information is provided to help you easily find the documentation on the appropriate message. The message documentation in Chapter 14, "Windows Messages," is divided into these categories. Therefore, to find the documentation on `BM_GETCHECK`, for example, simply look under the "Button Control Messages" category in Chapter 14 for the `BM_GETCHECK` message.

The other piece of information is provided in the Meaning column. This information provides a quick description of the message.

Message	*Category*	*Meaning*
BM_GETCHECK	Button Control	Determines whether a radio button or check box is checked
BM_GETSTATE	Button Control	Determines the state of a button control whenever the mouse button or space bar is pressed
BM_SETCHECK	Button Control	Places or removes the check mark from a radio button or check box

Message	*Category*	*Meaning*
BM_SETSTATE	Button Control	Highlights a check box or button
BM_SETSTYLE	Button Control	Modifies the button style
BN_CLICKED	Button Notification	Specifies that a button was clicked
BN_DOUBLECLICKED	Button Notification	Specifies that an owner draw or radio button was double-clicked
CB_ADDSTRING	Combo Box	Adds a string to the list box of a combo box
CB_DELETESTRING	Combo Box	Removes a string from the list box of a combo box
CB_DIR	Combo Box	Gets a list of files from the current directory and places the list in the combo box
CB_FINDSTRING	Combo Box	Searches for the first string from the list box of a combo box that matches the specified prefix
CB_GETCOUNT	Combo Box	Determines the number of items in the combo box
CB_GETCURSEL	Combo Box	Gets the item index of the current selection
CB_GETEDITSEL	Combo Box	Gets the starting and ending positions of the selected text in the edit control of a combo box
CB_GETITEMDATA	Combo Box	Gets the 32-bit value associated with an item in an owner draw combo box
CB_GETLBTEXT	Combo Box	Copies a string from a list box in a combo box to a buffer
CB_GETLBTEXTLEN	Combo Box	Determines the length of a string from a list box of a combo box
CB_INSERTSTRING	Combo Box	Inserts a string in a list box of a combo box
CB_LIMITTEXT	Combo Box	Specifies the maximum length of the text that can be entered in an edit control of a combo box

Message	*Category*	*Meaning*
CB_RESETCONTENT	Combo Box	Deletes the strings from a combo box
CB_SELECTSTRING	Combo Box	Selects the first string that has the specified prefix
CB_SETCURSEL	Combo Box	Selects a string and displays it in the list box of a combo box
CB_SETEDITSEL	Combo Box	Selects the text in the edit control within the specified starting and ending positions
CB_SETITEMDATA	Combo Box	Sets the 32-bit value associated with an item in an owner draw combo box
CB_SHOWDROPDOWN	Combo Box	Either shows or hides a drop-down list box in a combo box
CBN_DBLCLK	Combo Box Notification	Sent when a string was double-clicked
CBN_DROPDOWN	Combo Box Notification	Sent to the owner of the combo box when a list box is to be dropped down
CBN_EDITCHANGE	Combo Box Notification	Sent when the text in the edit control is modified
CBN_EDITUPDATE	Combo Box Notification	Specifies that the edit control will display altered text
CBN_ERRSPACE	Combo Box Notification	Sent when there is no more system memory
CBN_KILLFOCUS	Combo Box Notification	Specifies that the combo box no longer has the input focus
CBN_SELCHANGE	Combo Box Notification	Specifies that the selection was modified
CBN_SETFOCUS	Combo Box Notification	Specifies that the combo box received the input focus
DM_GETDEFID	Button Control	Gets the default push button's ID for a dialog box
DM_SETDEFID	Button Control	Modifies the default push button control ID for a dialog box
EM_CANUNDO	Edit Control	Indicates whether an edit control can respond to an EM_UNDO message

Message	*Category*	*Meaning*
EM_EMPTYUNDOBUFFER	Edit Control	Disables the undo capability of an edit control
EM_FMTLINES	Edit Control	Specifies whether the edit control should add or remove end-of-line characters from text that wraps around a line
EM_GETHANDLE	Edit Control	Gets the data handle of the buffer that stores the control window contents
EM_GETLINE	Edit Control	Gets a line from the edit control
EM_GETLINECOUNT	Edit Control	Gets the number of lines of text in the edit control
EM_GETMODIFY	Edit Control	Gets the setting of the modify flag for an edit control
EM_GETRECT	Edit Control	Gets the dimensions of the formatting rectangle of the edit control
EM_GETSEL	Edit Control	Gets the starting and ending positions of the current selection
EM_LIMITTEXT	Edit Control	Specifies the maximum number of bytes that the user can enter
EM_LINEFROMCHAR	Edit Control	Gets the line number of the line that contains the character at the specified position
EM_LINEINDEX	Edit Control	Gets the number of character positions that exist prior to the first character of a specified line
EM_LINELENGTH	Edit Control	Determines the length of a line from the text buffer for the edit control
EM_LINESCROLL	Edit Control	Scrolls the contents of the edit control a specified number of lines
EM_REPLACESEL	Edit Control	Replaces the current selection with the specified text

Message	*Category*	*Meaning*
EM_SETHANDLE	Edit Control	Specifies the text buffer that holds the contents of the edit control window
EM_SETMODIFY	Edit Control	Sets the modify flag for the specified edit control
EM_SETPASSWORDCHAR	Edit Control	Defines the password character displayed in an edit control with style ES_PASSWORD
EM_SETRECT	Edit Control	Sets the dimensions of the formatting rectangle for an edit control
EM_SETRECTNP	Edit Control	Sets the dimensions of the formatting rectangle for an edit control but does not repaint the control
EM_SETSEL	Edit Control	Selects the text within the specified starting and ending character positions
EM_SETTABSTOPS	Edit Control	Defines the tab stop settings for a multiline edit control
EM_SETWORDBREAK	Edit Control	Sent to a multiline edit control when the word-break function is replaced with a word-break function supplied by the application
EM_UNDO	Edit Control	Performs an “undo” of the last edit in an edit control
EN_CHANGE	Edit Control Notification	Indicates that an action has changed the content of the text
EN_ERRSPACE	Edit Control Notification	Specifies that an edit control is out of space
EN_HSCROLL	Edit Control Notification	Specifies that the horizontal scroll bar was clicked and is active
EN_KILLFOCUS	Edit Control Notification	Specifies that the edit control has lost the input focus
EN_MAXTEXT	Edit Control Notification	Specifies that the inserted text exceeds the limits for the edit control

Message	*Category*	*Meaning*
EN_SETFOCUS	Edit Control Notification	Specifies that the edit control has received the input focus
EN_UPDATE	Edit Control Notification	Specifies that the edit control will display altered text
EN_VSCROLL	Edit Control Notification	Specifies that the vertical scroll bar was clicked and is active
LB_ADDSTRING	List Box	Adds a string to the list box
LB_DELETESTRING	List Box	Removes a string from the list box
LB_DIR	List Box	Gets a list of files from the current directory and places the list of files in the list box
LB_FINDSTRING	List Box	Searches for a string in the list box that matches the prefix text
LB_GETCOUNT	List Box	Determines the number of items in a list box
LB_GETCURSEL	List Box	Gets the item index for the currently selected item
LB_GETHORIZONTALEXTENT	List Box	Gets the horizontal scroll width of a list box
LB_GETITEMDATA	List Box	Gets the 32-bit value associated with an item in an owner draw list box
LB_GETITEMRECT	List Box	Gets the coordinates of the rectangle binding the list box item
LB_GETSEL	List Box	Gets the selection state of a list box item
LB_GETSELCOUNT	List Box	Determines the number of items selected from a list box
LB_GETSELITEMS	List Box	Gets the item indexes of the selected items from a list box
LB_GETTEXT	List Box	Copies a string from a list box into a buffer
LB_GETTEXTLEN	List Box	Determines the length of a string from the list box
LB_GETTOPINDEX	List Box	Gets the item index for the first visible item in a list box
LB_INSERTSTRING	List Box	Inserts a string into the list box

Message	Category	Meaning
LB_RESETCONTENT	List Box	Deletes all the strings from a list box
LB_SELECTSTRING	List Box	Selects the first string that matches the specified prefix
LB_SELITEMRANGE	List Box	Selects one or more items from a list box
LB_SETCOLUMNWIDTH	List Box	Defines the column width in pixels for a multicolumn list box
LB_SETCURSEL	List Box	Selects a string and scrolls the string so that it can be seen in the list box
LB_SETHORIZONTALEXTENT	List Box	Defines the horizontal scroll width of a list box
LB_SETITEMDATA	List Box	Sets the 32-bit value associated with an item in an owner draw list box
LB_SETSEL	List Box	Defines the selection state of a string
LB_SETTABSTOPS	List Box	Defines the tab stops in a list box
LB_SETTOPINDEX	List Box	Sets the first visible item in a list box to the specified item index
LBN_DBLCLK	List Box Notification	Specifies that a string was double-clicked
LBN_ERRSPACE	List Box Notification	Specifies that there is no more system memory
LBN_KILLFOCUS	List Box Notification	Specifies that the list box has lost the input focus
LBN_SELCHANGE	List Box Notification	Specifies that the selection was changed
LBN_SETFOCUS	List Box Notification	Specifies that the list box has received the input focus
WM_ACTIVATE	Window Management	Sent whenever a window becomes active or inactive
WM_ACTIVATEAPP	Window Management	Sent if the window being activated doesn't belong to the same application as the previously active window

Message	*Category*	*Meaning*
WM_ASKCBFORMATNAME	Clipboard	Asks for the name of the CF_OWNERDISPLAY format
WM_CANCELMODE	Window Management	Sent when an application displays a message box and cancels the current system mode
WM_CHANGECBCHAIN	Clipboard	Sent to the members of the viewing chain when the chain has been modified
WM_CHAR	Input	Sent when a WM_KEYUP and a WM_KEYDOWN message are translated
WM_CHARTOITEM	Input	Sent in response to the WM_CHAR message by a list box with style LBS_WANTKEYBOARDINPUT
WM_CHILDACTIVATE	Window Management	Sent to a child window's parent window when the SetWindowPos function is used to move a child window
WM_CLEAR	Edit Control	Deletes the current selection
WM_CLOSE	Window Management	Sent when a window is closed
WM_COMMAND	Input	Sent when a menu item is selected, a control passes a message to its parent window, or an accelerator key is translated
WM_COMPACTING	System Information	Sent to top level windows when too much time is spent compacting memory, an indication that memory is low
WM_COMPAREITEM	Owner Draw Control	Compares two items to determine their relative position in a sorted owner draw list box or combo box
WM_COPY	Edit Control	Copies the current selection to the clipboard in CF_TEXT format
WM_CREATE	Window Management	Sent whenever the CreateWindow function is called

Message	*Category*	*Meaning*
`WM_CTLCOLOR`	Window Management	Sent to the parent window or to a control or message box whenever the control or message box is to be drawn
`WM_CUT`	Edit Control	Copies the current selection to the clipboard in `CF_TEXT` format and then deletes the selection from the control window
`WM_DEADCHAR`	Input	Sent when a `WM_KEYUP` message and a `WM_KEYDOWN` message are translated
`WM_DELETEITEM`	Owner Draw Control	Sent to the owner of an owner draw list box or combo box when a list box item is removed
`WM_DESTROY`	Window Management	Sent when a window is destroyed with the `DestroyWindow` function
`WM_DESTROYCLIPBOARD`	Clipboard	Sent when the contents of the clipboard are being destroyed
`WM_DEVMODECHANGE`	System Information	Sent to top level windows when device mode settings are modified
`WM_DRAWCLIPBOARD`	Clipboard	Sent as notification to the next application that the clipboard was modified
`WM_DRAWITEM`	Owner Draw Information	Indicates that an owner draw list or combo box needs redrawn
`WM_ENABLE`	Window Management	Sent whenever a window is enabled or disabled
`WM_ENDSESSION`	Window Management	Indicates whether the session is ended
`WM_ENTERIDLE`	Window Management	Sent to a window when a dialog box or menu is displayed and waiting for user response
`WM_ERASEBKGND`	Window Management	Sent whenever the window background needs erasing
`WM_FONTCHANGE`	System Information	Sent when font pool resources are modified

Message	*Category*	*Meaning*
WM_GETDLGCODE	Window Management	Sent to an input procedure associated with a control
WM_GETFONT	Control	Gets the font used by a control
WM_GETMINMAXINFO	Window Management	Gets the maximized window size, the minimum or maximum tracking size, and the maximized window position
WM_GETTEXT	Window Management	Gets the text for a window
WM_GETTEXTLENGTH	Window Management	Gets the length of the window text
WM_HSCROLL	Input and Scroll Bar	Sent when the horizontal scroll bar is activated
WM_HSCROLLCLIPBOARD	Clipboard	Sent to request horizontal scrolling for the CF_OWNERDISPLAY format
WM_ICONERASEBKGND	Window Management	Sent when the background of the icon needs to be erased
WM_INITDIALOG	Initialization	Sent before the dialog box is displayed
WM_INITMENU	Initialization	Sent to request the initialization of a menu
WM_INITMENUPOPUP	Initialization	Sent before a pop-up menu is displayed
WM_KEYDOWN	Input	Sent when a nonsystem key is pressed
WM_KEYUP	Input	Sent when a nonsystem key is released
WM_KILLFOCUS	Window Management	Sent just before a window loses the input focus
WM_LBUTTONDBLCLK	Input	Sent when the left mouse button is double-clicked
WM_LBUTTONDOWN	Input	Sent when the left mouse button is pressed
WM_LBUTTONUP	Input	Sent when the left mouse button is released
WM_MBUTTONDBLCLK	Input	Sent when the middle mouse button is double-clicked
WM_MBUTTONDOWN	Input	Sent when the middle mouse button is pressed

Message	*Category*	*Meaning*
WM_MBUTTONUP	Input	Sent when the middle mouse button is released
WM_MDIACTIVATE	MDI	Activates a child window
WM_MDICASCADE	MDI	Arranges child windows in a cascade fashion
WM_MDICREATE	MDI	Creates a child window
WM_MDIDESTROY	MDI	Closes a child window
WM_MDIGETACTIVE	MDI	Gets the active MDI child window
WM_MDIICONARRANGE	MDI	Arranges minimized child windows
WM_MDIMAXIMIZE	MDI	Maximizes an MDI child window
WM_MDINEXT	MDI	Makes the next child window active
WM_MDIRESTORE	MDI	Restores a child window
WM_MDISETMENU	MDI	Replaces the menu of the Windows pop-up menu, an MDI frame window, or both
WM_MDITILE	MDI	Arranges child windows in a tiled format
WM_MEASUREITEM	Owner Draw Control	Determines the dimensions of an owner draw combo box, list box, or menu item
WM_MENUCHAR	Window Management	Sent to the window that owns the menu when the menu mnemonic character input by the user doesn't match any mnemonic characters in the menu
WM_MENUSELECT	Window Management	Sent when a menu item is selected
WM_MOUSEACTIVATE	Input	Sent when a mouse button is pressed while the cursor is in an inactive window
WM_MOUSEMOVE	Input	Sent when the mouse is moved
WM_MOVE	Window Management	Sent when a window is moved

Message	*Category*	*Meaning*
WM_NCACTIVATE	Non-Client Area	Sent to a window when the caption or icon needs to be updated to reflect an active or inactive state
WM_NCCALCSIZE	Non-Client Area	Sent when the client area's size needs to be determined
WM_NCCREATE	Non-Client Area	Sent before the WM_CREATE message is sent when a window is created
WM_NCDESTROY	Non-Client Area	Sent after the WM_DESTROY message when a non-client area is destroyed
WM_NCHITTEST	Non-Client Area	Sent to the window containing the cursor whenever the mouse is moved
WM_NCLBUTTONDBLCLK	Non-Client Area	Sent when the left button is double clicked with the cursor in a non-client area
WM_NCLBUTTONDOWN	Non-Client Area	Sent when the left button is pressed with the cursor in a non-client area
WM_NCLBUTTONUP	Non-Client Area	Sent when the left button is released with the cursor in a non-client area
WM_NCMBUTTONDBLCLK	Non-Client Area	Sent when the middle button is double clicked with the cursor in a non-client area
WM_NCMBUTTONDOWN	Non-Client Area	Sent when the middle button is pressed with the cursor in a non-client area
WM_NCMBUTTONUP	Non-Client Area	Sent when the middle button is released with the cursor in a non-client area
WM_NCMOUSEMOVE	Non-Client Area	Sent when the mouse moves the cursor in a non-client area
WM_NCPAINT	Non-Client Area	Sent when the window border needs painting
WM_NCRBUTTONDBLCLK	Non-Client Area	Sent when the right button is double clicked with the cursor in a non-client area

Message	*Category*	*Meaning*
WM_NCRBUTTONDOWN	Non-Client Area	Sent when the right button is pressed with the cursor in a non-client area
WM_NCRBUTTONUP	Non-Client Area	Sent when the right button is pressed with the cursor in a non-client area
WM_NEXTDLGCTL	Control	Sent to the window function of a dialog box to modify the control focus
WM_PAINT	Window Management	Sent when a request to repaint a part of the application's window is made
WM_PAINTCLIPBOARD	Clipboard	Sent to request painting of the CF_OWNERDISPLAY format
WM_PAINTICON	Window Management	Sent when a request to repaint a part of the application's minimized window is made
WM_PALETTECHANGED	System Information	Sent to all windows when the system color palette is modified
WM_PARENTNOTIFY	Window Management	Sent to the parent of a child window when the child window is created or destroyed
WM_PASTE	Edit Control	Places the data from the control window at the position of the cursor
WM_QUERYDRAGICON	Window Management	Sent when a minimized window is about to be moved
WM_QUERYENDSESSION	Window Management	Sent when the End Session command is chosen
WM_QUERYNEWPALETTE	Window Management	Sent when a window is about to receive the input focus
WM_QUERYOPEN	Window Management	Sent when an icon is to be opened into a window
WM_QUIT	Window Management	Sent on request to terminate an application
WM_RBUTTONDBLCLK	Input	Sent when the right mouse button is double-clicked
WM_RBUTTONDOWN	Input	Sent when the right mouse button is pressed

Message	Category	Meaning
WM_RBUTTONUP	Input	Sent when the right mouse button is released
WM_RENDERALLFORMATS	Clipboard	Informs the clipboard owner that data in the clipboard must be rendered in all formats
WM_RENDERFORMAT	Clipboard	Instructs the clipboard owner to format the last data sent to the clipboard
WM_SETCURSOR	Input	Sent when the mouse input cannot be captured and the cursor has been moved
WM_SETFOCUS	Window Management	Sent after a window receives the input focus
WM_SETFONT	Control and Window Management	Modifies the font used by a control
WM_SETREDRAW	Window Management	Either sets or clears the redraw flag
WM_SETTEXT	Window Management	Sets the window text
WM_SHOWWINDOW	Window Management	Sent when a window is hidden or shown
WM_SIZE	Window Management	Sent when a window has been sized
WM_SIZECLIPBOARD	Clipboard	Sent to the clipboard owner when the clipboard application's window size is modified
WM_SPOOLERSTATUS	System Information	Sent from the Print Manager when a job is added to or removed from the print queue
WM_SYSCHAR	System	Sent when a WM_SYSKEYUP and a WM_SYSKEYDOWN message are translated
WM_SYSCOLORCHANGE	System Information	Sent to top level windows when the system color changes
WM_SYSCOMMAND	System	Sent when a command is selected from the System menu

Message	*Category*	*Meaning*
WM_SYSDEADCHAR	System	Sent when a WM_SYSKEYUP and a WM_SYSKEYDOWN message are translated
WM_SYSKEYDOWN	System	Sent when any keystroke sequence that includes the Alt key is pressed
WM_SYSKEYUP	System	Sent when any keystroke sequence that includes the Alt key is released
WM_TIMECHANGE	System Information	Sent when a application changes the system time
WM_TIMER	Input	Sent when the time limit for a timer expires
WM_UNDO	Edit Control	Performs an "undo" for the last action
WM_VKEYTOITEM	Input	Sent by a list box with LBS_WANTKEYBOARDINPUT style to the owner of the list box in response to a WM_CHAR message
WM_VSCROLL	Input and Scroll Bar	Sent when the vertical scroll bar is activated
WM_VSCROLLCLIPBOARD	Clipboard	Sent to request vertical scrolling for the CF_OWNDERDISPLAY format
WM_WININICHANGE	System Information	Sent when WIN.INI, the Windows initialization file, is modified

The Command-Line Compiler

This appendix serves as a reference to the command-line compiler. The command-line compiler provides direct control over the compilation process and is often called from a make file to develop Windows applications. The command-line compiler provided by Borland automatically compiles and links the specified files while invoking the Turbo Assembler, TASM, if it is needed to compile .ASM source files. The command-line compiler can be operated in either real or protected mode.

The command-line compiler is very flexible and Borland offers a range of options to control the compilation process. The following formats are used to invoke the command-line compiler.

Real Mode:

```
bcc [option [option...]] filename [filename...]
```

where:

`option` represents compiler options (can be none or several)

`filename` represents the file name(s) to be compiled and linked

Protected Mode:

```
bccx [option [option...]] filename [filename...]
```

where:

> `option` represents compiler options (can be none or several)
>
> `filename` represents the file name(s) to be compiled and linked

For example, `bccx test.c` would compile the file test.c by using the command-line compiler in protected mode.

Table C.1 lists the command-line compiler options.

***Table C.1.** Command-line compiler options.*

Option	*Meaning*
`@filename`	Use the response file name
`+filename`	Use the alternate configuration file specified in `filename`
`-1`	Generate 80186 instructions
`-1-`	Generate 8088/8086 instructions
`-2`	Generate 80286 protected-mode compatible instructions
`-A`	Use only ANSI keywords
`-A-` or `-AT`	Use Borland C++ keywords (the default)
`-AK`	Use only Kernighan and Ritchie keywords
`-AU`	Use only UNIX keywords
`-a`	Align word
`-a-`	Align byte (default)
`-B`	Compile and call the assembler to process in-line assembly code
`-b`	Make enums word-sized (default)
`-b-`	Make enum signed or unsigned
`-C`	Turn on nested comments
`-C-`	Turn off nested comments
`-c`	Compile to .OBJ, do not link
`-Dname`	Define the specified name to the string consisting of the null character
`-Dname=string`	Define the specified name to the specified string
`-d`	Merge duplicate strings on
`-d-`	Merge duplicate strings off (default)
`-Efilename`	Use the specified file name as the assembler

Option	Meaning
`-efilename`	Link and produce the specified file name
`-Fc`	Generate COMDEFs
`-Ff`	Create far variables automatically
`-Ff=size`	Create far variables automatically and set the threshold
`-Fm`	Enable `-Fc`, `-Ff`, and `-Fs` options
`-Fs`	Assume DS=SS in all memory models
`-f`	Emulate floating point (the default)
`-f-`	Don't do floating point
`-ff`	Do fast floating point (the default)
`-ff-`	Do ANSI floating point
`-f87`	Use 8087 instructions
`-f287`	Use 80287 instructions
`-G`	Optimize for speed
`-G-`	Optimize for size
`-gn`	Stop warnings after `n` messages
`-H`	Generate and use precompiled headers
`-H-`	Do not generate or use precompiled headers
`-Hu`	Use but do not generate precompiled headers
`-H=filename`	Set the name of the file for precompiled headers
`-h`	Use fast huge pointer arithmetic
`-Ipath`	Specify directories for include files
`-in`	Set significant identifier length to *n*
`-jn`	Stop errors after *n* messages
`-K`	Make the default character type unsigned
`-K-`	Make the default character type signed (the default)
`-k`	Turn on the standard stack frame (the default)
`-Lpath`	Directories for libraries
`-lx`	Pass option in *x* to the linker
`-l-x`	Suppress the option in `x` for the linker
`-M`	Instruct the linker to create a map file
`-mc`	Compile using the compact memory model
`-mh`	Compile using the huge memory model
`-ml`	Compile using the large memory model
`-mm`	Compile using the medium memory model

continues

Table C.1. continued

Option	Meaning
-mm!	Compile using the medium memory model; assume DS != SS
-ms	Compile using the small memory model
-ms!	Compile using the small memory model; assume DS != SS
-mt	Compile using the tiny memory model
-mt!	Compile using the tiny memory model; assume DS != SS
-N	Check for stack overflow
-n*path*	Specify output directory
-O	Optimize jumps
-O-	Do not optimize (the default)
-o*filename*	Compile source file to *filename*.obj
-P	Perform a C++ compile
-P*ext*	Perform a C++ compile and set the default extension to the extension specified in ext
-P-	Perform a C++ or C compile depending on the source file extension (the default)
-P-ext	Perform a C++ or C compile depending on the source file extension; set the default extension to the extension specified in *ext*
-p	Use Pascal calling convention
-p-	Use C calling convention (the default)
-Qe	Use all available EMS memory
-Qe-	Use no EMS memory
-Qx	Use all available extended memory
-Qx=*nnnn*	Reserve the number of Kbytes in *nnnn* for other programs
-Qx=*nnnn*,*yyyy*	Reserve *nnnn* Kbytes of extended memory for other programs and *yyyy* for the compiler
-Qx=,yyyy	Reserve *yyyy* Kbytes of extended memory for the compiler
-Qx-	Use no extended memory
-r	Use register variables
-r-	Do not use register variables
-rd	Keep only declared register variables in the registers
-S	Produce .ASM output
-T*string*	Pass the specified string as an option to TASM or the assembler specified with the -E option
-T-	Remove all assembler options
-U*name*	Undefine the specified name
-u	Generate underscores

Option	Meaning
-u-	Do not generate underscores
-V	Use smart C++ virtual tables
-Vf	Use far C++ virtual tables
-Vs	Use local C++ virtual tables
-V0, -V1	Use external and public C++ virtual tables
-v, -v-	Turn on source debugging
-vi, -vi-	Control the expansion of in-line functions
-W	Create an .OBJ for Windows with all functions exportable
-WD	Create an .OBJ for Windows to be linked as a .DLL with all function exportable
-WDE	Create an .OBJ for Windows to be linked as a .DLL with explicit export functions
-WE	Create an .OBJ for Windows with explicit export functions
-WS	Create an .OBJ for Windows that uses smart callbacks
-w	Display warnings
-w-	Do not display warnings
-w*xxx*	Allow the warning message in *xxx*
-w-*xxx*	Do not allow the warning message in *xxx*
-X	Disable compiler autodependency output
-Y	Enable overlay code generation
-Yo	Overlay the compiled files
-y	Turn on line numbers
-Z	Enable register usage optimization
-zA*name*	Specify code class
-zB*name*	Specify BSS class
-zC*name*	Specify code segment
-zD*name*	Specify BSS segment
-zE*name*	Specify far segment
-zF*name*	Specify far class
-zG*name*	Specify BSS group
-zH*name*	Specify far group
-zP*name*	Specify code group
-zR*name*	Specify data segment
-zS*name*	Specify data group
-zT*name*	Specify data class
-zX*	Use default name for X

Bibliography

Borland International. *Borland C++—Getting Started*. Scotts Valley, CA: Borland International, 1991.

Borland International. *Borland C++—Library Reference*. Scotts Valley, CA: Borland International, 1991.

Borland International. *Borland C++—Programmer's Guide*. Scotts Valley, CA: Borland International, 1991.

Borland International. *Borland C++—User's Guide*. Scotts Valley, CA: Borland International, 1991.

Borland International. *Borland C++—Whitewater Resource Toolkit*. Scotts Valley, CA: Borland International, 1991.

Microsoft Corporation. *Microsoft Windows Software Development Kit—Guide to Programming*. Redmond, WA: Microsoft Corporation, 1990.

Microsoft Corporation. *Microsoft Windows Software Development Kit—Reference Volume 1*. Redmond, WA: Microsoft Corporation, 1990.

Microsoft Corporation. *Microsoft Windows Software Development Kit—Reference Volume 2*. Redmond, WA: Microsoft Corporation, 1990.

Norton, Peter and Paul Yao. *Peter Norton's Windows 3.0 Power Programming Techniques*. New York: Bantam Computer Books, 1990.

Petzold, Charles. *Programming Windows: The Microsoft Guide to Writing Applications for Windows 3*. Redmond, WA: Microsoft Press, 1990.

Program Index

Index

Symbols

A

B

C

D

E

F

G

H

I

J-K

L

M

P

Q-R

S

T

U

V

W

X-Z

Sams—Covering The Latest In Computer And Technical Topics!

Audio

Advanced Digital Audio $39.95
Audio Systems Design and Installation $59.95
Compact Disc Troubleshooting and Repair . .$24.95
Handbook for Sound Engineers: The New Audio Cyclopedia, 2nd Ed. . .$99.95
How to Design & Build Loudspeaker & Listening Enclosures $39.95
Introduction to Professional Recording Techniques $29.95
The MIDI Manual $24.95
Modern Recording Techniques, 3rd Ed. $29.95
OP-AMP Circuits and Principles $19.95
Principles of Digital Audio, 2nd Ed. $29.95
Sound Recording Handbook $49.95
Sound System Engineering, 2nd Ed. $49.95

Electricity/Electronics

Active-Filter Cookbook $24.95
Basic Electricity and DC Circuits $29.95
CMOS Cookbook, 2nd Ed. $24.95
Electrical Wiring $19.95
Electricity 1-7, Revised 2nd Ed. $49.95
Electronics 1-7, Revised 2nd Ed. $49.95
How to Read Schematics, 4th Ed. $19.95
IC Op-Amp Cookbook, 3rd Ed. $24.95
IC Timer Cookbook, 2nd Ed. $24.95
RF Circuit Design $24.95
Transformers and Motors $29.95
TTL Cookbook $24.95
Understanding Digital Troubleshooting, 3rd Ed.$24.95
Understanding Solid State Electronics, 5th Ed. $24.95

Games

Master SimCity/SimEarth $19.95
Master Ultima $16.95

Hardware/Technical

First Book of Modem Communications $16.95
First Book of PS/1 . . . .$16.95
Hard Disk Power with the Jamsa Disk Utilities $39.95
IBM PC Advanced Troubleshooting & Repair $24.95
IBM Personal Computer Troubleshooting & Repair $24.95
Microcomputer Troubleshooting & Repair . .$24.95
Understanding Fiber Optics $24.95

IBM: Business

10 Minute Guide to PC Tools 7 . . . .$ 9.95
10 Minute Guide to Q&A 4 . . . .$ 9.95
First Book of Microsoft Works for the PC . . .$16.95
First Book of Norton Utilities 6 . . . .$16.95
First Book of PC Tools 7 . . . .$16.95
First Book of Personal Computing, 2nd Ed. . .$16.95

IBM: Database

10 Minute Guide to Harvard Graphics 2.3 . . . $9.95
Best Book of AutoCAD $34.95
dBASE III Plus Programmer's Reference Guide $24.95
dBASE IV Version 1.1 for the First-Time User $24.95
Everyman's Database Primer Featuring dBASE IV Version 1.1 . . . .$24.95
First Book of Paradox 3.5 . . . .$16.95
First Book of PowerPoint for Windows $16.95
Harvard Graphics 2.3 In Business $29.95

IBM: Graphics/Desktop Publishing

10 Minute Guide to Lotus 1-2-3 . . . .$ 9.95
Best Book of Harvard Graphics $24.95
First Book of Harvard Graphics 2.3 . . . . . .$16.95
First Book of PC Paintbrush $16.95
First Book of PFS: First Publisher $16.95

IBM: Spreadsheets/Financial

Best Book of Lotus 1-2-3 Release 3.1 . . . . $27.95
First Book of Excel 3 for Windows $16.95
First Book of Lotus 1-2-3 Release 2.3 . . . . $16.95
First Book of Quattro Pro 3 . . . . $16.95
First Book of Quicken In Business $16.95
Lotus 1-2-3 Release 2.3 In Business $29.95
Lotus 1-2-3: Step-by-Step $24.95
Quattro Pro In Business $29.95

IBM: Word Processing

Best Book of Microsoft Word 5 . . . . $24.95
Best Book of Microsoft Word for Windows . $24.95
Best Book of WordPerfect 5.1 . . . . $26.95
First Book of Microsoft Word 5.5 . . . . . . $16.95
First Book of WordPerfect 5.1 . . . . $16.95
WordPerfect 5.1: Step-by-Step $24.95

Macintosh/Apple

First Book of Excel 3 for the Mac $16.95
First Book of the Mac $16.95

Operating Systems/Networking

10 Minute Guide to Windows 3 . . . . $ 9.95
Best Book of DESQview $24.95
Best Book of Microsoft Windows 3 . . . . . $24.95
Best Book of MS-DOS 5 . . . . $24.95
Business Guide to Local Area Networks . . . $24.95
DOS Batch File Power with the Jamsa Disk Utilities $39.95
Exploring the UNIX System, 2nd Ed. $29.95
First Book of DeskMate $16.95
First Book of Microsoft Windows 3 . . . . . $16.95
First Book of MS-DOS 5 . . . . $16.95
First Book of UNIX $16.95
Interfacing to the IBM Personal Computer, 2nd Ed. $24.95
The Waite Group's Discovering MS-DOS, 2nd Edition $19.95
The Waite Group's MS-DOS Bible, 4th Ed. . $29.95
The Waite Group's MS-DOS Developer's Guide, 2nd Ed. $29.95
The Waite Group's Tricks of the UNIX Masters$29.95
The Waite Group's Understanding MS-DOS, 2nd Ed. $19.95
The Waite Group's UNIX Primer Plus, 2nd Ed.$29.95
The Waite Group's UNIX System V Bible . . $29.95
Understanding Local Area Networks, 2nd Ed. $24.95
UNIX Applications Programming: Mastering the Shell $29.95
UNIX Networking $29.95
UNIX Shell Programming, Revised Ed. . . . $29.95
UNIX: Step-by-Step $29.95
UNIX System Administration $29.95
UNIX System Security $34.95
UNIX Text Processing $29.95

Professional/Reference

Data Communications, Networks, and Systems $39.95
Handbook of Electronics Tables and Formulas, 6th Ed. $24.95
ISDN, DECnet, and SNA Communications . $49.95
Modern Dictionary of Electronics, 6th Ed. . . $39.95
Reference Data for Engineers: Radio, Electronics, Computer, and Communications, 7th Ed. $99.95

Programming

Advanced C: Tips and Techniques $29.95
C Programmer's Guide to NetBIOS $29.95
C Programmer's Guide to Serial Communications $29.95
Commodore 64 Programmer's Reference Guide $24.95
Developing Windows Applications with Microsoft SDK $29.95
DOS Batch File Power $39.95
Graphical User Interfaces with Turbo C++ . .$29.95
Learning C++ $39.95
Mastering Turbo Assembler $29.95
Mastering Turbo Pascal, 4th Ed. $29.95
Microsoft Macro Assembly Language Programming $29.95
Microsoft QuickBASIC Programmer's Reference $29.95
Programming in ANSI C $29.95
Programming in C, Revised Ed. $29.95
The Waite Group's BASIC Programming Primer, 2nd Ed. $24.95
The Waite Group's C Programming Using Turbo C++ $29.95
The Waite Group's C: Step-by-Step $29.95
The Waite Group's GW-BASIC Primer Plus .$24.95
The Waite Group's Microsoft C Bible, 2nd Ed. $29.95
The Waite Group's Microsoft C Programming for the PC, 2nd Ed. $29.95
The Waite Group's New C Primer Plus $29.95
The Waite Group's Turbo Assembler Bible . .$29.95
The Waite Group's Turbo C Bible $29.95
The Waite Group's Turbo C Programming for the PC, Revised Ed. $29.95
The Waite Group's Turbo C++Bible $29.95
X Window System Programming $29.95

Radio/Video

Camcorder Survival Guide . . . . $ 14.95
Radio Handbook, 23rd Ed. $39.95
Radio Operator's License Q&A Manual, 11th Ed. $24.95
Understanding Fiber Optics $24.95
Understanding Telephone Electronics, 3rd Ed. $24.95
VCR Troubleshooting & Repair Guide $19.95
Video Scrambling & Descrambling for Satellite & Cable TV $24.95

For More Information, See Your Local Retailer Or Call Toll Free

1-800-428-5331

All prices are subject to change without notice. Non-U.S. prices may be higher. Printed in the U.S.A.

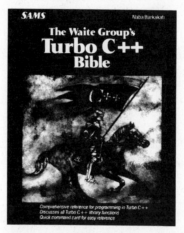

Sams' First Books Get You Started Fast!

"The First Book Series ... is intended to get the novice off to a good start, whether with computers in general or with particular programs ...."

The New York Times

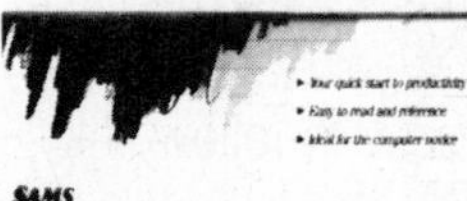

The First Book of WordPerfect 5.1
Kate Miller Barnes
275 pages, 7 3/8 x 9 1/4, $16.95 USA
0-672-27307-1

Look For These Books In Sams' First Book Series

The First Book of Excel 3 for the Mac
Christopher Van Buren
320 pages, 7 3/8 x 9 1/4, $16.95 USA
0-672-27328-4

The First Book of Excel 3 for Windows
Chrisopher Van Buren
320 pages, 7 3/8 x 9 1/4, $16.95 USA
0-672-27359-4

The First Book of Harvard Graphics
Jack Purdum
300 pages, 7 3/8 x 9 1/4, $16.95 USA
0-672-27310-1

The First Book of Lotus 1-2-3 Release 2.3
Alan Simpson & Paul Lichtman
330 pages, 7 3/8 x 9 1/4, $16.95 USA
0-672-27365-9

The First Book of Microsoft Windows 3
Jack Nimersheim
304 pages, 7 3/8 x 9 1/4, $16.95 USA
0-672-27334-9

The First Book of Microsoft Word 5.5, Second Edition
Brent Heslop & David Angell
320 pages, 7 3/8 x 9 1/4, $16.95 USA
0-672-27333-0

The First Book of Microsoft Word for Windows
Brent Heslop & David Angell
304 pages, 7 3/8 x 9 1/4, $16.95 USA
0-672-27332-2

The First Book of Microsoft Works for the PC
Debbie Walkowski
304 pages, 7 3/8 x 9 1/4, $16.95 USA
0-672-27360-8

The First Book of MS-DOS
Jack Nimersheim
272 pages, 7 3/8 x 9 1/4, $16.95 USA
0-672-27312-8

The First Book of Norton Utilities 6
Joseph Wikert, Rev. by Lisa Bucki
275 pages, 7 3/8 x 9 1/4, $16.95 USA
0-672-27384-5

The First Book of Paradox 3.5
Jonathan Kamin
320 pages, 7 3/8 x 9 1/4, $16.95 USA
0-672-27370-5

The First Book of PC Paintbrush
Deke McClelland
289 pages, 7 3/8 x 9 1/4, $16.95 USA
0-672-27324-1

The First Book of PC Tools 7
Gordon McComb
350 pages, 7 3/8 x 9 1/4, $16.95 USA
0-672-27371-3

The First Book of Personal Computing Second Edition
W.E. Wang & Joe Kraynak
275 pages, 7 3/8 x 9 1/4, $16.95 USA
0-672-27385-3

The First Book of PFS: First Publisher
Karen Brown & Robert Bixby
308 pages, 7 3/8 x 9 1/4, $16.95 USA
0-672-27326-8

The First Book of PowerPoint for Windows
Douglas Snyder
330 pages, 7 3/8 x 9 1/4, $16.95 USA
0-672-27356-X

The First Book of PROCOMM PLUS
Jack Nimersheim
250 pages, 7 3/8 x 9 1/4, $16.95 USA
0-672-27309-8

The First Book of PS/1
Kate Barnes
300 pages, 7 3/8 x 9 1/4, $16.95 USA
0-672-27346-2

The First Book of Q&A 4
Sandra E. Schnyder
272 pages, 7 3/8 x 9 1/4, $16.95 USA
0-672-27311-X

The First Book of Quattro Pro 3
Patrick Burns
300 pages, 7 3/8 x 9 1/4, $16.95 USA
0-672-27367-5

The First Book of Quicken in Business
Gordon McComb
300 pages, 7 3/8 x 9 1/4, $16.95 USA
0-672-27331-4

The First Book of the Mac
Carla Rose & Jay Rose
350 pages, 7 3/8 x 9 1/4, $16.95 USA
0-672-27355-1

The First Book of UNIX
Douglas Topham
300 pages, 7 3/8 x 9 1/4, $16.95 USA
0-672-27299-7

The First Book of WordPerfect for Windows
Kate Barnes
400 pages, 7 3/8 x 9 1/4, $16.95 USA
0-672-27343-8

SAMS

See your local retailer or call 1-800-428-5331.

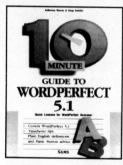

Sams' Series Puts You "In Business"

The *In Business* books have been specially designed to help business users increase their productivity and efficiency. Each book comes with a companion disk that contains templates for common business tasks, as well as tear-out quick references for common commands. In addition, the books feature Business Shortcuts—boxed notes and tips on how to improve the performance of the software. Regardless of the size of the business or the level of user, these books will teach you how to get the most out of your business applications.

Quattro Pro 3 In Business
Chris Van Buren
400 pages, 7 3/8 x 9 1/4, $29.95 USA
0-672-22793-2

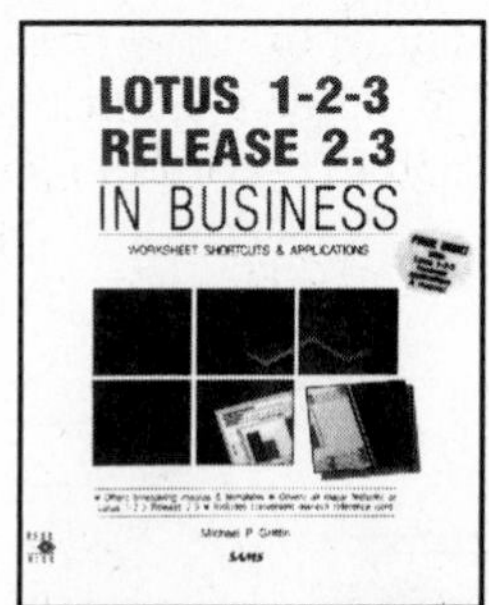

Lotus 1-2-3 Release 2.3 In Business
Michael Griffin
400 pages, 7 3/8 x 9 1/4, $29.95 USA
0-672-22803-3

Harvard Graphics 2.3 In Business
Jean Jacobson & Steve Jacobson
400 pages, 7 3/8 x 9 1/4, $29.95 USA
0-672-22834-3

Q&A 4 In Business
David B. Adams
400 pages, 7 3/8 x 9 1/4, $29.95 USA
0-672-22801-7

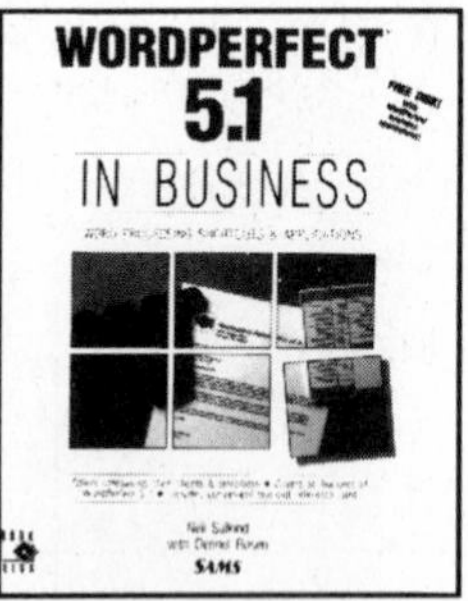

WordPerfect 5.1 In Business
Neil Salkind
400 pages, 7 3/8 x 9 1/4, $29.95 USA
0-672-22795-9

SAMS

See your local retailer or call 1-800-428-5331.

Companion Disk Offer!

Get the companion disk for this book on your choice of 5.25-inch or 3.5-inch disk. This offer provides you with all the files that you need to build the examples in this book using your Borland C++ compiler. The C and C++ source files, module definition files, project files, and resource files used for the examples in this book are included on the companion disk. To order your companion disk, send your name, address (complete with ZIP code), disk preference (specify either 5.25-inch or 3.5-inch disk), and a check or money order for $12.50 ($15 for foreign orders) to:

Borland Disk Offer
Code 1
MC Software
P.O. Box 115
Woodland, AL 36280-0115

If you prefer, you can simply copy this page, fill in the blanks, and send with the check or money order to the preceding address.

Cost Including Shipping and Handling:

$12.50 U.S. orders
$15.00 Foreign orders (U.S. dollars)

Disk Preference:

5.25-inch high-density (1.2M) ______
3.5-inch high-density (1.44M) ______

Payment Method:

Check ______
Money order ______

Name:____

Street Address: ________________________________

City: ____

State: ______ **Zip:** ___________________________

Check or money orders should be made payable to:

MC Software

Allow at least two weeks for delivery.

(This offer is made by MC Software.)